THE ESSENTIALS OF
ZEN BUDDHISM

The Library of Congress has catalogued this publication as follows:

Library of Congress Cataloging in Publication Data

Suzuki, Daisetz Teitaro, 1870-1966.
   The essentials of Zen Buddhism.

   Reprint of the 1962 ed.
   Includes bibliographies.
   1. Zen Buddhism. I. Title.
[BQ9265.4.S94 1973]   294.3'927   72-11306
ISBN 0-8371-6649-7

THE ESSENTIALS OF
Zen Buddhism

Selected from the Writings of
DAISETZ T. SUZUKI

Edited, and with an Introduction,
by BERNARD PHILLIPS

GREENWOOD PRESS, PUBLISHERS
WESTPORT, CONNECTICUT

COPYRIGHTS AND ACKNOWLEDGMENTS

Grateful acknowledgment is made to the following for permission to use copyright material in this volume:

RIDER & CO., London, for the use of copyright material by D. T. Suzuki from the following volumes and published here by special arrangement with them: *An Introduction to Zen Buddhism*, 1949; *Essays in Zen Buddhism, First Series*, 1949; *Essays in Zen Buddhism, Second Series*, 1950; *Essays in Zen Buddhism, Third Series*, 1953; *Living by Zen*, 1950.

HARPER & BROTHERS, New York, for "Human Values in Zen" by D. T. Suzuki from *New Knowledge in Human Values*, edited by A. H. Maslow, copyright, ©, 1959, by the Research Society for Creative Altruism.

THE OPEN COURT PUBLISHING COMPANY, Illinois, for "Zen Buddhism" by D. T. Suzuki from *Modern Trends in World Religions*, edited by J. M. Kitagawa, copyright, ©, 1959, by The Open Court Publishing Company.

BOLLINGEN FOUNDATION, INC., New York, for selections from *Zen and Japanese Culture* by D. T. Suzuki. Bollingen Series LXIV, copyright, ©, 1959, by Bollingen Foundation, Inc. Published for Bollingen Foundation, Inc. by Pantheon Books, Inc., New York, N.Y.

Acknowledgments for permission to quote are also made to the following: to *Monumenta Nipponica*, Tokyo, for "Zen Buddhism" by D. T. Suzuki in Vol. I, No. 1; to *Japan Quarterly*, Tokyo, for "The Oriental Way of Thinking" by D. T. Suzuki in Vol II, No. 1, and for "Zen in the Modern World" by D. T. Suzuki in Vol. V, No. 4; to *The Review of Religion*, New York, for "Enlightenment" by D. T. Suzuki in Vol. XVIII, Nos. 3–4; to Hōzōkan Press, Kyoto, for "The Essence of Buddhism" by D. T. Suzuki, and to Dr. Daisetz T. Suzuki for "Some Aspects of Zen Buddhism" from *Studies on Buddhism in Japan*, Vol. I, for "Zen Buddhism as Purifier and Liberator of Life" from *The Eastern Buddhist*, Vol. I, No. 1, and for "Living in the Light of Eternity."

Originally published in 1962 by E. P. Dutton & Co., Inc., New York

Reprinted with the permission of E. P. Dutton & Company, Inc.

Reprinted in 1973 by Greenwood Press, Inc., 51 Riverside Avenue, Westport, Conn. 06880

Library of Congress catalog card number 72-11306
ISBN 0-8371-6649-7

Printed in the United States of America

10 9 8 7 6 5 4

DEDICATED

TO

CORNELIUS CRANE

TABLE OF CONTENTS

INTRODUCTION

Zen Buddhism as Creative Religion

INTRODUCTION

ZEN BUDDHISM AS CREATIVE RELIGION

OF the current impact of Zen on the West it might perhaps be said that never before have so many evinced such interest in anything so little understood. Certainly, Zen tantalizes by its very inscrutability. Yet were Zen simply a thing opaque, how could it have evoked the eulogies of painters, psychiatrists, and philosophers? Sheer mystery has not the power permanently to attract, whereas it is just by its creative fusion of mystery and meaning that Zen speaks to the deepest level of man's being. Zen is neither purposeful nor wanton mystification; it is ultimately unfathomable because it is inexhaustible. Its elusiveness is the elusiveness ingredient in all that is alive, and the uniqueness of Zen is that it goes beyond books and beliefs to life itself.

The intent of Zen Buddhism is to bring man into union with life and with himself, or, in other words, to awaken in him the knowledge of *who he really is.* The unawakened man sees himself as in the world, but the world seems to him to be clearly something other than his own very self. This self he takes to be only a fragment of an unknown totality, a fragment now threatened, now supported by the other fragments with which it is in contact. He thus operates on things from a position which is external to them, and his dealings with life are only manipulations of its fragments. Because of this separation from life, his efforts at adjustment are never regulated by any sense of wholeness, and he is forever colliding with those portions of life which his piecemeal calculations had not envisaged.

His inner life exactly mirrors the outer fragmentation; his separation from all things is mysteriously matched by an alienation from himself as well. From whatever angle he would approach himself, he is not able to lay hands on his wholeness and to muster all of his being behind any project whatsoever. Whether he endeavors to express himself in word or in deed, he is never, as com-

mon parlance puts it, "all there," and so far as his responses have
been endorsed by only a portion of himself, they cannot but fall
short of perfect authenticity. No man can be wholehearted unless
he has come into his own wholeness. When the agent is not wholly
present in his action, then the action remains an appearance—an
"acting"—rather than a thing completely real.

Man's inner life and his dealings with the world are thus both
infected with unreality in the measure that he is separated from
himself and from his world. Both forms of estrangement, Buddhism
has always claimed, are tied to man's ignorance of his own true
being. It is from this state of alienation from life and ignorance of
self that Zen proposes to rescue him.

The unreal life is a life forever unconsummated. The man who
stands apart from things, unable to give himself to them, receives
payment in kind; because his relation to things is an external one,
these things, in turn, withhold their full reality from him. When
life is contemplated objectively, nowhere is there to be found anything that is free of limitations, nothing that fully satisfies the
yearning of the human heart. It is only when man's experience of
life is integral that it "means everything" to him; only when the
subject is not outside the object, where each lives in the other as
well as in itself—only then is life complete from moment to moment.
Otherwise, one remains imperfectly reconciled to life, somewhat
disappointed in one's share, and beset by the fear that even this
will one day be cut off by death. He who has not found his own
true being may clutch feverishly at fugitive satisfactions in the
endeavor to maximize his allotment. Or he may preach and practice stoic resignation, or look forward to some sort of posthumous
compensation for the shortcomings of finite existence. In all these
cases he is operating as a stranger in life, and he cannot in perfect
sincerity and wholeheartedness embrace life and say of it, as the
Creator Himself is supposed to have said, that it is exceedingly
good. Man's awareness of himself as something apart from life is
the symptom of his fallen condition, and until he overcomes it, he
must feel himself

>   . . . a stranger and afraid,
>   In a world I never made.

How does man come to be in this state of alienation from self and
estrangement from all that is? Why could not the Prodigal Son

stay at home and enjoy his father's bounty? Why had Adam to lose
Paradise? Why did Infinite Perfection create this world of im-
perfections? Shall we say that without the Fall there is no Redemption, without the departure there is no joyous homecoming,
without the finite infinity is only an abstraction? Zen is not prepared
to linger over the questions nor over any of the answers. If pressed
for a statement, Zen would only say, "Find your own way home,
and then you will understand the departure and the return."

To find one's way home would be to undo the Fall and to achieve
a re-entry into life. The outer world would then no longer be outside ourselves, and nothing would be seen as simply an ob-ject, i.e.,
as something which we re-ject or dis-own. In the union with life
which overcomes man's alienation, the universe becomes his very
own; he lives in it even as it lives in him. Life is no longer a collection of fragments externally and accidentally related, but a living
whole in which the parts retain their identity as parts and yet at
the same time are fully united with the whole. And the unity of
all things is reflected in the wholeness of his inner life. His left
hand knoweth what his right hand doeth, and his name is no longer
legion. With his energies no more diminished by the warfare of
the segments of his own being, man is then, for the first time, able
to give life his undivided attention from moment to moment. His
actions can then be truly characterized as wholeness responding
to wholeness, and his life is then no longer, as heretofore, a matter
of fragments pushing or being pushed by other fragments.

Such an unconditional union with life and with oneself is far
beyond anything that could be called acceptance or reconciliation.
To be reconciled to one's lot, to accept the universe, to try to make
a virtue of necessity—such attitudes remain on the plane of duality
where there is still a separation between the man and what he
adjusts to. Both acceptance and rejection are conditioned by
separation. Neither can be absolutely wholehearted. To-be-one-
with is something beyond acceptance and rejection or any kind of
affirmation and denial. What it signifies is love in the absolute sense
of the term, and the miracle of love is just this, that in defiance of
the laws of logic love transcends individuality even as it cherishes
and enhances individuality. Love overcomes separateness and yet
maintains it at the same time. Were the separateness something
final there could be no real contact and no love. Without the
separateness, on the other hand, there would be no poles for the
love to exist between. So that where love exists between A and B,

it can be truly said that although A is A and B is B, still, and at the same time, A is B and B is A. And this is the sort of loving union with life at which Zen aims, and which it achieves, and thus Zen may most descriptively be defined as the absolute love of life.

Perfect love casteth out all fear. When life is complete from moment to moment, where is there room for anxiety concerning the morrow? Anxiety is symptomatic of separateness from life; it is the fear that one may not attain what one hopes for or that one may lose what one momentarily clutches. Not that the life of love is without problems; challenge and response must always remain the warp and woof of life. It is only that where there is union with life the problems are real—not ego-projected—and the responses are creative and wholehearted, not forced or vacillating.

So he who lives in union with life must sooner or later die and face death. How does the man of Zen die? In absolute wholeheart-edness. He relates to death as he relates to life; death is not something that strikes him down from without, and hence it has no terrors for him. He is one with his dying as he is one with his living, and in some ineffable way he is beyond birth and death even as he is born and as he dies. Eternity, for Zen, is not a posthumous state of affairs. To live in eternity is to tap the infinity of the moment.

Man's fallen condition, his ignorance and his finitude, is not just his lack of information. His ignorance and his alienation, according to Buddhism, do not stem from a merely intellectual error which would be rectified by presenting him with a statement of the truth. It is his very being that is in error, indeed, the truth of the matter is that his being is constituted by the error. To overcome the error he must overcome himself, and the error will be vanquished only after a struggle unto death. Every level of love entails a dying and a resurrection, and the rebirth into the life of absolute love comes after what Zen calls the Great Death. No one is prepared to take that last step until he has first exhausted all his other resources, and finally stands emptied of all contrivances for meeting life. Only then will the need for reality drive him to the final abandoning of his self. The practice and discipline of Zen is to bring one to this point.

The Great Death is also the Great Awakening, and the existential awakening to one's true Self is called *enlightenment* (*satori*, in Japanese). It is the entry into the life of non-duality where one is no longer caught by the play of the opposites, where *self* is not set over against *other*, nor are ideals in conflict with realities. As love has degrees of depth, so does that union with life and with oneself which is called enlightenment. There is no final enlightenment, as there is no final perfection of love, for life itself is not final or finished. The true Zen person does not look upon *satori* as a momentary experience after which somehow all of life's problems will vanish. What vanishes is not life's problems, but man's exteriority vis-à-vis those problems. He now deals with all problems and with himself from within instead of from without—that is the great difference.

As he is now one with his tasks, they are not to him mere obstacles to be disposed of so that he may begin the business of "really living." His tasks *are* his life, and he lives in the Now, not in the abstract future. It is in the uncreative life that the doer is separated from what he does, and it is his divorce from life that makes him look before and after and pine for what is not. The creative artist does not value the final product above the process which created it, and the man of Zen makes a creative art of life itself, gives himself wholeheartedly to all its moments, and perceives no radical difference between means and ends.

The unenlightened person remains unknowing of his own rootage in life, and he thus confronts life as something quite other than himself. From his position of externality, he vacillates between two alternative modes of dealing with life, both uncreative and equally unsatisfying. As an idealist, his intent may be called sadistic; he would bend life to his will and compel it to take the shape of his idea for it. As a realist, he masochistically allows life to have its way with him; he is not prepared to oppose life in the name of any principle. Likewise, in coping with his own nature, he may try actively to retailor his own being in accordance with some ideal pattern, or he may be passively driven by his immediate impulses and passions without any effort to subdue them or even to channel them. In the one case, his life becomes effortful, tense, and angular; in the other case, it becomes an unstructured miscellany and threatens to dissipate into chaos. Neither manner of approach brings him to the condition of the enlightened man, whose relation to himself and to all life is creative and graceful. The enlightened man is neither fighting life nor passively submitting to it. He is one with life, and this being-one-with-life and the being-one-with-oneself are for Zen the very substance of the religious life.

As unity with life is not a static goal but a dynamic one, enlightenment does not signify the end of Zen practice, but only its real beginning. As enlightenment becomes ever deeper, Zen practice and everyday life become ever less distinguishable, which means that one's Zen and one's life are becoming realities, and are ceasing to be formalities alone. Religion can then no longer be thought of as a department within life, nor can Zen appear as a specific technique for achieving a particular goal. Reality, or the life of truth, is not a goal to be reached by a certain process. Unless the process be real, how shall it lead to reality as a goal? The real life, which is the religious life, emerges only where the goal is present in the process and where consummation is achieved at every moment. This is "Zen beyond Zen" about which nothing can any longer be said, for it is nothing special. The life of truth is nothing special and no label can be affixed to it. Reality itself is nameless, and where religion and life have become perfectly one there is no longer anything to be called Zen Buddhism. Zen is thus the only religion whose aim is to forget itself.

Zen Buddhism, in the last analysis, is not so much a religion as it is a pointing to the religious life itself. It is not concerned to defend a point of view or to propagate a set of beliefs *about* the absolute basis of life, but rather to lay hold on that absolute life itself. Its method is not to supply the mind with formal truths; it seeks only to help each person arrive at the existential discovery of his own true Self and thus to have him pass from the inauthentic life of formal posturing to the life of truth or the creative life. Zen is not an ideology but an ultimate therapy through which man comes into the possession of what is truly his own and attains spiritual freedom.

Other religions, of course, have also proclaimed that the truth would set man free, but for Zen this saving truth is the truth of one's own being, and, as such, it is concrete and personal and can never be enshrined in any formula which would be available to all and sundry. The truth of one's being must be grasped in and through one's being; it is a living truth and cannot be known abstractly or contemplated from the outside. No one can perceive it for another, no one can relate it to another—each must come to it by himself and through himself. Reality is inimitable, and the truth of one's own being cannot be patterned on that of another. Living truth must be forged, it cannot be followed. The Zen disciple who tries to win approval by quoting the master's own words only earns a blow from the master's staff.

That is to say the living truth is not a teaching, and one does not come by the truth of one's being simply through adhering to a teaching. Since there was a time when you were without the teaching, that teaching is something external to your being. The teaching is only something to which you cling, Zen would point out, something you try to absorb into yourself. But the very effort to heed the teaching indicates that it is something alien to your very self. A teaching is something general and abstract, and that is why Zen possesses no stock of teachings, no code, no creed. Zen has no truth to impose on the individual, for any truth of this sort would be an "imposition" and would fall short of being the kind of living truth which alone can confer reality and set men free. No truth that is imposed on an individual from without can be perfectly real for him, nor can such a truth ever evoke the unqualified endorsement of his entire being. The effort to conform to the specifications of a truth supposed to emanate from on high will never attain the proportions of a perfectly sincere response. The inevitable outcome of the futile effort to force oneself into the acceptance of what is not truly one's own is that sense of sin so conspicuous in the devotees of a supernatural deity.

If the living truth is not to be transmitted as a formal teaching, how, then, does one apprehend it? Not by any act of intellectual understanding, nor by any act of feeling, nor by the exercise of any faculty whatsoever. Man will never come to his wholeness through any partial response, and no fragment of man's being, neither his head nor his heart, can be the instrument of his salvation. Zen is not anti-intellectual any more than it is anti-emotional. It is in the strictest sense non-partisan, for it will not take sides with any of the parts of man's being, but is concerned only to arrive at his wholeness. Zen opposes the intellect and the feelings alike not as expressions of man's wholeness, but only as would-be usurpers of that wholeness.

As for the intellect, the farthest it can go is to understand why the reality of Zen is beyond its reach. In relation to the living truth of his own being, man's problem is not how to understand it, how to fix it as an intellectual possession, but rather how to be one with it, how to live out of it.

The intellect is by its nature "grasping," but it is only abstractions and not concrete realities that fall within its "grasp." The intellect understands when it has succeeded in fitting the unknown into a framework of familiar ideas. But every ideological framework is a limited structure, and therefore everything understandable is of limited content and potentiality. The intellect contacts not reality in its concreteness, but always only an abstracted portion of it. Intellection yields no more than a point of view, but never the living wholeness itself which is inexhaustibly fertile and allows for an infinity of possible points of view. In the deepest sense, therefore, "Know thyself" cannot mean "Understand thyself" (this is the limitation of psychoanalysis and of every merely psychological approach to the self). "Understand thyself" could mean only "Grasp one or several of the infinitely many aspects of thyself."

The wish to understand is the wish to possess, but nothing that is living admits of being possessed. Possession is a relation to an abstraction; you cannot approach anything living with the idea of possessing its living quality. If you try to make its living concreteness your own by an act of possession, you will merely kill it. Living things become ours not by being grasped, but by being loved. It is in the union of the spirit that living things become ours even as they remain themselves.

Life must be given the freedom to grow. So a living truth can never be fixated in a formula, in a creed, in a catechism. It is not an objective phenomenon that can be preserved in a treasure chest and passed on to one's heirs. When it is locked up in a strongbox, it quickly dies, and what remains is only the stench of death. There are, of course, embalming techniques that will keep the corpse from utter decay for an indefinite period, but embalming has not the power to revivify. This is the recurring tragedy in the history of religions. Again and again the living word is born into the world. Again and again it is treated as an objective commodity that can be grasped and enshrined forever in the form of a ritual, a creed, or an organization. But living truth soon loses its life when it is thus confined, that is, the forms capture only an abstracted portion of the living whole, but the living essence of things eludes every form or formulation. Zen alone, among the world's religions, makes no claim to the *possession* of the truth, for only Zen has clearly realized that living truth cannot be possessed. Any religion that believes it "has" the truth must be dealing only in abstract or formal truth.

The intellect can yield an understanding of life, indeed, many possible understandings of life, but it cannot bring man into union with life and with himself. For intellect, by its very nature, separates the subject from the object, the knower from what he knows. What the intellect grasps it objectifies; its relation to things is always "standoffish." This is true even when man tries to understand himself intellectually—he must stand outside himself to look at himself. He who looks and that at which he looks are never the same, and thus the effort to understand oneself in this way means that one has merely perpetuated the inner division in one's being and that one is no closer to overcoming one's alienation from oneself. (That is why no one can ever achieve wholeness with himself through psychoanalysis alone or through any merely psychological technique. Every psychological approach deals only with the self as objectified, and not with man's integral being in which there is no split between the self that knows and the self that is known as an object.) It is not by understanding ourselves that we unite with ourselves, Zen would say, but only plunging into ourselves. This demands a movement that is the exact opposite of what is required by an act of understanding.

For Zen, life itself is not something to be contemplated and understood objectively. To understand is to stand aside. The objective stance is motivated by the desire to dominate and to reduce to manageable proportions the object of knowledge. Understanding, unlike love, is a one-way relationship, an act of conquest in which I maintain my own being intact and remain the captain of all I survey. One gains the whole world by thus objectifying it, but one loses the soul of things, and what profit is there in it? It is what Mephistopheles offered Faust, what Satan constantly dangles before the eyes of all men: power at the expense of reality. To be related to the world objectively is to be related to it abstractly, and one's life is then increasingly pervaded by unreality. Is not this the ultimate reason for the vacuous quality characterizing so much of modern life? Technological society is the product of a purely abstract relation to life. Its "triumphs" are the work of intellect bent on conquest, and it is no wonder that the products of technology are in the end so deeply unsatisfying.

Life becomes real not as an exclusively intellectual product, but when it is created by wholeness responding to wholeness. The integral union with life cannot result from the fragmented, exteriorized, and abstract effort to dominate life either by physical or intellectual conquest. Reality is encountered not in the act of understanding but only in the act of giving oneself, that is of dying to one's position of exteriority to life. He who seeks to save his life of exteriority shall lose it and fall into unreality.

So far as Zen is none other than the life of truth itself, one cannot really be informed about Zen, one can only be transformed by Zen. He who seeks to be informed about Zen still thinks of Zen as an objective content which can be grasped from the outside. He who understands Zen no longer has Zen itself, but only some formula or formulation. Every such formula will enable him to answer certain questions about Zen, as a menu answers certain questions about the forthcoming dinner. But sooner or later there will come questions that are not answerable on the basis of the formula. Sooner or later whoever tries to live on the basis of his "understanding" of Zen or on the basis of any "understanding" of life will find himself colliding with reality. Reality is not a formula, and one must turn from the menu to the turkey if one would know its taste.

Most Westerners are long habituated to regarding the various religions abstractly in the fashion of a voter contemplating competing party platforms: the platforms are there in advance of the voter's decision. Each party is defined by the stand it professes to take in relation to certain principles and to concrete issues, and the voter has only to decide which party shall get his vote. Similarly, the religions of the world are commonly thought of as so many competing platforms of doctrines and precepts. The religious seeker has only to weigh their respective claims to truth and to affiliate himself with whichever one he concludes "has the truth." But Zen is not one of several possible truths which the mind may contemplate.

If one were to ask a Zen master whether Zen is true, the reply might come in the form of a question put to the questioner: Are you true? The reality of Zen and one's own reality cannot be separated. In the area of abstract or formal or objective truths, the being of the knower does not affect the truth of what is known. But where living truth is concerned, the relation of the knower to the truth is not an external one: the relation of the individual to the truth is itself part of the truth. The wish to know the truth without oneself entering into the truth is a wish that cannot be satisfied as far as the truth of Zen is concerned. Hence one cannot stand outside the living truth and inspect it. Absolute reality will not sit for its photograph.

The truth of Zen is nothing one can cling to or believe in. It is not possible to be *for* a living truth; one can only be *in* it. Partisanship is of the mind, which is always *outside* whatever it may be *for* or *against*. Where a religion stands for certain truths, it *ipso facto* stands outside them and it is defining itself in relation to abstractions. Zen would say that so long as you know what you stand for, you don't really stand for it, it is not yet truly yours, which means that your stance is to some degree a posturing. When you have really grasped the point there is no point to grasp. Absolute knowledge has nothing to know. Absolute faith has no object. A religion that calls for faith in something definite is not in touch with the Living God.

A truth that is definite is a truth that can be defined. Such a truth has a *finis*. But life itself being forever a matter of unfinished business, the truth that lives must be a truth that is unbounded, without a *finis*, in-finite rather than de-finite. Zen is not a doctrine, nor a set of ideas nor a position. It is not subsumable under any sort of "ism." It cannot be classified as either theism, atheism, or agnosticism. It is affiliated with no particular school of philosophy; it is no closer to idealism than to materialism. It has no view about the nature of reality; it formulates no system of ethics, propounds no political ideology.

The living substance of Zen is not any kind of canned goods attractively arrayed in a shopwindow in order to tempt the purchaser. Whatever it may put forth is not intended as a presentation of the objective content of Zen, and it is ultimately wrong to appeal to the words of any Zen master or any Zen text to corroborate one's understanding of Zen. Zen will be found not in the words themselves, but only in penetrating to the living source from which come these words and from which an infinity of other wordings could come. Otherwise, one has again only the outer form and not the inner reality itself. Zen, in short, is wholly of the spirit, and it does not admit of an objective transmission. It can be appropriated only creatively, and we shall have understood the Zen master's words only when we have entered into them in the way in which Beethoven's "Diabelli Variations" have "understood" the theme which he took from Diabelli.

The creative relation to life is the opposite of the abstract and external relation, for creativity is present only when the grasper and the grasped are one, when the creator has entered into his creation, where he has been molded even as he molds. It is the uncreative transaction which is merely manipulative and technical and where the being of the manipulator remains outside the process and unaffected by it. To say that Zen admits only of a creative appropriation is to say that it becomes available to us only as we give ourselves to it. There is no window-shopping possible in the realm of the spirit, and we cannot first look at Zen to see whether we should like to buy it. The substance of Zen does not exist apart from the creative act which appropriates it.

Zen is thus the only religion that demands creativity rather than conformity from its adherents, and which uncompromisingly rejects anything which they have begged or borrowed from a source other than themselves. Conformity can only be formal posturing; it can never be wholehearted assent. Zen urges man on to find what is truly his, for in that alone does he possess something which neither principalities nor powers nor Buddha nor God can remove from him. In his true Self alone does man attain an absolute grounding in life, and standing there he may embrace all life without fear.

The experience of most persons with religion could hardly have occasioned the suspicion that religion and creative living have anything whatsoever in common. Religion has most often served as a paradigm of the uncreative life, for in the overwhelming majority of its manifestations it has not encouraged individuality, freedom, and self-expression, but rather the opposites of these, namely, submission to authority, conformity to a law or a creed, the denying of self. The major religions of mankind, as they are understood and practiced, could hardly be described as calls to creativity.

If one thinks of religion as an attempt to conquer the hazards of finitude by cleaving to a truth or a reality beyond oneself, then the intent of Zen as a religion must remain unfathomable. One cannot be a Zen Buddhist in the way in which one may be a Christian or a Moslem. For there is no formal content which Zen holds up as embodying the ultimate truth about life and to which it asks the disciple to conform. Zen seeks reality, and reality is gained not in con-*form*-ity—which can only yield a correct *form*—but in creativity which goes beyond *form*-ality to reality. Zen has only one thing to say finally, and that is "To thine own self be true; thou canst not then be false to any man." Or "Be true to any man, thou canst not then be false to thine own self." Or "Be true to anything, thou canst not then be false to anything else." In short, "Be true," that is, "Be the living truth itself." "Be real, be reality itself." Or in the shortest possible terms, Zen would only say, "Be."

All of the procedures of Zen have the aim not of aligning man with a truth which transcends him but in awakening him to the living truth which is the Kingdom of Heaven within him. The life

of authenticity, the life of integrity, the life of holiness or wholeness, the life of truth, the life of reality, the creative life, the life
of freedom—all these are for Zen equivalent expressions designating
the same sort of life, which is, namely, the life emanating from and
endorsed by the totality of one's being which is not separate from
the totality of what is. This, for Zen, is the essentially religious life,
and its alternative is the partial life, the fragmented life, the life of
posturing and insincerity, the life that stands aside and will not
unite with things, the life that is uncreative and therefore un-holy
because it is un-*whole*-some.

Where Zen takes on the lineaments of a formal religion, it is yet
to be differentiated from other formal religions in this, that it gives
no sacramental significance to its pedagogical forms. Instead, it
constantly urges the disciple to penetrate its forms and to encounter the living reality. It exhorts him to discover who he really
is and so attain to the fullest and freest expression of himself. Its
goal is not the subordination of individuality in a common pattern
of formal belief. Other religions may proclaim the priesthood of all
believers, but Zen goes infinitely further in requiring of each that
he discover his own Buddhahood, that is, absolute reality. Other
faiths may confirm their devotees; Zen alone wishes to graduate
them. In the end, it is the only religion that has heeded Jehovah's
injunction to Pharaoh to "Let my people go," and it has dared to
remind Jehovah Himself that He must not claim exemption from
His own injunction.[1]

Whatever one may deem to be the historical relations between
Zen and that noble Indian who is the reputed founder of Buddhism,
it must be apparent that Zen cannot contemplate creating followers
of the Buddha. A follower is by definition an imitator, an epigone,
a conformist, in short, an uncreative spirit who is trying to hitch
a ride on the vehicle of another. For the Zen Buddhist, the religious

---

[1] If it be countered that as God is perfect, His omniscience must encom-
pass a knowledge of my individuality, and hence it is perfectly proper for
Him to legislate for me and for all His creatures, then Zen would reply that
God's knowledge must be less than perfect so far as it grasps me from a
position outside myself. If individuality is a reality and not just an appearance,
then the Divine Perfection must include my individuality, and not just
abstractly as an idea, but concretely. No word of God can express the full
truth of my individuality unless God is not other than my own true Self.
Otherwise His relation to me will be in some measure Procrustean, and His
decrees can never perfectly fit the measurements of my individuality.

life can never be simply an imitation of the Buddha. Truth of
being is inimitable. Whoever would copy its external forms, forgetting the individuality in which it is invariably rooted, finds himself forcing life to fit an abstraction. The Zen Buddhist is a follower
of the Buddha only in the respect that, like the Buddha, he is following no one, but only searching with might and main for the truth of
his being. The Buddha was a religious pioneer, not a Buddhist, and
so must all be pioneers who wish to live in the truth. Borrowed
plumage, Zen says, does not grow. If we would soar, we shall have
to sprout wings from our own living substance.

But if Zen is opposed to mere conformity, it is equally hostile to
mere nonconformity. The life of truth is to be gained neither
through conformity nor through nonconformity. Both alike imply a
divorce between man and that which he conforms to or rebels
against. Reality is attained in creativity, which is as removed from
nonconformity as it is from conformity since it emerges out of the
union of man and his object. When this is understood, it is evident
how far they are from grasping the intent of Zen who see it as a
call to anti-nomianism, or who imagine that the state of enlightenment is manifested only in those who are as different from the
ordinary as possible. Spiritual freedom is no closer to impulsive
spontaneity than it is to stale conformity. The assertion of the ego
is as unreal as its denial. Zen is beyond all these dualisms, and
nowhere does it recommend the expression of self in complete
indifference to the needs of others.

The truth that Zen seeks is not one thing as opposed to another,
for such a truth could never restore man to wholeness. Zen does
not take sides, for it does not want anything that is merely a side
of life or of the living truth. Whenever Zen seems to assert or deny
it is doing so merely provisionally or pedagogically. If it finds you
attached to A, Zen will assert not-A, not because it wishes to uphold the exclusive truth of not-A, but only to break your attachment to A. If you go on to cling to not-A, you completely miss the
point, and you will find that Zen is now once again asserting A.

So if Zen appears to oppose conformity in religion and in life, it
is not for the sake of asserting that there is a greater truth in being
a nonconformist. To be, to be the living truth is not to have one's
reality defined by something external. The conformist defines himself in relation to what he is for, the nonconformist in relation to
what he is against; both are but appendages to the abstractions
which they are for or against. Moreover, the conformist is aware of

his conformity against the background of actual or possible nonconformity; the nonconformist is aware of himself as against the
background of possible or actual conformity. So each defines himself in relation to his opposite, and thus each needs the other, if
only as a possibility, in order to grasp himself. But this means that
each is alienated from his true Self.

Every position is matched by an opposition, for positions are
only sides, and wherever there is a side, there is an opposite side.
Zen is not a position, nor is it a mere defiance of all positions. This
is the meaning of the advice that Zen gives that we are not to remain where there is a Buddha and we are to depart from the place
where there is no Buddha. Where there is a Buddha, living truth
has jelled into an objective form. Where there is no Buddha you
have sheer iconoclasm and nothing positive. Zen is beyond affirmation and denial. It is beyond the wisdom of security and the wisdom of insecurity. Creativity cannot be locked up in a formula,
neither is it synonymous with sheer impulsiveness.

Life calls for form, discipline, meaning, structure, universality,
but where these are overdone ossification sets in and death finally
ensues. Life needs naturalness, freedom, individuality, but where
these are absolutized, and there is nothing to balance these purely
centrifugal tendencies, the energies of life quickly dissipate. The
mystery of the creative act—which is the religious act—is that it
does not slight either of life's opposing requirements. In creativity
both form and matter, discipline and freedom, abstract universality and concrete particularity, meaning and embodiment are
perfectly fused—or, Zen would say, in a state of non-separation to
begin with. A want of creativity is manifested either by the formal
elements suppressing the matter and the individuality, or by a
chaotic bursting through of all forms in meaningless self-assertion.
The first peril attends all those who would absolutize the virtues
of classicism, the second, those who worship at the altar of
romanticism. Zen avoids both equally and urges us on to the
creative center from which both are falsely abstracted.

Creativity is neither classicist nor romanticist, and the creative
life, whether in the arts or elsewhere, is neither a stale adherence
to fixed patterns nor the apotheosis of individuality in defiance of
all constraining forms. The freedom which is defined only in relation to myself will be as unreal as the suppression of myself in the
name of something beyond myself. To conform to a form and to oppose a form are equally easy ways of evading life's call to creativity,

and, therefore, ultimately equally unsatisfying. Zen—which is the art of living creatively—calls for a transcendance of the dichotomy between self and not-self and thus of conformity and noncomformity. This dualism exists so long as man is alienated from life and from himself; it disappears when he enters into union with life and finds his Self.

The creative relation to the Buddha is neither a following nor a disobedience of the Buddha but a union with the spirit or the reality of the Buddha Nature. It is only in this way that one can avoid the twin evils of suppressing and of expressing individuality. It is only in this way that one comes to a basis on which one can be true to oneself and yet not be false to any man. This absolute basis is the true Self, and unless we possess it we had better not try to be true to ourselves. To be true to the momentary, relativistically conditioned, whimsical self is not Zen, for it is to separate from life, which is a movement opposite to what Zen requires. He who thinks that Zen is an invitation to anarchy is only trapped by another form—he is making a form of formlessness. To blind oneself to the long-range and common needs of man is to forget that my Self is not only my self but also my other, and it is to the Self that Zen bids us to be true.

Understanding this, we shall then know how to deal with the query: Does Zen have any moral principles? One may as well ask: Does Shakespeare have any literary principles? Does Bach have any musical principles? The answer is No—if the questions imply that one can produce real music, real literature, or real goodness by merely patterning one's production on any definable set of antecedent principles. The answer is Yes —if the questions imply that real music, real literature, or real goodness can be engendered by sheer impulsiveness. Creative reality is not less but more than anything that can be specified by principle, and Zen, therefore, comes not to destroy the Law but to fulfill it. Except the righteousness of the Zen seeker exceed that of the followers of principles and the breakers of principles, he can in no wise enter the Kingdom of Heaven. The Kingdom of Heaven is for creative spirits alone. Real goodness is creative goodness as real music is creative music.

For Zen, since the living truth is never to be found at either pole of any duality, there must be not one, but two equal and opposite ways of being immoral—that is untrue to life. One way is to try to subsume the infinite content of life under principles; the other

way is to do whatever you will whenever you will it. If the latter
sin against life is the one committed by the followers of Satan,
then is not the former the one to which the followers of the
Heavenly Father are prone? There is only one way to be moral and
that is to have transcended the dualism of rules and no rules and
to do the right thing at the right time in the right way, and this
calls for an act of creation in the living context. It is neither something that can be antecedently specified nor is it something to be
extemporized out of sheer spontaneity. Creative morality, that is
Zen, is beyond rules and no rules, and one comes to it only when
one finally gives up trying to cope with life from the outside. The
enlightened man who has entered into union with life resolves the
dualism of conformity vs. antinomianism, and only he can say
with Confucius: "I can do whatever my heart desires without con-
travening principles."

Life itself becomes an art only when we unite with it, as all
creativity emerges from the union of the artist and his task. So long
as man remains on the outside and attempts to grasp the truth
with his mind, he can only endlessly proliferate theories and points
of view which will never contain the living truth which he needs
to become whole. The truth that sets man free is not a "position,"
for all positions are finally "poses" which can never muster the
endorsement of man's entire being and which always remain external to the reality which they would grasp. Zen points to man's
being itself which is beyond every *this* or *that*, and it is just this
no-thing in every man that makes him feel insincere when he pretends that he is wholly identifiable as *this* or *that*.

The man who remains on the outside of life, content to in*spect*
it as a *spectator*, arrives at truths which are only *speculative* and
not living, and they will always be opposed by other points of view.
If he desires to get beyond points of view to the concrete reality of
life itself, he will have to relinquish his post as spectator and enter
into union with life. This is what Zen bids him to do. For Reality is
chaste and will not bare herself to strangers; she will give herself
only to him who is united with her in holy matrimony. This is
mysticism, to be sure; it is the wish of the mystic to overcome his
exteriority to life and to join in the life of things. Mysticism is the
art of living in union with life, and the living truth must be mystical truth. *Satori* is the mystical marriage with life.

So the Zen seeker after spiritual freedom is not on the lookout
for a true position, Zen is not a point of view, and the living truth

cannot be located in any position. Only the dead are fixed in position, and to take a position is to surrender the privileges and perils of the living for the secure fixity of the dead. Zen seeks simply the creative union with life, and in relation to this goal, every dogma, every creedal formulation, every ideology, every philosophical system represent a kind of heresy. For heresy is literally the choosing of a position, the taking of a side, i.e., the wish to reduce a living wholeness to one of its formulatable aspects. A life based on a point of view is a life immobilized around a partiality and thus bound to collide with other lives circumscribed by different partialities. The mark of every heresy is that it is opposed by other heresies, and this means that no heresy, that is no position as such, can be absolute. That alone is absolute which is confirmed in everything and by everything and which encounters no opposition anywhere, and this living truth is no point of view, but rather that from which all points of view are derivative and whose place they would usurp.

In his traditional religions, Western man has endeavored to achieve absolute anchorage in life through believing a certain set of ideas about himself, about his universe, and about that which is supposed to be the source of both. Since every set of ideas is limited and also fixed, sooner or later it proves to be incommensurate with the infinite content of life.

As the discrepancy between idea and actual experience begins to become manifest, two alternatives are open to the would-be believer: he may persist in clinging to the idea with unreasoning fanaticism, or he may begin to modify the idea. In the former event, he must deny life and experience in order to affirm the absolute truth of his idea; in the latter case, he is faithful to life and experience, but at the cost of surrendering his previous claim to an absolutely true idea, and then the religion which is based on this idea becomes ever less capable of providing the believer with strength and security.

In the warfare of science and religion, fundamentalist orthodoxy has chosen the first of these alternatives; the various forms of liberal theology have taken the second. Neither is able to meet the spiritual needs of modern man with integrity, for each possesses something that the other lacks. Only that religion can integrally satisfy the needs of modern man which gives to life an absolute underpinning, on the one hand, but which allows for the endless change, which is also of the essence of life, on the other hand. No religion committed to an idea, no religion comprising a definable teaching, no religion dedicated to a formulatable creed or code is in a position to do this. No formulation can be absolutely universal, for all formulations are conditioned by various relativities, and all formulations must periodically submit to revision in the light of man's growing experience. Life is forever a matter of unfinished business, and the living truth will not be covered by any formula. Zen claims absolute catholicity just because it is not entangled with concepts or formulae of any sort. Zen makes no historical claims nor is it rooted to any spot on the earth's surface. Its meaning is not confined to any particular set of categories or restricted by any limited perspectives. It may thus justifiably claim to be absolutely universal and to speak to all men everywhere who are concerned with achieving an ultimate grounding in life.

For a thousand years the West tried to center every department of life around the idea of God and to regulate every activity of life by principles derived from theology. But with the Renaissance came the revolt—in the name of individuality and self-expression—against the religious totalitarianism which would harness all of a life to a single idea. In ethics as in art, in education and in economics, in politics, in law, in literature and in music and philosophy, modern life is the rebellion of individuality against imposed form.

And yet no one can claim that modern man is altogether happy in his freedom and individuality, for these have been acquired by the negation of form and meaning, and thus it is no wonder that the feeling of life's meaninglessness is such a widespread symptom of our times. The freedom that modern man has achieved by his rebellion is not real or spiritual freedom; it is ultimately unsatisfying because it excludes its opposite, which means that it is only a half-truth or half-reality. Modern life is therefore as deficient as medieval life. In the Middle Ages, freedom and individuality were subordinated to ultimate meaning; in modern times, man possesses freedom, but life has lost its ultimate meaning. Each epoch has endeavored unsuccessfully to absolutize what is only half of man's total need. Human life requires both absolute freedom and absolute meaning in order to be fully real, and as long as man's integral need is denied, he will continue to vacillate from one pole to the other, absolutizing each half-truth in alternation.

No supernaturalistic religion can fulfill man's integral need, for every such religion is partisan and therefore partial by definition.

It does not accord metaphysical parity to the opposite poles of human life, but ever seeks reality and truth in the subordination of one pole to the other. Wherever God is thought of as confronting man, man's freedom is limited by God's will and law. Theistic religion pretends that life's need for absolute freedom can be denied, and that a life of truth can be achieved through conformity to the transcendent will of God. But, in fact, when man tries to subordinate himself to God, he always finds there is a Devil in his own breast who urges him to deny God and express himself. The Devil is God's polar counterpart and the champion of life's urge to freedom. The Devil is a half-reality, as God is, and each must be given his due. Where Thy will is other than my will, I shall never be able wholeheartedly to say "Thy will be done." It is not in His will that we shall find our peace, but only in that which is neither His nor ours but which simply *is*.

Neither the City of God nor the City of Satan is the true homeland of the human spirit, seeing that man can never sojourn for very long in either domain without feeling the call to visit the other. Neither in nature nor in supernature, neither in the finite nor in the infinite, neither in time nor in eternity, neither in the material nor in the ideal does life find its absolute grounding. The living truth will not be domiciled at one pole alone of any of these pairs of opposites. When Creator is set over against creature, when Heaven is elevated over earth, the ultimate meaning of life above its immediate content, then life becomes chained to an abstraction.

For Zen, holiness is synonymous with wholeness, and therefore Zen would negate neither life's need for absolute meaning (God) nor life's equally valid need for absolute freedom (Satan). Nor in the case of any of the pairs of opposites between which human life fluctuates would Zen wish to align itself with one side more than with the other. The intellect will never find any way of bridging these dualisms; to logic, A and not-A remain irreconcilably opposed. Hence the intellect can never solve man's ultimate existential problem—which is how to become real—that is, whole. So Zen directs man beyond the intellect to the living truth of his own Self in which these opposites have never been separated out.

Thus the existential resolution of the dualism of freedom and form is concretely exemplified in the lives of those who have achieved a deep enlightenment. It is the conspicuous absence of any kind of one-sidedness which gives to the Zen personality its elemental reality and which makes it at once attractive and unique.

In the main, Western man has been alternately drawn toward two opposite ideals of life—the one, characterized by Rabelaisian gusto and vitality and freedom from all inhibitions, lives by the motto "Do what you will"; the other, the life of the "saint," is characterized by inner strength and a yoking of all natural energies to the transcendent will of God. The fascination exerted by the enlightened Zen personality is just that it encompasses both these divergent modes of life. The true man, according to Zen, has both zestful freedom and inner substance, both strength and discipline on the one hand, and naturalness and spontaneity on the other hand. Such integrity can never result from forcing myself to do the will of God, nor can it come from merely following my own whims. It comes only when I am living out of my true Self, which is beyond all such dualisms. Then alone shall I know the service that is perfect freedom, and experience a life that is unconditionally meaningful and yet free of all constraint.

The life of the unenlightened can never be wholehearted, for it is perpetually fissured, or, as the Buddhist would say, based on the discrimination of opposites. Always he faces a choice of this or that, unable to have both and yet bound to learn sooner or later that each is incomplete without the other. His reason opposes his passions; his "higher" nature is at war with his "lower" nature; the "law in the members" conflicts with the "law of the mind." He would live for himself and also for others, yet he can find no way to do both. His desires conflict with his duties; wishing to serve God he is perennially tempted by the Devil. He would live for an ideal and yet he succumbs to the material. He pledges allegiance to Heaven, but cannot withstand the lure of earth and its pleasures. Whether he tries to be reflective or spontaneous, his actions are equally removed from authenticity. His life is a perpetual vacillation between opposite poles, and his very voice lacks the ring of reality, for it is prompted by no more than a part of himself at any time, and never has the backing of his entire being.

No ultimate peace can come to one who is thus fissured. Peace is but another name for the integrity of being which enables man to respond to life without inner conflict. A mind which is in pieces cannot be a mind at peace. Every dualistic recipe for achieving the peace that passeth understanding is predestined to failure, for it entails the futile attempt of one side of man to coerce the opposite side into a renunciation of its own needs. Man's real Self, Zen would say, is not to be sought in any dimension of himself, but only in

that from which every dimension—whether "higher" or "lower"—
is an abstraction. Man's real Self can only be his whole Self, and
that must not be identified with any of the warring factions which
he contains. Until he finds that living center of unity which is his
integral being, he will know neither peace nor sincerity.

The religions of the West are all dualistic, which means that they
accept these oppositions as ultimate and always seek for truth in
one direction as contrasted with its opposite. So Western religion
elevates reason over the passions, super-nature over nature, the
ideal over the material. It has made heaven more real than earth,
and has put God over all His creatures. But life itself will not for
very long submit to such Procrustean treatment, and the de-
valuated fragments periodically reassert themselves. So Western
religion has never been free of the struggle with materialism, secu-
larism, individualism, and the loyalty of the Western devotee has
always been divided.

Integrity is wholeness, not halfness. Holiness is holistic living,
not self-conquest. Spiritual freedom is unopposed response, not
self-control or self-restraint. Wholeheartedness can never even-
tuate from the resolution to slight what is metaphysically half of
reality. A mature religion must concede that both the "higher" and
the "lower," both the transcendent and the immediate, are equally
real, or rather equally unreal and abstract. A mature religion will
courageously confront the profound mystery embodied in the
split itself characteristic of human life, and will not seek salvation
through any of the fragments resulting from the split. For Zen
Buddhism, the split is the consequence of standing apart from life
and inspecting it objectively. The split is healed only through the
re-entry into life which contacts life's wholeness.

Philosophers, who are content with mere "points of view," may
label themselves as idealists or as materialists, as supernaturalists
or as naturalists. Zen seeks for an absolute which is a living whole
embracing all the pairs of opposites. So Zen sees the religious life
not as an opting for transcendent meaning in contrast to immediate
delights, but rather as the utterly concrete life which is not entangled in this insoluble dualism. "Deny thyself" must not mean
merely "Deny thy lower self," but also "Deny thy higher self"; not
merely "Deny thy impulsive or passionate self," but also "Deny
thy controlling will or rational self." In short, Zen would advise us
to deny all those fragments of Self which, whether they be called

"higher" or "lower," are only usurpers pretending to a throne which is not theirs.

Rather than becoming a party to the strife of systems, religion's true role is to heal the schism in man's soul by guiding him to that union with life which is beyond the dualities. The ultimate wisdom of Asia, brought to a focus in Zen Buddhism, is the perception that truth and reality must never be sought on the plane of opposition. What is absolute will not be found in one limited perspective as against another. Where there is opposition there is of necessity reciprocal limitation, and it is futile to seek Divinity in that which is no more real than its opposite. The apotheosis of transcendence, which has been the path mistakenly chosen by most of man's religions, is, in point of fact, an idolatrous substitute for authentic religion. For is it not the essence of idolatry to accord to what is less than the whole that devotion which is only to be rendered to the whole? As the ultimate psychotherapy, Zen steers man away from the idolatry inherent in every form of partisanship and directs his course to the living truth which is truly all in all and not just an aspect of life erroneously absolutized. The center of the circle is the focus of unity for all the radii; stand at the center and you comprehend all the radii together; move ever so slightly off center, and at once you must choose whether to stand on this radius or on that one. It is just man's off-centeredness which is his ultimate problem, and this is the problem which Zen takes up and solves.

Only he who lives from his whole Self can be called truly religious, and what characterizes the life of the enlightened soul is just that it has achieved creative wholeness. Such a life is graced with absolute freedom, for its movements are authored and authorized by the whole being and are in the deepest sense unopposed. Such a one will be conspicuously distinguishable from the individual whose religion is still enmeshed in duality and whose life is consequently marked by tenseness and incessant struggle as he strives in vain to subdue one half of himself to the other half. The Zen life is the life of wholeness responding to wholeness, or in other words, the life of absolute love, of unconditional union with all that is. To many Westerners it seems irresistibly real for this reason.

That the Occident has come to an awareness of the enormous spiritual heritage which is Zen Buddhism is almost entirely due to the labors of a single Japanese scholar. Dr. Daisetz Teitaro Suzuki

has striven for nearly seven decades to interpret the spirit of Far
Eastern religious thought to Westerners, and there is nothing to
indicate that without Suzuki's work anything like the present
world-wide interest in Zen would have yet developed. Prior to the
First World War the very name of Zen was hardly familiar to anyone outside Japan, and even in standard works on comparative
religion and on the history of Buddhism, Zen was either passed
over without mention or with at most a cursory reference. Suzuki's
writings during the twenties and the thirties laid the basis for the
amazing upsurge of interest in Zen which has occurred since the
end of the last war.

It was the Abbot Shaku Soyen of Engaku Monastery in Kamakura who was the first Zen personage to make his way to the West.
In 1893, Shaku Soyen, along with other notable representatives of
the world's faiths, participated in the World Parliament of Religions in Chicago. The Abbot was a substantial Zen figure, but
as he was unable to speak in English, his role at the Parliament
was overshadowed by the performance of Swami Vivekananda,
whose eloquence and dramatic personality made the greatest impression on the assemblage. However, one unenvisaged outcome
of Shaku Soyen's voyage was his meeting with Paul Carus, the
head of the Open Court Publishing Company, whom he interested
in Buddhism and with whom he continued to correspond after his
return to Japan. When Carus decided to publish a translation of
the *Tao Teh Ching*, he asked Shaku Soyen to send someone to help
with the translation. As a result, Daisetz Suzuki, a twenty-seven-
year-old disciple of the Abbot, was despatched to La Salle, Illinois.

The youngest of five children, Daisetz Suzuki was born on October 18, 1870. His father, a physician stemming from a line of physicians extending back for five or six generations, was also a Confucian
scholar and a minor writer who had published a short history of
Europe. Even as a child, the boy was impressed by his father's
writings and thought it would be a fine thing were he to become a
writer himself. The father's death, which occurred when Suzuki
was six, left the family in difficult financial circumstances. His
youth was passed in poverty, and though he managed to continue
in school up through the first year of higher middle school, he
finally was forced to drop out by virtue of his inability to pay the
slight tuition fee. For a year and a half thereafter he served as a
high-school teacher in a fishing village and taught English and other
subjects. Eventually, through the help of an elder brother who had

already got established, he was enabled to resume his education, and in 1891 he entered Waseda University and after six months transferred to Tokyo Imperial University.

His interest in Zen had been born a couple of years earlier in discussions with some of his high-school classmates.[2] These in turn had been influenced by one of their teachers who had studied Zen at Engaku Monastery. After Suzuki entered Tokyo University, he himself began to visit Engaku Monastery in nearby Kamakura and to study Zen under its Abbot, Imagita Kosen. The latter died after a year and was succeeded by Shaku Soyen, whose disciple Suzuki then became and with whom he continued to study until 1897 when he himself went to America to work for Paul Carus. During this period his first two published works appeared. The first, which came out in 1894, was a translation of *The Gospel of Buddha* which Paul Carus had compiled and a copy of which he had sent to Shaku Soyen. The second, completed two years later, was entitled *A New Interpretation of Religion* and was stimulated by a pamphlet which Shaku Soyen had brought back from the World Parliament of Religions and which contained a statement of what Buddhists were purported to believe.

Suzuki remained in the West for more than a decade, living mainly in La Salle and working as a translator, copy editor, and writer for the Open Court Publishing Company. During these years, he contributed articles and reviews to the *Monist*, translated the *Tao Teh Ching* as well as *Sermons of a Buddhist Abbot* and Aśvaghosha's *Discourse on the Awakening of Faith in the Mahayana*, and wrote his *Brief History of Early Chinese Philosophy* and his *Outlines of Mahayana Buddhism*. When Shaku Soyen returned to the United States in 1905 to work with a small group in San Francisco, Suzuki was invited there to serve as his interpreter. By a fortunate coincidence they finished their work and left San Francisco only a week before the earthquake. The two toured the eastern part of the United States, and after a meeting with President Theodore Roosevelt, went on to Europe for a short stay. While in England, Suzuki completed a translation into Japanese of Swedenborg's *Heaven and Hell* for the Swedenborg Society.

After his return to Japan in 1909, he became a professor of

[2] One of these was Kitaro Nishida, who remained Suzuki's lifelong friend and who eventually became Japan's greatest philosopher.

English at Peer's University in Tokyo and also at Tokyo Imperial University. He was married in 1911 to Beatrice Lane, an American woman, and for most of the following decade he lived in a house situated in the compound of Engaku Monastery where he continued his study of Zen with Shaku Soyen until the latter's death in 1919.

Suzuki's career as an interpreter of Zen Buddhism to the West did not really get under way until after he had passed the age of fifty. Though he had written an article on Zen for the Pali Text Society as early as 1906, and a series of short articles on Zen for a publication of the British Embassy in Tokyo during the war, his major contributions were all made after 1921. In that year he moved to Kyoto to become professor of the philosophy of religion at Otani College, and the same year he founded *The Eastern Buddhist* wherein there appeared many of the articles which were the bases for later books. His first book in English on Zen was the *Essays in Zen Buddhism* (First Series) which was published in 1927. This was followed by *Studies in the Laṅkāvatāra Sūtra*, *Essays in Zen Buddhism* (Second Series), *Essays in Zen Buddhism* (Third Series), *The Training of the Zen Buddhist Monk, An Introduction to Zen Buddhism, Manual of Zen Buddhism, Zen Buddhism and Its Influence on Japanese Culture,* and by other shorter studies. By 1936, his mounting international reputation brought him an invitation to participate in the World Congress of Faiths held in England under the presidency of Sir Francis Younghusband, and while there he also lectured on Zen at the Universities of London, Durham and Edinburgh as well as at Cambridge and Oxford.

His wife died in 1939, and during the subsequent war years Suzuki lived quietly in Kamakura, somewhat suspected by the Japanese secret police because of his long sojourn in the West, his marriage to an American, and his lack of enthusiasm for the war effort. After the war, Rider and Company began for the Buddhist Society in England the publication of his complete works in English, and in 1949, at the age of 79, Suzuki left Japan once again for what was to be another extended stay in the West. He went first to Hawaii for the East-West Philosophers' Conference, and continued on at the University of Hawaii for a year. The next year he taught at Claremont College in California and then went on a tour of American universities sponsored by the Rockefeller Foundation. In 1951, he moved to New York and remained there until 1957 as a professor of religion at Columbia University.

Since 1958, Suzuki has lived in Japan. It was during the ninth decade of his life that he witnessed the astonishing diffusion of interest in Zen throughout the world. The field he had so long cultivated had yielded an amazing harvest. Now over ninety years of age, he is still vigorous, and intellectually active, working steadily and anxious to complete as many translations of classical Zen texts as he may be able to in his remaining years. His bibliography includes about 100 books in Japanese, some 30 in English, and innumerable articles, pamphlets and monographs. As of the present, and with all the interest in Zen, there has not yet appeared any other writer who—by virtue of his training and experience in Zen, his mastery of the texts, his command of the requisite oriental and occidental tongues, and his familiarity with the thought of both East and West—can qualify as an authoritative interpreter of Zen to the world outside Japan. Of most of the recent writings on Zen it can be said that at best they are but paraphrases of Suzuki, and at worst sheer extemporization or imaginative extrapolation based either on Suzuki or on a limited contact with Zen or with some other form of Buddhism.

This book is intended to provide a comprehensive one-volume introduction to Zen Buddhism. It includes a substantial sampling of Suzuki's better known works and also items from sources not likely to have come to the attention of the general reader. The selections have been arranged with the idea of presenting as connected a treatment of the subject as is possible.

Is it necessary to warn the reader once more that the best book about Zen is only a book *about* Zen, but is *not* Zen itself? In the end, the substance of Zen must not be sought through any writings, and the great danger of reading too much about Zen is that one may arrive at an "understanding" of Zen. But when Zen is understood, it is no longer Zen that one has but only a conceptual facsimile thereof. Still, the beginner who is not in direct contact with the living tradition of Zen must needs turn to the written word for at least preliminary guidance, and one can only ask that the word be a living word and that it shall have emerged from a deep and sustained experience with the real thing.

I am sincerely grateful to the Zen Studies Society for the research grant which has enabled me to spend this past year in Japan studying Zen and preparing this volume. During the year I have lived almost as a member of Dr. Suzuki's household, and I have had the benefit of access to his private library and of numerous conversations with him. For all this, for the gift of his friendship to me over the past decade, and above all, for having opened my eyes to Zen, I owe him a debt which I shall never be able to repay. I also owe a great deal to the kindness and help of Dr. Suzuki's talented and dedicated assistant, Miss Mihoko Okamura, who has proofread all the extracts and has gone over the transliteration of foreign names to make them follow a uniform pattern. Miss Okamura has also prepared the comprehensive list of names and terms in Japanese or Chinese with their respective equivalents which appears as an appendix to this volume.

Finally, I wish thankfully to acknowledge the permission to quote from Dr. Suzuki's writings which I have received from the following: The Bollingen Foundation, Inc., *The Japan Quarterly, Review of Religion,* Harper and Brothers, Rider and Company, Open Court Publishing Company, *Monumenta Nipponica,* Hōzōkan Press, Sanseido Press, the Eastern Buddhist Society, and Dr. Daisetz T. Suzuki.

BERNARD PHILLIPS

THE ESSENTIALS OF
ZEN BUDDHISM

PART I

The General Sense of Zen

A special transmission outside the
    Scripture;
No dependence on words or letters;
Direct pointing at the Mind of man;
Seeing into one's Nature and the
    attainment of Buddhahood.

The Four Statements

1. *PRELIMINARY*[1]

BUDDHISM in its course of development has completed a form which distinguishes itself from its so-called primitive or original type—so greatly, indeed, that we are justified in emphasizing its historical division into two schools, Hinayana and Mahayana, or the Lesser Vehicle and the Greater Vehicle of salvation. As a matter of fact, the Mahayana, with all its varied formulae, is no more than a developed form of Buddhism and traces back its final authority to its Indian founder, the great Buddha Śākyamuni. When this developed form of the Mahayana was introduced into China and then into Japan, it achieved further development in these countries. This achievement was no doubt due to the Chinese and Japanese Buddhist leaders, who knew how to apply the principles of their faith to the ever-varying conditions of life and to the religious needs of the people. And this elaboration and adaptation on their part have still further widened the gap that had already been in existence between the Mahayana[2] and its

---

[1] *An Introduction to Zen Buddhism,* Rider & Co., 1949, pp. 31–37.

[2] To be accurate, the fundamental ideas of the Mahayana are expounded in the Prajñāpāramitā group of Buddhist literature, the earliest of which must have appeared at the latest within three hundred years of the Buddha's death. The germs are no doubt in the writings belonging to the so-called primitive Buddhism. Only their development, that is, a conscious grasp of them as most essential in the teachings of the founder, could not be effected without his followers actually living the teachings for some time through the variously changing conditions of life. Thus enriched in experience and matured in reflection, the Indian Buddhists came to have the Mahayana form of Buddhism as distinguished from its primitive or original form. In India, two Mahayana schools are known: the Mādhyamika of Nāgārjuna and the Vijñaptimātra or Yogācara of Asanga and Vasubandhu. In China more schools developed: the Tendai (T'ien-t'ai), the Kegon (Hua-yen), the Jōdo (Ching-t'u) the Zen (Ch'an), etc. In Japan we have besides these the Hokke, the Shingon, the Shin, the Ji, etc. All these schools or sects belong to the Mahayana wing of Buddhism.

3

more primitive type. At present the Mahayana form may be said not to display, superficially at least, those features most conspicuously characteristic of original Buddhism.

For this reason there are people who would declare that this branch of Buddhism is in reality no Buddhism in the sense that the latter is commonly understood. My contention, however, is this: anything that has life in it is an organism, and it is in the very nature of an organism that it never remains in the same state of existence. An acorn is quite different from a young oak with tender leaves just out of its protective shell, and even more so from a full-grown tree so stately and gigantic and towering up to the sky. But throughout these varying phases of change there is a continuation of growth and unmistakable marks of identity, whence we know that one and the same plant has passed through many stages of becoming. The so-called primitive Buddhism is the seed; out of it Far-Eastern Buddhism has come into existence with the promise of still further growth. Scholars may talk of historical Buddhism, but my subject here is to see Buddhism not only in its historical development but from the point of view of its still vitally concerning us as a quickening spiritual force in the Far East.

Among the many sects of Buddhism that have grown up especially in China and Japan, we find a unique order claiming to transmit the essence and spirit of Buddhism directly from its author, and this not through any secret document or by means of any mysterious rite. This order is one of the most significant in Buddhism, not only from the point of view of its historical importance and spiritual vitality, but from the point of view of its most original and stimulating manner of demonstration. The "Doctrine of the Buddha-heart (*buddhahṛidaya*)" is its scholastic name, but more commonly it is known as "Zen." That Zen is not the same as *dhyāna*, though the term Zen is derived from the Chinese transliteration (*ch'an-na; zenna* in Japanese) of the original Sanskrit, will be explained later on.

This school is unique in various ways in the history of religion. Its doctrines, theoretically stated, might seem to be those of speculative mysticism, but they are presented and demonstrated in such a manner that only those initiates who, after long training, have actually gained an insight into the system, can understand their ultimate signification. To those who have not acquired this penetrating knowledge, that is, to those who have not experienced Zen in their everyday active life, its teachings or rather its utter-

ances assume quite a peculiar, uncouth, and even enigmatical
aspect. Such people, looking at Zen more or less conceptually, consider Zen utterly absurd and ludicrous, or deliberately making
itself unintelligible in order to guard its apparent profundity
against outside criticism. But, according to the followers of Zen,
its apparently paradoxical statements are not artificialities contrived to hide themselves behind a screen of obscurity; they stem
simply from the fact that the human tongue is not an adequate
organ for expressing the deepest truths of Zen. The latter cannot
be made the subject of logical exposition; they are to be experienced in the inmost soul when they become for the first time intelligible. In point of fact, no plainer and more straightforward
expressions than those of Zen have ever been made by any other
branch of human experience. "Coal is black"—this is plain enough;
but Zen protests, "Coal is not black." This is also plain enough,
indeed, even plainer than the first positive statement when we
come right down to the truth of the matter.

Personal experience, therefore, is everything in Zen. No ideas are
intelligible to those who have no backing of experience. This is a
platitude. A baby has no ideas, for its mentality is not yet so
developed as to experience anything in the way of ideas. If it have
them at all, they must be something extremely obscure and blurred
and not in correspondence with realities. To get the clearest and
most efficient understanding of a thing, therefore, it must be
experienced personally. Especially when the thing is concerned
with life itself, personal experience is an absolute necessity. Without this experience, nothing relative to its profound working will
ever be accurately and therefore efficiently grasped. The foundation of all concepts is simple, unsophisticated experience. Zen
places the utmost emphasis upon this foundation-experience, and
it is around this that Zen constructs all the verbal and conceptual
scaffold which is found in its literature known as "Sayings" (*goroku,
yü-lu*). Though the scaffold affords a most useful means to reach
the inmost reality, it is still an elaboration and artificiality. We
lose its whole significance when it is taken for a final reality. The
nature of the human understanding compels us not to put too
much confidence in the superstructure. Mystification is far from
being the object of Zen itself, but to those who have not touched
the central fact of life Zen inevitably appears as mystifying. Penetrate through the conceptual superstructure and what is imagined

to be a mystification will at once disappear, and at the same time there will be an enlightenment known as *satori*.[3]

Zen, therefore, most strongly and persistently insists on an inner spiritual experience. It does not attach any intrinsic importance to the sacred sutras or to their exegeses by the wise and learned. Personal experience is strongly set against authority and objective revelation, and as the most practical method of attaining spiritual enlightenment, the followers of Zen propose the practice of *dhyāna*, known as *zazen*[4] in Japanese, of which Zen is the abbreviation.

A few words must be said here in regard to the systematic training by Zen of its followers in the attainment of the spiritual insight which has been referred to before as the foundation-experience of Zen. For this is where Zen pre-eminently distinguishes itself from other forms of mysticism. To most mystics such spiritual experience, so intensely personal, comes as something sporadic, isolated, and unexpected. Christians use prayer, or mortification, or contemplation so called, as the means of bringing this on themselves, and leave its fulfilment to divine grace. But as Buddhism does not recognize a supernatural agency in such matters, the Zen method of spiritual training is practical and systematic. From the beginning of its history in China, there has been such a tendency well marked; but, as time went on, a regular system has finally come into existence, and the Zen school at present has a thoroughgoing method for its followers to train themselves in the attainment of their object. Herein lies the practical merit of Zen. While it is highly speculative on the one hand, its methodical discipline on the other hand produces most fruitful and beneficial results on moral character. We sometimes forget its highly abstract character when it is expressed in connection with the facts of our everyday practical life; but here it is where we have to appreciate the real value of Zen, for Zen finds an inexpressibly deep thought even in holding up a finger, or in saying a "good morning" to a friend casually met on the street. In the eye of Zen the most practical is the most abstruse, and vice versa. All the system of discipline adopted by Zen is the outcome of this fundamental experience.

---

3 See below, Part III.

4 *Za* means "to sit," and *zazen* may be summarily taken as meaning "to sit in meditation." What it exactly signifies will be seen later in connection with the description of "The Meditation Hall" (*zendō; ch'an-t'ang*) in Part IV.

I said that Zen is mystical. This is inevitable, seeing that Zen is the keynote of Oriental culture; it is what makes the West frequently fail to fathom exactly the depths of the Oriental mind, for mysticism in its very nature defies the analysis of logic, and logic is the most characteristic feature of Western thought. The East is synthetic in its method of reasoning; it does not care so much for the elaboration of particulars as for a comprehensive grasp of the whole, and this intuitively. Therefore, the Eastern mind, if we assume its existence, is necessarily vague and indefinite, and seems not to have an index which at once reveals the contents to an outsider. The thing is there before our eyes, for it refuses to be ignored; but when we endeavor to grasp it in our own hands in order to examine it more closely or systematically, it eludes us and we lose its track. Zen is provokingly evasive. This is not due of course to any conscious or premeditated artifice with which the Eastern mind schemes to shun the scrutiny of others. The unfathomableness is in the very constitution, so to speak, of the Eastern mind. Therefore, to understand the East we must understand mysticism, that is, Zen.

It is to be remembered, however, that there are various types of mysticism, rational and irrational, speculative and occult, sensible and fantastic. When I say that the East is mystical, I do not mean that the East is fantastic, irrational, and altogether impossible to bring within the sphere of intellectual comprehension. What I mean is simply that in the working of the Eastern mind there is something calm, quiet, silent, undisturbable, which appears as if always looking into eternity. This quietude and silence, however, does not point to mere idleness or inactivity. The silence is not that of the desert shorn of all vegetation, nor is it that of a corpse forever gone to sleep and decay. It is the silence of an "eternal abyss" in which all contrasts and conditions are buried; it is the silence of God who, deeply absorbed in contemplation of His works past, present, and future, sits calmly on His throne of absolute oneness and allness. It is the "silence of thunder" obtained in the midst of the flash and uproar of opposing electric currents. This sort of silence pervades all things Oriental. Woe unto those who take it for decadence and death, for they will be overwhelmed by an overwhelming outburst of activity out of the eternal silence. It is in this sense that I speak of the mysticism of Oriental culture. And I can affirm that the cultivation of this kind of mysticism is principally due to the influence of Zen. If Bud-

dhism were to develop in the Far East so as to satisfy the spiritual
cravings of its people, it had to grow into Zen. The Indians are
mystical, but their mysticism is too speculative, too contemplative,
too complicated, and, moreover, it does not seem to have any real,
vital relation with the practical world of particulars in which we
are living. The Far-Eastern mysticism on the contrary is direct,
practical, and surprisingly simple. This could not develop into
anything else but Zen.

All the other Buddhist sects in China as well as in Japan bespeak
their Indian origin in an unmistakable manner. For their metaphysical complexity, their long-winded phraseology, their highly
abstract reasoning, their penetrating insight into the nature of
things, and their comprehensive interpretation of affairs relating to
life, are most obviously Indian and not at all Chinese or Japanese.
This will be recognized at once by all those who are acquainted
with Far-Eastern Buddhism. For instance, look at those extremely
complex rites as practised by the Shingon sect, and also at their
elaborate systems of "Mandala," by means of which they try to
explain the universe. No Chinese or Japanese mind would have
conceived such an intricate network of philosophy without being
first influenced by Indian thought. Then observe how highly
speculative is the philosophy of the Mādhyamika, the Tendai
(T'ien-t'ai), or Kegon (Hua-yen, Avatamsaka). Their abstraction
and logical acumen are truly amazing. These facts plainly show
that those sects of Far-Eastern Buddhism are at bottom foreign
importations.

But when we come to Zen after a survey of the general field of
Buddhism, we are compelled to acknowledge that its simplicity,
its directness, its pragmatic tendency, and its close connection
with everyday life stand in remarkable contrast to the other
Buddhist sects. Undoubtedly, the main ideas of Zen are derived
from Buddhism, and we cannot but consider it a legitimate development of the latter; but this development has been achieved
in order to meet the requirements peculiarly characteristic of the
psychology of the Far-Eastern people. The spirit of Buddhism has
left its highly metaphysical superstructure in order to become a
practical discipline of life. The result is Zen. Therefore, I make
bold to say that in Zen are found systematized or rather crystallized,
all the philosophy, religion, and life itself of the Far-Eastern people,
especially of the Japanese.

2. WHAT IS ZEN?[1]

BEFORE proceeding to expound the teaching of Zen at some length in the following pages, let me answer some of the questions which are frequently raised by critics concerning the real nature of Zen.

Is Zen a system of philosophy, highly intellectual and profoundly metaphysical, as most Buddhist teachings are?

It was stated in the Introduction that we find in Zen all the philosophy of the East crystallized, but this ought not to be taken as meaning that Zen is a philosophy in the ordinary application of the term. Zen is decidedly not a system founded upon logic and analysis. If anything, it is the antipode to logic by which I mean the dualistic mode of thinking. There may be an intellectual element in Zen, for Zen is the whole mind, and in it we find a great many things; but the mind is not a composite thing that is to be divided into so many faculties, leaving nothing behind when the dissection is over. Zen has nothing to teach us in the way of intellectual analysis; nor has it any set doctrines which are imposed on its followers for acceptance. In this respect, Zen is quite chaotic, if you choose to say so. Probably Zen followers may have sets of doctrines, but they have them on their own account, and for their own benefit; they do not owe the fact to Zen. Therefore, there are in Zen no sacred books or dogmatic tenets, nor are there any symbolic formulae through which an access might be gained into the signification of Zen. If I am asked, then, what Zen teaches, I would answer, Zen teaches nothing. Whatever teachings there are in Zen, they come out of one's own mind. We teach ourselves; Zen merely points the way. Unless this pointing is teaching, there is certainly nothing in Zen purposely set up as its cardinal doctrines or as its fundamental philosophy.

Zen claims to be Buddhism, but all the Buddhist teachings as propounded in the sutras and sastras are treated by Zen as mere waste paper whose utility consists in wiping off the dirt of intellect and nothing more. Do not imagine, however, that Zen is nihilism.

1 *An Introduction to Zen Buddhism*, pp. 38–47.

All nihilism is self-destructive, it ends nowhere. Negativism is sound as method, but the highest truth is an affirmation. When it is said that Zen has no philosophy, that it denies all doctrinal authority, that it casts aside all so-called sacred literature as rubbish, we must not forget that Zen is holding up in this very act of negation something quite positive and eternally affirmative. This will become clearer as we proceed.

Is Zen a religion? It is not a religion in the sense that the term is popularly understood; for Zen has no God to worship, no ceremonial rites to observe, no future abode to which the dead are destined, and, last of all, Zen has no soul whose welfare is to be looked after by somebody else and whose immortality is a matter of intense concern with some people. Zen is free from all these dogmatic and "religious" encumbrances.

When I say there is no God in Zen, the pious reader may be shocked, but this does not mean that Zen denies the existence of God; neither denial nor affirmation concerns Zen. When a thing is denied, the very denial involves something not denied. The same can be said of affirmation. This is inevitable in logic. Zen wants to rise above logic, Zen wants to find a higher affirmation where there are no antitheses. Therefore, in Zen, God is neither denied nor insisted upon; only there is in Zen no such God as has been conceived by Jewish and Christian minds. For the same reason that Zen is not a philosophy, Zen is not a religion.

As to all those images of various Buddhas and Bodhisattvas and Devas and other beings that one comes across in Zen temples, they are like so many pieces of wood or stone or metal; they are like the camellias, azaleas, or stone-lanterns in my garden. Make obeisance to the camellia now in full bloom, and worship it if you like, Zen would say. There is as much religion in so doing as in bowing to the various Buddhist gods, or as sprinkling holy water, or as participating in the Lord's Supper. All those pious deeds considered to be meritorious or sanctifying by most so-called religiously-minded people are artificialities in the eyes of Zen. It boldly declares that "the immaculate Yogins do not enter Nirvana and the precept-violating monks do not go to hell." This, to ordinary minds, is a contradiction of the common law of moral life, but herein lies the truth and life of Zen. Zen is the spirit of a man. Zen believes in his inner purity and goodness. Whatever is superadded or violently torn away, injures the wholesomeness of the spirit. Zen, therefore, is emphatically against all religious conventionalism.

Its irreligion, however, is merely apparent. Those who are truly religious will be surprised to find that after all there is so much of religion in the barbarous declaration of Zen. But to say that Zen is a religion in the sense that Christianity or Mohammedanism is would be a mistake. To make my point clearer, I quote the following. When Śākyamuni was born, it is said that he lifted one hand toward the heavens and pointed to the earth with the other, exclaiming: "Above the heavens and below the heavens, I alone am the Honored One!" Ummon Bun-en, founder of the Ummon School of Zen, comments on this by saying: "If I had been with him at the moment of his uttering this, I would surely have struck him dead with one blow and thrown the corpse into the maw of a hungry dog." What unbelievers would ever think of making such raving remarks over a spiritual leader? Yet one of the Zen masters following Ummon says: "Indeed, this is the way Ummon desires to serve the world, sacrificing everything he has, body and mind! How grateful he must have felt for the love of Buddha!"

Zen is not to be confounded with a form of meditation as practiced by "New Thought" people, or Christian Scientists, or Hindu Sannyāsins, or some Buddhists. *Dhyāna*, as ordinarily understood Zen, does not correspond to the practice as carried on in Zen. A man may meditate on a religious or philosophical subject while disciplining himself in Zen, but that is only incidental; the essence of Zen is not at all there. Zen purposes to discipline the mind itself, to make it its own master, through an insight into its proper nature. This getting into the real nature of one's own mind or soul is the fundamental object of Zen Buddhism. Zen, therefore, is more than meditation or *dhyāna* in its ordinary sense. The discipline of Zen consists in opening the mental eye in order to look into the very reason of existence.

To meditate a man has to fix his thought on something, for instance, on the oneness of God, or His infinite love, or on the impermanence of things. But this is the very thing Zen desires to avoid. If there is anything Zen strongly emphasizes, it is the attainment of freedom, that is, freedom from all unnatural encumbrances. Meditation is something artificially put on; it does not belong to the native activity of the mind. Upon what do the fowl of the air meditate? Upon what do the fish in the water meditate? They fly; they swim. Is not that enough? Who wants to fix his mind on the unity of God and man? or on the nothingness of this life? Who wants to be arrested in the daily manifestations of his life-

activity by such meditations as the goodness of a divine being or
the everlasting fire of hell?

We may say that Christianity is monotheistic, and the Vedanta
pantheistic; but we cannot make a similar assertion about Zen. Zen
is neither monotheistic nor pantheistic; Zen defies all such designations. Hence there is no object in Zen upon which to fix the
thought. Zen is a wafting cloud in the sky. No screw fastens it, no
string holds it; it moves as it lists. No amount of meditation will
keep Zen in one place. Meditation is not Zen. Neither pantheism
nor monotheism provides Zen with its subjects of concentration. If
Zen were monotheistic, it might tell its followers to meditate on the
oneness of things where all differences and inequalities, enveloped
in the all-illuminating brightness of the divine light, are obliterated.
If Zen were pantheistic it would tell us that every meanest flower in
the field reflects the glory of God. But what Zen says is: "After all
things are reduced to oneness, where would that One be reduced?"
Zen wants to have one's mind free and unobstructed; even the idea
of oneness or allness is a stumbling block and a strangling snare
which threatens the original freedom of the spirit.

Zen, therefore, does not ask us to concentrate our thought on
the idea that a dog is God, or that three pounds of flax are divine.
When Zen does this, it commits itself to a definite system of philosophy, and there is no more Zen. Zen just feels fire warm and ice
cold, because when it freezes we shiver and welcome fire. The feeling is all in all as Faust declares; all our theorization fails to touch
reality. But "the feeling" here must be understood in its deepest
sense or in its purest form. Even if we say that "This is the feeling"
Zen is no more there. Zen defies all concept-making. That is why
Zen is difficult to grasp.

Whatever meditation Zen may propose, then, will be to take
things as they are, to consider snow white and the raven black.
When we speak of meditation we in most cases understand its abstract character; that is, meditation is known to be the concentration of the mind on some highly generalized proposition, which is,
in the nature of things, not always closely and directly connected
with the concrete affairs of life. Zen perceives or feels, and does
not abstract nor meditate. Zen penetrates and is finally lost in the
immersion. Meditation, on the other hand, is outspokenly dualistic
and consequently inevitably superficial.

One critic[2] regards Zen as "the Buddhist counterpart of the 'Spiritual Exercises' of St. Ignatius Loyola." The critic shows a great inclination to find Christian analogies for things Buddhistic, and this is one of such instances. Those who have at all a clear understanding of Zen will at once see how wide of the mark this comparison is. Even superficially speaking, there is not a shadow of similitude between the exercises of Zen and those proposed by the founder of the Society of Jesus. The contemplations and prayers of St. Ignatius are, from the Zen point of view, merely so many fabrications of the imagination elaborately woven for the benefit of the piously-minded; and in reality, this is like piling tiles upon tiles on one's head, and there is no true gaining in the life of the spirit. We can say this, however, that those "Spiritual Exercises" in some ways resemble those meditations of Hinayana Buddhism, such as the Five Mind-quieting Methods, or the Nine Thoughts on Impurity, or the Six or Ten Subjects of Memory.

Zen is sometimes made to mean "mind-murder and the curse of idle reverie." This is the statement of Griffis, the well-known author of *Religions of Japan*.[3] By "mind-murder" I do not know what he really means, but does he mean that Zen kills the activities of the mind by making one's thought fix on one thing, or by inducing sleep? Mr. Reischauer in his book[4] almost endorses this view of Griffis by asserting that Zen is "mystical self-intoxication." Does he mean that Zen is intoxicated in the "Greater Self," so called, as Spinoza was intoxicated in God? Though Mr. Reischauer is not quite clear as to the meaning of "intoxication," he may think that Zen is unduly absorbed in the thought of the "Greater Self" as the final reality in this world of particulars. It is amazing to see how superficial some of the uncritical observers of Zen are! In point of fact, Zen has no "mind" to murder; therefore, there is no "mind-murdering" in Zen. Zen has again no "self" as something to which we can cling as a refuge; therefore, in Zen again there is no "self" by which we may become intoxicated.

The truth is, Zen is extremely elusive as far as its outward aspects are concerned; when you think you have caught a glimpse of it, it is no more there; from afar it looks so approachable, but as soon

[2] Arthur Lloyd: *Wheat Among the Tares*, p. 53.

[3] P. 255.

[4] *Studies of Buddhism in Japan*, p. 118.

as you come near it, you see it even farther away from you than before. Unless, therefore, you devote some years of earnest study to the understanding of its primary principles, it is not to be expected that you begin to have a generally fair grasp of Zen.

"The way to ascend unto God is to descend into one's self"— these are Hugo's words. "If thou wishest to search out the deep things of God, search out the depths of thine own spirit"—this comes from Richard of St. Victor. When all these deep things are searched out there is after all no "self." Where you can descend, there is no "spirit," no "God" whose depths are to be fathomed. Why? Because Zen is a bottomless abyss. Zen declares, though in a somewhat different manner: "Nothing really exists throughout the triple world; where do you wish to see the mind (or spirit =hsin)? The four elements are all empty in their ultimate nature, where could the Buddha's abode be?—but lo! the truth is unfolding itself right before your eye. This is all there is to it—and indeed nothing more!" A minute's hesitation and Zen is irrevocably lost. All the Buddhas of the past, present, and future may try to make you catch it once more, and yet it is a thousand miles away. "Mind-murder" and "self-intoxication" forsooth! Zen has no time to bother itself with such criticisms.

The critics may mean that the mind is hypnotized by Zen to a state of unconsciousness, and that when this obtains, the favorite Buddhist doctrine of emptiness (śūnyatā) is realized, where the subject is not conscious of an objective world or of himself, being lost in one vast emptiness, whatever this may be. This interpretation again fails to hit Zen aright. It is true that there are some such expressions in Zen as might suggest this kind of interpretation, but to understand Zen we must make a leap here. The "vast emptiness" must be traversed. The subject must be awakened from a state of unconsciousness if he does not wish to be buried alive. Zen is attained only when "self-intoxication" is abandoned and the "drunkard" is really awakened to his deeper self. If the mind is ever to be "murdered," leave the work in the hand of Zen; for it is Zen that will restore the murdered and lifeless one into a state of eternal life. "Be born again, be awakened from the dream, rise from the death, O ye drunkards!" Zen would exclaim. Do not try, therefore, to see Zen with the eyes bandaged.

I might multiply many such criticisms if it were necessary, but I hope that the above have sufficiently prepared the reader's mind for the following more positive statements concerning Zen. The basic idea of Zen is to come in touch with the inner workings of our being, and to do this in the most direct way possible, without resorting to anything external or superadded. Therefore, anything that has the semblance of an external authority is rejected by Zen. Absolute faith is placed in a man's own inner being. For whatever authority there is in Zen, all comes from within. This is true in the strictest sense of the word. Even the reasoning faculty is not considered final or absolute. On the contrary, it hinders the mind from coming into the directest communication with itself. The intellect accomplishes its mission when it works as an intermediary, and Zen has nothing to do with an intermediary except when it desires to communicate itself to others. For this reason, all the scriptures are merely tentative and provisory, there is in them no finality. The central fact of life as it is lived, is what Zen aims to grasp, and this in the most direct and most vital manner. Zen professes itself to be the spirit of Buddhism, but in fact it is the spirit of all religions and philosophies. When Zen is thoroughly understood, absolute peace of mind is attained, and a man lives as he ought to live. What more may we hope?

Some say that as Zen is admittedly a form of mysticism it cannot claim to be unique in the history of religion. Perhaps so; but Zen is a mysticism of its own order. It is mystical in the sense that the sun shines, that the flower blooms, that I hear at this moment somebody beating a drum in the street. If these are mystical facts, Zen is brimful of them. When a Zen master was once asked what Zen was, he replied: "Your everyday thought." Is this not plain and most straightforward? It has nothing to do with any sectarian spirit. Christians as well as Buddhists can practice Zen just as big fish and small fish are both contentedly living in the same ocean. Zen is the ocean, Zen is the air, Zen is the mountain, Zen is thunder and lightning, the spring flower, summer heat, and winter snow; nay, more than that, Zen is the man. With all the formalities, conventionalisms, and superadditions that Zen has accumulated in its long history, its central fact is very much alive. The special merit of Zen lies in this that we are still able to see into this ultimate fact without being biased by anything.

As has been said before, what makes Zen unique as it is practiced in Japan, is its systematic training of the mind. Ordinary mysticism has been too erratic a product and apart from one's ordinary life; this Zen has revolutionized. What was up in the heavens, Zen has brought down to earth. With the development of Zen, mysticism has ceased to be mystical; it is no more the spasmodic product of an abnormally endowed mind. For Zen reveals itself in the most uninteresting and uneventful life of a plain man of the street, recognizing the fact of living in the midst of life as it is lived. Zen systematically trains the mind to see this; it opens a man's eye to the greatest mystery as it is daily and hourly performed; it enlarges the heart to embrace eternity of time and infinity of space in its every palpitation; it makes us live in the world as if walking in the Garden of Eden; and all these spiritual feats are accomplished without resorting to any doctrines, but by simply asserting in the most direct way the truth that lies in our inner being.

Whatever else Zen may be, it is practical and commonplace and at the same time most living. An ancient master, wishing to show what Zen is, lifted one of his fingers, another kicked a ball, and a third slapped the face of his questioner. If the inner truth that lies deep in us is thus demonstrated, is not Zen the most practical and direct method of spiritual training ever resorted to by any religion? And is not this practical method also a most original one? Indeed, Zen cannot be anything else but original and creative because it refuses to deal with concepts but with living facts of life. When conceptually understood, the lifting of a finger is one of the most ordinary incidents in everybody's life. But when it is viewed from the Zen point of view it vibrates with divine meaning and creative vitality. As long as Zen can point out this truth in the midst of our conventional and concept-bound existence we must say that it has its reason for being.

The following quotation from a letter of Engo Bukkwa may answer, to a certain extent, the question asked in the beginning of this chapter, "What is Zen?"

"It is presented right to your face, and at this moment the whole thing is handed over to you. For an intelligent fellow, one word should suffice to convince him of the truth of it, but even then error has crept in. Much more so when it is committed to paper and ink, or given up to wordy demonstration or to logical quibble, then it slips farther away from you. The great truth of Zen is possessed by everybody. Look into your own being and seek it not through others. Your own mind is above all forms, it is free and quiet and sufficient; it eternally stamps itself in your six senses and four elements. In its light all is absorbed. Hush the dualism of subject and object, forget both, transcend the intellect, sever yourself from the understanding, and directly penetrate deep into the identity of the Buddha-mind; outside of this there are no realities. Therefore, when Bodhidharma came from the West, he simply declared: 'Directly pointing to one's own soul, my doctrine is unique, and is not hampered by the canonical teachings; it is the absolute transmission of the true seal.' Zen has nothing to do with letters, words, or sutras. It only requests you to grasp the point directly and therein to find your peaceful abode. When the mind is disturbed, the understanding is stirred, things are recognized, notions are entertained, ghostly spirits are conjured, and prejudices grow rampant. Zen will then forever be lost in the maze.

"The wise Sekisō Keisho said, 'Stop all your hankerings; let the mildew grow on your lips; make yourself like unto a perfect piece of immaculate silk; let your one thought be eternity; let yourself be like dead ashes, cold and lifeless; again let yourself be like an old censer in a deserted village shrine!'

"Putting your simple faith in this, discipline yourself accordingly; let your body and mind be turned into an inanimate object of nature like a stone or a piece of wood, when a state of perfect motionlessness and unawareness is obtained all the signs of life will depart and also every trace of limitation will vanish. Not a single idea will disturb your consciousness when lo! all of a sudden you will come to realize a light abounding in full gladsomeness. It is like coming across a light in thick darkness; it is like receiving treasure in poverty. The four elements and the five aggregates are no more felt as burdens; so light, so easy, so free you are. Your very existence has been delivered from all limitations; you have become open, light, and transparent. You gain an illuminating insight into the very nature of things which now appear to you as so many fairy-like flowers having no graspable realities. Here is manifested the unsophisticated self which is the original face of your being; here is shown all bare the most beautiful landscape of your birthplace. There is but one straight passage open and unobstructed through and through. This is so when you surrender all—your body, your life, and all that belongs to your inmost self. This is where you gain peace, ease, non-doing, and inexpressible delight. All the sutras and sastras are no more than communications of this fact; all the sages, ancient as well as modern, have exhausted their ingenuity and imagination to no other purpose than to point the way to this. It is like unlocking the door to a treasury; when the entrance is once gained, every object coming into your view is yours, every opportunity that presents itself is available for your use; for are they not, however multitudinous, all possessions obtainable within the original being of yourself? Every treasure there is but waiting your pleasure and utilization. This is what is meant by, 'Once gained, eternally gained, even unto the end of time.' Yet really there is nothing gained, what you have gained is no gain, and yet there is something truly gained in this."

3. ZEN BUDDHISM[1]

IN more than two centuries' quiet and steady development, since its introduction into China by Bodhidharma from the West, that is, from Southern India, where he was born as son of a royal family, Zen Buddhism established itself firmly, in the land of Confucianism and Taoism, as a teaching which claims to be,

> A special transmission outside the Scripture;
> No dependence on words or letters;
> Direct pointing at the Mind of man;
> Seeing into one's Nature and the attainment of Buddhahood.

By whom and exactly when this declaration in four lines was formulated to characterize the teaching of Zen Buddhism is not known. Tentatively, it was during the early part of the T'ang dynasty when Zen really began to take hold of the Chinese mind. The laying of its foundation is to be historically ascribed to Bodhidharma, but it was by Enō and his followers that it came to be recognized as a great spiritual power throughout the T'ang and all the following dynasties. They emphasized a great deal Zen's non-dependence upon the letter, that is, intellection, and its directly seizing upon the Mind itself which is Reality.

I now propose to analyze this four-line declaration and see what constitutes the essentials of Zen teaching.

In "A special transmission outside the Scripture" there are no implications whatever that point to the existence of an esoteric teaching in Buddhism, which came to be known as Zen. The phrase is simply identical with the following one which states Zen's non-dependence on the letter. Here "the letter" or "the Scripture" stands for conceptualism and all that the term implies—Zen abhors words and concepts and reasoning based on them. It thinks that we have been misled from the first rising of consciousness to resort

[1] *Monumenta Nipponica*, Vol. I, No. 1, pp. 48–57.

to ratiocination. We generally make too much of ideas and words thinking them to be facts themselves. They have so deeply entered, indeed, into the constitution of our being and we imagine that when we have them there is nothing more to be taken hold of in our experience. That is to say, words are everything, and experience is nothing, or at best secondary; and this is the way we have come to interpret life and consequently thereby to drain the sources of creative imagination.

Zen upholds, as every true religion does, direct experience of Reality. It aspires to drink from the fountain of life instead of merely listening to roundabout remarks concerning it. A Zen follower is not satisfied until he scoops with his own hands the living water of Reality which alone, he knows, will quench his thirst. The idea is well expressed in the *Gandavyūha-sūtra* (the Chinese version known as the forty-volume *Kegon*), thus:

"Sudhana asked: How does one come to this emancipation face to face? How does one get this realization?

"Sucandra answered: A man comes to this emancipation face to face when his mind is awakened to Prajñāpāramitā and stands in a most intimate relationship to it; for then he attains self-realization in all that he perceives and understands.

"Sudhana: Does one attain self-realization by listening to the talks and discourses on Prajñāpāramitā?

"Sucandra: That is not so. Why? Because Prajñāpāramitā sees intimately into the truth and reality of all things.

"Sudhana: Is it not that thinking comes from hearing and that by thinking and reasoning one comes to perceive what suchness is? And is this not self-realization?

"Sucandra: That is not so. Self-realization never comes from mere listening and thinking. O son of a good family, I will illustrate the matter by analogy. Listen! In a great desert there are no springs or wells; in the springtime or in the summer when it is warm, a traveller comes from the west going eastward; he meets a man coming from the east and asks him: I am terribly thirsty; pray tell where I can find a spring and a cool refreshing shade where I may drink, bathe, rest, and get thoroughly revived?

"The man from the east gives the traveller, as desired, all the information in detail, saying: When you go further east the road divides itself into two, right and left. You take the right one, and going steadily further on you will surely come to a fine spring and a refreshing shade. Now, son of a good family, do you think that the thirsty traveller from the west, listening to the talk about the spring and the shady trees, and thinking of going to that place as quickly as possible, can be relieved of thirst and heat and get refreshed?

"Sudhana: No, he cannot; because he is relieved of thirst and heat and gets refreshed only when, as directed by the other, he actually reaches the fountain and drinks of it and bathes in it.

"Sucandra: Son of a good family, even so with the Bodhisattva. By merely listening to it, thinking of it, and intellectually understanding it, you will never come to the realization of any truth. Son of a good family, the desert means birth and death; the man from the west means all sentient beings; the heat means all forms of confusion; thirst is greed and lust; the man from the east who knows the way is the Buddha or the Bodhisattva, who abiding in all-knowledge has penetrated into the true nature of all things and the reality of sameness; to quench the thirst and to be relieved of the heat by drinking of the refreshing fountain means the realization of the truth by oneself.

"Again, son of a good family, I will give you another illustration. Suppose the Tathāgata had stayed among us for another kalpa and used all kinds of contrivance, and, by means of fine rhetoric and apt expressions, had succeeded in convincing people of this world as to the exquisite taste, delicious odor, soft touch, and other virtues of the heavenly nectar; do you think that all the earthly beings who listened to the Buddha's talk and thought of the nectar, could taste its flavor?

"Sudhana: No, indeed; not they.

"Sucandra: Because mere listening and thinking will never make us realize the true nature of Prajñāpāramitā.

"Sudhana: By what apt expressions and skilful illustrations, then, can the Bodhisattva lead all beings to the true understanding of Reality?

"Sucandra: The true nature of Prajñāpāramitā as realized by the Bodhisattva—this is the true definite principle from which all his expressions issue. When this emancipation is realized he can aptly give expression to it and skilfully illustrate it."

From this it is evident that whatever apt expressions and skilful contrivances the Bodhisattva can make in his work among us, they must come out of his own experiences and also that, how believing we may be, we cannot cherish real faith until we experience it in our own lives and make it grow out of them.

Again, we read in the *Laṅkāvatāra-sūtra*: "The ultimate truth (*paramārtha*) is a state of inner experience by means of Noble Wisdom (*āryajñāna*), and as it is beyond the realm of words and discriminations it cannot be adequately expressed by them. Whatever is thus expressible is the product of conditional causation subject to the law of birth and death. The ultimate truth transcends the antithesis of self and not-self, and words are the products of antithetical thinking. The ultimate truth is Mind itself which is free from all forms, inner and outer. No words can therefore describe Mind, no discriminations can reveal it."

Discrimination is a term we quite frequently come across in Buddhist philosophy. It corresponds to intellection or logical reasoning. According to Buddhism, the antithesis of "A" and "not-A" is at the bottom of our ignorance as to the ultimate truth of existence, and this antithesis is discrimination. To discriminate is to be involved in the whirlpool of birth and death, and as long as we are thus involved, there is no emancipation, no attainment of Nirvana, no realization of Buddhahood.

We may ask: "How is this emancipation possible? And does Zen achieve it?"

When we say that a thing exists, or, rather, that we live, it means that we live in this world of dualities and antitheses. Therefore, to be emancipated from this world may mean to go out of it, or to deny it by some means if possible. To do either of these, is to put ourselves out of existence. Emancipation is then, we can say, self-destruction. Does Buddhism teach self-destruction? This kind of interpretation has often been advanced by those who fail to understand the real teaching of Buddhism.

But the fact is that this interpretation is not yet an "emancipated" one and fails to grasp the Buddhist logic of non-discrimination. This is where Zen properly comes in, asserting its own way of being "outside the Scripture" and "independent of the letter." The following *mondō* will illustrate my point.

Sekisō asked Dōgo: "After your passing, if somebody asks me about the ultimate truth of Buddhism, what should I say to him?"

Dōgo made no answer but called out to one of his attendants. The attendant answered, "Yes, master"; and the master said, "Have that pitcher filled with water." So ordering, he remained silent for a while, and then turning to Sekisō said, "What did you ask me about just now?" Sekisō repeated his question. Whereupon the master rose from his seat and walked away.

Sekisō was a good Buddhist student and no doubt understood thoroughly the teaching as far as his intellectual understanding went. What he wanted to know when he questioned his master concerning the ultimate truth of Buddhism was how to grasp it in the Zen way. The master was well aware of the situation. If he wished to explain the matter for Sekisō along the philosophical line of thought, he could of course give many citations from the Scripture and enter into the wordy explanations of them. But he was a Zen master, he knew the uselessness and fruitlessness of such a procedure. He called out his attendant, who immediately responded. He ordered him to fill the pitcher and the deed was immediately executed. He was silent for a while, for he had nothing further to say or to do. The ultimate truth of Buddhism could not go beyond this.

But Dōgo was kindhearted, indeed too kindhearted, and asked Sekisō what his question was. Sekisō was, however, not intelligent enough to see into the meaning of the entire transaction which had taken place right before his eyes. He stupidly repeated his question which was already answered. Hence the master's departure from the room. In fact, this abrupt departure itself told Sekisō all that the latter wished to know.

Some may say that this kind of answering leads the questioner nowhere, for he remains ignorant just as much as before, perhaps even worse than before. But does a philosophical or explanatory definition give the questioner any better satisfaction, that is, put him in any better position, as to the real understanding of the ultimate truth? He may in all likelihood have his conceptual stock of knowledge much augmented, but this augmentation is not the clearing up of his doubt, that is, the confirmation of his faith in Buddhism. Mere amassing of knowledge, mere stocking of time-worn concepts, is really suicidal in so far as real emancipation is taken into consideration. We are too used to so-called explanations, and have come to think when an explanation of a thing or a fact is given there is nothing more to ask about it. But the point is that there is no better explanation than actual experience and that actual experience is all that is needed in the attainment of Buddhahood. The object of the Buddhist life is to have it in actual actuality and in full abundance and this not loaded with explanatory notes.

To give another Zen way of treating this problem: Tokusan once remarked, "To ask is an error, but not to ask is also faulty."

This is tantamount to saying: "To be or not to be—that is the question." This questioning has indeed been the curse or the blessing of human consciousness ever since it came into existence. A monk came out of the congregation and proceeded to bow before Tokusan, as was customary for a disciple to do before he was about to ask instruction of the master. But Tokusan struck him without even waiting for him to finish his bowing. The monk naturally failed to understand him and made this protest, "I am just beginning to bow before you, O master, and why this striking?" The master lost no time in giving him this, "If I wait for your mouth to open it's too late."

From the so-called "religious" point of view, there is nothing in this, and for that matter in the previous *mondō*, that savors of piety, faith, grace, love, and so on. Where then is the religiosity of Zen Buddhism? I am not, however, going to discuss this question here. I only wish to remark that Buddhism, including Zen and all other schools, has a different set of terms wherewith its followers express their spiritual experience in accordance with their psychology and habits of thinking and feeling.

We now come to the second two lines of the Zen declaration: "Direct pointing at the Mind of man"; and "Seeing into one's Nature and the attainment of Buddhahood." What are "Mind," "Nature," and "Buddha?"

"Mind" here does not refer to our ordinarily functioning mind —the mind that thinks according to the laws of logic and feels according to the psychology described by the professors, but the Mind that lies underneath all these thoughts and feelings. It is *cittamātra,* the subject of talk in the *Laṅkāvatāra-sūtra.* This Mind is also known as Nature, i.e., Reality (*svabhāva*), that which constitutes the basis of all things. The Mind may be regarded as the last point we reach when we dig down psychologically into the depths of a thinking and feeling subject, while Nature is the limit of objectivity beyond which our ontology cannot go. The ontological limit is the psychological limit, and vice versa; for when we reach the one, we find ourselves in the other. The starting point differs: in the one we retreat inwardly as it were, but in the other we go on outwardly, and in the end we arrive at what might be called the point of identity. When we have the Mind, we have Nature: when Nature is understood, the Mind is understood; they are one and the same.

The one who has a thoroughgoing understanding of the Mind

and whose every movement is in perfect accordance with Nature is the Buddha—he who is enlightened. The Buddha is Nature personified. Thus we can say that all these three terms—Nature, Mind, and Buddha—are different points of reference; as we shift our positions, we speak in terms of respective orders. The ideal of Zen as expressed in its four-line declaration is directly to take hold of Reality without being bothered by any interrupting agency, intellectual, moral, ritualistic, or what not.

This direct holding of Reality is the awakening of *prajñā*, which may be rendered as transcendental wisdom. *Prajñā* awakened or attained is *prajñāpāramitā* (in Japanese *hannya-haramitsu*). This transcendental wisdom gives the solution to all the questions we are capable of asking about our spiritual life. Wisdom is not, therefore, the intellect in the ordinary sense; it transcends dialectics of all kinds. It is not the analytical process of reasoning, it does not work step by step, it leaps over the abyss of contradiction and mutual checking. Hence *pāramitā*, "reaching the other shore."

As the awakening of *prajñā* is the leaping over an intellectual impasse, it is an act of Will. Yet as it sees into Nature itself, there is a noetic quality in it. *Prajñā* is both Will and Intuition. This is the reason why Zen is associated strongly with the cultivation of the will power. To cut asunder the bonds of ignorance and discrimination is no easy task; unless it is done with the utmost exertion of the will, it can never be accomplished. To let go the hold of a solitary branch of the tree, called intellect, which outstretches over a precipice, and to allow ourselves to fall into a supposedly bottomless abyss—does this not require a desperate effort on the part of one who attempts to sound the depths of the Mind? When a Zen Buddhist monk was asked as to the depths of the Zen River while he was walking over a bridge, he at once seized the questioner and would have thrown him down into the rapids had not his friends hurriedly interceded for him. The monk wanted to see the questioner himself go down to the bottom of Zen and survey its depths according to his own measure. The leaping is to be done by oneself, all the help outsiders can offer is to let the one concerned realize the futility of such help. Zen in this respect is harsh and merciless, at least superficially so.

The monk just referred to as trying to throw the questioner overboard was a disciple of Rinzai, one of the greatest masters in in the T'ang history of Zen in China. When this monk asked the master what was the ultimate teaching of Buddhism, the master

came right down from his seat and taking hold of the monk, exclaimed, "Speak out! Speak out!" How could the poor bewildered
novice in the study of Zen speak, so unceremoniously seized by the
throat and violently shaken? In fact he wanted to see the master
"speak out" instead of his "speaking out," in regard to this question.
He never imagined his master to be so "direct." He did not know
what to say or what to do. He stood as if in ecstasy. It was only
when he was about to perform the deed of bowing before the
master, reminded by his fellow-monks, that a realization came
over him as to the meaning of the Scripture and the demand to
"speak out."

Even when an intellectual explanation is given, the understanding is an inner growth and not an external addition. This
must be much more the case with the Zen understanding. The basic
principle, therefore, underlying the whole fabric of Zen is directed
towards the growth or self-maturing of inner experience. Those
who are used to intellectual training or moral persuasion or devotional exercises would no doubt find in Zen discipline something
extraordinarily going against their expectations. But this is where
Zen is unique in the whole history of religion. Zen has indeed
developed along this line ever since the T'ang era when Baso and
Sekitō brought out fully the characteristic features of the Zen form
of Buddhism. The main idea is to live within the thing itself and
thus to understand it. What we in most cases do in order to understand a thing, is to describe it from outside, to talk about it objectively as the philosopher would have it, and try to carry out this
method from every possible point of observation except that of
inner assimilation or sympathetic merging. The objective method
is intellectual and has its field of useful application. Only let us
not forget the fact that there is another method which really gives
the key to an effective and all-satisfying understanding. The
latter is the method of Zen.

The following few examples will illustrate what the Zen method
is in the understanding of Buddhism. Zen, being a form of
Buddhism, has no specific philosophy of its own except what is
usually accepted by the Buddhists of the Mahayana school. What
makes Zen so peculiarly outstanding is its method, while the latter
is the inevitable growth of Zen's own attitude towards life and
truth.

Shōdai Erō who wished to know Zen came to Baso, and Baso asked, "What made you come here?"

"I wish to have Buddha-knowledge."

"No knowledge can be had of him, knowledge belongs to the Devil."

As the monk failed to grasp the meaning of this, the master directed him to go to Sekitō, a contemporary leader of Zen, who he suggested might enlighten the knowledge-seeking monk. When he came to Sekitō, he asked, "Who is the Buddha?"

"You have no Buddha-nature," the master gave his verdict.

"How about the animals?" demanded the monk.

"They have."

"Why not I?" Which was the natural question issuing from an extremely puzzled mind.

"Just because you ask."

This, it is said, opened the mind of Erō to the truth asserted by both Sekitō and Baso.

Superficially considered, there is no logical consistency in the remarks of these masters. Why does knowledge belong to the Devil? Why is not the monk endowed with the Buddha-nature when, according to Buddhist philosophy, it is taught that all beings are in possession of the Buddha-nature and that because of this fact they are all ultimately destined to attain Buddhahood. But that we are all Buddhas or that we are endowed with the Buddha-nature is the statement of a fact and not at all the inference reached by means of logical reasoning. The fact comes first and the reasoning follows, and not conversely. This being so, the Zen master desires to see his disciples come in actual personal touch with the fact itself and then to build up if they wish any system of thought based on their experience.

Shinrō, another monk, came to Sekitō and asked, "What is the idea of Bodhidharma's coming over to China from the west (that is, from India)?" This question was asked frequently in the early days of Zen history in China. The meaning is the same as asking, "What is the truth of Buddhism?"

Said Sekitō, "Ask the post standing there."

The monk confessed, "I fail to understand."

"My ignorance exceeds yours," said Sekitō.

The last remark made the monk realize the purport of the whole dialogue.

One or two more instances on ignorance follow. When Sekitō

saw Tokusan absorbed in meditation, Sekitō asked, "What are you doing there?"

"I am not doing anything," replied Tokusan.

"If so, you are sitting in idleness."

"Sitting in idleness is doing something."

"You say you are not doing anything," Sekitō pursued further; "but what is that anything which you are not doing?"

"Even the ancient sages know not," was the conclusion given by Tokusan.

Sekitō was one of the younger disciples of Enō and finished his study of Zen under Gyōshi, of Seigen. He was once asked by his monk, Dōgo, "Who has attained to the understanding of Enō's doctrine?"

"One who understands Buddhism."

"Have you then attained it?"

"No, I do not understand Buddhism."

The strange situation created by Zen is that those who understand it do not understand it, and those who do not understand it understand it—a great paradox, indeed, which runs throughout the history of Zen.

"What is the essential point of Buddhism?"

"Unless you have it, you do not understand."

"Is there any further turning when one thus goes on?"

"A white cloud is free to float about anywhere it lists—infinitely vast is the sky!"

To explain this in a more rational manner suited to our mortal intelligence, I may add: what Buddhism teaches is that all is well where it is; but as soon as one steps out to see if he is all right or not, an error is committed leading to an infinite series of negations and affirmations. To Eckhart every morning is "Good Morning" and every day a blessed day. This is our personal experience. When we are saved, we know what it is. However much we inquire about it, salvation never falls upon us.

A monk asks Sekitō, "What is emancipation?" "Who has ever put you in bondage?"

"What is the Pure Land?" "When did you ever get stained?"

"What is Nirvana?" "From whom did you get birth-and-death?"

The Mind, Nature, Buddha, or Buddha-nature—all these are so many ways of giving expression to the one idea, which is Great Affirmation. Zen proposes to bring it to us.

4. IS ZEN NIHILISTIC?[1]

In the history of Zen, Enō, traditionally considered the sixth patriarch of the Zen sect in China, cuts a most important figure. In fact, he is the founder of Zen as distinguished from the other Buddhist sects then existing in China. The standard set up by him as the true expression of Zen faith is this stanza:

> The Bodhi (True Wisdom) is not like the tree;
> The mirror bright is nowhere shining:
> As there is nothing from the first,
> Where does the dust itself collect?

This was written in answer to a stanza composed by another Zen monk who claimed to have understood the faith in its purity. His lines run thus:

> This body is the Bodhi-tree;
> The soul is like a mirror bright;
> Take heed to keep it always clean,
> And let no dust collect upon it.

They were both the disciples of the fifth patriarch, Gunin, and he thought that Enō rightly comprehended the spirit of Zen, and, therefore, was worthy of wearing his mantle and carrying his bowl as his true successor in Zen. This recognition by the master of the signification of the first stanza by Enō stamps it as the orthodox expression of Zen faith. As it seems to breathe the spirit of nothingness, many people regard Zen as advocating nihilism. The purpose of the present chapter is to refute this.

It is true that there are many passages in Zen literature which may be construed as conveying a nihilistic doctrine, for example,

[1] *An Introduction to Zen Buddhism,* pp. 48–57.

the theory of *śūnyatā* (emptiness).[2] Even among those scholars who are well acquainted with the general teaching of Mahayana Buddhism, some still cling to the view that Zen is the practical application of the *Sanron* (*san-lun*) philosophy, otherwise known as the Mādhyamika school. *Sanron* means, the "three treatises," which are Nāgārjuna's *Mādhyamika-śāstra* and *The Discourse of Twelve Sections,* and Deva's *Discourse of One Hundred Stanzas.* They comprise all the essential doctrines of this school. Nāgārjuna is thought to be its founder, and as the Mahayana sutras classified under the head of Prajñāpāramitā expound more or less similar views, the philosophy of this school is sometimes designated as the *prajñā* doctrine. Zen, therefore, they think, practically belongs to this class; in other words, the ultimate signification of Zen would be the upholding of the *śūnyatā* system.

To a certain extent, superficially at least, this view is justifiable. For instance, read the following:

"I come here to seek the truth of Buddhism," a disciple asked a master.

"Why do you seek such a thing here?" answered the master. "Why do you wander about, neglecting your own precious treasure at home? I have nothing to give you, and what truth of Buddhism do you desire to find in my monastery? There is nothing, absolutely nothing."

A master would sometimes say: "I do not understand Zen. I have nothing here to demonstrate; therefore, do not remain standing so, expecting to get something out of nothing. Get enlightened by yourself, if you will. If there is anything to take hold of, take it by yourself."

Again, "True knowledge *(bodhi)* transcends all modes of expression. There has been nothing from the very beginning which one can claim as having attained toward enlightenment."

Or, "In Zen there is nothing to explain by means of words, there is nothing to be given out as a holy doctrine. Thirty blows whether you affirm or negate. Do not remain silent; nor be discursive."

The question, "How can one always be with Buddha?" called out the following answer from a master: "Have no stirrings in your mind; be perfectly serene toward the objective world. To remain

---

[2] What the theory of *śūnyatā* really means is explained somewhat in detail in my *Essays in Zen Buddhism,* Series III, under "The Philosophy and Religion of the Prajñāpāramitā-sūtra" (pp. 234–323).

thus all the time in absolute emptiness and calmness, is the way
to be with the Buddha."

Sometimes we come across the following: "The middle way is
where there is neither middle nor two sides. When you are fettered
by the objective world, you have one side; when you are disturbed
in your own mind, you have the other side. When neither of these
exists, there is no middle part, and this is the middle way."

A Japanese Zen master who flourished several hundred years
ago, used to say to his disciples who would implore him to instruct
them in the way to escape the fetters of birth-and-death, "There is
no birth-and-death."

Bodhidharma, the first patriarch of the Zen sect in China, was
asked by Wu, the first Emperor (reigned A.D. 502–549) of the Liang
dynasty, as to the ultimate and holiest principle of Buddhism. The
sage is reported to have answered, "Vast emptiness and nothing
holy in it."

These are passages taken at random from the vast store of Zen
literature, and they seem to be permeated with the ideas of emptiness (*śūnyatā*), nothingness (*nāsti*), tranquillity (*śānti*), no-
thought (*acintā*), and other similar notions, all of which we may
regard as nihilistic or as advocating negative quietism.

A quotation from the *Prajñāpāramitā-hṛidaya-sūtra*[3] may prove
to be more astounding than any of the above passages. In fact, all
the sutras belonging to this *prajñā* class of Mahayana literature
are imbued thoroughly with the idea of *śūnyatā*, and those who
are not familiar with this way of thinking will be taken aback and
may not know how to express their judgment. This sutra, considered to be the most concise and most comprehensive of all the
prajñā sutras, is daily recited at the Zen monastery, in fact it is
the first thing the monks recite in the morning as well as before
each meal.

"Thus, Śāriputra, all things have the character of emptiness,
they have no beginning, no end, they are faultless and not faultless,
they are not perfect and not imperfect. Therefore, O Śāriputra,
here in this emptiness there is no form, no perception, no name,
no concepts, no knowledge. No eye, no ear, no nose, no tongue, no

---

[3] For the original Sanskrit, Genjō's Chinese translation, and a more literary
and accurate English rendering, see my *Essays*, Series III, pp. 215–233, where
the author gives his own interpretation of the signification of this important
sutra.

body, no mind. No form, no sound, no smell, no taste, no touch, no objects. . . . There is no knowledge, no ignorance, no destruction of ignorance. . . . There is no decay nor death; there are no four truths, viz., there is no pain, no origin of pain, no stoppage of pain, and no path to the stoppage of pain. There is no knowledge of Nirvana, no obtaining of it, no not-obtaining of it. Therefore, O Śāriputra, as there is no obtaining of Nirvana, a man who has approached the Prajñāpāramitā of the Bodhisattvas, dwells unimpeded in consciousness. When the impediments of consciousness are annihilated, then he becomes free of all fear, is beyond the reach of change, enjoying final Nirvana."

Going through all these quotations, it may be thought that the critics are justified in charging Zen with advocating a philosophy of pure negation, but nothing is so far from Zen as this criticism would imply. For Zen always aims at grasping the central fact of life, which can never be brought to the dissecting table of the intellect. To grasp this central fact of life, Zen is forced to propose a series of negations. Mere negation, however, is not the spirit of Zen, but as we are so accustomed to the dualistic way of thinking, this intellectual error must be cut at its root. Naturally Zen would proclaim, "Not this, not that, not anything." But we may insist upon asking Zen what it is that is left after all these denials, and the master will perhaps on such an occasion give us a slap in the face, exclaiming, "You fool, what is this?" Some may take this as only an excuse to get away from the dilemma, or as having no more meaning than a practical example of ill-breeding. But when the spirit of Zen is grasped in its purity, it will be seen what a real thing that slap is. For here is no negation, no affirmation, but a plain fact, a pure experience, the very foundation of our being and thought. All the quietness and emptiness one might desire in the midst of most active mentation lie therein. Do not be carried away by anything outward or conventional. Zen must be seized with bare hands, with no gloves on.

Zen is forced to resort to negation because of our innate ignorance (*avidyā*), which tenaciously clings to the mind as wet clothes do to the body. "Ignorance"[4] is all well as far as it goes, but it must not go out of its proper sphere. "Ignorance" is another name for

---

[4] This may be regarded as corresponding to Heraclitus' *Enantiodromia*, the regulating function of antithesis.

logical dualism. White is snow and black is the raven. But these belong to the world and its ignorant way of talking. If we want to get to the very truth of things, we must see them from the point where this world has not yet been created, where the consciousness of this and that has not yet been awakened and where the mind is absorbed in its own identity, that is, in its serenity and emptiness. This is a world of negations but leading to a higher or absolute affirmation—an affirmation in the midst of negations. Snow is not white, the raven is not black, yet each in itself is white or black. This is where our everyday language fails to convey the exact meaning as conceived by Zen.

Apparently Zen negates; but it is always holding up before us something which indeed lies right before our own eyes; and if we do not take it up, it is our own fault. Most people, whose mental vision is darkened by the clouds of ignorance, pass it by and refuse to look at it. To them Zen is, indeed, nihilism just because they do not see it. When Ōbaku Kiun was paying reverence to the Buddha in the sanctuary, a pupil of his approached and said: "When Zen says not to seek it through the Buddha, nor through the Dharma, nor through the Sangha, why do you bow to the Buddha as if wishing to get something by this pious act?"

"I do not seek it," answered the master, "through the Buddha, nor through the Dharma, nor through the Sangha; I just go on doing this act of piety to the Buddha."

The disciple grunted, "What is the use anyway of looking so sanctimonious?"

The master gave him a slap in the face, whereupon the disciple said, "How rude you are!"

"Do you know where you are?" exclaimed the master. "Here I have no time to consider for your sake what rudeness or politeness means." With this another slap was given.

Intelligent readers will see in this attitude of Ōbaku something he is anxious to communicate in spite of his apparent brusqueness to his disciple. He forbids outwardly, and yet in the spirit he is affirming. This must be comprehended if Zen is to be at all understood.

The attitude of Zen towards the formal worship of God may be gleaned more clearly from Jōshū's remarks given to a monk who was bowing reverently before Buddha. When Jōshū slapped the monk, the latter said: "Is it not a laudable thing to pay respect to Buddha?"

"Yes," answered the master, "but it is better to go without even a laudable thing."

Does this attitude savor of anything nihilistic and iconoclastic? Superficially, yes; but let us dive deep into the spirit of Jōshū out of the depths of which this utterance comes, and we will find ourselves confronting an absolute affirmation quite beyond the ken of our discursive understanding.

Hakuin, the founder of modern Japanese Zen, while still a young monk eagerly bent on the mastery of Zen, had an interview with the venerable Shōju. Hakuin thought that he fully comprehended Zen and was proud of his attainment, and this interview with Shōju was in fact intended to be a demonstration of his own high understanding. Shōju asked him how much he knew of Zen. Hakuin answered disgustingly: "If there is anything I can lay my hand on, I will get it all out of me." So saying, he acted as if he were going to vomit.

Shōju took firm hold of Hakuin's nose and said, "What is this? Have I not after all touched it?"

Let our readers ponder with Hakuin over this interview and find out for themselves what is that something which is so realistically demonstrated by Shōju.

Zen is not all negation, leaving the mind all blank as if it were pure nothing; for that would be intellectual suicide. There is in Zen something self-assertive, which, however, being free and absolute, knows no limitations and refuses to be handled in abstraction. Zen is a live fact, it is not like an inorganic rock or like an empty space. To come into contact with this living fact, nay, to take hold of it in every phase of life, is the aim of all Zen discipline.

Nansen was once asked by Hyakujō, one of his brother monks, if there was anything he dared not talk about to others. The master answered, "Yes."

Whereupon the monk continued, "What then is this something you do not talk about?"

The master's reply was, "It is neither mind, nor Buddha, nor matter."

This looks to be the doctrine of absolute emptiness, but even here again we observe a glimpse of something showing itself through the negation. Observe the further dialogue that took place between the two. The monk said:

"If so, you have already talked about it."

"I cannot do any better. What would you say?"

"I am not a great enlightened one," answered Hyakujō.

The master said: "Well, I have already said too much about it."

This state of inner consciousness, about which we cannot make any logical statement, must be realized before we can have any intelligent talk on Zen. Words are only an index to this state; through them we are enabled to get into its signification, but do not look to words for absolute guidance. Try to see first of all in what mental state the Zen masters are so acting. They are not carrying on all those seeming absurdities, or, as some might say, those silly trivialities, just to suit their capricious moods. They have a certain firm basis of truth obtained from a deep personal experience. There is in all their seemingly crazy performances a systematic demonstration of the most vital truth. When seen from this truth, even the moving of the whole universe is of no more account than the flying of a mosquito or the waving of a fan. The thing is to see one spirit working throughout all these, which is an absolute affirmation, with not a particle of nihilism in it.

A monk asked Jōshū, "What would you say when I come to you with nothing?"

Jōshū said: "Fling it down to the ground."

Protested the monk, "I said that I had nothing, what shall I let go?"

"If so, carry it away," was the retort of Jōshū.

Jōshū has thus plainly exposed the fruitlessness of a nihilistic philosophy. To reach the goal of Zen, even the idea of "having nothing" ought to be done away with. Buddha reveals himself when he is no more asserted; that is, for Buddha's sake Buddha is to be given up. This is the only way to come to the realization of the truth of Zen. So long as one is talking of nothingness or of the absolute, one is far away from Zen, and ever receding from Zen. Even the foothold of *śūnyatā* must be kicked off. The only way to get saved is to throw oneself right down into a bottomless abyss. And this is, indeed, no easy task.

"No Buddhas," it is boldly asserted by Engo, "have ever appeared on earth; nor is there anything that is to be given out as a holy doctrine. Bodhidharma, the first patriarch of Zen, has never come east, nor has he ever transmitted any secret doctrine through the mind; only people of the world, not understanding what all this means, seek the truth outside of themselves. What a pity that the thing they are so earnestly looking for is being trodden under their own feet. This is not to be grasped by the wisdom of all the sages. However, we see the thing and yet it is not seen; we hear it and yet it is not heard; we talk about it and yet it is not talked about; we know it and yet it is not known. Let me ask, How does it so happen?"

Is this an interrogation as it apparently is? Or, in fact, is it an affirmative statement describing a certain definite attitude of mind?

Therefore, when Zen denies, it is not necessarily a denial in the logical sense. The same can be said of an affirmation. The idea is that the ultimate fact of experience must not be enslaved by any artificial or schematic laws of thought, nor by any antithesis of "yes" and "no," nor by any cut-and-dried formulas of epistemology. Evidently Zen commits absurdities and irrationalities all the time; but this only apparently. No wonder it fails to escape the natural consequences—misunderstandings, wrong interpretations, and ridicules which are often malicious. The charge of nihilism is only one of these.

When Vimalakīrti asked Mañjuśrī what was the doctrine of non-duality as realized by a Bodhisattva, Mañjuśrī replied: "As I understand it, the doctrine is realized when one looks upon all things as beyond every form of expression and demonstration and as transcending knowledge and argument. This is my comprehension; may I ask what is your understanding?" Vimalakīrti, thus demanded, remained altogether silent. The mystic response, that is, the closing of the lips seems to be the only way one can get out of the difficulties in which Zen often finds itself involved, when it is pressed hard for a statement. Therefore, Engo, commenting on the above, has this to say:

"I say, 'yes,' and there is nothing about which this affirmation is made; I say, 'no,' and there is nothing about which this is made. I stand above 'yes' and 'no,' I forget what is gained and what is lost. There is just a state of absolute purity, a state of stark nakedness. Tell me what you have left behind and what you see before. A monk may come out of the assembly and say: 'I see the Buddha-hall and the temple gate before me, my sleeping cell and living room behind.' Has this man an inner eye opened? When you can assess him, I will admit that you really have had a personal interview with the ancient sages."

When silence does not avail, shall we say, after Engo, "The

gate of Heaven opens above, and an unquenched fire burns below?" Does this make clear the ultimate signification of Zen, as not choked by the dualism of "yes" and "no"? Indeed, as long as there remains the last trace of consciousness as to this and that, *meum et tuum,* none can come to a fuller realization of Zen, and the sages of old will appear as those with whom we have nothing in common. The inner treasure will remain forever unearthed.

A monk asked: "According to Vimalakīrti, one who wishes for the Pure Land ought to have his mind purified; but what is the purified mind?" Answered the Zen master: "When the mind is absolutely pure, you have a purified mind, and a mind is said to be absolutely pure when it is above purity and impurity. You want to know how this is to be realized? Have your mind thoroughly void in all conditions, then you will have purity. But when this is attained, do not harbor any thought of it, or you get non-purity. Again, when this state of non-purity is attained, do not harbor any thought of it, and you are free of non-purity. This is absolute purity." Now, absolute purity is absolute affirmation, as it is above purity and non-purity and at the same time unifies them in a higher form of synthesis. There is no negation in this, nor any contradiction. What Zen aims at is to realize this form of unification in one's everyday life of actualities, and not to treat life as a sort of metaphysical exercise. In this light all Zen "questions and answers" are to be considered. There are no quibblings, no playing at words, no sophistry; Zen is the most serious concern in the world.

Let me conclude this chapter with the following quotation[5] from one of the earliest Zen writings. Dōkō, a Buddhist philosopher and a student of the Vijñaptimātra (absolute idealism), came to a Zen master and asked.

"With what frame of mind should one discipline oneself in the truth?"

Said the Zen master: "There is no mind to be framed, nor is there any truth in which to be disciplined."

"If there is no mind to be framed and no truth in which to be disciplined, why do you have a daily gathering of monks who are studying Zen and disciplining themselves in the truth?"

The master replied: "I have not an inch of space to spare, and where could I have a gathering of monks? I have no tongue, and

5 This is taken from a work by Daiju Ekai, disciple of Baso.

how would it be possible for me to advise others to come to me?"

The philosopher then exclaimed: "How can you tell me a lie like that to my face?"

"When I have no tongue to advise others, is it possible for me to tell a lie?"

Said Dōkō despairingly, "I cannot follow your reasoning."

"Neither do I understand myself," concluded the Zen master.

5. *THE ORIENTAL WAY OF THINKING*[1]

"Thinking" is not, strictly speaking, the proper term for what I wish to express in this thesis, but as I do not know any other word I use it here provisionally and hope that when I finish this short paper the readers will comprehend what I am endeavoring to communicate to them.

I

"*Cogito ergo sum*" is Descartes' pronouncement and, I understand, modern philosophy in Europe starts from this. But in fact the opposite proposition is just as true: "*Sum ergo cogito.*" Because being is thinking and thinking is being. When a man declares, "I am," he is already thinking. He cannot assert his existence unless he goes through the process of thinking. Thinking precedes being. But without being how can a man begin thinking? Being must precede thinking. Without the eggs there are no chickens and without the chickens there are no eggs. This way of reasoning never brings the issue to a definite conclusion. But it is the game we are always indulging in, and we do not realize how wasteful we are of our mental energy. Being is thinking and thinking is being—to comprehend this proposition we need a different methodology in "thinking." This new methodology is "the Oriental way of thinking."

The "new" methodology which has been carried out by the Oriental mind runs contrariwise to the Western way. For Westerners, a thing either is or is not. When it is declared that it both is and is not, they reject the declaration as impossible. They would say we are born and therefore we are bound to die. But the Oriental mind works differently: We were never born and we never die. No birth and no death, no beginning and no ending—this is the

[1] *Japan Quarterly*, 1955, Vol. II, No. 1, pp. 51–58.

Oriental way of "thinking." To Westerners there must be a begin-
ning, God must create the world, in the beginning there is "the
Word." To us Orientals, everything goes otherwise: There is no
God, no creator, no beginning of things, no "Word," no "Logos,"
no "nothing." Westerners would then exclaim, "It is all nonsense!
It is absolutely unthinkable!" Orientals would say, "You are right.
As long as there is at all a 'thinking' you cannot escape getting into
the dilemma or the bottomless abyss of absurdity."

Now, our readers will see the "rationality" of my pronouncement: "No thinking of thinking is the Oriental way of thinking."

Let me give you an instance to illustrate my point.

In the T'ang period of Chinese history there was a Buddhist
monk who was troubled with the problem of birth and death, of
being and non-being, of good and evil. One day he accompanied his
master to offer condolences to one of the villagers where a death
took place. The monk, Zengen, knocked at the coffin and asked the
master, Dōgo, "Alive or dead?"

The master replied, "Alive? I would not say. Dead? I would not
say."

The monk said: "Why not say either way?"

The master persisted: "No saying either way."

On their way home, the monk who could not grasp what the
master meant asked, this time threateningly: "If you refuse to tell
me either way I will strike you, O master."

The master said, "Strike if you will. As to saying either way I
would not."

Zengen the monk struck, but to no avail. The master had something beyond thinking while Zengen strove hard to think it out.
Thinking always involves dividing, analyzing, running along the
road of dichotomy. In spite of the loving kindness of the master,
which was no doubt cherished towards his wretchedly tormented
disciple, he could not communicate his inner experience by means
of ordinary thinking. In reality the master's "not saying either way"
was a great saying directly expressing what was at the center of
the issue. But as long as the disciple's mind was working on the
plane of the dichotomous way of thinking, he could never come
to the master's experience. Strike or no strike, nothing will ever
come out of the master. The poor Zengen altogether failed to comprehend this.

After the master's death, Zengen visited another master called
Sekisō and presented him the same question, but the answer was

the same—"No saying either way." Zengen repeated, "Why not saying either way?" The master finished off, "No saying whatever!"

This, however, at once opened Zengen's mind, and how grateful he was to the unspeakable kindheartedness of the deceased master who resolutely repulsed his disciple's dichotomous approach to the truth.

One day Zengen was found walking up and down in the Dharma Hall with a spade on his shoulder. Sekisō the master asked, "What are you doing?"

Zengen answered, "I am searching for the late master's sacred bones."

Sekisō sarcastically remarked, "The surging waves are rolling over the ocean boundlessly extending and the white foam is washing the skies. Where would you be looking for the late master's sacred bones?"

"That is the very point where my efforts are concentrated," Zengen answered.

The difference between Zengen's way of thinking which is also generally ours and that of his two masters symbolizes the difference between East and West. The West thinks dichotomously. In fact thinking works in this way, for there is first of all the thinker himself who has an object before him of which he thinks. All the thinking we humans do proceeds in this manner. There is no escaping from this dualism. Birth and death, beginning and ending, creation and destruction, start from here. This may also be called the objective way of thinking, because by this method the thinking always goes away from the thinker. It starts with him and, therefore, he is always there; however far he may go he cannot make himself vanish away.

The Oriental way is to lose the thinker within the thinking. This is not the thinking in the ordinary sense of the term. That is why I say that there is no "thinking" in the Orient. That is why the masters are decisive in not giving Zengen any answer. They would express themselves either way, yes or no, to Zengen's asking if they could really do so. But the truth is that they could neither affirm nor negate. If they committed themselves either way, they would be sinning against their own inner experience. They had no choice but to continue declaring, "No saying either way." With them the thinker is the thinking. If they turned either way and said yes or no, the thinker is separated from his thought and the subjective integrating innerliness of the experience is destroyed.

The terms used here may look somewhat confusing or contradicting to our readers, for such terms as "subjective," "integrating," "innerliness," or "experience"—they all belong in the categories of thought which I say the Oriental way avoids. But the truth is that language is the most treacherous instrument the human mind has ever invented. We cannot live without resorting to this means of thought-communication, we are social beings; but if we once regard language as reality or experience itself, we commit a most grievous fault and take the finger for the moon itself which the finger is simply pointing at. Language is a double-edged sword; when it is not judiciously used, it kills not only the enemy but the wielder himself. The wise avoid this. They are always quite wary of language.

II

As I have not much time to be exhaustive on the subject let me confine myself to the exposition of the innerliness of experience which constitutes the gist of the Oriental way of "thinking."

When I say "I hear a sound," what I hear is not experientially a sound, it is "chū-chū" (the "twitter-twitter" of a sparrow) or "kah-kah" (the "caw-caw" of a crow). When I say "I see a flower" and declare it "to be beautiful," what I see is really not a beautiful flower, it is the yō-yō (freshness and beauty) and the shaku-shaku (brightness) in "Momo wa yō-yō tari, sono hana shaku-shaku tari,"[2] where the momo (peach) and its hana (flowers) are generalizations. We can say that even the "kah-kah" and the "chū-chū" or the "yō-yō" and "shaku-shaku" are as much generalized terms as the peach, the sparrow, or the crow. But there is this difference between the sparrow and the "chū-chū," or between the peach and the "yō-yō" or "shaku-shaku," that the sparrow or the peach points to an objective existence so called whereas the "chū-chū" or the "yō-yō" has no such objective reference, it is simply the expression given to one's experience as it takes place in the mind or somewhere in a region of no specifiable location.

Language always tends to hypostasize and the result is that whatever is expressed by means of language is not the real

[2] From the Book of Poetry, one of the five Chinese classics.

experience, but its idealized and, therefore, generalized and objectified representation of what is primarily experienced by the individual. The "*chū-chū*" or the "*kah-kah*" or "*yō-yō*" is the nearest
approach to such primal individual experiences. When they are
transformed into the sparrow or the crow or the peach, they are on
the general market where everybody can buy or sell as he wishes.
They become parts of public property, they altogether lose their
original personal flavor which makes them worthy of private
possession.

Language, we thus can say, has a double aspect, or rather that
our primal experience has two ways of expressing itself: one is
objective or towards the outside; while the other turns inwardly
and becomes subjective. But here we must remember that the
term "subjectivity" is not to be understood in its ordinary connotation. I intend to have it mean the innerliness of one's experience
which refuses to be intellectualized. For intellectualizing carries
on its analytical methodology endlessly and never comes to a conclusion or to a finality. This means that language and the intellect
are closely interrelated and that the intellect runs in the direction
opposite to subjectivity. The latter finds its mission as it were in
the deepening of the "*kah-kah*" or the "*chū-chū*" towards what is
at the back or the source of the experience. This means that the
methodology of subjectivity consists in returning to reality and not
in going away from it. The going away necessarily ends in dividing
reality infinitely and finding nothing to give one a restful seat or
an integrating point of identity.

The Western way is strong in generalization, which results in
the vaporization of reality. Reality consists in concretion and not
in generalization, though we must not take concretion for hypos-
tasization. For reality is not a substance in its objective sense. What
is generally known as an objective substance is a dreamy existence
which has after all no substance in it. The following conversation
which took place in ancient China between a government officer
and a Buddhist teacher will explain my point.

The officer known as Rikkō Taifu, quoting a Buddhist scholar
of the Six Dynasties Period, said: "It is wonderful that heaven-
and-earth is of the same root as myself and that the ten thousand
things are of the same substance as myself!" To this responded the
teacher, Nansen, by simply pointing at the flower in the courtyard
and without apparently referring to the oneness of things which
is implied in the statement made by the learned scholar-officer:

"O my friend, people of the world only dreamily look at this flower."

This *mondō* ("question and answer") is highly remarkable. The high government dignitary whose scholarly mind was trained in philosophical generalization dispersed reality into the misty transcendence of identity. The Buddhist master did not like it and instead of indulging in argumentation turned the officer's attention to the nearby object and told him not to turn it into a dream.

Superficially, this may sound like espousing materialism pure and simple. But those who know what is meant by concretion or subjectivism will understand the significance of the Buddhist point of view.

A commentator on this story makes the following remark:[3]

It is all very fine to say that the whole universe is no more than this Self and make this declaration: "When I am cold, heaven-and-earth is in the most thoroughgoing manner cold; when I am hot, heaven-and-earth is in the most thoroughgoing manner hot; when I assert, heaven-and-earth comes into existence in the most positive way; when I negate, heaven-and-earth is altogether annihilated; when I am right, heaven-and-earth is unconditionally in the right; when I am wrong, heaven-and-earth is unconditionally in the wrong." . . . As far as the logicalness of things is concerned, this declaration may be all very well. But if we stop here and do not know how to go further away, there would have been no chance for Sākyamuni to produce a bunch of flowers and for Bodhidharma to come to China across the Southern Seas. Nansen's remark just hits the nose of the philosopher at his sorest spot and breaks up in pieces the cozy corner where the philosopher thinks he is safely tucked in. It is like pushing a man over a ridge ten thousand feet high. When he is completely dead, he will have the chance to get resuscitated for once as a new man.

III

The resurrection of the dead, the awakening from the depths of the unconscious, the rising from a dream as a new man—this is turning towards the innerliness of the primary experience and

[3] This is taken from a Zen book known as the *Hekigan-shū*, case 40, whose author is Engo, of the Sung dynasty.

getting into the Oriental way of "thinking." As I said in the beginning, it is not "thinking" as we usually use the term, it is rather a form of feeling. But "feeling" will not do either, for the term is for states of consciousness. To reach the innerliness of experience we have to dig deeper into the source of consciousness, and feeling is not the instrument for this kind of work. It is still something intellectualized and wherever any form of intellectualization is traceable there can be no innerliness of Oriental subjectivity. The innerliness is something full of vitality; it is a concrete experience which refuses to be brought out to the superficiality of intellection.

What is needed here in the penetration of the innerliness of reality is a kind of existential intuition, and not the intellect, nor the feeling. Existential intuition is different from sense-intuition or from intellectual intuition, both of which are still on the objective plane of thinking and therefore require something standing against the subject. But in the case of what I call existential intuition there is no object, no subject, in the relativistic sense of the terms, there is only an absolute "is-ness" or rather "is" which cannot be defined as this or that. It is something which is not a something in which existential intuition takes place. When it sees itself as reflected in itself, there is an intuition, and it is from this intuition that the whole universe comes to existence. Meister Eckhart's statement will have to be understood in this sense: "In my birth all things were born; I was the origin of myself and all things. And I decide whether I and other things should exist or not." The statement is also in perfect correspondence to Buddha's declaration traditionally recorded to have been uttered by him when he came from his mother's body: "The heavens above and the earth below—I alone am the most honored one!" The intuition is a birth and with this birth comes the heaven and earth with all its multitudinousness of things. These sayings are really beyond the realm of intellectual rationalization.

Zen Buddhist literature is filled with such wild, irrational sayings that altogether go beyond our intellectual measurements. It is in the nature of existential intuition that it expresses itself along the line which runs directly opposite to that of intellectual objectification. Being so, it is inevitable that all that comes out of the intuition which may also be called primary is not to be caught up by the net of objectivity. A few more examples from Zen literature might be illuminating: Seppō once gave a sermon to the following effect:

Let every act of yours cover up the whole heaven-and-earth. Do not talk about the mysterious, do not talk about the Soul [or Mind] nor about the Nature [or Essence]. All of a sudden there comes out something altogether solitary. It is like a huge mass of fire. When you approach it your face is scorched. It is again like the famous ancient sword of Taia; when you try to touch it your life will be at stake; further, if you tarry and bide your time for thinking, you will be sorely left behind.[4]

Another sermon which is by Ummon, a younger contemporary of Seppō, has this: "Even when you instantly come to the realization that there is not a piece of fault to be discoverable in the whole field of heaven-and-earth, it is still at the stage of transmutation. When this becomes unnoticeable you are for the first time raised, but only halfway. If you wish to be raised in the entirety of your being you must realize that there is still one last way pointing further up. When this way is gained, the great activity presents itself where not a needle has room to insert itself and you have no need for anybody to whom you appeal for directions. [You are perfect master of yourself.]"

These statements are all cryptic expressions known only to those who have been initiated into the innerliness of reality. They are full of terms which defy our intellectual analysis. You must be plunged into the "mystery of being" if you wish to make them at all intelligible. This is not trying to mystify the matter. It is simply due to our looking for the truth in the wrong direction that we fail to grasp the situation.

Let me give you further quotations from the Buddhist tests which contain so much "spiritual" treasure we Orientals can and ought to be proud of. But at the same time the warning must be given you that the secret key is not found in the direction of objective verification but just in the opposite one.

During the period known as the Eshō persecution of Buddhism in the T'ang dynasty there was a recluse called Zendō who used to live in a rocky cave. He used to produce his staff[5] before people and say: "Such were all the Buddhas of the past, such will be all the Buddhas of the future, such are all the Buddhas of the present."

---

[4] The *Hekigan-shū*, case 22.

[5] The Buddhist monk generally carries a staff as he peregrinates from monastery to monastery in search of the truth.

Seppō also made use of his staff in giving expression to his primary experience. Lifting it up before his monks he declared: "This is just meant for the second and third grades of humanity." A monk came forward and said, "If you happen to meet the superior person what would you do?" Seppō threw the staff down and went away, leaving the inquisitive monk all alone.

Ummon criticized Seppō, saying, "He is destructive and altogether unmannerly." A monk approached him and asked, "What would you do if you were he?" Ummon took up his staff and gave him a hard beating.

Gonyō the Venerable, another teacher of the T'ang, raised his staff and asked a monk, "What is this?"

Said the monk, "I do not know, sir."

Gonyō reproved, "You do not know even a stick." He then erected it on the earth making a hole and said, "Do you understand?"

"No, sir, I do not."

The master said, "You do not even know what a hole is."

Gonyō now put it over the shoulder and said, "Do you now understand?"

"No, sir, I do not," was the response of the monk.

Gonyō said, "A home-made stick is carried over the shoulder; the presence of all people is disregarded; I go unhesitatingly among hundreds of thousands of mountains."

After giving all these references as to the way the staff is made use of in the demonstration of the innerliness of Oriental "thinking," Engo, the compiler of the Zen Buddhist text known as the *Hekigan-shū*, gives this remark:

Many questions are asked, but after all there is not much in the study [of Buddhism]. It is all due to your being concerned outwardly with the mountains and rivers and the great earth, and inwardly with the seeing, hearing, memorizing, and understanding, and also with Buddhahood as something you ought to try to attain, and with all beings whom you feel like saving from ignorance. Have all these concerns at once purged thoroughly out of your being, and then have your life, walking and standing, sitting and lying, innerized in a state of absolute identity. When this is realized you find that even when you are at the tip of a hair your world is as large as a triple chiliacosm, and that even when you are in the midst of sizzling water or a red-hot furnace your comfort is comparable to the land of happiness, and further that even when you are living among all kinds of precious stones and other treasures you feel as if you were under a straw-thatched roof surrounded by wild grasses and brambles.[6]

It is evident that such a life as is described here can never be the product of intellectualization. For intellectualization leads us nowhere but to an endless maze of entangling thistles. This surely cannot be our home of eternal peace.

To conclude: We all now know what has come out of Western sciences, dialectics, historical studies, and all kinds of intellectual analyses. Is it not high time to turn away at least for a while from all these employments and direct our attention to the Oriental way of "thinking"? However short and imperfect my presentation might have been, I hope I have demonstrated to a certain extent the fact that there is after all something in "the staff" so ominously produced by our predecessors whose eyes have penetrated into the inner darkness of reality.

---

[6] The *Hekigan-shū*, case 25.

6. ZEN A HIGHER AFFIRMATION[1]

SHUZAN SHŌNEN once held up his *shippe*[2] to an assembly of his disciples and declared: "Call this a *shippe* and you assert; call it not a *shippe* and you negate. Now, do not assert nor negate, and what would you call it? Speak, speak!"

One of the disciples came out of the ranks, took the *shippe* away from the master, and breaking it in two, exclaimed: "What is this?"

To those who are used to dealing with abstractions and high subjects, this may appear to be quite a trivial matter, for what have they, deep learned philosophers, to do with an insignificant piece of bamboo? How does it concern those scholars who are absorbed in deep meditation, whether it is called a bamboo stick or not, whether it is broken, or thrown on the floor? But to the followers of Zen this declaration by Shuzan is pregnant with meaning. Let us really realize the state of his mind in which he proposed this question, and we have attained our first entrance into the realm of Zen. There were many Zen masters who followed Shuzan's example, and, holding forth their *shippe,* demanded of their pupils a satisfactory answer.

To speak in the abstract, which perhaps will be more acceptable to most readers, the idea is to reach a higher affirmation than the logical antithesis of assertion and denial. Ordinarily, we dare not go beyond an antithesis just because we imagine we cannot. Logic has so intimidated us that we shrink and shiver whenever its name is mentioned. The mind made to work, ever since the awakening of the intellect, under the strictest discipline of logical dualism, refuses to shake off its imaginary cangue. It has never occurred to us that it is possible for us to escape this self-imposed intellectual limitation; indeed, unless we break through the antithesis of "yes"

[1] *An Introduction to Zen Buddhism,* pp. 66–73.

[2] A stick about one and a half feet long, made of split bamboo bound with rattan. To be pronounced *ship-pei.*

and "no," we can never hope to live a real life of freedom. And the soul has always been crying for it, forgetting that it is not after all so very difficult to reach a higher form of affirmation, where no contradicting distinctions obtain between negation and assertion. It is due to Zen that this higher affirmation has finally been reached by means of a stick of bamboo in the hand of the Zen master.

It goes without saying that this stick thus brought forward can be any one of myriads of things existing in this world of particulars. In this stick we find all possible existences and also all our possible experiences concentrated. When we know it—this homely piece of bamboo—we know the whole story in a most thoroughgoing manner. Holding it in my hand I hold the whole universe. Whatever statement I make about it is also made of everything else. When one point is gained, all other points go with it. As the Avataṃsaka (Kegon) philosophy teaches, "The One embraces All, and All is merged in the One. The One is All, and All is the One. The One pervades All, and All is in the One. This is so with every object, with every existence." But, mind you, here is no pantheism, nor the theory of identity. For when the stick of bamboo is held out before you, it is just the stick, there is no universe epitomized in it, no All, no One; even when it is stated that "I see the stick" or that "Here is a stick" we all miss the mark. Zen is no more there, much less the philosophy of the Avataṃsaka.

I spoke of the illogicalness of Zen in one of the preceding chapters; the reader will now know why Zen stands in opposition to logic, formal or informal. It is not the object of Zen to look illogical for its own sake, but to make people know that logical consistency is not final, and that there is a certain transcendental statement that cannot be attained by mere intellectual cleverness. The intellectual groove of "yes" and "no" is quite accommodating when things run their regular course; but as soon as the ultimate question of life comes up, the intellect fails to answer it satisfactorily. When we say "yes," we assert, and by asserting we limit ourselves. When we say "no," we deny, and to deny is exclusion. Exclusion and limitation, which after all are the same thing, murder the soul; for is it not the life of the soul that lives in perfect freedom and in perfect unity? There is no freedom or unity in exclusion or in limitation. Zen is well aware of this. In accordance with the demands of our inner life, therefore, Zen takes us to an absolute realm wherein there are no antitheses of any sort.

We must remember, however, that we live in affirmation and not in negation, for life is affirmation itself; and this affirmation must not be the one accompanied or conditioned by a negation, such an affirmation is relative and not at all absolute. With such an affirmation life loses its creative originality and turns into a mechanical process grinding forth nothing but soulless flesh and bones. To be free, life must be an absolute affirmation. It must transcend all possible conditions, limitations, and antitheses that hinder its free activity. When Shuzan held forth his stick of bamboo, what he wanted his disciples to understand was to have them realize this form of absolute affirmation. Any answer is satisfactory if it flows out of one's inmost being, for such is always an absolute affirmation. Therefore, Zen does not mean a mere escape from intellectual imprisonment, which sometimes ends in sheer wantonness. There is something in Zen that frees us from conditions and at the same time gives us a certain firm foothold, which, however, is not a foothold in a relative sense. The Zen master endeavors to take away all footholds from the disciple which he has ever had since his first appearance on earth, and then to supply him with one that is really no foothold. If the stick of bamboo is not to the purpose, anything that comes handy will be made use of. Nihilism is not Zen, for this bamboo stick or anything else cannot be done away with as words and logic can. This is the point we must not overlook in the study of Zen.

Some examples will be given for illustration. Tokusan used to swing his big stick whenever he came out to preach in the hall, saying, "If you utter a word I will give you thirty blows; if you utter not a word, just the same, thirty blows on your head." This was all he would say to his disciples. No lengthy talk on religion or morality; no abstract discourse, no hair-splitting metaphysics; on the contrary, quite roughshod riding. To those who associate religion with pusillanimity and sanctimoniousness, the Zen master must appear a terribly unpolished fellow. But when facts are handled as facts without any intermediary, they are generally rude things. We must squarely face them, for no amount of winking or evading will be of any avail. The inner eye is to be opened under a shower of thirty blows. An absolute affirmation must rise from the fiery crater of life itself.

Hōen of Gosozan once asked: "When you meet a wise man on your way, if you do not speak to him or remain silent, how would you interview him?" The point is to make one realize what I call

an absolute affirmation. Not merely to escape the antithesis of
"yes" and "no," but to find a positive way in which the opposites
are perfectly harmonized—this is what is aimed at in this question.
A master once pointed to a live charcoal and said to his disciples: "I
call this fire, but you call it not so; tell me what it is." The same
thing here again. The master intends to free his disciples' minds
from the bondage of logic, which has ever been the bane of
humanity.

This ought not to be regarded as a riddle proposed to puzzle
you. There is nothing playful about it; if you fail to answer, you
are to face the consequences. Are you going to be eternally chained
by your own laws of thought, or are you going to be perfectly
free in an assertion of life which knows no beginning or end? You
cannot hesitate. Grasp the fact or let it slip—between these there
is no choice. The Zen method of discipline generally consists in
putting one in a dilemma, out of which one must contrive to escape, not through logic indeed, but through a mind of higher order.

Yakusan studied Zen first under Sekitō and asked him: "As to
the three divisions and twelve departments of Buddhism, I am not
altogether unacquainted with them, but I have no knowledge whatever concerning the doctrine of Zen as taught in the South.[3] Its
followers assert it to be the doctrine of directly pointing at the
mind and attaining Buddhahood through a perception of its real
nature. If this is so, how may I be enlightened?" Sekitō replied,
"Assertion prevails not, nor does denial. When neither of them is
to the point, what would you say?" Yakusan remained meditative
as he did not grasp the meaning of the question. The master then
told him to go to Baso, who might be able to open the monk's eye
to the truth of Zen. Thereupon, the monk Yakusan went to the new
teacher with the same problem. His answer was, "I sometimes
make one raise the eyebrows, or wink, while at other times to do
so is altogether wrong." Yakusan at once comprehended the ultimate purport of this remark. When Baso asked, "What makes you
come to this?" Yakusan replied, "When I was with Sekitō, it was
like a mosquito biting at an iron bull." Was this a satisfactory
reason or explanation? How strange this so-called affirmation!

Rikō, a high government officer of the T'ang dynasty, asked
Nansen: "A long time ago a man kept a goose in a bottle. It grew

[3] Zen, in contradistinction to the other Buddhist schools, originated in the
southern provinces of China.

larger and larger until it could not get out of the bottle any more; he did not want to break the bottle, nor did he wish to hurt the goose; how would you get it out?" The master called out, "O Officer!" to which Rikō at once responded: "Yes!" "There, it is out!" This was the way Nansen produced the goose out of its imprisonment. Did Rikō get his higher affirmation?

Kyōgen Chikan[4] said: "Suppose a man climbing up a tree takes hold of a branch by his teeth, and his whole body is thus suspended. His hands are not holding anything and his feet are off the ground. Now another man comes along and asks the man in the tree as to the fundamental principle of Buddhism. If the man in the tree does not answer, he is neglecting the questioner; but if he tries to answer he will lose his life; how can he get out of his predicament?" While this is put in the form of a fable, its purport is like those already mentioned. If you open your mouth trying to affirm or to negate, you are lost. Zen is no more there. But merely remaining silent will not do either. A stone lying there is silent, a flower in bloom under the window is silent, but neither of them understands Zen. There must be a certain way in which silence and eloquence become identical, that is, where negation and assertion are unified in a higher form of statement. When we attain to this we know Zen.

What then is an absolute affirmative statement? When Hyakujō Ekai wished to decide who would be the next chief of Ta-kuei-shan monastery, he called in two of his chief disciples, and producing a pitcher, which a Buddhist monk generally carries about him, said to him: "Do not call it a pitcher but tell me what it is." The first one replied: "It cannot be called a piece of wood." The abbot did not consider the reply quite to the mark; thereupon the second one came forward, lightly pushed the pitcher down, and without making any remark quietly left the room. He was chosen to be the new abbot who afterwards became "the master of one thousand and five hundred monks." Was this upsetting a pitcher an absolute affirmation? You may repeat this act, but you will not necessarily be regarded as understanding Zen.

Zen abhors repetition or imitation of any kind, for it kills. For the same reason, Zen never explains but only affirms. Life is fact and no explanation is necessary or pertinent. To explain is to apologize and why should we apologize for living? To live—is that

---

4 A younger contemporary of Isan Rēiyū (771–853).

not enough? Let us then live, let us affirm! Herein lies Zen in all
its purity and in all its nudity as well.

In the monastery of Nansen Fugwan, monks of the eastern wing
quarrelled with those of the western wing over the possession of a
cat. The master seized it and lifting it before the disputing monks,
said: "If any of you can say something to save the poor animal, I
will let it go." As nobody came forward to utter a word of affirmation, Nansen cut the object of dispute in two, thus putting an end
forever to an unproductive quarrelling over "yours" and "mine."
Later on Jōshū came back from an outing and Nansen put the case
before him, and asked him what he would have done to save the
animal. Jōshū without further ado took off his straw sandals and
putting them on his head went out of the room. Seeing this, Nansen
exclaimed, "If you were here at the time you would have saved
the cat."

What does all this mean? Why was a poor innocent creature
sacrificed? What has Jōshū's placing his sandals over his head to
do with the quarrelling? Did Nansen mean to be irreligious and
inhuman by killing a living being? Was Jōshū really a fool to play
such a strange trick? And then "absolute denial" and "absolute affirmation"—are these really two? There is something fearfully
earnest in both these actors, Jōshū and Nansen. Unless this is
apprehended, Zen is, indeed, a mere farce. The cat certainly was
not killed to no purpose. If any of the lower animals is ever to attain Buddhahood, this cat was surely the one so destined.

The same Jōshū was once asked by a monk: "All things are reducible to the One, where is this One to be reduced?" The master's
reply was: "When I was in Ch'ing district, I had a monk's robe made
that weighed seven *chin*." This is one of the most noted sayings
ever uttered by a Zen master. One may ask, "Is this what is meant
by an absolute affirmation? What possible connection is there between a monk's robe and the oneness of things?" Let me ask: You
believe that all things exist in God, but where is the abode of God?
Is it in Jōshū's seven-*chin* cassock? When you say that God is here,
He can no more be there; but you cannot say that He is nowhere,
for by your definition God is omnipresent. So long as we are
fettered by the intellect, we cannot interview God as He is; we
seek Him everywhere but He ever flies away from us. The intellect
desires to have Him located, but it is in His very nature that He
cannot be limited. Here is a great dilemma ever put to the intellect,
and it is an inevitable one. How shall we find the way out? Jōshū's

priestly robe is not ours; his way of solution cannot be blindly followed, for each of us must beat out his own track. If someone comes
to you with the same question, how will you answer it? And are
we not at every turn of life confronted with the same problem?
And is it not ever pressing for an immediate and most practical
solution?

Gutei's[5] favorite response to any question put to him was to
lift one of his fingers. His little boy-attendant imitated him, and
whenever the boy was asked by strangers as to the teaching of the
master, he would lift his finger. Learning of this, the master one
day called the boy in and cut off his finger. The boy in fright and
pain tried to run away, but was called back, when the master held
up his finger. The boy tried to imitate the master, as was his wont,
but the finger was no more there, and then suddenly the significance of it all dawned upon him. Copying is slavery. The latter
must never be followed, only the spirit is to be grasped. Higher
affirmations live in the spirit. And where is the spirit? Seek it in
your everyday experience.

We read in a sutra: There was an old woman on the east side of
the town who was born when the Buddha was born, and they lived
in the same place throughout all their lives. The old woman did
not wish to see the Buddha; if he ever approached she tried in
every way to avoid him, running up and down, hiding herself
hither and thither. But one day finding it impossible to flee from
him, she covered her face with her hands, and lo, the Buddha appeared between each of her ten fingers. Let me ask, Who is this
old lady?

Absolute affirmation is the Buddha, you cannot fly away from
it, for it confronts you at every turn, but somehow you do not
recognize it until, like Gutei's little boy, you lose a finger. It is
strange, but the fact remains that we are like "those who die of
hunger while sitting beside the rice bag," or rather like "those who
die of thirst while standing thoroughly drenched in the midst of
the river." One master goes a step further and says that "We are
the rice itself and the water itself." If so, we cannot truthfully say
that we are hungry or thirsty, for from the very beginning nothing
has been wanting in us. A monk came to Sōzan Honjaku, asking
him to be charitable as he was quite destitute. Sōzan called out:
"O my venerable sir!" to which the monk immediately responded.

[5] A disciple of Kōshū Tenryū, of the ninth century.

Then said Sōzan, "You have already had three big bowlfuls of rich home-made *chiu* (liquor) and yet you insist that it has never yet wetted your lips!" Perhaps we are all like this poor opulent monk; when we are already quite filled up, we never realize the fact.

To conclude, here is another of the innumerable statements that abound in Zen literature, absolutely affirming the truth of Zen. Seihei asked Suibi Mugaku: [6]

"What is the fundamental principle of Buddhism?"

"Wait," said Suibi, "when there is no one around I will tell you."

After a while Seihei repeated the request, saying, "There is no one here now; pray enlighten me."

Coming down from his chair, Suibi took the anxious inquirer into the bamboo grove, but said nothing. When the latter pressed for a reply, Suibi whispered, "How high these bamboos are! And how short those over there!"

[6] "The Transmission of the Lamp" (*Dentō-roku*), Vol. XV.

7. ZEN BUDDHISM[1]

ZEN'S approach to Reality, when broadly stated, is to reverse all trends, ancient as well as modern, which have been going through the history of human thinking, and pull them backward to their source, or starting point. It is not a Copernican revolution, but a far more radical turning. Zen wants to see everything overturned to its very foundation, and to have it make a new start on that overturned foundation. My statement will be quite contrary to what you may expect; I hope you will therefore make up your minds to leave behind whatever mental equipment you have, for it will be of no use in the world of Zen. It is like Dante's *Divine Comedy*; we have to abandon all our hopes, wishes, ambitions, whatever they are, when we are about to enter the gate of hell. For in the world of Zen we are all to be naked, thoroughly shorn of all the trappings we have put on ourselves since the very beginning of creation.

A certain Zen master lived in the Sung dynasty. This Zen master appeared on the pulpit and wanted to give a sermon to his congregation. His sermon started like this: "Last night I thought of a good sermon that I might give this morning. But as I stand before you, I cannot recall what it was, however much I strive." He paused for a while and then said, "Now let me pray to the god of memory and see if I can remember." Then he said something like this, "O Lord, have mercy on me!" (This is a Christian prayer, you may say, and how would a Zen master utter such a thing? I answer, God is not so discriminating as we are.) When he recited this prayer his memory revived, and he said, "Now I remember what I wanted to say. If you ask me what Zen is, I would say, 'How stupid you are to ask about Zen! You are Zen itself. You are somewhat like a fish in the water, and, being thirsty, asking for water. How stupid you are!' " (In fact, every one of us is.)

[1] *Modern Trends in World Religions*, Kitagawa, J. M., editor, Open Court, 1959, pp. 261–279.

Saying this, the master came down from the pulpit without any further remark.

A sermon like this, to be sure, is far from being satisfactory, especially to modern intellectuals. Everything would have to be defined, conceptualized, generalized and expressed in a wordy argumentative fashion. But the Zen masters are a very strange set of people. They will never give you the so-called direct answer you are hoping for. But all the answers the masters give are, in fact, most direct. It is those who hear the answers that take them in an indirect way, and strive to conceptualize them. As long as there is conceptualization there is no Zen. Zen, thus, has nothing to do with language. This language we use at the moment is to be understood as mere language and not conceptually or abstractly.

In some ways Zen appears to be automatic. If someone asks a Zen master, "What is Zen?" the master would answer, "Zen." "What is Buddha?" "Buddha." "What is Reality?" "Reality." He is like a parrot, repeating the question one is asking.

Again, if one says, "Master, I don't understand what you say." Then, the master would answer, "I don't understand any better than you." He may add, "If you wish to understand really, ask the wall, ask the table, ask within yourself, and you will find the answer awaiting you."

If you are a Christian or a Confucian or a Taoist, you may ask, "What is Tao, or God?" The master would say, "Tao or God is on the other side of the fence." Then the questioner may retort, "O Master, that is the road leading to the city. What I wish to know is the real absolute Tao, or God." "As for the great highway (*tao*), that goes straight to Chang-an." (Chang-an used to be the capital of China in the T'ang dynasty. Nowadays we may say, "All roads lead to Rome, or to Washington, D.C.") In this way, the Zen master may appear to evade the very question the disciple or questioner wishes to have answered. But the point is that the very desire to know is already a deviation from "the highway." What the master wants you to do is to go back to "the highway" instead of going farther and farther astray. Hence his remark: The highway is right here.

Another way to define Zen might be as follows: A monk asks the master, "What is Zen?" or "What does Zen teach?" If this takes place in the monastery, the master may point to a stretch of lawn, all green, while a slight, gentle rain tenderly makes it greener.

Another way of expressing the above: There is generally a flag or a pennant in the monastery courtyard. When the master is about to answer the questioning monk he notices it fluttering as the breeze passes. He calls the monk's attention to the pennant and says, "See how it sways gently, this way and that way." Coming down from the pulpit he makes no further remark.

"This is all so mystifying," you will say. "Zen is a very strange thing. Zen leads us to a mystery, to a labyrinth, from which we are not told how to extricate ourselves. Instead of a solution, you are leading us into a network of complexities." Perhaps you are perfectly in the right. The fact is, as long as we were in the Garden of Eden we had no questions, no complexities of any kind. All went on without inciting us to question. But once a question is raised, it is like poking a stick into the beehive. Thousands of inmates are disturbed and will reward us with their poisonous stings, which may finally kill us unless we find the way to deal with them.

Perhaps it is best not to ask, not to talk. But if we don't ask or talk, where will we be? Should we ask, or should we not ask? Zen would, however, say: "If you want to ask, ask; if you don't, don't. Either will do; both will do."

"This is sheer contradiction," you will excitedly remonstrate.

And the Zen master would retort complacently, "There is no contradiction whatever."

The other day I heard a Hassidic story of a Rabbi telling one of his followers, "Life is like a wheel." The follower, taking it to heart, thought life was a wheel. After some years the Rabbi came again and told the follower, "Life is like a straight line." Then that man did not know what to think. I do not know what the Rabbi had in his mind when he made these apparently conflicting statements which put his follower in an utterly confused state of mind. But whatever interpretation the Hassidic tradition may offer, from my point of view the Rabbi is in the right in every way, for life is a wheel and life is a straight line. Sometimes it goes straight, sometimes it goes in a broken line, and sometimes it goes any old way. Life has no definitely conceptualizable pattern which it follows. It has its own inner reason eluding our human ways of imprisoning it.

When Meister Eckhart met a beggar by chance and greeted him with a "Good morning," the beggar retorted, "What morning is not a good morning?" The beggar seems to have been quite enlightened, for no doubt every morning is a good morning, every day is a good day. Whether we greet each other "good morning," "good evening," or "good night," life goes on smoothly, peacefully, and happily. Nowadays, we seem to have forgotten this kind of *goodness* and try to evaluate everything according to the categories of good and evil.

In Zen the "good" has no moral implications, it has no ethical connotation; it is just *good* and no more. When God created the world and all was done, He said, "It is good." This "good," to be sure, has no moral meaning. In the same way, the Zen people say, "Every day is a good day." There is no moral judgment implied. It is simply *good*. The day may be stormy, or unlucky, but it is just as *good*, and all other references are to be dropped.

So Zen may be thought as being morally indifferent to all that goes under the name of good or evil, to what happens to us, to what happens to the world, and to what happens to all mankind. Zen seems to be quite indifferent, quite unconcerned about the human situation generally. If Zen is so indifferent and so unconcerned, then we have no use for it, especially at a time like ours when we are tending toward mutual destruction, even toward the annihilation of humanity. What then is the use of talking about Zen?

In 1957, a conference of psychoanalysts took place in Mexico, and I was invited to tell them how Zen is related to their study and practice. I do not pretend to know much about psychoanalysis, psychology, or psychotherapy, but I said this: "You seem to speak very much about fear and insecurity, freedom and spontaneity, and the problem of what is the real self. If you wish to know how Zen is related to your subject, I can tell you that Zen offers to get rid of all these feelings—of fears, anxieties, insecurity, frustration —and make you free, really free, from these inhibiting ideas or imaginations, or whatever they are called. Zen is able to give you freedom, but to get Zen, to be really free, spontaneous, and to really have, as the Bible says, the truth that will make you free, the truth of freedom, one might say, you must go beyond psychology. Going beyond psychology means reversing the position of psychology. Psychology today knows only how to study its subject matter objectively; it is still a science. What Zen aims to have it do is to take a reverse course: to approach the matter *subjectively*. To be truly rid of the above symptoms psychology or psychoanalysis will be of no help to you; you must come to Zen."

We hear and talk a great deal, particularly the psychologists, about spontaneity and about being spontaneous. But what they are talking about is a childlike spontaneity, an animal spontaneity, which is by no means the spontaneity and freedom of an adult human being. The truly human freedom and spontaneity must have long transcended this childish state of mind. It is true that there is spontaneity, a kind of freedom, in early life. But that is not the freedom of the really matured man! As long as he is unable to give up his childish freedom, he will need the help of a psychologist; but he can never expect to be free and spontaneous if he does not go through years, perhaps many decades, of self-discipline, at the end of which he will have reached the status of a fully matured manhood.

Confucius is recorded to have said: At fifteen one begins to study or to learn. (I must remind you, this is not reading books, but reflecting on life, on reality itself.) Then at thirty, he knows where he stands. (That is to say, he acquires a certain insight into the meaning of life.) At forty, he is no longer confused. (He knows where to go, and does not go astray.) At fifty, he knows his heavenly vocation. At sixty, his ears are ready to listen to whatever is said to him. (He no longer needs to resist or to assert himself; everything is all right, everything is *good*.) At seventy, he acts as his mind wills and does not go beyond the norm. (This corresponds to St. Augustine's idea, "Love God and do as you will." Confucius had no Augustinian God, but as far as the experience itself is concerned, St. Augustine's statement corresponds to that of Confucius.)

In Zen there is a similar saying. There was a master in recent Japan—that is, about two hundred and fifty years ago—who said:

> While living,
> Be a dead man,
> Be thoroughly dead—
> And behave as you like,
> And all's well.

To "love God" is a more positive way of expressing the experience than to "be dead while living." But whether it is positive or negative, there is little difference in the fundamental way of feeling reality. Confucius, the Zen master, and the Christian saint walk on the same road, hand in hand.

You may now say, "I should like to hear something more approachable, more tangible. None of this seems to be close enough to me." But the Zen master insists that nothing is closer than this. Most ordinary people want something more rational, more logical, or more amenable to our ordinary intelligence and reason.

The philosophers try to solve this problem in their own way, and some say it is "pure experience." Zen is something very close to pure experience. It is somewhat like "consciousness in general" or "universal consciousness." It also might approach Jung's "collective unconscious." However, instead of "collective," I am tempted to call it "cosmic" unconscious, as more aptly suiting my understanding of reality. But Jung is a psychologist and does not like to go beyond his province. The scientists are a strange group of human beings. They limit not only the field of their studies, but also the extent of their human interests. They seem to think that being scientists means they cannot be anything else. But they are human beings first, and as such I should like to see them try hard to understand what the ultimate Reality or Life is. Their devotion to a life of intellectualization cripples them, for they refuse to study life in its totality. It's a great pity. Why not smash through these boundaries they have set up for themselves? If there is a bottomless abyss beyond their boundaries let them jump over it, or better, jump right into it. They are always afraid of peering down over the edge to see how deep the abyss is. "There is no bottom—we are afraid—we can't go another step further." Modern philosophers, too, are sometimes like the scientists and say, "Well, we must come to a decision, but we cannot decide." Thus they speak of life being empty and having no meaning. Confucius would say, "You limit yourself." Accordingly, both scientists and philosophers limit themselves, hesitating to go ahead and trembling before the "emptiness."

What is needed here is not the "courage to be" but a kind of desperately venturesome spirit that makes one risk his whole being. This risk I speak of is far from gambling; it is falling with intents and purposes into the abyss of emptiness from which one has no idea of ever returning to life again. If one is at all conscious of there being rocks beneath to receive him, he is not yet "thoroughly dead," and will have no chance of return. You climb toward the top of the pole, and when you have reached the very top, just let yourself go. You can't go any further with your own effort. "When you let go, you find yourself filling up the ten quarters," says an old Zen master. As long as you cling to the pole you will never be able to transcend yourself. Many fear and say, "That is quite a dangerous thing to do. If I do what you say, I shall lose my life completely." But you must lose your life once. If you lose it once, you will not lose it again. On the contrary, you will live for the first time.

In the Bible we read, "Knock and the door will be opened unto you." But this "door" will never be opened unto you by knocking upon it gingerly. The knock most decisively is a knock of desperation. The whole being must thrust itself against the door. And then the door opens by itself. No one opens it. It is neither your weight nor your strength; it opens quite by itself. In fact, ironically, there *was* no door from the very beginning. As long as we do not use our strength in its entirety, as long as we falteringly hesitate, we can never reach the point where our entire being becomes desperately involved. Only to such a being will the door be opened—the door that is no door.

There lives on the island of Hawaii a simple woman who is a devotee of the Pure Land sect of Buddhism (Shin-shū) and who had an extraordinary experience. In essence, this is what she says:

We are all destined for Hell.
We were taught that we are all committers of original sin,
We are all bound for Hell.
How terrifying!
I hesitated to jump into Hell,
Because I did not know what Hell would be like.
I lingered and lingered,
But there was no other way but to jump in.
I plunged in.
And lo, there was no burning fire to greet me,
But the lotus flower gently receiving me.
After this, I am no more afraid of Hell,
Nor am I hankering for Paradise.
I will now go anywhere—Paradise or Hell.
Wherever Buddha wants me I am ready to go.

Is this not quite expressive? It is really the essence of all religious experience. Religious experience is, in Japanese, *sono-mama* or sometimes *kono-mama*, which means "taking things as they are." The Chinese would say *shih-mo* or *chih-mo*, meaning "such" or "so." The Christian expression would be "let Thy will be done." Christianity is somehow always associated with a personality as in their use of the word "Thy." In "Thy will be done," however, "Thy" may be a person or a thing or an entity, and the "will" is the will that issues from somewhere beyond our own limited will. Here comes in the Shin-shū doctrine of the "other power" (*tariki*). "To take things as they are"—this is the basic experience or the general consciousness underlying all these expressions.

Buddhism is often regarded as being pantheistic. This must be corrected. Buddhism is absolutely not pantheistic. Buddhism stands in itself and is not to be subsumed under any such category. Pantheism is apt to ignore differences, while Buddhism does not. Differences are differences and as such they remain. But there is something in the particular differences which makes them most intimately related to each other, as if they all come from one source. Buddhists, therefore, say: The differences are as they are and are yet reducible to the One, but where is the One to return? The One is the Many and the Many is the One, but never as in pantheism.

Likewise, Indian philosophy talks about the *advaita,* which means non-duality. This immediately brings up the question: Is it monism, is it oneness? No, it is not one, either. It is neither one nor two. If it is one, we must have two. (Two means many in this case.) We may then say, in philosophical terms, that the *advaita* points to "pure experience," as William James has it. I see a flower, that is one experience; I hear a song, that is another particular experience. "Pure experience" is something which runs through all these particular experiences. When we say this we make a scientific abstraction; but in Zen experience when I see a flower, that particular experience is at the same time pure experience. Pure experience, therefore, is not something that can be extracted from each particular experience and then be synthetically concocted in a test tube. For there is no such entity to be known as "pure experience." The experience is in this way conceptually abstracted from each particular experience in order to facilitate our understanding. Thus, each particular experience is pure experience. There is no special kind of experience which can be designated as pure experience.

Some philosophers talk about the "concrete universal" as an attempt to describe the nature of ultimate Reality. Whatever we call this ultimate Reality, the universal concrete or the concrete universal, as long as we do not go beyond the mere fact of designation, conceptualization, whether psychologically or ontologically, we can never reach the end of our existential research. We must have language, but it is this language that keeps us from reaching Reality itself; it is language that stands between Reality and ourselves and misleads us by making us think the pointing finger more real than the moon to which it points.

To manage language properly is a very difficult thing indeed. Without language we cannot live even for a day, but at the same time language is a curse of human life. Just because we have given a name to something, we think the name is the thing itself and forget that it is a mere sign, devised for the sake of convenience. Names are handy; we can carry them all in a little pocketbook. But the realities are not so squeezable. Language is like a map. We spread the map of the world before us and we smugly pretend to know its experience. But the real earth is the one we tread upon inch after inch, mile after mile, with our two feet. Instead we like to measure the map with instruments of our own invention, this way and that way, and then we become involved in contradictions. We struggle and struggle to extricate ourselves from contradictions, but in so doing we create more, and sink deeper and deeper into the well of endless conflicts.

As for reality, it must be taken with naked hands, not with the gloves of language, idealization, abstraction, or conceptualization. Semantics is an excellent study in its own way, but for approaching Reality the semanticists are sadly underequipped. Reality can be handled only by Reality. This means we must put away completely all our beautiful structures, philosophical, theological, or otherwise, at least for a while. As Carlyle writes in his *Sartor Resartus,* we must be shorn of all kinds of raiment and "spiritual" trappings too, and stand before Reality in stark nakedness. Only then will Reality permit itself to be realized by us. Dressing ourselves is all right, but then we become too conscious of something other than ourselves—I mean our surroundings. No objection is made to social-mindedness, but rather to our becoming controlled and enslaved by those exterior things. Our modern society is especially successful in leading us further and further away from our true selves with all kinds of distractions. Among the baneful influences we have today which come to us from every direction I count logic, abstraction, overintellectualization, linguistic studies, etc. I mean baneful only in the sense that they reign supreme in our minds as being the only tools for reaching Reality.

The question now arises, how then would you express this primary experience which is Reality? If language is of no use, how can we communicate our experience to others? We are all social beings and like to communicate to others what we experience. Without language, how can this be done?

I do not wish to deny the function of language in our social life, but I should like to state that we are to *use* language and not to be used by it. This is our most important consideration. We invent all sorts of machinery for various purposes, and then make ourselves its slaves. Lewis Mumford says, "Modern man is the victim of the very instruments he values most." Language is one such instrument. The following will give us an idea as to how a Zen master makes free use of language.

A monk asked the master, "Discarding all languages, negations, affirmations, all possible expressions, how may we take hold of Reality itself?"

The master said, "I am tired today and I cannot answer that. Go to one of my disciples. He will be able to give you the answer."

So the monk, obediently following his instruction, went to the elder monk and asked the same question. The elder monk said, "Did you ask our master?"

Said the disciple, "Yes, it was he who directed me to come to you."

The elder's answer was: "I have a cold today, you had better go to my fellow monk who will be able to explain it to you."

The monk again set out for the third one. The third monk said, "As to that, I cannot say anything."

The monk then went back to the master to report all the adventures he had had with the disciples. Then the master said, "The first disciple's head is gray; the second disciple's head is dark."

Was there any form of communication among these words? The questioning monk was evidently sincere enough to wish to know Reality, but what about the three? From the ordinary point of view they did not seem to be at all serious-minded. Were they really so, or not?

To give another instance: There was a monk who accompanied the teacher on his walk. When the master noticed a flock of geese flying in the sky, he asked, "Where are they flying?"

The disciple said, "Flown away!" The master then turned around and taking hold of the disciple's nose twisted it. The monk felt pain and cried out, "Oh, Master, it hurts."

"There!" said the master. "They are not flown away."

The next day, the master appeared in the pulpit, and the disciple-monk whose nose was pinched came out of the congregation and rolled up the matting which is generally spread before the master. The rolling of the mat signifies that the sermon is over and the whole gathering is to disperse. The master, noticing the monk's

untimely deed—untimely because the sermon had not yet started—
silently came down from the pulpit and went back to his quarters.
The disciple followed him. The master turned toward him and
said, "How was it that you rolled up the matting even before I had
begun my talk?"

The monk replied, "You pinched my nose yesterday and it hurt."

"Where did you have your mind yesterday?"

"The nose no longer hurts today."

"Now you really know what's what, young man."

The monk bowed profoundly.

The monk went back to his quarters and wept.

A fellow-monk anxiously asked, "What is the matter with you?"

The weeping monk answered, "Go to the master and ask him what
is the matter with me." The fellow-monk saw the master and asked
after his friend. But the master told him to return to the weeping
monk and find out for himself. Obediently the perplexed monk
came back to ask his friend again. This time the latter burst into
hearty laughter. All the more mystified, the inquiring monk asked,
"What is the matter with you? What does this all mean? A while
ago I found you bitterly weeping, and now you are laughing. I
cannot understand at all."

The laughing one replied, "A while ago I was weeping, now I
am laughing."

Some people think that Zen is abstract, intangible and nonsensical. But it is not so. So far we have seen nothing abstract.
Indeed everything is most concrete, factual and a matter of everyday occurrence. "The wind bloweth where it listeth." The streamer
flutters as the breeze passes by. The master is just as susceptible
to any kind of bodily ailment as anyone else. Even after his Zen
experience which came upon him by having his nose pinched, the
monk weeps and laughs. When we go on like this, things grow
more puzzling and bewildering.

Here is another incident, which took place in the life of Rinzai,
one of the great figures in the early history of Zen in China. Rinzai
was an outstanding Zen master of the ninth century and the
founder of the Zen school which bears his name. Once he was
asked to give a sermon to a group of intellectuals of the day. He
began: "Today, having been invited by the government and other
officials, I stand here before you. It is in accordance with social
convention. As for Zen, to give a talk on it, I cannot even begin to
open my mouth. There is no room in Zen to put your foot in or on

it. But I will do my best to demonstrate, in compliance with the wish of this august audience, what Zen is. If any of you wish to come up and cross swords with me you are at liberty, and then I will testify as to whether you have had a Zen experience or not. I will be your witness."

This challenge was accepted by one monk who began by asking, "What is the essence of Zen Buddhism?" To this the master gave a hearty "Kwatz!" (a kind of meaningless exclamation). The monk quietly bowed. The master said, "Well, you are somewhat worth talking with."

A Buddhist scholar then came forth to ask, "We have all kinds of scripture—the scripture of the three baskets (*tripiṭaka*) and of the twelve divisions. Have they not already explained what the Buddha-nature is? What is the use of trying to talk further about Zen?"

Rinzai said, "You have never weeded your garden. You had better attend to that before you come here."

The scholar went on, "Buddha cannot deceive us."

The master queried, "Where is Buddha?" The scholar remained silent. The master continued, "Don't try to cheat me in the presence of an august personage. Clear away quickly lest you should prevent others from coming to question me." Thus the scholar was dismissed unceremoniously.

One could relate innumerable anecdotes such as these, with little or no further clarification of the problem; so let us simply conclude with a reiteration of some earlier statements about Zen. Zen is the reversal of the ordinary way of thinking, and this reversal implies negation and contradiction. We say, ordinarily, A is A but never not-A or B. Zen, however, would deny this, saying that A is not-A, and, furthermore, that because of A being not-A, A is A. This is the puzzling dialectic of Zen, you may say. There is also what may be termed Zen behaviorism. When the nose is pinched it hurts. When the head aches the Zen man does not feel up to talking. When a bird sings, he hears it and knows that it is a nightingale. When he walks on the mountain pass and detects a fragrance in the air he recognizes it as the laurel in bloom. What differentiates the Zen man from most of us is that the former is conscious of all these facts of our everyday experience being related to the totality of being.

PART II

The Origins of Zen

"What is the meaning of the First
Patriarch's coming from the West?"
"Why don't you ask about your own
mind?"

The Transmission of the Lamp

1. ENLIGHTENMENT[1]

ACCORDING to my way of interpreting Buddhism, it revolves around Buddha's enlightenment experience. *Buddha* means "the enlightened one," and "enlightenment" is *bodhi*. Both *Buddha* and *bodhi* come from the same root, *budh*, "to wake," "to become aware of," etc. Buddha is an awakened one, one who is awakened from a life of relativity or conditionality. What he teaches is *bodhi*, "enlightenment," or *sambodhi*, "the perfect enlightenment that knows no equal."

Buddha's doctrine is based on his enlightenment, and its purpose to make every one of us attain this enlightenment, so that Buddhism would not remain as something which stands outside oneself and does not concern one personally. Buddha was a consistent personalist and strongly urged his followers to value their personal experience and not merely to rely on authority or a superior personality. Each was exhorted to exert himself for his own emancipation. We read in the *Dhammapada*:

By oneself, indeed, is evil done; by oneself is one injured. By oneself is evil left undone; by oneself is one purified. Purity and impurity belong to oneself. No one purifies another (v. 165).[2]

This may be considered altogether too individualistic, but, after all, you have to sip your own glass of water when you are thirsty. You cannot get any proxy to do your work in Heaven or Hell. Enlightenment must be personally experienced. Buddhism does not, therefore, consist in Buddha's teaching based on his enlightenment which his followers are told just to swallow even before they can taste it, each by his own personal experience. For this reason, to

[1] *The Review of Religion*, Vol. XVIII, Nos. 3–4, pp. 133–144.

[2] *The Dhammapada*, tr. by S. Radhakrishnan (London, 1950), p. 114.

study Buddhism we must, above all, find out what the perfect enlightenment is.

Let us first inquire then how Buddha came to his enlightenment experience. How did he achieve it? Like all other Indian saints or philosophers, his foremost concern was to be emancipated from the bondage of birth and death, to be liberated from the shackles of existence. As far as existence is conditioned, it always binds us to something, and the binding means tension. This is the human situation in which we all are. And there is something in every one of us who reflects at all on the actualities of existence which constantly urges us to transcend them. We long for immortality, for eternal life, for absolute freedom, for liberation. Buddha was exceptionally sensitive in this respect. He wanted to be liberated from the bondage of existence by all possible means.

This longing, or desire, or urge is quite human and comes from our being able to reflect on our own situation, to become conscious of our surroundings, inner as well as outer, and to detach ourselves from the life we live. This longing, when translated into metaphysical terms, is our probing into the ultimate significance of reality. This probing presents itself in the form of the following questions: Is life worth living? What is the meaning of life? Whence do we come and whither do we go? What is this self who raises all these questions? Is there any outside agent who handles this universe to satisfy his whims? And so on.

All these and many other questions of a similar nature, however varied they may appear, all issue from one and the same fundamental source. They are all inquiries concerning the ultimate destiny of life, the significance of reality. So we can resolve all these questions into one and say: What is reality? Philosophers and so-called religious-minded people may have their own approach to this final question. And Buddhists, especially Zen Buddhists, have theirs too, which is different from that of philosophers and also from that of the religious-minded. Most of those people try to solve the problem as it is presented to them, that is, objectively. They would take up the problem as it is asked and try to answer it in the way it is given to them.

Buddhists, on the other hand, strive to reach the source or origin itself from whence the problem issues and to see how it came to be asked at all. When the question "What is reality?" is given, instead of taking up the question as such, they go to the questioner himself. The question therefore ceases to be an abstract one; the person, the living person, is brought in. He is full of life, and so is the question, which now is no longer abstract and impersonal but vitally concerns the questioner himself. When a disciple asks, "What is the Buddha-nature or reality?" the master would counter-question and demand, "Who are you?" or "Where do you get the question?" Sometimes the master may call the questioner's name, and when the monk responds, "Yes, master," the master may re-main silent for a while and ask, "Do you understand?" The monk would confess his inability to understand. The master's verdict then would be, "A good-for-nothing fellow!"

The Buddhist idea is that the question is never to be separated from the questioner. So long as they are kept separate, there will be no solution coming the way of the questioner.

How did the question ever come to be asked? How did the questioner ever take it into his head to ask the question? The ques-tioning is possible only when the questioner separates himself from reality. He stands outside of it, he detaches himself from it, looks at it and asks the question, "What is this?" This is the privilege allowed only to us humans; the animals have nothing of the sort; they just live reality. There is no question whatever for them. They are neither happy nor unhappy. They just take things as they come. But it is different with us. We know how to put ourselves outside actualities, and reflect upon them and ask all kinds of questions about them. And thereby we torment ourselves or sometimes amuse ourselves. However, when the question is of vital concern to us, we are far from being amused. It is, indeed, our privilege to be tormented, and therefore it must also be our privilege to be blessed. This can never be so with the animals.

A monk asked Nansen, "I am told that all the Buddhas of the past, present, and future do not know that 'it' is there while the cat and the ox do know. How is this possible?"

The master said, "Before the Buddha entered the Deer Park he knew something of 'it.' "

The monk asked, "How about the animals knowing 'it'?"

Nansen retorted, "How could you suspect them?"

This idea is that whatever we may mean by "it," "it" is no longer there when we ask about "it" as if "it" were something which can be sought outside ourselves. Every one of us lives "it," and, when we separate ourselves from "it" by asking about it, the result is that we now go out of ourselves and get lost. This is like the centipede which was unable to move any more, because it reflected upon itself to find out how it managed all its legs, one after another, without being hampered or confused. The trouble comes from this separation of questioner and question.

However, the separation of the question from the questioner is quite a natural thing with human beings, for we are so constituted as to have to ask questions everywhere and at every moment of our lives. But, at the same time, this constant questioning is the source of the most agonizing situation into which we so deeply put ourselves. The Buddhist contention is that the solution can never come out of this separation. The separation is needed to ask the question, but the separation is not the key to the solution. On the contrary, it keeps one away from the solution.

To solve the question is to be one with it. When this oneness takes place in its deepest sense, the solution comes out of the identity by itself, without the questioner's trying to solve the question. The question solves itself then. This is the position taken by Buddhists toward the solution of the question, "What is reality?" That is to say, when the questioner ceases to be outside the question, when they are one, then they return to the original situation in which they were. That is, when they return to the very beginning of things when there was yet no dichotomy of subject and object—the time before the separation took place, before there was the creation of the world—this is the time the solution is possible in one's actual experience, and not in the form of a logical demonstration.

When I say this, the reader may ask: When you say "before the dichotomization of subject and object" or "before God created the world," that means "before we were born" or "before any question comes out of ourselves." If this be the case, we have no questions to ask, hence no solution of any kind. Not only this, the enlightenment itself ceases to have any meaning whatever, for all is reduced to absolute emptiness where there was yet no God, no creation, no ourselves, and therefore no questions. This is not a solution but an annihilation.

The trouble is that I have been inadvertently leading the reader in the wrong direction, that is, I have been misleading him and putting him into the very maze out of which my object was to rescue him. For the reader here is preparing for his own funeral rites. What I wanted to do was to take him out of any sort of questioning, arguing, reasoning, etc., so that he would be absolutely free—free from all analytical disputations. This is possible only when the questioner is identified with the question, or when his whole being turns into a great question mark which covers the beginning of the world to its end. This is a matter of experience and not of argumentation. This is the point Buddha reached after six years of hard thinking and strenuous ascetic discipline. My point will become clearer as we go on.

In any event, Buddhists strongly emphasize the experience of enlightenment, out of which alone comes the solution of all problems. As long as there is an intellectual separation going on in one form or another, the question will never be answered. Whatever answer we may have will be no answer in the true sense of the word, for it will come as postulate and not as an actual answer. The basic answer which touches, or, rather, threatens the very existence of ourselves is no idle one.

The separation of subject and object means the raising of the question, and it is answered not intellectually but experientially, for it is in the nature of the intellect that its answer always calls forth a further series of questions and so can never be final. Besides, an intellectual solution, if it can ever be had, always remains intellectual and never touches one's own being. The intellect is peripheral and dichotomous. In one sense, we can say that the question of reality is answered already even before it is asked, but this will not be understood on the intellectual plane, for this goes beyond it.

While the question and the separation are inseparably linked together, the questioning really means that reality wishes to know itself, and to know itself it was necessary for reality to divide itself into questioner and question. This being the case, the answer must come out of reality itself before the separation took place. This means that the answer lies where the questioner and the question were still one. The question came after the separation; there was no question before the separation. Therefore, when we go where the question has never been raised, there is naturally no question, and where there is no question, there is naturally no answer. This realm of no questioning and answering is where there is a final solution. Hence a Zen philosopher's declaration that the answer is given even before the question is asked.

The question is asked, "What is God?" and the Zen master will say, "Who are you?"

Q. "Can or will Christ save me?"

A. "You are not yet saved."

Q. "Is Buddha really enlightened?" Or "What is enlightenment?"
A. "You are not enlightened."
Q. "What message did Bodhidharma bring from India?"
A. "Where are you this moment?"

There was a high government officer in ancient China who was interested in Zen. He once said to a Zen master,

"A man kept a young goose in a jar. It grew bigger and the jar became too small for it. Now the problem is, How can it be safely extricated without breaking the jar?"

The master called the officer by his name, and the officer replied, "Yes, master."

Immediately then the master said, "There, the goose is out!"

The fact is that the answer always goes along with the question, for the questioning is the answering. But, at the same time, we must remember that unless the question is asked no answer will be forthcoming.

Jōshū once asked Nansen, "What is the Tao?" (The Tao here we may take as standing for reality.)

Nansen: "Your everyday mind[3] is the Tao."

Jōshū: "Does it need any specific disciplinary orientation?"[4]

Nansen: "No, when you try to orient yourself, you turn against it."

Jōshū: "But if one does not, how does one know it to be Tao?"

Nansen: "The Tao does not belong to knowledge, nor does it belong to not-knowing. To know is delusion, not to know is indifference (*wu-chi, avyākṛita*). When you attain the Tao which is

---

[3] "Everyday mind" is in Chinese *p'ing-ch'ang hsin. P'ing-ch'ang* means "usual," "ordinary," "everyday," and *hsin* is "mind" "heart," "thought," or "consciousness." The combination is, therefore, "a state of mind in which one ordinarily is." The Buddhist scholars may designate this as "a state of suchness," "reality as it is," or simply "as-it-is-ness." When a monk asked a master, "What is meant by one's everyday thought (or consciousness)?" the master answered, "I eat when hungry; I drink when thirsty." This is a kind of instinctive unconscious life where there is no intellectual or reflective calculation. If we stop here, there will be no human life whose characteristic feature is a highly developed consciousness. To be conscious and yet to be unconscious—this then is "one's everyday mind."

[4] *Ch'ü-hsiang* in Chinese. Literally, it means "turning toward," "intentional direction." The above translation may sound too modern, but the idea is there.

beyond all shadow of doubt, you will realize that it is like the great void so limitlessly expanding, so vastly empty, and no more room is left there for right and wrong."

The Tao is the perfect enlightenment, and what we can state about the Tao will also apply to the enlightenment. When you turn toward it, that is, when a question is asked about it, it is no longer there where the questioner looks. But if you do not search for it, if you do not specifically direct your attention toward it in order to locate it, it will never come within your grasp. The Tao is beyond the reach of logical comprehension, beyond the ken of intellection. All this means that the enlightenment will never be attained as long as you are on this side of the stream.

This I would call the logic of enlightenment. It is when this "logic" is understood that we can, more intelligently than before, approach the question of the enlightenment experience Buddha had, from which Buddhism with all its later developments not only in India but in China starts.

It was for this reason that Buddha could never solve his problem so long as he grappled with it at the level of a dichotomous separation, so long as the questioner was kept apart from the question itself. This meant that Buddha always saw his question dangling before him, of which he wished somehow to make a satisfactory disposition. The story of Buddha is a typical example of what man's quest after reality or truth goes through before he can arrive at a final solution.

In the quest of truth we generally start with the study of philosophy, for the unfolding of our reasoning powers is synchronous with our reflection on reality. We first study the history of thought and see what all those ancient wise men had to say about the problem, which also troubled them immensely. Buddha followed a similar procedure. What he did first, after leaving his home life, was to go to the forest and see the most learned men of his day. This, however, failed to be satisfactory. Philosophy, by its nature, is unable to take us back to where the question has not yet been asked, for this is demanding too much of philosophy, which has its own limitations. It may give us a distant and not at all clarified view of reality itself, but it is possible that the nearer we approach the further it fades away. It is simply tantalizing. It was quite natural for Buddha that he had finally to leave his teachers.

He now tried ascetic discipline. Most of us somehow think that by curbing the claims of the flesh the mind is purified and ready to see the truth as it is. But self-mortification treats the self, the questioner, as a kind of enemy who is to be defeated and crushed. The enemy always stands before the questioner. However desperately the questioner may struggle in this deadly battle, the enemy will never be vanquished; for, so long as the self or the questioner is alive, he will create a new enemy and have to fight him. The killing of the enemy does not mean the saving of the self or the answering of the question. The self is maintained only when there is a not-self which is an enemy. The self is the creator of the enemy. The questioner is always a questioner, a question-creator.

In ascetic training the questioner is the self. The self is then made to face what is not the self, that is, the enemy, and this enemy is to be disposed of by any means. But the enemy can never be conquered so long as there is the self. The self is never left alone; it always wants something against which it can assert itself, to prove its power, to show itself as something of all-importance. The self loses its selfhood when there are no other selves over which it must demonstrate itself. Asceticism is a form of pride or self-assertion.

Ascetic discipline or moral training can never go beyond the self, but, unless we go beyond the self, there is no chance to get the solution of the problem with which we started our quest for reality. The self must be thoroughly forsaken and emptied of everything that savors of selfhood, that is, of the opposition of self and not-self.

Buddha found this in the most practical way. One day, he wished to stand up from his seat and failed because, from lack of proper nourishment, he was too feeble to support himself. He had been trying to subsist on a minimum amount of food so that his body would be too weak to assert itself. The end was attained, for the body became too weak and could not maintain itself. But the problem of reality and truth remained unsolved just as before; torturing the flesh was not the way to the solution. He then thought, "If he has to die, the questioner dies away with the question still unsolved."

He began to take food and recover his former health and strength, so that he could carry on his inquiries into the all-absorbing question. But how should he proceed now? The intellect failed to give him an answer, and the ascetic mortification was not of much avail. He did not know what to do. He was at a complete loss, but the urge to get a solution to his question was stronger than ever. If his had been a lesser and weaker mind, it might have collapsed under the weight of the situation. Cornered, as it were, into this situation, his whole being reacted against it. He now felt that he had no question to solve, no self to stand up against an enemy. His self, his intellect, indeed, his whole being was poured into the question. That is to say, he now became the question itself. The differentiation of questioner and question, of self and not-self, disappeared, and there was just one undivided *unknown*. He was buried in this *unknown*.

There was then, as we may picture to ourselves, no Śākyamuni the questioner, no ego-conscious self, no question set before his intellect and threatening his existence, and along with them no heavens sheltering him, no earth supporting him. If we could have stood beside Buddha at that time and looked into his being, we might have detected there nothing but one big question mark occupying the entire universe. This was the state of his mind, if we can say that he then had any kind of mind. He had been in this state for some little time, when he happened to look up and see the morning star. The beams of light emanating from the star struck his eyes, and it was this incident that brought his entire consciousness back to its ordinary key. The question that had troubled him so persistently and so harassingly now disappeared altogether. Everything acquired a new significance. The whole world now appeared to him in a new light. The following is said to have been his utterance:

> Thro' many a birth in *saṃsāra* wandered I,
> Seeking but not finding, the builder of this house.
> Sorrowful is repeated birth.
>
> O house-builder! you are seen. You shall build no house again.
> All your rafters are broken, your ridge-pole is shattered.
> To dissolution goes the mind.
> The end of craving have I attained.[5]

What makes a man feel that he has been going through many a cycle of births and deaths is due to his clinging to the idea of an individual ego-substance (*ātman*). When this idea is dispelled as he

[5] *The Dhammapada*, tr. by Narada Thera (Columbo, 1946). p. 26, vv. 153–54.

sees into its nature, which is unreal, transient, and conditional, and not at all self-existing, he will no longer be attached to it; for all its rafters, beams, and ridge-pole are now completely destroyed and will never be reconstructed. They were all the products of a dualistic way of thinking. This vanishing of dualism is "dissolution" which is "emptiness" (śūnyatā). "Dissolution," however, may not be a good term for visaṅkhāra. Visaṅkhāra means the "disappearance of things conditionally existing" (saṅkhāra). According to Buddhist scholars, this phenomenal world is an "aggregate" existence made up of conditions, and not a self-existing reality (ātman). When the mind is said to have attained "dissolution," it means that the mind has entered into a state of "absolute emptiness" (śūnyatā), that it is completely free from all conditionalities, that it is "Transcendence."[6] In other words, the mind gains its ultimate reality, being now above birth and death, self and not-self, good and evil. "I am absolute conqueror." This idea is asserted in the following verse (gātha), which is also regarded as Buddha's utterance at the time of his enlightenment:

All-vanquishing, all-knowing, lo! am I,
from all wrong thinking wholly purged and free.

All things discarded, cravings rooted out,
—whom should I follow?—I have found out all.

No teacher's mine, no equal. Counterpart
to me there's none throughout the whole wide world.

The Arhat am I, teacher supreme,
utter Enlightenment is mine alone;
unfever'd calm is mine, Nirvana's peace.[7]

The "all-vanquishing" or "all-conquering" one is never to be conquered by anybody. He is absolute. He knows no defeat, because he is above all forms of opposition. He is altogether unique. Then he is "all-knowing." This does not mean that he knows things individually, singly, one after another. This is the ordinary knowl-

---

[6] This is a term used by Karl Jaspers for Being-in-itself. The citta (mind) free from the Aggregates (skandha) is the "Transcendence of the world."

[7] Further Dialogues of Buddha, Part I, tr. by Lord Chalmers, p. 121.

edge we have at the level of relativity and finitude. The knowledge possessed by the all-knowing one is what I call *"prajñā*-intuition," a knowledge of all things in their totality and unity, the knowledge that lies at the foundation of all individual knowledge. It is that which makes our relative knowledge possible; therefore, it is wholly purged and free from "all wrong thoughts." This kind of knowledge is possessed only by the one in whom there is no division between questioner and question, that is, by Buddha, the Enlightened One.

We must realize that without this enlightenment experience, as I have tried to relate it, as the greatest event in the life of Buddha, there could never have been a religion known as Buddhism. Everything, then, that we connect with the name of Buddhism must go back to this experience of Buddha's, and whenever we encounter any difficulty in the study and understanding of Buddhist teachings we must seek its ultimate solution in Buddha's enlightenment experience. A Buddha is no Buddha without his enlightenment. So is Buddhism no Buddhism without basing itself on the meaning of Buddha's "perfect enlightenment." Thus we can see in what way Buddhism distinguishes itself from all other religions.

That the enlightenment is the very foundation of Buddhism, regardless of its wide range of ramifications as it spread out all over Asia, is seen from the fact that even in the Pure Land doctrine, which calls itself the teaching based on "the other-power" and is apparently against the spirit of "the self-power" doctrine as promulgated by the founder of Buddhism, the enlightenment idea nevertheless forms its basis. Because the Pure Land became possible by Amida's first attaining the *anuttara-samyak-sambodhi*, "incomparable supreme enlightenment," and all that follows from its establishment is no more than the inner unfolding of the enlightenment experience of Amida. While we have to elucidate in more detail what is meant by "the other-power," the main purpose of our rebirth into the Pure Land is the attainment of the perfect enlightenment in this blessed realm where all conditions are most favorably arranged for it. From this we can see that even the Pure Land doctrine, which is generally considered so remote from the "original" teaching of Buddha, is also, after all, the doctrine of enlightenment. Those who find it difficult to attain enlightenment here and now are persuaded to get or, rather, assured of getting it in their next life by being born into Amida's land.

We now know, I hope, what it was that was experienced by Buddha under the Bodhi tree on the bank of the Nairañjanā about twenty-five centuries ago. The next step in the study of Buddhism will be to find out what the contents of the perfect enlightenment are which makes us "all-conquering" as well as "all-knowing."

2. ENLIGHTENMENT AND IGNORANCE[1]

STRANGE though it may seem, the fact is that Buddhist scholars are engrossed too much in the study of what they regard as the Buddha's teaching and his disciples' exposition of the Dharma, so called, while they neglect altogether the study of the Buddha's spiritual experience itself. According to my view, however, the first thing we have to do in the elucidation of Buddhist thought is to inquire into the nature of this personal experience of the Buddha, which is recorded to have presented itself to his inmost consciousness at the time of Enlightenment (*sambodhi*). What the Buddha taught his disciples was the conscious outcome of his intellectual elaboration to make them see and realize what he himself had seen and realized. This intellectual outcome, however philosophically presented, does not necessarily enter into the inner essence of Enlightenment experienced by the Buddha. When we want, therefore, to grasp the spirit of Buddhism, which essentially develops from the content of Enlightenment, we have to get acquainted with the signification of the experience of the founder—experience by virtue of which he is indeed the Buddha and the founder of the religious system which goes under his name. . . .

Here, then, arises the most significant question in the history of Buddhism. What was it in this experience that made the Buddha conquer Ignorance (*avidyā*) and freed him from the defilements (*āsrava*)? What was the insight or vision he had into things, which had never been presented to his mind? Was it his doctrine of universal suffering due to thirst (*tṛiṣṇā*) and grasping (*upādāna*)? Was it his causation theory by which he traced the source of pain and suffering to ignorance?

It is quite evident that his intellectual activity was not the efficient cause of Enlightenment. "Not to be grasped by mere logic" (*atarkavacana*) is the phrase we constantly encounter in Buddhist

[1] *Essays in Zen Buddhism*, (First Series), Rider & Co., 1949, pp. 118–162.

literature, Pali and Sanskrit. The satisfaction the Buddha experienced in this case was altogether too deep, too penetrating, and too far-reaching in result to be a matter of mere logic. The intellectual solution of a problem is satisfying enough as far as the blockage has been removed, but it is not sufficiently fundamental to enter into the depths of our soul-life. All scholars are not saints and all saints are by no means scholarly. The Buddha's intellectual survey of the Law of Origination (*pratītya-samutpāda*), however perfect and thoroughgoing, could not make him so completely sure of his conquest over ignorance, pain, birth, and defilements. Tracing things to their origin or subjecting them to a scheme of concatenation is one thing, but to subdue them, to bring them to subjection in the actuality of life, is quite another thing. In the one the intellect alone is active, but in the other there is the operation of the will—and the will is the man. The Buddha was not the mere discoverer of the Twelvefold Chain of Causation, he took hold of the chain itself in his hands and broke it into pieces so that it would never again bind him to slavery.

His insight reached the bottom of his being and saw it really as it was, and the seeing was like the seeing of your own hand with your own eyes—there was no reflection, no inference, no judgment, no comparison, no moving either backward or forward step by step, the thing was seen and that was the end of it, there was nothing to talk about, nothing to argue, or to explain. The seeing was something complete in itself—it did not lead on to anything inside or outside, within or beyond. And it was this completeness, this finality, that was so entirely satisfying to the Buddha, who now knew that the chain was found broken and that he was a liberated man. The Buddha's experience of Enlightenment therefore could not be understood by referring it to the intellect which tantalizes but fails to fulfil and satisfy.

The Buddha's psychological experience of life as pain and suffering was intensely real and moved him to the very depths of his being, and in consequence the emotional reaction he experienced at the time of Enlightenment was in proportion to this intensity of feeling. All the more evident, therefore, it is that he could not rest satisfied with an intellectual glancing or surveying of the facts of life. In order to bring a perfect state of tranquillity over the waves of turmoil surging in his heart, he had to have recourse to something more deeply and vitally concerned with his inmost being. For all we can say of it, the intellect is after all a

spectator, and when it does some work it is as a hireling for better
or for worse. Alone it cannot bring about the state of mind designated as enlightenment. The feeling of perfect freedom, the feeling
that *"aham hi araha loke, aham satthā anuttaro,"* could not issue
from the consciousness of an intellectual superiority alone. There
must have been in the mind of the Buddha a consciousness far
more fundamental which could only accompany one's deepest
spiritual experience.

To account for this spiritual experience the Buddhist writers exhaust their knowledge of words relating to the understanding,
logical or otherwise. "Knowledge" (*vijjā*), "understanding" (*pajā-
nanā*), "reason" (*ñana*), "wisdom" (*paññā*), "penetration" (*ab-
hisameta*), "realization" (*abhisambuddha*), "perception" (*sañ-
janam*), and "insight" (*dassana*),[2] are some of the terms they use.
In truth, so long as we confine ourselves to intellection, however
deep, subtle, sublime, and enlightening, we fail to see into the gist
of the matter. This is the reason why even the so-called primitive
Buddhists who are by some considered positivists, rationalists, and
agnostics, were obliged to assume some faculty dealing with things
far above relative knowledge, things that do not appeal to our
empirical ego.

The Mahayana account of Enlightenment as is found in the
Lalita-vistara (chapter on "Abhisambodhana") is more explicit as
to the kind of mental activity or wisdom which converted the Bodhisattva into the Buddha. For it was through *"ekacittakṣaṇa-sam-
yukta-prajñā"* that supreme perfect knowledge was realized
(*abhisambuddha*) by the Buddha. What is this *prajñā?* It is the
understanding of higher order than that which is habitually exercised in acquiring relative knowledge. It is a faculty both intellectual and spiritual, through the operation of which the soul is enabled
to break the fetters of intellection. The latter is always dualistic inasmuch as it is cognizant of subject and object, but in the *prajñā*
which is exercised "in unison with one-thought-viewing" there is
no separation between knower and known, these are all viewed
(*īkṣhana*) in one thought (*ekacitta*), and Enlightenment is the outcome of this. By thus specifying the operation of *prajñā*, the Maha-

---

[2] *The Mahāvyutpatti,* CXLII, gives a list of thirteen terms denoting the
act of comprehending with more or less definite shades of meaning: *buddhi,
mati, gati, mata, drishtam, abhisamitāvi, samyagavabodha, supratividdha,
abhilakshita, gatimgata, avabodha, pratyabhijñā,* and *menire.*

yanists have achieved an advance in making clearer the nature
of *sambodhi:* for when the mind reverses its usual course of working and, instead of dividing itself externally, goes back to its
original inner abode of oneness, it begins to realize the state of
"one-thought-viewing" where Ignorance ceases to scheme and the
Defilements do not obtain.

Enlightenment we can thus see is an absolute state of mind in
which no "discrimination" (*parikalpita* or *vikalpa*), so called, takes
place, and it requires a great mental effort to realize this state of
viewing all things "in one thought." In fact, our logical as well as
practical consciousness is too given up to analysis and ideation;
that is to say, we cut up realities into elements in order to understand them; but when they are put together to make the original
whole, its elements stand out too conspicuously defined, and we
do not view the whole "in one thought." And as it is only when
"one thought" is reached that we have Enlightenment, an effort is
to be made to go beyond our relative empirical consciousness,
which attaches itself to the multitudinosity and not to the unity of
things. The most important fact that lies behind the experience of
Enlightenment, therefore, is that the Buddha made the most
strenuous attempt to solve the problem of Ignorance and his utmost will-power was brought forth to bear upon a successful issue
of the struggle.

We read in the *Kaṭha Upaniṣad:* "As rain water that has fallen
on a mountain ridge runs down on all sides, thus does he who sees
a difference between qualities run after them on all sides. As pure
water poured into pure water remains the same, thus, O Gautama,
is the self of a thinker who knows." This pouring pure water into
pure water is, as we have it here, the "viewing all qualities in one
thought" which finally cuts off the hopelessly entangling logical
mesh by merging all differences and likenesses into the absolute
oneness of the knower (*jñānin*) and the known (*jñeya*). This, however, in our practical dualistic life, is a reversion, a twisting, and a
readjustment.

Eckhart, the great German mystic, is singularly one with the
"one-thought-viewing" of things as done by Buddhists when he
expresses his view thus: "Das Auge darin ich Gott sehe, ist dasselbe
Auge, darin Gott mich sieht. Mein Auge und Gottes Auge ist ein
Auge und ein Gesicht und ein Erkennen und eine Liebe."[3] The

---

[3] Franz Pfeiffer, p. 312, Martensen, p. 29.

idea of reversion is more clearly expressed in Jacob Boehme's simile of the *"umgewandtes Auge"* with which God is recognized.

Enlightenment, therefore, must involve the will as well as the intellect. It is an act of intuition born of the will. The will wants to know itself as it is in itself, *yathābhūtam dassana,* free from all its cognitive conditions. The Buddha attained this end when a new insight came upon him at the end of his ever-circulatory reasoning from decay and death to Ignorance and from Ignorance to decay and death, through the twelve links of the *Pratītya-samutpāda.* The Buddha had to go over the same ground again and again, because he was in an intellectual impasse through which he could not move further on. He did not repeat the process, as is originally imagined, for his own philosophical edification.

The fact was that he did not know how to escape this endless rotation of ideas; at this end there was birth, there was decay and death, and at the other end there was Ignorance. The objective facts could not be denied, they boldly and uncomfortably confronted him, while Ignorance balked the progress of his cognitive faculty moving further onward or rather inward. He was hemmed in on both sides, he did not know how to find his way out, he went first this way and then that way, forever with the same result—the utter inutility of all his mental labor. But he had an indomitable will; he wanted, with the utmost efforts of his will, to get into the very truth of the matter; he knocked and knocked until the doors of Ignorance gave way: and they burst open to a new vista never before presented to his intellectual vision. Thus he was able to exclaim to Upaka, the naked ascetic, whom he happened to meet on his way to Benares after Enlightenment:

> All-conqueror I, knower of all,
> From every soil and stain released,
> Renouncing all, from craving ceased,
> Self-taught; whom should I Master call?
>
> That which I know I learned of none,
> My fellow is not on the earth.
> Of human or of heavenly birth
> To equal me there is not one.

I truly have attained release,
The world's unequalled teacher I,
Alone, enlightened perfectly,
I dwell in everlasting peace.[4]

When we speak of Enlightenment or Illumination we are apt to think of its epistemological aspect and to forget the presence of a tremendous will-power behind it—the power in fact making up the entire being of an individual. Especially as in Buddhism the intellect stands forth prominently, perhaps more than it ought to, in the realization of the ideal Buddhist life, scholars are tempted to ignore the significance of the will as the essentially determinate factor in the solution of the ultimate problem. Their attention has thus been directed too much toward the doctrine of the *Pratītya-samutpāda* or the *Ārya-satya*, which they considered constituted the final teaching of Buddhism. But in this they have been sadly at fault, nor have they been right in taking Buddhism for a sort of ethical culture, declaring that it is no more than a system of moral precepts (*śīla*), without a soul, without a God, and consequently without a promise of immortality. But the true Buddhist ideas of Ignorance, Causation, and Moral Conduct had a far deeper foundation in the soul-life of man. Ignorance was not a cognitive ignorance, but meant the darkness of spiritual outlook. If Ignorance were no more than cognitive, the clearing up of it did not and could not result in Enlightenment, in freedom from the Fetters and Defilements, or Intoxicants as some Pali scholars have them. The Buddha's insight penetrated the depths of his being as the will, and he knew what this was, *yathābhūtam*, or in its *tathābhāva* (thatness or suchness), he rose above himself as a Buddha supreme and peerless. The expression "*Anuttara-samyak-sambodhi*" was

---

[4] Translated by Bhikkhu Sīlācāra. The original Pali runs as follows:
　　Sabbābhibhū sabbavidū 'ham asmi,
　　Sabbesu dhammesu anūpalitto,
　　Sabbaṁjaho tanhākknaye vimutto,
　　Sayaṁ abhiññāya kam uddiseyaṁ.
　　Na me ācariyo atthi, sadiso me na vijjati,
　　Sadevakasmiṁ lokasmiṁ na 'tthi me paṭpuggalo.
　　Ahaṁ hi arahā loke, ahaṁ satthā anuttaro,
　　Eko, 'mhi sammasambuddho, sītibhūto 'smi, nibbuto.
　　　　　　　　　　　　　　　　　　　Dīgha-Nikāya, XXVI.

thus used to designate this pre-eminently spiritual knowledge realized by him.

Ignorance, which is the antithesis of Enlightenment, therefore acquires a much deeper sense here than that which has hitherto been ascribed to it. Ignorance is not merely not knowing or not being acquainted with a theory, system or law; it is not directly grasping the ultimate facts of life as expressive of the will. In Ignorance knowing is separated from acting, and the knower from that which is to be known; in Ignorance the world is asserted as distinct from the self; that is, there are always two elements standing in opposition. This is, however, the fundamental condition of cognition, which means that as soon as cognition takes place there is Ignorance clinging to its every act. When we think we know something, there is something we do not know. The unknown is always behind the known, and we fail to get at this unknown knower, who is indeed the inevitable and necessary companion to every act of cognition. We want, however, to know this unknown knower, we cannot let this go unknown, ungrasped without actually seeing what it is; that is, Ignorance is to be enlightened. This involves a great contradiction, at least epistomologically. But until we transcend this condition there is no peace of mind, life grows unbearable.

In his search for the "builder" (gahākara), the Buddha was always accosted by Ignorance, an unknown knower behind knowing. He could not for a long time lay his hands on this one in a black mask until he transcended the dualism of knower and known. This transcending was not an act of cognition, it was self-realization, it was a spiritual awakening and outside the ken of logical reasoning, and therefore not accompanied by Ignorance. The knowledge the knower has of himself, in himself—that is, as he is to himself— is unattainable by any proceedings of the intellect which is not permitted to transcend its own conditions. Ignorance is brought to subjection only by going beyond its own principle. This is an act of the will. Ignorance in itself is no evil, nor is it the source of evil, but when we are ignorant of Ignorance, of what it means in our life, then there takes place an unending concatenation of evils. Tṛiṣṇā (craving) regarded as the root of evil can be overcome only when Ignorance is understood in its deeper and proper signification.

Therefore, it betrays a shortsightedness on the part of Buddhist scholars when they relegate Ignorance to the past in trying to explain the rationale of the Twelvefold Chain of Causation (*Pratītya-samutpāda*)[5] from the temporal point of view. According to them the first two factors (*aṅgāni*) of the *Pratītya-samutpāda* belong to the past, while the following eight belong to the present and the last two to the future. Ignorance, from which starts the series of the *Nidāna*, has no time-limits, for it is not of time but of the will, as is Enlightenment. When time-conception enters, Enlightenment, which is negatively the dispelling of Ignorance, loses all its character of finality, and we begin to look around for something going beyond it. The fetters would ever be tightening around us, and the defilements would be our eternal condition. No gods would sing of the Awakened One as "a lotus unsoiled by the dust of passion, sprung from the lake of knowledge; a sun that destroys the darkness of delusion; a moon that takes away the scorching heat of the inherent sins of existence."[6]

If Enlightenment made the whole universe tremble in six different ways as is recorded in the sutras, Ignorance over which it finally prevailed must have as much power, though diametrically opposed to it in value and virtue, as Enlightenment. To take Ignorance for an intellectual term and then to interpret it in terms of time-relation, altogether destroys its fundamental character as the first in the series of the Twelve *Nidāna*. The extraordinary power wielded by the Buddha over his contemporaries as well as posterity was not entirely due to his wonderful analytical acumen, though we have to admit this in him; it was essentially due to his spiritual greatness and profound personality, which came from his will-power penetrating down into the very basis of creation. The vanquishing of Ignorance was an exhibition of this power which therefore was invincible and against which Mara with all his hosts was utterly powerless either to overwhelm or to entice. The failure to see into the true meaning of Ignorance in the system of the *Pratītya-samutpāda* or in the *Āryasatya* will end unavoidably in misconstruing the essential nature of Enlightenment and consequently of Buddhism.

---

[5] Ordinarily, the Chain runs as follows: 1. Ignorance (*avidyā*); 2. Disposition (*saṃskāra*); 3. Consciousness (*vijñāna*); 4. Name and Form (*nāma-rūpa*); 5. Six Sense-organs (*saḍāyatana*); 6. Touch (*sparśa*); 7. Feeling (*vedanā*); 8. Desire (*tṛṣṇā*); 9. Clinging (*upādāna*); 10. Becoming (*bhāva*); 11. Birth (*jāti*); and 12. Old Age and Death (*jarāmaraṇam*).

[6] *The Buddhacarita*, Book XIV.

In the beginning, which is really no beginning and which has no spiritual meaning except in our finite life, the will wants to know itself, and consciousness is awakened, and with the awakening of consciousness the will is split in two. The one will, whole and complete in itself, is now at once actor and observer. Conflict is inevitable; for the actor now wants to be free from the limitations under which he has been obliged to put himself in his desire for consciousness. He has in one sense been enabled to see, but at the same time there is something which he, as observer, cannot see. In the trail of knowledge, Ignorance follows with the inevitability of fate, the one accompanies the other as shadow accompanies object, no separation can be effected between the two companions. But the will as actor is bent on going back to his own original abode where there was yet no dualism, and therefore peace prevailed. This longing for the home, however, cannot be satisfied without a long, hard, trying experience. For the thing once divided in two cannot be restored to its former unity until some struggle is gone through with. And the restoration is more than a mere going back, the original content is enriched by the division, struggle, and resettlement.

When first the division takes place in the will, consciousness is so enamored of its novelty and its apparent efficiency in solving the practical problems of life that it forgets its own mission, which is to enlighten the will. Instead of turning its illuminating rays within itself—that is, toward the will from which it has its principle of existence—consciousness is kept busy with the objective world of realities and ideas; and when it tries to look into itself, there is a world of absolute unity where the object of which it wishes to know is the subject itself. The sword cannot cut itself. The darkness of Ignorance cannot be dispelled because it is its own self. At this point the will has to make a heroic effort to enlighten itself, to redeem itself, without destroying the once-awakened consciousness or rather by working out the principle lying at the basis of consciousness. This was accomplished as we see in the case of the Buddha, and he became more than mere Gautama, he was the Awakened One and the Exalted and supremely Enlightened. In willing there is really something more than mere willing, there is thinking and seeing. By this seeing, the will sees itself and is thereby made free and its own master. This is knowing in the most fundamental sense of the term and herein consists the Buddhist redemption.

Ignorance prevails as long as the will remains cheated by its own offspring or its own image, consciousness, in which the knower always stands distinguished from the known. The cheating, however, cannot last, the will wishes to be enlightened, to be free, to be by itself. Ignorance always presupposes the existence of something outside and unknown. This unknown outsider is generally termed ego or soul, which is in reality the will itself in the state of Ignorance. Therefore, when the Buddha experienced Enlightenment, he at once realized that there was no *ātman*, no soul-entity as an unknown and unknowable quantity. Enlightenment dispelled Ignorance and with it all the bogies conjured up from the dark cave of ego disappeared. Ignorance in its general use is opposed to knowledge, but from the Buddhist point of view, in which it stands contrasted to Enlightenment, it means the ego (*ātman*), which is so emphatically denied by the Buddha. This is not to be wondered at, seeing that the Buddha's teaching centered in the doctrine of Enlightenment, the dispelling of Ignorance.

Those who see only the doctrine of non-*ātman* in Buddhism, and fail to inquire into the meaning of Enlightenment, are incapable of appreciating the full significance of the Buddha's message to the world. If he simply denied the existence of an ego-entity from the psychological point of view after reducing it into its component factors, scientifically he may be called great as his analytical faculties stood far above those of his contemporaries in this respect; but his influence as a spiritual leader would not have reached so far and endured so long. His theory of non-*ātman* was not only established by a modern scientific method, but essentially was the outcome of his inner experience. When Ignorance is understood in the deeper sense, its dispelling unavoidably results in the negation of an ego-entity as the basis of all our life-activities. Enlightenment is a positive conception, and for ordinary minds it is quite hard to comprehend it in its true bearings. But when we know what it means in the general system of Buddhism, and concentrate our efforts in the realization of it, all the rest will take care of themselves, such as the notion of Ego, Ignorance, Fetters, Defilements, etc. "Moral conduct," "contemplation," and "higher understanding"—all these are meant to bring about the desired end of Buddhism; that is, Enlightenment. The Buddha's constant reiteration of the theory of causation, telling his disciples how, when this is cause, that is effect, and how, when cause disappears, effect also disappears, is not primarily to get them acquainted with a kind of formal logic, but to let them see how Enlightenment is causally related to all human happiness and spiritual freedom and tranquillity.

So long as Ignorance is understood as logical inability to know, its disappearance can never bring out the spiritual freedom to which even the earliest known literature of Buddhism makes so frequent and so emphatic allusions. . . .

Enlightenment or the dispelling of Ignorance, which is the ideal of the Buddhist life, we can see now most clearly, is not an act of the intellect, but the transforming or remodelling of one's whole being through the exercise of the most fundamental faculty innate in every one of us. Mere understanding has something foreign in it and does not seem to come so intimately into life. If Enlightenment had really such a tremendous effect on our spiritual outlook as we read in the sutras, it could not be the outcome of just getting acquainted with the doctrine of Causation. Enlightenment is the work of *prajñā*, which is born of the will which wants to see itself and to be in itself. Hence the Buddha's emphasis on the importance of personal experience; hence his insistence on meditation in solitude as the means of leading to the experience. Meditation, through which the will endeavors to transcend the condition it has put on itself in the awakening of consciousness, is therefore by no means the simple act of cogitating on the theory of Origination or Causation, which forever moves in a circle, starting from Ignorance and ending in Ignorance. This is the one thing that is most needed in Buddhism. All the other metaphysical problems involve us in a tangled skein, in a matted mass of thread.

Ignorance is thus not to be got rid of by metaphysical means but by the struggle of the will. When this is done, we are also freed from the notion of an ego-entity which is the product or rather the basis of Ignorance, on which it depends and thrives. The ego is the dark spot where the rays of the intellect fail to penetrate, it is the last hiding-lair of Ignorance, where the latter serenely keeps itself from the light. When this lair is laid bare and turned inside out, Ignorance vanishes like frost in the sun. In fact, these two are one and the same thing, Ignorance and the idea of ego. We are apt to think that when Ignorance is driven out and the ego loses its hold on us, we have nothing to lean against and are left to the fate of a dead leaf blown away hither and thither as the wind listeth. But this is not so; for Enlightenment is not a negative idea meaning simply the absence of Ignorance. Indeed, Ignorance is the negation of Enlightenment and not the reverse. Enlightenment is affirmation in the truest sense of the word, and therefore it was stated by the Buddha that he who sees the Dharma sees the Buddha, and he who sees the Buddha sees the Dharma, and again that he who wants to see the Buddha ought not to seek him in form, nor in voice, etc. When Ignorance ruled supreme, the ego was conceived to be a positive idea, and its denial was nihilistic. It was quite natural for Ignorance to uphold the ego where it found its original home. But with the realization of Enlightenment, the whole affair changes its aspect, and the order instituted by Ignorance is reversed from top to bottom. What was negative is now positive, and what was positive now negative. Buddhist scholars ought not to forget this revaluation of ideas that comes along with Enlightenment. Since Buddhism asserts Enlightenment to be the ultimate fact of Buddhist life, there is in it nothing negativistic, nothing pessimistic.

3. *HISTORY OF ZEN BUDDHISM FROM BODHIDHARMA TO ENŌ (HUI-NENG)*[1]
(A.D. 520–A.D. 713)

MY intention here is not to make a thoroughly critical and scientific study of the history of Zen Buddhism; for this presupposes some knowledge of the development of Buddhism in China, and there are, as far as my knowledge extends, no textbooks on the subject, which are accessible to readers of this book. The main object of the present essay will therefore be to acquaint them first with the traditional history of Zen as it is told by its followers both in Japan and China. Its critical investigation will follow when readers are in a degree prepared for the task.

The traditional origin of Zen in India before its introduction into China, which is recorded in Zen literature, is so mixed with legends that no reliable facts can be gathered from it. In the days when there was yet no critical study of anything and when things, especially relating to religion, were believed in a wholesale manner, we could not expect anything else. It may now be too late to try to unravel the mysteries enveloping the origin of Zen in India except in a general and logical way from the historical facts already known concerning the development of Mahayana Buddhism. In fact, Zen Buddhism, as was already discussed, is the product of the Chinese mind, or rather the Chinese elaboration of the Doctrine of Enlightenment. Therefore, when we want to narrate the history of Zen, it may be better in some respects not to go to India but to stay in China and study the psychology and philosophy of her people and the surrounding conditions that made it possible for Zen to achieve a successful growth in the land of the celestials, always remembering that it is a practical interpretation of the Doctrine of Enlightenment.

Some scholars may, however, object to this kind of treatment

---

[1] *Essays in Zen Buddhism* (First Series), pp. 163–228.

of the subject, on the ground that if Zen is at all a form of
Buddhism, or even the essence of it as is claimed by its followers,
it cannot be separated from the general history of Buddhism in
India. This is quite true, but as far as facts are concerned, Zen
as such did not exist in India—that is, in the form as we have it
today; and therefore when we try to go beyond China to trace its
origin and development, the only way open to us will be the one
I have followed in my previous essays collected here. That is to
say, we must consider Zen the Chinese interpretation of the
Doctrine of Enlightenment, which is expounded in all Buddhist
literature, most intensively in the Mahayana and more or less provisionally in the Hinayana. As time went on this doctrine steadily
grew to occupy the minds of the Buddha's followers and to control
the course of development of Buddhist thought generally; for was
it not through Enlightenment that Guatama became the Buddha,
the Enlightened One? And is it not the object of Buddhism to follow the footsteps of its founder in the attainment of final emancipation? But the Chinese adherents of Buddhism [2] or the upholders
of Enlightenment did not wish to swallow Indian Buddhism undigested. The practical imagination of the Chinese people came
thus to create Zen, and developed it to the best of their abilities to
suit their own religious requirements.

When we compare Zen as a finished product with the Doctrine
of Enlightenment, as the latter began to unfold itself in primitive
Buddhism, we find a wide and seemingly impassable gap between
the two. This was, however, naturally to be expected. Let us consider the following facts. In the beginning the Buddha was somewhat
timid to disclose the entire secrets of the reason of Buddhahood,
thinking that his disciples were not quite capable of following
every step he had taken himself. The feeling he first had after
Enlightenment governed him almost throughout the entire course
of his earthly life. It was this: that the Perfect Supreme Enlightenment attained by him was too exalted an object for sentient
beings to strive after, and that even when it was disclosed to them
they would not fully comprehend it but might defile it to their own
demerit. Did he not even think of passing into Nirvana right after
Enlightenment? His whole life, in spite of the advice of the
Brahmadeva, seems to have been controlled by this feeling—the

---

[2] Used to designate the school which upholds the Doctrine of Enlightenment (sambodhi).

reluctance to reveal the entirety of his inmost self-realization (*pratyātmajñāna*, according to the terminology of the *Laṅkāvatāra*). In point of fact, the Buddha himself might have communicated what he realized to all his disciples unreservedly, but the impression we get from the Āgama or Nikāya literature is that he was actually reluctant to do so. At least this was the way the earlier writers of the canonical books attempted to represent their master whatever their motives might be. This being the case, the idea of Enlightenment was not brought forward so fully and conspicuously in Hinayana literature as at once to command our attention. But as I pointed out, this idea lies only superficially buried among the other and less-important ideas, and can easily be made manifest by logically and psychologically following up the course of events related in the canonical writings concerning the Enlightenment of the Buddha.

The earlier writers conceived the Fourfold Noble Truth or the Twelvefold Chain of Causation, or the Eightfold Path of Righteousness to be the central teaching of Buddhism, which also included on the psychological side the theory of non-ego (*anātman*). But when we reflect, both philosophically and from the Zen point of view, on the life of the Buddha and on the ultimate principle of Buddhahood, we cannot help thinking of his Enlightenment as the most significant and most essential and most fruitful part of Buddhism. Therefore, what the Buddha really wished to impart to his disciples must be said to have been the Doctrine of Enlightenment in spite of the Hinayanistic interpretation or understanding of what is known as early Buddhism. But so long as Buddhism flourished in India, this central idea of Enlightenment did not make very much further development than is expounded in most of the Mahayana sutras. It was only after Bodhidharma, who brought it to China, that the idea took root there and grew up to what we designate now specifically as the Zen school of Buddhism. The history of Zen, therefore, properly speaking or in its narrower sense, may best be regarded as beginning in China. The Indian soil was too metaphysical, too rich in romantic imagination, for Zen to grow as such in its pure form.

While the attainment of Buddhahood or Arhatship was the ultimate goal of his teaching, the Buddha was practical and always close to the facts of life and insisted in his ordinary sermons on a life regulated by moral rules. Nor had he any desire to disclose intellectually or metaphysically the content of Enlightenment which must be experienced but cannot be explained. He never neglected to emphasize the significance of self-realization, for Nirvana or Enlightenment was to be attained personally through one's own efforts in one's own inner consciousness. The Fourfold Noble Truth or the Twelvefold Chain of Causation or the Theory of Non-ego was an intellectual guide to the realization of the Buddhist life. Such teaching could not have any practical meaning except as finally leading to Enlightenment.

The Buddha never thought that his followers would come to lay the entire stress of his teaching on these intellectual structures which could not stand by themselves without being supported by an inner spirit. The Eightfold Path of Righteousness was an ethical guide to Enlightenment, and as such it was regarded by the Buddha. Those who have no higher insight into his teaching than reading a moral signification in it take it for a kind of ethical culture and no more. They think that Buddhism is a positivism as philosophy and its Brotherhood (Sangha) a body of moral ascetics. They praise the Buddha as the originator of a scientific religious system free from spiritualistic superstitions which so frequently and abundantly grow around religion. But we know better because these comments are not in full accord with the teaching of the Buddha, for they only reflect one side of it and fail to take an inner and comprehensive view of the whole field. If these critics took up the practice of dhyāna as constituting the essence of Buddhism along with the above considerations, they may be said to have come nearer to the goal; but even this dhyāna is a form of spiritual exercise which will prepare the way to the final realization of nirvāṇa. Dhyāna in itself does not distinguish Buddhism from the other philosophico-religious systems which existed in India in the day of the Buddha. Therefore, to understand Zen as expressing the Doctrine of Enlightenment, which is the reason of Buddhism, we must wait for the rise of the Mahayana. And when this was introduced into China by Bodhidharma, it grew up to what we now know by the name of Zen Buddhism.

I

The legendary story of the origin of Zen in India runs as follows: Śākyamuni was once engaged at the Mount of the Holy Vulture in preaching to a congregation of his disciples. He did not resort to any lengthy verbal discourse to explain his point, but simply lifted before the assemblage a bouquet of flowers which was presented to him by one of his lay-disciples. Not a word came out of his mouth. Nobody understood the meaning of this except the old venerable Mahākāśyapa, who quietly smiled at the master, as if he fully comprehended the purport of this silent but eloquent teaching on the part of the Enlightened One. The latter perceiving this opened his golden-tongued mouth and proclaimed solemnly, "I have the most precious treasure, spiritual and transcendental, which this moment I hand over to you, O venerable Mahākāśyapa!"

Orthodox Zen followers generally blindly take this incident to be the origin of their doctrine, in which, according to them, is disclosed the inmost mind of the Buddha as well as the secret of the religion. As Zen claims to be the inmost essence of Buddhism and to have been directly transmitted by the Buddha to his greatest disciple, Mahākāśyapa, its followers naturally look for the particular occasion when this transmission took place between the master and the disciple. We know in a general way that Mahākāśyapa succeeded the Buddha as the leader of the Faith, but as to his special transmission of Zen, we have no historical records in the Indian Buddhist writings at present in our possession. This fact is, however, specially mentioned for the first time, as far as we know, in a Chinese Zen history called "The Records of the Spread of the Lamp," compiled by Ri Shunkyoku, in 1029, and also in "The Accounts of the Orthodox Transmission of the Dharma," compiled by Kaisū in 1064, where this incident is only referred to as not quite an authentic one historically. In "The Records of the Transmission of the Lamp," written in 1004, which is the earliest Zen history now extant, the author does not record any particular event in the life of the Buddha regarding the Zen transmission. As all the earlier histories of Zen are lost, we have at present no means to ascertain how early the Zen tradition started in China. Probably it began to be talked about among the Zen followers when their religion had been well established in China late in the eighth century.

In those days there must have been some necessity to invent such a legend for the authorization of Zen Buddhism; for as Zen grew in strength the other schools of Buddhism already in existence grew jealous of its popular influence and attacked it as having no authorized records of its direct transmission from the founder of Buddhism, which was claimed by the devotees of Zen. This was the case especially when the latter made so light of the doctrinal teaching discussed in the sutras and sastras, as they thought that the ultimate authority of Zen issued out of their own direct personal experience. In this latter they were quite insistent; but they were not, nor could they be, so critical and independent as to ignore altogether the authority of historical Buddhism, and they wanted somehow to find the record that the Buddha handed Zen over to Mahākāśyapa and from Mahākāśyapa on to the twenty-eighth patriarch, Bodhidharma, who became the first patriarch of Zen in China. A line of twenty-eight Indian patriarchs thus came to be established by Zen historians, while, according to other schools, there were only twenty-three or twenty-four patriarchs after the founder. When the historians had the need for the special transmission of Zen from the Buddha to Mahākāśyapa, they felt it necessary to fill up the gap between the twenty-third or twenty-fourth patriarch and Bodhidharma himself, who according to them was the twenty-eighth.

From the modern critical point of view it does not matter very much whether Zen originated with Bodhidharma in China or with the Buddha in India, inasmuch as Zen is true and has an enduring value. And again from the historian's point of view, which tries scientifically to ascertain the source of development resulting in Zen Buddhism, it is only important to find a logical connection between the Mahayana Doctrine of Enlightenment in India and its practical application by the Chinese to the actualities of life; and as to any special line of transmission in India before Bodhidharma as was established by the Zen devotees, it is not a matter of much concern nor of great importance. But as soon as Zen is formulated into an independent system, not only with its characteristic features but with its historically ascertainable facts, it will be necessary for the historians to trace its line of transmission complete and not interrupted; for in Zen, as we shall see later, it is of the utmost importance for its followers to be duly certified or approved by the masters as to the genuineness or orthodox character of their realization. Therefore, as long as Zen is the product of the Chinese soil from the Indian seed of Enlightenment as I take it, no special line of transmission need be established in India unless it is in a general logical manner such as was attempted in my previous essays.

The twenty-eight patriarchs of Zen regarded by its followers as the orthodox line of transmission are as follows:

1. Śākyamuni
2. Mahākāśyapa
3. Ānanda
4. Śaṇavāsa
5. Upagupta
6. Dhṛitika
7. Micchaka
8. Buddhanandi
9. Buddhamitra
10. Bhikshu Pārśva
11. Puṇyayaśas
12. Aśvaghosha
13. Bhikshu Kapimala
14. Nāgārjuna

15. Kāṇadeva
16. Ārya Rāhulata
17. Saṃghanandi
18. Saṃghayaśas
19. Kumāralāta
20. Jayata
21. Vasubandhu
22. Manura
23. Haklenayaśas
24. Bhikshu Siṃha
25. Vāśasita
26. Puṇyamitra
27. Prajñātara
28. Bodhidharma[3]

To be consistent with the view that Zen was a "special transmission from the Buddha outside of his doctrinal teaching," Zen historians have extended this transmission even beyond Śākyamuni; for, according to tradition prevalent already among early Buddhists, there were at least six Buddhas prior to the Buddha of the present kalpa who was the Muni of the Śākyas; and these several Buddhas had each to leave a *gātha* of "Dharma transmission" which is systematically preserved in Zen history. Now if the six Buddhas of the past had their *gātha*, why not those patriarchs between Śākyamuni and Bodhidharma, all inclusively? Or, if any one of them had at all any kind of *gātha*, why not the rest of them too? So, they have all bequeathed their *gātha* of transmission regularly prefaced with the words, "I now hand over to you the eye-treasure of the Great Law, which you will guard and ever be mindful of." No doubt they are fictitious productions of the historical imagination which was so highly exercised by the early writers of Zen history, evidently inspired by an extraordinary zeal for their orthodox faith.

The translators of these patriarchal verses are, according to the author of the "Records of the Right Transmission," Shikyōryōrō of the First Wei dynasty, and Narenyasha, of the Eastern Wei;

[3] It should be noted that Bodhidharma, listed here as the twenty-eighth patriarch of Zen in India, is also considered the first patriarch of Zen in China.

the former came from Middle India and the latter from Kabul. Their book, known as the "Account of Succession in the Law," disappeared after the repeated persecutions carried out by the reigning dynasties, but the stories of these patriarchs were quoted at least in the two books, the *Pao-lin Ch'uan* and the *Shêng-chou Chi*, both compiled prior to the "Transmission of the Lamp," in which they are referred to. But they too were lost some time after Kaisū in the Sung dynasty. Therefore at present the "Transmission of the Lamp" is the earliest history of Zen, where the twenty-eight patriarchs and their verses of law transmission are recorded in detail.

To quote as samples two of the six Buddhas' *gātha*, the first Buddha Vipaśyin declares:

> This body from within the Formless is born,
> It is like through magic that all forms and images appear:
> Phantom beings with mentality and consciousness have no
>   reality from the very beginning;
> Both evil and happiness are void, have no abodes.

The *gātha* of the sixth Buddha, Kāśyapa, who just preceded the Muni of the Śākyas, runs thus:

> Pure and immaculate is the nature of all sentient beings;
> From the very beginning there is no birth, no death;
> This body, this mind—a phantom creation it is;
> And in phantom transformation there are neither sins nor
>   merits.

When the Buddha belonging to the present age ordered Mahā-kāśyapa to be the orthodox transmitter of the Good Law, he uttered the following verse:

> The Dharma is ultimately a dharma which is no-dharma;
> A dharma which is no-dharma is also a dharma;
> As I now hand this no-dharma over to thee;
> What we call the Dharma, the Dharma—where after all is
>   the Dharma?

The sixth patriarch, Dhṛitika, has:

Penetrate into the ultimate truth of mind,
And we have neither things nor no-things;
Enlightened and not-enlightened—they are the same;
Neither mind nor things there is.

The twenty-second patriarch, Manura, gave his view thus:

The mind moveth with the ten thousand things:
Even when moving, it is serene.
Perceive its essence as it moveth on,
And neither joy nor sorrow there is.

In these *gāthas* we notice the teaching generally characteristic of Mahayana Buddhism as it prevailed in India. As I said before, as far as the doctrinal side of Buddhism was concerned, Zen had nothing particularly to offer as its own; for its raison d'être consists in its being a spiritual experience and not in its being a special system of philosophy or of certain dogmas conceptually synthesized. We have Zen only when the Mahayana Buddhist speculation is reduced to the actual things of life and becomes the direct expression of one's inner life. And this did not come to pass until Buddhism was transplanted into China and made there to grow nourished by a people whose practical turn of mentality refused to swallow the Indian tradition undigested. The form of thought as adopted in the so-called patriarchal verses did not appeal to the Chinese mind. When they got into the thought itself, they wished to express it in their own way, they wished to live the thought as was natural to them, and not to hoard it as something imported from abroad and not inherently belonging to their psychology.

When Bodhidharma gave his full sanction to his disciples, he is supposed to have composed the following *gātha*:

The original reason of my coming to this country
Was to transmit the Law in order to save the confused;
One flower with five petals is unfolded,
And the bearing of fruit will by itself come.

By this "bearing of fruit" did Bodhidharma prophesy the full development of Zen later in China? The "five petals" are supposed to mean the five Zen Fathers in China after Dharma when Zen came to be recognized as a branch of Buddhism with a message of its own. Whether this *gātha* was really a prophetic one by Bodhidharma himself, or whether it was composed by some Zen historian after the sixth patriarch Enō, we have no means to decide. The one thing certain historically is that Bodhidharma's teaching began to be naturalized in China about two hundred years after him and assimilated by her people in a manner best suited to their mental idiosyncrasies. Zen in the form we have it today could not mature anywhere outside China. India was too metaphysical, or too given up to mystic imagination. It was the home for the Yuishiki (Yogācāra), the Shingon (Mantra school), the Kegon (Avataṃsaka), or the Sanron (Śūnyatā or Mādhyamika). As for Zen, it needed a mind which had already been deeply steeped in the Laotzŭan ideas and feelings and yet could not detach itself from the details of daily life. Aloofness, romanticism, a certain practical temperament, and yet an even, steady, well-balanced character—these were needed to develop Zen to its present form. That is to say, if Mahayana Buddhism, as was expounded by Nāgārjuna and Aśvaghosha, and in the *Vimalakīrti, Prajñāpāramitā*, and other sutras, especially in the *Laṅkāvatāra*, were not worked upon by Chinese genius, Zen as such could not at all have come into existence.

It may not altogether be out of place here to show by concrete examples how much the Indian method diverges from the typically Chinese one in demonstrating the truth of Zen Buddhism. As I have repeatedly illustrated, Buddhism, whether early or later, is a religion of freedom and emancipation, and the ultimate aim of its discipline is to release the spirit from its possible bondage so that it can act freely in accordance with its own principles. This is what is meant by non-attachment (*apratishṭita-cittam*). The idea is negative inasmuch as it is concerned with untying the knots of the intellect and passion, but the feeling implied is positive, and the final object is attained only when the spirit is restored to its original activity. The spirit knows its own way, and what we can do is to rid it of all the obstacles our ignorance has piled before it. "Throw them down" is therefore the recurring note in the Buddhist teaching.

The Indian Buddhist way of impressing the idea is this: a Brahman named Black-nails came to the Buddha and offered him two huge flowering trees which he carried each in one of his hands through his magical power. The Buddha called out, and when the

Brahman responded the Buddha said, "Throw them down!" The Brahman let down the flowering tree in his left hand before the Buddha. The latter called out again to let them go, whereupon Black-nails dropped the other flowering tree in the right hand. The Buddha still kept up his command. Said the Brahman: "I have nothing now to let go. What do you want me to do?"

"I never told you to abandon your flowering plants," said the Buddha, "what I want you to do is to abandon your six objects of sense, your six organs of sense, and your six consciousnesses. When these are all at once abandoned and there remains nothing further to be abandoned, it is then that you are released from the bondage of birth-and-death."

In contrast to this plain, though somewhat roundabout, talk of the Buddha, the following case of Jōshū Jūshin is direct and concise and disposes of the matter in a most unequivocal manner. A monk came and asked the master, "How is it when a man brings nothing with him?"

"Throw it away!" was Jōshū's immediate response.

"What shall he throw down when he is not burdened at all?"

"If so, carry it along!"

The Zen masters delight in paradoxes, and Jōshū's remark here is a typical one.

The problem of emancipation is important, but the still more important one is, "Who or what is the Buddha?" When this is mastered, Buddhism has rendered its full service. What did the Indian philosophers think of the Buddha? There was an old lady who lived at the time of the Buddha. She was born at the same time as the Buddha himself and lived in the eastern part of the city. She had a singular aversion against the Buddha and never wished to see him. Whenever he passed by she would run away. But whichever way she turned she would encounter him, east or west. She covered her face with her hands, and lo! she saw the Buddha between her fingers. This is beautiful and illuminating. What follows is the Zen way of treating the subject: A monk came to Enkan Saian, a disciple of Baso, and asked, "What is the original body of Vairocana?"

Said the master, "Would you mind passing that water-pitcher over to me?"

The monk handed it to the master as asked. Then the master requested him to put it back where he got it. The monk did so. But not getting any answer as he thought to his first question, he

asked again, "What is the original body of Vairocana Buddha?"
The master expressed his regret, saying, "Long it is since the departure of the old Buddha!"

These two instances will suffice to illustrate where the Chinese
Zen mind deviates from the Indian.

II

The history of Zen dates with the coming of Bodhidharma
(Bodai-daruma) from the west, A.D. 520. He came to China with
a special message which is summed up in the following lines:

> A special transmission outside the Scripture;
> No dependence on words or letters;
> Direct pointing at the Mind of man;
> Seeing into one's Nature and the attainment of Buddhahood.

These four lines as describing the principles of Zen teaching as
distinguished from other schools of Buddhism already in existence
in China were formulated later and not by Bodhidharma himself.
We cannot exactly tell who was the real author, as we have no
definite information on this subject. One historian, Sōkan, who
compiled from the T'ien-t'ai point of view a Buddhist history entitled "The Rightful Lineage of the Sākya Doctrine" in 1237, as-
scribes it to Nansen Fugwan; probably the formula originated in
those days when Baso, Hyakujō, Ōbaku, Sekitō, and Yakusan were
flourishing in the "West of the River" and in the "South of the
Lake." Since then they have been regarded as characteristically
Zen, and it was Bodhidharma who breathed this spirit into the
minds of the Chinese Buddhists. The latter had more or less been
given up, on the one hand, to philosophizing, and, on the other
hand, to practicing contemplation. They were not acquainted
with the direct method of Zen which was to see straightway into
the truth of Enlightenment and attain Buddhahood without going
through so many stages of preparation prescribed by the scholars.

Our knowledge of the life of Bodhidharma comes from two
sources. One, which is the earliest record we have of him, is by
Dōsen in his "Biographies of the High Priests" which was compiled
early in the T'ang dynasty, A.D. 645. The author was the founder

of a Vinaya sect in China and a learned scholar, who, however, was living before the movement of the new school to be known as Zen came into maturity under Enō, the sixth patriarch, who was nine years old when Dōsen wrote his *Biographies*. The other source is "The Records of the Transmission of the Lamp," A.D. 1004, compiled by Dōgen early in the Sung dynasty. This was written by a Zen monk after Zen had received full recognition as a special branch of Buddhism, and contains sayings and doings of its masters. The author often refers to some earlier Zen histories as his authorities, which are, however, lost now, being known by the titles only.

It is quite natural that these two accounts of the life of Bodhidharma should vary at several points. The first was written when Zen was not yet fully established as a school, and the second by one of the Zen masters. In the first, Bodhidharma, the founder of Zen, is treated as one of the many other Buddhist priests eminent in various fields as translators, commentators, scholars, Vinaya followers, masters of meditation, possessors of miraculous virtues, etc., and Bodhidharma could not naturally occupy in such a history any very prominent position distinguishing him from the other "high priests." He is described merely as one of those "masters of meditation" whose conception of *dhyāna* did not differ from the old traditional one as was practiced by the Hinayana followers.

Dōsen did not understand the message of Bodhidharma in its full signification, though he could read in it something not quite of the so-called "practice of meditation." And therefore it is sometimes argued by scholars that there is not much of Zen in Dōsen's account of Bodhidharma worthy of its first Chinese promulgator and that therefore Bodhidharma could not be so regarded as is claimed by the followers of the Zen school of Buddhism. But this is not doing justice to Zen, nor to Dōsen, who never thought of writing a Zen history before Zen came to be known as such. Dōsen could not be a prophetic historian. While the biographical history of Dōgen contains much that is to be discredited as regards the life of Bodhidharma, especially that part of his life before he came to China, we have reason to believe that the greater part of Dōgen's account of Bodhidharma's doings after his arrival in China is historical. In this latter respect Dōsen must be taken as complementing Dōgen. It is not quite in accord with the spirit of fair critical judgment to be partial to one authority at the expense of the other without duly weighing all the historically known circumstances that contributed to the making of these histories.

According to Dōsen, Bodhidharma left many writings or sayings which were apparently still in circulation at the time of the
author of the *Biographies of the High Priests,* but the only authentic writing of the Zen founders at present in our possession is a
very short one, which is preserved in Dōsen's "Biographies," as well
as in Dōgen's "Records." There are some other essays ascribed to
Bodhidharma,[4] but most of those, though deeply imbibing the
spirit of Zen, are spurious except one which I am inclined to think
to be genuinely his. It is entitled "On the Pacification of the Soul."
Together with the first one, which is generally known under the
title "The Meditation on Four Acts," we have just two pieces of
writing handed down as Bodhidharma's. Though I do not think
that "The Meditation on Four Acts" could be the best possible
specimen of writing to be bequeathed by the founder of Zen,
which will admit us straightway into the very essence of Zen, I
will give here an English translation of it as the most reliable essay
of Bodhidharma, the first patriarch of Zen in China.

There are two versions, as I said before, of the writing, the one
in the "Biographies" and the other in the "Records," and they do not
quite agree with each other in some points. The main drift is the
same, but in detail they vary. The question now is: which is the
more original one? Chronologically the "Biographies" were compiled earlier than the "Records," but the latter presupposes some
earlier writings which were utilized for its compilation. We have
no means to ascertain the reliability of the documents thus made
use of, and then the authority of the "Biographies" is not absolute.
Therefore the only profitable method of judging the respective
merit of the two versions is to compare them from the literary
point of view and see what light such comparison will shed on the
nature of each. The result I have reached is that the author of the
"Biographies" used the one preserved in the "Records," which is
more faithful to the original if there were any such besides this very
version. The reason for this conclusion is that Bodhidharma's writing appears much improved after the editing of Dōsen, the author
of the "Biographies"; for he had to edit it for his own purposes. Thus
edited, Bodhidharma's writing is now in a better style; that is,
more concise, more to the point, and more refined. For this reason
the following translation is made from Dōgen's "Records" in which

---

4 "Six Essays" by Bodhidharma is the book in which the so-called writings
of Bodhidharma are collected.

the author had every reason to reproduce the original as it stood.

[Bodhidharma], the Teacher of the Law, was the third son of a great Brahman king in South India, of the Western Lands. He was a man of wonderful intelligence, bright and far-reaching; he thoroughly understood everything that he ever learned. As his ambition was to master the doctrine of the Mahayana, he abandoned the white dress of a layman and put on the black robe of monkhood, wishing to cultivate the seeds of holiness. He practiced contemplation and tranquillization, he knew well what was the true significance of worldly affairs. Inside and outside he was transpicuous; his virtues were more than a model to the world. He was grieved very much over the decline of the orthodox teaching of the Buddha in the remoter parts of the earth. He finally made up his mind to cross over land and sea and come to China and preach his doctrine in the kingdom of Wei. Those that were spiritually inclined gathered about him full of devotion, while those that could not rise above their own one-sided views talked about him slanderingly.

At the time there were only two monks called Dōiku and Eka, who while yet young had a strong will and desire to learn higher things. Thinking it a great opportunity of their lives to have such a teacher of the Law in their own land, they put themselves under his instruction for several years. Most reverently they followed him, asked questions to be enlightened, and observed his directions well. The Teacher of the Law was moved by their spirit of sincerity and disciplined them in the true path, telling them, 'This is the way to obtain peace of mind,' and 'This is the way to behave in the world,' 'This is the way to live harmoniously with your surroundings,' and 'This is the *upāya* (means).' These being the Mahayana ways to keep the mind tranquil, one has to be on guard against their wrongful applications. By this mental pacification *pi-kuan*[5] is meant; by this behavior, the Four Acts; by this harmony with things, the protection from slander and ill-disposition; and by this *upāya*, detachment.

Thus I[6] have briefly stated the story of what follows.

[5] *Hekkwan* in Japanese. This is the most significant phrase in Bodhidharma's writing. I have left it untranslated, for later this will be explained fully.

[6] The author of this story or prefatory note is Donrin, who, according to Dr. Tokiwa, of Tokyo Imperial University, was a learned scholar partaking in the translation of several Sanskrit works. He is also mentioned in connection with Eka in the biography of the latter by Dōsen. If Donrin were more of a

There are many ways to enter the Path, but briefly speaking they are of two sorts only. The one is "Entrance by Reason" and the other "Entrance by Conduct." By "Entrance by Reason" we mean the realization of the spirit of Buddhism by the aid of the scriptural teaching. We then come to have a deep faith in the True Nature which is one and the same in all sentient beings. The reason why it does not manifest itself is due to the overwrapping of external objects and false thoughts. When one, abandoning the false and embracing the true, and in simpleness of thought abides in *pi-kuan*, one finds that there is neither selfhood nor otherness, that the masses and the worthies are of one essence, and firmly holds on to this belief and never moves away therefrom. He will not then be guided by any literary instructions, for he is in silent communion with the principle itself, free from conceptual discrimination, for he is serene and not-acting. This is called "Entrance by Reason."

By "Entrance by Conduct" is meant the Four Acts in which all other acts are included. What are the four? 1. How to requite hatred; 2. To be obedient to karma; 3. Not to seek after anything; and 4. To be in accord with the Dharma.

1. What is meant by "How to requite hatred"? Those who discipline themselves in the Path should think thus when they have to struggle with adverse conditions: During the innumerable past ages I have wandered through multiplicity of existences, all the while giving myself to unimportant details of life at the expense of essentials, and thus creating infinite occasions for hate, ill-will, and wrongdoing. While no violations have been committed in this life, the fruits of evil deeds in the past are to be gathered now. Neither gods nor men can foretell what is upon me. I will submit myself willingly and patiently to all the ills that befall me, and I will never bemoan or complain. In the Sutra it is said not to worry over ills that may happen to you. Why? Because through intelligence one can survey (the whole chain of causation). When this thought arises, one is in concord with the principle because he makes the best use of hatred and turns it into the service in his advance toward the Path. This is called the "way to requite hatred."

2. By "being obedient to karma" is meant this: There is no self (*ātman*) in whatever beings that are produced by the interplay of

---

scholar as we can see by this identification than a genuine Zen master, it was quite natural for him to write down this "Meditation on Four Acts," which mainly appeals as it stands to the scholarly interpretation of Zen. While the doctrine of *pi-kuan* is emphatically Zen, there is much in the "Meditation" that lends itself to the philosophizing of Zen.

Karmic conditions; pain and pleasure we suffer are also the results of our previous action. If I am rewarded with fortune, honor, etc., this is the outcome of my past deeds which, by reason of causation, affect my present life. When the force of karma is exhausted, the result I am enjoying now will disappear; what is then the use of being joyful over it? Gain or loss, let us accept karma as it brings us the one or the other; the spirit itself knows neither increase nor decrease. The wind of gladness does not move it, as it is silently in harmony with the Path. Therefore this is called "being obedient to karma."

3. By "not seeking after anything" is meant this: Men of the world, in eternal confusion, are attached everywhere to one thing or another, which is called seeking. The wise, however, understand the truth and are not like the vulgar. Their minds abide serenely in the uncreated while the body turns about in accordance with the laws of causation. All things are empty and there is nothing desirable and to be sought after. Wherever there is the merit of brightness there follows the demerit of darkness. This triple world where one stays too long is like a house on fire; all that has a body suffers, and who would ever know what is rest? Because the wise are thoroughly acquainted with this truth, they never get attached to anything that becomes, their thoughts are quieted, they never seek. Says the Sutra: Wherever there is seeking, there you have sufferings; when seeking ceases you are blessed. Thus we know that not to seek is verily the way to the truth. Therefore I preach to you not "to seek after anything."

4. By "being in accord with the Dharma" is meant that the reason which we call the Dharma, in its essence is pure, and that this reason is the principle of emptiness in all that is manifested, as it is above defilements and attachments, and as there is no Self or Other in it. Says the Sutra: In the Dharma there are no sentient beings, because it is free from the stains of being; in the Dharma there is no Self because it is free from the stain of selfhood. When the wise understand this truth and believe in it, their conduct will be "in accordance with the Dharma."

As the Dharma's essence has no desire to possess, the wise are ever ready to practice charity with their body, life, property, and they never begrudge, they never know what an ill grace means. As they have a perfect understanding of the threefold nature of emptiness they are above partiality and attachment. Only because of their will to cleanse all beings of their stains, they come among them as of them, but they are not attached to the form. This is known as the inner aspect of their life. They, however, know also how to benefit others, and again how to glorify the path of enlightenment. As with the virtue of charity, so with the other five virtues [in the Prajñāpāramita]. That the wise practice the six virtues of perfection is to get rid of confused thoughts, and yet they are not conscious of their doings. This is called "being in accord with the Dharma."

The doctrine of the Two Entrances is evidently taken from the *Vajrasamādhi-sūtra;*[7] and that of the Four Acts is an amplification of the second form of Entrance as is expounded in the Sutra. A comparison with the passage from it will make this point clear at once:

Said the Buddha: The two entrances are "Entrance by Reason" and "Entrance by Conduct." "Entrance by Reason" means to have a deep faith that all sentient beings are identical in essence with the true nature which is neither unity nor multiplicity; only it is beclouded by external objects. The nature in itself neither departs nor comes. When a man in singleness of thought abides in *chüeh-kuan,* he will clearly see into the Buddha-nature, of which we cannot say whether it exists or exists not, and in which there is neither selfhood nor otherness. He will also find that the nature is the same both in the masses and in the worthies. He thus firmly holds the ground of the diamond-heart and never moves away therefrom; he is serene and not-doing, and free from conceptual discrimination. This is called "Entrance by Reason."

"Entrance by Conduct" means not to be unsteady and reclining in mind and not to be in its shadows changing like a stream. Wherever you are, let your thought be serene and not be seeking after anything. Let it be like unto the great earth unmoved even in a raging storm. Giving up all thoughts of egoism in your heart, save all beings and let them cross over to the other shore. There are no births, no signs, no clinging, no abandoning; in the mind of a Bodhisattva there is no going-out, no coming-in. When this mind which neither goes out nor comes in enters into that which is never entered into, it is called entering. This is the way the Bodhisattva enters into the Dharma. The Dharma is not empty in form, and the Dharma of non-emptiness is not to be put aside as nonentity. Why? The Dharma that is not nonentity is filled with virtues. It is neither mind nor shadows, it is pure in its suchness.

In comparing these two texts the reader will be impressed with

---

[7] Translated into Chinese during the Northern Liang dynasty, which lasted from A.D. 397 to 439. The translator's name is lost.

the most important and most striking change Bodhidharma made in his quotation, which is the substituting of *pi-kuan* for *chüeh-kuan*. *Pi* ordinarily means "wall" or "precipice," and is often found in combination with *li*, "standing," in such phrases as *pi li wan jên*, to describe an unscalable wall, or figuratively to represent the attitude, for instance, of Acala-Vidyārāja standing straight up. What was the reason of Bodhidharma's changing *chüeh*, "to awaken," or "to be enlightened" into a word which apparently has no organic relation to the following *kuan*, "to perceive," or "to contemplate"? The novel combination is a very important one, for it alters the sense of the whole context in which it occurs.

Dōsen, the author of the "Biographies", refers to Bodhidharma's *Ta-ch'êng pi-kuan*, "Mahayanistic wall-contemplation," in his commentary notes to Zen, as the most meritorious work Bodhidharma achieved in China. For this reason he is often spoken of as the *Pi-kuan* Brahman—that is, wall-contemplating Brahman—and in Japan the monks belonging to the Sōtō school of Zen are supposed to follow the example of the founder of their religion when they keep up the practice of sitting facing the wall while meditating. But this is evidently a superficial interpretation of the phrase *pi-kuan*; for how could mere wall-gazing start a revolutionary movement in the Buddhist world as is implied in Dōsen's life of Bodhidharma?[8] How could such an innocent practice provoke a terrible opposition among scholars of those days? To my view, *pi-kuan* has a far deeper meaning, and must be understood in the light of the following passage in the "Records," which is quoted from a work known as the *Pieh Chi*, meaning some special document of prior existence:

The master first stayed in the Shōrinji monastery for nine years, and when he taught the second patriarch, it was only in the following way: "Externally keep yourself away from all relationships, and, internally, have no pantings (or hankerings, *ch'uan*) in your heart;[9] when your

---

[8] We read in Dōsen's "Biographies" that wherever Bodhidharma stayed he taught people in his Zen doctrine, but as the whole country at the time was deeply plunged into scholastic discussions, there was a great deal of slanderous talk against meditation when they learned of Bodhidharma's message.

[9] Is it possible that this passage has some reference to the *Vajrasamādhi* where Bodhisattva Mahābala speaks of a "flaccid mind" and a "strong mind"? The former which is possessed by most common people "pants" (or gasps

mind is like unto a straight-standing wall you may enter into the Path." Eka tried variously to explain (or to discourse on) the reason of mind, but failed to realize the truth itself. The master simply said, "No! No!" and never proposed to explain to his disciple what was the mind-essence in its thoughtless state (that is, in its pure being).

(Later) said Eka, "I know now how to keep myself away from all relationships."

"You make it a total annihilation, do you not?" queried the master.

"No, master," replied Eka, "I do not make it a total annihilation."

"How do you verify your statement?"

"For I know it always in a most intelligible manner, but to express it in words—that is impossible."

Thereupon, said the master, "That is the mind-essence itself transmitted by all the Buddhas. Harbor no doubts about it."

In fact, this passage sums up the special message contained in Bodhidharma's teaching, and in it we may get an adequate answer as to the exact meaning of *pi-kuan*. The term must have been a novel one in his day, and the originality of his views really lay in the creative sense of the one word "*pi*." It was so concrete, so graphic, and there was nothing abstract and conceptual about it. Hence Dōsen's special reference to Bodhidharma's teaching as the *Ta-ch'êng pi-kuan* (Mahayanistic wall-contemplation). While there was nothing specifically Zen in his doctrine of "Two Entrances and Four Acts," the teaching of *pi-kuan*, wall-contemplation, was what made Bodhidharma the first patriarch of Zen Buddhism in China.

The author of the "Rightful Transmission of the Śākya Doctrine" interprets *pi-kuan* as meaning the state of mind where "no external dusts get in." This may be all right, but we are not told where he finds the authority for this way of understanding. Had he in mind Bodhidharma's remark to Eka as recorded in the document known

---

or hankers) very much, and prevents them from successfully attaining to the *tathāgata-dhyāna*, while the "strong mind" is characteristic of one who can enter upon the realm of reality (*bhūtakoṭi*). So long as there are "pantings" (or gaspings) in the mind, it is not free, it is not liberated, and cannot identify itself with the suchness of reason. The mind must be "strong" or firm and steady, self-possessed and concentrating, before it is ready for the realization of *tathāgata-dhyāna*—a *dhyāna* going far beyond the reach of the so-called four *dhyānas* and eight *samādhis*.

as *Pieh Chi?* In any event the underlying meaning of the "wall-contemplation" must be found in the subjective condition of a Zen master, which is highly concentrated and rigidly exclusive of all ideas and sensuous images. To understand the phrase *pi-kuan* as simply meaning "wall-gazing" will be sheer absurdity. If the specific message of Bodhidharma as the founder of Zen in China is to be sought anywhere in the writings of his, which are still in existence, it must be in this "Mahayanistic wall-contemplation."

Besides this writing, which is the only one left by Bodhidharma in our possession at present, we have the *Laṅkāvatāra-sūtra,* and *Vajrasamādhi-sūtra,* and *Vajracchedikā-sūtra,* through which we can also have a glimpse into the central teaching of Bodhidharma. Zen, unlike other schools of Buddhism, has no particular sutras to be called the "foundation canon" on which its followers would base the principal tenets of their school; but Bodhidharma recommended the *Laṅkāvatāra* to his first disciple Eka, as containing the teaching most intimately related to Zen, and after him this scriptural writing came to be studied chiefly by Zen scholars. As to the importance of the *Vajrasamādhi* as expounding the philosophy of Zen, we can easily understand it from Bodhidharma's own reference to the sutra in his writing as was already pointed out.

With regard to the *Vajracchedikā-sūtra,* most people think of it as having nothing to do with Zen prior to the fifth patriarch, Gunin; for it was he who, for the first time, introduced it among his own disciples, while Bodhidharma himself made no allusion whatever to this, one of the most popular Buddhist texts in China. But according to Enō's Preface to the *Vajracchedikā,* which is still preserved, "ever since the coming-west of Bodhidharma he wanted to propagate the meaning of this sutra and lead people to understand the Reason and to see into the Nature." If this were actually the case, Bodhidharma, to say the least, must have had some knowledge of this sutra from the very beginning of his career in China, and the connection in a way between this and Zen must have been more fundamental than that between the *Laṅkāvatāra* and Zen. The prevalent notion then that the *Vajracchedikā* came only in vogue after Gunin and Enō must be revised. Whatever this may be, the *Laṅkāvatāra* is too difficult material for popular consumption, and it was natural that this sutra came to be gradually superseded by the *Vajracchedikā* as Zen gained more in power and influence. As one of the sutras belonging to the *Prajñāpāramitā* class of Buddhist literature, the teaching of the *Vajracchedikā* was comparatively simple and had something much akin to the Laotzŭan ideas of emptiness and non-doing. It was not hard for the average Chinese to follow its philosophy of Śūnyatā; in fact this agreed well with a certain aspect of Chinese thought.[10]

However, with Zen followers all literature was like a finger pointing at the moon, and there was not much in itself that will actually lead one to the seeing of one's own inner nature; for this seeing was a realization which must be attained by one's own personal efforts apart from the mere understanding of letters. All Buddhist sutras including the Laṅkāvatāra, Vajrasamādhi, and Vajracchedikā could not be of much help to the really earnest seeker of the truth, so long as his idea is to grasp the naked facts with his own un-gloved hands. This was possible only when his own inner consciousness opened by itself, from within, through his whole-souled efforts. Literature is helpful only when it indicates the way, it is not the thing itself.

The earlier part of Bodhidharma's life while in India, as narrated in the "Records," may be discredited as containing a large dose of fiction, but the latter part of it cannot so easily be disposed of. This is where it supplements the story in Dōsen's "Biographies," which was written by a good historian, however, who did not know anything about the future development of Zen. According to the "Records" then, the first great personage Bodhidharma had an interview with when he came to China was the king of Liang, the greatest Buddhist patron of the time. And the interview took place in the following manner:

The Emperor Wu of Liang asked Bodhidharma:

"Ever since the beginning of my reign I have built so many

---

10 In this connection I wish to make some remarks against certain scholars who consider the philosophy of Śūnyatā to be the foundation of Zen. Such scholars fail utterly to grasp the true purport of Zen, which is first of all an experience and not a philosophy or dogma. Zen can never be built upon any set of metaphysical or psychological views; the latter may be advanced after the Zen experience has taken place, but never before. The philosophy of the Prajñāpāramitā can never precede Zen, but must always follow it. Buddhist scholars like those at the time of Bodhidharma are too apt to identify teaching and life, theory and experience, description and fact. When this confusion is allowed to grow, Zen Buddhism will cease to yield an intelligent and satisfactory interpretation. Without the fact of Enlightenment under the Bodhi-tree near the Nairañjanā, no Nāgārjunas could ever hope to write a single book on the Prajñā philosophy.

temples, copied so many sacred books, and supported so many monks and nuns; what do you think my merit might be?"

"No merit whatever, sire!" Bodhidharma bluntly replied.

"Why?" demanded the Emperor, astonished.

"All these are inferior deeds," thus began Bodhidharma's significant reply, "which would cause their author to be born in the heavens or on this earth again. They still show the traces of worldliness, they are like shadows following objects. Though they appear actually existing, they are no more than mere nonentities. As to a true meritorious deed, it is full of pure wisdom and is perfect and mysterious, and its real nature is beyond the grasp of human intelligence. Such as this is not to be sought after by any worldly achievement."

The Emperor Wu thereupon asked Bodhidharma again, "What is the first principle of the holy doctrine?"

"Vast emptiness, and there is nothing in it to be called holy, sire!" answered Bodhidharma.

"Who is it then that is now confronting me?"

"I know not, sire!"

The answer was simple enough, and clear enough too, but the pious and learned Buddhist Emperor failed to grasp the spirit pervading the whole attitude of Bodhidharma.

Seeing that there was no further help to be given to the Emperor, Bodhidharma left his dominion and retired into a monastery in the state of Wei, where he sat quietly practicing the "wall-contemplation," it is said, for nine long years, until he came to be known as the *Pi-kuan* Brahman.[11]

One day a monk Shinkō (later Eka) visited him and most earnestly implored him to be enlightened in the truth of Zen, but Bodhidharma paid no attention. Shinkō was not to be disappointed, for he knew that all the great spiritual leaders of the past had gone through with many a heartrending trial in order to attain the final object of their aspiration. One evening he stood in the midst of the snow waiting for Bodhidharma to notice him when at last the fast-falling snow buried him almost to his knees.

---

[11] As I stated before, there is a confusion between Bodhidharma's *mien-pi* habit of sitting and his doctrine of the *pi-kuan* meditation. The confusion dates quite early, and even at the time of the author of the "Records" the original meaning of *pi-kuan*, wall-contemplation, must have been lost.

Finally, the master turned back and said, "What do you wish me to do for you?"

Said Shinkō, "I am come to receive your invaluable instructions; pray open your gate of mercy, and extend your hand of salvation to this poor suffering mortal."

"The incomparable doctrine of Buddhism," replied Bodhidharma, "can be comprehended only after a long, hard discipline and by enduring what is most difficult to endure, and by practicing what is most difficult to practice. Men of inferior virtue and wisdom are not allowed to understand anything about it. All the labors of such ones will come to naught."

Shinkō at last cut off his left arm with the sword[12] he was carrying, and presented it before the teacher as a token of his sincerity in the desire to be instructed in the doctrine of all the Buddhas. Said Bodhidharma, "This is not to be sought through another."

"My soul is not yet pacified. Pray, master, pacify it."

"Bring your soul here, and I will have it pacified."

Shinkō hesitated for a moment but finally said, "I have sought it these many years and am still unable to get hold of it!"

"There! it is pacified once for all." This was Bodhidharma's sentence.[13]

Bodhidharma then gave him the name Eka.

Nine years passed, and Bodhidharma wished to return to his native country. He called in all his disciples before him, and said, "The time is come for me to depart, and I want to see what your attainments are."

"According to my view," said Dōfuku, "the truth is above affirmation and negation, for this is the way it moveth."

[12] Sometimes this man is said to be a civilian and sometimes a soldier embracing Confucianism.

[13] As one can readily see, this story is more or less fictitious. I mean Shinkō's standing in the snow and cutting off his arm in order to demonstrate his earnestness and sincerity. Some think that the snow story and that of self-mutilation do not belong to that of Shinkō, but are borrowed from some other sources, as Dōsen makes no reference to them in his book. The loss of the arm was due to a party of robbers who attacked Shinkō after his interview with Bodhidharma. We have no way to verify these stories either way. The whole setting, however, is highly dramatic, and there must have been once in the history of Zen some necessity to interweave imagination largely with facts, whatever they may be.

Bodhidharma said, "You have got my skin."

Next came in the nun, Sōji, and said, "As I understand it, it is like Ānanda's viewing the Buddhaland of Akshobhya: it is seen once and never again."

Bodhidharma said, "You have got my flesh." .

Dōiku was another disciple who presented his view, saying: "Empty are the four elements and nonexistent the five *skandhas*. According to my view, there is not a thing to be grasped as real."

Bodhidharma said, "You have got my bone."

Finally, Eka—that is, Shinkō, reverently bowing to the master, kept standing in his seat and said nothing.

Bodhidharma then announced, "You have my marrow."[14]

Mystery envelops the end of Bodhidharma's life in China; we do not know how, when, and where he passed away from this earth. Some say that he was poisoned by his rivals, others say that he went back to India, crossing the desert, and still others report that he came over to Japan. In one thing they all agree, which is this: he was quite old, being, according to Dōsen, over one hundred and fifty years at his death.

III

After Bodhidharma, Eka (487–593) was the chief exponent of Zen Buddhism. He was already a learned scholar before he came to his teacher for instruction, not only in the Chinese classics but in Buddhist lore. No amount of learning, however, satisfied him; indeed he seems to have had a sort of enlightenment in his way, which he wanted to have Bodhidharma corroborate. After he left the master he did not at once begin his preaching, hiding himself among the lower strata of society. He evidently shunned being

---

[14] According to Keisō, the author of the "Right Transmission of the Law," Bodhidharma has here followed Nāgārjuna in the anatomy of Zen-understanding. For Nāgārjuna says in his famous commentary on the *Prajñā-pāramitā-sūtra*, "Moral conduct is the skin, meditation is the flesh, the higher understanding is the bone, and the mind subtle and good is the marrow."

"This subtle mind," says Keisō, is what is secretly transmitted from the Buddha to his successors in the faith. He then refers to Chigi of the Sui dynasty, who regards this mind as the abode of all the Buddhas and as the middle way in which there is neither unity nor multiplicity and which can never be adequately expressed in words.

looked up to as a high priest of great wisdom and understanding. However, he did not neglect quietly preaching the Dharma whenever he had an occasion. He was simply quiet and unassuming, refusing to show himself off. But one day when he was discoursing about the Dharma before a temple gate, there was another sermon going on inside the temple by a resident priest, learned and honored. The audience, however, left the reverend lecturer inside and gathered around the street monk, probably clad in rags and with no outward signs of ecclesiastical dignity. The high priest got angry over the situation. He accused the beggar monk to the authorities as promulgating a false doctrine, whereupon Eka was arrested and put to death. He did not specially plead innocent but composedly submitted, saying that he had according to the law of karma an old debt to pay up. This took place in A.D 593, and he was one hundred and six years old when he was killed.

According to Dōsen, Eka's eloquence flowed directly from his heart, and was not encrusted with learning or scholarly discourse. While he was preaching in an important city on the meaning of Zen, those who could not rise above "the letter that killeth" took his teaching for heresy, as the words of a devil devoid of sense. Especially among them a master of meditation called Dōkan, who had about one thousand followers about him, at once assumed an offensive attitude toward Eka. He sent one of his disciples to the Zen exponent, perhaps to find out what kind of man he really was. As soon as the disciple learned what was the teaching of the so-called heretic, he was so deeply impressed by this man that he was converted into a Zen advocate. Dōkan despatched another of his followers to call the first one back, but he followed the example of the predecessor. Several other messengers were sent one after another, but the result was altogether discouraging. Later, when Dōkan happened to meet his first messenger, he asked: "How was it that I had to send for you so many times? Did I not open your eye after taking pains so much on my part?" The former disciple, however, mystically answered: "My eye has been right from the first, and it was through you that it came to squint." This stirred the master's ire, and it was through his machination, writes Dōsen, that Eka had to suffer official persecution.

This story taken from Dōsen's "Biographies" varies from that in Dogen's "Records," but they both agree in making Eka a martyr at the hands of his enemy. There is no doubt that in the Zen teaching of Bodhidharma and his first Chinese disciple, Eka, there was something that was unintelligible to most of the Buddhists of the time who had been trained either in the abstract metaphysics or in the tranquillizing exercises, or in the mere morality, of Buddhism. The exponents of Zen then must have emphasized the truth to be awakened in one's inner consciousness, even at the expense of the canonical teaching as is variously elucidated in the sutras and sastras, many of which in translations had already been in circulation. This must have excited the conservatists and literalists.

Like Bodhidharma, Eka did not leave any literary writing, though we know from their biographies that both had their sermons collected and in the case of Eka "classified,"[15] whatever this may mean. The following preserved extracts, however, may throw light on the teaching of Eka. A lay-disciple called Kō wrote a letter to Eka: "Shadow follows a body and echo rises from a sound. He who in pursuit of the shadow tires out the body, does not know that the body produces the shadow; and he who attempts to stop an echo by raising his voice, does not understand that the voice is the cause of the echo. (In a similar way) he who seeks Nirvana by cutting desires and passions is to be likened to one who seeks a shadow apart from its original body; and he who aspires to Buddhahood thinking it to be independent of the nature of sentient beings is to be likened to one who tries to listen to an echo by deadening its original sound. Therefore, the ignorant and the enlightened are walking in one passageway; the vulgar and the wise are not to be differentiated from each other. Where there are no names, we create names, and because of these names judgments are formed. Where there is no theorizing, we theorize, and because of this theorizing, disputes arise. They are all phantom creations and not realities, and who knows who is right and who is wrong? They are all empty, no substantialities have they, and who knows what is and what is not? So we realize that our gain is not real gain and our loss not real loss. This is my view and may I be enlightened if I am at fault."

To this Eka answered: "You have truly comprehended the

---

[15] According to this, there must have been a special volume of sermons, and letters by Eka, which were compiled evidently by his disciples and admirers before they were put down in writing and thoroughly revised by the author himself. In the case of Bodhidharma too, according to Dōsen, his sayings were apparently in circulation in the day of Dōsen, that is, early in the T'ang dynasty.

Dharma as it is; the deepest truth lies in the principle of identity. It is due to one's ignorance that the mani-jewel is taken for a piece of brick, but lo! when one is suddenly awakened to self-enlightenment it is realized that one is in possession of the real jewel. The ignorant and the enlightened are of one essence, they are not really to be separated. We should know that all things are such as they are. Those who entertain a dualistic view of the world are to be pitied, and I write this letter for them. When we know that between this body and the Buddha there is nothing to separate one from the other, what is the use of seeking after Nirvana (as something external to ourselves)?"

Next to Eka came Sōsan (d. 606), who succeeded as the third patriarch. The interview between master and disciple took place in this manner: A layman of forty troubled with *fêng-yang*[16] according to the "Records," came to Eka and asked:

"I am suffering from *fêng-yang;* pray cleanse me of my sins."

"Bring your sins here," said Eka, "and I will cleanse you of them."

The lay-disciple was silent for a while but finally said, "As I seek my sins, I find them unattainable."

"I have then finished cleansing you altogether. You should thenceforth take refuge in the Buddha, Dharma, and Saṃgha (Brotherhood), and abide therein."

"As I stand before you, O master," asked Sōsan, "I know that you belong to the Brotherhood, but pray tell me what are the Buddha and the Dharma?"

Replied the master: "Mind is the Buddha, Mind is the Dharma; and the Buddha and the Dharma are not two. The same is to be said of the Brotherhood."

This satisfied the disciple, who now said, "Today for the first time I realize that sins are neither within nor without nor in the middle; just as Mind is, so is the Buddha, so is the Dharma; they are not two."[17]

---

[16] Understood by some to be leprosy.

[17] In the *Vimalakīrti,* chapter iii, "The Disciples," we have the following: "Do not worry about the sins you have committed, O monks," said Vimalakīrti. "Why? Because sins are in their essence neither within nor without nor in the middle. As the Buddha taught us, all things are defiled when Mind is defiled; all things are pure when Mind is pure; and Mind is neither within nor without nor in the middle. As is Mind, so are sins and defilements, so are all things—they never transcend the suchness of truth."

He was then ordained by Eka as a Buddhist monk, and after this he fled from the world altogether, and nothing much of his life is known. This was partly due to the persecution of Buddhism carried on by the Emperor of the Northern Chou dynasty. It was in the twelfth year of K'ai-huang, of the Sui dynasty (A.D. 592), that he found a disciple worthy to be his successor. His name was Dōshin. He asked the master:

"Pray show me the way to deliverance."

"Who has ever put you in bondage?"

"Nobody."

"If so," said the master, "why should you ask for deliverance?"

This put the young novice on the way to final enlightenment, which he attained after many years' study under the master. When Sōsan thought that the time was ripe to consecrate him as his successor in the faith, he handed him, as the token of the rightful transmission of the Law, the robe which had come down from Bodhidharma, the first patriarch of Zen in China. He died in A.D. 606. While much of his life is obscure, his thought is gleaned from a metrical composition known as *Shinjinmei* or "Inscribed on the Believing Mind," which is one of the most valuable contributions by the masters to the interpretation of Zen teaching. Here follows a somewhat liberal translation of the poem:

Inscribed on the Believing Mind[18]

The Perfect Way knows no difficulties
Except that it refuses to make preference:

18 *Hsin* is one of those Chinese words which defy translation. When the Indian scholars were trying to translate the Buddhist Sanskrit works into Chinese they discovered that there were five classes of Sanskrit terms which could not be satisfactorily rendered into Chinese. We thus find in the Chinese Tripitaka such words as *prajña, bodhi, buddha, nirvāṇa, dhyāna, bodhisattva,* etc., almost always untranslated; and they now appear in their original form among the technical Buddhist terminology. If we could leave *hsin* with all its nuance of meaning in this translation, it would save us from the many difficulties that face us, in its English rendering. For *hsin* means mind, heart, soul, spirit—each singly as well as all inclusively. In the present composition by the third patriarch of Zen it has sometimes an intellectual connotation, but at other times it can properly be done by "heart." But as the predominant note of Zen Buddhism is more intellectual than anything else, though not in the sense of being logical or philosophical, I decided here to translate *hsin* as "mind" rather than as "heart."

Only when freed from hate and love,
It reveals itself fully and without disguise.

A tenth of an inch's difference,
And heaven and earth are set apart:
If you want to see it manifest,
Take no thought either for or against it.

To set up what you like against what you dislike—
This is the disease of the mind:
When the deep meaning [of the Way] is not understood
Peace of mind is disturbed and nothing is gained.

[The Way is] perfect like unto vast space,
With nothing wanting, nothing superfluous:
It is indeed due to making choice
That its suchness is lost sight of.

Pursue not the outer entanglements,
Dwell not in the inner void;
When the mind rests serene in the oneness of things,
The dualism vanishes by itself.

And when oneness is not thoroughly understood,
In two ways loss is sustained—
The denial of reality may lead to its absolute negation,
While the upholding of the void may result in contradicting itself.
Wordiness and intellection—
The more with them the further astray we go;
Away therefore with wordiness and intellection,
And there is no place where we cannot pass freely.[19]

When we return to the root, we gain the meaning;
When we pursue the external objects, we lose the reason.
The moment we are enlightened within,
We go beyond the voidness of a world confronting us.

[19] This means: When the absolute oneness of things is not properly understood, negation as well as affirmation will tend to be a one-sided view of reality.
When Buddhists deny the reality of an objective world, they do not mean
that they believe in the unconditioned emptiness of things; they know that
there is something real which cannot be done away with. When they uphold
the doctrine of void, this does not mean that all is nothing but an empty hol-
low, which leads to a self-contradiction. The philosophy of Zen avoids the
error of one-sideness involved in realism as well as in idealism.

Transformations going on in an empty world which confronts us,
Appear real all because of Ignorance:
Try not to seek after the true,
Only cease to cherish opinions.

Tarry not with dualism,
Carefully avoid pursuing it;
As soon as you have right and wrong,
Confusion ensues, the mind is lost.

The two exist because of the one,
But hold not even to this one;
When the one mind is not disturbed,
The ten thousand things offer no offence.

When no offense is offered by them, they are as if not existing;
When the mind is not disturbed, it is as if there is no mind.
The subject is quieted as the object ceases,
The object ceases as the subject is quieted.

The object is an object for the subject,
The subject is a subject for an object:
Know that the relativity of the two
Rests ultimately on the oneness of the void.

In the oneness of the void the two are one,
And each of the two contains in itself all the ten thousand things:
When no discrimination is made between this and that,
How can a one-sided and prejudiced view arise?

The Great Way is calm and large-minded,
Nothing is easy, nothing is hard:
Small views are irresolute,
The more in haste the tardier they go.

Clinging never keeps itself within bounds,
It is sure to go in the wrong way:
Let go loose, and things are as they may be,
While the essence neither departs nor abides.

Obey the nature of things, and you are in concord with the Way,
Calm and easy and free from annoyance;
But when your thoughts are tied, you turn away from the truth,
They grow heavier and duller and are not at all sound.

When they are not sound, the soul is troubled;
What is the use of being partial and one-sided then?
If you want to walk the course of the One Vehicle,
Be not prejudiced against the six sense-objects.

When you are not prejudiced against the six sense-objects,
You in turn identify yourself with enlightenment;
The wise are non-active,
While the ignorant bind themselves up;
While in the Dharma itself there is no individuation,
They ignorantly attach themselves to particular objects.
It is their own minds that create illusions—
Is it not the greatest of self-contradictions?

Ignorance begets the dualism of rest and unrest,
The enlightened have no likes and dislikes:
All forms of dualism
Are ignorantly contrived by the mind itself.
They are like unto visions and flowers in the air:
Why should we trouble ourselves to take hold of them?
Gain and loss, right and wrong—
Away with them once for all!

If an eye never falls asleep,
All dreams will by themselves cease:
If the mind retains its oneness,
The ten thousand things are of one suchness.
When the deep mystery of one suchness is fathomed,
All of a sudden we forget the external entanglements:
When the ten thousand things are viewed in their oneness,
We return to the origin and remain what we are.

Forget the wherefore of things,
And we attain to a state beyond analogy:
Movement stopped is no movement,
And rest set in motion is no rest.
When dualism does no more obtain,
Even oneness itself remains not as such.

The ultimate end of things where they cannot go any further,
Is not bound by rules and measures:
The mind in harmony (with the Way) is the principle of identity
In which we find all doings in a quiescent state;

Irresolutions are completely done away with,
And the right faith is restored to its native straightness;
Nothing is retained now,
Nothing is to be memorized,
All is void, lucid, and self-illuminating,
There is no stain, no exertion, no wasting of energy—
This is where thinking never attains,
This is where the imagination fails to measure.

In the higher realm of True Suchness
There is neither "other" nor "self":
When a direct identification is asked for,
We can only say, "Not two."[20]

In being not two all is the same,
All that is is comprehended in it:
The wise in the ten quarters,
They all enter into this absolute faith.

This absolute faith is beyond quickening (time) and
        extension (space).
One instant is ten thousand years;
No matter how things are conditioned, whether with "to be"
        or "not to be,"
It is manifest everywhere before you.

The infinitely small is as large as large can be,
When external conditions are forgotten;
The infinitely large is as small as small can be,
When objective limits are put out of sight.

What is is the same with what is not,
What is not is the same with what is:
Where this state of things fails to obtain,
Be sure not to tarry.

One in all,
All in one—
If only this is realized,
No more worry about your not being perfect!

---

[20] I.e., *Tat tvam asi.*

The believing mind is not divided,
And undivided is the believing mind—
This is where words fail,
For it is not of the past, future, or present.

Under Dōshin (580–651), the fourth patriarch, Zen was divided
into two branches. The one known as Gozuzen (Niu-t'ou Ch'an) did
not live long after the passing of its founder, Hōyū, who lived at
Mount Niu-t'ou, and is considered not belonging to the orthodox
line of Zen. The other branch was headed by Gunin, who is regarded by historians as the fifth patriarch, and it is his school that
has survived. He came to the master when he was still a mere boy,
and what pleased his master at their interview was the way he
answered. When Dōshin asked what was his family name (*Hsing*),
he said:

"I have a nature (*hsing*), and it is not an ordinary one."
"What is that?"
"It is the Buddha-nature (*fu-hsing*)."
"Then you have no name?"
"No, master," said the boy, "for it is empty in its nature." Here
is a play of words; the characters denoting "family name" and that
for "nature" are both pronounced *hsing*. When Dōshin was referring to the "family name" the young follower took it for "nature"
purposely, whereby to express his view by a figure of speech.

Dōshin's interview with Hōyū, the founder of the Gozu school
of Zen, was significant, showing where their views differed and
how the one came to be converted into the orthodox understanding
of Zen. It was during the Chen-kuan era of the T'ang dynasty
that Dōshin, learning of the presence of an extraordinary saintly
man in the Niu-t'ou mountains, decided to see who he could be.
When Dōshin came to a Buddhist temple in the mountains he
inquired after the man and was informed of a lonely anchorite who
would never rise from his seat nor salute people even when they
were approaching him. When Dōshin proceeded farther into the
mountains he saw him as he was told, sitting quietly and paying no
attention to the presence of a stranger. He then asked the hermit
what he was doing here. "I am contemplating on Mind," was the
reply.

Dōshin then demanded: "What is he that is contemplating?
What is Mind that is contemplated?"

Hōyū was not prepared to answer such questions. Thinking that the visitor was a man of deep understanding, he rose from the seat and saluting him asked who he was. When he found that the visitor was no other personage than Dōshin himself, whose reputation he was not ignorant of, he thanked him for the visit. They were now about to enter a little hut near by where they might talk about religion, when Dōshin saw some wild animals such as tigers and wolves wandering about the place, and he threw up his hands as if he were greatly frightened. Hōyū remarked, "I see this is still with you."

The fourth patriarch responded at once, "What do you see yet?" No answer came from the hermit. After a while the patriarch traced the character "Buddha" (*fu*) on the stone on which Hōyū was in the habit of sitting in meditation. Seeing it, the latter looked as if shocked. Said the patriarch, "I see this is still with you." But Hōyū failed to see the meaning of this remark and earnestly implored to be instructed in the ultimate teaching of Buddhism. This was done, and Hōyū became the founder of the Gozu school of Zen Buddhism.

Dōshin died at the age of seventy-two, A.D. 651.

Gunin (602–675), the fifth patriarch, came from the same province as his predecessor, Ch'i-chou, now in the district of Hu-pei. His temple was situated in Huang-mei Shan (Yellow Plum Mountain), where he preached and gave lessons in Zen to his five hundred pupils. He is claimed by some to have been the first Zen master who attempted to interpret the message of Zen according to the doctrine of the *Vajracchedikā-sūtra*. Though I cannot quite agree with this view, for the reason already referred to elsewhere, we can consider the fifth patriarch the beginning of a turning in the history of Zen, which opened up to a full view under the sixth patriarch, Enō. Until now the Zen followers had kept quiet, though working steadily, without arresting public attention; the masters had retired either into the mountains or in the hurly-burly of the world where nobody could tell anything about their doings. But the time had at last come for a full proclamation of Zen, and Gunin was the first who appeared in the field preparing the way for his successor, Enō.

Beside this orthodox line of patriarchs there were some sporadic expositors of Zen throughout the sixth and the seventh centuries. Several of them are mentioned, but there must have been many

more such who were either altogether forgotten or not at all known
to the world. The two best known are Hōshi (418–514) and Fukyo
(497–569); and their lives are recorded in the "Records" as "adepts
in Zen but not appearing in the world, though well-known at the
time." This is a strange phrasing, and it is hard to know definitely
what "not appearing in the world" means. Usually it applies to
one who does not occupy any recognized position in an officially
registered monastery. But of those classed under this heading
there is one at least to whom the designation does not properly
apply; for Chigi was a great high priest occupying an influential
ecclesiastical post in the Sui dynasty. Whatever this was, those
recorded here did not belong to the orthodox Zen school. The
Tendai (T'ien-t'ai) followers object to seeing two of their fathers,
Eshi and Chigi, mentioned as "adepts in Zen but not appearing
in the world, though well-known at the time." They think that
these two are great names in the history of their school and ought
not to be so indifferently referred to in the records of the Zen
masters. But from the Zen point of view this classification is justifiable for the reason that the Tendai, except in its metaphysics, is
another current of Zen started independently of the line of Bodhidharma, and if this were allowed to take a more practical course of
development it should surely have resulted in Zen as we have it
now. But its metaphysical side came to be emphasized at the expense of the practical, and for this reason the Tendai philosophers
were ever at war with the Zen, especially with the ultra-left wing,
which was inflexible in denouncing an appeal to ratiocination and
literary discoursing and sutra learning. In my view the Tendai is
a variation of Zen and its first promulgators may justly be classed
as Zen masters, though not of the pedigree to which belong Sekitō,
Yakusan, Baso, Rinzai, et al.

While there were thus in the sixth and seventh centuries some
other lines of Zen about to develop, the one started by Bodhidharma was uninterruptedly carried on by Eka, Sōsan, Dōshin, and
Gunin, who proved to be the most fruitful and successful. The
differentiation of two schools under the fifth patriarch, by Enō
and Jinshū, helped the further progress of pure Zen by eliminating
unessential or rather undigested elements. That the school of Enō
survived the other proves that his Zen was in perfect accord with
Chinese psychology and modes of thinking. The Indian elements
which had been found attached to the Zen of Bodhidharma and
his successors down to Enō were something grafted and not native

to Chinese genius. And therefore when Zen came to be fully established under Enō and his followers, it had nothing further to obstruct its free development until it became almost the only ruling power in the Chinese world of Buddhism. We must carefully watch how Enō came to be Gunin's successor and where he differed from the rival school under the Jinshū.

IV

Enō (638–713) came from Hsin-chou in the southern part of China. His father died when he was yet young. He supported his mother by selling wood in town. When one day he came out of a house where he sold some fuel, he heard a man reciting a Buddhist sutra. The words deeply touched his heart. Finding what sutra it was and where it was possible to get it, a longing came over him to study it with the master. The sutra was the "Diamond Sūtra" (*Vajracchedikā-sūtra*) and the master was the fifth patriarch residing at Yellow Plum in Ch'i-chou. Enō somehow managed to get money enough for the support of his aged mother while he was gone.

It took him about a month to reach Yellow Plum, where he at once proceeded to see Gunin at the head of five hundred monks (sometimes said to be seven or even ten hundred). At the first interview the fifth patriarch asked,

"Where do you come from? and what do you want here?"

"I am a farmer from Hsin-chou and wish to become a Buddha."

"So you are a Southerner," said the patriarch, "but the Southerners have no Buddha-nature; how could you expect to attain Buddhahood?"

This, however, did not discourage the bold seeker after the truth, for he at once responded: "There may be Southerners and Northerners, but as far as Buddha-nature goes, how could you make such a distinction in it?"

This pleased the master very much. Enō was given an office as rice-pounder for the Brotherhood. More than eight months, it is said, he was employed in this menial labor, when the fifth patriarch wished to select his spiritual successor from among his many disciples. One day he made an announcement that any one who could prove his thorough comprehension of the religion would be given the patriarchal mantle and proclaimed as his legitimate heir.

Jinshū (d. 706), who was the most learned of all the disciples and thoroughly versed in the lore of his religion, and who was therefore considered by his brethren in the faith to be in possession of an unqualified right to the honor, composed a stanza expressing his view, and posted it on the outside wall of the meditation hall. It read:

> This body is the Bodhi tree,
> The soul is like a mirror bright;
> Take heed to keep it always clean,
> And let not dust collect on it.

All those who read these lines were greatly impressed, and secretly cherished the idea that the author of this *gātha* would surely be awarded the prize. But when they awoke the next morning they were surprised to see another written alongside of it, which ran as follows:

> The Bodhi is not like the tree,
> The mirror bright is nowhere shining;
> As there is nothing from the first,
> Where can the dust itself collect?

The writer of these lines was an insignificant layman in the service of the monastery, who spent most of his time in pounding rice and splitting wood for the Brotherhood. He had such an unassuming air that nobody ever thought much of him, and therefore the entire community was now set astir to see this challenge made upon its recognized authority. But the fifth patriarch saw in this unpretentious monk a future leader of mankind, and decided to transfer to him the robe of his office. He had, however, some misgivings concerning the matter; for the majority of his disciples were not enlightened enough to see anything of deep religious intuition in the lines by the rice-pounder, Enō: and if he were publicly awarded the honor they might do him harm. So the fifth patriarch gave a secret sign to Enō to come to his room at midnight, when the rest of the Brotherhood was fast asleep. Then he gave him the robe as insigne of his authority and in acknowledgement of his unsurpassed spiritual attainment, and with the assurance that the future of their faith would be brighter than ever. The patriarch then advised him that it would be wise for him to hide his own light under a bushel until the proper time arrived for his public appearance and active propaganda, and also that the robe which was handed down from Bodhidharma as the sign of faith should no more be given up to Enō's successors, because Zen was now fully recognized by the outside world in general and there was no more necessity to symbolize the faith by the transference of the robe. That night Enō left the monastery.

This narrative is taken from the literature left by the followers of the sixth patriarch and is naturally partial in his favor. If we had another record left by Jinshū and his school, the account here reproduced might materially differ. In fact, we have at least one document telling Jinshū's relation to Gunin. It is the memorial inscription on his gravestone written by Chōsetsu, one of his lay-disciples. In this inscription Jinshū is referred to as the one to whom the Dharma has been transmitted from his master, Gunin. Judging from this, the patriarchal authority of Enō was not an undisputed one at the time, or the orthodox order of succession was not settled until some time later, when the school of Enō had been well established in authority over all the other schools of Zen that might have been existing then. Unfortunately, this memorial inscription does not give any further information concerning Enō's relation to Gunin, but even from the above narrative we can gather certain facts of importance which will shed light on the history of Zen.

First, what necessity was there to make Enō an unlearned rustic in contrast with the erudition and wide information ascribed to Jinshū? Or was Enō really such an ignoramus as could not read anything written? But the *Fa-pao-t'an-ching*, a collection of his sermons, contains passages quoted from such sutras as the *Nirvāṇa, Vajracchedikā, Laṅkāvatāra, Saddharma-puṇḍarīka, Vimalakīrti, Amitābha,* and *Bodhisattva-sīla-sūtra.* Does this not evince the fact that the author was not altogether unacquainted with Mahayana literature? Probably he was not a learned scholar as compared with Jinshū, but in the narratives of his life we can trace some systematic effort to make him more unlettered than he actually was. What, let me ask, do we read in this attempt at the hand of the editors? In my opinion this emphasizing of the contrast between the two most eminent disciples of the fifth patriarch was at the same time the emphasizing of the real character of Zen as independent of learning and intellectuality. If Zen is, as its followers claim, a "special transmission outside the scriptural teaching," the understanding of it must be possible even for the unlettered and unphilosophizing.

The greatness of Enō as a Zen master is all the more enhanced. This was in all likelihood the reason why the sixth patriarch was unreasonably and sometimes even dramatically made unlettered.

Secondly, why was not the patriarchal robe transferred beyond Enō? If Gunin advised him to keep it with him, what does the advice really imply? That the life of the possessor of the robe would be threatened points to the fact that there was a dispute among the disciples of Gunin. Did they regard the robe as the symbol of patriarchal authority? But what advantages, material or spiritual, accrued from the ownership of it? Did the teaching of Bodhidharma come now to be believed as the genuine transmission of the Buddha? And for that reason did the robe really cease to signify anything relative to the truth of Zen? If so, when Bodhidharma first declared his special mission as teacher of Zen, was he looked upon as a heretic and persecuted accordingly? The legend that he was poisoned by his rival teachers from India seems to corroborate this. At all events, the question of the robe is deeply connected with the status of Zen teaching among the various schools of Buddhism at the time, and also with its firmer hold on the popular minds than ever before.

Thirdly, the secrecy observed in all the transactions between Gunin and Enō concerning the transmission of the Dharma naturally arrests our attention. To raise the rice-pounder, who is not even an ordained monk, to the rank of a patriarch, though only in name, to succeed a great master who stands at the head of several hundred disciples, seems to be a real cause for envy and jealousy and even for hatred. But if one were really enlightened enough to take charge of the important position of spiritual leadership, could not a combined effort of master and pupil withstand all the opposition? Perhaps even enlightenment could not stand against human passions so irrational and elemental. I cannot, however, help imagining an attempt on the part of the biographers of Enō at the dramatization of the whole scene. I am very likely mistaken, and there might have been some historical conditions of which we are now ignorant due to the lack of documents.

Three days after the flight of Enō from the Yellow Plum Mountain, the news of what had happened in secret became noised abroad throughout the monastery, and a party of indignant monks, headed by one named Myō-jōza, pursued the fugitive, Enō, who, in accordance with his master's instructions, was silently leaving the Brotherhood. When he was overtaken by the pursuers while crossing a mountain pass far from the monastery, he laid down his robe on a rock near by and said to the monk, Myō-jōza: "This robe symbolizes our patriarchal faith and is not to be carried away by force. Take this along with thee, however, if thou so desirest."

Myō-jōza tried to lift it, but it was as heavy as a mountain. He halted, hesitated, and trembled with awe. At last he said: "I come here to obtain the faith and not the robe. O my brother monk, pray dispel my ignorance."

Said the sixth patriarch: "If thou comest for the faith, stop all thy hankerings. Think not of good, think not of evil, but see what at this moment thy own original face doth look like, which thou hadst even prior to thy own birth."

Being thus demanded, Myō-jōza at once perceived the fundamental truth of things, which hitherto he had sought in things without. He now understood everything, as if he had taken a cupful of cool water and tasted it to his own satisfaction. Out of the immensity of his feeling he was literally bathed in tears and perspiration, and most reverently approaching the patriarch he saluted him and asked, "Besides this hidden sense as is embodied in these significant words, is there anything which is secret?"

The patriarch answered: "In what I have shown to thee there is nothing hidden. If thou reflectest within thyself and recognizest thine own face, which was before the world, secrecy is in thyself."

Whatever historical circumstances surrounded Enō in those remote days, it is certain that in this statement, "to see one's own face even before one was born," we find the first proclamation of the new message, which was destined to unroll a long history of Zen and to make Enō really worthy of the patriarchal robe. We can see here what a new outlook Enō has succeeded in opening to the traditional Indian Zen. In him we do not recognize anything of Buddhism as far as phraseology goes, which means that he opened up his own way of presenting the truth of Zen after his original and creative experience. Prior to him the Zen experience had some borrowings, either in wording or in method, to express itself. To say "You are the Buddha," or "You and the Buddha are one," or "The Buddha is living in you," is too stale, too flat, because too abstract and too conceptual. They contain deep truth but are not concrete nor vivifying enough to rouse our dormant souls from insensibility. They are filled up too much with abstractions and learned phraseology. Enō's simple-mindedness, not spoiled by learning and philosophizing, could grasp the truth at firsthand.

Hence the unusual freshness in the way he handled the problem.
We may come to this again later.

V

Gunin died, A.D. 675, four years[21] after the Dharma was transmitted to Enō. But Enō never started his mission work until some
years later, for in accordance with the advice of his master he lived
a secluded life in the mountains. One day he thought that it was
time for him to go out in the world. He was now thirty-nine years
old, and it was in the first year of I-fêng (A.D. 676) during the
T'ang dynasty. He came to Fa-hsing temple in the province of
Kuang, where a learned priest, Inshū, was discoursing on the
Nirvāṇa-sūtra. He saw some monks arguing on the fluttering
pennant; one of them said, "The pennant is an inanimate object
and it is the wind that makes it flap." Against this it was remarked
by another monk that "Both wind and pennant are inanimate
things, and the flapping is an impossibility." A third one protested,
"The flapping is due to a certain combination of cause and condition"; while a fourth one proposed a theory, saying, "After all there
is no flapping pennant, but it is the wind that is moving by itself."
The discussion grew quite animated when Enō interrupted with
the remark, "It is neither wind nor pennant but your own mind
that flaps." This at once put a stop to the heated argument. The
priest-scholar, Inshū, was greatly struck by the statement of Enō,
so conclusive and authoritative. Finding out very soon who this
Enō was, Inshū asked him to enlighten him on the teaching of the
master of Yellow Plum Mountain. The gist of Enō's reply was as
follows:

"My master had no special instruction to give; he simply insisted
upon the need of our seeing into our own Nature through our own
efforts; he had nothing to do with meditation, or with deliverance.
For whatever can be named leads to dualism, and Buddhism is not
dualistic. To take hold of this non-duality of truth is the aim of
Zen. The Buddha-nature of which we are all in possession, and
the seeing into which constitutes Zen, is indivisible into such oppositions as good and evil, eternal and temporal, material and

[21] There is, however, a variation from five years to fifteen years according
to different authorities.

spiritual. To see dualism in life is due to confusion of thought; the wise, the enlightened, see into the reality of things unhampered by erroneous ideas."

This was the beginning of Enō's career as Zen master. His influence seems to have been immediate and far-reaching. He had many disciples numbering thousands. He did not, however, go around preaching and proselytizing. His activities were confined in his own province in the south, and the Pao-lin monastery at Ts'ao-ch'i was his headquarters. When the Emperor learned that Enō succeeded Gunin as one of Bodhidharma's spiritual descendants in the faith of Zen, he sent him one of his Court officials with an imperial message, but Enō refused to come up to the capital, preferring to stay in the mountains. The messenger, however, wished to be instructed in the doctrine of Zen, that he might convey it to his august master at Court. Said Enō in the main as follows:

"It is a mistake to think that sitting quietly in contemplation is essential to deliverance. The truth of Zen opens by itself from within and it has nothing to do with the practice of *dhyāna*. For we read in the *Vajracchedikā* that those who try to see the Tathāgata in one of his special attitudes, as sitting or lying, do not understand his spirit, and that the Tathāgata is designated as Tathāgata because he comes from nowhere and departs nowhere, and for that reason he is the Tathāgata. His appearance has no whence, and his disappearance no whither, and this is Zen. In Zen, therefore, there is nothing to gain, nothing to understand; what shall we then do with sitting cross-legged and practicing *dhyāna*? Some may think that understanding is needed to enlighten the darkness of ignorance, but the truth of Zen is absolute in which there is no dualism, no conditionality. To speak of ignorance and enlightenment, or of *bodhi* and *kleśa* (wisdom and passions), as if they were two separate objects which cannot be merged in one, is not Mahayanistic. In the Mahayana every possible form of dualism is condemned as not expressing the ultimate truth. Everything is a manifestation of the Buddha-nature, which is not defiled in passions, nor purified in enlightenment. It is above all categories. If you want to see what is the nature of your being, free your mind from thought of relativity and you will see by yourself how serene it is and yet how full of life it is."

While Enō was working for the cause of Zen in the south, Chōsetsu, representing another school, was active in the north. Before he was converted into Buddhism he was a learned Confucian and thus destined from the start to cut a different figure, compared with his brother-disciple, Enō. The Emperor Wu of the T'ang dynasty was one of the devoted followers of Jinshū, and naturally around him were gathered a large number of courtiers and government officers. When the Emperor Chung-tsung came to the throne, A.D. 685, he was all the more treated with reverence, and it was Chōsetsu, one of the state ministers, who inscribed a biographical sketch and eulogy on the memorial stone erected over his grave when he died. One of his sermons recorded reads:

> The teaching of all the Buddhas
> In one's own Mind originally exists:
> To seek the Mind without one's Self,
> Is like running away from the father.

He died in A.D. 706, seven years prior to Enō. His school, known as the Northern in contrast to Enō's Southern school, prospered in the north far better than the latter did in the south. But when Baso (d. 788) and Sekitō (700–790) began their active propaganda in the south and finally established the foundations of Zen teaching, Jinshū's school failed to find able successors and finally disappeared altogether, so that all the records we have of it come from the rival school. It thus came to pass that Enō, and not Jinshū, was recognized as the sixth patriarch of Zen Buddhism in China.

The difference between the Southern and Northern school of Zen is one inherent in human mind; if we call the one intellectual or intuitional, the other would be regarded as pragmatical. The reason why the Southern school is known as "abrupt" or "instant" (*yugapad*) against the "gradual" (*kramavṛittya*) school of the north is because it upholds that the coming of enlightenment is instantaneous, and does not allow any gradation as there are no stages of progress in it; whereas the Northern school emphasizes the process of arriving at enlightenment which is naturally gradual, requiring much time and concentration. Enō was a great advocate of absolute idealism, while Jinshū was a realist and refused to ignore the world of particulars where time rules over all our doings. An idealist does not necessarily ignore the objective aspect of reality, but his eyes are always fixed at one point which stands by itself, and his surveyings are done from this absolute point. The doctrine of abruptness is thus the result of looking at the multi-

tudinousness of things in absolute unity. All true mystics are followers of the "abrupt" school. The flight from the alone to the
alone is not, and cannot be, a gradual process. The teaching of
Jinshū is to be heeded as practical advice to those who are actually
engaged in the study of Zen, but it fails to describe the character
of the experience known as "the seeing into one's own Nature,"
which was the special message of Enō as distinguished from those
of the other Buddhist schools. That the school of Jinshū could not
survive as a branch of Zen was natural enough, for Zen could not
be anything else but an instantaneous act of intuition. As it opens
up all of a sudden a world hitherto undreamed of, it is an abrupt
and discrete leaping from one plane of thought to another. Jinshū
missed the ultimate object of Zen when he emphasized the process
to reach the end. As a practical adviser he was excellent and full
of merit.

The ideas of instantaneity and gradation in the realization of
the truth of Zen originally come from the *Laṅkāvatāra* (Nanjō's
edition, p. 55), where this distinction is made in regard to cleansing
one's mind of its stream of ideas and images. According to the
sūtra, this cleansing is in one sense gradual but in another abrupt
or instantaneous. When it is regarded as like the ripening of a
fruit, the modelling of a vessel, the growing of a plant, or the
mastering of an art, which takes place gradually and in time, it is
an act of gradual process; but when it is comparable to a mirror
reflecting objects, or to the *ālaya* reproducing all mental images,
the cleansing of mind takes place instantaneously. Thus the sutra
recognizes the two types of minds: with some the cleansing to a
state of enlightenment can be obtained gradually after a long
practice of meditation, perhaps through many a successive life;
but to others it may come all of a sudden, even without previously
conscious efforts. The division of the two schools as regards the
abrupt realization of enlightenment is based not only on the
statements in the sūtra but ultimately on facts of psychology. The
point at issue, however, was not a question of time; whether enlightenment took place as an act of one moment or not ceased to
concern them; for the difference now developed into that of their
general philosophical attitude and outlook toward the fact of
enlightenment itself. The question of physical time has thus turned
into that of psychology in its more profound aspect.

When process is emphasized, the end is forgotten, and process
itself comes to be identified with end. When a disciple of Jinshū

came to Enō to be instructed in Zen, he asked what was the teaching of Jinshū, and the disciple informed him thus: "My master
usually teaches us to stop the working of our minds and to sit
quietly in meditation for a long time at a stretch, without lying
down." To this Enō responded, "To stop the working of mind and
to sit quietly in meditation is a disease and not Zen, and there is
no profit whatever to be gained from a long sitting." Then he gave
him the following gātha:

> While living, one sits up and lies not,
> When dead, one lies and sits not;
> A set of ill-smelling bones!
> What is the use of toiling and moiling?

This shows exactly where Enō stands in relation to his rival Jinshū
who is so taken up with the practical details of the process of Zen.
Those two gātha inscribed on the monastery wall at Yellow Plum
Mountain while they were yet under the tutorship of Gunin are
eloquent enough to bring out the characterist c features of the two
schools.[22]

When Enō further asked the monk from the north as to the
teaching of his teacher in regard to morality (śila), meditation
(dhyāna), and wisdom (prajñā), the monk said, "According to my
master Jinshū, morality consists in not doing anything that is bad;
wisdom in reverently practicing all that is good; and meditation in
purifying the heart."

Replied Enō: "My view is quite different. All my teaching issues
from the conception of Self-nature, and those who assert the
existence of anything outside it betray their ignorance of its nature.
Morality, meditation, and wisdom—all these are forms of Self-nature. When there is nothing wrong in it, we have morality; when it
is free from ignorance, it is wisdom; and when it is not disturbed,
it is meditation. Have a thorough understanding once for all as to
the being of Self-nature, and you know that nothing dualistic obtains in it; for here you have nothing to be particularly dis-

---

[22] These accounts, whether truly historical or not, concerning the contro-
versy between the two leaders of Zen early in the T'ang dynasty prove how
heated was the rivalry between the north and the south. "The Platform Sutra
on the Treasure of the Law" (Fa-pao-t'an-ching) appears as if written with
the sole object of refuting the opponents of the "abrupt" school.

tinguished as enlightenment, or ignorance, or deliverance, or knowledge, and yet from this nothingness there issues a world of particulars as objects of thought. For him who has once had an insight into his own Nature, no special posture as a form of meditation is to be recommended; everything and anything is good to him, sitting, or lying, or standing. He enjoys perfect freedom of spirit, he moves along as he feels, and yet he does nothing wrong, he is always acting in accord with his Self-nature, his work is play. This is what I call 'the seeing into one's own Nature'; and this seeing is instantaneous as much as the working is, for there is no graduating process from one stage to another."

VI

Some of the sermons of the sixth patriarch are preserved in the book known as the "Platform Sutra on the Treasure of the Law" (Fa-pao-t'an-ching). The title "Sutra" has generally been given to writings ascribed to the Buddha or those somehow personally connected with him, and that a collection of the sermons of Hui-nêng has been so honored shows what a significant position he occupies in the history of Chinese Buddhism. The *Platform Sutra* has a reference to the famous ordination platform erected by Guṇabhadra, the first translator of the *Laṅkāvatāra*, of the Liu-sung dynasty, A.D. 420–479. At the time of the erection during the Liang dynasty, as well as later, it was prophesied by Chiyaku (according to another authority by Paramārtha) that some years later a Bodhisattva in the flesh would be ordained on this platform and deliver sermons on the Buddha's "spiritual seal." Thus the "Platform Sutra" means orthodox teaching of the Zen given from this platform.

The sermons here preserved are mere fragments of those delivered during the thirty-seven years of Enō's active missionary life. Even of these fragments how much is to be regarded as genuine and authoritative is a question to which we cannot at present give a definite answer, as the book seems to have suffered the vicissitudes of fate, partly showing the fact that the Zen message of the sixth patriarch was extraordinary in many respects so as to arouse antagonism and misunderstanding among Buddhists. When this antagonism later reached its climax, it is reported that the book was burned up as against the genuine teaching of Buddhism. Except a few sentences and passages, however, which can at once be rejected as spurious, we may take the "Platform Sutra" on the whole as expressing the spirit and teaching of the sixth patriarch of Zen.

The principal ideas of Enō, which make him the real Chinese founder of Zen Buddhism, may be summed up as follows:

1. We can say that Zen has come to its own consciousness in Enō. While Bodhidharma brought it from India and successfully transplanted it in China, it did not fully realize its special message at the time. More than two centuries were needed before it grew aware of itself and knew how to express itself in the way native to the Chinese mind; the Indian mode in which its original teaching had been expressed, as was the case with Bodhidharma and his immediate disciples, had to give way as it were to become truly Chinese. As soon as this transformation or transplantation was accomplished in the hands of Enō, his disciples proceeded at once to work out all its implications. The result was what we have as the Zen school of Buddhism. How then did Enō understand Zen?

According to him Zen was the "seeing into one's own Nature." This is the most significant phrase ever coined in the development of Zen Buddhism. Around this Zen is now crystallized, and we know where to direct our efforts and how to represent it in our consciousness. After this the progress of Zen Buddhism was rapid. It is true that this phrase occurs in the life of Bodhidharma in the "Transmission of the Lamp," but it is in the part of his life on which we cannot put much reliance. Even if the phrase was actually used by Bodhidharma it was not necessarily considered by him the essence of Zen as distinguishing itself from other schools of Buddhism. Enō, however, was fully aware of its signification, and impressed the idea unequivocally upon the minds of his audience. When he made his first declaration of Zen for the benefit of Inshū, the statement was quite unmistakable: "We talk of seeing into our own nature, and not of practicing *dhyāna* or obtaining liberation." Here we have the gist of Zen, and all his later sermons are amplifications of this idea.

By "Nature" he understood Buddha-nature, or, more particularly from the intellectual point of view, *prajñā*. He says that this *prajñā* is possessed by every one of us, but owing to the confusion of thought we fail to realize it in ourselves. Therefore we must be instructed and properly guided by an adept in Zen Buddhism, when we shall open a spiritual eye and by ourselves see into the Nature. This Nature knows no multiplicity, it is absolute oneness, being the same in the ignorant as well as in the wise. The difference comes from confusion and ignorance. People talk so much, think so much of *prajñā*, but fail altogether to realize it in their own minds. It is like talking about food all day; however much we may talk we forever remain hungry. You may explain the philosophy of *śūnyatā* for ten thousand years, but so long as you have not yet seen into your nature it is absolutely of no avail. There are again some people who regard Zen as consisting in sitting quietly with an empty mind devoid of thoughts and feelings. Such know not what *prajñā* is, what mind is. It fills the universe and never rests from work. It is free, creative, and at the same time it knows itself. It knows all in one and one in all. This mysterious working of *prajñā* issues from your own Nature. Do not depend upon letters but let your own *prajñā* illumine within yourself.

2. The inevitable result of it was the "abrupt" teaching of the Southern school. The seeing is an instant act as far as the mental eye takes in the whole truth at one glance—the truth which transcends dualism in all form; it is abrupt as far as it knows no gradations, no continuous unfolding. Read the following passage from the "Platform Sutra," in which the essentials of the abrupt doctrine are given:

When the abrupt doctrine is understood there is no need of disciplining oneself in things external. Only let a man always have a right view within his own mind, no desires, no external objects will ever defile him. This is the seeing into his Nature. O my friends, have no fixed abode inside or outside,[23] and your conduct will be perfectly free and unfettered. Take away your attachment and your walk will know no obstructions whatever. . . . The ignorant will grow wise if they abruptly get an understanding and open their hearts to the truth. O my friends, even the Buddhas will be like us common mortals when they have no

[23] This is a constant refrain in the teaching of the *Prajñāpāramitā-sūtras*—to awaken one's thought where there is no abode whatever. When Jōshū called on Ungo, the latter asked, "O you, old wanderer! how is it that you do not seek an abiding place for yourself?" "Where is my abiding place?" "There is an old temple ruin at the foot of this mountain." "That is a fitting place for your old self," responded Jōshū. Later, he came to Shūyusan, who asked him the same question, saying, "O you, old wanderer! why don't you get settled?" "Where is the place for me to get settled?" "Why, this old wanderer doesn't know even where to get settled for himself." Said Jōshū, "I have been engaged these thirty years in training horses, and today I have been kicked around by a donkey!"

enlightenment, and even we mortals will be Buddhas when we are enlightened. Therefore we know that all things are in our own minds. Why do we not then instantly see into our own minds and find there the truth of Suchness? In the "Sutra on the Moral Conduct of the Bodhisattva" we read that we are all pure in our Self-nature, and that when we know our own minds we see into this nature and all attain to Buddhahood. Says the *Vimalakīrti-sūtra*, "An instant opening leads us into the Original Mind." O my good friends, while under my master Gunin I realized the truth the moment I heard him speak and had an instant (i.e., abrupt) glimpse into the true essence of Suchness. This is the reason why I now endeavor by means of this doctrine to lead truth-seekers to an instant (i.e., abrupt) realization of *bodhi*. When you by yourselves look into your minds, you perceive at once what the Original Nature is. . . .

Those who know by themselves do not look for anything external. If they adhere to the view that liberation comes through external aid, through the office of a good, wise friend, they are entirely at fault. Why? There is a knower in your own mind, and it is this that makes you realize the truth by yourselves. When confusion reigns in you and false views are entertained, no amount of teaching by others, good, wise friends of yours, will be of use for your salvation. When, on the other hand, your genuine *prajñā* shines forth, all your confused thoughts will vanish in an instant. Knowing thus what your Self-nature is, you reach Buddhahood by this single understanding, one knowledge.

3. When the seeing into Self-nature is emphasized and intuitive understanding is upheld against learning and philosophizing, we know that as one of its logical conclusions the old view of meditation begins to be looked down on as merely a discipline in mental tranquillization. And this was exactly the case with the sixth patriarch. Since the beginning of Buddhism there have been two currents of thought concerning the meaning of meditation: the one was, like Arāda and Udraka, who were the two teachers of the Buddha, to take it for suspending all psychic activities or for wiping consciousness clean of all its modes; and the other was to regard meditation simply as the most efficacious means for coming in touch with the ultimate reality. This fundamental difference of views with regard to meditation was a cause of the unpopularity at first of Bodhidharma among the Chinese Buddhists, scholars, and *dhyāna*-masters of the time. It was also a factor of divergence between the Gozu school of Zen and the orthodox teaching of the fourth patriarch, as well as between the Northern and the

Southern schools of Zen Buddhism after the fifth patriarch. Enō, the sixth patriarch, came out as a strong advocate of intuitionalism and refused to interpret the meaning of *dhyāna* statically, as it were. For the mind, according to him, at the highest stage of meditation was not a mere being, mere abstraction devoid of content and work. He wanted to grasp something which lay at the foundation of all his activities mental and physical, and this something could not be a mere geometrical point, it must be the source of energy and knowledge. Enō did not forget that the will was after all the ultimate reality and that enlightenment was to be understood as more than intellection, more than quietly contemplating the truth. The mind or Self-nature was to be apprehended in the midst of its working or functioning. The object of *dhyāna* was thus not to stop the working of Self-nature but to make us plunge right into its stream and seize it in the very act. His intuitionalism was dynamic. In the following dialogues both Enō and his disciples are still using the older terminology, but the import of this parley is illustrative of the point I want to specify.

Genkaku first studied Tendai philosophy and later while reading the *Vimalakīrti* he discovered his Self-nature. Being advised to see the sixth patriarch in order to have his experience certified or testified to, he came to Ts'ao-ch'i. He walked round the master three times, and erecting his staff straight stood before him. Said the master, "Monks are supposed to observe three hundred rules of conduct and eighty thousand minor ones; whence comest thou, so full of pride?"

"Birth-and-death is a matter of grave concern, and time waits for nobody!" said the Tendai philosopher.

"Why dost thou not grasp that which is birthless and see into that which is timeless?" the master demanded.

"Birthless is that which grasps, and timeless is that which sees into."

"That is so, that is so," agreed the master.

When this was over, Genkaku came to Enō again in the full attire of the Buddhist monk, and reverently bowing to the master wished to take leave of him.

Said the master, "Why departest thou so soon?"

"There is from the very beginning no such thing as movement, and then why talkest thou of being soon?"

"Who knows that there is no movement?" retorted the master.

"There," exclaimed Genkaku, "thou makest a judgment thyself!"

"Thou truly comprehendest the intent of that which is birthless."

"How could the birthless ever have an intent?" Genkaku asked.

"If there were no intent, who could ever judge?"

"Judgments are made with no intent whatever." This was the conclusion of Genkaku.

The master then expressed his deep appreciation of Genkaku's view on the subject, saying, "Well thou hast said!"

Chikō was an adept in meditation, which he studied under the fifth patriarch. After twenty years' discipline he thought he well understood the purport of meditation or *samādhi*. Gensaku, learning of his attainment, visited him, and said, "What are you doing there?"

"I am entering into a *samādhi*."

"You speak of entering, but how do you enter into *samādhi*—with a thought-ful mind or with a thought-less mind? If you say with a thought-less mind, all non-sentient beings such as plants or bricks could attain *samādhi*. If you say with a thought-ful mind, all sentient beings could attain it."

"When I enter into *samādhi*," said Chikō, "I am not conscious of either being thought-ful or being thought-less."

"If you are conscious of neither, you are right in *samādhi* all the while; why do you then talk at all of entering into it or coming out of it? If, however, there is really entering or coming out, it is not Great Samādhi."

Chikō did not know how to answer. After a while he asked who was Gensaku's teacher and what was his understanding of *samādhi*.

Said Gensaku, "Enō is my teacher, and according to him (the ultimate truth) lies mystically serene and perfectly quiet; substance and function are not to be separated, they are of one Suchness. The five *skandhas* are empty in their nature, and the six sense-objects have no reality. (The truth knows of) neither entering nor going out, neither being tranquil nor disturbed. *Dhyāna* in essence has no fixed abode. Without attaching yourself to an abode, be serene in *dhyāna*. *Dhyāna* in essence is birthless; without attaching yourself to the thought of birth (-and-death), think in *dhyāna*. Have your mind like unto space and yet have no thought of space." Thus learning of the sixth patriarch's view on *samādhi* or *dhyāna*, Chikō came to the master himself and asked to be further enlightened. Said the patriarch: "What Gensaku told you is true. Have your mind like unto space and yet entertain in it no thought of emptiness. Then the truth will have its full activity un-

impeded. Every movement of yours will come out of an innocent
heart, and the ignorant and the wise will have an equal treatment
in your hands. Subject and object will lose their distinction, and
essence and appearance will be of one suchness. (When a world
of absolute oneness is thus realized) you have attained to eternal
samādhi."

To make the position of the sixth patriarch on the subject of
meditation still clearer and more definite, let me quote another
incident from his "Platform Sutra". A monk once made reference to
a *gātha* composed by Garin which read as follows:

> I, Garin, know a device
> Whereby to blot out all my thoughts:
> The objective world no more stirs the mind,
> And daily matures my enlightenment!

Hearing this, the sixth patriarch remarked: "That is no Enlightenment but leads one into a state of bondage. Listen to my *gātha*:

> I, Enō, know no device,
> My thoughts are not suppressed:
> The objective world ever stirs the mind,
> And what is the use of maturing enlightenment?

These will be sufficient to show that Enō, the sixth patriarch,
was on the one hand no quietist, nor nihilist advocating the doctrine of absolute emptiness, while on the other hand he was no
idealist either, in the sense of denying an objective world. His
dhyāna was full of action, yet above a world of particulars, so long
as it was not carried away by it and in it.

4. Enō's method of demonstrating the truth of Zen was purely
Chinese and not Indian. He did not resort to abstract terminology
nor to romantic mysticism. The method was direct, plain, concrete, and highly practical. When the monk Myō-jōza came to him
and asked for instruction, he said, "Show me your original face before you were born." Is not the statement quite to the point? No
philosophic discourse, no elaborate reasoning, no mystic imagery,
but a direct unequivocal dictum. In this the sixth patriarch cut
the first turf and his disciples quickly and efficiently followed in
his steps. Notice how brilliantly Rinzai made use of this method
in his sermon on a "true man of no title."

To give another instance. When Enō saw Ejō of Nangaku, he said, "Whence comest thou?" which was followed by "What is it that so cometh?" It took Ejō eight long years to answer the question satisfactorily. Afterward this way of questioning became almost an established form of greeting with Zen masters.

Nan-in asked a newly arrived monk, "Whence comest thou?"

"I am from Han-shang."

Said the master, "You are at fault as much as I am."

Kyōgen asked Sanshō, "Whence comest thou?"

"From Rinzai."

"Bringest thou his sword?"

Sanshō took up his seat-cloth (*zagu*) and struck Kyōgen across his mouth and went away. Bokujū asked a monk, "Whence comest thou?"

"From Yang-shan."

"Thou art a liar!" was the verdict of the master. Another time he asked another monk, "Whence comest thou?"

"From west of the river, sir."

"How many sandals has thou worn out?" This monk had evidently a gentler treatment.

This difference of method between the Indian and the Chinese often raised the question as to the difference, if there be any, between the "Tathāgata Dhyāna" and the "Patriarchal Dhyāna." For instance, when Kyōgen showed his song of poverty to Kyōzan, the latter said, "You understand the Tathāgata Dhyāna but not yet the Patriarchal Dhyāna." When asked about the difference, Bokujū replied, "The green mountains are green mountains, and the white clouds are white clouds."

VII

Enō died in A.D. 713, while the T'ang dynasty was enjoying its halcyon days and Chinese culture reached the highest point in its history. A little over one hundred years after the passing of the sixth patriarch, Ryū Sōgan, one of the most brilliant literati in the history of Chinese literature, wrote a memorial inscription on his tombstone when he was honored by the Emperor Hsien-tsung with the posthumous title, Great Mirror (*tai-chien*), and in this we read: "In a sixth transmission after Bodhidharma there was Tai-chien. He was first engaged in menial labor and servile work. Just a few

words from the master were enough and he at once understood
the deepest meaning conveyed in them. The master was greatly
impressed, and finally conferred on him an insigne of faith. After
that he hid himself in the Southern district; nobody heard of him
again for sixteen years, when he thought the time was ripe for
him to come out of the seclusion. He was settled at Ts'ao-ch'i [24] and
began to teach. The number of disciples is said once to have
reached several thousands.

"According to his doctrine, non-doing is reality, emptiness is the
truth, and the ultimate meaning of things is vast and immovable.
He taught that human nature in its beginning as well as in the end
is thoroughly good and does not require any artificial weeding-
out, for it has its root in that which is serene. The Emperor Chung-
tsung heard of him and sent his courtier twice asking him to appear at Court, but failed to get him out. So the Emperor had his
words instead which he took for his spiritual guidance. The teaching (of the sixth patriarch) in detail is generally accessible today;
all those who talk at all about Zen find their source of information
in Ts'ao-ch'i."

After Enō Zen was split up into several schools, two of which
have survived even down to this day, in China as well as in Japan.
The one represented by Gyōshi of Seigen (d. 740) continues now
as the Sōtō school of Zen, and the other, coming down the line of
Ejō of Nangaku (677–744), is now represented by the Rinzai
school. Though much modified in various aspects, the principle
and spirit of Zen Buddhism is still alive as it was in the days of
the sixth patriarch, and as one of the great spiritual heritages of
the East it is still wielding its unique influence, especially among
cultured people in Japan.

[24] This is the name of the place where Enō had his Zen headquarters.

PART III

The Enlightenment Experience

"What is the essential point of
Buddhism?"
"Unless you have it, you do not
understand."

The Transmission of the Lamp

1. ON SATORI—THE REVELATION OF
A NEW TRUTH IN ZEN BUDDHISM[1]

THE essence of Zen Buddhism consists in acquiring a new viewpoint of looking at life and things generally. By this I mean that if we want to get into the inmost life of Zen, we must forego all our ordinary habits of thinking which control our everyday life, we must try to see if there is any other way of judging things, or rather if our ordinary way is always sufficient to give us the ultimate satisfaction of our spiritual needs. If we feel dissatisfied somehow with this life, if there is something in our ordinary way of living that deprives us of freedom in its most sanctified sense, we must endeavor to find a way somewhere which gives us a sense of finality and contentment. Zen proposes to do this for us and assures us of the acquirement of a new point of view in which life assumes a fresher, deeper, and more satisfying aspect. This acquirement, however, is really and naturally the greatest mental cataclysm one can go through with in life. It is no easy task, it is a kind of fiery baptism, and one has to go through the storm, the earthquake, the overthrowing of the mountains, and the breaking in pieces of the rocks.

This acquiring of a new point of view in our dealings with life and the world is popularly called by Japanese Zen students "satori" (*wu* in Chinese). It is really another name for enlightenment (*anuttara-samyak-sambodhi*), which is the word used by the Buddha and his Indian followers ever since his realization under the Bodhi tree by the river Nairañjanā. There are several other phrases in Chinese designating this spiritual experience, each of which has a special connotation, showing tentatively how this phenomenon is interpreted. At all events there is no Zen without satori, which is indeed the alpha and omega of Zen Buddhism. Zen devoid of satori is like a sun without its light and heat. Zen may lose all its literature,

---

[1] *Essays in Zen Buddhism* (First Series), pp.. 229–266.

all its monasteries, and all its paraphernalia; but as long as there is satori in it it will survive to eternity. I want to emphasize this most fundamental fact concerning the very life of Zen; for there are some even among the students of Zen themselves who are blind to this central fact and are apt to think when Zen has been explained away logically or psychologically, or as one of the Buddhist philosophies which can be summed up by using highly technical and conceptual Buddhist phrases, Zen is exhausted, and there remains nothing in it that makes it what it is. But my contention is, the life of Zen begins with the opening of satori (*k'ai wu* in Chinese).

Satori may be defined as an intuitive looking into the nature of things in contradistinction to the analytical or logical understanding of it. Practically, it means the unfolding of a new world hitherto unperceived in the confusion of a dualistically-trained mind. Or we may say that with satori our entire surroundings are viewed from quite an unexpected angle of perception. Whatever this is, the world for those who have gained a satori is no more the old world as it used to be; even with all its flowing streams and burning fires, it is never the same one again. Logically stated, all its opposites and contradictions are united and harmonized into a consistent organic whole. This is a mystery and a miracle, but according to the Zen masters such is being performed every day. Satori can thus be had only through our once personally experiencing it.

Its semblance or analogy in a more or less feeble and fragmentary way is gained when a difficult mathematical problem is solved, or when a great discovery is made, or when a sudden means of escape is realized in the midst of most desperate complications; in short, when one exclaims "Eureka! Eureka!" But this refers only to the intellectual aspect of satori, which is therefore necessarily partial and incomplete and does not touch the very foundations of life considered as one indivisible whole. Satori as the Zen experience must be concerned with the entirety of life. For what Zen proposes is the revolution, and the revaluation as well, of oneself as a spiritual unity. The solving of a mathematical problem ends with the solution, it does not affect one's whole life. So with all other particular questions, practical or scientific, they do not enter the basic life-tone of the individual concerned. But the opening of satori is the remaking of life itself. When it is genuine—for there are many simulacra of it—its effects on one's moral and spiritual life are revolutionary, and they are enhancing, purifying, as well as exacting. When a master was asked what constituted Buddha-hood, he answered, "The bottom of a pail is broken through." From this we can see what a complete revolution is produced by this spiritual experience. The birth of a new man is really cataclysmic.

In the psychology of religion this spiritual enhancement of one's whole life is called "conversion." But as the term is generally used by Christian converts, it cannot be applied in its strict sense to the Buddhist experience, especially to that of the Zen followers; the term has too affective or emotional a shade to take the place of satori, which is above all noetic. The general tendency of Buddhism is, as we know, more intellectual than emotional, and its doctrine of enlightenment distinguishes it sharply from the Christian view of salvation; Zen as one of the Mahayana schools naturally shares a large amount of what we may call transcendental intellectualism, which does not issue in logical dualism. When poetically or figura-tively expressed, satori is "the opening of the mind-flower," or "the removing of the bar," or "the brightening up of the mind-works."

All these tend to mean the clearing up of a passage which has been somehow blocked, preventing the free, unobstructed opera-tion of a machine or a full display of the inner works. With the re-moval of the obstruction, a new vista opens before one, boundless in expanse and reaching the end of time. As life thus feels quite free in its activity, which was not the case before the awakening, it now enjoys itself to the fullest extent of its possibilities, to attain which is the object of Zen discipline. This is often taken to be equivalent to "vacuity of interest and poverty of purpose." But according to the Zen masters the doctrine of non-achievement con-cerns itself with the subjective attitude of mind which goes beyond the limitations of thought. It does not deny ethical ideals, nor does it transcend them; it is simply an inner state of consciousness with-out reference to its objective consequences.

As to the opening of satori, all that Zen can do is to indicate the way and leave the rest all to one's own experience; that is to say, following up the indication and arriving at the goal—this is to be done by oneself and without another's help. With all that the master can do, he is helpless to make the disciple take hold of the thing unless the latter is inwardly fully prepared for it. Just as we cannot make a horse drink against his will, the taking hold of the ultimate reality is to be done by oneself. Just as the flower blooms out of its inner necessity, the looking into one's own nature must be the outcome of one's own inner overflowing. This is where Zen is so personal and subjective, in the sense of being inner and creative. In the Āgama or Nikāya literature we encounter so frequently such phrases as "*Atta-dīpā viharatha atta-saraṇā anaññasaraṇā*," or "*sayaṃ abhiññā*," or "*Diṭṭha-dhammo patta-dhammo vidita-dhammo pariyogāḷha-dhammo aparappaccayo satthu sāsane*"; they show that enlightenment is the awakening, within oneself and not depending on others, of an inner sense in one's consciousness, enabling one to create a world of eternal harmony and beauty—the home of Nirvana.

I said that Zen does not give us any intellectual assistance, nor does it waste time in arguing the point with us; but it merely suggests or indicates, not because it wants to be indefinite, but because that is really the only thing it can do for us. If it could, it would do anything to help us come to an understanding. In fact Zen is exhausting every possible means to do that, as we can see in all the great masters' attitudes toward their disciples. When they are actually knocking them down, their kindheartedness is never to be doubted. They are just waiting for the time when their pupils' minds get ripened for the final moment. When this is come, the opportunity of opening an eye to the truth of Zen lies everywhere. One can pick it up in the hearing of an inarticulate sound, or listening to an unintelligible remark, or in the observation of a flower blooming, or in the encountering of any trivial everyday incident such as stumbling, rolling up a screen, using a fan, etc. These are all sufficient conditions that will awaken one's inner sense. Evidently a most insignificant happening, and yet its effect on the mind infinitely surpasses all that one could expect of it. A light touch of an ignited wire, and an explosion shaking the very foundations of the earth. In fact, all the causes of satori are in the mind. That is why when the clock clicks, all that has been lying there bursts up like a volcanic eruption or flashes out like a bolt of lightning.[2] Zen calls this "returning to one's own home"; for its followers will declare: "You have now found yourself; from the very begin-

2 The lightning simile in the *Kena Upaniṣad* (IV, 30), as is supposed by some scholars, is not to depict the feeling of inexpressive awe as regards the nature of Brahman, but it illustrates the bursting out of enlightenment upon consciousness. "A—a—ah" is most significant here.

ning nothing has been kept away from you. It was yourself that closed the eye to the fact. In Zen there is nothing to explain, nothing to teach, that will add to your knowledge. Unless it grows out of yourself, no knowledge is really of value to you; borrowed plumage never grows."

So far the phenomenon called satori in Zen Buddhism has been treated as constituting the essence of Zen, as the turning point in one's life which opens the mind to a wider and deeper world, as something to be gleaned even from a most trivial incident of everyday life. I wish to close this essay by making a few general remarks in the way of recapitulation on the Buddhist experience known as satori.

1. People often imagine that the discipline of Zen is to induce a state of self-suggestion through meditation. This is not quite right. As we can see from the various instances above cited, satori does not consist in producing a certain premeditated condition by intensely thinking of it. It is the growing consciousness of a new power in the mind, which enables it to judge things from a new point of view. Ever since the unfoldment of consciousness we have been led to respond to the inner and outer conditions in a certain conceptual and analytical manner. The discipline of Zen consists in upsetting this artificially constructed framework once for all and in remodelling it on an entirely new basis. The older frame is "Ignorance" (*avidyā*) and the new one "Enlightenment" (*sambodhi*). It is evident therefore that meditating on a metaphysical or symbolical statement which is a product of our relative consciousness plays no part in Zen.

2. Without the attainment of satori no one can enter into the mystery of Zen. It is the sudden flashing of a new truth hitherto altogether undreamed of. It is a sort of mental catastrophe taking place all at once after so much piling of matters intellectual and demonstrative. The piling has reached its limit and the whole edifice has now come to the ground, when behold a new heaven is opened to your full survey. Water freezes suddenly when it reaches a certain point, the liquid has turned into a solidity, and it no more flows. Satori comes upon you unawares when you feel you have exhausted your whole being. Religiously this is a new birth, and, morally, the revaluation of one's relationship to the

world. The latter now appears to be dressed in a different garment which covers up all the ugliness of dualism, which is called in Buddhist phraseology delusion (*māyā*) born of reasoning (*tarka*) and error (*vikalpa*).

3. Satori is the *raison d'être* of Zen, and without which Zen is no Zen. Therefore every contrivance (*upāya*), disciplinary or doctrinal, is directed toward the attainment of satori. Zen masters could not remain patient for satori to come by itself; that is, to come sporadically and at its own pleasure. They earnestly seek out some way to make people deliberately or systematically realize the truth of Zen. Their manifestly enigmatical presentations of it were mostly to create a state of mind in their disciples, which would pave the way to the enlightenment of Zen. All the intellectual demonstrations and exhortatory persuasions so far carried out by most religious and philosophical leaders failed to produce the desired effect. The disciples were led further and further astray. Especially when Buddhism was introduced into China with all its Indian equipment, with its highly metaphysical abstractions, and in a most complicated system of moral discipline, the Chinese were at a loss how to grasp the central point of the doctrine of Buddhism, Bodhidharma, Enō, Baso, and other masters noticed the fact. The natural outcome was the proclamation of Zen; satori was placed above sutra-reading and scholarly discussion of the sastras, and it came to be identified with Zen. Zen therefore without satori is like pepper without its pungency. But at the same time we must not forget that there is such a thing as being too conscious of satori, which is indeed to be detested.

4. This emphasizing in Zen of satori above everything else makes the fact quite significant that Zen is not a system of *dhyāna* as practiced in India and by other schools of Buddhism than the Zen. By *dhyāna* is understood popularly a kind of meditation or contemplation; that is, the fixing of thought, especially in Mahayana Buddhism, on the doctrine of emptiness (*śūnyatā*). When the mind is so trained as to be able to realize the state of perfect void in which there is not a trace of consciousness left, even the sense of being unconscious having departed—in other words, when all forms of mental activity are swept clean from the field of consciousness, which is now like a sky devoid of every speck of cloud, a mere broad expanse of blue—*dhyāna* is said to have reached its perfection. This may be called ecstasy or trance, but it is not Zen. In Zen there must be a satori; there must be a general mental up-

heaval which destroys the old accumulations of intellectuality and
lays down a foundation for a new faith; there must be the awakening of a new sense which will review the old things from an angle
of perception entirely and most refreshingly new. In *dhyāna* there
are none of these things, for it is merely a quieting exercise of the
mind. As such it has doubtless its own merits, but Zen ought not to
be identified with such a *dhyāna*. The Buddha therefore got dissatisfied with his two Sankhya teachers, in whose teaching the
meditations were so many stages of self-abstraction or thought-
annihilation.

5. Satori is not seeing God as He is, as may be contended by
some Christian mystics. Zen has from the very beginning made
clear its principal thesis, which is to see into the work of creation
and not interview the Creator Himself. The latter may be found
then busy moulding His universe, but Zen can go along with its
own work even when He is not found there. It is not depending on
His support. When it grasps the reason of living a life, it is satisfied.
Hōen of Gosozan used to produce his own hand and asked his
disciples why it is called a hand. When one knows the reason,
there is satori and one has Zen. Whereas with the God of mysticism
there is the grasping of a definite object, and when you have God,
what is not God is excluded. This is self-limiting. Zen wants absolute freedom, even from God. "No abiding place" means that;
"Cleanse your mouth even when you utter the word 'Buddha'"
amounts to the same thing. It is not that Zen wants to be morbidly
unholy and godless, but that it knows the incompleteness of a
name. Therefore when Yakusan was asked to give a lecture, he did
not say a word, but instead came down from the pulpit and went
off to his own room. Hyakujō merely walked forward a few steps,
stood still, and opened his arms—which was his exposition of the
great principle of Buddhism.

6. Satori is the most intimate individual experience and therefore cannot be expressed in words or described in any manner. All
that one can do in the way of communicating the experience to
others is to suggest or indicate, and this only tentatively. The one
who has had it understands readily enough when such indications
are given, but when we try to have a glimpse of it through the
indices given we utterly fail. We are then like the man who says
that he loves the most beautiful woman in the world and yet who
knows nothing of her pedigree or social position, of her personal
name or family name, knows nothing of her individuality physical

as well as moral. We are again like the man who puts up a staircase
in a place where four crossroads meet, to mount up thereby into
the upper story of a mansion, and yet who knows not just where
that mansion is, in the east or west, in the north or south. The
Buddha was quite to the point when he thus derided all those
philosophers and vain talkers of his day, who merely dealt in abstractions, empty hearsay, and fruitless indications. Zen therefore
wants us to build the staircase right at the front of the very palace
into whose upper story we are to mount up. When we can say
"This is the very personality, this is the very house," we have the
satori interviewed face to face and realized by oneself. (*Ditthe va
dhamme sayam abhiññā sacchikatvā.*)

7. Satori is not a morbid state of mind, a fit subject for abnormal
psychology. If anything it is a perfectly normal state of mind.
When I speak of a mental upheaval, one may be led to consider
Zen something to be shunned by ordinary people. This is a mistaken view of Zen, unfortunately often held by prejudiced critics.
As Nansen declared, it is your "everyday thought." When later a
monk asked a master[3] what was meant by "everyday thought," he
said,

> Drinking tea, eating rice,
> I pass my time as it comes;
> Looking down at the stream, looking up at the mountains,
> How serene and relaxed I feel indeed!

It all depends upon the adjustment of the hinge whether the
door opens in or out. Even in the twinkling of an eye, the whole
affair is changed, and you have Zen, and you are as perfect and
normal as ever. More than that, you have in the meantime acquired something altogether new. All your mental activities are
now working to a different key, which is more satisfying, more
peaceful, and fuller of joy than anything you ever had. The tone
of your life is altered. There is something rejuvenating in it. The
spring flowers look prettier, and the mountain stream runs cooler
and more transparent. The subjective revolution that brings out
this state of things cannot be called abnormal. When life becomes
more enjoyable and its expanse is as broad as the universe itself,

[3] Hōji Bunkin, a disciple of Hofuku Juten (d. 928).

there must be something in satori quite healthy and worth one's striving after its attainment.

8. We are supposedly living in the same world, but who can tell the thing we popularly call a stone lying before this window is the same thing to all of us? According to the way we look at it, to some the stone ceases to be a stone, while to others it forever remains a worthless specimen of a geological product. And this initial divergence of views calls forth an endless series of divergencies later in our moral and spiritual lives. Just a little twisting, as it were, in our modes of thinking, and yet what a world of difference will grow up eventually between one another! So with Zen, satori is this twisting, or rather screwing, not in the wrong way, but in a deeper and fuller sense, and the result is the revelation of a world of entirely new values.

Again, you and I sip a cup of tea. The act is apparently alike, but who can tell what a wide gap there is subjectively between you and me? In your drinking there may be no Zen, while mine is brim full of it. The reason is, the one moves in the logical circle and the other is out of it; that is to say, in one case rigid rules of intellection so called are asserting themselves, and the actor even when acting is unable to unfetter himself from these intellectual bonds; while in the other case the subject has struck a new path and is not at all conscious of the duality of his act; in him life is not split into object and subject or into acting and acted. The drinking at the moment to him means the whole fact, the whole world. Zen lives and is therefore free, whereas our "ordinary" life is in bondage; satori is the first step to freedom.

9. Satori is enlightenment (*sambodhi*). So long as Buddhism is the doctrine of enlightenment, as we know it to be, from its earliest as well as from its later literature, and so long as Zen asserts satori to be its culmination, satori must be said to represent the very spirit of the Buddhist teaching. When it announces itself to be the transmission of the Buddha-*citta* (*fu-hsin*) not dependent upon the logical and discursive exposition in the canonical writings, either Hinayana or Mahayana, it is by no means exaggerating its fundamental characteristic as distinguished from the other schools of Buddhism that have grown up in Japan and China. Whatever this may be, there is no doubt that Zen is one of the most precious and in many respects the most remarkable spiritual possessions bequeathed to Eastern people. Even when it is considered the

Buddhist form of speculative mysticism not unknown to the West in the philosophy of Plotinus, Eckhart, and their followers, its complete literature alone since the sixth patriarch, Enō, so well preserved, is worth the serious study of scholars and truth-seekers. And then the whole body of the *kōan* systematically grading the progress of the spiritual awakening is the wonderful treasure in the hands of the Zen monks in Japan at present.

2. CHIEF CHARACTERISTICS OF SATORI[1]

DAIE was a great advocate of satori, and one of his favorite sayings was, "Zen has no words; when you have satori, you have everything." Hence his strong arguments for it, which came, as has already been shown, from his own experience. Until then, he was quite ready to write a treatise against Zen in which he planned to disclaim everything accredited to Zen by its followers. His interview with his master Engo, however, crushed all his former determination, making him come out as a most intense advocate of the Zen experience. As I go on with this study of the *kōan* exercise, I shall have many occasions to make further references to Daie. In the meantime I wish to enumerate some of the most salient features of satori, which will later help us understand the role of *kōan* in the whole structure of Zen.

1. *Irrationality*. By this I mean that satori is not a conclusion to be reached by reasoning, and defies all intellectual determination. Those who have experienced it are always at a loss to explain it coherently or logically. When it is explained at all, either in words or gestures, its content more or less undergoes a mutilation. The uninitiated are thus unable to grasp it by what is outwardly visible, while those who have had the experience discern what is genuine from what is not. The satori experience is thus always characterized by irrationality, inexplicability, and incommunicability.

Listen to Daie once more: "This matter [i.e., Zen] is like a great mass of fire; when you approach it your face is sure to be scorched. It is again like a sword about to be drawn; when it is once out of the scabbard, someone is sure to lose his life. But if you neither fling away the scabbard nor approach the fire, you are no better than a piece of rock or of wood. Coming to this pass, one has to be quite a resolute character full of spirit."[2] There is nothing here

---

[1] *Essays in Zen Buddhism* (Second Series), Rider & Co., 1950, pp. 30–36.

[2] Daie's sermon at the request of Ri Senkyō.

suggestive of cool reasoning and quiet metaphysical or epistemological analysis, but of a certain desperate will to break through an
insurmountable barrier, of the will impelled by some irrational or
unconscious power behind it. Therefore, the outcome also defies
intellection or conceptualization.

2. *Intuitive Insight.* That there is noetic quality in mystic experiences has been pointed out by James in his *Varieties of Religious Experience,* and this applies also to the Zen experience known
as satori. Another name for satori is *kenshō* (*chien-hsing*), meaning "to see essence or Nature," which apparently proves that there
is "seeing" or "perceiving" in satori. That this seeing is of quite a
different quality from what is ordinarily designated as knowledge
need not be specifically noticed. Eka is reported to have made this
statement concerning his satori which was confirmed by Bodhidharma himself: "[As to my satori], it is not a total annihilation;
it is knowledge of the most adequate kind; only it cannot be expressed in words." In this respect Jinne was more explicit, for he
says that "the one character *chi* (knowledge) is the source of all
mysteries (*myō*)."[3]

Without this noetic quality satori will lose all its pungency, for
it is really the reason of satori itself. It is noteworthy that the
knowledge contained in satori is concerned with something universal and at the same time with the individual aspect of existence.
When a finger is lifted, the lifting means, from the viewpoint of
satori, far more than the act of lifting. Some may call it symbolic,
but satori does not point to anything beyond itself, being final as
it is. Satori is the knowledge of an individual object and also that
of Reality which is, if I may say so, at the back of it.

3. *Authoritativeness.* By this I mean that the knowledge realized
by satori is final, that no amount of logical argument can refute it.
Being direct and personal it is sufficient unto itself. All that logic
can do here is to explain it, to interpret it in connection with other
kinds of knowledge with which our minds are filled. Satori is thus
a form of perception, an inner perception, which takes place in the
most interior part of consciousness. Hence the sense of authoritativeness, which means finality. So, it is generally said that Zen is

---

[3] Shūmitsu in "Zen Masters and Disciples." *Myō* is a difficult term to
translate; it often means "exquisiteness," "indefinable subtlety." In this case
myō is the mysterious way in which things are presented to this ultimate
knowledge.

like drinking water, for it is by one's self that one knows whether it is warm or cold. The Zen perception being the last term of experience, it cannot be denied by outsiders who have no such experience.

4. *Affirmation.* What is authoritative and final can never be negative. For negation has no value for our life, it leads us nowhere; it is not a power that urges, nor does it give one a place to rest. Though the satori experience is sometimes expressed in negative terms, it is essentially an affirmative attitude toward all things that exist; it accepts them as they come along regardless of their moral values. Buddhists call this *kṣānti,* "patience," or more properly "acceptance," that is, acceptance of things in their suprarelative or transcendental aspect where no dualism of whatever sort avails.

Some may say that this is pantheistic. The term, however, has a definite philosophic meaning and I would not see it used in this connection. When so interpreted the Zen experience exposes itself to endless misunderstandings and "defilements." Daie says in his letter to Myōsō: "An ancient sage says that the Tao itself does not require special disciplining, only let it not be defiled. I would say: To talk about mind or nature is defiling; to talk about the unfathomable or the mysterious is defiling; to practice meditation or tranquillization is defiling; to direct one's attention to it, to think about it is defiling; to be writing about it thus on paper with a brush is especially defiling. What then shall we have to do in order to get ourselves oriented, and properly apply ourselves to it? The precious Vajra-sword is right here and its purpose is to cut off the head. Do not be concerned with human questions of right and wrong. All is Zen just as it is, and right here you are to apply yourself." Zen is Suchness—a grand affirmation.

5. *Sense of the Beyond.* Terminology may differ in different religions, and in satori there is always what we may call a sense of the Beyond; the experience indeed is my own but I feel it to be rooted elsewhere. The individual shell in which my personality is so solidly encased explodes at the moment of satori. Not, necessarily, that I get unified with a being greater than myself or absorbed in it, but that my individuality, which I found rigidly held together and definitely kept separate from other individual existences, becomes loosened somehow from its tightening grip and

melts away into something indescribable, something which is of quite a different order from what I am accustomed to. The feeling that follows is that of a complete release or a complete rest—the feeling that one has arrived finally at the destination. "Coming home and quietly resting" is the expression generally used by Zen followers. The story of the prodigal son in the *Saddharmapuṇḍarīka*, in the *Vajrasamādhi*, and also in the New Testament points to the same feeling one has at the moment of a satori experience.

As far as the psychology of satori is considered, a sense of the Beyond is all we can say about it; to call this the Beyond, the Absolute, or God, or a Person is to go further than the experience itself and to plunge into a theology or metaphysics. Even the "Beyond" is saying a little too much. When a Zen master says, "There is not a fragment of a tile above my head, there is not an inch of earth beneath my feet," the expression seems to be an appropriate one. I have called it elsewhere the Unconscious, though this has a psychological taint.

6. *Impersonal Tone.* Perhaps the most remarkable aspect of the Zen experience is that it has no personal note in it as is observable in Christian mystic experiences. There is no reference whatever in Buddhist satori to such personal and frequently sexual feelings and relationships as are to be gleaned from these terms: flame of love, a wonderful love shed in the heart, embrace, the beloved, bride, bridegroom, spiritual matrimony, Father, God, the Son of God, God's child, etc. We may say that all these terms are interpretations based on a definite system of thought and really have nothing to do with the experience itself. At any rate, alike in India, China, and Japan, satori has remained thoroughly impersonal, or rather highly intellectual.

Is this owing to the peculiar character of Buddhist philosophy? Does the experience itself take its colors from the philosophy or theology? Whatever this is, there is no doubt that in spite of its having some points of similitude to the Christian mystic experience, the Zen experience is singularly devoid of personal or human colorings. Chōben, a great government officer of the Sung dynasty, was a lay-disciple of Hōsen of Chiang-shan. One day after his official duties were over, he found himself leisurely sitting in his office, when all of a sudden a clash of thunder burst on his

ear, and he realized a state of satori. The poem he then composed
depicts one aspect of the Zen experience:

> Devoid of thought, I sat quietly by the desk in my
>   official room,
> With my fountain-mind undisturbed, as serene as
>   water;
> A sudden clash of thunder, the mind-doors burst
>   open,
> And lo, there sitteth the old man in all his homeliness.

This is perhaps all the personal tone one can find in the Zen experience, and what a distance between "the old man in his homeliness"
and "God in all His glory," not to say anything about such feelings
as "the heavenly sweetness of Christ's excellent love," etc.! How
barren, how unromantic satori is when compared with the Christian mystic experiences!

Not only satori itself is such a prosaic and non-glorious event,
but the occasion that inspires it also seems to be unromantic and
altogether lacking in super-sensuality. Satori is experienced in connection with any ordinary occurrence in one's daily life. It does
not appear to be an extraordinary phenomenon as is recorded in
Christian books of mysticism. Someone takes hold of you, or slaps
you, or brings you a cup of tea, or makes some most commonplace
remark, or recites some passage from a sutra or from a book of
poetry, and when your mind is ripe for its outburst, you come at
once to satori. There is no romance of love-making, no voice of the
Holy Ghost, no plenitude of Divine Grace, no glorification of any
sort. Here is nothing painted in high colors, all is gray and extremely unobtrusive and unattractive.

7. *Feeling of Exaltation.* That this feeling inevitably accompanies satori is due to the fact that it is the breaking up of the
restriction imposed on one as an individual being, and this breaking up is not a mere negative incident but quite a positive one
fraught with signification because it means an infinite expansion
of the individual. The general feeling, though we are not always
conscious of it, which characterizes all our functions of consciousness, is that of restriction and dependence, because consciousness
itself is the outcome of two forces conditioning or restricting each
other. Satori, on the contrary, essentially consists in doing away
with the opposition of two terms in whatsoever sense—and this

opposition is the principle of consciousness as before mentioned, while satori is to realize the Unconscious which goes beyond the opposition.

To be released of this, therefore, must make one feel above all things intensely exalted. A wandering outcast maltreated everywhere not only by others but by himself finds that he is the possessor of all the wealth and power that is ever attainable in this world by a mortal being—if this does not give him a high feeling of self-glorification, what could? Says a Zen master, "When you have satori you are able to reveal a palatial mansion made of precious stones on a single blade of grass; but when you have no satori, a palatial mansion itself is concealed behind a simple blade of grass."

Another Zen master, evidently alluding to the *Avataṃsaka*, declares: "O monks, lo and behold! A most auspicious light is shining with the utmost brilliancy all over the great chiliacosm, simultaneously revealing all the countries, all the oceans, all the Sumerus, all the suns and moons, all the heavens, all the lands—each of which number as many as hundreds of thousands of koṭi. O monks, do you not see the light?" But the Zen feeling of exaltation is rather a quiet feeling of self-contentment; it is not at all demonstrative, when the first glow of it passes away. The Unconscious does not proclaim itself so boisterously in the Zen consciousness.

8. *Momentariness.* Satori comes upon one abruptly and is a momentary experience. In fact, if it is not abrupt and momentary, it is not satori. This abruptness (*tun*) is what characterizes the Enō school of Zen ever since its proclamation late in the seventh century. His opponent Jinshū was insistent on a gradual unfoldment of Zen consciousness. Enō's followers were thus distinguished as strong upholders of the doctrine of abruptness. This abrupt experience of satori, then, opens up in one moment an altogether new vista, and the whole of existence is appraised from quite a new angle of observation.

3. PSYCHOLOGICAL ANTECEDENTS OF SATORI PRIOR TO THE KŌAN SYSTEM[1]

HERE I wish to examine what are these psychological equipments or antecedents that lead up to satori. As we have already seen, this state or what may be called Zen consciousness comes on in connection with the most trivial incidents such as the raising of a finger, uttering a cry, reciting a phrase, swinging a stick, slapping a face, and so on. As the outcome is apparently incongruous with the occasion, we naturally presume some deep-seated psychological antecedents which are thereby abruptly brought to maturity. What are these antecedents? Let us examine a few of the classical cases of satori as recorded in the annals of Zen.

1. The story of the interview of Eka with Bodhidharma, the first patriarch of Zen in China, is somewhat veiled with historical inaccuracies and suffers much from its dramatic treatment, but even with these disadvantages we still have an intelligent account of the interview, for historical accuracy is not always the necessary condition for determining what actually took place. Whatever literary treatment the event receives later on also helps us to understand the situation. We may well remember that the imagination often depicts so-called facts psychologically more truthfully than the historian's objective testimony.

According to "The Transmission of the Lamp" Eka was a liberal-minded, open-hearted sort of person, thoroughly acquainted with Confucian and Taoist literature, but always dissatisfied with their teaching because they seemed to him not quite thoroughgoing. When he heard of Bodhidharma coming from India, he went to Shao-lin-ssŭ where the master stayed. He hoped for the opportunity to talk with him on the subject upon which he wished to be enlightened, but the master was always found sitting silently facing the wall.

[1] *Essays in Zen Buddhism* (Second Series), pp. 37–51.

Eka reflected: "History gives examples of ancient truth seekers, who were willing, for the sake of enlightenment, to have the marrow extracted from their bones, their blood spilled to feed the hungry, to cover the muddy road with their hair, or to throw themselves into the mouth of a hungry tiger. What am I? Am I not also able to give myself up on the altar of truth?"

On the ninth of December of the same year, he stood in the fast-falling snow and did not move until the morning when the snow had reached his knees. Bodhidharma then took pity on him and said, "You have been standing in the snow for some time, and what is your wish?"

Replied Eka, "I am come to receive your invaluable instruction; pray open the gate of mercy and extend your hand of salvation to this poor suffering mortal."

Bodhidharma then said: "The incomparable teaching of the Buddha can be comprehended only after a long and hard discipline and by enduring what is most difficult to endure and by practicing what is most difficult to practice. Men of inferior virtue and wisdom who are lighthearted and full of conceit are not able even to set their eyes on the truth of Buddhism. All the labor of such men is sure to come to nought."

Eka was deeply moved, and in order to show his sincerity in the desire to be instructed in the teachings of all the Buddhas, he cut off his left arm with a sword he carried and presented it before the quietly meditating Bodhidharma. Thereupon, the master remarked, "You are not to seek this [truth] through others."

"My soul is not yet pacified. Pray, Master, pacify it."

"Bring your soul here and I will have it pacified," said Bodhidharma.

After a short hesitation Eka finally confessed, "I have sought it for many years and am still unable to take hold of it."

Here Daie makes the comment: "Eka well understood the situation in which he found himself after studying all the scriptures, and it was good of him that he gave the master a straightforward answer. The 'thing,' he knew, was not to be sought after with a purpose, or without a purpose; nor was it to be reached by means of words, nor by mere quietude; nor was it to be logically grasped, nor illogically explained. It was nowhere to be encountered nor was it to be inferred from anything; no, not in the five Skandhas, not in the eighteen Dhatus. He did well in answering this way."

"There! Your soul is pacified once and for all," Bodhidharma confirmed.

This confirmation on the part of the master at once opened Eka's eye of satori. Daie again remarks: "It was like the dragon getting into water, or the tiger leaning against the rock. At that moment Eka saw not the master before him, nor the snow, nor the mind that was reaching out for something, nor the satori itself which took possession of his mind. All vanished away from his consciousness, all was emptiness. So it was said that 'Loneliness reigns here, there is not a soul in the monastery of Shao-lin.' But did Eka remain in this emptiness? No, he was awakened abruptly to a new life. He threw himself down over the precipice, and lo, he came out fully alive from certain death. And surely he felt then the cold snow piled up in the temple court. As before, his nose rested above his upper lip."

The characteristic points I wish to notice in the case of Eka are: that he was a learned scholar; that he was not satisfied with mere scholarship but wished to grasp something innerly; that he was most earnest in his search for an inmost truth which would give peace and rest to his soul; that he was prepared to sacrifice anything for the purpose; that he devoted some years to the hard task of locating his soul so-called, for evidently he thought in accordance with the traditional view that there was a "soul" at the center of his being and that when it was grasped he would attain the desired end; that while Eka's interview with Bodhidharma is narrated as if it were an event of one day or one evening, it is possible that some days or months of intense mental lucubration took place between it and the master's exhortation; that the statement "I have not been able to take hold of my soul" was not a plain statement of fact but meant that the whole being of Eka was thrown down, that is, he had reached here the end of his life as an individual existence conscious all the time of its own individuality; that he was dead unto himself when the master's remark unexpectedly revived him—this can be seen from the remark as above cited, "Loneliness reigns here, there is not a soul in the monastery of Shao-lin."

This "loneliness" is an absolute loneliness in which there is no dualistic contrast of being and non-being. The cry—for it was a cry and not a proposition—that "there is no soul to be taken hold of" could not be uttered until this state of absolute loneliness was reached. It was also just because of this realization that Eka was able to rise from it upon Bodhidharma's remarking, "Pacified then is your soul!" When we carefully and sympathetically follow the course of events that led up to Eka's satori, we naturally have to fill up the gaps in the record of his life in the way here proposed. My point of view will become clearer as we proceed.

2. The case of Enō, who is regarded now as the sixth patriarch of Zen in China, presents some contrasts to that of Eka so long as Enō is made out to be an unlearned peddler. This treatment given to Enō is in a way interesting as it reveals a certain tendency among followers of Zen who ignore learning and the study of sutras. In Enō's case, however, there was a historical background which made him stand against his rival, Jinshū, who was noted for his wide knowledge and scholarship. In reality, Enō was not such an ignoramus as his followers wanted him to appear, for his sermons known as the "Platform Sutra" contain many allusions to Buddhist literature. All we can say of him as regards his learning is that he was not so erudite as Jinshū. According to history, his first knowledge of Zen came from the *Vajracchedikā*. While he was peddling wood and kindling he overheard one of his patrons read that sutra. This inspired him and he decided to study Zen teachings under Gunin, the fifth patriarch of Zen. When he saw the master, the latter asked:

"Where do you come from? What do you want here?"

"I am a farmer from Hsin-chou and wish to become a Buddha."

"So you come from the south," said the master. "But the southerners have no Buddha-nature in them; how could you expect to be a Buddha?"

Enō protested, "There are southerners and there are northerners, but as to Buddha-nature, no distinction is to be made between them."

If Enō had had no preliminary knowledge or experience of Buddhism he could not have answered like that. He worked under Gunin in the granary of the monastery as a rice cleaner and not as a regular monk, and remained there for eight months. One day the fifth patriarch, wishing to decide on his successor, wanted to see how much of his teaching was understood by his followers, who numbered about five hundred. He therefore requested that each of them compose a poem expressing his understanding of the teaching. The poem composed by Jinshū, the most scholarly of his five hundred disciples, ran as follows:

> This body is the Bodhi tree,
> The soul is like a mirror bright;
> Take heed to keep it always clean,
> And let not dust collect upon it.

Enō was not satisfied with it and composed another which was inscribed beside the learned Jinshū's:

> The Bodhi is not like the tree,
> The mirror bright is nowhere shining;
> As there is nothing from the beginning,
> Where can the dust collect itself?[2]

So far as we can judge by these poems alone, Enō's is in full accord with the doctrine of Emptiness as taught in the *Prajñā-pāramitā-sūtra*, while Jinshū's, we may say, has not yet quite fully grasped the spirit of Mahayana Buddhism. Enō's mind, thus, from the first developed along the line of thought indicated in the *Vajracchedikā* which he learned even before he came to Gunin. But it is evident that he could not have composed the poem without having experienced the truth of Emptiness in himself. The first inspiration he got from the *Vajracchedikā* made him realize the presence of a truth beyond this phenomenal world. He came to Gunin, but it required a great deal of trained intuitive power to get into the spirit of the *Prajñāpāramitā*, and even with the genius of Enō this could not have been accomplished very easily. He must have worked very hard while cleaning rice to have delved so successfully into the secrets of his own mind.

The eight months of menial work were by no means all menial;[3]

[2] According to the Tun-huang MS. copy of the "Platform Sūtra," the third line reads: "The Buddha-nature is ever pure and undefiled." This book, compiled by Enō's disciples, has suffered a somewhat vicissitudinous fate, and the current edition differs very much from such ancient copies as the Tun-huang MS. and the Japanese edition recently recovered at the Kōshōji monastery, Kyoto.

[3] Is it not illuminating to note that Enō passed his life in a most prosaic and apparently non-religious employment while in the monastery, working up his mind to develop into the state of satori? He did not repeat the name of Buddha, he did not worship the Buddha according to the prescribed rules of the monastery life, he did not confess his sins and ask for pardon through

a great spiritual upheaval was going on in the mind of Enō. The reading of Jinshū's poem gave him the occasion for giving utterance to his inner vision. Whatever learning, insight, and instruction he had had before were brought finally into maturity and culminated in the poem which was the living expression of his experience. His *Vajracchedikā* thus came to life in his own being. Without actually experiencing the *Prajñāpāramitā*, Enō could not have made the statement which he made to Myō-jōza, one of his pursuers after he left Gunin. When Myō-jōza wanted to be enlightened, Enō said, "Think not of good, think not of evil, but see what at the moment thy own original features are, which thou hadst even before coming into existence."

The points which I wish to note in the case of Enō are:

a. He was not a very learned man though he was in fact well acquainted with several Mahayana sutras. He was decidedly not one of those scholars who could write recondite and well-informed commentaries on the sutras and sastras. His main idea was to get into the true meaning of a text.

b. The text which first attracted his attention was the *Vajracchedikā*, which was very likely most popular in his day. This sutra belongs to the *Prajñāpāramitā* group. It is not a philosophical work but contains deep religious truths as they represented themselves to the Indian Mahayanist genius. They are expressed in such a way as to be almost incomprehensible to ordinary minds, as they often seem contradictory to one another, as far as their logical thoroughness is concerned. Writers of the *Prajñāpāramitā* sutras are never tired of warning their readers not to get alarmed with their teachings, which are so full of audacious statements.

The object of Enō's coming to Gunin was to study Zen and to breathe the spirit of the *Prajñāpāramitā*, and not to turn the rice mill or to chop wood. But there is no doubt that he did a great deal of thinking within himself. Gunin must have noticed it and given him occasional instructions privately as well as publicly, for we cannot think that all his five hundred pupils were left to them-

---

the grace of God, he did not throw himself down before a Buddha and offer most ardent prayers to be relieved of the eternal bond of transmigration. He simply pounded his rice so that it could be ready for his Brotherhood's consumption. This ultra commonplaceness of Enō's role in the monastery life is the beginning of the Zen discipline which distinguishes itself remarkably from that of other Buddhist communities.

selves to understand the deep meaning of the *Vajracchedikā,* or the *Laṅkāvatāra,* or any other Zen literature. He must have given them frequent discourses on Zen, during all of which time Enō's mind was maturing.

d. It is probable that Jinshū's poem was the occasion for Enō to bring out to the surface all that was revolving about in his deep consciousness. He had been seeking for ultimate truth, or to experience in himself the final signification of the *Prajñāpāramitā.* Jinshū's poem, which went against its significance, produced in Enō's mind a contrary effect and opened up a more direct way to the *Prajñāpāramitā.*

3. Tokusan, who is noted for his swinging a staff, was also a student of the *Vajracchedikā* before he was converted to Zen. Different from his predecessor Enō, he was very learned in the teaching of the sutra and was extensively read in its commentaries, showing that his knowledge of the *Prajñāpāramitā* was more systematic than Enō's. He heard of this Zen teaching in the south, according to which a man could be a Buddha by immediately taking hold of his inmost nature. This he thought could not be the Buddha's own teaching, but the Evil One's, and he decided to go down south. In this respect his mission again differed from that of Enō. The latter wished to get into the spirit of the *Vajracchedikā* under the guidance of the fifth patriarch, while Tokusan's idea was to destroy Zen if possible. They were both students of the *Vajracchedikā,* but the sutra inspired them in ways diametrically opposite. Tokusan's psychology reminds us of that of St. Paul as he walked under the summer sun along the road to Damascus.

Tokusan's first objective was Lung-t'an, where resided a Zen master. On his way to the mountain he stopped at a teahouse where he asked the woman keeper to give him some refreshments. "Refreshment" is *tien-hsin* in Chinese, meaning, literally, "to punctuate the mind." Instead of setting out the requested refreshments for the tired monk-traveller, the woman asked, "What are you carrying on your back?"

He replied, "They are commentaries on the *Vajracchedikā.*"

"They are indeed!" said the woman. "May I ask you a question? If you can answer it to my satisfaction, you will have your refreshments free; but if you fail, you will have to go somewhere else."

To this Tokusan agreed.

The woman keeper of the teahouse then proposed the following: "I read in the *Vajracchedikā* that the mind is obtainable neither in the past, nor in the present, nor in the future. If so, which mind do you wish to punctuate?"

This unexpected question from an apparently insignificant country woman completely upset the knapsackful scholarship of Tokusan, for all his knowledge of the *Vajracchedikā* together with its various commentaries gave him no inspiration whatever. The poor scholar had to go without his lunch. Not only this, but he also had to abandon his bold enterprise to defeat the teachers of Zen; for when he was no match even for the keeper of a roadside teahouse, how could he expect to defeat a professional Zen master? Even before he saw the master of Lung-t'an, he was certainly made to think more about his self-imposed mission.

When Tokusan saw the master of Lung-t'an, he said, "I have heard people talk so much of Lung-t'an [Dragon's Pool], yet as I see it, there is no dragon here, nor any pool."

The master quietly replied, "You are indeed in the midst of Lung-t'an."

Tokusan finally decided to stay at Lung-t'an and to study Zen under the guidance of its master. One evening he was sitting outside the room quietly and yet earnestly in search of the truth. The master said, "Why do you not come in?"

"It is dark," replied Tokusan.

Whereupon the master lit a candle and handed it to the disciple. When Tokusan was about to take it, the master blew it out. This suddenly opened his mind to the truth of Zen teaching. Tokusan bowed respectfully.

"What is the matter with you?" asked the master.

"After this," Tokusan asserted, "whatever propositions the Zen masters may make about Zen, I shall never again cherish a doubt about them."

The next morning Tokusan took out all his commentaries on the *Vajracchedikā*, once so valued and considered so indispensable that he had to carry them about with him wherever he went, committed them to the flames, and turned them all into ashes.

The case of Tokusan shows some characteristic points differing much from those of the preceding case. Tokusan was learned not only in the *Vajracchedikā* but in other departments of Buddhist philosophy such as the *Abhidharmakośa* and the *Yogācāra*. But in the beginning he was decidedly against Zen, and the object of his coming out of the Shu district was to annihilate it. This, at any rate, was the motive that directed the surface current of his conscious-

ness; as to what was going on underneath, he was altogether unaware of it. The psychological law of contrariness was undoubtedly
in force and was strengthened as against his superficial motive
when he encountered a most unexpected opponent in the form of
a teahouse keeper. His first talk with the Zen master concerning
the Dragon's Pool completely crushed the hard crust of Tokusan's
mentality, releasing all the forces deeply hidden in his consciousness. When the candle was suddenly blown out, all that was
negated prior to this incident unconditionally reasserted itself. A
complete mental cataclysm took place. What had been regarded
as most precious was now not worth a straw.

Afterward, when Tokusan himself became a master, he used to
say to an inquirer, "Whether you say 'yes,' you get thirty blows;
whether you say 'no,' you get thirty blows just the same."

A monk asked him, "Who is the Buddha?"

"He is an old monk of the Western country."

"What is enlightenment?"

Tokusan gave the questioner a blow, saying, "You get out of
here; do not scatter dirt around us!"

Another monk wished to know something about Zen, but Tokusan roared, "I have nothing to give, begone!"

What a contrast this is to all that had been astir in Tokusan's
mind before his arrival at Lung-t'an! It does not require much
imagination to see what sort of a mental revolution was going on
in Tokusan's mind after his interview with the woman keeper of
the teahouse, and especially when he was sitting with his master,
outwardly quiet but inwardly so intensely active as to be oblivious
of the approach of darkness.

4. Rinzai was a disciple of Ōbaku and the founder of the school
that bears his name. His Zen experience presents some interesting
features which may be considered in a way typically orthodox in
those days when the *kōan* system of Zen discipline was not yet in
vogue. He had been studying Zen for some years under Ōbaku
when the head monk asked, "How long have you been here?"

"Three years, sir."

"Have you ever seen the master?"

"No, sir."

"Why don't you?"

"Because I do not know what question to ask him."

The head monk then told Rinzai, "You go and see the master
and ask, 'What is the principle of Buddhism?' "

Rinzai saw the master as he was told and asked, "What is the principle of Buddhism?" Even before he could finish the question, Ōbaku gave him several blows.

When the head monk saw him coming back from the master, he inquired about the result of the interview.

Said Rinzai sorrowfully, "I asked him and was beaten with many blows."

The monk told him not to be discouraged but to go again to the master.

Rinzai saw Ōbaku three times, but each time the same treatment was accorded to him, and poor Rinzai was not any the wiser.

Finally Rinzai thought it best to see another master and the head monk agreed. The master directed him to go to Daigu.

When Rinzai came to Daigu, the latter asked, "Where do you come from?"

"From Ōbaku."

"What instruction did he give you?"

"I asked him three times about the ultimate principle of Buddhism and each time he gave me several blows without any instructions. I wish you would tell me what fault I committed."

Daigu said, "No one could be more thoroughly kindhearted than that dotard master, and yet you want to know where you were faulty."

Thus reprimanded, Rinzai's eye was opened to the meaning of Ōbaku's apparently unkind treatment. He exclaimed, "After all there is not much in Ōbaku's Buddhism!"

Daigu at once seized Rinzai's collar and said: "A while ago you said you could not understand and now you declare that there is not much in Ōbaku's Buddhism. What do you mean by that?"

Rinzai, without saying a word, punched Daigu's ribs three times with his fist.

Daigu loosened his hold on Rinzai and remarked, "Your teacher is Ōbaku; I am not at all concerned with the whole business."

Rinzai returned to Ōbaku, who asked him, "How is it that you are back so soon?"

"Because your kindness is much too grandmotherly."

Ōbaku said, "When I see that fellow, Daigu, I will give him twenty blows."

"Don't wait to see him," said Rinzai, "have it now!" So saying, he gave the old master a good slap.

The old master laughed heartily.

What attracts our attention in the present case is Rinzai's silence for three years, not knowing what to ask the master. This appears to me to be full of significance. Did he not come to Ōbaku to study Zen Buddhism? If so, what had he been doing before the head monk advised him to see the master? And why did he not know what to ask him? And, finally, what made him so thoroughly transformed after seeing Daigu? To my mind Rinzai's three years under Ōbaku were spent in a vain attempt to grasp by thinking it out— the final truth of Zen. He knew full well that Zen was not to be understood by verbal means or by intellectual analysis, but still by thinking he strove for self-realization. He did not know what he was really seeking or where his mental efforts were to be directed. Indeed, if he had known the what and the where, it would have to be said that he was already in possession of something definite, and one who is in possession of something definite is not far from truly understanding Zen.

It was when Rinzai was in this troubled state of mind, wandering about on his spiritual pilgrimage, that the head monk from his own experience perceived that the time had come for him to give some timely advice to this wornout truth seeker. He gave Rinzai an index whereby he might successfully reach the goal. When Rinzai was roughly handled by Ōbaku, he was not surprised nor was he angered; he simply failed to understand what the blows indicated, and was grieved. On his way to Daigu he must have pondered the subject with all the mental powers at his command. Before he was told to ask the master concerning the ultimate truth of Buddhism, his troubled mind was reaching out for something to lean on; his arms, as it were, were stretched out in every direction to grasp something in the dark. When he was in this desperate situation, a pointer came to him in the form of "thirty blows," and Daigu's remark about a "kindhearted dotard master," which finally led him to grasp the object at which all the pointers had been directed. If it had not been for the three years of intense mental application and spiritual turmoil and vain search for the truth, this crisis could never have been reached. So many conflicting ideas, lined with different shades of feelings, had been in *mêlée* but suddenly their tangled skein was loosened and arranged itself in a new and harmonious order.

4. FACTORS DETERMINING THE ZEN EXPERIENCE[1]

FROM the above examples chosen rather at random from the earlier history of Zen in China, I wish to observe the following main facts concerning the Zen experience: (1) There is a preliminary intellectual equipment for the maturing of Zen-consciousness; (2) There is a strong desire to transcend oneself, by which is meant that the true student of Zen must aspire to go beyond all the limitations that are imposed upon him as an individual being; (3) A master's guiding hand is generally found there to open the way for the struggling soul; and (4) A final upheaval takes place from an unknown region, which goes under the name of "satori."

1. That the content of the Zen experience is largely intellectual is easily recognizable, and also that it shows a decided non-theistic or pantheistic tendency, if the theological terms, though with a great deal of reservation, are at all applicable here. Bodhidharma's demand: "Bring your own soul and I will have it pacified"; Enō's, "Think not of good, nor of evil, and at that very moment what are your original features?"; Nangaku's, "When it is said to be a somewhat, one altogether misses the mark"; Baso's, "I will tell you what, when you drink up in one draught all the water of the Western Lake"—all these utterances are characteristically non-sentimental, "non-religious," and, if anything, simply highly enigmatical, and to a certain extent intellectual, though of course not in the technical sense. Compared with such Christian expressions as "the glory of God," "love of God," "the Divine Bride," etc., the Zen experience must be judged as singularly devoid of human emotions. There is in it, on the contrary, something that may be termed cold scientific evidence or matter-of-factness. Thus in the Zen consciousness we can almost say that what corresponds to the Christian ardor for a personal God is lacking.

[1] *Essays in Zen Buddhism* (Second Series), pp. 52–62.

181

The Zen followers are not apparently concerned with "trespasses," "repentance," "forgiveness," etc. Their mentality is more of a metaphysical type, but their metaphysics consists not of abstractions, logical acuteness, and hair-splitting analysis, but of practical wisdom and concrete sense facts. And this is where Chinese Zen specifically differs from Indian Mahayana *dhyāna*. Enō is generally considered, as was mentioned before, not to be especially scholarly, but his mind must have been metaphysical enough to have grasped the import of the *Vajracchedikā*, which is brimful of high-sounding metaphysical assertions. When he understood the *Prajñāpāramitā-sūtra*, the highly philosophical truth contained in it was turned into the practical question of "Your original features even prior to your birth," and then into Baso's "drinking up the whole river in one draught," etc.

That Zen masters were invariably students of philosophy in its broadest sense, Buddhist or otherwise, before their attention was directed to Zen, is suggestive. I say here "Buddhist philosophy" in the strict sense of the term, for it is not the result of reasoning; especially such a doctrine as that of Emptiness is not at all the outcome of intellectual reflection, but simply the statement of direct perception in which the mind grasps the true nature of existence without the intermediary of logic. In this way *"sarvadharmāṇām śūnyatā"* is declared.

Those who study Buddhism only from its "metaphysical" side forget that this is no more than deep insight, that it is based on experience, and not the product of abstract analysis. Therefore, when a real truth-seeker studies such sutras as the *Laṅkāvatāra* or the *Vajracchedikā*, he cannot lightly pass over those assertions which are made here so audaciously and unconditionally; in fact he is dazzled, taken aback, or becomes frightened. But still there is a certain power in them which attracts him in spite of himself. He begins to think about them, he desires to come in direct touch with the truth itself, so that he knows that he has seen the fact with his own eyes. Ordinary books of philosophy do not lead one to this intuition because they are no more than philosophy; whatever truth philosophy teaches is exhausted within itself, and fails to open up a new vista for the student. But in the study of Buddhist sutras which contain the utterances of the deepest religious minds, one is inwardly drawn into the deeper recesses of consciousness; and finally one becomes convinced that those utterances really touch the ground of Reality.

What one thinks or reads is always qualified by the preposition "of," or "about," and does not give us the thing itself. Not mere talk about water, nor the mere sight of a spring, but an actual mouthful of it gives the thirsty complete satisfaction. But a first acquaintance with the sutras is needed to see the way pointed and know where to look for the thing itself. Without this pointing we may be at a loss how and where to concentrate our efforts. Therefore say the sutras, "I am both the director or leader and the truth itself."

We can thus see that the antecedent that leads to the Zen experience is not adoration, obedience, fear, love, faith, penitence, or anything that usually characterizes a good Christian soul; but it is a search for something that will give mental peace and harmony by overruling contradictions and joining tangled threads into one continuous line. Every Zen aspirant feels this constant and intense seeking for mental peace and wholeness. He generally manages to have an intellectual understanding of some sort concerning himself and the world, but this invariably fails to satisfy him thoroughly, and he feels an urge to go on deeper so that the solid ground of Reality is finally reached.

Tokusan, for example, was content with a conceptual grasp of the doctrine of Emptiness while he was studying the *Prajñāpāramitā*, but when he heard of the southern teaching his peace was disturbed. His apparent motive for going down to the south was to smash the heretical Zen, but he must have felt all the time a hidden sense of uneasiness in his deeper consciousness though he was apparently determined to suppress the feeling by his reasoning. He failed in this, for the thing which he wished to suppress suddenly raised its head, perhaps to his great discomfort, when he was challenged by the woman keeper of the teahouse. Finally, at Lung-t'an the blowing out of a lighted candle placed him where he was to be from the very beginning. Consciously, he never had any idea as to this final outcome, for nothing could be planned out in this matter of Zen experience. After this, that is, after the attainment of Zen intuition, the swinging of a staff was thought by him to be the only necessary thing in directing his followers to the experience of Zen.

He never prayed, he never asked for the forgiveness of his sins, he never practiced anything that popularly goes under the name of religious deeds;[2] for the bowing to the Buddha,[3] the offering of incense, the reading of the sūtras, and saying the *nembutsu*[4]—these were practiced just because they had been practiced by all the Buddhas, and manifestly for no other reason. This attitude of the Zen master is evidenced by the remarks of Ōbaku[5] when he was asked as to the reason of these pious acts.

2. This intense seeking[6] is the driving force of Zen consciousness. "Ask and it shall be given you; seek and ye shall find; knock and it shall be opened unto you." This is also the practical instruction leading up to the Zen experience. But as this asking or seeking is altogether subjective and the biographical records of Zen do not give much information in this regard, especially in the earlier periods of Zen history, its importance is to be inferred from various circumstances connected with the experience. The presence and intensity of this seeking or inquiring spirit were visible in Eka when he was said to have stood for some time in the snow, so great was

[2] When Jōshū was asked what constituted the deeds to be properly performed by a monk, he said, "Be detached from deeds."

[3] A monk came to Jōshū and said, "I am going as a pilgrim to the South, and what advice would you be good enough to give?" Said the master, "If you go South, pass quickly away from where the Buddha is, nor do you stay where there is no Buddha."

[4] A monk asked Takkan of Kinzan, "Do you ever practice the *nembutsu* ('reciting the name of the Buddha')?" The master replied, "No, I never do." "Why do you not?" "For I am afraid of polluting the mouth."

[5] When Ōbaku was at Enkan's monastery, an imperial prince still in exile was among the Brotherhood serving as a novitiate. When the prince one day noticed Ōbaku bowing to the Buddha in the Buddha Hall, he remarked, "We are told not to seek [the truth] through Buddha, nor through the Dharma, nor through the Brotherhood (*sangha*). How is it that you keep on bowing to Buddha? What do you want from him?" Ōbaku answered, "Not to seek [the truth] through Buddhas, nor through the Dharma, nor through the *sangha*—that is all right. Yet I go on bowing to Buddha this way." The prince-novitiate retorted, "What is the use of bowing after all?" Ōbaku gave him a slap. The latter remarked, "How rough you are!" Ōbaku roared, "Where do you think we are? Is there any room here to make any comment, rough or fine?" So saying, he gave the novitiate another slap. And the novitiate ran away.

[6] This "seeking" is technically known as *kufū* (*kung-fu*).

his desire to learn the truth of Zen. The biographers of Enō emphasize his lack of learning, make much of his poem on "Emptiness," and neglect to depict his inner life during the months he was engaged in cleaning rice. His long and hazardous traveling from the south to the monastery where Gunin resided must have been a great undertaking in those days, the more so when we know that he was only a poor farmer's boy. His reading of the *Vajracchedikā*, or his listening to it as recorded in his biography, must have stirred up a very strong desire to know really what it all meant. Otherwise, he would not have dared such a venturesome journey; and thus, while working in the granary, his mind must have been in a great state of spiritual excitement, being most intensely engaged in the search for truth.

In the case of Rinzai, he did not even know what to ask of the master. If he had known, things probably would have gone much easier with him. He knew that there was something wrong with him, for he felt dissatisfied with himself; he was searching for some unknown reality, he knew not what. If he could define it, this meant that he had already come to its solution. His mind was just one great question-mark with no special object; as his mind was, so was the universe; just the mark, and nowhere to affix it, as there was yet nothing definite anywhere.

This groping in the dark must have lasted for some time in a most desperate manner. It was indeed this very state of mind that made him ignorant as to what specific question he might place before his master. He was not in this respect like Enō who already had a definite proposition to solve, even before he came to Gunin; for his problem had been the understanding of the *Vajracchedikā*. Enō's mind was perhaps the simpler and broader, while Rinzai like Eka was already too intellectually "tainted," as it were; and all they felt was a general uneasiness of mind, as they knew not how to cut asunder all the entanglements which were made worse by their very learning. When the head monk told Rinzai to ask the master about "the fundamental principle of Buddhism," it was a great help, indeed, for now he had something definite to take hold of. His general mental uneasiness was brought to an acute point especially when he was repulsed with "thirty blows." The fruit of his mental seeking was maturing and ready to fall on the ground.

The final shaking—quite a severe one, it must be admitted—was given by Ōbaku. Between this shaking and the final fall under Daigu, Rinzai's question-mark pointed to one concrete fact where all his three years of accumulated efforts were most intensely concentrated. Without this concentration he could not have exclaimed, "There is not much after all in the Buddhism of Ōbaku!"

It may not be inopportune to say a few words concerning autosuggestion with which the Zen experience is often confused. In autosuggestion there is no intellectual antecedent, nor is there any intense seeking for something, accompanied by an acute feeling of uneasiness. In autosuggestion a definite proposition is given to the subject, which is accepted by him unquestioningly and wholeheartedly. He has a certain practical result in view, which he desires to produce in himself by accepting the proposition. Everything is here from the first determined, prescribed, and suggested.

In Zen there is an intellectual quest for ultimate truth which the intellect fails to satisfy; the subject is urged to dive deeper under the waves of the empirical consciousness. This diving is beset with difficulties because he does not know how and where to dive. He is at a complete loss as to how to get along, until suddenly he somehow hits a spot that opens up a new field of vision. This mental impasse, accompanied by a steady, untiring, and wholehearted "knocking," is a most necessary stage leading to the Zen experience. Something of the psychology of autosuggestion may be working here as far as its mechanical process is concerned, but the entire form into which this psychology is fitted to work is *toto caelo* different from what is ordinarily understood by that term.

The metaphysical quest which was designated as an intellectual antecedent of Zen consciousness opens up a new course in the life of a Zen student. The quest is attended by an intense feeling of uneasiness, or one can say that the feeling is intellectually interpreted as a quest. Whether the quest is emotionally the sense of unrest, or whether the unrest is intellectually a seeking for something definite—in either case the whole being of the individual is bent on finding something upon which he may peacefully rest. The searching mind is vexed to the extreme as its fruitless strivings go on, but when it is brought up to an apex it breaks or it explodes and the whole structure of consciousness assumes an entirely different aspect. This is the Zen experience. The quest, the search, the ripening, and the explosion—thus proceeds the experience.

This seeking or quest is generally done in the form of meditation which is less intellectual (*vipaśyanā*) than concentrative (*dhyāna*). The sitter sits cross-legged after the Indian fashion as directed in the tract called *Tso-ch'an I*, "How to Sit and Meditate."

In this position, which is regarded by Indians and Buddhists generally as being the best bodily position to be assumed by the Yogins, the seeker concentrates all his mental energy in the effort to get out of this mental impasse into which he had been led. As the intellect has proved itself unable to achieve this end, the seeker has to call upon another power if he can find one. The intellect knows how to get him into this cul-de-sac, but it is singularly unable to get him out of it.

At first the seeker knows of no way of escape, but get out he must by some means, be they good or bad. He has reached the end of the passage and before him there yawns a dark abyss. There is no light to show him a possible way to cross it, nor is he aware of any way of turning back. He is simply compelled to go ahead. The only thing he can do in this crisis is simply to jump, into life or death. Perhaps it means certain death, but living he feels to be no longer possible. He is desperate, and yet something is still holding him back; he cannot quite give himself up to the unknown.

When he reaches this stage of *dhyāna,* all abstract reasoning ceases; for thinker and thought no longer stand contrasted. His whole being, if we may say so, is thought itself. Or perhaps it is better to say that his whole being is "no-thought" (*acitta*). We can no longer describe this state of consciousness in terms of logic or psychology. Here begins a new world of personal experiences, which we may designate "leaping," or "throwing oneself down the precipice." The period of incubation has come to an end.

It is to be distinctly understood that this period of incubation, which intervenes between the metaphysical quest and the Zen experience proper, is not one of passive quietness but of intense strenuousness, in which the entire consciousness is concentrated at one point. Until the entire consciousness really gains this point, it keeps up an arduous fight against all intruding ideas. It may not be conscious of the fighting, but an intense seeking, or a steady looking down into the abysmal darkness, is no less than that. The one-pointed concentration (*ekāgra*) is realized when the inner mechanism is ripe for the final catastrophe. This takes place, if seen only superficially, by accident, that is, when there is a knocking at the eardrums, or when some words are uttered, or when some unexpected event takes place, that is to say, when a perception of some kind goes on.

We may say that here a perception takes place in its purest and simplest form, where it is not at all tainted by intellectual analysis or conceptual reflection. But an epistemological interpretation of Zen experience does not interest the Zen Yogin, for he is ever intent upon truly understanding the meaning of Buddhist teachings, such as the doctrine of Emptiness or the original purity of the Dharmakāya, and thereby gaining peace of mind.

3. When the intensification of Zen consciousness is going on, the master's guiding hand is found helpful to bring about the final explosion. As in the case of Rinzai, who did not even know what question to ask of Ōbaku, a student of Zen is frequently at a loss what to do with himself. If he is allowed to go on like this, the mental distraction may end disastrously. Or his experience may fail to attain its final goal, since it is liable to stop short before it reaches the stage of the fullest maturity. As frequently happens,. the Yogin remains satisfied with an intermediate stage, which from his ignorance he takes for finality. The master is needed not only for encouraging the student to continue his upward steps but to point out to him where his goal lies.

As to the pointing, it is no pointing as far as its intelligibility is considered. Ōbaku gave Rinzai "thirty blows," the master of Lung-T'an blew out the candle, and Enō demanded Myō-jōza's original form even before he was born. Logically, all these pointers have no sense, they are beyond rational treatment. We can say that the pointers have no earthly use as they do not give us any clue from which we can start our inference. But inasmuch as Zen has nothing to do with ratiocination, the pointing need not be a pointing in its ordinary sense. A slap on the face, a shaking one by the shoulder, or an utterance will most assuredly do the work of pointing when the Zen consciousness has attained a certain stage of maturity.

The maturing on the one hand, therefore, and the pointing on the other must be timely; if the one is not quite matured, or if the other fails to do the pointing, the desired end may never be experienced. When the chick is ready to come out of the eggshell, the mother hen knows and pecks at it, and lo, there jumps out a second generation of the chicken family.

We can probably state in this connection that this pointing or guiding, together with the preliminary more or less philosophical equipment of the Zen Yogin, determines the content of his Zen consciousness, and that when it is brought up to a state of full maturity it inevitably breaks out as Zen experience. In this case, the experience itself, if we can have it in its purest and most original form, may be said to be something entirely devoid of colorings of any sort, Buddhist or Christian, Taoist or Vedantist. The experience may thus be treated wholly as a psychological event which has nothing to do with philosophy, theology, or any special religious teaching. But the point is whether, if there were no philosophical antecedent or religious aspiration or spiritual unrest, the experience could take place merely as a fact of consciousness.

The psychology, then, cannot be treated independently of philosophy or a definite set of religious teachings. That the Zen experience takes place at all as such, and is formulated finally as a system of Zen intuitions, is principally due to the master's guiding, however enigmatical it may seem; for without it the experience itself is impossible.

This explains why the confirmation of the master is needed regarding the orthodoxy of the Zen experience, and also why the history of Zen places so much stress on the orthodox transmission of it. So we read in the "Platform Sutra" of Enō:

Genkaku (d. A.D. 713) was particularly conversant with the teaching of the Tendai school on tranquillization (*samatha*) and contemplation (*vipaśyanā*). While reading the *Vimalakīrti*, he attained an insight into the ground of consciousness. Gensaku, a disciple of the patriarch, happened to call on him. They talked absorbingly on Buddhism, and Gensaku found that Genkaku's remarks were in complete agreement with those of the Zen Fathers, though Genkaku himself was not conscious of it. Gensaku asked, "Who is your teacher in the Dharma?" Genkaku replied: "As regards my understanding of the sutras of the Vaipulya class I have for each its regularly authorized teacher. Later while studying the *Vimalakīrti*, by myself I gained an insight into the teaching of the Buddha-mind, but I have nobody yet to confirm my view." Gensaku said, "No confirmation is needed prior to Bhīshmasvararāja,[7] but after him those who have satori by themselves with no master "belong to the naturalistic school heterodoxy." Genkaku asked, "Pray you testify." Gensaku said, however: 'My words do not carry much weight. At Ts'ao-ch'i the sixth patriarch is residing now, and people crowd

[7] *Wei-yin-wang*. This may be considered to mean "prior to the dawn of consciousness" or "the time before any systematic teaching of religion started."

upon him from all quarters to receive instruction in the Dharma. Let us go over to him" . . .[8]

4. If the intensified Zen consciousness does not break out into the state of satori, we can say that the intensification has not yet attained its highest point; for when it does there is no other way left to it than to come to the final *dénouement* known as satori. This fact, as we have already seen, has been specially noticed by Daie as characterizing the Zen experience. For, according to him, there is no Zen where there is no satori. That satori came to be recognized thus as the Zen experience *par excellence* at the time of Daie and even previously, and that Daie and his school had to uphold it so strongly against some tendencies which grew up among Zen followers and threatened to undermine the life of Zen, prove that the development of the *kōan* exercise was something inevitable in the history of Zen consciousness—so inevitable indeed that if this failed to develop Zen itself would have ceased to exist.

[8] This whole passage does not occur in the Tun-huang MS. It is probable that it was added at a much later date. But this fact does not affect the force of the argument advanced by Gensaku.

5. THE PSYCHOLOGICAL ANTECEDENT AND THE CONTENT OF THE ZEN EXPERIENCE[1]

SINCE the early days of Zen, its practice has been mistakenly regarded as that of mere quietism or a kind of technics of mental tranquillization. Hence Enō's expostulation about it and Nangaku's warning to Baso. The sitting cross-legged is the form of Zen, while inwardly the Zen consciousness is to be nursed to maturity. When it is fully matured, it is sure to break out as satori, which is an insight into the Unconscious. There is something noetic in the Zen experience, and this is what determines the entire course of Zen discipline. Daie was fully conscious of this fact and was never tired of upholding it against the other school.

That satori or Zen experience is not the outcome of quiet sitting or mere passivity, with which Zen discipline has been confused very much even by the followers of Zen themselves, can be inferred from the utterances or gestures that follow the final event. How shall we interpret Rinzai's utterance, "There is not much in the Buddhism of Ōbaku"? Again, how about his punching the ribs of Daigu? These evidently show that there was something active and noetic in his experience. He actually grasped something that met his approval.

There is no doubt that he found what he had all the time been searching for, although at the moment when he began his searching he had no idea of what it meant—for how could he? If he remained altogether passive, he could never have made such a positive assertion. As to his gesture, how self-assuring it was, which grew out of his absolute conviction! There is nothing whatever passive about it.[2]

---

[1] *Essays in Zen Buddhism* (Second Series), pp. 62–71.

[2] One day St. Francis was sitting with his companions when he began to groan and said, "There is hardly a monk on earth who perfectly obeys his superior." His companions much astonished said, "Explain to us, Father, what is perfect and supreme obedience." Then, comparing him who obeys to a

The situation is well described by Dai-ō Kokushi when he says: "By 'a special transmission outside the sutra-teaching' is meant to understand penetratingly just one phrase by breaking both the mirror and the image, by transcending all forms of ideation, by making no distinction whatever between confusion and enlightenment, by paying no attention to the presence or the absence of a thought, by neither getting attached to nor keeping oneself away from the dualism of good and bad. The one phrase which the follower of Zen is asked to ponder (kung-fu) and find the final solution of is 'Your own original features even before you were born of your parents.

"In answering this one ought not to cogitate on the meaning of the phrase, nor try to get away from it; do not reason about it, nor altogether abandon reasoning; respond just as you are asked and without deliberation, just as a bell rings when it is struck, just as a man answers when he is called by name. If there were no seeking, no pondering, no contriving as to how to get at the meaning of the phrase, whatever it may be, there would be no answering—hence no awakening."

While it is difficult to determine the content of Zen experience merely by means of those utterances and gestures which involuntarily follow the experience—which is, indeed, a study in itself—I give in the appendices some of them which are culled indiscriminately from the history of Zen. Judging from these utterances, we can see that all these authors have had an inner perception, which put an end to whatever doubts and mental anxieties from which they may have been suffering; and further, that the nature of this

---

corpse, he said: "Take a dead body and put it where you will, it will make no resistance: when it is in one place it will not murmur; when you take it away from there it will not object; put it in a pulpit, it will not look up but down; wrap it in purple and it will only look doubly pale." (Paul Sabatier's *Life of St. Francis*, pp. 260–61.) While it is difficult to tell what is the real purport of this, it may appear as if St. Francis wished his monks to be literally like a corpse; but there is something humorous about the remark when he says, "Put it in a pulpit. . . ." The Zen Buddhist would interpret it as meaning to keep one's mind in a perfect state of perspicuity which perceives a flower as red and a willow tree as green, without putting anything of its own confused subjectivity into it. A state of passivity, indeed, and yet there is also fullness of activity in it. A form of passive activity, we may call it.

inner perception did not allow itself to be syllogistically treated, as it had no logical connection with what has preceded it.

Satori as a rule expresses itself in words which are not intelligible to the ordinary mind; sometimes the expression is merely descriptive of the experience-feeling, which naturally means nothing to those who have never had such feelings within themselves. So far as the intellect is concerned, there is an unsurpassable gap between the antecedent problem and its consequent solution; the two are left logically unconnected. When Rinzai asked about the ultimate principle of Buddhism, he was given thirty blows by his master Ōbaku. After he had attained satori and understood the meaning of his experience, he merely said, "There is not much in Ōbaku's Buddhism." We are left ignorant as to what this "not much" really is. When this "what" was demanded by Daigu, Rinzai simply poked his ribs.

These gestures and utterances do not give the outsider any clue to the content of the experience itself. They seem to be talking in signs. This logical discontinuity or discreteness is characteristic of all Zen teaching. When Seihei was asked what the Mahayana was, he said, "The bucket-rope." When asked about the Hinayana, he replied: "The coin-string"; about the moral impurities (*āsrava*), "The bamboo-basket"; about the moral purities (*anāsrava*), "The wooden dipper." These answers are apparently nonsensical, but from the Zen point of view they are easily digested, for the logical discontinuity is thereby bridged over. The Zen experience evidently opens a closed door revealing all the treasures behind it. It suddenly leaps over to the other side of logic and starts a dialectics of its own.

Psychologically, this is accomplished when what is known as "abandonment," or "throwing oneself over the precipice," takes place. This "abandonment" means the moral courage of taking risks; it is plunging into the unknown which lies beyond the topography of relative knowledge. This unknown realm of logical discontinuity must be explored personally; and this is where logic turns into psychology, it is where conceptualism has to give way to life-experience.

We cannot, however, "abandon" ourselves just because we wish to do so. It may seem an easy thing to do, but after all it is the last thing any being can do, for it is done only when we are most thoroughly convinced that there is no other way to meet the situation. We are always conscious of a tie, slender enough to be sure, but how strong when we try to cut it off! It is always holding us back when we wish to throw ourselves at the feet of an all-merciful One, or when we are urged to identify ourselves with a noble cause or anything that is grander than mere selfishness. Before being able to do this there must be a great deal of "searching," or "contriving," or "pondering."[3] It is only when this process is brought to maturity that this "abandoning" can take place. We can say that this "contriving" is a form of purgation.

When all the traces of egotism are purged away, when the will-to-live is effectively put down, when the intellect gives up its hold on the discrimination between subject and object, then all the contrivances cease, the purgation is achieved, and the "abandonment" is ready to take place.[4]

All Zen masters are, therefore, quite emphatic about completing the whole process of "contriving and searching." For an abandonment to be thoroughgoing, it is necessary for the preliminary process to be also thoroughgoing. The masters all teach the necessity of going on with this "searching" as if one were fighting against a deadly enemy, or "as if a poisonous arrow were piercing a vital part of the body, or as if one were surrounded on all sides by raging flames, or as if one had lost both his parents, or as if one were disgraced owing to one's inability to pay off a debt of a thousand pieces of gold."

Shōichi Kokushi, the founder of Tōfukuji monastery, advises one to "think yourself to be down an old deep well; the only thought you then have will be to get out of it, and you will be desperately engaged in finding a way of escape; from morning to evening this one thought will occupy the entire field of your consciousness." When one's mind is so fully occupied with one single thought,

---

[3] The Christians would say, "a great deal of seeking, asking, and knocking."

[4] James gives in his *Varieties of Religious Experience* (pp. 321 *ff*.) the story of Antoinette Bourignon, who, finding her spiritual obstacle in the possession of a penny, threw it away and started her long spiritual journey thus absolutely free from earthly cares. "A penny" is the symbol of the last thread of egotism which so effectively ties us up to a world of relativity. Slender though the thread is, it is sufficiently strong for all of us. The cutter is given to the student of Zen in the shape of a *kōan*, as will be seen later on.

strangely or miraculously there takes place a sudden awakening within oneself. All the "searching and contriving" ceases, and with it comes the feeling that what was wanted is here, that all is well with the world and with oneself, and that the problem is now for the first time successfully and satisfactorily solved. The Chinese have the saying, "When you are in an impasse, there is an opening." The Christians teach, "Man's extremity is God's opportunity."

The main thing to do when a man finds himself in this mental extremity is to exhaust all his powers of "searching and contriving," which means to concentrate all his energy on one single point and see the farthest reach he can make in this frontal attack. Whether he is pondering a knotty problem of philosophy, or mathematics, or contriving a means of escape from oppressive conditions, or seeking a passage of liberation from an apparently hopeless situation, his empirical mind, psychologically speaking, is taxed to its limit of energy; but when the limit is transcended a new source of energy in one form or another is tapped.

Physically, an extraordinary amount of strength or endurance is exhibited to the surprise of the man himself; morally, often on a battlefield a soldier manifests great courage, performing deeds of audacity; intellectually, a philosopher, if he is a really great one, clears up a new way of looking at Reality; religiously, we have such spiritual phenomena as conversion, conformation, reformation, salvation to the Christians, and satori, enlightenment, intuition, *parāvṛitti*, etc., to the Buddhists.

All these various orders of phenomena are explainable, as far as psychology goes, by the same law; accumulation, saturation, and explosion. But what is peculiar to the religious experience is that it involves the whole being of the individual, that it affects the very foundation of his character. And besides, the content of this experience may be described in the terminology of either Christian faith or Buddhist philosophy, according to the nature of its antecedents, or according to the surroundings and education of the particular individual concerned. That is, he interprets the experience in conformity to his own intellectual resources, and to him this interpretation is the best and the only plausible one to be given to the facts in hand.

He cannot accept them in any other light, for to do so will be the same as rejecting them as illusive and devoid of meaning. As

Buddhism has no such creeds as are cherished by Christians, who are Christians because of their intellectually conforming themselves to the theology and tradition of their forefathers, Buddhists give their religious experience an altogether different coloring. Especially to Zen followers such terms as divine grace, revelation, mystic union, etc., are foreign and sound quite unfamiliar. No matter how closely psychologically related one experience may be to the other, Buddhist or Christian, it begins to vary widely as soon as it is subsumed under categories of the Christian or the Buddhist ideology.

As stated before, the antecedents of the experience are thus designated by Zen masters altogether differently from those of the Christian mystics. Stigmata, ligature, expurgation, road of the cross, the anguish of love, etc.—all such terms have no meaning in Zen experience. The antecedents required by the latter are concentration, accumulation, self-forgetting, throwing oneself down the precipice, going over to the other side of birth-and-death, leaping, abandonment, cutting off what precedes and what follows, etc. There is here absolutely nothing that may be called religious by those who are familiar only with the other set of phraseology.

To make clearer this psychological process of "self-forgetting" and "cutting off both the past and the future," let me cite some of the classical examples.

The monk Jō came to Rinzai and asked, "What is the essence of Buddhism?" Rinzai came down from his straw chair, seized the monk, gave him a slap, and let him go. Jō stood still.

A monk nearby said, "O Jō, why don't you make a bow?" Jō was about to bow when he came to a realization.

This is the brief statement in the language of Rinzai of the event that happened to Jō. Brief though it is, we can gather from it all that is essential, all that we need to know concerning Jō's Zen experience. First of all, he did not come to Rinzai casually. There is no doubt that his question was the outcome of a long pondering and an anxious search after the truth. Before the *kōan* system was yet in vogue, Zen followers did not definitely know how to ask a question, as we saw in the case of Rinzai.

Intellectual puzzles are everywhere, but the difficulty is to produce a question which is vital and on which depends the destiny of the questioner himself. When such a question is brought to light, the very asking is more than half the answering. Just a little move-ment on the part of the master may be sufficient to open up a new life in the questioner. The answer is not in the master's gesture or speech; it is in the questioner's own mind which is now awakened. When Jō asked the master about the essence of Buddhism, the question was no idle one; it came out of his inmost being, and he never expected to have it answered intellectually.

When he was seized and slapped by the master, he was probably not at all surprised, in the sense that he was taken aback and at a loss what to do; but he was surprised in this sense that he was entirely put out of the beaten track of logic where he was most likely still lingering, although he was not conscious of it himself. He was carried away from the earth where he used to stand and to which he seemed to be inevitably bound; he was carried away he knew not where, only that he was now lost to the world and to himself. This was the meaning of his "standing still." All his former efforts to find an answer to his question were put to naught; he was at the edge of the precipice to which he clung with all his remaining strength, but the master relentlessly pushed him over. Even when he heard the voice of the attending monk calling out to him, he was not fully awakened from his stupefaction. It was only when he was about to make the usual bows that he recovered his sense—the sense in which logical discontinuity was bridged over and in which the answer to his question was experienced with-in himself—the sense in which he read the ultimate meaning of all existence, having nothing further to seek.

This *dénouement,* however, could not have been attained had it not been preceded by the regular course of concentration, accu-mulation, and abandonment. If Jō's question had been an ab-stract and conceptual one which had no roots in his very being, there could not have been truth and ultimacy in his understanding of the answer.

To give another illustration which will be illuminating when con-sidered in connection with Jō, Ummon (died 949) was the founder of the school bearing his name. His first master was Bokujū, who had urged Rinzai to ask Ōbaku concerning the essence of Buddhism. Ummon was not satisfied with his knowledge of Buddhism which had been gained from books, and came to Bokujū to have a final settlement of the intellectual balance-sheet with him. Seeing Ummon approach the gate, Bokujū shut it in his face. Ummon could

not understand what it all meant, but he knocked and a voice
came from within:

"Who are you?"

"My name is Ummon. I come from Chih-hsing."

"What do you want?"

"I am unable to see into the ground of my being and most
earnestly wish to be enlightened."

Bokujū opened the gate, looked at Ummon, and then closed it.
Not knowing what to do, Ummon went away. This was a great
riddle, indeed, and some time later he came back to Bokujū. But he
was treated in the same way as before. When Ummon came for a
third time to Bokujū's gate, his mind was firmly made up, by
whatever means, to have a talk with the master. This time as soon
as the gate was opened he squeezed himself through the opening.
The intruder was at once seized by the chest and the master demanded: "Speak! Speak!" Ummon was bewildered and hesitated.
Bokujū, however, lost no time in pushing him out of the gate again,
saying, "You good-for-nothing fellow!" As the heavy gate swung
shut, it caught one of Ummon's legs, and he cried out: "Oh! Oh!"
But this opened his eyes to the significance of the whole proceeding.

It is easy to infer from this record that Ummon's Zen experience
had a long and arduous preliminary course, although there is in
the record no allusion to his psychological attitude toward the
whole affair. His "searching and contriving" did not of course begin
with this experience; it came to an end when he called on Bokujū.
He knew no means of escape from the dilemma in which he found
himself; his only hope was centered in Bokujū. But what answer
did he get from the master? To be looked at and shut out—what
relation could this have to his earnest questioning about his inner
self?

On his way home he must have pondered the new situation to
the limit of his mental capacity. This pondering, this searching
must have been intensified by his second visit to the master, and
on the third visit it was fast approaching a culmination, and most
naturally ended dramatically. When he was requested by Bokujū
to speak out if he had anything to say, to utter a word if there
was something that required expression, his Zen consciousness became fully matured, and only a touch was needed to change it into an awakening. The needed touch came in the form of an intense
physical pain. His cry, "Oh! Oh!" was at the same time the cry
of satori, an inner perception of his own being, whose depth

now for the first time he has personally sounded so that he could really say, "I know, for I am it!" I say here that the physical pain in Ummon's case is not to be understood as having any essential significance; it merely took place at an opportune moment for his Awakening.

(This psychological process has been depicted here somewhat conjecturally, but it will grow more convincing later when the psychology of the *kōan* exercise is described according to the various records left by the masters, and also according to the directions given by them to their devotees.)

6. SATORI[1]

SATORI obtains when eternity cuts into time or impinges upon time, or, which is the same thing after all, when time emerges from eternity. Time means *shabetsu*, differentiation and determination, while eternity is *byōdō*, all that is not *shabetsu*. Eternity impinging upon time will then mean that *byōdō* and *shabetsu* interpenetrate each other, or to use Kegon terminology, the interfusion of *ri* (the universal) and *ji* (the individual). But as Zen is not interested so much in conceptualization as in "existential thinking" so called, satori is said to take place when consciousness realizes a state of "one thought." "One thought," *ichinen* in Japanese and *ekakṣaṇa* in Sanskrit, is the shortest possible unit of time. Just as English-speaking people say "quick as thought," thought, i.e., *nen*, represents an instant, i.e., time reduced to an absolute point with no durability whatever. The Sanskrit *kṣaṇa* means both thought and instant. When time is reduced to a point with no durability, it is "absolute present" or "eternal now." From the point of view of existential thinking, this "absolute present" is no abstraction, no logical nothingness; it is, on the contrary, alive with creative vitality.

Satori is the experience of this fact. Buddhist scholars often define *ichinen*, "one thought," as a point of time which has neither the past nor the future, that is to say, *ichinen* is where eternity cuts into time, and when this momentous event takes place it is known as satori.

It now goes without saying that satori is not stopping the flow of consciousness, as is sometimes erroneously contended. This error comes from taking *samādhi* as preliminary to the experience of satori and then confusing *samādhi* with the suspension of thoughts—a psychological state of utter blankness, which is another word for death. Eternity has a death-aspect, too, as long as it remains in itself, that is, as long as it remains an abstraction like other generalized ideas.

[1] *Living by Zen*, Rider & Co., 1950, pp. 46–88.

Eternity to be alive must come down into the order of time where it can work out all its possibilities, whereas time left to itself has no field of operation. Time must be merged into eternity, when it gains its meaning. Time by itself is non-existent very much in the way that eternity is impotent without time. It is in our actual living of eternity that the notion of time is possible. Each moment of living marks the steps of eternity. To take hold of eternity, therefore, consciousness must be awakened just at the very moment when eternity lifts its feet to step into time. This moment is what is known as the "absolute present" or "eternal now." It is an absolute point of time where there is no past left behind, no future waiting ahead. Satori stands at this point, where potentialities are about to actualize themselves. Satori does not come out of death, it is at the very moment of actualization. It is in fact the moment itself, which means that it is life as it lives itself.

The bifurcation of reality is the work of the intellect; indeed it is the way in which we try to understand it in order to make use of it in our practical life. But this is not the way to understand reality to the satisfaction of our hearts. The bifurcation helps us to handle reality, to make it work for our physical and intellectual needs, but in truth it never appeals to our inmost needs. For the latter purpose reality must be taken hold of as we immediately experience it. To set it up, for instance, in space and time, murders it. This is the fundamental mistake we have committed in the understanding of reality. At the beginning of the intellectual awakening we thought we achieved a grand feat in arranging reality within the frame of time and space. We never thought this was really preparing for a spiritual tragedy.

Things are made to expand in space and to rise and disappear in time; a world of multitudes is now conceived. Spatially, we are unable to see the furthest limits; temporally, we desire to fix the beginning and end of things, which, however, defy the efforts of our scientists and philosophers. We are thus kept prisoners in the system of our own fabrication. And we are most discontented prisoners, kicking furiously against the fates. We have systematized things by means of space and time, but space and time are terribly disturbing ideas.

Space is not time, time is not space; infinite expansion cannot be made to harmonize with perpetual transformation; the spatial conception of the world tends to keep things stabilized in the Absolute, while its temporal interpretation keeps us in a most uneasy frame of mind. We crave for something eternal and yet we are forever subjected to states of transience. A life of sixty or seventy years is not at all satisfying, and all the work we can accomplish during these short intervals does not amount to much.

Take nations instead of individuals; their time-allowance may be longer, but what difference do they make in cycles of millenniums? Cultures are more enduring and seem to have some worth. But if we are encompassed in vastness of space and endlessness of time, what are they with all the philosophers, artists, and with all the generals and strategists? Are they not all like vanishing foam or shooting stars?

Men of satori are not, however, worried about these things. For satori stands firmly on the Absolute Present, Eternal Now, where time and space are coalesced and yet begin to get differentiated. They lie there dormant, as it were, with all their futurities and possibilities; they are both there rolled up with all their achievements and unfoldments. It is the privilege of satori, sitting in the Absolute Present, quietly to survey the past and contemplate the future. How does the Zen master enjoy this privilege, we may ask?

The following story will help to make us acquainted with the Zen master's way of leading his disciples to the lively content of the Absolute Present.

Baso was walking one day with Hyakujō, one of his pupils. Seeing a flock of wild geese flying across the sky, he said, "What are they?"

Answered Hyakujō, "They are wild geese, master."

Baso asked again, "Whither are they flying?"

"They are all gone now."

Baso turned toward Hyakujō and gave a twist to his nose. Feeling much pain, Hyakujō gave a suppressed cry.

Baso immediately pursued, "Are they really gone?"

This awakened Hyakujō to a state of satori, and the experience was demonstrated on the following day when the master mounted the platform to give his congregation a talk on Zen. Hyakujō came forward and began to roll up the matting which is generally spread before the master for his disciples to make their bows to him. This rolling up as a rule means the end of the session. Baso came down from his seat and left for his room.

Hyakujō was called in, and Baso said, "When I have not said a word why did you roll up the matting?"

Hyakujō said, "Yesterday you were kind enough to give my nose a twist which pained me very much."

"Where is your mind wandering today?"

"The nose does not hurt me any more today."

"You have indeed a deep insight into the matter of 'this day,'" was Baso's testimony.

"This day" here means the Absolute Present and corresponds to Ummon's "The Fifteenth Day." "This day" or "today" is *konnichi* in Japanese, for which a more expressive term is often used by the Zen masters, that is, *sokkon*. *Soku* is a difficult term to translate; it means "just this," or abstractly, "self-identity"; *sokkon*, therefore, is "this very moment" and the master would often demand, "What is the matter of this very moment?"

When Baso twisted Hyakujō's nose his idea was to make his disciple awake to the fact of the Absolute Present, and not to be just concerned with flying birds. The birds are in space and fly in time; you look at them and you put yourself immediately in space-relations; you observe that they are flying, and this at once confines you in the frame of time. As soon as you are in the system of time and space, you step off the Absolute Present, which means that you are no more a free, self-regulating spirit, but a mere man, karma-fettered and logically-minded. Satori never comes out of such existence. Hence Baso's boundless love which prompted him to give a twist to Hyakujō's nose. The pain itself had nothing to do with Hyakujō's satori itself. The incident afforded him an opportunity to break up the framework of consciousness, which vigorously and tyrannically places the mind under the rules of space and time and consequently of logical conceptualization.

The master's business is to take away these shackles from the disciple's mind. He does this generally by means of negations or contradictions, proposing "to see a rainfall suspended," or "not to call a fan a fan, or a spade a spade." This may still have a trace of intellection, but the twisting of the nose, or the kicking at the chest, or the shaking by the collar is something utterly unheard of in the annals of spiritual discipline. But its effectiveness has repeatedly and fully been proved by the Zen masters.

It is interesting to cite the sequence of the Hyakujō incident, for it was quite dramatic. When he returned to his own quarters from his interview with Baso in regard to the rolling-up of the matting he was found to be crying aloud. A brother monk anxiously inquired what was the matter with him. But Hyakujō said, "You go

to the master and find out for yourself what is the matter with me."
The brother monk went to Baso and asked about Hyakujō. Baso
said, "You go back to him and find it out directly from him." The
brother monk came back to Hyakujō and asked him about it again.
But Hyakujō, instead of answering him, burst into a roar of laughter. The monk was nonplused. "A while ago you were crying, and
how is it that you are laughing now?" Hyakujō was nonchalant
and said, "I was crying before, but I am now laughing."

Undoubtedly, Hyakujō must have undergone a deep psychological change since his nose was pinched by his master Baso. He
evidently realized that there was another life than that which is
under the enthralment of the time-concept, that is, generally found
ruminating over the frustrations of the past and looking forward,
full of anguish, to events yet to happen.

The Hyakujō now crying, now laughing, does not lose sight of
the Absolute Present. Before his satori his crying or laughing was
not a pure act. It was always mixed with something else. His unconscious consciousness of time urged him to look forward, if not
thinking of the past. As the result, he was vexed with a feeling of
tension, which is unnecessarily exhausting. His mind was never
complete in itself; it was divided, torn to pieces, and could not be
"one whole mind" (*isshin* or *ichinen*). It lost its resting-place,
balance, stillness. Most modern minds are, therefore, neurotics,
victims of logical confusion and psychological tension.

In "Our Sense of the Present," an article in the *Hibbert Journal*,
April number, 1946, the author, Ethel M. Rowell, refers to "a
stillness which abides in the present, and which we can experience
here and now." This stillness, this timeless time, is "the instant
made eternity," that is, it is the moment infinitely expanding—"one
moment, one and infinite." The writer's characterization of the
sense of the Present is very informing in its connection with satori
as explained in this chapter. But she does not go very far beyond
describing the sense itself. "Ultimately a sense of the Present is
perhaps a reflection in us of the presence of Him who is always
present, who himself is the eternity at the heart of the present, 'the
still point of the turning world.' And to learn to rest in the present
is perhaps a first step toward the 'practice of the presence of
God.'"

This is tentative enough, but does not open up to a satori. The mere feeling for the Present is not enough to make one leap into the eternity and self-sufficiency of the Present. The feeling still leaves something dualistic, whereas satori is the Absolute Present itself. And because of this, the experience goes along with every other experience growing out of the serialistic conception of time. Hence Hyakujō's remarks: "It pained me yesterday but it does not today," "I am laughing now though I was crying a little while ago." Out of such daily experience as pain and no-pain, crying and laughing, human consciousness weaves a time-continuum, and regards it as reality.

When this is accomplished, the procedure is now reversed, and we begin to build up our experiences on the screen of time. Serialism comes first now, and we find our lives miserably bound by it. The Absolute Present is pushed back; we are no more conscious of it. We regret the past and worry about the future. Our crying is not pure crying, nor is our laughing pure laughing. There is always something else mixed up with it; that is, the Present has lost its innocence and absoluteness. The future and the past overlay the present and suffocate it. Life is now suffocated, maimed and crippled.

A Vinaya[2] teacher once asked a Zen master:

"How do you discipline yourself in your daily life?"

The master said: "When I am hungry I eat, when I feel tired I sleep."

Teacher: "That is what everybody generally does. Could he be said to be disciplining himself as much as yourself?"

Master: "No, not in the same way."

Teacher: "Why not the same?"

Master: "When they eat, they dare not eat, their minds are filled with all kinds of contrivances. Therefore, I say, not the same."

E. M. Rowell cites in her article the story of a London woman after an air raid during the war: "After a night of blitz a woman was seen to come repeatedly to the door of her battered little house and to look anxiously up and down the street. An official approached her. "Can I do anything to help you?" She answered,

---

2 *Vinaya* in Sanskrit means "rules of moral discipline," forming one of the three departments of the Buddhist teaching: Sutras, which are Buddha's personal discourses, Vinaya, rules laid down by Buddha for his disciples of various grades; and Abhidharma, philosophical treatises dealing with Buddhist thought.

"Well, have you seen the milkman anywhere about? My man always likes his early cup of tea." And the author adds: "The past was hostile, the future unreliable, but the companionable present was there with her. Life was precarious, but—her husband wanted his early cup of tea!"

The only difference between the Zen master who ate and slept heartily and the London woman who wanted milk for her husband's early cup of tea is that the one had satori while the other was just an ordinary human; the one deeply looked into the secrets of the Absolute Present which is also "this present little instant" of everybody and of the whole world, while most of us, including the other, are experiencing it and have a feeling for it, but have not yet had any satori about it.

We read in the Bible (Matt. vi, 34): "Take therefore no thought for the morrow; for the morrow shall take thought for the things of itself. Sufficient unto the day is the evil thereof." The idea expressed here by Jesus exactly corresponds to the Zen conception of the Absolute Present. Zen has its own way of presenting the idea, and its satori may seem remote from the Christian feeling. But when Christians stand all naked, shorn of their dualistic garments, they will discover that their God is no other than the Absolute Present itself.

They generally think of Him as putting on so many ethical and spiritual appendages, which in fact keep Him away from them; they somehow hesitate to appear before Him in their nakedness, that is, to take hold of Him in the Absolute Present. The Christian sense of the Absolute Present does not come to a focus and crystallize, as it were, into a satori; it is too diffused, or still contains a residue of time-serialism.

Zen has several names for satori as it is observed in its relationship with various fields of human experience. Some of them are "the mind that has no abode," "the mind that owns nothing," "the homeless mind," "the unattached mind," "mindlessness," "thoughtlessness," "the one mind." These designations all refer to the popular conception of "mind," and Zen strongly denies its existence as reality. But this denial is not the outcome of rationalization, being based on actual experience. The dualistic notion of mind or thought and matter has been the bane of human consciousness, and we have been prevented from properly understanding ourselves. For this reason, Zen is most emphatic in its insistence on "mindlessness," and this not proved syllogistically but as a matter of fact. To clear consciousness of any trace of attachment to the mind-concept, Zen proposes various practical methods, one of which is, according to Daiju Ekai, a disciple of Baso, as follows: [3]

If you wish to have a clear insight into the mind that has no abode, you have it at the very moment when you are sitting [in the right mood of meditation]. Then you see that the mind is altogether devoid of thoughts, that it is not thinking of ideas, good or evil.

Things past are already past, and when you do not pursue them, the past mind disappears by itself, together with its contents. As to things that are to come, have no hankerings after them, do not have them conjured up in imagination. Then the future mind will disappear by itself with all its possible contents. Things that are at this moment before your mind are already here. What is important in regard to things generally is not to get attached to them. When the mind is not attached, it raises no thoughts of love or hate, and the present mind will disappear by itself with all its contents.

When your mind is thus not contained in the three divisions of time [past, future, and present], it can be said that the mind is not in time [i.e., it is in a state of timelessness].

If the mind should be stirred up, do not follow the stirrings, and the following-up mind will by itself disappear. When the mind abides with itself, do not hold on to this abiding, and the abiding mind will by itself disappear. Thus when the no-abiding mind obtains, this is abiding in no-abode.

When you have a clear cognizance of this state of mind, your abiding mind is just abiding and yet not abiding at all in any particular abode. When it is not abiding it is not conscious of any particular abode to be known as no-abiding. When you have thus a clear insight into the state of consciousness not abiding anywhere [that is, when it is not fixed at any particular object of thought], you are said to have a clear insight into the original mind. This is also known as seeing into one's own being. The mind that has no abode anywhere is no other than the Buddha-mind.

This no-abiding mind is the Absolute Present, for it has no abode anywhere in the past, or in the future or in the present; the mind is

[3] From "Essentials of the Abrupt Awakening" (*Tongo Yōmon Ron*), by Daiju Ekai.

decidedly not what it is commonly understood to be by those not yet awakened to satori.

Daiju says somewhere else in his book "Abrupt Awakening" that "when the mind penetrates through This Instant, what is before and what is after are manifested at once to this mind; it is like the past Buddhas at once facing the future Buddhas; the ten-thousand things [concur] simultaneously; so say the Sutras. Where all things are known in one thought, this is the spiritual field, for all-knowledge is attained here." All these things are possible only when one's mind is awakened to the Absolute Present, not as a logical conclusion, but as satori consciousness.

Here is an interesting story of an old woman keeping a teahouse at the foot of the Lung-t'an monastery in Li-chou. Tokusan, who later became noted for his staff, dropped in at the teahouse by the roadside while on pilgrimage in search of a good Zen master. He was a scholar of the *Vajracchedikā sūtra* ("Diamond Sutra"), but hearing of Zen, which taught that the mind itself was Buddha, he could not accept it and wanted to interview a Zen student. Shouldering his precious commentary on the sutra, he left his abode in Szŭ-ch'uan.

He asked the old woman to serve him a *ten-jin*. *Ten-jin* means refreshments, but literally "punctuating the mind." She asked what was in his rucksack. He said, "This is a commentary on the 'Diamond Sutra.'"

The old woman resumed: "I have a question to ask you. If your answer is satisfactory I will serve you refreshments free. If otherwise, you will have to go somewhere else."

Tokusan said, "Well, I am ready."

The question was this: "According to the 'Diamond Sutra,' we have, 'The past mind is unattainable, the present mind is unattainable, the future mind is unattainable.' Now, which mind is it you want to punctuate?"

This baffled the scholar, and the old woman made him go somewhere else for his refreshments.

I do not know how *ten-jin*, literally "punctuating the mind," came to mean refreshments, but the old woman made a very pungent use of the character, *jin* or *shin* (mind), to put the proud scholar's mind at the impasse. Whatever this be, how should we understand the statement in the "Diamond Sutra"? What does the mind past, present, and future mean? What is the signification of "unattainable"?

When satori obtains in the Absolute Present, all these questions solve themselves. The mind or consciousness, serially divided and developed in time, always escapes our prehension, is never "attainable" as to its reality. It is only when our unconscious consciousness, or what might be called super-consciousness, comes to itself, is awakened to itself, that our eyes open to the timelessness of the present in which and from which divisible time unfolds itself and reveals its true nature.

Tokusan, still uninitiated in the mystery of satori at the time of his interview with the old lady of the teahouse, could not understand what her question purported. His conception of time was gained from his pet commentary by Seiryō, which meant that his understanding could not go beyond logical reasonableness; the distance between this and satori was immeasurable, for the difference was not one of calculability, but of order, of quality, of value. The gap between satori and rationality could never be bridged by concept-making and postulation, or abstract reasoning or anything belonging to the order of intellect (*vijñāna*), but by an absolute negation of the reason itself, which means "an existential leap."

Another name for satori is *kenshō*, "seeing into one's own Nature." This may suggest the idea that there is what is known as Nature or Substance making up one's being, and that this Nature is seen by somebody standing against it. That is to say, there is one who sees and there is another which is seen, subject and object, master and guest. This view is the one generally held by most of us, for our world is a rational reconstruction which keeps one thing always opposing another, and by means of this opposition we think, and our thinking in turn is projected into every field of experience; hence this dichotomous world multiplying itself infinitely.

Kenshō, on the contrary, means going against this way of thinking and putting an end to all forms of dualism. This really means reconstructing our experience from its very foundation. What Zen attempts is no other than the most radical revolution of our world-view.

The rationalistic way of dissolving contradictory concepts is to create a third concept in which they can be harmoniously set up. To find out such a new concept is the work taken up by the philosopher. While it is a great question whether he can finally succeed in discovering an all-embracing and all-uniting and all-harmonizing concept, we cannot stop short of arriving at such a result as far as our intellect is concerned. Endless and fruitless may be our efforts, but we shall have to go on this way.

The Zen way has taken an altogether different course, diametrically opposed to the logical or philosophical method. It is not that Zen is defiantly antagonistic to the latter, for Zen is also ready to recognize the practical usefulness of the intellect and willing to give it the proper place it deserves. But Zen has advocated another method of reaching the finality of things, where the spirit lies at rest with itself as well as with the world at large. It tells us to retreat to our inner self in which no bifurcation has yet taken place. Ordinarily, we go out of ourselves to seek a place of ultimate rest. We walk on and on until we reach God, who is at the head of a long, tedious series of bifurcations and unifications.

Zen takes the opposite course and steps backward, as it were, to reach the undifferentiated continuum itself. It looks backward to a point before the world with all its dichotomies has yet made its debut. This means that Zen wants us to face a world into which time and space have not yet put their cleaving wedges. What kind of experience is this? Our experience has always been conditioned by logic, by time, and by space. Experience will be utterly impossible if it is not so conditioned. To refer to experience free from such conditions is nonsensical, one may say. Perhaps it is, so long as we uphold time and space as real and not conceptually projected. But even when these basic conditions of experience are denied, Zen talks of a certain kind of experience. If this be really the case, Zen experience must be said to take place in the timelessness of the Absolute Present.

Do not ask how this is possible, for its possibility has been all the time demonstrated by Zen. We must remember that the realm of Zen is where no rationality holds good; in fact it supplies the field of operation for it; we can say that with the Zen experience all the rationalistic superstructure finds its solid basis.

Incidentally we may remark that the Christian view of the world starts with "the tree of knowledge," whereas the Buddhist world is the outcome of Ignorance (*avidyā*). Buddhists, therefore, negate the world as the thing most needed for reaching the final abode of rest. Ignorance is conquered only when the state of things prior to Ignorance is realized, which is satori, seeing into one's own nature as it is by itself, not obscured by Ignorance. Ignorance is the beginning of knowledge, and the truth of things is not to be attained by piling knowledge upon knowledge, which means no more, no less, than intensifying Ignorance.

From this Buddhist point of view Christians are all the time rushing into Ignorance when they think they are increasing the amount of knowledge by logical acumen and analytical subtlety. Buddhists want us to see our own "original face" even before we were born, to hear the cry of the crow even before it was uttered, to be with God even before He commanded light to be. Christians take God and His light as things irrevocable, imperatively imposed upon them, and start their work of salvation under these limitations. Their "knowledge" always clings to them, they cannot shake this shackle off; they become victims of logic and rationality. Logic and rationality are all very well, Buddhists say, but the real spiritual abode, according to Buddhists, is found only where logic and rationality have not yet made their start, where there is yet no subject to assert itself, no object to be taken hold of, where there is neither seer nor the seen, which is "seeing into one's own Nature."

Satori, or the "seeing into one's own Nature," is frequently confused with nothingness or emptiness, which is a pure state of negativity. Superficially, this seems to be justifiable. For, logically speaking, the mind awakened to the timelessness of time has no content, does not convey any sense of actual experience. As to "seeing into one's own Nature," if this means a state of consciousness where there is neither the seeing subject nor the object seen, it cannot be anything else but a state of pure emptiness, which has no significance whatever for our everyday life, which is full of frustrations and expectations and vexations. This is true as far as our dualistic thinking is concerned. But we must remember that Zen deals with the most fundamental and most concrete experience lying at the basis of our daily living. Being an individual experience and not the conclusion of logical reasoning, it is neither abstract nor empty. On the contrary, it is most concrete, and filled with possibilities.

If satori were a mere empty abstraction or generalization it could not be the basis of the ten thousand things. Rationalization goes upward, getting rid of multiplicities step by step, and finally reaches a point which has no width, no breadth, merely indicating a position. But satori digs downward under the ground of all existence in order to reach the rock which is an undifferentiated whole. It is not something floating in the air, but a solid substantial entity, though not in the sense of an individual sense-object.

In conformity with the common-sense way of thinking, Zen frequently uses terms which are liable to be misunderstood. Thus the term "Nature" affords good opportunity for misinterpretation. We are apt to take it for something underlying a phenomenal sense-object, though existing in a much more subtle way, but satori does not consist in seeing such a subtle object; for in the satori seeing there is neither subject nor object; it is at once seeing and not seeing; that which is seen is that which sees, and vice versa. As subject and object are thus one in the satori seeing, it is evident that it is not seeing in the ordinary dualistic sense. And this has led many superficially-minded people to imagine that Zen's seeing is seeing into the Void, being absorbed in contemplation, and not productive of anything useful for our practical life.

The great discovery we owe Buddhism, and especially Zen, is that it has opened for us the way to see into the suchness of things, which is to have an insight into "the originally pure in essence and form which is the ocean of transcendental *prajñā*-knowledge," as Gensha says in one of his sermons. "The originally pure" is "a stillness which abides in the present."

Buddhists use the word "pure" in the sense of absolute, and not in that of freedom from dirt and external matters. "The originally pure" means that which is unconditioned, undifferentiated, and devoid of all determinations; it is a kind of super-consciousness in which there is no opposition of subject and object, and yet there is a full awareness of things that are to follow as well as things already fulfilled. In a sense "the originally pure" is emptiness, but an emptiness charged with vitality. Suchness is, therefore, the two contradictory concepts, emptiness and not-emptiness, in a state of self-identity. Suchness is not their synthesis but their self-identity as concretely realized in our everyday experience.

What we have to remember here is that the concept of suchness is not the result of rationalistic thinking about experience but just a plain direct description of it. When we see a white flower we describe it as white; when it is a red one, we say it is red. This is simply a factual statement of the senses; we have not reasoned about redness or whiteness, we just see things red or white, and declare them so. In a similar way, Zen sees with its satori-eye things as they are in themselves, i. e., they are seen as such—such as they are, no more, no less, and Zen says so.

We as human beings, Zen proclaims, cannot go any further than this. Science and philosophy will say that our senses are not reliable; nor is the intellect; they are not to be depended upon as the absolutely trustworthy instrument of knowledge, and, therefore, that the Zen view of suchness cannot be regarded either as the last source of authority. This analogy, however, does not hold good in the case of Zen, because the satori-seeing cannot be classed under the same category as the sense information. In satori there is something more, though this something is something absolutely unique and can be appreciated only by those who have had its experience.

This, it is true, is the case with all feelings: the feeling that you are an absolutely unique individuality, the feeling that the life you are enjoying now absolutely belongs to you, or the feeling that God is giving this special favor to you alone and to nobody else. But all these feelings ultimately refer to one definite subject known as "I" which is differentiated from the rest of the world. Satori is not a feeling, nor is it an intellectual act generally designated as intuition. Satori is seeing into one's own Nature; and this "Nature" is not an entity belonging to oneself as distinguished from others; and in the "seeing" there is no seer, there is nothing seen; "Nature" is the seer as well as the object seen. Satori is "mindlessness," "one absolute thought," "the absolute present," "originally pure," "emptiness," "suchness," and many other things.

According to the Zen master, our sense experience alone is not enough; nor is intellection, if we wish to sound the bottomless abyss of reality; satori must be added to it, not mechanically or quantitatively, but chemically, as it were, or qualitatively. When we hear a bell or see a bird flying, we must do so by means of a mind christened by satori, that is to say, we then hear the bell even prior to its ringing, and see the bird even prior to its birth. Once the bell rings or the bird flies, they are already in the world of the senses, which means that they are differentiated, subject to intellectual analysis and synthesis, which means in turn that "the originally pure" has been adulterated, leading to further and further adulterations, that there is no longer "the full moon of suchness" as seen by Buddhist poets, but one now thickly veiled with threatening clouds. Suchness is synonymous with pureness.

Zen masters wish us to see into that unconscious consciousness which accompanies our ordinary dualistically-determined consciousness. The "unconscious" so called here is not the psychological unconscious, which is regarded as making up the lowest stratum of our mind, probably accumulated ever since we began to become conscious of our own existence. "The unconscious" of the Zen master is more logical or epistemological than psychological; it is a sort of undifferentiated knowledge, or knowledge of non-distinction, or transcendental *prajñā*-knowledge.

In Buddhism generally two forms of knowledge are distinguished; the one is *prajñā* and the other is *vijñāna*. *Prajñā* is all-knowledge (*sarvajña*), or transcendental knowledge, i.e., knowledge undifferentiated. *Vijñāna* is our relative knowledge in which subject and object are distinguishable, including both knowledge of concrete particular things and that of the abstract and universal. *Prajñā* underlies all *vijñāna*, but *vijñāna* is not conscious of *prajñā* and always thinks it is sufficient in itself and with itself, having no need for *prajñā*. But it is not from *vijñāna*, relative knowledge, that we get spiritual satisfaction. However much of *vijñāna* we may accumulate, we can never find our abode of rest in it, for we somehow feel something missing in the inmost part of our being, which science and philosophy can never appease.

Science and philosophy do not apparently exhaust Reality; Reality contains more things than that which is taken up by our relative knowledge for its investigation. What is still left in Reality, according to Buddhism, turns toward *prajñā* for its recognition. *Prajñā* corresponds to "unconscious consciousness" already referred to. Our spiritual yearnings are never completely satisfied unless this *prajñā* or knowledge is awakened, whereby the whole field of consciousness is exposed, inside and outside, to our full view. Reality has now nothing to hide from us.

The Zen master's life-efforts are concentrated in awakening this *prajñā*, unconscious consciousness, knowledge of non-distinction, which, like a vision of will-o'-the-wisp, unobtrusively, tantalizingly, and constantly shoots through the mind. You try to catch it, to examine it on your palm, to name it definitely, so that you can refer to it as a definitely determined individual object. But this is impossible because it is not an object of dualistically-disposed intellectual treatment.

Prajñā is not, however, that dark consciousness of the brute or child which is waiting for development and clarification. It is, on the contrary, that form of consciousness which we can attain only after years of hard seeking and hard thinking. The thinking, again, is not to be confused with mere intellection; for it must be, to use the terminology of Kierkegaard, existential thinking and not dialectical reasoning. The Zen consciousness thus realized is the highest form of consciousness.

7. SOME ASPECTS OF ZEN BUDDHISM[1]

I

THE most important practical and, yet in a way, philosophical task of every Mahayana Buddhist is squarely to meet the question of sameness and difference, unity and diversity, *byōdō* and *shabetsu*,[2] and to solve it in his own fashion and to his own inner satisfaction. This is not an intellectual work imposed upon him, for he is not always supposed to have an intellect equal to the task—even the great philosophers find it very hard indeed to probe the problem successfully and to the fulfilment of their logical requirements. What the Buddhist is asked to do is to solve the problem in a practical way. That is to say, he is to have his troubled heart thoroughly quieted and at rest as to the meaning of his life. Philosophically speaking, sameness in difference and difference in sameness, or, to use Buddhist terminology, *byōdō* in *shabetsu* and *shabetsu* in *byōdō*, or, more directly, *byōdō soku shabetsu* and *shabetsu soku byōdō*—this is the formula given out by the Buddhist philosophers for the solution of the problem, and if the Buddhist only has an insight into its truth, complete contentment will by itself come to his heart. What he actually needs is this contented state of mind in which he can meet every possible occurrence great and small in his life. Philosophy is not necessarily his concern. It is only when his inner mind is analyzed by the philosopher that the latter finds here the realization of the principle of *byōdō soku shabetsu shabetsu soku byōdō*. No practical Buddhists hold forth this abstract principle before them as the problem for solution. They simply find themselves troubled in a strange and annoying manner and wish

---

[1] *Studies on Buddhism in Japan*, 1939, Vol. I, pp. 1–35.

[2] Byōdō means literally "evenness and equalness" and stands for the Sanskrit *samatā*, and *shabetsu* "disagreement and separateness," and its corresponding Sanskrit is *bheda*.

217

to be delivered from it. After a great deal of spiritual struggle they finally find themselves mysteriously released from the bond which has been the source of their constant annoyance. When later they, if at all philosophically inclined, examine themselves, their release is disclosed to have been along the line of *byōdō soku shabetsu* and *shabetsu soku byōdō*. This is a kind of dialectical interpretation given to the inner personal experience which has taken place prior to the interpretation or expression. The experience dumb in itself is now said to have found its mouthpiece. This is what I mean by the practical solution of the great problem which besets us in every walk of our life. I only wish here to emphasize the fact that the solution is an inner personal experience and not an intellectual one.

In Zen Buddhism this practical solution is called satori, corresponding to "the establishment of faith" (*shinjin ketsujō*) in the teaching of the Pure Land school of Buddhism. The attainment or "opening" of satori is thus the object of Zen discipline. Without satori there is no Zen, that is, without seeing into the truth of *byōdō soku shabetsu* and *shabetsu soku byōdō,* Zen loses its raison d'être. However fine and plausible the talk or argument may be which we can advance about the truth, there is no Zen in it unless there is satori underlying it. Zen goes directly against the conceptual understanding of it. There is nothing mysterious about satori. The Zen masters would say: when we see an apple, we know at once and in a most convincing manner that it is an apple and not a table. No amount of argument against this conviction will ever succeed in repudiating it; satori is a kind of inner sense perception.

As satori is not thus the outcome of intellection the Zen masters avoid the use of conceptual language, using concrete terms instead and illustrating the truth by imageries and paradoxes. At first sight their sermons or dialogues (*mondō*) are almost nonsensical, they yield no intelligible meaning as far as their logical process of reasoning is applicable. But after some time of intensely concentrated pondering on the statement, one comes all of a sudden upon its meaning, and realizes that the Zen masters are after all giving us facts as they actually see them with no idea of mystifying them.

Here I wish to make a remark about what may be termed Zen methodology known as *mondō*. The Zen truth is characteristically developed by this method. *Mondō* literally means "questioning-and-answering." The master or the disciple asks a question or drops a remark which is taken up by the other side; the *mondō* may then come abruptly to an end. As it is not meant dialectically to develop the sense contained in the question or statement, this abrupt ending is natural. A *mondō* sometimes goes on a little further than this, but rarely beyond a fourth or fifth exchange of views. As far as the truth itself is concerned, just the lifting of a finger or a coughing is enough to demonstrate it. But a demonstration always goes beyond itself, it points to something else, and the *mondō* rises out of this fact. The wheel of truth is never known in its suchness until it "revolves," and from this revolution starts a questioning-and-answering. When this initial movement is understood, the whole truth is realized including the "wheel" itself. But let it remain ungrasped at the source of its movement and any amount of dialoguing will be sheer superfluity. Zen has therefore a *mondō* and not a dialogue.

The following selections from the *Hekigan-shū* (*Pi-yen Chi*) considered "The First Book of Zen Buddhism" will illustrate what has been pointed out in the foregoing statements as regards the nature and content of Zen experience. The key to the understanding of these *mondō* is naturally to have a satori whereby the truth of *byōdō soku shabetsu* or *shabetsu soku byōdō* is made to reveal itself, and this not in a metaphysical or an intellectual way as these abstract terms may suggest, but in the most concrete and practical way, so that the truth is perceived while taking up your cup of tea, or while defending yourself against the onslaught of a deadly foe, or while witnessing the destruction of a whole city by an earthquake or by the enemy's bursting shells. The *mondō* that follow may look innocent enough and to some too abstract and transcendental. But as the object of Zen discipline is to get in touch personally with the "Perfect Way" and to live it, what looks innocent or abstract is full of threatening reality.

2

Jōshū Jūshin of the T'ang dynasty used to give the following sermon: "'The Perfect Way is not difficult, only it abhors selecting-and-choosing.' As soon as something is asserted, there is a selecting-and-choosing, there is a lucid blankness; but I am not in that lucid blankness. Do you, however, pay regard to it, or not?"

This sermon is based on Sōsan's well-known poem on "The Believing Mind." Sōsan is the third patriarch of Zen Buddhism in China and the poem begins with these lines:

> The Perfect Way is not difficult,
> Only it abhors selecting-and-choosing.
> Let there be neither love nor hate,
> And all will be boundless, lucid blankness.

This may require explanation. The "Perfect Way" is the highest truth or reality, to realize which is the object of Zen discipline, in fact, of all religion and philosophy. Those acquainted with Chinese history of thought know well what the Way or Tao means, which corresponds to some extent to the Western conception of Logos. Now, Sōsan declares that there is nothing difficult in the nature of the Perfect Way, nor in our understanding of it; but as long as our mind is confused with ideas of opposition resulting from selecting-and-choosing, such as love and hate, good and bad, right and wrong, truth and falsehood, beauty and ugliness, it is unable to see into the Way itself. Oppositions and contradictions, and consequently an endless series of complications all starting from selecting-and-choosing, put our minds in utter confusion, but when this confusion is cleared away, all becomes lucid because there is nothing to obstruct the inner eye's surveying the boundless blankness of the Absolute, that is, of the Perfect Way. What is to be noted here is that the Way is not mere blankness, an absence of all distinctions, where nothingness conceived negatively rules, but there is a lucidity in it whereby a world of multiplicities is illumined. This is why Jōshū declares that "I am not in that lucid blankness." If he stays there, his Way is no more perfect or absolute, it becomes conditioned, it becomes an idea, and subjects itself to the laws governing the world of particulars. But if he does not keep his eye on the lucid blankness, he is mixed up in the melee of conditions. To strike the balance as it were is necessary and this not ideationally. Hence Jōshū's last sentence: "Do you pay regard to it or not?" His pupils are now urged to see with their own eyes into the secret of *byōdō soku shabetsu* and *shabetsu soku byōdō*.

We can say that *byōdō* here corresponds to the lucid blankness of Jōshū while *shabetsu* is selecting-and-choosing. The truth of Zen is to have both at one stroke *byōdō* and *shabetsu* or selecting-and-choosing and lucid blankness.

"At one stroke" is a psychological expression. Logically speaking, this experience is to discover a third term bridging the two contradicting or opposing ideas, *byōdō* and *shabetsu*. One may ask if there could be any third term that would connect *byōdō* and *shabetsu*. This is where the philosopher is working hard to give expression to the idea, while the Zen master would simply say, "You find it by yourself, and know what it is. If you do, speak, speak!" When you "speak," he rests with it, and as to interpreting the experience he leaves it to the philosopher.

Soku (*chi* in Chinese), the connecting particle, is a kind of sign of identity, showing that the relation between the two terms, *byōdō* and *shabetsu*, is one of identity. But this idea of identity as existing between *byōdō* and just *shabetsu* is not to the point and is apt to lead to a misapprehension. While the Buddhist philosophers are quite painstaking to define the relation between the two ideas by saying not only *byōdō soku shabetsu* but *shabetsu soku byōdō*, the relation is not properly that of identity. You cannot just place *shabetsu* over *byōdō*, or conversely, and say that they coincide. It is more than identity, it goes beyond geometry; can we say that it is a kind of moving or living identity, in which each particular retaining its particularity is yet more than itself so that there is a state of universal interpenetration or interchangeability among all particulars? It is a very elusive relationship when one attempts to give it verbal definition. This is why Zen avoids abstraction and conceptualism.

Jōshū thus in his sermon does not use such abstract terms as *byōdō* and *shabetsu*, his terminology is much closer to our daily experiences, "selecting-and-choosing" is what we are practicing every day. "Lucid blankness" is somewhat mystical but it is an experience familiar to students of Yoga or Zen, and much prized and held dear by some of them. Jōshū wishes on the one hand to keep them away from this thought, this hankering after blankness, and on the other hand from being swallowed up in the surging waves of particular phenomena. His question may not be of much consequence, and you can answer it readily from the conceptual point of view, I believe. But what he wants is to see his pupils in a practical and living way realize the truth, and if they really realized it, they could demonstrate the experience in a most convincing manner and therefore entirely satisfyingly to the master. Let us see if his pupils succeeded.

One of the monks stood up and counter-questioned his master: "If you are not in the lucid blankness, to what do you pay regard?"

This counter-questioning clearly shows that the questioner has entirely missed the point the master wished to direct his attention to. He took the master literally and logically, for he is quite right in proposing this counter-question as far as the superficial sense of Jōshū's remark is concerned. If the master himself is not in the lucid blankness what does he wish his pupils to hold dear? "Lucid blankness" is the principle of sameness where all differences are merged into the One. To take hold of this One is generally considered to be the objective of Zen or general Buddhist discipline. But Jōshū says that he is not with the One and to all appearance wants his pupils to walk away from it. Is this right? The monk utterly failed to locate the whereabouts of the master. Hence his counter-questioning sadly betraying the absence in him of the spirit of Zen.

The master's answer was,

"I know not either."

The answer is quite significant. It has nothing to do with agnosticism. The master is no ignoramus. He knows perfectly well, but his knowledge is not of the same order as the knowledge we have of things relative. His knowledge of the lucid blankness in relation to selecting-and-choosing is not to be measured by the ordinary standard we use in the realm of logic and discrimination, though this does not mean that it is altogether mystical and lost in obscurantism. To those who have no experience along this line, it is an absurdity. The monk never expected such an answer from the master, which is really no answer. Naturally this further question:

"If you know not, why do you say that you are not in the lucid blankness?"

Unfortunately, the monk is altogether moving on a different plane; he and his master are using apparently the same language, but the meaning each attaches to it has nothing in common with the other. Unless the monk effects a leap from his plane to that of the master, this *mondō* will never come to a consummation desired. Jōshū's final remark is: "Enough with your asking! Make your bow now, and retire!"

Has the monk really finished his asking? From his point of view he seems to have plenty of questioning yet to do. Jōshū knows that, but from Jōshū's point of view all the questioning the monk can make in this connection is exhausted; for further arguing cannot do anything good except repeating without an end the same old question. But once let the monk rise from the position he so obstinately holds and all will be clear. "I know not either" showed the way for the monk how to rise; but if this could not be made use of, no further exchange of words would be needed. Or we can say this: the monk's last question or rather argument "When you know not, why do you say that you are not in the lucid blankness?" is the question all the intelligent minds are ever asking and yet none of them have come to a final solution with all their intelligence. This fact is significant. There must be another approach to the question; probably the question itself is the answer. When an answer is sought outside the question, it leads nowhere, that is to say, one comes back to the original question after going through a round of all possible answers. Jōshū had the same experience and has finally come to the conclusion that the interrogation itself is the affirmation. We intelligently ask, "Why?" or "What?" or "Whence?" or "Whither?" expecting the answer in a form of affirmation; but the answer is in the question itself. To "Why?" we answer, "Why?!" with an exclamation mark added, though not in surprise, nor with any sense of doubt.

"I do not know either." "Enough with your questioning! Make your bow now, and retire!" Unless we shift our position of selecting-and-choosing to a higher or broader plane of thought where *prajñā* has her abode, we shall never be able to see into Jōshū's mind and grasp the outcome of his two statements.

The whole *mondō* is reproduced below in order to have an integral survey of it.

Jōshū used to give this sermon: "The Perfect Way is not difficult, only it abhors selecting-and-choosing. As soon as something is asserted, there is a selecting-and-choosing, there is a lucid blankness; but I am not in that lucid blankness. Do you, however, pay regard to it, or not?"

A monk rose from the rank and asked, "If you are not in the lucid blankness, to what do you pay regard?"

Jōshū said, "I know not either."

The monk pursued, "If you know not, why do you say that you are not in the lucid blankness?"

Jōshū concluded, "Enough with your asking! Make your bow now, and retire!"

Secchō, of the Sung dynasty, who selected the one hundred cases of Zen *mondō* for the *Hekigan-shū*, has his commentary verse attached to the above, which literally translated is as follows:

> The Perfect Way is not difficult,
> Every word, every phrase uttered is that.
> Manyness of the One,
> Non-duality of the Two.
> In the sky, as the sun rises the moon sets;
> Before the railings, the high mountains and the refreshing waters.
> When consciousness is all gone in your dried-up skull, where is the feeling of joy?
> Yet the dragon's singing is heard not quite silenced in the dead forest.
> Difficult! Difficult!
> Selecting-and-choosing and lucid blankness—use your own eyes to see.

Let me give you a paraphrase of these lines which are, I am sure, hardly intelligible to most readers of this paper. "The Perfect Way is not difficult"—so it is declared by the third patriarch and heartily endorsed by Jōshū. But really it is not at all so difficult as we may imagine; for every word and every phrase we may utter is in accord with the Perfect Way itself. Not only when it is asserted but even when it is negated, the Perfect Way lies before you in its completeness, neither hurt nor helped. How is this? When you affirm the One, multiplicities are found included in it. The One is one only when there are the Many. The One is the Many. When you speak of the Two, subject and object, mind and matter, noesis and noema, God and the world, Buddha and Sarvasattva, they are not really two, nor are they one. Do you want to see into the secrets of this paradox? Look up toward the heavens, and you see the sun rise in the morning as the moon fades away behind the dawning clouds. Look out from the window of your retreat among the mountains far away from human habitation. How deep the valley lies before you! and how refreshingly cool the stream runs! The secrets are no secrets here, all is manifest. But if you still confess your inability to decipher them, I will tell you what to do now. Have your mind thoroughly purged of all prepossessed ideas, feelings, imaginations, and other sundries rising out of the fundamental prejudice known as "selecting-and-choosing": let your so-called consciousness be like unto a dried-up skull where not a speck of life principle is left pulsating; and when this is carried out to perfection, lo and behold, there you hear the singing of the dragon even in the midst of the dead forest of the unconscious where you thought all vitality gone and no greenness at sight. A mysterious scene of resuscitation has taken place, for a new life has now come up, the phoenix has risen out of the ashes, the lotus blooms forth from the flaming fire. This is the Zen revelation. Difficult indeed this! Let those who have an eye to see, see into the fountainhead of things and realize by themselves where the selecting-and-choosing takes its rise and where the lucid blankness spreads itself before them! They will then understand what is meant by *byōdō soku shabetsu* and *shabetsu soku byōdō*.

Engo, who is the commentator on the *Hekigan-shū*, adds: When a state of absolute oneness (*byōdō*) is realized, you perceive as before a mountain as mountain, and a river as river, heaven as heaven, and earth as earth; and yet heaven is sometimes earth, and earth heaven, a mountain is not a mountain, a river is not a river. How is it so? How is it possible that "A" is at once "A" and "not-A?" How do we escape this contradiction? Engo does not seem to be troubled at all with the irrationality, for he quietly proceeds to say that "When the wind comes, trees are stirred; when the waves are high, the boat is lifted up; spring is for germination, summer for growth, autumn for harvesting, and winter for reservation." This is generally the way the Zen masters synthesize as it were all logical contradictions.

The reference to the skull and to the dragon singing in Secchō's versified commentary as above cited is derived from the following *mondō*:

A monk asked Kyōgen, "What is the Way?"

Kyōgen replied, "The singing dragon in the dead tree."

Monk: "Who is the man walking in the Way?"

Kyōgen: "An eye glaring in the skull."

Later this monk came to Sekisō and asked: "What is meant by the singing dragon in the dead tree?"

Sekisō: "A feeling of joy is still here."

Monk: "What is meant by a glaring eye in the skull?"

Sekisō: "Consciousness is still here."

The monk again called on Sōzan and proposed the same question: "What is meant by the singing dragon in the dead tree?"

Sōzan: "The pulsation is not interrupted."

Monk: "What is meant by a glaring eye in the skull?"

Sōzan: "Not thoroughly dried up."

Monk: "Who hears it?"

Sōzan: "The whole universe resounds with it, and there is none who hears it not."

Monk: "What melody is it that is sung by the dragon?"

Sōzan: "It is an unknown melody, but those who hear it are lost to themselves."

The dried-up skull and the dead tree or forest stand as symbols for a state of absolute oneness to which all particulars have been reduced. What Zen experiences, however, is not the skull or the dead wood of oneness in which no life is moving. The skull must have an eye, a living, glaring eye whereby it surveys a world of particulars; the dead tree must give shelter to a singing dragon whose music can be heard throughout the chiliacosm. But, some may ask, why an eye in the skull instead of in this living body? Why the dragon in the dead tree instead of in the clouds bearing thunder and lightning? To understand this, we have for once to go through Zen experience ourselves, for it is only when we reach the darkest abyss of unconsciousness that we become aware of the working of the cosmic process wherein we are provided with an eye and can listen to the snorting dragon.

3

In order to further elucidate the nature of the Perfect Way which was one of Jōshū's favorite topics of sermon, the following are selected again from the *Hekigan-shū*, in which there are altogether four *mondō* relative to the same subject. Each *mondō* approaches it from a different angle and is in the shrewdest manner and yet most artlessly handled by the master. While those who have an eye to see can see where the master is, the uninitiated are naturally at a loss what to make of his apparently most elusive treatment of the topic.

A monk came up to Jōshū and asked: "[It is said that] the Perfect Way is not difficult, only it abhors selecting-and-choosing. What happens then when there is no selecting-and-choosing?"

Jōshū: "Above the heavens and below the heavens, I alone am the honored one!"

Monk: "This is still a selecting-and-choosing."
Jōshū: "O you philistine! Where is the selecting-and-choosing!"
The monk remained silent.

In this *mondō* we can see that as far as reasoning is concerned the monk's question is quite to the point. All our reasoning starts from "selecting-and-choosing" as the Chinese Zen masters have it, and reflection is the prerogative of the human mind. What will become of it if there is no selecting-and-choosing? Either we fall back to the original chaos of the unconscious, or we go beyond the plane of intellection. How do we escape this dilemma? As long as we are what we are, there must be a way to solve it. The monk in question here, however, does not fully understand where Jōshū is and pursues him along the line of logicality. Even when the answer is given squarely expressing the truth of no-selecting-and-choosing the monk is unable to see it. He expostulates but the master knows better. He seems to mean when he declares, "Above the heavens and below the heavens I alone am the honored one," that here is reality not at all affected by the logic of selecting-and-choosing. This is the utterance legendarily ascribed to Śākyamuni himself when he came out of his mother's womb. It is really a statement of absolute affirmation, and it is only when this is thoroughly understood that one comes to the realization of the Perfect Way. With the monk, however, it was not so, for he was still groping in the maze of words and ideas. As long as one stays on this plane, it is impossible for him to scale the height where minds like Jōshū's are. It is not difficult, on the other hand, to come down so to speak from the height of absolute affirmation to the level of relativity and contradiction, because the latter gains its meaning only when it is referred to the Absolute. The monk remains a philistine with all his intellectual ingenuity inasmuch as he is a juggler of ideas.

Secchō's versified comment may be regarded as referring either personally to Jōshū or to the Perfect Way itself:

[He or it] resembles the unfathomability of the ocean
And the unscalability of the mountain.
The mosquito plays [to no purpose] with the typhoon raging through
   the air;
The ant labors [in vain] to shake a pillar of iron.
Selecting! Choosing!
Look at the cloth-drum hanging on the eaves!

The Perfect Way is beyond all modes of measurement, any attempt at measuring is like a mosquito going against a hurricane or an ant trying to shake the steel construction. If we take Secchō as commenting on Jōshū's position, we can say this: the monk is the ant and the mosquito, and how can he expect to cope with a giant like Jōshū? At any rate, all our endeavors to reach an ultimate conclusion by means of selecting-and-choosing are altogether useless as a drum fitted with cloth instead of leather: however much we may beat it no audible response issues. From another point of view, however, the value of the cloth-drum may be said to consist in its very valuelessness. Things belonging to this world of particulars are useful, and modern people vie with one another to make them work more efficiently, and the outcome of it all is this state of unrest and strain as we are at present experiencing. "The Perfect Way," I am sure, "is not difficult," nor is it so nervous as we are.

In order to make the whole *mondō* more intelligible and palatable, if this is possible, to our readers, I add here a few words intended to be explanatory. As long as we are living in this world of opposites, we cannot do away with selecting-and-choosing which is indeed the essence of human intellect. To do away with selecting-and-choosing therefore inevitably means to go to annihilation, the negation of all things presented to our senses, outer and inner. The monk's question is quite a natural one which all of us are likely to ask if we are told that annihilation is the Perfect Way. Being a Zen adept, Jōshū never argues, but simply asserts, and his statement is conclusive enough, we can never expect to go any further than that. In spite of apparent annihilation implied in the erasure of selecting-and-choosing, the fact that "I am," or, to quote Buddha and Jōshū again, "Above the heavens and below the heavens, I alone am the honored one," remains indisputably true; for when the monk talks to me, I give him the answer. This fact is the most mysterious one and the most solemn and dignifying one, too. If you fail to realize it, you are quite a commonplace personality. "Before Abraham was, I am"—this is the Christian way of expressing the same fact, and the Christians are asked to grasp the meaning of it. If they fail, they are philistines just as much as Jōshū's monk questioner. "I am"—this is not the outcome of selecting-and-choosing. Engo comments here "The mountains crumble, the rocks split," before this fact.

4

There was still another monk trying to tackle the old master Jōshū on the problem of the Perfect Way. He said: "'The Perfect Way is not difficult, only it abhors selecting-and-choosing. Is this not a favorite hiding-place for some masters, where however they find themselves imprisoned?"

Jōshū's reply was: "Once I was asked about it five years ago, and ever since I have not been able to answer it."

This *mondō* gives us some points to reflect upon. We have for once to realize that whatever statement we can make about the Perfect Way or final reality or the Absolute is bound to miss the mark, for it is always *about* the thing and not the thing itself. However eloquently and however minutely we may describe an apple, no amount of description can go any further than the limits ascribed to a description, for description cannot be fact.

When the pointing finger is taken for the moon, what ensues is more than a comedy of error. If a master takes refuge always in the statement that "the Perfect Way is not difficult . . ." and does not know further what to do with it, he digs his own grave and is buried alive in it. Absolute affirmation must be dynamic and not static, therefore not dead; it must bloom forth as a perfect flower in the garden of complexities. It must have vitality and creativity; the singing dragon must dance out of the dead forest. "Selecting-and-choosing" must evolve from the very midst of no-selecting-and-choosing, that is, of the lucid blankness. *Byōdō soku shabetsu* and *shabetsu soku byōdō* must be a living fact and not a mere verbal inane assertion. To hide oneself in it and to look wise is not the Perfect Way of the Zen masters. If one at all claims to be an adept in Zen, he must know how to be more than just verbose. The monk's question hits the mark hard. If it were addressed to somebody else, he might feel very much perplexed; but the man standing before the monk was Jōshū himself, one of the greatest Zen masters, especially great in the use of the tongue. Engo justly comments that if not for a master of Jōshū's caliber and experience the gauntlet must have been found very heavy indeed to take up. See, however, how nonchalantly Jōshū comes out of the trap so cleverly set against him. His innocent answer, apparently a kind of apologetic confession, keeps the monk's mouth effectively closed forever. "I was once asked about it five years ago, and ever since I have not been able to answer it." Is this an apology, or a confession, or an evasion? If not, what can the statement be? What was it that put the impudent monk to silence?

This is what makes some people say that Zen is difficult to understand. So it is indeed. What looks like an apology is really one of the most straightforward statements one can make about the Absolute. Jōshū is not a dialectician, he is not used to debating, he always talks directly to the point, and therefore no one can go around or beyond his remark. It is final, your rejection or acceptance must be wholehearted, there is no halfway meeting. As Engo says, there is no crack in Jōshū through which one can insert an edge of controversial argumentation.

Although quite unnecessary I may add a few words here. Jōshū confesses that for the past five years he has been at work to find a good answer to the question any intelligent mind might come to ask, but in vain. In truth, all wise men, since of old, since the dawn of consciousness in the universe, have been asking the same question over and over again, and what final words have they been able to give? Except this, "I know not." It is indeed the final word one can ever give to the riddle of the world. But, mind you, it is not the confession of ignorance from the intellectual point of view, from the point of view of selecting-and-choosing. Superficially it confesses ignorance, but to be ignorant in this wise is the consummation of wisdom, of super-intellection. Being so, the "I know not" is altogether satisfying to the most seriously inquiring mind, there is nothing negative about it, it is absolute affirmation in spite of its grammatical form. A Zen master was asked, "What is the most phenomenal event in the whole world?" The master gave this as an answer; "I sit here alone in this mountain." This is an affirmation; but is there any difference, as far as the ultimate meaning is concerned, between the negative "I know not" and the affirmative "I sit here"? "I sit here by myself" is indeed the most phenomenal event, and do you know the reason of it? "No, I know not," but "I am" just the same. Wonderful indeed this! Another Zen master seeing a monk approach opened the gate widely and greeted him with this query: "What is this?" The greeting was returned with the same note, "What is this?" Whereupon the master nodded and retired into his room. What more can we say than "I sit here all by myself"; "What's this?" "I know not"? What else can we do than the nodding and returning to the study? All this points to the same fact, to the same truth, to the same experience; and when one of these statements or doings is understood, the rest follow in the steps.

There was a recluse philosopher in the Tōsu monastery whose name was Sōdō. He was deeply involved in the task of discovering the "Perfect Way" under the guidance of Secchō the master. Finally, he succeeded in the work, and when one day the master asked him about it, Sōdō the recluse simply shouted, "O you this beast!" Is this not outrageous—to answer like this to his master's civil inquiry? But we can remark that it is possible only for him who had real experience to behave before the master so insolently, and that it is the latter indeed who is really satisfied with the disciple's wholly ignoring the conventionalism of our worldly life.

The behavior of this lunatic recluse monk was in other ways too altogether out of the common run. When he went out to attend religious ceremonies he used to carry out his wornout sandals and the sutras together as one bundle in his *kaṣāya*. When asked, "What is your family usage?" he would answer, "A pair of sandals wrapped up in the *kaṣāya!*" *The kaṣāya* (*kesa* in Japanese) is a robe signifying the holiness of the wearer's profession, while the sandals, though highly necessary for practical purposes and by no means despicable, are usually classed with things dirty and valueless especially when they are wornout ones. So the recluse has now made one bundle of these two contradicting objects, carrying them on his shoulder triumphantly. This may be regarded as symbolizing his absolute affirmation. When he was further asked as to the ultimate meaning of his strange bundle of synthesis, he would say, "Barefooted I go down the mountain." Evidently he does not stay with his affirmation or abide in his "lucid blankness," he is active enough occasionally to leave his mountain retreat in order to perform religious work in the village below.

Secchō's comment on Jōshū here reads:

> The royal elephant snorts,
> The intrepid lion roars.
> A talk devoid of flavor
> Effectively shuts one's mouth.
> South and North, East and West;
> The Raven[3] flies, the Hare[3] leaps.

[3] The Raven symbolizes the sun and the Hare the moon.

Secchō's laconic style requires interpretation. Jōshū's "apology" is compared here to the snorting of the elephant and to the roaring of the lion. There is nothing faint and apologetic about Jōshū when he refers to his inability of extricating himself from the dilemma. In truth, his statement transcends all verbal quibbles, there is no point in it which one can take hold of; being devoid of all flavor it beggars all description, no one can make any assertion about it. And yet there extends before us immensity of space in all directions, north and south, east and west, and again there flows an endless stream of time with the sun and moon, now rising, now setting—and this not mere repetition but an infinitely varying creation. Secchō's ode as before applies to the Perfect Way itself as well as to Jōshū who is the master hand in conducting Zen mondō.

5

We now come to the fourth and last mondō by Jōshū in reference to the Perfect Way as recorded in the Hekigan-shū. A monk asks: "'The Perfect Way is not difficult, only it abhors selecting-and-choosing.' As soon as something is asserted, there is a selecting-and-choosing. What would you do then for others?"

This monk is again after Jōshū trying to get him cornered. If he says this or that, he commits the fault of selecting-and-choosing, he is caught in his own trap. The monk is no green hand. Jōshū, however, is not to be so easily palmed off on. He most artlessly retorts, "Why don't you quote at full length?"

Jōshū's sermon as we have seen above has something more, but the monk has not quoted the passage in full. Hence Jōshū's demand, and this demand has on the face of it no intrinsic connection with the monk's request for information. But from the Zen point of view there is something far deeper than what is merely superficial and verbal. We must try to read into Jōshū's inner life, which, liberated from shackles of intellection, moves on the plane of no-selecting-and-choosing. This monk was however not an ordinary one, he was able to say this: "My memory fails to go further." Apparently a plain statement of fact, for he did not try to carry out his argumentativeness any further. But Jōshū knew well what this monk was after and where his general mental attitude tended. The master fell back upon his original theme, and said:

"Only this—'The Perfect Way is not difficult, only it abhors select-ing-and-choosing.'"

As is repeatedly remarked, Zen is not to be understood accord-ing to the ordinary rules of logic, or to the literal sense of words as they are uttered. We must try to investigate the mental attitude of the master which he holds toward life and the world. In other words, we must plunge as far as we can by means of imagination into the mental and spiritual atmosphere wherein he moves. We must abandon our habitual selecting-and-choosing which thwarts every step we make in our daily life. This is in fact doing violence to our accustomed way of dealing with ourselves and the world. We may not think this possible, for it is the giving up of the life we all live since the beginning of the world. But this is what is demanded by the Zen master of those who desire to be in his com-pany. Instead of restoring to intellection, therefore, we must strive to discover a new route to the realm of Zen experience. This may be said to correspond to the Christian revelation of divine truth. The discovery of the new route is indeed a revelation. Zen experi-ence is revealed truth.

To come back to the *mondō* under consideration, the final state-ment given by Jōshū is no more than the repetition of the original couplet, but what the monk wished was decidedly not the repeti-tion, for this does not lead him anywhere, he is made to stay where he was. From his position which is the outcome of selecting-and-choosing, this is most unsatisfactory. When he said: "What will you do if you are to help others to the understanding of Zen? You cannot avoid getting into the mess of selecting-and-choosing. How do you then make the Perfect Way manifest before others?", he no doubt expected Jōshū to perform some dialectical wonders. But Jōshū was a great Zen master and knew perfectly well how to deal with the difficulty which is essentially logical and not on the plane of Zen. If the monk, however, failed to see into the meaning of the repetition given out by the master he would have to de-vote another ten years to the study of Zen. For the repetition here is not really a repetition, it bears altogether a new meaning apart from the literal one. The meaning is to be sought in the general mental attitude of Jōshū himself which controls all his behavior and makes him utter those "nonsensical ejaculations." So we can see that the repetition goes beyond phrasing, and that it is really a reflection of Jōshū's Zen mind which is to be intuited here. When this is done, the monk will find his eyes replaced by a new pair the existence of which he was never aware of before. So Engo aptly notes here: Jōshū has effected this surgical operation without making use of scalpels and scissors and also without premeditation. The work has been carried out so perfectly naturally. The final remark given by Jōshū is not to be taken, continues Engo, "as affirming or negating anything, nor as going beyond affirmation and negation. It is really outside the four [logical] propositions, it refuses to be defined by any amount of negations. Why? Because when we come to the matter of Zen it is like unto a flash of lightning or the issuing of sparks when the stone is struck, no time is to be lost, the fact must be instantly grasped; a slightest wavering or dallying and you find yourself eternally lost."

Secchō's commentary verse is as terse as ever, and may be construed as referring either to Jōshū personally or to the Perfect Way itself which goes through all "selecting-and-choosing" as well as through the "lucid blankness."

> The water pouring fails to soak;
> The wind blowing fails to penetrate.
> He steps like the tiger, moves like the dragon;
> He makes spirits cry and gods weep.
> The head is three feet long—who is he?
> He stands on one leg facing you in silence.

Secchō's Reality is a queer-looking creature, with the head three feet long, standing on one leg, and squarely gazing on you. In this description of the Absolute Secchō has a precedent in the ancient master who gave this answer to a monk who asked about the Buddha: "The head measures three feet in length and the neck two inches." This being so extraordinarily formed is naturally endowed with a body which water fails to drown, fire to burn, and wind to smash to pieces. Its strength is abnormal too, and even the gods and spirits ask mercy before it as its supernatural powers are beyond conception. This is the meaning of Secchō's versified comment on Jōshū's *mondō* as given above. It is equally applicable to the Perfect Way itself and to Jōshū's Zen mind, for the two are practically the same thing. But, from the common-sense point of view, what an extraordinary description! That which no physical forces can crush and to which even the gods have to bow stands before you with a head as long as three feet (how definite!), silently, and on one leg (why one?). Is this not the most amazing event which can take place under the sun? What does Secchō the poet really mean? Engo says that in this couplet Secchō has in the veriest manner depicted Jōshū and that those who wish to live the life of Jōshū are to dig a sense out of it. But Engo, when in his playful challenging mood, complements: "What a monster! What a holy man from nowhere! Do you see him? Be gone! Shrink away! O this wild beast! We cannot let you go unnoticed. So here goes a slap!"

One can say that all these are poetical exaggerations and have nothing to do with the understanding of genuine Zen. To a certain extent that is true. But when genuine Zen is understood the "exaggerations" or "absurdities" will become intelligible too. Let us only note here that in the history of Zen thought in China Secchō marks the culmination of this poetic tendency of giving expression to Zen experience.

6

As far as the philosophy of Zen experience is concerned, the following verse by Banzan, a disciple of Baso gives the gist of it as well as the third patriarch's "Inscription on the Believing Mind."

> The Mind is, like the moon, full and solitary,
> Its Light swallows up the ten thousand things.
> It is not that the Light illumines the Field,
> Nor is the Field in existence [apart from the Light].
> Both the Light and the Field are forgotten,
> And what is that [which is still left behind]?

"Which is still left behind" has been supplied in order to make the intended meaning complete from the logical point of view. The Zen masters would leave the line as it stands in the original and let students fill the lacuna by themselves. For the object of Zen discipline is to come personally in touch with the Mind which is at the root of all existences. This Mind is however to be distinguished from our individual minds, as the latter belong to the world as much as "the ten thousand things." The Mind is Light, full and solitary, enveloping the totality of things. This Mind-Light is, however, not a dualistic existence standing against its object of illumination which Banzan calls the "Field"; nor is the Field a separate existence reflecting the light of the Mind. When both Light and Field, subject and object, the one and the many, are "forgotten," most philosophers imagine that nothing is left behind, that there is a total annihilation, a state of absolute nothingness or emptiness or, as Jōshū would have it, "lucid blankness." But with Zen masters it is not so, there is a third term, the Mind, which does not belong to the categories of any philosophical system, but which, while all inclusive, is not something set apart from the world of particulars. Students of Zen are required to realize it in the fashion of sense perception and not intellectually, that is, conceptually; they are intuitively to grasp it and not to understand it as a concept needed to complete a system. The Mind is to be perceived in a way somewhat similar to that in which a sense object is perceived.[4] Whatever dialectics needed for the confirmation of the fact are to be advanced after the experience and not before.

The following verse by Yōka runs along the same line of thought and expresses the Zen experience as was personally gone through by the poet, and is not a conceptual abstract statement:

> The mind is an organ of thought and objects are set against it:
> The two are like marks on the surface of the mirror;
> When the dirt is removed, the light begins to shine.
> Both mind and objects being forgotten, Ultimate Nature
> reveals itself true.

Whatever name we may give to this Ultimate Nature, it is the Light, it is the Mind, it is the Mirror, it is the Perfect Way, it is the Buddha, Dharmakāya, and Reality, which is realizable only by transcending the dialectics of selecting-and-choosing.

This transcending, according to Zen, is brought about when the following advice is most truthfully observed:

---

[4] This is not quite to the point. To make it clearer another article is to be written, and it is in fact a very important aspect of Zen experience.

> Be detached, be detached!
> Be most thoroughly detached!
> Even when you come to a pass where no further detachment
>   is possible,
> Be still detached, and detached for ever more!

By "detachment" here the author means to get rid of every possible trace of ratiocination, or, psychologically speaking, to dig down to the lowest strata of consciousness and to go deeper yet even through the bottomless abyss of the unconscious.

> Be detached, be detached!
> Be thoroughly detached!
> What then?
> The pine is green,
> And white is the snow.

Below is another stanza by a Zen master depicting the same experience of detachment and awakening—for detachment must finally come to an awakening:

> Reasoning comes to an end, imaginations and calculations
>   are forgotten:
> To what can this be compared? There's no analogy whatever.
> The moon shining overhead all night this frosty night
> Has at last quietly, without my knowing when, set over the
>   valley yonder.
> The branches already heavily loaded with fruit bend further
>   down as the monkey climbs.
> Walking along the narrow winding path among the faraway
>   mountains, one feels as if gone astray.
> Raising my head, I happen to notice over there the faint
>   lingering glow of the autumn,
> And realize that the sun naturally sets to the west of my
>   residence.[5]

[5] By Hōgen Moneki.

The main point touched upon in the above-cited stanzas is that there is what may be designated as Mind or Light or Ultimate Nature, which "swallows up" this world of dualities but which is no separate reality in existence. Our relativistic way of thinking or viewing things generally is apt to make us set up a third concept as bridging the gap between the one and the many, the perceiving and the perceived, the mind and the ten thousand things, "the Light" and "the Field," "lucid blankness" and "selecting-and-choosing." As far as logic and human consciousness are concerned, this third term may be useful and most convenient, but Zen insists that there is no reality corresponding to it—a reality as is conceived in this world of particulars. It abides in and with them, and yet it is perceived as not conditioned by them. When you are asked to pick it up or bring it out before us, you cannot very well do it. Nor does the idea of a universal apply to it, for it is not in the realm of logic. You may declare such an elusive and illusory thing to be altogether non-existent and therefore of no practical value whatever. Yet the strangest experience of ours is that all our thinking and feeling point to it, and that when we take hold of it, though naturally not in the way we take hold of a particular object, we are singularly satisfied and fulfil the "naked intent stretching into God"—an expressive phrase used by the author of the *Cloud of Unknowing*. Such a variety of names has been given by Zen masters and Buddhist philosophers to this mysterious inconceivable "thing." The masters, however, have not been content by any means with mere naming, which affords abundant chances to all forms of misunderstanding. This experience they wanted to be transferred on to their pupils, they wanted the latter to experience the same experience they had with themselves. To do this they have been exhausting whatever means that came their way, verbal, poetic, symbolic, gesticulatory (though this is not a good term), personal, or "actional." In the verse last quoted, Hōgen alludes to the moon in the frosty night quietly setting over the valley yonder, or to the monkey trying to pick the fruit off the bending branch, or to the evening sun casting its parting glow near his mountain retreat. When reasoning has come to its end, when no dialectic is able to transmit his inner experience livingly, when the experience itself is to be awakened in another mind, what can the master do except depict the views he is familiar with in his quiet monastery?

To further illustrate this impasse and the way out, I give another *mondō* from the *Hekigan-shū*, this time in the form of a question which the master himself answers:

Ummon used to give this to his disciples for twenty years, which none could answer:

"Every one of us is endowed with the Light. When you try to have a look at it perfect darkness prevails. What is the Light in your possession?"

As none ever ventured to say a word, Kōrin finally asked the master to give his own view. Ummon said: "The refectory, the monastery gate." Again he gave this: "It's better even for good things not to happen."

The "perfect darkness" of Ummon may be considered somewhat corresponding to a "Cloud of Unknowing" or to "Divine Darkness," though we have to be on guard not to get Buddhist thought confused with the Christian, for there are some fundamental differences between the two systems of thought. The Light declared by Ummon to be in possession of every one of us shines through our sense organs and in our consciousness, but it is not something distinct from those organs whereby it is made to reveal itself, nor can it be said that it is identical with them. In a way it is both transcendental and immanent, because it "swallows up" all things and yet it is neither in them nor outside them. Human phraseology has no adequate term to define the exact position of the Light in our experiences for the very reason that all our experiences are possible by virtue of it. It cannot be extracted as the chemist does with his elements from "the ten thousand things." When we try to seize it or to bring it out in the light, it is no more there. It defies analysis, it does not allow the passage of any kind of light, whereby it can be singled out and pointed at by us saying, "Look, here it is! This is what is understood by Ummon's 'perfect darkness.'"

This being so, is it then absolutely impossible to acquaint others with the presence of the Light which is of the weightiest significance in the study of Zen? Ummon's "The refectory, the monastery gate" is one way whereby we can have a glimpse into the "perfect darkness." His second remark helps to make this glimpse still clearer. "It is better even for good things not to happen." The idea is: Even when you say "yes" or "no" you already commit yourself to a statement, and to make any statement about a thing which in its nature forbids this is to do violence to it. Vimalakīrti's silence seems to be after all the best way to lead us to the understanding of the perfect darkness.

Sampei Gichū, one of the T'ang masters, expresses the same idea in the following verse:

> "It" is with our seeing and hearing, yet "it" is not that,
> Nor is "it" something distinct which can be presented to
>   you as such.
> When you understand this, all is well with you:
> As to substance and function, you may talk of their oneness
>   as well as of their separateness.

Reference here to "substance" and "function" follows the usual methodology of Buddhist thought. The Light or "It," though no definite term is here used, may be regarded as substance or as function or as neither; the main thing is to have an understanding, a nodding, or a smiling to oneself.

Secchō's commentary verse here has great mystifying effect as much as Ummon's original theme:

> Self-illumining, each solitary light arranges itself in
>   order;
> For your sake, he opens one passageway:
> The trees shorn of their flowers are altogether bare.
> Look into it, and nobody fails to see it—
> Seen? No, not seen?
> Riding backward on an ox one enters into the Buddha-hall.

As we can see here and elsewhere, the uniqueness of Zen philosophy consists in offering us such expressions as, for instance, Ummon's "The refectory, the monastery gate," or Secchō's "Riding backward on an ox one enters into the Buddha-hall," whereby the adepts tax their ingenuity heavily to communicate their understanding of the perfect darkness. For the darkness, after all, yields something of itself to those who seek, to those who knock, to those who feel "a naked intent stretching into God."

Zen and philosophy may be referring to the same experiences, for even philosophy cannot do away with them, in fact it is an intellectual attempt to interpret all our experiences; but they do not use the same language, because what Zen aims at is to make others live facts themselves by most direct methods. Conceptualization is not in the program of Zen, Zen wants to make a concrete demonstration of its experiences within the human limits of representation. The demonstration or representation may vary, sometimes verbal and poetic, sometimes personal and realistic or "actional." When it is verbal, it does not follow the usual method of reasoning and it is in this that Zen deviates from philosophy. What has already been stated about Zen in the preceding pages sufficiently shows that it is so. Inasmuch as Zen avoids "selecting-and-choosing" and yet does not abide in "the lucid blankness" of the Absolute, it cannot help but adopt a unique method of its own and express itself in words altogether unintelligible to ordinary intellects. By the personal and realistic or "actional" method, it is meant that in Zen boxing the ears, slapping the face, kicking, swinging the staff, stretching the bow, beating the drum, holding forth a finger, and many another exhibition of a personality are freely resorted to. The reason is: all our experiences start from the body, from the activity of the sense organs including consciousness, and as it is Zen that tries to understand the meaningless meaning of this activity or movement, Zen naturally employs the method that would direct our attention to the movement itself instead of to that which reflects on it.

To make this point clearer, let me cite one concrete instance and see wherein this personal or "actional" method consists. Indeed, in the history of religious experience no such demonstrations or expressions or expediencies have been practiced as we observe recorded in the annals of Zen.

Rinzai once gave this short sermon: "There is one true man with no title who presides over the reddish fleshly mass of yours. He is all the time coming in and out through your sense organs; you who have not testified to this, look, look!"

A monk came out of the rank and asked, "Who is this true man with no title?"

Rinzai came down from his straw chair and taking hold of the monk said, "Speak, speak!"

The monk hesitated, whereupon the master let him go, saying, "What a worthless piece of stick is this true man with no title!" and returned to his own quarters.

When this *mondō* or "incident" is conceptually interpreted, the one true man here referred to may be taken as meaning the soul or spirit as it is popularly understood, and Rinzai by saying "Look! Look!" called the monk's attention to it. He evidently wished to have them realize it in themselves. "Look! Look!" let me notice, is significant; what Rinzai wants us to have is our personal experience of this "one true man" himself as he functions over and through our senses, and not merely making statements about him. Now comes forward a monk who tries to see the master commit himself to a verbal interpretation of the whole situation. But Rinzai is a Zen master, and not a schoolteacher, nor a preacher of the gospel. He comes down from his chair and seizing the monk personally demands, "Speak! Speak!" By this Rinzai wished to see the monk's "one true man with no title" act. To "speak" does not mean to move your lips but to act with your whole being, to see your entire personality move forward with everything that pertains to it. When Rinzai took hold of the monk, Rinzai's entire "man" unreservedly asserted himself, and this he also wanted to see in his monk. The latter miserably failed, because his mind was wandering on the plane of relative dualistic consciousness and was naturally at a loss how to respond to the master's call. Seeing this Rinzai gave his final judgment: "What a useless piece of stick!" "The one true man" was found dead in the monk. No doubt Rinzai and also the monk could have made some assertion conceptually regarding the inner man functioning with and through their sense organs. But all concepts are mediated, being results of dualistic reflection, while Zen is averse to all forms of mediation. The action of the inner man is thus likened to a flash of lightning: it disappears as soon as it is perceived, there is no interruption, no hesitancy, no apology, it moves so swiftly that one almost feels as if nothing happened. So it is stated by Ummon: "Every one has the Light within himself, but as soon as he looks at it there reigns perfect darkness." To come across this kind of inner experience is the sole object of Zen discipline. No amount of verbal discussion, therefore, no logical acuteness, no intellectual subtlety will probe the deep secrets of Zen. Rinzai's reference to the "one true man" in every one of us may appear at first sight and also from the conventional point of view to be an assertion on the relative plane of consciousness, but that it was not so is unmistakably recognized from his behavior which followed the monk's questioning. All Zen movement or activity is to be understood not as our common sense or intellect wants to understand it but as it were from the reverse side of it; we must first enter into the experience itself in order to be one with it, to become the actor or creator himself, to move along with the stream, and not to be the onlooker. Rinzai's directness, or, as it may be called, his personal rudeness—the seizing of the person of the questioner, the peremptory demand, and the final defamatory remark—is really the kindliest and most adequate method of instruction a Zen master can ever give to his pupils.

7

When this direct personal method is not inwardly grasped, the other method which is verbal will also be utterly unintelligible. This has already been well illustrated though from a different point of view in the first part of this paper. That the verbal method is just as unintelligible as the "actional" is quite in accord with the character of Zen discipline. As has been repeatedly observed, Zen has no deliberate intention to distinguish itself from intellection or our common-sense way of thinking and reasoning, but it is altogether due to Zen experience that Zen has created its own unique unparalleled methods of self-expression and also of instruction. Zen is not satisfied with the philosophical methodology; besides every one of us cannot be expected to be a philosopher; whereas anybody can be a student of Zen if only he applies himself assiduously to the work, guided by his inner urge after the truth. The following *mondō* also culled from the *Hekigan-shū* gives us an insight into a kind of Zen theology in which we may say that the relation of God to the world is discussed.

Enkan Saian, who was one of the disciples of Baso, of the T'ang dynasty, one day asked his attendant to bring him the rhinoceros fan.[6] But the attendant reported that the fan was torn to pieces. The master demanded then, "Bring me the rhinoceros itself if the fan is broken to pieces." The attendant gave no answer. Engo, commentator of the *Hekigan-shū*, remarks here: Enkan the old master knew even before his asking that the fan had been torn to pieces and was of no practical use. In his asking for it there was an ulterior motive, he wanted to open the way for his attendant to the truth of Zen experience. The attendant failed to see the

---

[6] A fan whose frame is made of the rhinoceros horn.

point and answered, "The fan is torn to pieces." The master who was kindhearted enough to make use of every available opportunity pursued him, demanding the rhinoceros itself. What would he really do with the animal? His idea was simply to find out if the monk had the faintest perception of the truth implied in his request.

This *mondō* did not stop with the attendant's silence, it evoked further comments on the part of the contemporary Zen masters. Tōsu Daidō said, "I wouldn't mind producing him, but I am afraid his horn may not be complete." On this Secchō comments, "I want your animal with an incomplete horn."

Sekisō said, "If I give him back to the master, none will be left with me." Secchō's comment was, "Yes, the rhinoceros is still here!"

Shifuku drew a circle and in it inscribed the character "*niu*," representing the animal. To this Secchō gave the following: "Why not bring him out?"

Hofuku said, "The master is growing old, and it would be well if somebody else were available to serve him [I am sorry that I cannot please him]." Secchō commented on this "Unfortunately, it is much ado for nothing."

This last master seems to have pleased Engo the best, for he remarks: "Hofuku's words are quite appropriate. The first three masters' statements are rather easy to see, but Hofuku's have a deeper meaning. Secchō perfectly understands the point, hence his comment, 'Unfortunately, it is much ado for nothing!' Formerly, when I was with Kei the librarian, my understanding of Hofuku did not go beyond rationalism. I then thought: 'The master is losing his mind due to senility; when he has the head he forgets the tail. A while ago he wanted the fan, and now he is after the rhinoceros. A man of such irrationality is hard to serve.'"

It may not be difficult to interpret the first three masters on the intellectual plane, they yield so to speak to a conceptual treatment; but the last master shows us no logical seam along which a knife of reasoning may be applied. Secchō's "Much ado for nothing" refers to the meaninglessness of Hofuku's position, or it may be better to state that Hofuku has completely annihilated himself. No "self" is left in him, he is humbleness itself, all that he does or says comes out of this emptied selfhood, no utilitarianism is here, he lives in a realm of absolute values, which is of no-value and where all doings are no-doings. Secchō's versified comment reads:

The rhinoceros fan has been in use for ever so many years;
But when a question is asked, utter ignorance prevails all
  around.
The refreshing breeze through infinite space, and the
  rhinoceros with its horn perfectly formed—
All these are like the rainy clouds passing, and who can
  lay hold of them?

Engo now adds: Each one of us is in possession of the rhinoceros
fan, and by virtue of that we go through every hour of our life.
How is it that when we ask about it we are to confess our complete
ignorance—Ummon's perfect darkness? Not only Enkan's attendant, but all the four masters who have wisely given each his answer according to his light really know nothing about it. Does
Secchō the author of the versified comment then know? When
Mujaku called on Monju, he was treated to tea. Raising the
tea cup made of glass, Monju asked, "Do you have this in the
South?" Mujaku said, "No, we have it not." "What do you use then
for tea?" Mujaku remained silent. When the meaning of this *kōan*
is understood, then you will realize what a refreshing breeze rises
out of your rhinoceros fan and also what a splendid horn decorates
the head of the animal. The comments given by the four masters of
old are indeed like the morning clouds and evening showers which
once passed are not to be taken hold of again.

Enkan's rhinoceros fan, Monju's tea cup, Secchō's morning
clouds and evening showers, and all other doings and sayings recorded in the history of Zen thought—none of them are to be taken
hold of again; they are forever passing; when we think we have
taken hold of them, they are no more there, for what is left in our
hands is a conceptual carcass, quite dead. Something more than intellectual categories is needed to get, for instance, into Hofuku's
remark: "Master, you are growing old, and it would be well if
somebody else were available to serve you. [As to myself, I am so
sorry I am unable to please you."]

8

A life of meaninglessness or purposelessness is what characterizes the entire course of Zen discipline, and it is because of this
that the Perfect Way is declared to be not at all difficult. Indeed,

without the selecting-and-choosing this world of particulars disappears, for reflection and discrimination are the condition of all our experiences, which, when no expressions are given to them, are the same as non-existent. The principle, therefore, of *shabetsu soku byōdō* and *byōdō soku shabetsu* is to be fully realized in order to see what it is which makes all the Zen masters of the past labor so painstakingly and also so vigorously exercise themselves as we have seen above. But there is still one thing we have to recall, which is that Zen is the art of reading into the reason of one's own being and that as this has no assignable end, no definable meaning, there is no finality in the art, we cannot exhaust its depths. Even when we come to a realization, we may find it to be still in need of, shall we say, improvement, as it is capable of infinite progress.

Let Nansen and Hyakujō conclude:

Nansen once visited Hyakujō and Hyakujō asked: "Is there anything (*Dharma*) about which sages of old found nothing could be predicated even for the sake of others?"

Nansen: "Yes, there is."

Hyakujō: "What is that about which they found nothing could be predicated?"

Nansen: "It is neither Mind nor Buddha nor a thing."

Hyakujō: "Predicated!"

Nansen: "This is as far as I can go. How about you?"

Hyakujō: "I am not a great master, and how can I know whether there is anything about which something can be predicated, or not?"

Nansen: "I fail to understand."

Hyakujō: "There, indeed something has been predicated!"

To make this *mondō* more intelligible to the average reader, I may add a word about the Chinese character *shuo*, or *setsu* in Japanese, on which the whole "discussion" revolves. The character *setsu* which I translated here "to predicate" has several meanings: "to narrate," "to preach," "to tell," "to make a statement about," "to persuade," etc. In the present *mondō* it means "to give a definition to," or simply "to assert something" about any object or idea or experience. In whatever sense it may be taken, the idea involved here is that as soon as you make a sentence, for example, "A is B," something is predicated about "A" whereby the subject is limited and becomes one of "the ten thousand things." If, therefore, "A" is really something beyond the plane of relativity, even to say "A," i.e., "A is A," is to negate "A"; but if nothing is predicated about "A," how can we know that there is even a thing or *Dharma* called "A"? An endless series of negations is also predicating something about "A." But the most annoying or most harassing fact is that this "A" persistently presses itself into our consciousness, demanding recognition in some form, and yet when a recognition is given to it, it hides away from our view refusing to accept any predicates. To make it somehow amenable to human understanding, philosophy makes use of dialectic and Zen appeals to concrete personal experience.

PART IV

The Practice and Discipline of Zen

If you strive after Buddhahood by
any conscious contrivances, your
Buddha is indeed the source of
eternal transmigration

Rinzai

1. THE MEDITATION HALL AND THE
IDEALS OF THE MONKISH DISCIPLINE[1]

I

To get a glimpse into the practical and disciplinary side of Zen, we have to study the institution known as the Meditation Hall. It is an educational system quite peculiar to the Zen sect. Most of the main monasteries belonging to this sect are provided with Meditation Halls, and in the life of the Zen monk more than anywhere else we are reminded of that of the Buddhist Brotherhood (*samgha*) in India. This system was founded by the Chinese Zen master, Hyakujō, more than one thousand years ago. Until his time the monks used to live in monasteries belonging to the Vinaya sect, which were governed by a spirit not quite in accordance with the principles of Zen. As Zen flourished more and more and its followers increased in number and in influence, there was need for its own institution, exclusively devoted to the promotion of its objects. According to Hyakujō, the Zen monasteries were to be neither Hinayanistic nor Mahayanistic, but they were to unite the disciplinary methods of both schools in a new and original manner, best suited to the realization of the Zen ideals, as they were conceived by the masters of the earlier days.

The original book compiled by Hyakujō giving detailed regulations of the Zen monastery was lost. The one we have now was compiled during the Yüan dynasty from the actual life in the monastery at the time, which was supposed to be a faithful continuation of the old institution, though naturally with some modifications and transformations due to historical exigencies. This book was compiled under the auspices of the reigning Emperor Shun, and is known as *Chokushu Shingi* ("The Imperial Edition of the Regulations in the Zen Monastery"). In Japan the Zen monasteries have never been established on a grand scale as in China,

[1] *Essays in Zen Buddhism* (First Series), pp. 314–362.

and as a result all the regulations as detailed in the Imperial Edition were not practiced. But their spirit and all that was applicable to Japanese life and conditions were adopted. The ideals of Zen life were never lost sight of anywhere.

But before I proceed further I wish to speak briefly of one of such ideals set before the eyes of all Zen students, for it is really the most important and noteworthy feature in the monastery life of Zen. It is indeed this that distinguishes Zen from the other Buddhist schools originated in China, and is to be considered most characteristically Zen, at the same time animating its long history. By this I mean the notion of work or service. Hyakujō left the guiding principle of his life, which is pre-eminently the spirit of the Meditation Hall: "No work, no eating." When he was thought too old to work in the garden (his daily occupation besides lecturing and educating the monks in Zen), the disciples hid all his garden implements, as he would not listen to their repeated oral remonstrances. He then refused to eat, saying, "No work, no eating."

At all the Meditation Halls work is thus considered a vital element in the life of a monk. It is altogether a practical one, and chiefly consists in manual labor, such as sweeping, cleaning, cooking, fuel-gathering, tilling the farm, or going about begging in the villages far and near. No work is considered beneath their dignity, and a perfect feeling of brotherhood and democracy prevails among them. However hard, or mean from the ordinary point of view, a work may be, they will not shun it. They believe in the sanctity of manual labor. They keep themselves busy in every way they can; they are no idlers as some of the so-called monks or mendicants are, physically at least, as in India, for instance.

We can see in this sanctification of work the practical attitude of the Chinese mind well reflected. When I said that Zen was the Chinese interpretation of the doctrine of enlightenment, the Zen conception of work did not essentially or theoretically enter into my conclusion. But from the practical point of view work is such an integral part of the Zen life now that the one cannot be conceived as independent of the other. In India the monks are mendicants; when they meditate they retire into a quiet corner away from worldly cares; and inasmuch as they are supported economically by their secular devotees, they do not propose to work in any menial employment such as Chinese and Japanese Zen monks are used to. What saved Zen Buddhism from deteriorating into quietism or mere intellectual gymnastics, which was more or less the fate befalling other schools of Buddhism, was surely due to the gospel of work. Apart from its psychological value, it proved an efficient agency in preserving the health and sanity of Zen Buddhism throughout its long history of growth.

Whatever may be this historical importance of work, Hyakujō must have had a profound knowledge of human psychology when he made work the ruling spirit of the monastery life. His idea of "No work, no eating"[2] did not necessarily originate from an economic or ethical valuation of life. His sole motive was not that nobody deserved his daily bread if he did not earn it with the sweat of his brow. True, there is a virtue in not eating the bread of idleness, and there have been so many Buddhists since the early days of Buddhism who thought it a most disgraceful thing to be living on others' earnings and savings, that Hyakujō's object, while it might have been unconsciously conceived, was more psychological in spite of his open declaration, "No work, no eating." It was to save his monks from mental inactivity or an unbalanced development of mind which too often results from the meditative habit of the monkish life.

When the muscles are not exercised for the execution of spiritual truths, or when the mind and body are not put to practical test, the severance generally issues in inimical results. As the philosophy of Zen is to transcend the dualistic conception of flesh and spirit, its practical application will naturally be, dualistically speaking, to make the nerves and muscles the ready and absolutely obedient servants of the mind. "The spirit is willing but the flesh is weak" will not do. Whatever religious truth there is in this latter statement, psychologically it comes from the lack of a ready channel between mind and muscles. Unless the hands are habitually trained to do the work of the brain, the blood ceases to circulate evenly throughout the body, it grows congested especially in the brain. The result will be not only an unsound condition of the body generally, but a state of mental torpidity in which ideas presented are like wafting clouds. One may be awake and yet the mind is filled with the wildest dreams and visions which are not at all related to realities of life. Fantasies are fatal to Zen, and those who practice Zen think-

[2] Literally, "A day [of] no work [is] a day [of] no eating." Cf. II Thessalonians 3: 10: "If any would not work, neither should he eat." It is noteworthy that St. Francis of Assisi made this the first rule of his Brotherhood

ing it a form of meditation are too apt to be visited upon by this insidious enemy. Hyakujō's insistence upon manual work has saved Zen from falling into the pitfall of antinomianism or from becoming a hallucinatory mode of mind.

Apart from these psychological considerations, there is a moral reason which ought not to escape attention in our estimate of Hyakujō's wisdom in instituting work as a vital part of Zen life. For the soundness of ideas must be tested finally by their practical application. If they fail in this—that is, if they cannot be carried out in everyday life producing lasting harmony and satisfaction, giving benefit to all concerned—to oneself as well as to others—no ideas can be said to be sound and practical. While physical force alone is no standard in judging the value of ideas, the latter, however logically consistent, have no reality when they are not joined to life. Especially in Zen, abstract ideas that do not convince one in practical living are of no value whatever. Conviction must be gained through experience and not through abstraction, which means that conviction alone has no solid basis; only when it is efficiently acted out in life can it be considerable. Moral assertion or "bearing witness" ought to be over and above an intellectual judgment; that is to say, the truth must be the product of one's living experiences. An idle reverie is not their business, the Zen followers will insist. They sit quietly and practice zazen[3] to reflect on whatever lessons they have gained while working. They are against chewing the cud all the time, putting into action whatever reflections they have made during hours of quiet-sitting and testing their validity in the vital field of practicality. If Zen had not insisted on acting its ideas, the institution would have long before this sunk into a mere somniferous and trance-inducing system, and all the treasure thoughtfully hoarded by the masters in China and Japan would have been cast away as heaps of rotten stuff.

---

[3] *Tso-ch'an* is one of those compound Buddhist terms made of Sanskrit and Chinese. *Tso* is Chinese meaning "to sit," while *ch'an* stands for *dhyāna* or *jhana*. The full transliteration of the term is *ch'an-na*, but for brevity's sake the first character alone has been in use. The combination of *tso-ch'an* comes from the fact that *dhyāna* is always practiced by sitting cross-legged. This posture has been considered by the Indians the best way of sitting for a long while in meditation. In it, according to some Japanese physicians, the center of gravitation rests firmly in the lower regions of the body, and when the head is relieved of an unusual congestion of blood the whole system will work in perfect order and the mind be put in suitable mood to take in the truth.

Perhaps unwittingly supported by these reasons, the value of work or service has been regarded by all Zen followers as one of their religious ideals. No doubt the idea was greatly enforced by the characteristic industry and practicalness of the Chinese people by whom Zen was mainly elaborated. If there is any one thing that is most emphatically insisted upon by the Zen masters as the expression of their faith, it is serving and doing work for others; not ostentatiously, but quietly and without announcement. Says Eckhart, "What a man takes in by contemplation he must pour out in love." Zen would say, "pour it out in work," meaning by work the active and concrete realization of love. Tauler made spinning and shoemaking and other homely duties gifts of the Holy Ghost; Brother Lawrence made cooking sacramental; George Herbert wrote:

> Who sweeps a room as to thy laws
> Makes that and the action fine.

These are all expressive of the spirit of Zen, as far as its practical side is concerned. Mystics are thus all practical men; they are far from being visionaries whose souls are too absorbed in things unearthly or of the other world to be concerned with their daily life. The common notion that mystics are dreamers and stargazers ought to be corrected, as it has no foundation in facts. Indeed, psychologically there is a most intimate and profound relationship between a practical turn of mind and a certain type of mysticism; the relationship is not merely conceptual or metaphysical. If mysticism is true its truth must be a practical one, verifying itself in every act of ours, and, most decidedly, not a logical one, to be true only in our dialectics. Sings a Zen poet Hō-koji:[4]

---

[4] He was the noted Confucian disciple of Baso, and his wife and daughter were also devoted Zen followers. When he thought the time had come for him to pass away, he told his daughter to watch the course of the sun and let him know when it was midday. The daughter hurriedly came back and told the father that the sun had already passed the meridian and was about to be eclipsed. Hō came out, and while he was watching the said eclipse, she went in, took her father's own seat, and passed away in meditation. When the father saw his daughter already in Nirvana, he said, "What a quick-witted girl she is!" Hō himself passed away some days later.

> How wondrously supernatural,
> And how miraculous this!
> I draw water, and I carry fuel!

II

The Meditation Hall (zendō), as it is built in Japan, is generally a rectangular building of various size according to the number of monks to be accommodated. One at Engakuji,[5] Kamakura, was about 36 feet by 65 feet. The floors, about eight feet wide and three feet high, are raised along the longer sides of the building, and an empty space is left in the middle throughout the entire length of the Hall. This space is used for practicing an exercise known as kinhin, which means literally "sutra-walking." The space allotted to each monk on the tatami floor does not exceed one mat, three by six feet, where he sits, meditates, and sleeps at night. The bedding for each is never more than one large wadded quilt, summer or winter. He has no regular pillow except that which is temporarily made up by himself out of his own private possessions. These latter, however, are next to nothing: for they are kesa (kaṣāya in Sanskrit) and koromo (priestly robe), a few books, a razor, and a set of bowls, all of which are put up in a box about thirteen by ten by three and a half inches. In travelling this box is carried in front supported with a sash about the neck. The entire property thus moves with the owner. "One dress and one bowl, under a tree and on a stone" was the graphical description of the monkish life in India. Compared with this, the modern Zen monk must be said to be abundantly supplied. Still, his wants are reduced to a minimum, and no one can fail to lead a simple, perhaps the simplest, life if he models his after that of the Zen monk.

The desire to possess is considered by Buddhism to be one of the worst passions mortals are apt to be obsessed with. What, in fact, causes so much misery in the world is a strong impulse of acquisitiveness. As power is desired, the strong always tyrannize over the weak: as wealth is coveted, the rich and poor are always crossing their swords of bitter enmity. International wars rage,

---

[5] This historical temple was unfortunately destroyed by the earthquake of 1923, with many other buildings.

social unrest ever goes on, unless the impulse to have and hold is completely uprooted. Cannot a society be reorganized upon an entirely different basis from what we have been used to seeing from the beginning of history? Cannot we ever hope to stop the amassing of wealth and the wielding of power merely from the desire for individual or national aggrandizement? Despairing of the utter irrationality of human affairs, the Buddhist monks have gone to the other extreme and cut themselves off even from reasonable and perfectly innocent enjoyments of life. However, the Zen ideal of putting up the monk's belongings in a tiny box a little larger than a foot square and three inches high is their mute protest, though so far ineffective, against the present order of society.

In this connection it will be of interest to read the admonition left by Daitō the National Teacher (1282–1337) to his disciples. He was the founder of Daitokuji, Kyoto, in 1326, and is said to have spent about one-third of his life, which was not a very long one, among the lowest layers of society under the Gojō bridge, begging his food, doing all kinds of menial work, and despised by the so-called respectable people of the world. He did not care for the magnificence of a prosperous and highly honored temple life led by most Buddhist priests of those days, nor did he think much of those pious and sanctimonious deeds that only testify to the superficiality of their religious life. He was for the plainest living and the highest thinking. The admonition reads:

"O you, monks, who are here in this mountain monastery, remember that you are gathered for the sake of the religion and not for the sake of clothes and food. As long as you have shoulders [that is, the body] you shall have clothes to wear, and as long as you have a mouth you shall have food to eat. Be ever mindful, throughout the twelve hours of the day, to apply yourselves to the study of the Unthinkable. Time passes like an arrow; never let your minds be disturbed by worldly cares. Ever, ever be on the lookout. After my wandering away, some of you may have fine temples in prosperous conditions, towers and halls and holy books all decorated in gold and silver, and devotees may noisily crowd into the grounds; some may pass hours in reading the sutras and reciting the dharanis, and, sitting long in contemplation, may not give themselves up to sleep; they may, eating once a day and observing the fast days, and throughout the six periods of the day, practice all the religious deeds.

"Even when they are thus devoted to the cause, if their thoughts are not really dwelling on the mysterious and intransmissible Way of the Buddhas and Fathers, they may yet come to ignore the law of moral causation, ending in a complete downfall of the true religion. Such all belong to the family of evil spirits; however long my departure from the world may be, they are not to be called my descendants. Let, however, there be just one individual, who may be living in the wilderness in a hut thatched with one bundle of straw and passing his days by eating the roots of wild vegetables cooked in a pot with broken legs; but if he single-mindedly applies himself to the study of his own [spiritual] affairs, he is the very one who has a daily interview with me and knows how to be grateful for his life. Who should ever despise such a one? O monks, be diligent, be diligent."[6]

In India the Buddhist monks never eat in the afternoon. They properly eat only once a day, as their breakfast is no breakfast in the sense that an English or American breakfast is. So the Zen monks, too, are not supposed to have any meal in the evening. But the climatic necessity in China and Japan could not be ignored, and they have an evening meal after a fashion; but to ease their conscience it is called "medicinal food (yüeh-shih))." The breakfast, which is taken very early in the morning, while it is still dark, consists of rice gruel and pickled vegetables (tsukemono).

The principal meal at 10 A.M. is rice (or rice mixed with barley), vegetable soup, and pickles. In the afternoon, at four, they have only what is left of the dinner—no special cooking is done. Unless they are invited out or given an extra treat at the house of some generous patrons, their meals are such as above described, year in, year out. Poverty and simplicity are their motto.

One ought not, however, to consider asceticism the ideal life of Zen. So far as the ultimate signification of Zen is concerned, it is neither asceticism nor any other ethical system. If it appears to advocate either the doctrine of suppression or that of detachment, the supposed fact is merely on the surface; for Zen as a school of Buddhism more or less inherits the odium of a Hindu discipline.

[6] In those monasteries which are connected in some way with the author of this admonition, it is read or rather chanted before a lecture or *teishō* begins.

The central idea, however, of the monkish life is not to waste, but to make the best possible use of things as they are given us, which is also the spirit of Buddhism in general. In truth the intellect, imagination, and all other mental faculties as well as the physical objects surrounding us, our own bodies not excepted, are given us for the unfolding and enhancing of the highest powers possessed by us as spiritual entities and not merely for the gratification of our individual whims or desires, which are sure to conflict with and injure the interests and rights asserted by others. These are some of the inner ideas underlying the simplicity and poverty of the monkish life.

III

As there is something to be regarded as peculiarly Zen in the table manners of the monks, some description of them will be given here.

At mealtimes a gong is struck, and the monks come out of the Meditation Hall in procession carrying their own bowls to the dining room. The low tables are laid there all bare. They sit when the leader rings the bell. The bowls are set—which, by the way, are made of wood or paper and well lacquered. A set consists of four or five dishes, one inside the other. As they are arranging the dishes and the waiting monks go around to serve the soup and rice, the *Prajñāpāramitā-hṛidaya-sūtra*[7] is recited, followed by the "Five Meditations" on eating, which are: "First, of what worth am I? Whence is this offering? Secondly, accepting this offering, I must reflect on the deficiency of my virtue. Thirdly, to guard over my own heart, to keep myself away from faults such as covetousness,

---

[7] I must not forget to mention that after the reading of the *Hṛidaya-sūtra* the following names of the Buddhas and others are invoked: 1. Vairocana-Buddha in his immaculate Body of the Law; 2. Vairocana-Buddha in his perfect Body of Bliss; 3. Sākyamuni-Buddha in his infinite manifestations as Body of Transformation; 4. Maitreya-Buddha, who is to come in some future time; 5. All the Buddhas past, present, and future in the ten quarters of the world; 6. The great holy Bodhisattva Mañjuśri; 7. The great morally perfect Bodhisattva Samantabhadra; 8. The great compassionate Bodhisattva Avalokiteśvara; 9. All the venerable Bodhisattva-mahāsattvas; and 10. Mahāprajñāpāramitā.

etc.—this is the essential thing. Fourthly, this food is taken as good medicine in order to keep the body in a healthy condition. Fifthly, to ensure spiritual attainment this food is accepted." After these "Meditations" they continue to think about the essence of Buddhism, "The first mouthful is to cut off all evils; the second mouthful is to practice every good; the third mouthful is to save all sentient beings so that everybody will finally attain to Buddhahood."

They are now ready to take up their chopsticks, but before they actually partake of the sumptuous dinner, the demons or spirits living somewhere in the triple world are remembered; and each monk taking out about seven grains from his own bowl offers them to those unseen, saying, "O you, demons and other spiritual beings, I now offer this to you, and may this food fill up the ten quarters of the world and all the demons and other spiritual beings be fed therewith."

While eating quietude prevails. The dishes are handled noiselessly, no word is uttered, no conversation goes on. Eating is a serious affair with them. When a second bowl of rice is wanted, the monk folds his hands before him. The monk waiter notices it, comes round with the rice receptacle called *ohachi*, and sits before the hungry one. The latter takes up his bowl and lightly passes his hand around the bottom before it is handed to the waiter. He means by this to take off whatever dirt that may have attached itself to the bowl and that is likely to soil the hand of the serving monk. While the bowl is filled, the eater keeps his hands folded. If he does not want so much, he gently rubs the hands against each other, which means "Enough, thank you."

Nothing is to be left when the meal is finished. The monks eat up all that is served them, "gathering up of the fragments that remain." This is their religion. After a fourth helping of rice, the meal generally comes to an end. The leader claps the wooden blocks and the serving monks bring hot water. Each diner fills the largest bowl with it, and in it all the smaller dishes are neatly washed, and wiped with a piece of cloth which each monk carries. Now a wooden pail goes around to receive the slops.[8] Each monk

---

[8] When the slop-basin goes around, spiritual beings are again remembered: "This water in which my bowls were washed tastes like nectar from heaven. I now offer this to the numerous spirits of the world: may they all be filled and satisfied! *Om, Ma-ku-ra-sai* (in Chinese, *mo-hsui-lo-hsi*) *Svāhā!*"

gathers up his dishes and wraps them up once more, saying, "I have now finished eating, and my physical body is well nourished: I feel as if my will power would shake the ten quarters of the world and dominate over the past, present, and future: turning both the cause and the effect over to the general welfare of all beings, may we all unfailingly gain in powers miraculous!" The tables are now empty as before except those rice grains offered to the spiritual beings at the beginning of the meal. The wooden blocks are clapped, thanks are given, and the monks leave the room in orderly procession as they came in.

IV

Their industry is proverbial. When the day is not set for study at home, they are generally seen, soon after breakfast, about half-past five in summer and about half-past six in winter, out in the monastery grounds, or in the neighboring villages for begging, or tilling the farm attached to the *zendō*. They keep the monastery, inside as well as outside, in perfect order. When we sometimes say, "This is like a Zen monastery," it means that the place is kept in the neatest possible order. When begging they go miles away. Commonly, attached to a *zendō* there are some patrons whose houses the monks regularly visit and get a supply of rice or vegetables. We often see them along the country road pulling a cart loaded with pumpkins or potatoes. They work as hard as ordinary laborers. They sometimes go to the woods to gather kindling or fuel. They know something of agriculture, too. As they have to support themselves in these ways, they are at once farmers, laborers, and skilled workmen. For they often build their own Meditation Hall under the direction of an architect.

These monks are a self-governing body. They have their own cooks, proctors, managers, sextons, masters of ceremony, etc. In the days of Hyakujō there seem to have been ten such offices, though the details are not now known, due to the loss of his *Regulations*. While the master or teacher of a *zendō* is its soul, he is not directly concerned with its government. This is left to the senior members of the community, whose characters have been tested through many years of discipline. When the principles of Zen are discussed, one may marvel at their deep and subtle metaphysics, if there are any, and imagine what a serious, pale-faced, head-drooping, and world-forgetting group of thinkers these monks are. But in their actual life they are, after all, common mortals engaged in menial work, but they are cheerful, cracking jokes, willing to help one another, and despising no work which is usually considered low and not worthy of an educated hand. The spirit of Hyakujō is ever manifest among them.

It was not only the monks' that worked but the master himself shared their labor. This was according to Hyakujō to cooperate in and equalize the work among all concerned without distinction of rank. Therefore the master together with his disciples tilled the farm, planted trees, weeded the garden, picked tea-leaves, and was engaged in all other kinds of manual work. Making use of such opportunities, he gave them practical lessons in the study of Zen, and the disciples, too, did not fail to appreciate his instructions.

When Jōshū was sweeping the courtyard a monk asked him, "How does a speck of dust come into this holy ground?" To this Jōshū answered, "Here comes another!" On another occasion, when the master was found again sweeping the ground, Ryū, a minister of state, paid a visit to the temple and said to the master gardener, "How is it that a great wise man like you has to sweep off the dust?"

"It comes from the outside,"[9] replied Jōshū.

When Nansen was working outdoors with his monks, Jōshū, who was told to watch over a fire, suddenly cried out: "Fire! Fire!" The alarm made all the monks rush back to the dormitory hall. Seeing this, Jōshū closed the gate and declared, 'If you could say a word the doors would be opened." The monks did not know what to say. Nansen, the master, however, threw the key into the hall through a window. Thereupon Jōshū flung open the gate.

While working on the farm a monk happened to cut an earthworm in twain with his spade, whereupon he asked the master Chōsha, "The earthworm is cut in twain and both parts are still wriggling: in which of them is the Buddha-nature present?" The master said, "Have no illusion!" But the monk insisted, "I cannot help this wriggling, sir." "Don't you see that fire and air elements have not yet been dispersed?"

[9] This question of dust reminds one of Berkeley's remark, "We have just raised a dust and then complain we cannot see."

When Shiko and Shōkō were out gardening, a similar thing happened, and Shōkō asked the master concerning the real life of the earthworm. Without answering him, the master took up the rake, first struck the one end of the worm, then the other, and finally the space between the two. He then threw down the rake and went away.

One day Ōbaku was weeding with a hoe, and seeing Rinzai without one, asked, "How is it that you do not carry any hoe?"

Answered Rinzai, "Somebody has carried it away, sir."

Thereupon, Ōbaku told him to come forward as he wanted to discuss the matter with him.

Rinzai stepped forward.

Said Ōbaku, lifting his hoe, "Only this, but all the world's unable to hold it up."

Rinzai took the hoe away from the master and lifted it up, saying, "How is it that it is now in my own hands?"

Ōbaku remarked, "Here is a man doing a great piece of work today!" He then returned to his own room.

Another day, observing Rinzai resting on a hoe, Ōbaku said to him, "Are you tired?"

Rinzai replied, "I have not even lifted my hoe, and how should I be tired?"

Ōbaku then struck him. Rinzai, however, snatching the stick away from the master, pushed him down. Ōbaku called out to the Ino[10] (*karmadāna*) to help him up from the ground. The Ino responded to the call and helped the master up, saying, "Why do you permit this crazy fellow's rudeness?" As soon as the master was again on his feet, he struck the Ino. Rinzai then began to dig the earth and made this announcement, "In other places they cremate, but here you will all be buried alive."

The story of Isan and Kyōzan, while they were out picking tea-leaves, has already been told in one of the preceding essays. Zen history, indeed, abounds with such incidents as here referred to, showing how the masters try to discipline their pupils on every possible occasion. The events of daily life, manifestly trivial on the surface, thus handled by the masters, grow full of signification. At any rate all these *mondō* most eloquently illustrate the whole trend of the monastery life in olden days, where the spirit of work and

---

[10] The office of managing director in the monastery.

service was so thoroughly and harmoniously blended with the high thinking on matters deeply spiritual.

V

The monks thus develop their faculties all round. They receive no literary—that is, formal—education usually gained from books and abstract instruction; their discipline and knowledge are practical and efficient. The basic principle of the *zendō* life is "learning by doing." They despise the so-called soft education, which is like those predigested foods meant for the convalescent. When a lioness gives birth to her cubs, it is proverbially believed that after three days she will push them down over a deep precipice to see if they can climb back to her. Those that fail this trial are not worthy of her race. Something of this kind is aimed at by the Zen master, who will treat the monks with every manner of seeming unkindness. The monks have not enough clothes to put on, not enough food to indulge in, not enough time to sleep, and, to cap these, they have plenty of work to do, menial as well as spiritual.

The outer needs and the inward aspirations, if they work on harmoniously and ideally, will finally end in producing fine characters well trained in Zen as well as in the real things of life. This unique system of education, which is still going on at every *zendō*, is not so well known among the laity even in this country. And then the merciless tides of modern commercialism leave no corner uninvaded. Before long the solitary island of Zen may be found buried, as is everything else, under the waves of sordid materialism. The monks themselves are beginning not to understand the great spirit of the successive masters. Though there are some aspects in the monastic education which may be improved, its highly religious and reverential feeling must be preserved if Zen is to remain alive.

Theoretically, the philosophy of Zen transcends the whole range of discursive understanding, and is not bound by rules of antithesis. But to say this is placing Zen on very slippery ground, and there are many who fail to walk erect. When there is a fall, the result is sometimes disastrous. Like some of the medieval mystics, Zen students may turn into libertines, losing control over themselves. History is a witness to this, and psychology can readily explain the process of such degeneration. Therefore, says a Zen master, "Let one's ideal rise as high as the crown of Vairocana (the highest divinity), while his life may be so full of humility as to make him prostrate before an infant's feet." Which is to say, "If any man desire to be first, the same shall be last of all, and servant of all." Therefore, the monastery life is minutely regulated and the details are enforced in strict obedience to the spirit already referred to. Humility, poverty, and inner sanctification—these ideals of Zen are what saves Zen from sinking into the level of the medieval antinomians. Thus we can see how the *zendō* discipline plays a great part in the teachings of Zen and their practical application to our daily life.

When Tanka stopped at Erinji of the Capital, the cold was so severe that he took one of the Buddha-images enshrined there and made a fire for himself. The keeper of the shrine, seeing this, was greatly exercised.

"How dare you burn up our wooden Buddha?"

Said Tanka, who was looking for something in the ashes with his stick, "I am gathering the holy *śarīra*[11] in the ashes."

"How," said the keeper, "do you expect to find *śarīras* by burning a wooden Buddha?"

"If there are no *śarīras* to be found in it, may I have the remaining two Buddhas for my fire?" retorted Tanka.

The shrine keeper later lost his eyebrows for remonstrating against the apparent impiety of Tanka, while the Buddha's wrath never was visited upon the latter.

Though one may doubt its historical occurrence, the story is a notable one, and all the Zen masters agree as to the higher spiritual attainment of the Buddha-desecrating Tanka. When later a monk asked a master about Tanka's burning a Buddha's statue, the master said:

"When cold we sit around the hearth of fire."

"Was he then at fault or not?"

"When hot, we go to the bamboo grove by the stream," was the answer.

I quote another comment on the story, as this is one of the most significant subjects in the study of Zen. When Suibi Mugaku, a

---

[11] *Shê-lî* is some indestructible substance, generally in pebble form, supposedly found in the body of a saint when it is cremated.

disciple of Tanka, was making offerings to the Arhats, probably carved in wood, a monk came up and asked, "Tanka burned a wooden Buddha and how is it that you make offerings to these Arhats?"

The master said, "Even when it was burned, it could not be burned up; and as to my making offerings, I do as I please."

"When these offerings are made to the Arhats, would they come to receive them, or not?"

"Do you eat every day, or not?" the master demanded. As the monk remained silent, the master declared, "Intelligent ones are hard to find!"

Whatever the merit of Tanka from the purely Zen point of view, there is no doubt that such deeds as his are to be regarded as highly sacrilegious and to be avoided by all pious Buddhists. Those who have not yet gained a thorough understanding of Zen may go all lengths to commit every manner of crime and excess, even in the name of Zen. For this reason the regulations of the monastery are rigid that pride of heart may depart and the cup of humility be drunk to the dregs.

When Shukō of the Ming dynasty was writing a book on the ten laudable deeds of a monk, one of those high-spirited, self-assertive fellows came to him, saying, "What is the use of writing such a book when in Zen there is not an atom of a thing to be called laudable or not?" The writer answered, "The five aggregates (*skandha*) are entangling, and the four elements (*mahābhūta*) grow rampant, and how can you say there are no evils?" The monk still insisted, "The four elements are ultimately empty and the five aggregates have no reality whatever." Shukō, giving him a slap on his face, said, "So many are merely learned; you are not the real thing yet; give me another answer." But the monk made no answer and went off filled with anger. "There," said the master, "why don't you wipe the dirt off your own face?" In the study of Zen the power of an all-illuminating insight must go hand in hand with a deep sense of humility and meekness of heart.

Let me cite, as one instance in teaching humility, the experience which a new applicant monk is made to go through when he first approaches the Meditation Hall. The applicant may come duly equipped with certificates of his qualifications and with his monkish paraphernalia consisting of such articles as are already mentioned, but the *zendō* authorities do not admit him into their company at once. Generally, some formal excuse will be told him: that their establishment is not rich enough to take in another monk, or that the Hall is already too full. If the applicant quietly retires with this, there will be no place for him anywhere, not only in the *zendō* of his choice, but in any other throughout the land. For he will meet similar refusals everywhere. If he wants to study Zen at all, he is not to be discouraged by such excuses.

The persistent applicant will now seat himself at the entrance porch. Putting his head down on the box which he carries in front of him, he calmly waits there. Sometimes a strong morning or evening sun shines right over the recumbent monk on the porch, but he keeps on in this attitude without stirring. When the dinner hour comes he asks to be admitted and fed. This is granted, for no Buddhist monasteries will refuse food and lodging to a travelling monk. After eating, however, the novice goes out again on the porch, and continues his petition for admittance. No attention will be paid him until the evening, when he asks for lodging. This being granted as before, he takes off his travelling sandals, washes his feet, and is ushered into a room reserved for such purposes. But most frequently he finds no bedding there, for a Zen monk is supposed to pass his night in deep meditation. He sits upright all night, evidently absorbed in the contemplation of a *kōan*. On the following morning he goes out as on the previous day to the entrance hall and resumes the same posture as before, expressive of an urgent desire to be admitted. This may go on for three to five or even seven days. The patience and humility of the new applicant are tried thus hard until finally he will be taken in by the authorities, who, apparently moved by his earnestness and perseverance, will try somehow to accommodate him.

This procedure is growing somewhat a formal affair, but in olden days, when things were not yet settled into a mere routine, the applicant monk had quite a hard time, for he would actually be driven out of the monastery by force. We read in the biographies of the old masters of still harder treatments mercilessly dealt out to them.

The Meditation Hall is regulated with militaristic severity and precision to cultivate such virtues as humility, obedience, simplicity, and earnestness in the monkish hearts that are ever prone to follow indiscriminately the extraordinary examples of the old masters, or that are liable to put in practice in a crude and undigested manner the high doctrines of a Śūnyatā philosophy such as is expounded in the Prajñāpāramitā class of Mahayana literature.

A partial glimpse of such life we have already gained in the description of the table manners as above.

VI

There is a period in the monastic life exclusively set apart for mental discipline, and not interrupted by any manual labor except such as is absolutely needed. It is known as great *sesshin* (*chieh-hsin*)[12] and lasts a week, taking place once a month during the seasons called the "Summer Sojourn" and the "Winter Sojourn." The summer sojourn begins in April and ends in August, while the winter one begins in October and ends in February. *Sesshin* means "collecting or concentrating the mind." While this period is lasting the monks are confined at the *zendō*, get up earlier than usual, and sit further into the night. There is a kind of lecture every day during the period. Textbooks are used, the most popular of which are the *Hekigan-shū* and *Rinzai-roku*, these two being considered the most fundamental books of the Rinzai school. The *Rinzai-roku* is a collection of sermons and sayings of the founder of the Rinzai Zen sect. The *Hekigan-shū*, as has been noted elsewhere, is a collection of one hundred Zen "cases" of "themes" with critical annotations and poetical comments. It goes without saying that there are many other books used for the occasion. To an ordinary reader, such books generally are a sort of *obscurum per obscurius*. After listening to a series of lectures he is left in the lurch as ever. Not necessarily that they are too abstruse, but that the reader is still wanting in insight into the truth of Zen.

The lecture is a solemn affair. Its beginning is announced by a striking of the bell. As the master appears in the hall what is known as *teishō* (*t'i-ch'ang*) [13] takes place. While the master is offering to

[12] It is not known how early this *sesshin* originated in the history of the *zendō*. It is not mentioned in Hyakujo's "Regulations." Most probably it was not started in China, but in Japan from the time of Hakuin. The sojourn period generally being a "stay-at-home" season, the monks do not travel, but practice *sesshin* and devote themselves to the study of Zen; but in the week specially set up as such, the study is pursued with the utmost vigor.

[13] *Tei* means "to carry in hand," "to show forth," or "manifest," and *shō* "to recite." Thus by a *teishō* the old master is revived before the congregation and his discourses are more or less vividly presented to view. It is not merely explaining or commenting on the text.

the Buddha and to his departed master, the monks recite a short
dharaṇī-sūtra called *Daihishu*,[14] which means "the *dharaṇī* of great
compassion." Being a Chinese transliteration of the Sanskrit original, mere recitation of the sūtra does not give any intelligent sense.
Probably the sense is not essential in this case; the assurance is
sufficient that it contains something auspicious and conducive to
spiritual welfare. What is more significant is the way in which it
is recited. Its monotone, punctuated with a wooden timekeeper
known as *mokugyo* (Wooden Fish), prepares the mind of the audience for the coming event. After the *dharaṇī*, which is recited
three times, the monks read in chorus generally the exhortatory
sermon left by the founder of the monastery. In some places
Hakuin's "Song of Zazen" is chanted. The following are translations
of Hakuin and of Musō Kokushi,[15] whose last exhortatory sermon
is one of the most popular.

Musō Kokushi's Exhortatory Sermon

I have three kinds of disciples: those who, vigorously shaking off all
entangling circumstances, and with singleness of thought apply themselves to the study of their own [spiritual] affairs, are of the first class.
Those who are not so single-minded in the study, but, scattering their
attention, are fond of book learning, are of the second. Those who, cover-
ing their own spiritual brightness, are only occupied with the dribblings
of the Buddhas and Fathers, are called the lowest. As for those whose
minds are intoxicated by secular literature and who are engaged in
establishing themselves as men of letters, they are simply laymen with
shaven heads, they do not belong even to the lowest. As regards those
who think only of indulging in food and sleep and give themselves up
to indolence—could such be called members of the Black Robe? They

---

[14] *Dharaṇī* is a Sanskrit term which comes from the root *dhṛi*, meaning "to
hold." In Buddhist phraseology, it is a collection, sometimes short, sometimes long, of exclamatory sentences which are not translated into other
languages. It is not therefore at all intelligible when it is read by the monks
as it is done in the Chinese and Japanese monasteries. But it is supposed to
"hold" in it in some mysterious way something that is most meritorious and
has the power to keep evil ones away. Later, *dharaṇī* and *mantram* have
grown confused with one another.

[15] The founder of Tenryūji, Kyoto. He is known as "Teacher of Seven Em-
perors" (1274–1361).

are truly, as designated by an old master, clothes racks and rice bags. Inasmuch as they are not monks, they ought not to be permitted to call themselves my disciples and enter the monastery and sub-temples as well; even a temporary sojourn is to be prohibited, not to speak of their application as student monks. When an old man like myself speaks thus, you may think he is lacking in all-embracing love, but the main thing is to let them know of their own faults, and, reforming themselves, to become growing plants in the patriarchal gardens.

Hakuin's Song of Meditation

All sentient beings are from the very beginning the Buddhas:
It is like ice and water;
Apart from water no ice can exist.
Outside sentient beings, where do we seek the Buddhas?
Not knowing how near the Truth is,
People seek it far away,—what a pity!
They are like him who, in the midst of water,
Cries in thirst so imploringly;
They are like the son of a rich man
Who wandered away among the poor.
The reason why we transmigrate through the six worlds
Is because we are lost in the darkness of Ignorance;
Going astray further and further in the darkness,
When are we able to get away from birth-and-death?

As regards the Meditation practiced in the Mahayana,
We have no words to praise it fully.
The Virtues of Perfection such as charity and morality,
And the invocation of the Buddha's name, confession, and ascetic
    discipline,
And many other good deeds of merit,—
All these issue from the practice of Meditation.
Even those who have practiced it for one sitting
Will see all their evil karma wiped clean;
Nowhere will they find the evil paths,
But the Pure Land will be near at hand.
With a reverential heart, let them to this Truth
Listen even for once,
And let them praise it, and gladly embrace it,
And they will surely be blessed most infinitely.

For such as, reflecting within themselves,
Testify to the truth of Self-nature,
To the truth that Self-nature is no-nature,
They have really gone beyond the ken of sophistry.
For them opens the gate of the oneness of cause and effect,
And straight runs the path of non-duality and non-trinity.
Abiding with the Not-particular in particulars,
Whether going or returning, they remain for ever unmoved;
Taking hold of the Not-thought in thoughts,
In every act of theirs they hear the voice of the truth.
How boundless the sky of *samādhi* unfettered!
How transparent the perfect moonlight of the Fourfold Wisdom!
At that moment what do they lack?
As the Truth eternally calm reveals itself to them,
This very earth is the Lotus Land of Purity,
And this body is the body of the Buddha.

The lecture lasts about an hour. It is quite different from an ordinary lecture on a religious subject. Nothing is explained, no arguments are set forward, no apologetics, no reasonings. The master is supposed simply to reproduce in words what is treated in the textbook before him. At the end, the Four Great Vows are repeated three times, and the monks retire to their quarters. The vows are:

However innumerable sentient beings are, I vow to save them all;
However inexhaustible our evil passions are, I vow to exterminate them;
However immeasurable the holy doctrines are, I vow to study them;
However inaccessible the path of Buddhas is, I vow to attain it.

VII

During the *sesshin,* they have, besides lectures, what is known as *sanzen.*[16] To do *sanzen* is to go to the master and present one's views on a *kōan* for his critical examination. On those days when a special *sesshin* is not going on, the interviews will probably take place twice a day, but during the period of thought collection—

16 *San-chan* literally means "to attend or study Zen."

which is the meaning of *sesshin*—the monk is to see the master four or five times a day. This seeing the master does not take place openly,[17] for each monk is required to come up individually to the master's room, where the interview goes on in a most formal and solemn manner. When the monk is about to cross the threshold of the master's room, he makes three bows, prostrating himself on the floor. He now enters the room keeping his hands folded, palm to palm, before the chest, and when he comes near the master he sits down and makes another bow. Once in the room, all worldly convention is disregarded. If absolutely necessary from the Zen point of view, blows may be exchanged. To make manifest the truth of Zen with all sincerity of heart is the sole consideration here, and everything else receives only a subordinate attention. Hence this elaborate formalism. The presentation over, the monk retires in the same way as before. One *sanzen* for over thirty monks will occupy more than one hour and a half, and this is the time of the utmost tension for the master, too. To have this four or five times a day must be a kind of ordeal for the master himself, if he is not of robust health.

An absolute confidence is placed in the master as far as his understanding of Zen goes. But if the monk has sufficient reason to doubt the master's ability, he may settle it personally with him at the time of *sanzen*. This presentation of views, therefore, is no idle play for either of the parties concerned. It is indeed a most serious affair, and because it is so the discipline of Zen has a great moral value outside its philosophy. How serious this is may be guessed from the famous interview between the Venerable Shōju and Hakuin, father of modern Zen in Japan.

One summer evening when Hakuin presented his view to the old master, who was cooling himself on the veranda, the master said, "Stuff and nonsense." Hakuin echoed, loudly and rather satirically, "Stuff and nonsense!" Thereupon the master seized him, struck him several times, and finally pushed him off the veranda. It was soon after the rainy weather, and poor Hakuin rolled in the mud and water. Having recovered himself after a while, he

---

[17] Formerly, this was an open affair, and all the *mondō* (askings and answerings) took place before the whole congregation, as is stated in the "Regulations" of Hyakujō. But, later, undesirable results followed, such as mere formalism, imitations, and other empty nonsenses. In modern Zen, therefore, all *sanzen* is private, except on formal occasions.

came up and reverentially bowed to the teacher, who then remarked again, "O you, denizen of the dark cavern!"

Another day Hakuin felt that the master did not know how deep
his intuition of Zen was and decided to have a settlement with him
anyhow. As soon as the time came Hakuin entered the master's
room and soon exhausted all his ingenuity in contest with him. He
had made up his mind not to give way an inch of ground this time.
The master was furious, and finally taking hold of Hakuin gave
him several slaps and forced him off the porch again. He fell several
feet at the foot of the stone wall, where he remained for a while
almost senseless. The master looked down and heartily laughed at
the poor fellow. This brought Hakuin back to consciousness. He
came up again all in perspiration. The master, however, did not
release him yet and stigmatized him as ever with, "O you, denizen
of the dark cavern!"

Hakuin grew desperate and thought of leaving the old master
altogether. When one day he was going about begging in the
village, a certain incident[18] made him all of a sudden open his
mind's eye to the truth of Zen, hitherto completely shut off from
him. His joy knew no bounds and he came back in an exalted state
of mind. Even before he crossed the front gate, the master recognized him and beckoned to him, saying, "What good news have
you brought back today? Come right in, quick, quick!" Hakuin
told him of his experience. The master tenderly stroked him on
the back and said, "You have it now, you have it now." After this,
Hakuin was never called names.

Such was the training the father of modern Japanese Zen had to
go through. How terrible the old Shōju seems when pushing
Hakuin off the stone wall! But how motherly when the disciple,
after so much ill-treatment, finally came out triumphantly! There
is nothing lukewarm in Zen. It expects one to penetrate into the
very depths of truth, and the truth can never be grasped until one

[18] While thus going around, he came to a house where an old woman refused to give him any rice; he continued to stand in front of it, looking as
if he heard nothing. His mind was intensely concentrated on the subject which
concerned him most. The woman got angry at his apparent persistence and
she struck him with the broom she was using and told him to depart at once.
The heavy broom smashed his large monkish hat and knocked him to the
ground. He lay there for a while, but when he came to his senses everything
became clear and transparent to him.

comes back to one's native nakedness shorn of all trumperies, intellectual or otherwise. Each slap dealt by Shōju stripped Hakuin of his insincerities. We are each living under so many casings which have nothing to do with our inmost self. To reach the latter, and to gain the real knowledge of ourselves, the masters resort to methods seemingly inhuman. In this case, however, there must be absolute faith in the truth of Zen and in the master's perfect understanding of it. The lack of this faith will also mean the same in one's own spiritual possibilities. So exclaims Rinzai: "O you, men of little faith! How can you ever expect to fathom the depths of the ocean of Zen?"

VIII

In the life of the *zendō* there is no fixed period of graduation as in a school education. With some, graduation may not take place even after his twenty years of boarding there. But with ordinary abilities and a large amount of perseverance and indefatigability, one is able to probe into every intricacy of the teachings of Zen within a space of ten years.

To practice the principle of Zen, however, in every moment of life—that is, to grow fully saturated with its spirit—is another question. One life indeed may be too short for this, for it is said that even Śākyamuni and Maitreya are yet in the midst of self-training.

To be a perfectly qualified master, a mere understanding of the truth of Zen is not sufficient. One must go through a period which is known as "the long maturing of the sacred womb." The term must have originally come from Taoism; nowadays it means, broadly speaking, living a life harmonious with the understanding. Under the direction of a master, a monk may finally attain to a thorough knowledge of all the mysteries of Zen; but this is more or less intellectual, though in the highest possible sense. The monk's life, in and out, must grow in perfect unison with this attainment. To do this a further training is necessary, for what he has gained at the *zendō* is after all the pointing of the direction where his utmost efforts have to be put forth. But it is not at all imperative now to remain in the *zendō*. On the contrary, his intellectual attainments must be further put on trial by coming into actual contact with the world. There are no prescribed rules for this "maturing." Each one acts on his own discretion in the accidental circumstances in which he may find himself. He may retire into the mountains and live as a solitary hermit, or he may come out into the "market" and be an active participant in the affairs of the world. The sixth patriarch is said to have been living among the mountaineers for fifteen years after leaving the fifth patriarch. He was not known in the world until he came out to a lecture by Inshū. Chū, the National Teacher, spent forty years in Nan-yang and did not show himself in the capital. But his holy life became known far and near, and at the urgent request of the Emperor he finally left his hut. Isan spent several years in the wilderness, living on nuts and befriending monkeys and deer. However, he was found out, big monasteries were built about his anchorage, and he became master of 1,500 monks. Kanzan, the founder of Myōshinji, Kyoto, retired in Mino Province, and worked as day-laborer for the villagers. Nobody recognized him until one day an accident brought out his identity and the court insisted on his founding a monastery in the capital. Hakuin became the keeper of a deserted temple in Suruga which was his sole heritage in the world. We can picture to ourselves the scene of its dilapidations when we read this: "There were no roofs and the stars shone through at night. Nor was there any floor. On rainy days it was necessary to put on a rain-hat and a pair of high *geta* when anything took place in the main part of the temple. All the property attached to it was in the hands of the creditors, and the priestly belongings were mortgaged to the merchants." This was the beginning of Hakuin's career.

There are many other notable ones; the history of Zen abounds with such instances. The idea, however, is not to practice asceticism, it is the "maturing," as they have properly designated, of one's moral character. Many serpents and adders are waiting at the porch, and if one fails to trample them down effectively they raise their heads again and the whole edifice of moral culture built up in vision may collapse even in one day. Antinomianism is also the pitfall for Zen followers against which a constant vigil is needed.

IX

In some respects, no doubt, the kind of education prevailing at the *zendō* is behind the times. But its guiding principles such as simplification of life, not wasting a moment idly, self-independence, and what they call "secret virtue," are sound for all ages. Especially this last is one of the most characteristic features of Zen discipline. "Secret virtue" means practicing goodness without any thought of recognition, neither by others nor by oneself. The Christians may call this the doing of "Thy Will." I plunge into the water to save a child from drowning. What was to be done was done. No more thought is needed; I walk away not turning back. A cloud passes, and the sky is as blue and as broad as ever. Zen calls it a "deed without merit," and compares it to the work of a man who tried to fill a well with snow.

This is the psychological aspect of "secret virtue." Religiously considered, it is to regard and use the world reverentially and gratefully, feeling as if one were carrying on one's shoulders all the sins of the world. An old woman asked Jōshū, "I belong to the sex that is hindered in five ways from attaining Buddhahood; and how can I ever be delivered from them?" Answered the master, "O let all other people be born in heaven and let me, this humble self, alone continue suffering in this ocean of pain!" This is the spirit of the true Zen student. There is another story illustrating the same spirit of long-suffering. The district of Jōshū[19] where this Zen master's monastery was situated, and where he got his popular title, was noted for a fine stone bridge. A monk one day came up to the master and asked, "We hear so much of the splendid stone bridge of Jōshū, but what I see here is nothing but a miserable old log bridge."

Jōshū retorted, "You only see the log bridge, and fail to see the stone bridge of Jōshū."

"What then is the stone bridge?"

"Horses go over it, asses go over it," Jōshū replied.

This seems to be but a trivial talk about a bridge, but considered from the innermost way of looking at such cases, there is a great deal of truth touching the center of one's spiritual life. We may inquire as to the kind of bridge represented here. Was Jōshū speaking only of a bridge in his monastery? Let each one of us reflect and see if we are not in possession of "a bridge" over which pass not only horses and asses, men and women, carts heavy and light, but the entire universe complete with its insanities and morbidities; a bridge which is not only thus passed over but quite

[19] The masters are often known by the name of the monastery or by the district in which the monastery is located.

frequently trampled on and even cursed at but which suffers patiently and uncomplainingly.

But this spirit of self-suffering is not to be understood in the Christian sense that man must spend all his time in prayer and mortification for the absolution of sin. A Zen monk has no desire to be absolved from sin, for this has still the idea of the self, the ego, and Zen is free from egotism. The Zen monk wishes to save the world from the misery of Ignorance, and as to his own "sin" he lets it take care of itself, as he knows it is not inherent in his nature. For this reason it is possible for him to be one of those who are described as "they that weep as though they wept not; and they that rejoice as though they rejoiced not; and they that buy as though they possessed not; and they that use this world as not abusing it."

Says Christ, "When thou doest alms, let not thy left hand know what thy right hand doeth; that thine alms may be in secret." This is a "secret virtue" of Buddhism. But when He goes on to say that "thy Father who seeth in secret shall recompense thee," there we see a deep cleavage between Buddhism and Christianity. So long as there is any thought of anybody, whether he be God or Devil, knowing of your doings, Zen would say, "You are not yet one of us." Deeds that are accompanied by such thought are not "merit-less deeds," but full of tracks and shadows. If a Spirit is tracing you, he will in no time get hold of you and make you account for what you have done. The perfect garment shows no seams, inside and outside; it is one complete piece and nobody can tell where the work began and how it was woven. In Zen, therefore, there ought not to be left any trace of consciousness after the doing of alms, much less the thought of recompense even by God. The Zen ideal is to be "the wind that bloweth where it listeth, and the sound of which we hear but cannot tell whence it cometh and whither it goeth."

Resshi, the Chinese philosopher, describes this frame of mind in a figurative manner as follows: "I allowed my mind without restraint to think of whatever it pleased and my mouth to talk about whatever it pleased; I then forgot whether the 'this and not-this' was mine or other's, whether the gain and loss was mine or other's: nor did I know whether Rōshōshi was my teacher, and whether Hakkōshi was my friend. In and out, I was thoroughly trans-formed; and then it was that the eye became like the ear, and the ear like the nose, and the nose like the mouth; and there was nothing that was not identified. The mind was concentrated, and the form dissolved, and the bones and flesh all thawed away: I did not know where my form was supported, where my feet were treading; I just moved along with the wind, east and west, like a leaf of a tree detached from the stem, I was not conscious whether I was riding on the wind or the wind riding on me."[20]

X

Zen followers disapprove of Christians—even mystics—being too conscious of God who is the creator and supporter of all life and all being. The attitude in Zen toward the Buddha is that of a complete identification of the self with the object of thought. This is the reason why they loath to hear the word Buddha or Zen mentioned in their discourse, not because they are anti-Buddha, but because there is nothing especially to be so designated. Listen to the gentle remonstrance given by Goso Hōen to his disciple Engo:

"You are all right, but you have a trivial fault." Engo asked two or three times what that fault was. Said the master, "You have too much of Zen."

"Why," protested the disciple, "if one is studying Zen, don't you think it a natural thing to speak it? Why is it to be despised?"

Replied Goso, "When it is an ordinary everyday conversation, it is somewhat better."

A monk happened to be there with them, who asked, "Why do you specially hate talking about Zen?"

"Because it turns one's stomach," was the master's verdict.

[20] The wind is probably one of the best imageries to get us into the idea of non-attachment or *Sūnyatā* philosophy. The New Testament has at least one allusion to it: "The wind bloweth as it listeth," and here we see the Chinese mystic making use of the wind to depict his inner consciousness of absolute identity, which is also the Buddhist notion of the void. Now compare the following passage from Eckhart: Darum ruft die Braue auch weiter: "Weiche von mir, mein Geliebter, weiche von mir": "Alles, was irgend der Darstellung fähig ist, das halte ich nicht für Gott. Und so fliehe ich vor Gott, Gottes wegen!"—"Ei, wo ist dann der Seele Bleiben?"—"Auf den Fittichen der Winde!" (Büttner, *Meister Eckeharts Schriften und Predigten*, Erster Band, p. 189.) "So fliehe ich vor Gott, Gottes wegen," reminds us of a Zen master who said, "I hate even to hear the name of the Buddha." From the Zen point of view, "Gottes wegen" may better be left out.

Rinzai's way of expressing the idea is quite violent and revolutionary. Those uninitiated in the methods of Zen would find the following passages horrifying, but we can see how earnestly he feels about the falsehoods of the world and how unflinchingly he faces up against them. His hands may be compared to Jehovah's in trying to destroy the idols and causing the images to cease. Rinzai endeavors to strip one's spirit of its last raiment of falsehood.

"O you, followers of Truth, if you wish to obtain an orthodox understanding [of Zen], do not be deceived by others. Inwardly or outwardly, if you encounter any obstacles, lay them low without delay. If you encounter the Buddha, slay him; if you encounter the Patriarch, slay him; if you encounter the Arhat or the parent or the relative, slay them all without hesitation: for this is the only way to deliverance. Do not get yourselves entangled with any object, but stand above, pass on, and be free. As I see those so-called followers of Truth all over the country, there are none who come to me free and independent of objects. In dealing with them, I strike them down any way they come. If they rely on the strength of their arms, I cut them right off; if they rely on their eloquence, I shut them up; if they rely on the sharpness of their eyes, I will hit them blind. There are none who have presented themselves before me all alone, all free, all unique. They are invariably found caught by the idle tricks of the old masters. I have really nothing to give you; all that I can do is to cure you of the diseases and deliver you from bondage.

"O you, followers of Truth, show yourselves here independent of all objects, I want to weigh the matter with you. For the last five or ten years I have waited in vain for such, and there are none such yet. They are all ghostly existences, ignominious gnomes haunting the woods or bamboo groves, they are elfish spirits of the wilderness. They are madly feeding on heaps of filth. O you, mole-eyed, why are you wasting all the pious donations of the devout! Do you think you deserve the name of a monk, when you are still entertaining such a mistaken idea [of Zen]? I tell you, no Buddhas, no holy teachings, no disciplining, no testifying! What can you seek in a neighbor's house? O you, mole-eyed! You are putting another head over your own! What do you lack in yourselves? O you, followers of Truth, what you are making use of at this very moment is none other than what makes a Patriarch or a Buddha. But you do not believe me, and seek it outside. Do not commit yourselves to an error. There are no realities outside, nor is there anything inside you may lay your hands on. You stick to the literal meaning of what I say to you, but far better it is to have all your hankerings stopped, and be "doing nothing"[21] etc., etc.

This was the way Rinzai wanted to wipe out all trace of God-consciousness from the mind of a truth-seeker. How he wields Thor-like his thunderbolt of harangue!

XI

The state of mind in which all traces of conceptual consciousness are wiped out is called poverty by the Christian mystics, and Tauler's definition is "Absolute poverty is thine when thou canst not remember whether anybody has ever owed thee or been indebted to thee for anything; just as all things will be forgotten by thee in the last journey of death."

The Zen masters are more poetic and positive in their expression of the feeling of poverty, they do not make a direct reference to things worldly. Sings Mumon:

> Hundreds of spring flowers; the autumnal moon;
> A refreshing summer breeze; winter snow:
> Free thy mind of all idle thoughts,
> And for thee how enjoyable every season is!

Or according to Shuan of Nantai:

> At Nantai I sit quietly with an incense burning,
> One day of rapture, all things are forgotten,
> Not that mind is stopped and thoughts are put away,
> But that there is really nothing to disturb my serenity.

This is not to convey the idea that he is idly sitting and doing nothing in particular; or that he has nothing else to do but to enjoy the cherry blossoms fragrant in the morning sun, or the lonely moon white and silvery; he may be in the midst of work, teaching pupils, reading the sutras, sweeping and farming as the masters in the past have done, and yet his own mind is filled with transcend-

---

[21] *Buji (wu-shih)* may correspond to the biblical "Take no thought for the morrow, for the morrow shall take thought for things of itself. . . ."

ental bliss and quietude. He is living in God, as Christians may say. ·All hankerings of the heart have departed, there are no idle thoughts clogging the flow of life activity, and thus he is empty and poverty-stricken. As he is poverty-stricken, he knows how to enjoy the "spring flowers" and the "autumnal moon." When worldly riches are amassed in his heart, no room is left there for such celestial enjoyments. The Zen masters are wont to speak positively about their contentment and unworldly riches. Rather than to say they are empty-handed, they talk of the natural sufficiency of things about them. Yōgi, however, refers to his deserted habitation where he found himself to be residing as keeper. One day he ascended the lecturing chair in the Hall and began to recite his own verse:

> My dwelling is now here at Yōgi; the walls and roof, how
>   weather-beaten!
> The whole floor is covered white with snow crystal,
> Shivering down the neck, I am filled with thoughts.

After a pause he added the fourth line:

> How I recall the ancient masters whose habitat was no
>   better than the shade of a tree!

Kyōgen is seemingly more direct in his allusion to poverty:

> Last year's poverty was not yet perfect;
> This year poverty is poverty indeed;
> Poverty last year left room for a gimlet's point,
> But this year the gimlet too has gone.

Later, a master called Koboku Gen commented on this song of poverty by Kyōgen in the following verse:

> "Neither a gimlet's point nor the room of it," some sing;
>   but this is not yet real poverty:
> As long as one is conscious of having nothing, there still
>   remains the guardian of poverty.
> I am lately poverty-stricken in all conscience,
> For from the very beginning I do not see even the one that
>   is poor.

Ummon was not poverty-stricken, but lean and emaciated, for when a monk asked him what were the special features of his school, the master answered, "My skin is dry and my bones protruding." Corpulence and opulence have never been associated with spirituality, at least in the East. As a matter of fact, they are not inconsistent ideas; but the amassing of wealth under our economic conditions has always resulted in producing characters that do not go very well with our ideals of saintliness. Perhaps our too emphatic protest against materialism has done this. Thus not to have anything, even the remnant of wisdom and virtue, has been made the object of Buddhist life. As true Bodhisattvas are above even purity and virtuousness, how much more so they would be above petty weaknesses of human being! When the Buddhists are thus cleansed of all these, they will truly be poverty-stricken and thin and transparent.

The aim of Zen discipline is to attain to the state of "non-attainment" when technically expressed. All knowledge is an acquisition and accumulation, whereas Zen proposes to deprive one of all one's possessions. The spirit is to make one poor and humble—thoroughly cleansed of inner impurities. Learning, on the contrary, makes one rich and arrogant. Because learning is earning, the more learned, the richer, and therefore "in much wisdom is much grief; and he that increaseth knowledge increaseth sorrow." It is, after all, "vanity and a striving after wind." Zen will heartily endorse this too. Says Lao-tzŭ, "Scholars gain every day while the Taoists lose every day." [22] The consummation of this kind of loss is "non-attainment," which is poverty. Poverty in another word is emptiness, śūnyatā. When the spirit is all purged of its filth accumulated from time immemorial, it stands naked, with no raiments, with no trappings. It is now empty, free, genuine, assuming its native authority. And there is a joy in this, not that kind of joy which is liable to be upset by its counterpart, grief, but an absolute joy which is "the gift of God," which makes a man "enjoy good in all his labor," and from which nothing can be taken, to which nothing can be added, but which shall stay forever. Non-attainment, therefore, in Zen is a positive conception, and not privative. The Buddhist modes of

---

22 The full passage is: "He who seeks learnedness gets daily enriched. He who seeks the Tao is daily made poor. He is made poorer and poorer until he arrives at non-action (wu-wei). With non-action, there is nothing that he cannot achieve."

thinking often differ from those of the West, and Christian readers are taken aback at the idea of emptiness and at the too unconditioned assertion of idealism. Singularly, all mystics, Buddhist or no, agree in their idea of poverty as being the end of spiritual development.

All the training of the monk in the *zendō*, in theory as well as in practice, is based on the notion of "meritless deed." Poetically, this idea is expressed as follows:

> The bamboo shadows sweep over the stairs,
> But the dust remains unstirred;
> The moonlight penetrates the depth of the pool,
> But the water shows no trace.

When this is expressed in the more Indian and technical terms on the *Laṅkāvatāra-sūtra,* it is as follows:

"Habit energy is not separated from mind, nor is it together with mind; though enveloped in habit energy, mind has no marks of difference.

"Habit energy, which is like a soiled garment produced by *manovijñāna,* keeps mind from shining forth, though mind itself is a robe of the utmost purity.

"I state that the *ālaya* is like empty space, which is neither existent nor non-existent; for the *ālaya* has nothing to do with being or no-being.

"Through the transformation of *manovijñāna,* mind is cleansed of foulness; it is enlightened as it now thoroughly understands all things: this I preach." [23]

XII

The monastery life is not all working and sitting quietly meditating on the *kōan.* There is something of intellectual life, in the form of lecturing, as has already been referred to. Anciently, however, there was no regular *sesshin,* and all the lecturing or giving sermons to the congregation was carried out on the feast days, memorial days, or on other auspicious occasions such as receiving visitors, honorably discharging the officials, or completing given

[23] *The Laṅkāvatāra,* p. 296.

pieces of work. Every available opportunity was thus used intellectually to enlighten earnest seakers of the truth. These discourses, sermons, exhortations, and short, pithy remarks so characteristic of Zen are recorded in its literature, the bulk of which consists of nothing more. While claiming to be above letters, Zen is filled with them.

To my mind the Chinese language is pre-eminently adapted for Zen; it is probably the best medium of expression for Zen as far as its literary side alone is thought of. Being monosyllabic, the language is terse and vigorous, and a single word conveys much meaning in it. While vagueness of sense is perhaps an unavoidable shortcoming, Zen knows how to avail itself of it, and the very vagueness of the language becomes a most powerful weapon in the hand of the master. He is far from wanting to be obscure and misleading, but a well-chosen monosyllable grows when it falls from his lips into a most pregnant word loaded with the whole system of Zen. Ummon is regarded as the foremost adept in this direction. To show how extremely laconic were his sayings:

When he was asked what was the sword of Ummon, he replied, "Hung!"

"What is the one straight passage to Ummon?"

"Most intimate!"

"Which one of the *trikāya* [Three Bodies of Buddha] is it that will sermonize?"

"To the point!"

"I understand this is said by all the old masters, that when you know the truth, all the karma hindrances are empty from the beginning; but if you do not, you have to pay all the debts back. I wonder if the second patriarch knew of this or not."

Replied the master, "Most certainly!"

"What is the eye of the true Dharma?"

"Everywhere!"

"When one commits patricide, or matricide, one goes to the Buddha to confess the sin; however, if one murders a Buddha or Patriarch, where should one go for confession?"

"Exposed!"

"What is the Tao [path, way, or truth]?"

"Walk on!"

"How is it that without the parent's consent one cannot be ordained?"

"How shallow!"

"I cannot understand."

"How deep!"

"What kind of phrase is it that does not cast any shadow?"

"Revealed!"

"How do you have an eye in a question?"[24]

"Blind."

Just one syllable, and the difficulties are disposed of. The Zen master generally does not indulge in circumlocution; if the speaker is direct and plain he is direct in hitting the point and plain in expressing his thoughts without encumbering appendages. For these the Chinese language is eminently suited. Brevity and forcefulness are its specific qualities, for each single syllable is a word and often a complete sentence. A string of nouns with no verbs or connectives is often sufficient to express a complex thought. Chinese literature is thus full of trenchant epigrams and pregnant aphorisms. The words are unwieldy and disconnected; they are like so many pieces of rock with nothing cementing them one to another. They do not present themselves as organic. Each link in the chain has a separate independent existence. But as each syllable is pronounced the effect is irresistible. Chinese is a mystic language par excellence.

As terseness and directness are the life of Zen, its literature is full of idiomatic and colloquial expressions. The Chinese are partisan to classic formalism, and scholars and philosophers knew only to express themselves in elegant and highly polished style. Consequently most of what is left to us in ancient Chinese literature is this classicism. Hardly any popular and colloquial lore had come

---

[24] Not an ordinary question asking enlightenment, but one that has a point in it showing some understanding on the part of the inquirer. All those questions already quoted must not be taken in their superficial or literary sense. They are generally metaphors. For instance, when one asks about a phrase having no shadow, he does not mean any ordinary ensemble of words known grammatically as such, but an absolute proposition whose verity is so beyond a shadow of doubt that every rational being will at once recognize it as true on hearing it. Again, when a reference is made to murdering a parent or a Buddha, it has really nothing to do with such horrible crimes. As we have in Rinzai's sermon, the murdering is transcending the relativity of a phenomenal world. Ultimately, therefore, this question amounts to the same thing as asking "Where is the one to be reduced, when the many are reduced to the one?"

down to posterity; whatever we have of it is from the T'ang and the Sung dynasties and is to be sought in the writings of the Zen masters. It is an irony of fate that those who so despised the use of letters to convey truth became the bearers and transmitters of ancient popular idioms and expressions discarded as unworthy and vulgar by the classical writers. The reason, however, is plain. The Buddha preached in the vernacular; so did Christ. The Greek, Sanskrit, and even Pali texts are all later elaboration when the faith began to grow stale, and scholasticism had the chance to assert itself. Then the living religion turned into an intellectual system and had to be translated into a highly but artificially polished, and therefore stilted, formalism. Zen consciously opposed this sort of refinement and chose to use the language close to the heart of the people.

The Zen masters made effort to avoid the technical nomenclature of Buddhist philosophy. Not only did they discuss such subjects as appealed to a plain man, but in making use of his everyday language the central ideas of Zen were being expressed in the most effective way possible. In this way, their literature became a unique repository of ancient wisdom. In Japan, too, when Hakuin modernized Zen he profusely utilized slangy phrases, colloquialisms, and even popular songs. A neological tendency in Zen is inevitable, seeing that it is creative and refuses to express itself in the worn-out, lifeless language of scholars and stylists. But as a result, even learned students of Chinese literature these days are unable to understand its writings, and their spiritual meanings as well. Thus has Zen literature come to constitute a unique class of literary work in China, standing by itself outside the main bulk of classical literature.

As I said elsewhere, Zen became truly the product of the Chinese mind by thus creating a unique influence in the history of Chinese culture. As long as Indian influence predominated, Zen could not be free from the speculative abstraction of Buddhist philosophy, which meant that Zen was not Zen in its specialized sense. Some scholars think that there is no Zen in the so-called primitive Buddhism and that the Buddha was not at all the author of Zen. But we must all remember that such critics are entirely ignoring the fact that religion, when transplanted, adapts itself to the genius of the people among whom it is introduced, and that unless it does so it gradually dies out, proving that there was no life-giving soul in that religion. Zen has claimed from the beginning of its history in

China that it is transmitting the spirit and not the letter of the Buddha, by which we understand that Zen, independent of traditional Buddhist philosophy including its terminology and modes of thinking, wove out its own garment from within just as the silkworm weaves its own cocoon. Therefore the outer garment of Zen is original, befitting itself wonderfully well, and there are no patchings on it nor any seams either: Zen is truly the traditional celestial robe.

XIII

Taking it all in all, Zen is emphatically a matter of personal experience; if anything can be called radically empirical, it is Zen. No amount of reading, no amount of teaching, and no amount of contemplation will ever make one a Zen master. Life itself must be grasped in the midst of its flow, to stop it for examination and analysis is to kill it, leaving its cold corpse to be embraced. Therefore, everything in the Meditation Hall and every detail of its disciplinary curriculum is so arranged as to bring this idea into the most efficient prominence. The unique position maintained by the Zen sect among other Mahayana schools in Japan and China throughout the history of Buddhism in the Far East is no doubt due to the institution known as the Meditation Hall or *zendō*.

2. THE GROWTH OF THE KŌAN SYSTEM AND ITS SIGNIFICATION[1]

WHAT the *kōan* proposes to do is to develop artificially or systematically in the consciousness of the Zen followers what the early masters produced in themselves spontaneously. It also aspires to develop this Zen experience in a greater number of minds than the master could otherwise hope for. Thus the *kōan* tended to the popularization of Zen and at the same time became the means of conserving the Zen experience in its genuineness. Aristocratic Zen was now turned into a democratic, systematized and, to a certain extent, mechanized Zen. No doubt it meant to that extent a deterioration; but without this innovation Zen might have died out a long time before. To my mind it was the technique of the *kōan* exercise that saved Zen as a unique heritage of Far-Eastern culture.

In order to understand a little better the circumstances which necessitated the rise of *kōan,* let me quote one or two of the masters who lived in the eleventh century. From them we can see that there were at least two tendencies that were at work undermining Zen. One was the doctrine and practice of absolute quietude, and the other was, the habit of intellection that was everywhere impressed upon Zen from the outside. Absolute quietism, which the masters were never tired of combating, was mistakenly regarded from the outset of Zen history as the essence of Zen teaching; but this tendency somehow inevitably attached itself to Zen practice.

As to the intellectual understanding of Zen, the outsiders as well as some Zen advocates are constantly practicing it against the experience of Zen. There is no doubt that herein lurks its most deadly enemy. If they are not effectually put down they are sure to raise their heads again and again, especially when Zen shows any symptoms of decline. Shinjō Kokumon says in one of his sermons, "As far as Zen is concerned, experience is all in all. Anything not based

1 *Essays in Zen Buddhism* (Second Series), pp. 83–91.

upon experience is outside Zen. The study of Zen, therefore, must grow out of life itself; and satori must be thoroughly penetrating. If anything is left unexhausted there is an opening to the world of devils.

"Did not an ancient master say that numberless corpses are lying on the smooth, level ground, and also that they are really genuine ones who have passed through thickets of briars and brambles? Nowadays most people are led to imagine that Zen reaches its ultimate end when all the functions of body and mind are suspended, and concentration takes place in one single moment of the present in which a state of eternity-in-one-moment prevails— a state of absolute cessation, a state like an incense burner in an old roadside shrine, a state of cold aloofness.

"It is most unfortunate that they are unable to realize that this state of concentration, however desirable, when one becomes attached to it hinders the attainment of a true inner perception and the manifestation of the light which is beyond the senses."

Daie says in a letter to Shinnyo Dōnin who was one of his monk disciples: "There are two forms of error now prevailing among followers of Zen, laymen as well as monks. The one thinks that there are wonderful things hidden in words and phrases, and those who hold this view try to learn many words and phrases. The second goes to the other extreme, forgetting that words are the pointing finger, showing one where to locate the moon. Blindly following the instruction given in the sutras, where words are said to hinder the right understanding of the truth of Zen and Buddhism, they reject all verbal teachings and simply sit with eyes closed, letting down the eyebrows as if they were completely dead. They call this quiet-sitting, inner contemplation, and silent reflection. Not content with their own solitary practices, they try to induce others also to adopt and practice this wrong view of Zen. To such ignorant and simple-minded followers they would say, 'One day of quiet-sitting means one day of progressive striving.'

"What a pity! They are not at all aware of the fact that they are planning for a ghostly life. Only when these two erroneous views are done away with is there a chance for real advancement in the mastery of Zen. For we read in the sutra that while one should not get attached to the artificialities and unrealities which are expressed by all beings through their words and language, neither should one adopt the other view which rejects all words indiscriminately, forgetting that the truth is conveyed in them when they are properly understood, and further, that words and their meanings are neither different nor not different, but are mutually related so that the one without the other is unintelligible. . . ."

There are many other passages expressing similar views in the sayings and discourses of the Zen masters of Daie's day besides those given by him, and from them we can conclude that if Zen were left to its own course, it would surely have degenerated either into the practice of quiet-sitting and silent contemplation, or into the mere memorizing of the many Zen sayings and dialogues. To save the situation and to plan for a further healthy development of Zen, the Zen masters could do nothing better than introduce the innovation of the *kōan* exercises.

What is a *kōan?*

A *kōan*, according to one authority, means "a public document setting up a standard of judgment," whereby one's Zen understanding is tested as to its correctness. A *kōan* is generally some state-ment made by an old Zen master, or some answer of his given to a questioner. The following are some that are commonly given to the uninitiated:

1. A monk asked Tōsan, "Who is the Buddha?"
"Three *chin* of flax."

2. Ummon was once asked, "When not a thought is stirring in one's mind, is there any error here?"
"As much as Mount Sumeru."

3. Jōshū answered, "*Mu!*" (*Wu*) to a monk's question, "Is there Buddha-nature in a dog?" *Mu* literally means "not" or "none," but when this is ordinarily given as a *kōan*, it has no reference to its literal signification; it is "*Mu*" pure and simple.

4. When Myo-jōza the monk overtook the fugitive Enō, he wanted Enō to give up the secret of Zen. Enō replied, "What are your original features which you have even prior to your birth?"

5. A monk asked Jōshū, "What is the meaning of the first pa-triarch's visit to China?"
"The cypress tree in the front courtyard."

6. When Jōshū came to study Zen under Nansen, he asked, "What is the Tao (or the Way)?"
Nansen replied, "Your everyday mind, that is the Tao."

7. A monk asked, "All things are said to be reducible to the One, but where is the One to be reduced?"

Jōshū answered, "When I was in the district of Ch'ing I had a robe made that weighed seven *chin*."

8. When Hō-koji the old Zen adept first came to Baso in order to master Zen, he asked, "Who is he who has no companion among the ten thousand things of the world?"

Baso replied, "When you swallow up in one draught all the water in the Western River, I will tell you."

When such problems are given to the uninitiated for solution, what is the object of the master? The idea is to unfold the Zen psychology in the mind of the uninitiated, and to reproduce the state of consciousness, of which these statements are the expression. That is to say, when the *kōan* are understood the master's state of mind is understood, which is satori and without which Zen is a sealed book.

In the beginning of Zen history a question was brought up by the pupil to the notice of the master, who thereby gauged the mental state of the questioner and knew what necessary help to give him. The help thus given was sometimes enough to awaken him to realization, but more frequently than not puzzled and perplexed him beyond description, and the result was an ever-increasing mental strain or "searching and contriving" on the part of the pupil, of which we have already spoken in the foregoing pages. In actual cases, however, the master would have to wait for a long while for the pupil's first question, if it were coming at all. To ask the first question is to be more than half the way to its own solution, for it is the outcome of a most intense mental effort for the questioner to bring his mind to a crisis. The question indicates that the crisis is reached and the mind is ready to leave it behind. An experienced master often knows how to lead the pupil to a crisis and to make him successfully pass it. This was really the case before the *kōan* exercise came in vogue, as was already illustrated by the examples of Rinzai, Nangaku, and others.

As time went on there grew up many mondō which were exchanged between masters and pupils. And with the growth of Zen literature it was perfectly natural now for Zen followers to begin to attempt an intellectual solution or interpretation of them. The "questions-and-answers" ceased to be experiences and intuitions of Zen consciousness, and became subjects of logical inquiry. This was disastrous, yet inevitable. Therefore the Zen master who wished for the normal development of Zen consciousness and the vigorous growth of Zen tradition would not fail to recognize rightly the actual state of things, and to devise such a method as to achieve finally the attainment of the Zen truth.

The method that would suggest itself in the circumstances was to select some of the statements made by the old masters and to use them as pointers. A pointer would then function in two directions: (1) To check the working of the intellect, or rather to let the intellect see by itself how far it can go, and also that there is a realm into which it as such can never enter; (2) To effect the maturity of Zen consciousness which eventually breaks out into a state of satori.

When the *kōan* works in the first direction there takes place what has been called "searching and contriving." Instead of the intellect, which taken by itself forms only a part of our being, the entire personality, mind and body, is thrown out into the solution of the *kōan*. When this extraordinary state of spiritual tension, guided by an experienced master, is made to mature, the *kōan* works itself out into what has been designated as the Zen experience. An intuition of the truth of Zen is now attained, for the wall against which the Yogin has been beating hitherto to no purpose breaks down, and an entirely new vista opens before him. Without the *kōan* the Zen consciousness loses its pointer, and there will never be a state of satori. A psychological impasse is the necessary antecedent of satori. Formerly, that is, before the days of the *kōan* exercise, the antecedent pointer was created in the consciousness of the Yogin by his own intense spirituality. But when Zen became systematized owing to the accumulation of Zen literature in the shape of "questions-and-answers," the indispensability of the *kōan* had come to be universally recognized by the masters.

The worst enemy of Zen experience, at least in the beginning, is the intellect, which consists and insists in discriminating subject from object. The discriminating intellect, therefore, must be cut short if Zen consciousness is to unfold itself, and the *kōan* is constructed eminently to serve this end.

On examination we at once notice that there is no room in the *kōan* to insert an intellectual interpretation. The knife is not sharp enough to cut the *kōan* open and see what are its contents. For a *kōan* is not a logical proposition but the expression of a certain mental state resulting from the Zen discipline. For instance, what logical connection can there be between the Buddha and "three *chin* of flax"? or between the Buddha-nature and "*Mu*"? or between the secret message of Bodhidharma and "a cypress tree"? In a noted Zen textbook, the *Hekigan-shū*, Engo gives the following notes concerning the "three *chin* of flax," showing how the *kōan* was interpreted by those pseudo-Zen followers who failed to grasp Zen:

"There are some people these days who do not truly understand this *kōan;* this is because there is no crack in it to insert their intellectual teeth. By this I mean that it is altogether too plain and tasteless. Various answers have been given by different masters to the question, 'What is the Buddha?' One said, 'He sits in the Buddha Hall.' Another said, 'The one endowed with the thirty-two marks of excellence.' Still another, 'A bamboo-root whip.' None, however, can excel Tōsan's 'three *chin* of flax' as regards its irrationality, which cuts off all passage of speculation. Some comment that Tōsan was weighing flax at the moment, hence the answer. Others say that it was a trick of equivocation on the part of Tōsan; and still others think that as the questioner was not conscious of the fact that he was himself the Buddha, Tōsan answered him in this indirect way.

"Such (commentators) are all like corpses, for they are utterly unable to comprehend the living truth. There are still others, however, who take the 'three *chin* of flax', as the Buddha (thus giving it a pantheistic interpretation). What wild and fantastic remarks they make! As long as they are beguiled by words, they can never expect to penetrate into the heart of Tōsan, even if they live to the time of Maitreya Buddha. Why? Because words are merely a vehicle on which the truth is carried. Not comprehending the meaning of the old master, they endeavor to find it in his words only, but they will find therein nothing to lay their hands on. The truth itself is beyond all description, as is affirmed by an ancient sage, but it is by words that the truth is manifested.

"Let us, then, forget the words when we gain the truth itself. This is done only when we have an insight through experience into that which is indicated by words. The 'three *chin* of flax' is like the royal thoroughfare to the capital: when you are once on it every step you take is in the right direction. When Ummon was once asked what was the teaching that went beyond the Buddhas and the patriarchs, he said, 'Dumpling.' Ummon and Tōsan are walking the same road hand in hand. When you are thoroughly cleansed of all the impurities of discrimination, without further ado the truth will be understood. Later the monk who wanted to know what the Buddha was went to Chimon and asked him what Tōsan meant by 'three *chin* of flax.' Said Chimon, 'A mass of flowers, a mass of brocade.' He added, 'Do you understand?' The monk replied, 'No.' 'Bamboos in the South, trees in the North,' was the conclusion of Chimon."

Technically speaking, the *kōan* given to the uninitiated is intended "to destroy the root of life," "to make the calculating mind die," "to root out the entire mind that has been at work since eternity," etc. This may sound murderous, but the ultimate intent is to go beyond the limits of intellection, and these limits can be crossed over only by exhausting oneself once for all, by using up all the psychic powers at one's command. Logic then turns into psychology, intellection into conation and intuition. What could not be solved on the plane of empirical consciousness is now transferred to the deeper recesses of the mind. So, says a Zen master, "Unless at one time perspiration has streamed down your back, you cannot see the boat sailing before the wind." "Unless once you have been thoroughly drenched in perspiration you cannot expect to see the revelation of a palace of pearls on a blade of grass."

The *kōan* refuses to be solved under any easier conditions. But once solved it is compared to a piece of brick used to knock at a gate; when the gate is opened the brick is thrown away. The *kōan* is useful as long as the mental doors are closed, but when they are opened it may be forgotten. What one sees after the opening will be something quite unexpected, something that has never before entered even into one's imagination. But when the *kōan* is re-examined from this newly acquired point of view, how marvellously suggestive, how fittingly constructed, although there is nothing artificial here!

3. PRACTICAL INSTRUCTIONS REGARDING THE KŌAN EXERCISE[1]

THE following are some of the practical suggestions that have been given by Zen masters of various ages, regarding the *kōan* exercise; and from them we can gather what a *kōan* is expected to do toward the development of Zen consciousness, and also what tendency the *kōan* exercise has come to manifest as time goes on. As we will see later on, the growth of the *kōan* exercise caused a new movement among the Zen masters of the Ming dynasty to connect it with the *nembutsu*,[2] that is, the recitation of the Buddha-name. This was owing to the presence of a common denominator between the psychological mechanism of the *kōan* exercise and the recitation of the Buddha-name.

A Zen master of early Sung gives the following instruction in the study of Zen:

"O you brother monks! You may talk glibly and perhaps intelligently about Zen, about Tao, and scoff at the Buddhas and patriarchs; but when the day comes to reckon up all your accounts, your lip-Zen will be of no avail. Thus far you have been beguiling others, but today you will find that you have been beguiling yourselves. O you brother monks! While still strong and healthy in body try to have a real understanding as to what Zen is. After all it is not such a difficult thing to take hold of the lock; but simply because you have not made up your minds to die in the last ditch, if you do not find a way to realization, you say, 'It is too difficult; it is beyond my power.' It is absurd! If you are really men of will, you will find out what your *kōan* means. A monk once asked Jōshū, 'Has a dog the Buddha-nature?' to which the master answered, '*Mu!*' Now devote yourselves to this *kōan* and try to find its mean-

---

[1] *Essays in Zen Buddhism* (Second Series), pp. 91–100.

[2] *Nien-fu*. Literally, "thinking of the Buddha."

297

ing. Devote yourselves to it day and night, whether sitting or lying, whether walking or standing; devote yourselves to its solution during the entire course of the twelve periods. Even when dressing or taking meals, or attending to your natural wants, have your every thought fixed on the *kōan*. Make resolute efforts to keep it always before your mind. Days pass, years roll on, but in the fullness of time when your mind is so attuned and recollected there will be a sudden awakening within yourselves—an awakening into the mentality of the Buddhas and the patriarchs. You will then, for the first time, and wherever you may go, never again be beguiled by a Zen master."[3]

Ian Shin of Busseki monastery gives this advice:

"The old saying runs, 'When there is enough faith, there is enough doubt which is a great spirit of inquiry, and when there is a great spirit of inquiry there is an illumination.' Have everything thoroughly poured out that has accumulated in your mind—learning, hearing, false understanding, clever or witty sayings, the so-called truth of Zen, Buddha's teachings, self-conceit, arrogance, etc. Concentrate yourself on the *kōan*, of which you have not yet had a penetrating comprehension. That is to say, cross your legs firmly, erect your spinal column straight, and paying no attention to the periods of the day, keep up your concentration until you grow unaware of your whereabouts, east, west, south, north, as if you were a living corpse.

"The mind moves in response to the outside world and when it is touched it knows. The time will come when all thoughts cease to stir and there will be no working of consciousness. It is then that all of a sudden you smash your brain to pieces and for the first time realize that the truth is in your own possession from the very beginning. Would not this be great satisfaction to you in your daily life?"

Daie was a great *kōan* advocate of the twelfth century. One of his favorite *kōan* was Jōshū's *"Mu,"* but he had also one of his own. He used to carry a short bamboo stick which he held forth before an assembly of monks, and said: "If you call this a stick, you affirm; if you call it not a stick, you negate. Beyond affirmation and negation what would you call it?" In the following extract from

[3] From the "Breaking Through the Zen Frontier Gate" (*Zenkan Sakushin, ch'an-kuan-ts'ê-chin*).

his sermons titled *Daie Fusetsu*,[4] compiled by Sokei, 1190, he gives still another *kōan* to his gardener monk, Jōkyō.

The truth (*Dharma*) is not to be mastered by mere seeing, hearing, and thinking. If it is, it is no more than the seeing, hearing, and thinking; it is not at all seeking after the truth itself. For the truth is not in what you hear from others or learn through the understanding. Now keep yourself away from what you have seen, heard, and thought, and see what you have within yourself. Emptiness only, nothingness, which eludes your grasp and to which you cannot fix your thought. Why? Because this is the abode where the senses can never reach. If this abode were within the reach of your senses it would be something you could think of, something you could have a glimpse of; it would then be something subject to the law of birth and death.

The main thing is to shut off all your sense organs and make your consciousness like a block of wood. When this block of wood suddenly starts up and makes a noise, that is the moment you feel like a lion roaming about freely with nobody disturbing him, or like an elephant that crosses a stream not minding its swift current. At that moment there is no fidgeting, nothing doing, just this and no more. Says Heiden the Elder:

> The celestial radiance undimmed,
> The norm lasting for ever more;
> For him who entereth this gate,
> No reasoning, no learning.

You should know that it is through your seeing, hearing, and thinking[5] that you enter upon the path, and it is also through the seeing, hearing, and thinking that you are prevented from entering. Why? Let you be furnished with the double-bladed sword that destroys and resuscitates life where you have your seeing, hearing, and thinking, and you will be able to make good use of the seeing, hearing, and thinking. But if the sword that cuts both ways, that destroys as well as resuscitates, is missing, your seeing, hearing, and thinking will be a great stumbling-block, which will cause you to prostrate again and again on the ground. Your truth eye will be completely blinded; you will be walking in complete darkness, not knowing how to be free and independent. If you want,

---

[4] *Ta-hui P'u-shuo.*

[5] Abbreviated for "the seen, heard, thought, and known."

however, to be the free master of yourself by doing away with your seeing, hearing, and thinking, stop your hankering monkey-like mind from doing mischief; keep it quietly under control; keep your mind firmly collected regardless of what you are doing—sitting or lying, standing or walking, remaining silent or talking; keep your mind like a line stretched taut; do not let it slip out of your hand. Just as soon as it slips out of your control you will find it in the service of the seeing, hearing, and thinking. In such a case is there any remedy? What remedy is applicable here?

A monk asked Ummon, "Who is the Buddha?" "The dried-up dirt-cleaner." This is the remedy; whether you are walking or sitting or lying, let your mind be perpetually fixed on this "dirt-cleaner." The time will come when your mind will suddenly come to a stop like an old rat who finds himself in a cul-de-sac. Then there will be a plunging into the unknown with the cry, "Ah! this!" When this cry is uttered you have discovered yourself. You find at the same time that all the teachings of the ancient worthies expounded in the Buddhist Tripitaka, the Taoist Scriptures, and the Confucian Classics, are no more than commentaries upon your own sudden cry, "Ah! this!"

Daie was never tired of impressing upon his disciples the importance of having satori which goes beyond language and reasoning and which bursts out in one's consciousness by overstepping the limits of consciousness. His letters and sermons are filled with advice and instructions directed toward this end. I quote one or two of them. That he was so insistent on this point proves that Zen in his day was degenerating to a form of mere quietism on the one hand and on the other to the intellectual analysis of the kōan left by the old masters.

"The study of Zen must end in satori. It is like a holiday race-boat which is ordinarily put away in some quiet corner, but which is designed for winning a regatta. This has been the case with all the ancient masters of Zen, for we know that Zen is really won only when we have satori. You have to have satori somehow, but you will never get what you want by trying to be quiet with yourself, by sitting like a dead man. Why? Does not one of the patriarchs say that when you attempt to gain quietness by suppressing activity your quietness will all the more be susceptible to disturbance? However earnestly you may try to quiet your confused mind, the result will be altogether contrary to what you expect to realize so long as your reasoning habit continues.

"Abandon, therefore, this reasoning habit; have the two characters, 'birth' and 'death,' pasted on your forehead, and fix your attention exclusively on the following *kōan*, as if you were oppressed under the obligation of a very heavy debt. Think of the *kōan* regardless of what you are doing, regardless of what time of the day it is, day or night. A monk asked Jōshū, 'Has a dog the Buddha-nature, or not?' Said Jōshū, '*Mu!*' Collect your thoughts upon this '*Mu!*' and see what is contained in it. As your concentration goes on you will find the *kōan* altogether devoid of taste, that is, without any intellectual clue whereby to fathom its content. Yet in the meantime you may have a feeling of joy stealing into your heart, which, however, is soon followed by another feeling, this time a feeling of disquietude. Paying no attention to this interweaving of emotions, exert yourself to go ahead with the *kōan*, when you will become aware that you have pushed yourself like the old rat into a blind alley. A turning back will then be necessary, but this can never be accomplished by the weak-minded, who are ever faltering and hesitating."

In another place Daie says: "Just steadily go on with your *kōan* every moment of your life. If a thought rises, do not attempt to suppress it by conscious effort; only renew the attempt to keep the *kōan* before the mind. Whether walking or sitting, let your attention be fixed upon it without interruption. When you begin to find it entirely devoid of flavor, the final moment is approaching; do not let it slip out of your grasp. When all of a sudden something flashes out in your mind, its light will illuminate the entire universe, and you will see the spiritual land of the Enlightened Ones fully revealed at the point of a single hair, and the great wheel of the Dharma revolving in a single grain of dust."[6]

Kūkoku Keiryō[7] has a similar advice for monks. He says:

"Jōshū's '*Mu!*', before you have penetrated into its meaning, is like a silver mountain or an iron wall (against which you stand nonplused). But as you go on with '*Mu!*' day after day trying to get into its content, and do not give even a moment's rest to your-

---

[6] Daie's passages are taken from a collection of his letters, sermons, discourses, and sayings known as his *Fusetsu*, *Goroku*, and *Sho*. He was very well acquainted with the *Avataṃsaka* (or *Gaṇḍavyūha*), and there are many allusions by him to its teachings, as we find in this last sentence here.

[7] Still living in 1466.

self, the supreme moment will inevitably come upon you, just as a flood makes its own channel; and then you will see that the iron wall and the silver mountain were not, after all, very formidable. The main point is not to put any reliance on learning, but to put a stop to all hankering, and to exert yourself to the utmost to solve the great problem of birth-and-death. Do not waste your time by merely thinking of 'Mu!' as if you were no more than a simpleton; make no attempt to give a false solution to it by means of speculation and imagination. Resolutely put yourself, heart and soul, into the unraveling of the problem of 'Mu!' When suddenly, as you let go of your hold, there comes a grand overturning of the whole system of consciousness, and for the first time you realize in a most luminous manner what all this finally comes to."

The author of *The Mirror for Zen Students*[8] confirms all that has already been quoted, and describes fully the psychology of the *kōan* exercise.

"What is required of Zen devotees is to see into the phrase[9] that liveth and not into the one which is dead. Try to search for the sense of the *kōan* you have, putting your whole mental strength into the task like the mother hen sitting on her eggs, like a cat trying to catch a rat, like a hungry one eagerly looking everywhere for food, like a thirsty one seeking for water, like a child thinking of its mother. If you exert yourself as seriously and as desperately as that, the time will surely come when the sense of the *kōan* will dawn upon you.

"There are three factors making for success in the study of Zen: (1) great faith, (2) great resolution, and (3) great spirit of inquiry. When any one of these is lacking it is like a cauldron with a broken leg, it limps. At all moments of your life, regardless of what you are doing, exert yourself to see into the meaning of Jōshū's 'Mu.' Keep

8 Compiled by Tai-in, a Korean Zen master of the Ming era (A.D. 1368–1650). The book appeared in 1579.

9 That is, *ku*. The Zen masters generally distinguish two kinds of *ku;* the live one and the dead one. By the "live *ku*" are meant such statements as give no clues whatever to their rational interpretations but put an end to the functioning of the empirical consciousness; whereas the "dead *ku*" are those that lend themselves to logical or philosophical treatment and therefore that can be learned from others and committed to memory. This according to Tai-in.

the *kōan* always before your mind and never release the spirit of inquiry. As the inquiry goes on steadily and uninterruptedly you will come to see that there is no intellectual clue in the *kōan*, that it is altogether devoid of sense as you ordinarily understand that word, that it is entirely flat, devoid of taste, has nothing appetizing about it, and that you are beginning to have a certain feeling of uneasiness and impatience. When you come to this state it is the moment for you to cast aside the scabbard, throw yourself down into the abyss, and by so doing lay a foundation for Buddhahood.

"Do not think that the meaning of the *kōan* is at the moment of your holding it up for solution; do not reason about it or exercise your imagination over it; do not wait for satori to come over you by clearing your mind of its confused ideas; only collect yourself on the unintelligibility of the *kōan* over which the mind evidently has no control.[10] You will finally find yourself like an old rat getting into the farthest corner of the barn where it suddenly perceives by veering clear round the way of escape. To measure the *kōan* by an intellectual standard, as you ordinarily do with other things, to live your life up and down in the stream of birth-and-death, to be al-

---

[10] Tai-in cautions his *kōan* students on the following ten points: (1) Do not calculate according to your imagination; (2) Let not your attention be drawn where the master raises his eyebrows or twinkles his eyes; (3) Do not try to extract meaning from the way the *kōan* is worded; (4) Do not try to demonstrate on the words; (5) Do not think that the sense of the *kōan* is to be grasped where it is held out as an object of thought; (6) Do not take Zen for a state of mere passivity; (7) Do not judge the *kōan* with the dualistic standard of *yu* (*asti*) and *wu* (*nasti*); (8) Do not take the *kōan* as pointing to absolute emptiness; (9) Do not ratiocinate on the *kōan;* and (10) Do not keep your mind in the attitude of waiting for satori to turn up. The *kōan* exercise is confused with so-called meditation, but from all these warnings given by an old master regarding the exercise it is evident that Zen is not an exercise in meditation or in passivity. If Zen is to be properly understood by its students, Eastern and Western, this characteristic aspect of it must be fully comprehended. Zen has its definite object, which is "to open our minds to satori," as we say, and in order to bring about this state of consciousness a *kōan* is held out before the mental eye, not to meditate on, nor to keep the mind in a state of receptivity, but to use the *kōan* as a kind of pole with which to leap over the stream of relativity to the other side of the Absolute. And the unique feature of Zen Buddhism is that all this is accomplished without resorting to such religious conceptions as sin, faith, God, grace, salvation, a future life, etc.

ways assailed by feelings of fear, worry, and uncertainty, all this is owing to your imagination and calculating mind. You ought to know how to rise above the trivialities of life, in which most people are found drowning themselves. Do not waste time asking how to do it, just put your whole soul into the business. It is like a mosquito biting at an iron bull; at the very moment the iron absolutely rejects your frail proboscis, you for once forget yourself, you penetrate, and the work is done."

Sufficient authorities have now been quoted to show where lies the function of the *kōan* in bringing about what is known as satori, and also to show what the Zen master had in mind when he first began to exercise the minds of his disciples toward the maturing of their Zen consciousness. In the way of summary I conclude this part of the present chapter with a passage from the writings of Hakuin, who is father of the modern Japanese Rinzai school of Zen. In this we will see how the psychology of Zen has been going on without much change for more than a thousand years, since the days of Enō and his Chinese followers.

If you want to get at the unadulterated truth of egolessness, you must once for all let go your hold and fall over the precipice, when you will rise again newly awakened and in full possession of the four virtues of eternity, bliss, freedom, and purity, which belong to the real ego. What does it mean to let go of your hold on the precipice? Suppose a man has wandered out among the remote mountains, where no one else has ever ventured. He comes to the edge of a precipice unfathomably deep, the rugged rock covered with moss is extremely slippery, giving him no sure foothold; he can neither advance nor retreat, death is looking at him in the face. His only hope lies in holding on to the vine which his hands have grasped; his very life depends on his holding on to it. If he should by carelessness let go his hold, his body would be thrown down to the abyss and crushed to pieces, bones and all.

It is the same with the student of Zen. When he grapples with a *kōan* single-handedly he will come to see that he has reached the limit of his mental tension, and he is brought to a standstill. Like the man hanging over the precipice he is completely at a loss what to do next. Except for occasional feelings of uneasiness and despair, it is like death itself. All of a sudden he finds his mind and body wiped out of existence, together with the *kōan*. This is what is known as "letting go your hold." As you become awakened from the stupor and regain your breath it is like drinking water and knowing for yourself that it is cold. It will be a joy inexpressible.

To recapitulate: The innovation of the *kōan* exercise was inevitable owing to the following circumstances:

1. If the study of Zen had run its natural course it would soon have come to its own extinction owing to the aristocratic nature of its discipline and experience.

2. As Zen gradually exhausted its creative originality in two or three hundred years of development after the time of Enō, the sixth patriarch, it found that a new life must be awakened in it, if it were to survive, by using some radical method which would vigorously stir up the Zen consciousness.

3. With the passing of the age of creative activity there was an accumulation of materials known as "stories" (*hua-t'ou*), or "conditions" (*chi-yüan*), or "questions-and-answers" (*wên-ta*), which made up the bulk of Zen history; and this tended to invite intellectual interpretation, ruinous to the maturing of the Zen experience.

4. The rampant growth of Zen quietism since the beginning of Zen history most dangerously threatened the living experience of Zen. The two tendencies, quietism or the school of "silent illumination," and intuitionalism or the school of noetic experience, had been from the beginning, covertly if not openly, at war with each other.

Because of these conditions, the *kōan* exercise adopted by the Zen masters of the tenth and the eleventh centuries was designed to perform the following functions:

1. To popularize Zen in order to counteract native aristocracy which tended to its own extinction;

2. To give a new stimulus to the development of Zen consciousness, and thus to accelerate the maturing of the Zen experience;

3. To check the growth of intellectualism in Zen;

4. To save Zen from being buried alive in the darkness of quietism.

From the various quotations which have been given concerning the *kōan* exercise, the following psychic facts may be gathered:

1. The *kōan* is given to the student first of all to bring about a highly wrought-up state of consciousness.

2. The reasoning faculty is kept in abeyance, that is, the more

superficial activity of the mind is set at rest so that its more central and profounder parts which are found generally deeply buried can be brought out and exercised to perform their native functions.

3. The affective and conative centers which are really the foundations of one's personal character are charged to do their utmost in the solution of the *kōan*. This is what the Zen master means when he refers to "great faith" and "great spirit of inquiry" as the two most essential powers needed in the qualification of a successful Zen devotee. The fact that all great masters have been willing to give themselves up, body and soul, to the mastery of Zen, proves the greatness of their faith in ultimate reality, and also the strength of their spirit of inquiry known as "seeking and contriving," which never suspends its activity until it attains its end, that is, until it has come into the very presence of Buddhatā itself.

4. When the mental integration thus reaches its highest mark there obtains a neutral state of consciousness which is erroneously designated as "ecstasy" by the psychological student of the religious consciousness. This Zen state of consciousness essentially differs from ecstasy in this: Ecstasy is the suspension of the mental powers while the mind is passively engaged in contemplation; the Zen state of consciousness, on the other hand, is the one that has been brought about by the most intensely active exercise of all the fundamental faculties constituting one's personality. They are here positively concentrated on a single object of thought, which is called a state of oneness (*ekāgra*). It is also known as a state of *daigi,* or "fixation."[11]

This is the point where the empirical consciousness with all its contents both conscious and unconscious is about to tip over its borderline, and get noetically related to the Unknown, the Beyond, the Unconscious. In ecstasy there is no such tipping or transition, for it is a static finality not permitting further unfoldment. There is nothing in ecstasy that corresponds to "throwing oneself down the precipice," or "letting go the hold."

5. Finally, what at first appears to be a temporary suspense of all psychic faculties suddenly becomes charged with new energies hitherto undreamed of. This abrupt transformation has taken place quite frequently by the intrusion of a sound, or a vision, or a form of motor activity. A penetrating insight is born of the inner depths

---

11 *Ta-i* in Chinese, *Essays in Zen Buddhism* (First Series), p. 254.

of consciousness, as the source of a new life has been tapped, and with it the *kōan* yields up its secrets.

A philosophical explanation of these psychic facts is offered by Zen Buddhists in the following manner. It goes without saying that Zen is neither psychology nor philosophy, but that it is an experience charged with deep meaning and laden with living, exalting contents. The experience is final and its own authority. It is the ultimate truth, not born of relative knowledge, that gives full satisfaction to all human wants. It must be realized directly within oneself: no outside authorities are to be relied upon. Even the Buddha's teachings and the master's discourses, however deep and true they are, do not belong to one so long as they have not been assimilated into his being, which means that they are to be made to grow directly out of one's own living experiences. This realization is called satori. All *kōans* are the utterances of satori with no intellectual mediations; hence their uncouthness and incomprehensibility.

The Zen master has no deliberate scheme on his part to make his statements of satori uncouth or logically unpalatable; the statements come forth from his inner being, as flowers burst out in springtime, or as the sun sheds its rays. Therefore to understand them we have to be like flowers or like the sun; we must enter into their inner being. When we reproduce the same psychic conditions, out of which the Zen masters have uttered these *kōan*, we shall know them. The masters thus avoid all verbal explanations, which only serve to create in the minds of their disciples an intellectual curiosity to probe into the mystery. The intellect being a most obtrusive hindrance, or rather a deadly enemy, at least in the beginning of Zen study, it must be banished for a while from the mind. The *kōan* is, indeed, a great baffler to reasoning. For this reason, Zen is ever prone to give more value to the psychic facts than to conceptualism. As the facts are directly experienced and prove quite satisfactory, they appeal irresistibly to the "seeking and contriving" mind of the Zen follower.

As facts of personal experience are valued in Zen, we have such *kōan* as Ummon's "dried up dirt-cleaner," of Jōshū's "cypress tree," Tōsan's "three *chin* of flax," etc., which are all familiar incidents in everyone's life. Compared with the Indian expressions such as "All is empty, unborn, and beyond causation" or "The whole universe is contained in one particle of dust," how homely the Chinese are! Owing to this fact, Zen is better designed to exclude the intellect and to lead our empirical consciousness to its deeper sources. If a noetic experience of a radically different order is to be attained, which sets all our strivings and searchings at rest, something that does not at all belong to the intellectual categories is to be devised. More precisely speaking, something illogical, something irrational, something that does not yield itself to an intellectual treatment is to be the special feature of Zen. The *kōan* exercise was thus the natural development of Zen consciousness in the history of human strivings to reach the ultimate. By means of the *kōan* the entire system of our psychic apparatus is made to bear upon the maturing of the satori state of consciousness.

4. THE IMPORTANCE AND THE FUNCTION
OF THE SPIRIT OF INQUIRY[1]

As has already been stated, the preparatory equipment of the Zen devotee before he takes up the *kōan* exercise is:

1. To awaken a most sincere desire to be delivered from the bondage of karma, from the pain of birth and death;

2. To recognize that the aim of the Buddhist life consists in attaining enlightenment, in maturing a state of consciousness known as satori;

3. To realize the futility of all intellectual attempts to reach this aim, that is, to solve in a most living manner the ultimate problem of existence;

4. To believe that the realization of satori means the awakening of Buddha-nature which lies deeply buried in all minds;

5. To be in possession of a strong spirit of inquiry which will ever urge a man to experience within himself the presence of Buddha-nature. Without this fivefold equipment he may not hope to carry out the *kōan* exercise successfully to its end.

Even when he is thus mentally qualified, he may not believe the *kōan* to be the most efficient means to reach the goal. It may be that he is more attracted to the Shingon or Tendai method of discipline, or to the recitation of the Buddha's name as in the Pure Land sects, or to the repetition of the *daimoku* as in the Nichiren sect. This is where what may be termed his religious idiosyncrasies rule, which are due to his previous karma. In this case, he cannot be a successful follower of Zen, and his emancipation will have to be effected in some other way.

Even among Zen followers there are some who are no believers in the *kōan*, regarding it as something artificially contrived; indeed, they go even further and declare satori itself to be a sort of excrescence which does not properly belong to the original system

[1] *Essays in Zen Buddhism* (Second Series), pp. 117–135.

of Zen. Most Japanese adherents of the Sōtō school of Zen belong
to this class of kōan denouncers. This divergence of views as to the
efficacy of the kōan exercise and the experience of satori comes
rather from the differences of philosophical interpretation given
to Zen by the followers of the Sōtō and the Rinzai. As far as the
practice of Zen is concerned, both are descendants of Bodhidharma
and Enō.

However this may be, one must believe in the kōan if he is to
be disciplined in it and awakened by it to satori. Now the question is: How is a kōan—at least the first kōan—to be brought up
into the field of consciousness so as to occupy its center when one
undertakes to solve its meaning? It evidently has no logical connotation, for its express purpose is to cut off every passage to
speculation and imagination. For instance, when "Mu" is given to
a Zen Yogin, how is he expected to deal with it? There is no doubt
that he is not to think about it, for no logical thinking is possible.
"Mu" does not yield any meaning inasmuch as it is not to be
thought of in connection with the dog, nor for that matter with
the Buddha-nature, either; it is "Mu" pure and simple. The kōan
neither denies nor asserts the presence of Buddha-nature in the
dog, although Jōshū used the "Mu" on being asked about the
Buddha-nature. When the "Mu" is given as a kōan to the uninitiated, it stands by itself; and this is exactly what is claimed from
the beginning by Zen masters, who have used it as an eye-opener.

So with "the cypress tree." It is simply "the cypress tree," and
has no logical connection with the question: "What is the idea
of the first patriarch's visit to China?" Nor does it at all refer to
the pantheistic view of existence, which is sometimes thought to
be the world conception of the Buddhists. This being the case,
what mental attitude shall we take toward the kōan when it is given
us as the key to the secrets of Zen?

Generally, the Chinese characters used in describing the mental
attitude toward a kōan are: teiki, teizei, teitetsu, ko, meaning, "to
lift," "to hold up," "to raise"; kan, "to see," "to regard," "to hold
before the eye"; san, "to be concerned with," "to be in," "to consult," "to refer to"; sankyū or taikyū "to investigate," "to inquire
into"; kufū, "to seek a clue," "to search for a solution," "to exercise
one's mind on a subject"; gai, "to examine." All these terms purport
to mean "to keep a kōan continually before one's mental eye so as
to make one endeavor to find a clue to its secrets."

These two processes, the holding up and the striving, may be considered one; for the sole object of holding up a *kōan* before the mind is to see into its meaning. As this goes on, the meaning searched after objectively in "*Mu*," "cypress tree," or "three *chin* of flax," exfoliates itself, not from the *kōan* indeed, but from within the Yogin's own mind. This is the moment when the *kōan* becomes perfectly identified with the searching and striving mind, and the meaning yields itself through this identification.

It may not thus be proper to say that the *kōan* is understood, for at the moment of understanding there is no *kōan* separate from the mind. Nor is it proper to assert that it is the mind that understands itself, for the understanding is a reflection, an aftermath; a mind is the reconstruction of the understanding. There is as yet no judgment here, no subject, no predicate; there is simply the exclamation, "Ah!" The Chinese terms used in this connection are quite graphic: "one outbursting cry." The moment is thus: "the bursting of the bag," "the breaking up of the tar casket," "a sudden snapping," "a sudden bursting," "the bursting of the bamboo with a crack," "the breaking up of the void," etc.

The word "concentration" has been used very much in the *kōan* exercise, but, in fact, concentration is not the main point, though it inevitably follows. The thing most essential in the exercise is the will to get into the meaning—we have at present no suitable expression—of the *kōan*. When the will or the spirit of inquiry is strong and constantly working, the *kōan* is necessarily kept without interruption before the eye, and all the other thoughts that are not at all cogent are naturally swept off the field of consciousness. This exclusion and sweeping off are a byproduct, they are more or less accidental. This is where the *kōan* exercise is distinct from mere concentration and also from the Indian form of *dhyāna*, that is, meditation, abstraction, or thought cessation.

Two forms of concentration may be distinguished now: the one brought about as it were mechanically, and the other resulting inevitably, but in essence accidentally, from the intensification of an inquiring spirit. When concentration followed by identification is once attained either way, it necessarily ends in the final outburst of satori. But genuine Zen always requires the presence of a spirit of inquiry, as is shown in the following quotations.

Daie, who was one of the earlier advocates of the *kōan*, was always emphatic about this point; for we find references to it everywhere in his discourses *Daie Fusetsu*. Consider such statements as the following: "Single out the point where you have been in doubt all your life and put it upon your forehead." "Is it a holy one, or a commonplace one? Is it an entity, or a non-entity? Press your question to its very end. Do not be afraid of plunging yourself into a vacuity: find out what it is that cherishes the sense of fear. Is it a void, or is it not?"

Daie never advises us just to hold up a *kōan* before the mind; he tells us, on the contrary, to make it occupy the very center of attention by the sheer strength of an inquiring spirit. When a *kōan* is backed up by such a spirit, it is, he says, "like a great consuming fire which burns up every insect of idle speculation that approaches it." Without this stimulating spirit of inquiry philosophically colored, no *kōan* can be made to hold up its position before the consciousness. Therefore, it is almost a common-sense saying among Zen masters to declare that, "In the mastery of Zen the most important thing is to keep up a spirit of inquiry; the stronger the spirit the greater will be the satori that follows; there is, indeed, no satori when there is no spirit of inquiry; therefore begin by inquiring into the meaning of a *kōan*."

According to Kōhō Gemmyō,[2] we have this:

"The *kōan* I ordinarily give to my pupils is: 'All things return to the One; where does the One return?' I make them search after this. To search after it means to awaken a great inquiring spirit for the ultimate meaning of the *kōan*. The multitudinousness of things is reducible to the One, but where does this One finally return? I say to them: Make this inquiry with all the strength that lies in your personality, giving yourself no time to relax in this effort. In whatever physical position you are, and in whatever business you are employed, never pass your time idly. Where does the One finally return? Try to get a definite answer to this query. Do not give yourself up to a state of doing nothing; do not exercise your fantastic imagination, but try to bring about a state of perfect identification by pressing your spirit of inquiry forward, steadily, and uninterruptedly. You will be then like a person who is critically ill, having no appetite for what you eat or drink. Again you will be like an idiot, with no knowledge of what is what. When your searching spirit comes to this stage, the time has come for your mental flower to burst out."

2 1238–1295.

Koin Jōkin, late in the fifteenth century, has this to say regarding the *kōan* exercise:

" 'Searching and contriving' (*kufū*) may best be practiced where noise and confusion do not reach; cut yourself off from all disturbing conditions; put a stop to speculation and imagination; and apply yourself wholeheartedly to the task of holding on to your *kōan*, never letting it go off the center of consciousness, whether you are sitting or lying, walking or standing still. Never mind in what condition you are placed, whether pleasing or disagreeable, but try all the time to keep the *kōan* in mind, and reflect within yourself who it is that is pursuing the *kōan* so untiringly and asking you this question so unremittingly.

"As you thus go on, intensely in earnest, inquiring after the inquirer himself, the time will most assuredly come to you when it is absolutely impossible for you to go on with your inquiry, as if you had come to the very fountain of a stream and were blocked by the mountains all around. This is the time when the tree together with the entwining wisteria breaks down, that is, when the distinction of subject and object is utterly obliterated, when the inquiring and the inquired are fused into one perfect identity. Awakening from this identification, there takes place a great satori that brings peace to all your inquiries and searchings."

Tenki Zui's [3] advice to students of Zen is this:

"Have your minds thoroughly washed off of all cunning and crookedness, sever yourselves from greed and anger which rise from egotism, and let no dualistic thoughts disturb you any longer so that your consciousness is wiped perfectly clean. When this purgation is effected, hold up your *kōan* before the mind: 'All things are resolvable into the One, and when is this One resolved? Where is it really ultimately resolved?'

"Inquire into this problem from beginning to end, severally as so many queries, or undividedly as one piece of thought, or simply inquire into the whereabouts of the One. In any event, let the whole string of questions be distinctly impressed upon your consciousness so as to make it the exclusive object of attention. If you allow any idle thought to enter into the one solid, uninterruptible chain of inquiries, the outcome will ruin the whole exercise.

"When you have no *kōan* to be held before your minds, there will be no occasion for you to realize a state of satori. To seek

3 From Unsei Shukō's "Biographies of the Famous Zen Masters of Ming."

satori without a *kōan* is like boiling sands which will never yield nourishing rice.

"The first essential thing is to awaken a great spirit of inquiry and strive to see where the One finally resolves itself. When this spirit is kept constantly alive so that no chance is given to languor or heaviness or otioseness to assert itself, the time will come to you without your specially seeking it when the mind attains a state of perfect concentration. That is to say, when you are sitting, you are not conscious of the fact; so with your walking or lying or standing, you are not at all conscious of what you are doing; nor are you aware of your whereabouts, east or west, south or north; you forget that you are in possession of the six senses; the day is like the night, and vice versa. But this is still midway to satori, and surely not satori itself. You will have yet to make another final and decided effort to break through this, a state of ecstasy, when the vacuity of space will be smashed to pieces and all things reduced to perfect evenness. It is again like the sun revealing itself from behind the clouds, when things worldly and superworldly present themselves in perfect objectivity."

According to Sozan Jōki: [4]

"It is necessary for the uninitiated to have a kind of tool wherewith to take hold of Zen; and it is for this reason that they are told to practice the *nembutsu*, that is, to be thinking of the Buddha. The Buddha is no other than Mind, or rather, that which desires to see this Mind. Where does this desire, this thought take its rise? From the Mind, we all say. And this Mind is neither a mind, nor a Buddha, nor a something. What is it then?

"To find it out, let them abandon all that they have accumulated in the way of learning, intellection, and knowledge; and let them devote themselves exclusively to this one question, 'Who is it that practices the *nembutsu* (*namu-amida-butsu*)?' Let this inquiring spirit assert itself to the highest degree. Do not try to reason it out; do not assume a state of mere passivity for satori to come by itself; do not allow yourself to cherish false thoughts and imaginations; do not let ideas of discrimination assert themselves. When your striving and seeking are constant, permitting no breaks and interruptions, your *dhyāna* will naturally be matured, and your inquiring spirit (*gidan*) brought up to the inevitable crisis. You will then see that *nirvāna* and *samsara*, the land of purity and

---

[4] Shukō's "Biographies."

the land of defilement, are mere idle talk, and that there is from the beginning nothing requiring explanation or commentary, and further that Mind is not a somewhat belonging to the realm of empirical consciousness and therefore not an object of mental comprehension."[5]

Dokuhō Kizen[6] who flourished in the latter half of the fifteenth century used to advocate strongly the awakening of an inquiring spirit, as is seen in the following passage:[7]

"If you are determined to escape birth and death, a great believing heart is first of all to be awakened and great vows to be established. Let this be your prayer: So long as the *kōan* I am holding this moment is not solved, so long as my own face which I have even prior to my birth is not seen, so long as the subtle deeds of transmigration are not destroyed, I make up my mind most resolutely not to abandon the *kōan* given me for solution, not to keep myself away from truly wise teachers, and not to become a greedy pursuer of fame and wealth; and when these determinations are deliberately violated, may I fall in the evil paths. Establishing this vow, keep a steady watch over your heart so that you will be a worthy recipient of a *kōan*.

"When you are told to see into the meaning of '*Mu*' the essential thing to do in this case is to let your thought be focused on the 'why' of the Buddha-nature being absent in the dog. When the *kōan* deals with the oneness of all things, let your thought be fixed on the 'where' of this oneness. When you are told to inquire into the sense of the *nembutsu*, let your attention be principally drawn on the 'who' of the *nembutsu*. Thus, turning your light of reflection inwardly, endeavor to enter deeply into a spirit of in-

---

[5] J. *fukatoku*, C. *pu-k'o-tê*, S. *anupalabdha*.

[6] His stanza on the Zen experience is recorded in Shukō's "Biographies of the Famous Zen Masters of Ming":

> "Here rules an absolute quietness, all doings subside;
> Just a touch, and lo, a roaring thunder-clap!
> A noise that shakes the earth, and all silence;
> The skull is broken to pieces, and awakened I am. from the dream!"

[7] Quoted in the "Breaking Through the Zen Frontier Gate." (*Zenkan Sakushin*).

quiry. If you feel that you are not gaining strength in this exercise, repeat the whole *kōan* as one complete piece of statement from the beginning to the end. This orderly pursuance of the *kōan* will help you to raise your spirit of inquiry as to the outcome of it. When this spirit is kept alive without interruption and most sincerely, the time will come to you when you perform, even without being aware of it, a somersault in the air. After experiencing this you may come back to me and see how my blows are dealt out."

Kūkoku Keiryō[8] seems to·be an advocate of the *nembutsu* as well as the *kōan*, but as far as he advises his pupils to exercise themselves on a *kōan*, he upholds the spirit of inquiry to be the sustaining force in the exercise. For he says that the *kōan* is to be "silently inquired into," that the "*Mu*" is to be "made lucid" by "furiously" attending to it; that students of Zen should apply themselves to this thought, "This mind is kept working while the body continues its Māyā-like existence, but where is it to rest when the dead body is cremated?" To find out where the oneness of things ultimately lies, the student must reflect within himself and inquire into the problem so as to locate definitely its whereabouts.[9]

All these masters belonging to late Yüan and early Ming, when the *kōan* system became a definitely settled method in the mastery of Zen, agree in keeping up a strong inquiring spirit as regards the meaning of the *kōan* or the spirit itself that thus inquires. The *kōan* is not just to be held up before the mind as something that gathers up like a magnet all one's mental energies about it; the holding must be sustained and nourished by the strong undercurrent of spiritual energy without whose backing the holding becomes mechanical and Zen loses its creative vitality.

We may question: Why is not the mechanical method also in full accord with the spirit of Zen? Why is the inquiring method to be preferred? Why is it necessary to keep up the spirit of inquiry

---

[8] From Shukō's "Biographies."

[9] Shukō comments on Keiryō's view of the *nembutsu:* When the question is concerned with the *nembutsu,* Keiryō, is not so particular about cherishing a spirit of inquiry as was generally done in his day. For he states in one of his letters that while, according to the master Udon, one is advised to inquire into the "who" of the *nembutsu,* this inquiring form of *nembutsu* is not absolutely necessary, for just to practice it in one's ordinary frame of mind will be enough.

throughout the *kōan* exercise? Has it anything to do with the nature of satori itself that emerges from the exercise? The reason why the masters have all emphasized the importance of the inquiring spirit is, in my view, owing to the fact that the *kōan* exercise started first to reproduce the Zen consciousness, which had grown up naturally in the minds of the earlier Zen devotees. Before these earlier men had taken to the study of Zen, they were invariably good students of Buddhist philosophy; indeed, they were so well versed in it that they finally became dissatisfied with it; for they came to realize that there was something deeper in its teachings than mere analysis and intellectual comprehension. The desire to penetrate behind the screen was quite strong in them.

What is the Mind, or the Buddha-nature, or the Unconscious that is always posited behind the multitudinousness of things, and is felt to be within ourselves? They desired to grasp it directly, intuitively, as the Buddhas of the past had done. Impelled by this desire to know, which is the spirit of inquiry, they reflected within themselves so intensely, so constantly, that the gate was finally opened to them, and they understood. This constant knocking at the gate was the antecedent condition that always seemed to be present and resulted in the maturing of their Zen consciousness.

The object of the exercise is to bring about this intense state of consciousness, in a sense artificially, for the masters could not wait for a genius to rise spontaneously,[10] and therefore sporadically, from among their less spiritually-equipped brothers. Unless the aristocratic nature of Zen was somewhat moderated, so that even men of ordinary capacity could live the life of a Zen master, Zen itself might rapidly disappear from the land where Bodhidharma and his followers had taken such special pains to make its root strike in deeply. Zen was to be democratized, that is, systematized.

Honei Ninyū[11] says in one of his sermons: "Shouldering a bag,

10 According to Kūkoku Keiryō: "Anciently, there were probably some who had satori without resorting to the *kōan* exercise, but there are none nowadays who can ever attain satori without strenuously applying themselves to the exercise."

11 Disciple of Yōgi Hōe; before he became a Zen devotee he was a great scholar of Tendai philosophy. When he came to Secchō, who was a great figure in the Ummon school of Zen, the master at once recognized in him a future Zen master. To stimulate him, Secchō addressed him sarcastically, "O you great college professor!" The remark stung Honei to the quick, and he

holding a bowl, I have been pilgrimaging for more than twenty years all over the country and visited more than a dozen masters of Zen. But at present I have no special attainment to call my own. If I have, I can tell you, I am not much better than a piece of rock devoid of intelligence. Nor had those reverend masters of Zen whom I visited any special attainment which might benefit others. Ever since I remain a perfect ignoramus with no knowledge of anything, with no intelligence to understand anything. I am, however, satisfied with myself. Inadvertently carried by the wind of karma I find myself at present in the country of Chiang-ning, and have been made to preside over this humble monastery and to lead others, mixing myself with people of the world. Here thus as a host I serve all the pilgrims coming from various parts of the country. There is enough of salt, sauce, porridge, and rice with which to feed them sufficiently. My time, thus engaged, is passed quietly, but as to the truth of Buddhism there is not even a shadow of it to dream of."

If all Zen masters held themselves on to this exalted view of Zen Buddhism, who would ever be able to succeed them and uninterruptedly transmit to posterity their experience and teaching? Sekiden Hōkun says:[12]

> Very few indeed there are who can walk the path of
>   our Fathers!
> In depth and steepness it surpasses an abysmal pit;
> Uselessly I extend the hand to help the passengers;
> Let the moss in my front court grow as green as it
>   chooses.

[12] From his *Sayings*, Vol. II.

---

determined to surpass in Zen even this great master. When he finally became a master, he appeared in the pulpit and said: "Behold, I am now in the tongue-pulling hell!" So saying, he was seen as if pulling out his tongue with his own hand and exclaimed: "Oh! Oh! This hell is meant for liars." Another time, seeing his attendant monk offering incense to the Buddha, preparatory to a regular discourse to be given by the master, he said, "Monks, my attendant has already given you a sermon," and without another word came down from the pulpit.

This view of Zen is what we must expect, of course, of a genuine Zen master, but when the moss of the Zen courtyard is never disturbed by the footsteps of any human beings, what will become of Zen? The path must be made walkable, to a certain extent at least; some artificial means must be devised to attract some minds who may one day turn out to be true transmitters of Zen.[13]

The rise of the *kōan* exercise was altogether a natural growth in the history of Zen. Being so, the function of a first *kōan* must be to reproduce as it were artificially the same state of consciousness that was experienced by the earlier masters in a more spontaneous way. This means to bring the spirit of inquiry into a point of concentration or "fixation." The *kōan* shows no logical clue to take hold of in an intellectual and discursive manner, and therefore an uninitiated Yogin has to turn away from logic to psychology, from ideation to personal experience, from what is his own only superficially to his inmost being.

The *kōan* does not, indeed, make light of reasoning, that is, it does not try to check it by force; but as the *kōan* stands before the Yogin like "an iron wall and a silver mountain" against any advance of speculation or imagination, he has no choice but to abandon reasoning. He must find some other means of approach. He cannot yield up his spirit of inquiry, for it is that which makes him stronger and more determined than ever to break through the iron wall. When the *kōan* is properly presented, it never crushes this spirit but gives it greater stimulation.

It was because of this inquiring mind that the earlier Zen devotees became dissatisfied with all the intellectual explanations of things, and that they came finally to a master and knew what they wanted of him. Without this perpetual urge from within, they might have remained well contented with whatever philosophical teachings were given them in the sutras and sastras. This urge from within was thus never to be ignored even when the *kōan* exercise came to replace the more spontaneous rise of Zen consciousness. *Sanshin* or *gijō*, which is no other than this urge or this inquiring spirit, is therefore now always kept in the foreground in the study of Zen. The master's advice: "See where you are going to rest after death, after cremation"; or "Exerting all

---

[13] That Zen was something unapproachable from its first appearance in China can easily be gathered from the legend that Bodhidharma kept up his lonely, silent meditation for nine years.

your mental energies, inquire into the final abode where the oneness of things returns"; or "Awaken a great spirit of inquiry and
see where the One returns; do not let this spirit vacillate or falter";
or "See what kind of mental attitude it is, see what meaning is
yielded here, be decided to search out all that is contained therein"; or "Ask of your self, inquire into your self, pursue your self,
investigate within your self, and never let others tell you what it
is, nor let it be explained in words."

When a Yogin grapples with the *kōan* in this manner, he is ever
alive to the spirit of Zen, and so is the *kōan*. As the problem is a
living one and not at all a dead one, satori which follows must
also be a really living experience.

Metaphysically stated, we can say that a persistent appeal to
the spirit of inquiry is based on a firm faith in the working of
Buddha-nature in every individual being. It is in fact this Buddha-
nature itself that leads us to inquire into the abode of the One.
The keeping up of an inquiring spirit in Zen devotees means no
less than the self-assertion of Buddha-nature. Hence the statement
that "the greater the faith the stronger the spirit of inquiry, and the
stronger the spirit of inquiry the deeper the attainment of satori."[14]

Faith and an inquiring spirit are not contradictory terms, but
are complementary and mutually conditioning. The reason why
the old masters were so persistent in keeping up a great spirit of
inquiry in the *kōan* exercise becomes now intelligible. Probably
they were not conscious of the logic that was alive behind their
instruction. The presence of Buddha-nature could only be recognized by a perpetual knocking at a door, and is not this knocking
an inquiring into? The Chinese character which I have rendered
"spirit of inquiry" literally means "to doubt" or "to suspect," but in
the present case "to inquire" will be more appropriate. Thus *daigi*
(*ta-i*) will mean "great mental fixation resulting from the utmost
intensification of an inquiring spirit."

Hakuin writes in one of his letters, in which he treats of the
relative merits of the *nembutsu* and the *kōan:* "In the study (of
Zen) what is most important is the utmost intensification of an inquiring spirit. Therefore, it is said that the stronger the inquiring
spirit, the greater the resulting satori, and that a sufficiently strong
spirit of inquiry is sure to result in strong satori. Further, accord-

[14] Quoted by Busseki Ian Shin in a Zen history entitled *Hui-yüan hsü-lioh.*
(Egen Zokuryaku.)

ing to Engo, the greatest fault (with Zen devotees) is the lack of an inquiring spirit over the *kōan*. When their inquiring spirit reaches its highest point of fixation there is a moment of outburst. If there are a hundred of such devotees, nay a thousand of them, I assure you, every one of them will attain the final stage. When the moment of the greatest fixation presents itself, they feel as if they were sitting in an empty space, open on all sides and extending boundlessly; they do not know whether they are living or dead; they feel so extraordinarily transparent and free from all impurities, as if they were in a great crystal basin, or shut up in an immense mass of solid ice; they are again like a man devoid of all sense; if sitting, they forget to rise, and if standing, they forget to sit.

"Not a thought, not an emotion is stirred in the mind which is now entirely and exclusively occupied with the *kōan* itself. At this moment they are advised not to cherish any feeling of fear, to hold no idea of discrimination, but to go on resolutely ahead with their *kōan*, when all of a sudden they experience something akin to an explosion, as if an ice basin were shattered to pieces, or as if a tower of jade had crumbled, and the event is accompanied with a feeling of immense joy such as never before has been experienced in their lives. . . . Therefore, you are instructed to inquire into the *kōan* of '*Mu*' and see what sense there is in it. If your inquiring spirit is never relaxed, always intent on '*Mu*' and free from all ideas and emotions and imaginations, you will most decidedly attain the stage of great fixation. . . . This is all due to the presence of an inquiring spirit in you; for without that the climax will never be reached, and, I assure you, an inquiring spirit is the wings that bear you on to the goal."[15]

One of the practical reasons why the mechanical method of holding the *kōan* which is not accompanied by a spirit of inquiry is disclaimed by the masters is that the devotee's mind becomes concentrated on mere words or sounds. This, however, may not be an altogether bad thing, as we may see later on, only that we cannot be sure of reaching, as maintained by Hakuin and others, the stage of the greatest fixation prior to the outburst of satori.

The presence of an inquiring spirit paves the way much more readily and surely to satori, because satori is what gives satisfaction to the inquiring spirit, but chiefly because the inquiring spirit awakens the faith which lies at the basis of our being. The Zen

[15] From Hakuin's work known as *Orategama*.

masters say, "Where there is faith (*shin, hsin*), there is doubt (*gi, i,*)" that is, where there is faith, there is an inquiring spirit, for doubting is believing. Let it be remarked that doubting or inquiring in Zen does not mean denying or being skeptical, it means desiring to see, to come in direct contact with the object itself, putting aside all that stands between the seer and the object. The devotee as yet has no idea as to the what of the object he wishes to see, but he believes in its existence or presence within himself. Mere description or intellectual explanation does not satisfy him, his faith is not thereby confirmed. The desire for confirmation, to see his faith solidly or absolutely established, as in the case of sense perception, means the awakening of an inquiring spirit, and the importance of this is steadily maintained by Zen masters. If so, the mechanical repetition of the *kōan* must be said not to be in accord with the spirit of Zen.

In a book called "Hakuzan's Admonitions Regarding the Study of Zen,"[16] which belongs to late Ming, the question of an inquiring spirit (*gijō, i-ch'ing*) is discussed in detail. The following is an abstract.

In striving (*kufū*) to master Zen, the thing needed is to cherish a strong desire to destroy a mind subject to birth and death. When this desire is awakened, the Yogin feels as if he were enveloped in a blazing fire. He wants to escape it. He cannot just be walking about, he cannot stay quietly in it, he cannot harbor any idle thoughts, he cannot expect others to help him out. Since no moment is to be lost, all he has to do is to rush out of it to the best of his strength and without being disturbed by the thought of the consequence.

Once the desire is cherished, the next step is more technical in the sense that an inquiring spirit is to be awakened and kept alive, until the final moment of solution arrives. The inquiry is concerned with the whence of birth and the whither of death, and to be constantly nourished by the desire to rise above them. This is impossible unless the spirit of inquiry is matured and breaks itself out to a state of satori.

The method of maturing consists chiefly in:

1. Not caring for worldly things.
2. Not getting attached to a state of quietude.
3. Not being disturbed by pluralities of objects.

[16] *Hakuzan Oshō Sanzen Keigo* (*Po-shan Ho-shang san-ch'an ching-yü*). Mui Ganrai (1575–1630) is the author.

4. Being constantly watchful over oneself, behaving like a cat who is after a mouse.

5. Concentrating one's spiritual energy on the *kōan*.

6. Not attempting to solve it intellectually where there are no such cues in it.

7. Not trying to be merely clever about it.

8. Not taking it for a state of doing-nothing-ness.

9. Not taking a temporary state of transparency for finality.

10. Not reciting the *kōan* as if it were the *nembutsu* practice or a form of *dharaṇī*.

When these cautions are properly followed, the Yogin is sure to bring the spirit of inquiry to a state of maturity. If not, not only the spirit refuses to be awakened, but the Yogin is liable to get into wrong ways and will never be able to rise above the bondage of birth and death, that is, to realize the truth of Zen.

The wrong ways into which the Yogin may fall are:

1. Intellectualism, wherein the *kōan* is forced to yield up its logical contents.

2. A pessimistic frame of mind whereby the Yogin shuns such environments as are unfavorable to quiet contemplation.

3. Quietism, by which he tries to suppress ideas and feelings in order to realize a state of tranquillization or perfect blankness.

4. The attempt to classify or criticize according to his own intellectualistic interpretation all the *kōan* left by the ancient masters.

5. The understanding that there is something inside this body of the various combinations, whose intelligence shines out through the several sense organs.

6. And which by means of the body functions to perform deeds good or bad.

7. Asceticism, in which the body is uselessly subjected to all forms of mortification.

8. The idea of merit by the accumulation of which the Yogin desires to attain Buddhahood or final deliverance.

9. Libertinism, in which there is no regulation of conduct, moral or otherwise.

10. Grandiosity and self-conceit.

These, in short, are the ways of those whose spirit of inquiry is not sincere and therefore not in accordance with the spirit of the *kōan* exercise.

It is by means of this "spirit of inquiry" that we finally attain Hakuin's *daigi*, "great fixation" or "a state of oneness," where a mountain is not seen as such, nor a sheet of water as such, for the reason that pluralities lose their meaning and appear to the Yogin in their aspect of sameness. But that too is merely a stage in his progress toward the final realization, in which a mountain is a mountain and a sheet of water a sheet of water. When this state of great fixation is held as final, there will be no upturning, no outburst of satori, no penetration, no insight into Reality, no severing the bonds of birth and death.

PART V

The Life of Freedom in Zen

While living
Be a dead man,
Be thoroughly dead—
And behave as you like,
And all's well.

Bunan

1. ZEN BUDDHISM AS PURIFIER AND LIBERATOR OF LIFE[1]

ZEN in its essence is the art of seeing into the nature of one's own being, and it points the way from bondage to freedom. By making us drink right from the fountain of life, it liberates us from all the yokes under which we finite beings are usually suffering in this world. We can say that Zen liberates all the energies properly and naturally stored in each of us, which are in ordinary circumstances cramped and distorted so that they find no adequate channel for activity.

This body of ours is something like an electric battery in which a mysterious power latently lies. When this power is not properly brought into operation, it either grows moldy and withers away or is warped and expresses itself abnormally. It is the object of Zen, therefore, to save us from going mad or being crippled. This is what I mean by freedom, giving free play to all the creative and benevolent impulses inherently lying in our hearts. Generally, we are blind to the fact that we are in possession of all the necessary faculties to make us happy and loving toward one another. All the struggles we see around us come from this ignorance. Zen, therefore, wants us to open a "third eye," as Buddhists call it, to the hitherto undreamed-of region shut away from us through our own ignorance. When the cloud of ignorance disappears, the infinity of the heavens is manifested, where we see for the first time into the nature of our own being. We then know the signification of life, it is no longer blind striving, nor is it a mere display of brutal forces. While we know not definitely the ultimate purport of life, there is something in it that makes us feel infinitely blessed in the living of it and remain quite rested with it in all its evolution, without raising questions or entertaining pessimistic doubts.

When we are still full of vitality and not yet awakened to the knowledge of life, the seriousness of life's conflicts is for the mo-

[1] *The Eastern Buddhist*, Vol. I, No. 1, pp. 13–37.

ment in a state of quiescence. But sooner or later the time will come to face life squarely and solve its most perplexing and pressing riddles. Says Confucius, "At fifteen my mind was directed to study, and at thirty I knew where to stand." This is one of the wisest sayings by the Chinese sage. Psychologists will agree to this statement of his; for, generally, fifteen is about the age youth begins to look around in earnest and inquire into the meaning of life. All the spiritual powers hitherto securely hidden in the subconscious part of the mind break out almost simultaneously. When this breaking out is too precipitous and violent, the mind often loses its balance; in fact, many cases of nervous prostration reported during adolescence are chiefly due to this loss of the mental equilibrium. Usually the effect is not grave and the crisis may pass without leaving deep markings. In some characters, either through their inherent tendencies or the influence of environment upon their plastic constitution, the spiritual awakening stirs them to the very depths of their personality. This is the time they will be asked to choose between the "Everlasting No" and the "Everlasting Yea." This choosing is what Confucius means by "study"—the deeply delving into the mysteries of life.

Normally, the outcome of the struggle is the "Everlasting Yea," or "Let thy will be done"; for life is, after all, a form of affirmation, however negatively it might be conceived by the pessimists. Nevertheless, there are times in life when our too sensitive minds turn in the other direction and make us exclaim with Andreyev in *The Life of Man:* "I curse everything that you have given. I curse the day on which I was born. I curse the day on which I shall die. I curse the whole of my life. I fling everything back at your cruel face, senseless Fate! Be accursed, be forever accursed! With my curses I conquer you. What else can you do to me? . . . With my last thought I will shout into your asinine ears: Be accursed, be accursed!" This is a terrible indictment of life, it is a complete negation of life, it is a most dismal picture of the destiny of man on earth. Buddhists aptly speak of "Leaving no trace," for we know nothing of our future except that we all die away, including the very earth from which we have come. There are certainly things justifying pessimism.

Life, as most of us live it, is a struggle. As long as life is a form of struggle, it cannot be anything but suffering. Does not a struggle mean the impact of two conflicting forces, each trying to get the upper hand of the other? If life's battle is lost, the outcome is death, and death is the fearsomest thing in the world. Even when death be conquered, one is left alone, and the loneliness is more unbearable than the struggle itself. There is no turning away. One may not be conscious of this, and may go on indulging in momentary pleasures that are afforded by the senses. But this being unconscious does not in the least alter the facts of life. However insistently the blind may deny the existence of the sun, they cannot annihilate it.

The first of Buddha's "Fourfold Noble Truths" states that life is pain. Did not everyone of us come to this world screaming and in a way protesting? To be ejected from a warm, soft womb into cold and prohibitive surroundings was surely a painful incident, to say the least. Growth is always attended with pain. Teething is a painful process. Puberty is accompanied by a mental as well as physical disturbance. The growth of the organism called society is as well marked with painful cataclysms, and we are constantly witnessing its birth throes. We may calmly reason that this is all inevitable, that inasmuch as every reconstruction means the destruction of the old regime, we cannot help going through a painful operation. But cold, intellectual analysis does not alleviate the harrowing feelings we undergo. The pain inflicted on our nerves is ineradicable.

This process, however, is providential. For the more you suffer the deeper grows your character, and with the deepening of your character you read the more penetratingly into the secrets of life. Great artists, religious leaders, and social reformers have come out of the intensest struggles which they fought bravely, frequently in tears and with bleeding hearts. Unless you eat your bread in sorrow, you cannot taste of real life. Mencius says that when Heaven wants to perfect a great man it tries him in every possible way until he comes out triumphantly from all his painful experiences.

To me Oscar Wilde seems always posing or striving for an effect, and though he is considered an artist of standing, there is something about him that repels me. Yet even he exclaims in his *De Profundis:* "During the last few months I have, after terrible difficulties and struggles, been able to comprehend some of the lessons hidden in the heart of pain. Clergymen and people who use phrases without wisdom sometimes talk of suffering as a mystery. It is really a revelation. One discerns things one never discerned before. One approaches the whole of history from a different standpoint."

You can observe what sanctifying effects his prison life produced on his character. Had he gone through a similar trial in the beginning of his career, he might have produced far greater works than those we have of him at present.

We are too ego-centered. The ego shell in which we live is the hardest thing to outgrow. We seem to carry it all the time from childhood up to the time we die. We are, however, given chances to break through this shell, and the first and greatest of them is when we reach adolescence. This is the first time the ego comes to recognize the "other," or the awakening of sexual love. An ego, entire and undivided, now begins to feel a split in itself. Love hitherto dormant lifts its head and causes a great commotion. For the love now stirred demands at once the assertion and the annihilation of the ego. Love makes the ego lose itself in the object it loves, and yet at the same time it wants to have the object as its own. This is a contradiction, and a struggle that is a tragedy of life. This elemental feeling must be one of the divine agencies whereby man is urged to advance in his upward walk. God gives tragedies to perfect man. The greatest bulk of literature ever produced in this world is but the harping on the same string of love, and we never seem to grow weary of it. But this is not what we are concerned with here. I want to emphasize that through the awakening of love we get a glimpse into the infinity of things, and that this glimpse urges youth to Romanticism or to Rationalism according to his temperament and environment and education.

When the ego shell is broken and the "other" is taken into its own body, we can say that the ego has denied itself or that the ego has taken its first steps toward the infinite. Religiously, here ensues an intense struggle between the finite and the infinite, between the intellect and a higher power, or, more plainly, between the flesh and the spirit. This is the problem of problems that has driven many a youth into the hands of Satan. The struggle to be fought in sincerity may go on up to the age of thirty, when Confucius "knew where to stand." The religious consciousness is then fully awakened, and all the possible ways of escaping from the struggle or bringing it to an end are most earnestly sought in every direction. Books are read, lectures are attended, sermons are greedily taken in, and various religious exercises or disciplines are tried.

How does Zen solve the problem of problems?

In the first place, it proposes the solution by directly appealing to facts of personal experience and not to book knowledge. The nature of one's own being where apparently rages the struggle between the finite and the infinite is to be grasped by a faculty beyond the intellect. For Zen says it is the latter that first made us raise the question which it could not answer by itself, and that therefore it is to be put aside to make room for something higher and more enlightening. The intellect has a peculiarly disquieting quality about it. Though it raises questions to disturb the serenity of the mind, it is too frequently unable to give ultimate answers to them. It upsets the blissful peace of ignorance and yet it does not restore the former state of rest. Because it points out ignorance, it is often considered illuminating, whereas the fact is that it disturbs, not always bringing light on its path. It is not final, it waits for something higher than itself for the solution of the questions it raises regardless of consequences. Were it able to bring rest and order for us settling the matter once for all, an Aristotle or a Hegel would have sufficed with a single system of philosophy. But the history of thought proves that each new structure raised even by a man of extraordinary intellect is sure to be torn down by the succeeding ones. This constant tearing down and building up are all right as far as philosophy itself is concerned, for the inherent nature of the intellect demands this kind of activity. But when it comes to the question of life itself we cannot wait for the ultimate solution to be offered by the intellect. We cannot suspend even for a moment our life activity in order that philosophy may unravel its mysteries. Mysteries or no, live we must. The hungry cannot wait until a complete analysis of food is obtained and the nourishing value of each element is determined. Scientific knowledge of food for the dead will be of no use whatever. Zen therefore does not rely on the intellect for the solution of its deepest problems.

By personal experience it is meant to plunge right into the fact firsthand and not to come to it through an intermediary. Its favorite analogy is: to point at the moon a finger is needed, but woe to those who take the finger for the moon; a basket is welcome to carry our fish home, but when the fish are safely on the table why should we eternally bother ourselves with the basket? Here stands the fact, and let us grasp it with naked hands lest it should slip away—this is what Zen proposes to do. As nature abhors a vacuum, Zen abhors anything coming between the fact and ourselves. According to Zen, there is no struggle in the fact itself such as between the finite and the infinite, between the flesh and the spirit.

These are idle distinctions fictitiously designed by the intellect for its own interest. Those who take them seriously or those who try to read them into the very fact of life are those who take the finger for the moon. When we are hungry we eat; when we are sleepy we lay ourselves down; and where does the infinite or the finite come in here? Are not we complete in ourselves and each in himself? Life as it is lived suffices. It is only when the disquieting intellect steps in and tries to murder it that we stop living and imagine ourselves to be short of or in something. The intellect has its usefulness in its proper sphere, but it must not interfere with the flowing of the life stream. The fact of flowing must under no circumstances be arrested or meddled with; for the moment your hands are dipped into it, its transparency is disturbed, it ceases to reflect your image which you have had all the time and will continue to have to the end of time.

Almost corresponding to the "Four Maxims" of the Nichiren Sect, Zen has its own four statements:

> A special transmission outside the Scripture;
> No dependence on words or letters;
> Direct pointing at the Mind of man;
> Seeing into one's Nature and the attainment of Buddhahood.

This sums up all that is claimed by Zen as religion. Of course we must not forget that there is a historical background to this bold pronunciamento. At the time of the introduction of Zen into China, most of the Buddhists were addicted to the discussion of highly metaphysical questions, contented with merely observing the ethical precepts laid down by the Buddha and leading a lethargic life entirely absorbed in the contemplation of the evanescence of things worldly. They missed apprehending the great fact of life itself, which flows altogether outside of these vain exercises of the intellect or of the imagination. Bodhidharma and his successors recognized this pitiful state of affairs. Hence their proclamation as above cited. In a word, they mean that Zen has its way of pointing to the nature of one's own being, and that when this is done one attains to Buddhahood, in which all the contradictions and disturbances caused by the intellect are entirely harmonized in a unity of higher order.

For this reason Zen never explains but indicates, it does not appeal to circumlocution nor generalization. It always deals with facts, concrete and tangible. Seen from the world of logic, Zen may be full of contradictions and repetitions. But as it stands above all things, it goes serenely on its own way. As a Zen master aptly puts it, "carrying his homemade cane on the shoulder, he goes right among the mountains." It does not challenge logic, it simply walks its path of facts, leaving all the rest to their own fates. It is only when logic forgetting its place and functions tries to step into the track of Zen that it loudly proclaims its principles and forcibly drives out the intruder. The intellect is not despised for it is often utilized for the cause of Zen itself. To show some examples of Zen's direct dealing with the fundamental facts of existence, the following are selected:

Rinzai once delivered a sermon, saying: "Over a mass of reddish flesh there sits a true man who has no title; he is all the time coming in and out from your sense organs. If you have not yet testified to the fact, Look! Look!" A monk came forward and asked, "Who is this true man of no title?" Rinzai came right down from his straw chair and taking hold of the monk exclaimed: "Speak! Speak!" The monk remained irresolute, not knowing what to say, whereupon the master, letting him go, remarked, "What worthless stuff is this true man of no title!" Rinzai then went straight back to his room.

Rinzai was noted for his "rough" and direct treatment of his disciples. He never liked the roundabout dealings which characterized the methods of a lukewarm master. He must have inherited this directness from his own teacher Ōbaku, by whom he was struck three times for asking what the fundamental principle of Buddhism was. It goes without saying that Zen has nothing to do with mere striking or roughly shaking the questioner. If you take this as constituting the essentials of Zen, you would commit the same gross error as one who took the finger for the moon. As in everything else, but most particularly in Zen, all its outward manifestations or demonstrations must never be regarded as final. They just indicate the way where to look for the facts. Therefore, these indicators are important, we cannot do well without them. But once caught in them unawares, they are like entangling meshes, we are doomed; for Zen can never thus be comprehended. Zen does not try to ensnare you in the net of logic or of words. What Zen warns is not to be caught in them. Therefore, Rinzai grasps with his naked hands what is directly presented to us all. If a third eye of ours is opened undimmed, we shall know in an unmistakable manner where Rinzai is driving us. We have first to get right into the very spirit of the master and interview the inner man. No amount of wordy explanations will ever lead us into the nature of our own selves. The more you explain, the further astray it goes. It is like trying to catch your own shadow. You run after it and it runs with you at an identical pace. When you realize it, you read deep into the spirit of Rinzai or Ōbaku, and their kindheartedness will begin to be appreciated.

Ummon the great master had to lose one of his legs in order to get an insight into the life principle from which the whole universe takes rise, including his own humble existence. He visited his teacher Bokujū, who was a senior disciple of Rinzai under Ōbaku, three times before he was admitted to see him. The master asked, "Who are you?" "I am Bun-en,"[2] answered the monk. When the truth-seeking monk was allowed to go inside the gate, the master took hold of him by the collar and demanded: "Speak! Speak!" Ummon hesitated, whereupon the master pushed him out of the gate, saying, "Oh, you good-for-nothing fellow!"[3] While the gate was hastily shut, one of Ummon's legs was caught and broken. The intense pain resulting from this apparently awakened the poor fellow to the greatest fact of life. He was no more a solicitous, pity-begging monk; the realization now gained paid more than enough for the loss of his leg. Says Confucius, "If a man understands the Tao in the morning, it is well with him even when he dies in the evening." Some would feel indeed that truth is of more value than mere vegetative or animal living. But, alas, there are so many living corpses wallowing in the mud of ignorance and sensuality.

This is where Zen is most difficult to understand. Why this sarcastic vituperation? Why this seeming heartlessness? What fault had Ummon to deserve the loss of his leg? He was a poor truth-seeking monk, earnestly anxious to be enlightened by the master. Was it really necessary for the master to shut him out three times, and when the gate was half opened to close it again so violently, so inhumanly? Was this the truth of Buddhism Ummon was so eager to get? But the outcome of all this singularly was what was desired by both of them. As to the master, he was satisfied to see the disciple attain an insight into the secrets of his being; and as

---

[2] His name. Ummon is the monastery where he later became a master.

[3] Literally, "an old clumsy gimlet of the Ch'in dynasty."

regards the disciple he was most grateful for what was done to
him. Evidently, Zen is the most irrational, inconceivable thing in
the world. And this is why Zen is not subject to logical analysis or
to intellectual treatment. It is to be directly and personally experienced by each of us in his 'inner being. Just as two stainless
mirrors reflect each other, the fact and our own spirits must stand
facing each other with no intervening agents. When this is done we
are able to seize upon the living, pulsating fact itself.

Freedom is an empty word until this happens. The first object
was to escape the bondage in which all finite beings find themselves, but if we do not cut asunder the very chain of ignorance
that binds us hands and feet, where shall we look for deliverance?
And this chain of ignorance is wrought of nothing else but the intellect and sensuous infatuation, which cling tightly to every
thought we may have, to every feeling we may entertain. They are
hard to get rid of, they are like wet clothes as is aptly expressed
by the Zen masters. "We are born free and equal." Whatever this
may mean socially or politically, Zen maintains that it is absolutely
true in the spiritual domain, and that all the fetters and manacles
we seem to be carrying about us are put on later through ignorance of the true condition of existence. All the treatments, sometimes literary and sometimes physical, which are liberally and kind-
heartedly given by the masters to inquiring souls, are intended to
regain the original state of freedom. And this is never really realized until we once personally experience it through our own efforts,
independent of any ideational representation. The ultimate standpoint of Zen is that we have been led astray through ignorance to
find a split in our own being, that there was from the very beginning no need for a struggle between the finite and the infinite, that
the peace we seek so eagerly has been here all the time. Sotōba
(Su Tung-p'o), the noted Chinese poet and statesman, expresses
the idea in the following verse:

> Misty rain on Mount Lu,
> And waves surging in Chê-chiang;
> When you have not yet been there,
> Many a regret surely you have;
> But once there and homeward you wend,
> And how matter-of-fact things look!
> Misty rain on Mount Lu,
> And waves surging in Chê-chiang.

Seigen Ishin also asserts, "Before a man studies Zen, to him mountains are mountains and waters are waters; after he gets an insight into the truth of Zen through the instruction of a good master, mountains are not mountains and waters are not waters; but after this when he really attains to the abode of rest, mountains are once more mountains and waters are waters."

Bokujū was once asked, "We have to dress and eat every day, and how can we escape from all that?"

The master replied, "We dress, we eat."

"I do not understand you," said the questioner.

"If you don't understand put your dress on and eat your food."

Zen thus deals in concrete facts and does not indulge in generalization. I do not wish to add legs to a painted snake, but if I may add my philosophical comments on Bokujū's, I say this. We are all finite, we cannot live out of time and space; inasmuch as we are earth-created, there is no way to grasp the infinite, how can we deliver ourselves from the limitations of existence? This is perhaps the idea put in the first question of the monk, to which the master replies: Salvation must be sought in the finite itself, there is nothing infinite apart from finite things; if you seek something transcendental, that will cut you off from this world of relativity, which is the same thing as the annihilation of yourself. Salvation cannot be had at the cost of your own existence. If so, put your dress on and eat your food, and find your way of freedom in this dressing and eating. This was too much for the questioner, who, therefore, confessed himself as not understanding the meaning of the master. Therefore, the latter continued: Whether you understand or not, just the same go on living in the finite, with the finite; for you die if you stop eating and keeping yourself warm on account of your aspiration for the infinite. No matter how you struggle, *nirvāṇa* is to be sought in the midst of *saṃsāra* (birth-and-death). Whether an enlightened Zen master or an ignoramus neither can escape the so-called laws of nature. When the stomach is empty, both are hungry; when it snows, both have to put on an extra flannel. I do not, however, mean that they are both material existences, they are what they are, regardless of their conditions of spiritual development. As the Buddhist scriptures have it, the darkness of the cave itself turns into enlightenment when a torch of spiritual insight burns. It is not that a thing called darkness is first taken out and another thing known by the name of enlightenment is carried in later, but that enlightenment and darkness are substantially one and the same thing from the very beginning; the change from the one to the other has taken place inwardly or subjectively. Therefore the finite is the infinite, and vice versa. These are not two separate things, though we are compelled to conceive them intellectually. This is the idea, logically interpreted, contained in Bokujū's answer given to the monk. The mistake consists in our splitting into two what is really and absolutely one. Is not life one as we live it, before we apply the murderous knife of intellect to it?

On being requested by the monks to deliver a sermon, Hyakujō Nehan told them to work on the farm, after which he would give them a talk on the great subject of Buddhism. They did as they were told, and came to the master for a sermon, when the latter, without saying a word, merely extended his open arms toward the monks. Perhaps there is after all nothing mysterious in Zen. Everything is open to your full view. If you eat your food and keep yourself cleanly dressed and work on the farm to raise your rice or vegetables, you are doing all that is required of you on this earth, and the infinite is realized in you. How realized? When Bokujū was asked what Zen was he recited a Sanskrit phrase from a sutra, "Mahāprajñāpāramitā!"[4] The inquirer acknowledged his inability to understand the purport of the strange phrase, and the master put a comment on it, saying:

> My robe is all worn out after so many years' usage.
> And parts of it in shreds loosely hanging have been
>   blown away to the clouds.

Is the infinite after all such a poverty-stricken mendicant?

One thing in this connection we cannot afford to lose sight of— that is, the peace of poverty (for peace is only possible in poverty) is obtained after a fierce battle with the entire strength of your personality. A complacency gleaned from idleness or from a *laissez-faire* attitude of mind is a thing most to be abhorred. There is no Zen in this, but sloth and mere vegetation. The battle must rage in its full vigor and masculinity. Without this, whatever peace obtains is a simulacrum, and it has no deep foundation, the first storm encountered will dash it to the ground. Zen is quite emphatic about this. The moral virility found in Zen, apart from its mystic flight,

---

[4] *Makahannyaharamita!* in Japanese.

comes from the fighting of the battle of life courageously and undauntedly.

From the ethical point of view, therefore, Zen may be considered a discipline aiming at the reconstruction of character. Our ordinary life only touches the fringe of personality, it does not cause a commotion in the deepest parts of the soul. Even when the religious consciousness is awakened, most of us lightly pass it over. We thus live on the superficiality of things. We may be clever and bright but what we produce lacks depth and sincerity, and does not appeal to the inmost feelings. Some are utterly unable to create anything except makeshifts or imitations betraying their shallowness of character and want of spiritual experience. While Zen is primarily religious, it also molds our moral character. It may be better to say that a deep spiritual experience is bound to effect a change in the moral structure of one's personality.

How is this so?

The truth of Zen is such that when we want to comprehend it penetratingly we must undergo a great struggle, sometimes a long and exacting constant vigilance. To be disciplined in Zen is no easy task. A Zen master once remarked that the life of a monk can be attained only by a man of great moral strength, and that even a minister of the state may not be expected to become a successful monk. A minister of the state in China was considered to be the greatest achievement a man could ever hope for in this world. Not that a monkish life requires the austere practice of asceticism, but that it implies the raising of one's spiritual powers to their highest notch. The utterances and activities of the great Zen masters have come from this elevation. They are not intended to be enigmatic or driving us to confusion. They are the overflowing of a soul filled with deep experiences. Therefore, unless we are ourselves elevated to the same height as the masters, we cannot gain the same commanding views of life.

Says Ruskin:

And be sure also, if the author is worth anything, that you will not get at his meaning all at once—nay, that at his whole meaning you will not for a long time arrive in any wise. Not that he does not say what he means, and in strong words, too; but he cannot say it all and what is more strange, will not, but in a hidden way and in parable, in order that he may be sure you want it. I cannot see quite the reason of this, nor analyze that cruel reticence in the breasts of wise men which makes them always hide their deeper thought. They do not give it to you by way of help, but of reward, and will make themselves sure that you deserve it before they allow you to reach it.

And this key to the royal treasury of wisdom is given us only after patient and painful moral struggle.

The mind is ordinarily chock full with all kinds of intellectual nonsense and passional rubbish. They are of course useful in their own ways in our daily life. There is no denying that. But it is chiefly because of these accumulations that we are made miserable and groan under the feeling of bondage. Each time we want to make a movement, they fetter us, they choke us, and cast a heavy veil over our spiritual horizon. We feel as if we are constantly living under restraint. We long for naturalness and freedom, yet we do not seem to attain them. The Zen masters know this, for they too have gone through the same experiences. They want to have us rid ourselves of these wearisome burdens which we really do not have to carry in order to live a life of truth and enlightenment. Thus they utter a few words and demonstrate with action that, when rightly comprehended, will deliver us from the oppression and tyranny of these intellectual accumulations. But the comprehension does not come to us so easily. Being so long accustomed to the oppression, the mental inertia becomes hard to remove. In fact it has gone down deep into the roots of our own being, and the whole structure of personality is often to be overturned. The process of reconstruction is stained with tears and blood. But the height the great masters have climbed cannot otherwise be reached; the truth of Zen can never be attained unless it is attacked with the full force of one's being. The passage is strewn with thistles and brambles, and the climb is slippery in the extreme. It is no pastime but the most serious task in life; no idlers will ever dare attempt it. It is indeed a moral anvil on which your character is tempered. To the question, "What is Zen?" a master gave this answer, "Boiling oil over a blazing fire." This scorching experience we have to go through before Zen smiles on us and says, "Welcome home."

One of these utterances by the Zen masters that will stir a revolution in our minds is this: Hō-koji, formerly a Confucian, asked Baso, "What kind of man is he who does not keep company with any thing?" Replied the master, "I will tell you when you have swallowed up in one draught all the waters in the West River." What an irrelevant reply to the most serious question one can ever raise in the history of thought! It sounds almost sacrilegious when we know how many souls there are who go down under the weight of this question. But Baso's earnestness leaves no room for doubt, as is quite well known to all the students of Zen. In fact, the rise of Zen after the sixth patriarch, Enō, was due to the brilliant career of Baso, under whom there arose more than eighty fully-qualified masters, and Hō-koji, who was one of the foremost lay disciples of Zen, earned a well-deserved reputation as the Vimalakīrti of Chinese Buddhism. A talk between two such veteran Zen masters could not be an idle sport. However easy and even careless it may appear, there is hidden in it a most precious gem in the literature of Zen. We cannot tell how many students of Zen were made to sweat and weep because of the inscrutability of Baso's statement.

To give another instance: a monk asked the master Keishin of Chōsha, "Where has Nansen gone after his death?"

Replied the master, "When Sekitō was still in the order of young novitiates, he saw the sixth patriarch."

"I am not asking about the young novitiate. What I wish to know is, where is Nansen gone after his death?"

"As to that," said the master, "it makes one think."

The immortality of the soul is another big question. The history of religion is built upon this one question, one may almost say. Everybody wants to know about life after death. Where do we go when we pass away from this earth? Is there really another life? or is the end of this the end of all? While there may be many who do not worry themselves as to the ultimate significance of the solitary, "companionless" One, there are none perhaps who have not once at least in their lives asked themselves concerning their destiny after death. Whether Sekitō when young saw the sixth patriarch or not does not seem to have any inherent connection with the departure of Nansen. The latter was the teacher of Chōsha, and naturally the monk asked him whither the teacher finally passed. Chōsha's answer is no answer from the ordinary rules of logic. Hence the second question, but still a sort of equivocation from the lips of the master. What does this "making one think" explain? From this it is apparent that Zen is one thing and logic another. When we fail to make this distinction and expect of Zen to give us something logically consistent and intellectually illuminating, we altogether misinterpret the signification of Zen. Did I not state in the beginning that Zen deals with facts and not with generalizations? This is the very point where Zen goes straight to the foundations of personality. The intellect does not lead us there; for we do not live in the intellect, but in the Will. Brother Lawrence says (*The Practice of the Presence of God*) "that we ought to make a great difference between the acts of the understanding and those of the will: that the first were comparatively of little value, and the others, all."

Zen literature is brim full of such statements, which seem to have been uttered casually and innocently, but those who know will testify to the fact that all these utterances dropped so naturally from the lips of the masters are as potent as deadly poisons, that when they are once taken in they cause such violent pain as to make one's intestines wriggle nine times and more, as the Chinese would express it. But it is only after pain and turbulence that all the internal impurities are purged and one is reborn with a new outlook on life. It is strange that Zen grows intelligible only when these mental struggles are gone through. But the fact is that Zen is an experience actual and personal, and not a knowledge to be gained by mere analysis or comparison. "Do not talk poetry except to a poet; only the sick know how to sympathize with the sick." This explains the whole situation. Our minds are to be matured to be in tune with those of the masters. Let this be accomplished, and when one note is struck, the whole symphony is born. And what Zen does for us is to prepare our minds to be yielding and appreciative recipients of old masters. Psychologically, Zen thus releases whatever energies we may have in store, of which we are not conscious in ordinary circumstances.

2. HUMAN VALUES IN ZEN[1]

WE are requested to say something objective, something scientific, in regard to human values. But I am afraid I have nothing to say which is so characterized. The fact is that I am not a scholar, I am just a plain, ordinary layman deeply interested in the advance and enhancement of human culture in general. It is for this reason that I may be permitted to express my humble view concerning the promotion of "unselfish behavior." As to its "causes and conditions," I am sure there are many able speakers who have been carrying on their investigations and may have something objective and scientific and highly contributive to human welfare. It is not mine to follow their examples.

The point I wish to make is that there is something "new," though not scientific or objective perhaps, in the way of evaluating human behavior. The fact is that this something "new" is really not at all new, it is very ancient, and its being ancient makes it new because there is nothing new under the sun and what is old is new when it is viewed from an angle hitherto neglected.

All the values in the broad field of human activity may be stamped as old and dilapidated and even worn out in the sense that ever since the dawn of civilization we have been talking about them constantly. And because of this constant talk, the values inestimably valuable are weatherbeaten and have lost their freshness and consequently their viability.

One way to resuscitate them is to re-evaluate them and see what is that which ultimately constitutes their value. When we do this we discover that all values come from unselfish motives. Any act with its base in an egoistic source is bad, hateful, and ugly, and goes against the general welfare of humanity. Egoism is thus always found at the basis of such an act. The ego is the mischief-maker. Even when we do something, objectively speaking, good and benefiting all of us, the act may not be judged as gen-

---

[1] *New Knowledge in Human Values*, A. H. Maslow (ed.), Harper, 1959, pp. 94–105.

uinely good if we find the shadow of ego lurking behind it.

Roughly speaking, values have two aspects: subjective and objective, and I like to emphasize the subjective, and state that a value is valueless when it is not subjectively free from an egoistic impulse. In terms of Taoism or Mahayana Buddhism, the value is a value when it is a no-value. Psychologically, when all the values are shut up in the depths of the unconscious or in the limbo of oblivion, we have the values in their genuine form. Lao-tzŭ says that what can be designated as this or that is not Tao. Tao is nameless. The very moment you say, "It is good," the good loses its goodness. The really good is just so, and no more, no less. The good is just-so-ness. So with the rest of human values.

When God saw the world created in response to His fiat, "Let there be light," He said, "It is good." This "good" has nothing to do with any human way of evaluating things. The "good" is the isness of things, it is not something added to them from an external source. If it is, it is valueless. Anything of value is something inherent in it. When a thing is genuinely in its isness, it is valuable. A painted beauty is no beauty. The beautiful need not claim itself to be beautiful, it stands before us and we all know it is beautiful.

Some may say that this kind of beauty or goodness or truth is not human but divine and that we are asked to talk about human values. But I should like to ask if there is anything that is divine which is not at the same time human. The human and the divine are one, for what is humanly valuable is so only because it is divine. This is the reason why I say that the old is new and the new is old.

Bashō (1644–94), the founder of the modern Japanese poetical form known today as *haiku*, had this to utter when he saw Mount Yoshino covered with cherry blossoms:

> What a sight!
> What a sight!
> Nothing more!
> Mount Yoshino, flower-bedecked![2]

[2] Another translation:
> Wonderful!
> Wonderful!
> Only this!
> Mount Yoshino flowering!

Shakespeare also has something to this effect: "O wonderful, wonderful, and most wonderful wonderful!"

A feeling when at its highest and deepest refuses to be wordy. It utters—and not coherently. To be wordy and coherent and logical is the function of the intellect. The feeling—especially what I like to call primary, that is, what we feel even before any designation or differentiation could have taken place, the sheer feeling of being just-so, even before our intellectual discrimination made its start in our consciousness—this is what I like to be understood as the primary feeling.

Some again may protest, "How presumptuous and arrogant you are, to confuse what is divine and what is human!"

But I protest on my part: "How self-degrading you are not to identify what is human with what is divine!" How can we exist even for a moment without being divine? That we are at all is of God, we owe everything to God. Even not to be of God is of God. How can we escape from being of God? Things are humanly valuable just because they are of God.

When we pursue this line of thought, everything we judge to be of value, to be meaningful, to be worth preserving or conserving as humanly desirable, is all of God. Human values so called then acquire a new, fresh, and inspiring significance.

Love is regarded by every one of us as a great force remolding and ameliorating the structure of human community. There are no thinkers or religious leaders who do not emphasize the importance of Love in our communal life. Love corresponds to the Buddhist idea of *mahākaruṇā*, and according to Buddhists the Buddha-heart is no other than *mahākaruṇā* itself. *Mahākaruṇā* is equivalent to *agape* as distinguished from *eros*.

Christians would say *eros* is mixed up with egoistic interests. To purge it of all such impurities the ego must be sacrificed, that is, crucified, and then regenerated. Crucifixion and resurrection symbolize it.

In this respect Buddhism differs from the Christian doctrine. For Buddhists tell us that there is from the beginning no ego and therefore that there is no need of crucifying it. This is known as the doctrine of non-ego or *nirātman* or *anatta*. When we realize that the *ātman* is *non-existent*, *mahākaruṇā* asserts itself, as *mahākaruṇā* constitutes the Buddha-heart, and the Buddha-heart is no other than the human heart.

Apparently, there is much misunderstanding about the doctrine of *anatta* which is construed as negativistic. The misunderstanding, in fact, rises from grammar. The prefix *a* or *an* is deprivative. But the *anatta* is not to be interpreted from the purely linguistic point of view, for the doctrine is based on an existential experience. The denial of the ego does not stop just with the denial. Experience goes much more deeply and is more informative of reality than linguistics. Even when the ego is found non-existent, as an entity, life goes on as ever, regardless of our conceptual turmoil. Even when Buddha is reported to have found "the house builder" who is no more to build him a house, and further, even when it is said that his "mind has gone to an utter dissolution and all his desires are destroyed," he never ceased to keep up his activities as the great teacher of the Dharma (truth), which is still alive together with his personality even after his entrance into *parinirvāṇa* more than twenty-four centuries ago. I like to ask, "What is that which thus continues to be living among us?"

This cannot be anything else but Life, that is, Love, or *mahākaruṇā*. As long as the conceptual delusion of an ego entity subsists, *mahākaruṇā* remains dormant, it invariably finds itself beclouded by the delusive ego, and its activity is refracted, warped. In spite of this, it occasionally breaks through the clouds of egotism, and deeds of pure altruism are performed to the wonderment of the agent himself. This is why Mencius upholds human nature to be inherently good, free from ego-centered impulses. "Creative altruism" is not something foreign to human beings. The creativity is obstructed only when intellection grows too rampantly and unwarrantedly.

A modern Japanese Zen master tells us:

> While living
> Be a dead man,
> Be thoroughly dead—
> And behave as you like,
> And all's well.

This is a most significant saying and directly points to the creative altruistic way of living. Probably there is nothing new in this Zen master's advice. I do not think there is, and yet how refreshingly new it is! We all love to live, to be alive, and yet are we really living? We may be living in a way, but not as we ought to, as human beings honorable and dignified. We can readily understand what a miserable life each one of us is leading when we reflect within ourselves, or when we read our daily papers.

We must die once while living and live a new life. Paradise must be lost and regained. It's a good thing that God once chased us out of the Garden of Eden because of our eating the fruit of knowledge. We must eat another fruit of knowledge which nullifies, òr rather revivifies in its own way, the effect of the first fruit. The first fruit killed us. Being killed, we must not stay killed, we must revive. This is possible when we eat a second fruit of knowledge, which is a new knowledge tapping the source of creativity.

There are two Zen stories which I wish to quote in connection with "human values" or with "creative altruism," for, according to my view, the stories illuminatingly point out where lies the new way of living.

There was a great Zen master in China during the T'ang dynasty. He is said to have lived one hundred and twenty years, and his name was Jōshū. In the monastery compounds where he resided there was a stone bridge reputed all over the empire. Once a visiting monk asked the master, "We hear so much of your stone bridge, but as I see it it is no more than a rickety old log bridge."

Jōshū answered, "You just see the log bridge and do not see the stone one."

The monk asked, "What then is the stone bridge?"

"Horses pass over it, asses pass over it," was the reply.

Not only horses and asses, but in these days automobiles of any description pass over it. The bridge is solidly built, as solidly as the earth itself. The wise and the stupid, the rich and the poor, the noble and the humble, the young and the old—they all walk on it in full confidence, with the feeling of utmost security as if they were the earth itself.

Two monks were engaged in a heated discussion about the ultimate truth that does not permit equivocation. The question arose whether the Tathāgata ever indulged in ambiguities. One said that his words can never be ambiguous. The other then asked, "What are the Tathāgata's words?"

The first monk answered, "How could the deaf hear them?"

The second one remarked, "Sure enough, you have fallen into a secondary stage."

"What then are the Tathāgata's words?"

The question was immediately followed by this: "Have a cup of tea, O my brother monk."

"Have a cup of tea" is one of the favorite phrases of the Zen monks in Japan as well as in China. When a visitor comes it is customary to treat him to a cup of tea, it is an act of courtesy in our daily life. Once a Chinese Zen master of the tenth century was asked, "What is the temple (saṅghārāma)?"

"Just this."

"What is the person in the temple?"

"What?! What!?"

"What will you do when a visitor calls on you?"

"Have a cup of tea."

Such an epigrammatic dialogue known as mondō, "question-and-answer," illustrates a typical weltanschauung and lebens-anschauung of the Zen master. Take "the temple" for the objective world, and "the person" for the subject, and "the visitor's calling" for human situation, and the whole mondō will begin to assume a much greater significance than a monkish life in the mountain retreat.

Some may object after reading the two Zen stories here cited, saying: "You may be all right as far as individuals are concerned, but how about our social, or communal, or international life? We as individuals on the whole seem to be decent, well-behaving, orderly, law-abiding, trustworthy, but as soon as we live as a group in whatever form it may take, we lose all the fine qualities we have shown as individuals, and the devil, or whatever devilishness is still alive in every one of us perhaps, lifts his head and most violently asserts himself. This we all know. How should we deal with this ugly fact?"

This is indeed the crux of our modern world situation. I have been long wrestling with the problem, but so far I have not been able to solve it. All that I can say at present is: whatever form our group life may take, its constituents are individuals after all. Let, therefore, the constituent individuals be thoroughly purged of all their defiled ingredients and have their individual mahākaruṇā regain its original purity and work out its way without being hindered by our human overintellectualization. For this purpose, my two Zen stories are to be thoroughly, experientially studied and assimilated into our daily life.

We all know the story of the Prodigal Son. There is a similar story in a Buddhist sutra known as the "Lotus Gospel." Probably they come from the same original source. What interests me here is that whatever wanderings a man may have to go through he invariably longs for his home and wants to return. The lost paradise is to be regained. Otherwise, we have no security. It is strange that we have to lose in order to gain. Time loses itself in the infinity and returns to itself again. We are historical beings and as such we go through all the vicissitudes of an historical being. But we are so made as to transcend history in order to secure the Pure Land of eternal happiness. History cannot be denied, but to be really an historical being man is to go beyond history. History is time. As long as he is in time, he is enslaved by his future as well as his present. He cannot help being the plaything of all kinds of affective disturbances, among which we may specify such things as recollection and anticipation. He then can never be master of himself. Without being master of himself he can never be free and creative.

The Prodigal Son is a miserable creature during his wanderings. But the time comes upon him when he suddenly realizes that his home is nowhere else but in his wanderings. In fact, he has been carrying his home all the time on his shoulders throughout his long, long wanderings and wayfarings. With this realization his past and his future crystallize themselves, as it were, in his absolute present, he is the eternal now, he stands in the "here-now," he is master of himself. He is no more a creature. Yes, he is a creature and yet not a creature, for while his creatureliness does not go beyond the superficial realm of objectivity, he is yet no more in it, he has gone beyond it. That is to say, he is back to himself and is in himself, he stands in his "here-now," he is not a slave to anybody or anything, but a master and lord of the universe, the storehouse of infinite possibilities.

As limited beings we have to talk in terms of time and history, and this is where logicians and linguists have their special field of study. But we are more than that, we also belong to the realm of eternals. And as such we are entitled to resort to experiences attainable in it. The thing, however, which we ought not to forget is that the infinity is not something distinguishable from the finite and thus in possession of an independent entity—which makes it one of the finite. While it may not be quite exact to say that the infinite is the finite, the infinite is not to be regarded as a kind of quiddity existing as such in the finite. After all, finite and infinite are words conceptually distinguishable, and therefore subject to ambiguities.

In our actual life no such things take place, and those who have an experience in this field know at once what the monk meant when he told his monk friend to have a cup of tea. From the ordinary conceptual point of view, we may expostulate, "What has the absolute truth to do with sipping a cup of tea?" The Zen master will answer: "It is from this sipping that creative altruism makes its start, and if anything new can come out of human values it is from the cup of tea taken by the two monks."

After writing so far, I think of another possible objection coming from the audience, which is: "So far so good, perhaps, Mr. Speaker, but your talk lacks precision. The stone bridge which is trodden by the lame as well as by the athlete, and a cup of tea which is sipped not only by two friendly monks but by each one of us in his daily life—in what logical connection does the bridge or the tea stand to the issue which is the chief concern of today's Conference? Can't you give us a precise position you take in the discussion?"

To answer this, I am afraid, will take more time than we can afford here. But this much I can say: the word "precise," along with other cognate terms, belongs to the field of sciences, dealing with things subject to quantitative measurements, and those terms themselves, strictly speaking, are only approximately definite. The sciences limit themselves, and within these limits they can talk about definability and verifiability. Once beyond them, all the scientific or logical terminology will lose its value, and we have to resort to expressions paradoxical or contradictory or nonsensical or full of absurdities. And the strange fact is that it is those extraordinary expressions that will more "precisely," or more definitively, tell the experiences belonging to the realm of ultimate reality.

It is not exact to call those experiences intuitional in its usual sense. Lacking a more appropriate English term "intuition" is used with the following reservation: for instance, in the case of Zen the experience is not between subject and object, but it is of a something which is neither subject nor object becoming conscious of itself.

Probably to make the matter more intelligible to our Christian audience, I may be allowed to resort to Christian terminology. The experience referred to is God becoming conscious of Himself, or the Godhead objectifying Himself as creator God. To explain further: when God was in Himself, something happened, humanly speaking, and He willed to create the world. It is in fact better to say that God could not help willing to create the world; in God, necessity and free will are one; and when this willing took place in Him, He became conscious of Himself. This is the Zen experience.

I am going into theology, I'm afraid. I have many more things to say in this connection to avoid possible misunderstandings. But I must stop with this remark:

There is, after all, nothing new under the sun. The oldest is the newest and the newest is the oldest.

While preparing this paper, I received a kind of memorandum released, I believe, for the press with the date of September 29 (Sunday), 1957, in which I note the following (in abstract): "The old ways of handling the great problems of modern times are insufficient and altogether inadequate. We are here to attack them 'scientifically' and find the new ways of applying the new additional knowledge thus gained to the solution of the multitude of personal and social complexities which confront us now as the outcome of the advancing technology and industrialization."

In view of these statements, my presentation so far may seem to have nothing to do with the scientific treatment of the problems we are required to solve in a new way. It may further appear to be a kind of "exhortation" or a bit of "*a priori* thinking" as is condemned by the Program Committee. I am fully conscious of my paper not containing anything toward constructing a science of human values. I have no time, however, to justify my position; I only wish to say a few words more about "knowledge" or sciences generally.

There is no doubt this is the age of reason and technology, but at the same time we all know that it is not science and technology that will solve the problems confronting or rather threatening us these days so ominously. Before this fact, science and technology are utterly helpless. They are, on the contrary, fiercely fanning up the flames of war between nations, between races, between cultures. We talk about peace, disarmament, mutual confidence, reconciliation, and many other things, and yet we are not even to stop the testing of nuclear weapons, when we are fully aware of the fact that any substantial increase in nuclear explosions is surely a great danger not only to the human race but to all living beings. We claim that the defense measures are needed for prevention of war, but did they ever stop war? Are we not all the more bending our scientific and technological ingenuities toward the possible event of a war of mutual extermination? In many ways we seem to be rational and farsighted enough, but reason never keeps us within limits of rationality. When we want to break through reason, we do it quite readily regardless of science and technology. We make use of them to promote irrationality.

What moves human beings is decidedly not science and the rationality of human nature; nor does the scientific treatment of anything and whatever knowledge accruing therefrom help us in any practical way to solve the problems such as we are facing at present. To believe in them is a modern superstition.

If science or knowledge per se can *do* anything, let the scientist or the learned man take the reins of government and see if he accomplishes anything. It is the man and not his knowledge that does things. I do not know exactly how old world history is. But, for the sake of argument, let it be ten thousand years. During this time we have accumulated a large amount of knowledge, and our ways of living have made wonderful advances. But are we better men and women than those brothers and sisters of, say, two thousand years ago, in Europe or in China or India? Essentially, human nature has not changed. One instance will suffice to prove this. How did we behave before and during World War II? And how are we behaving after it?

If science and knowledge and technology and industrial civilization can accomplish anything in the way of alleviating any kind of tension we are feeling at present on all sides, let us find some means whereby all the leading statesmen of all nations, beginning with Eisenhower and Khrushchev, come to this school of science and technology and after three or four years of study go back to their respective positions and resume their business as before. What can we expect of them then? Do we not know that we'll be facing the same state of affairs as before? As long as the man himself does not go through a transformation no amount of science and knowledge will improve the human situation in which we all are at this moment. The politicians, individually, may be good, respectable men, but when they are at the head of a group, small or large, the leaders are no more leaders, they are democrats. They follow the masses whose mentality requires ages to be lifted up above the level of mediocrity.

Let us, therefore, be patient and wait another one thousand, or two thousand, or even a million, years, for that matter, but in the meantime work steadily, continuously, and with all our moral and spiritual resources toward improving human nature basically. For this purpose, the best method is to follow, individually and collectively, the old ways of discipline. This is also, I am sure, the new method of enhancing the sense of creative altruism.

3. *LIVING IN THE LIGHT OF ETERNITY*[1]

I

ETERNITY is, as a philosopher defines it, "an infinite extent of time, in which every event is future at one time, present at another, past at another."[2]

This is an interesting definition, no doubt, but what is "infinity"? "No beginning and no end?" What is time that has no beginning and no end? Time cannot be defined without eternity nor eternity without time. Is eternity time going on forever in two directions, past-ward and future-ward? Is time eternity chopped to pieces or numbers?

Let us see whether a symbolic representation of eternity is more amenable to our understanding or imagination. What would a poet, for instance, say about it?

> I saw Eternity the other night,
> Like a great ring of pure and endless light,
>   All calm, as it was bright,
>   And round beneath it, Time, in hours, days, years
> Driven by the spheres,
>   Like a vast shadow moved, in which the world
> And all her train were hurled.[3]

Henry Vaughan's lines, as Bertrand Russell points out,[4] are evidently suggested by Plato's *Timaeus* in which Plato states:

[1] *Living in the Light of Eternity*, Pendle Hill, 1954.

[2] *The Dictionary of Philosophy*, edited by Dagobert D. Runes (New York: Philosophical Library), p. 97.

[3] Henry Vaughan, "The World."

[4] *History of Western Philosophy*, p. 144.

Now the nature of the ideal being was everlasting, but to bestow this attribute in its fulness upon a creature was impossible. Wherefore He God resolved to have a moving image of eternity, and when He set in order the heaven, He made this image eternal but moving according to number, while eternity itself rests in unity; and this image we call time. For there were no days and nights and months and years before the heaven was created, but when He constructed the heaven He created them also.[5]

Further, Plato goes on to say that the heaven and time are so closely knit together that if one should dissolve the other might also be dissolved:

Time, then, and the heaven came into being at the same instant in order that, having been created together, if ever there was to be a dissolution of them, they might be dissolved together. It was framed after the pattern of the eternal nature, that it might remember this as far as was possible; for the pattern exists from eternity, and the created heaven has been, and is, and will be, in all time.

The heaven is eternity; and "the sun and moon and the five stars" are "the forms of time, which imitate eternity and revolve according to a law of number," and the moving images of the eternal essence which alone "is" and is not subject to becoming. What we see with our sense is not the heaven itself, the original eternal being itself, which is only in God's mind. If we wish, therefore, "to live in the light of eternity" we must get into God's mind. "Is this possible?" one may ask. But the question is not the possibility of achieving this end, but its necessity; for otherwise we cannot go on living even this life of ours though bound in time and measurable in days and nights, in months and years. What is necessary, then, must be possible. When the Eternal negated itself to manifest itself in "the forms of time," it assuredly did not leave the forms helpless all by themselves; it must have entered into them though negated. When the Eternal negated itself into the moving, changing, sensible forms of time, it hid itself in them. When we pick them up, we must see "the shoots of everlastingness" in them.

5 *Dialogues of Plato,* translated by B. Jowett (London: Oxford University Press), Vol. III, p. 456. Published in the United States by Random House.

"Was" and "will be" must be in "is." What is finite must be carrying in it, with it, everything belonging to infinity. We who are becoming in time, therefore, must be able to see that which eternally "is." This is seeing the world as God sees it, as Spinoza says, "*sub specie aeternitatis.*"

Eternity may be regarded as a negation as far as human finitude is concerned, but inasmuch as this finitude is always changing, becoming, that is, negating itself, what is really negative is the world itself and not the eternal. The eternal must be an absolute affirmation which our limited human understanding defines in negative terms. We must see the world in this affirmation, which is God's way of seeing the world, seeing everything as part of the whole. "Living in the light of eternity" cannot be anything else.

B. Jowett, translator of Plato, writes in his introduction to *Timaeus*:

Not only Buddhism, but Greek as well as Christian philosophy, show that it is quite possible that the human mind should retain an enthusiasm for mere negations. . . . Eternity or the eternal is not merely the unlimited in time but the truest of all being, the most real of all realities, the most certain of all knowledge, which we nevertheless only see through a glass darkly.

The enthusiasm Jowett here refers to is not "for mere negations" or for things which are "seen only through a glass darkly"; it cannot come out of the human side of finitude; it must issue from eternity itself, which is in the finitude, indeed, and which makes the finitude what it is. What appears to be a mere negation from the logical point of view is really the is-ness of things. As long as we cannot transcend the mere logicality of our thinking, there will be no enthusiasm of any kind whatever in any of us. What stirs us up to the very core of our being must come from the great fact of affirmation and not from negation.

II

Buddhism is generally considered negativistic by Western scholars. There is something in it which tends to justify this view, as we observe in Nāgārjuna's doctrine of "Eight No's":

> There is no birth,
> Nor is there death;
> There is no beginning,
> Nor is there any ending;
> Nothing is identical with itself,
> Nor is there any diversification;
> Nothing comes into existence,
> Nor does anything go out of existence.[6]

What he aims at by negating everything that can be predicated of the *Dharma* (Ultimate Reality) is to bring out thereby what he terms the Middle Way. The Middle Way is not sheer nothingness, it is a something that remains after every possible negation. Its other name is the Unattainable, and the *Prajñāpāramitā-sūtra* teach the doctrine of the Unattainable. I will try to illustrate what it means in order to clarify the deeper implications of this contradictory statement.

Tokusan[7] of T'ang dynasty, China, was a learned scholar versed in this doctrine. He was not satisfied with the Zen form of Buddhist teaching which was then rapidly gaining power, especially in the south of China. Wishing to refute it he came out of Szŭ-ch'uan in the southwestern part of China.

His objective was to visit a great Zen monastery in the district of Li-yang. When he approached it he thought of refreshing himself with a cup of tea. He entered a teahouse by the roadside and ordered some refreshments. Seeing the bundle he was carrying on his back, the old lady who happened to be the teahouse keeper asked what it was.

Tokusan said, "This is Seiryō's great commentary on the "Diamond Sutra," a portion of the great *Prajñāpāramitā-sūtra.*"

"I have a question. If you answer it I shall be glad to serve you the refreshments free of charge. Otherwise, you will have to go elsewhere."

"What is your question?" the monk asked.

"According to the 'Diamond Sutra,' 'The past mind is unattainable, the future mind is unattainable, and the present mind is unattainable.' If so, what is the mind which you wish to punctuate?"

---

6 The *Mādhyamika-śastra*, "Treatise on the Middle Way."

7 790–865.

An explanation is needed here. In Chinese, "refreshments," *tien-hsin*, literally means "punctuating the mind." I do not know how the term originated. The teahouse keeper making use of "the mind" associated with "refreshments" quoted the sutra in which the mind in terms of time is said to be "unattainable" in any form, either past, present, or future. If this is the case, the monk cannot be said to have any "mind" which he wishes to "punctuate." Hence her question.

Tokusan was nonplused. He had not prepared for such questions while studying the sutra along the conventional line of conceptual interpretation. He could not give an answer and was obliged to go without his tea. Those who do not know how to transcend time will naturally find it difficult to attain *nirvāṇa* which is eternity.

The unattainability of *nirvāṇa* comes from seeking it on the other shore of becoming as if it were something beyond time or birth-and-death (*saṃsāra*). *Nirvāṇa* is *saṃsāra* and *saṃsāra* is *nirvāṇa*. Therefore, eternity, *nirvāṇa*, is to be grasped where time, *saṃsāra*, moves on. The refreshments cannot be taken outside time. The taking is time. The taking is something attainable, and yet it goes on in something unattainable. For without this something unattainable all that is attainable will cease to be attainable. This paradoxicality marks life.

Time is elusive, that is, unattainable. If we try to take hold of it by looking at it from the outside, we cannot even take ordinary refreshments. When time is caught objectively in a serialism of past, present, and future, it is like trying to catch one's own shadow. This is negating eternity constantly. The unattainable must be grasped from the inside. One has to live in it and with it. While moving and changing, one must become the moving and changing. Emerson in "Brahma" sings of the eternal as "one" in the changing and moving forms of time:

> They reckon ill who leave me out;
>   When me they fly, I am the wings;
> I am the doubter and the doubt,
>   And I the hymn the Brahmin sings.

Where "the doubter and the doubt" are one, there is Brahma as "the pattern of the eternal nature," which is God Himself. When "the doubter and the doubt" are separated and placed in the serialism of time, the dichotomy cuts into every moment of life, darkening forever the light of eternity.

"Living in the light of eternity" is to get into the oneness and allness of things and to live with it. This is what the Japanese call "seeing things *sono-mama*"[8] in their suchness, which in William Blake's terms is to "hold infinity in the palm of your hand, and eternity in an hour."

To see things as God sees them, according to Spinoza, is to see them under the aspect of eternity. All human evaluation is, however, conditioned by time and relativity. It is ordinarily difficult for us humans "to see a world in a grain of sand, and a heaven in a wild flower." To our senses, a grain of sand is not the whole world, nor is a wild flower in a corner of the field a heaven. We live in a world of discrimination and our enthusiasm rises from the consideration of particulars. We fail to see them "evenly" or "uniformly" as Meister Eckhart tells us to do, which is also Spinoza's way, Blake's way, and other wise men's way, East and West. Tennyson must have been in a similar frame of consciousness when he plucked a wild flower out of the crannied wall and held it in his hand and contemplated it.[9]

III

However difficult this way of looking at the world is, the strange thing to most of us, or rather the wonderful thing, is that once in a while we transcend the temporal and relativistic point of view. It is then that we realize that life is worth living, and that death is not the end of all our strivings, and furthermore that what Buddhists call "thirst" (*tṛiṣṇā*) is more deeply rooted than we imagine, as it grows straight out of the root of *karuṇā*.[10]

Let me cite Bashō, a Japanese *haiku* poet of the eighteenth century:

---

[8] In the "as-it-is-ness" of things.

[9] "Flower in the Crannied Wall."

[10] "Compassion." One may say it is the Buddhist equivalent of love.

Yoku mireba   [When] closely inspected,
Nazuna hana saku   Nazuna in bloom
Kakine kana   [Under] the hedge!

The *nazuna* is a small flowering wild plant. Even when in bloom it is hardly noticeable, having no special beauty. When the time comes, it blooms, fulfilling all that is required of a living being as ordered at the beginning of creation. It comes directly from God as does any other form of being. There is nothing mean about it. Its humble glory surpasses all human artificiality. But ordinarily we pass by it and pay not the slightest attention. Bashō at the time must have been strangely impressed by its blooming under a thickly growing hedge, modestly lifting its tender head hardly discernible from the rest. The poet does not at all express his emotions. He makes no allusions whatever to "God and man," nor does he express his desire to understand "What you are root, and all, and all in all." He simply looks at the *nazuna* so insignificant and yet so full of heavenly splendor and goes on absorbed in the contemplation of "the mystery of being," standing in the midst of the light of eternity.

At this point it is important to note the difference between East and West. When Tennyson noticed the flower in a crannied wall he "plucked" it and held it in his hand and went on reflecting about it, pursuing his abstract thought about God and man, about the totality of things and the unfathomability of life. This is characteristic of Western man.

His mind works analytically. The direction of his thinking is toward the externality or objectivity of things. Instead of leaving the flower as it is blooming in the cranny, Tennyson must pluck it out and hold it in his hand. If he were scientifically minded, he would surely bring it to the laboratory, dissect it, and look at it under the microscope; or he would dissolve it in a variety of chemical solutions and examine them in the tubes, perhaps over a burning fire. He would go through all these processes with anything, mineral or vegetable, animal or human. He would treat the human body, dead or alive, with the same innocence or indifference as he does a piece of stone. This is also a kind of seeing the world in the aspect of eternity or rather in the aspect of perfect "evenness."

When the scientist finishes (though the "when" of this is unpredictable) his examination, experimentation, and observation, he will indulge in all forms of abstract thinking: evolution, heredity, genetics, cosmogony. If he is still more abstract minded, he may extend his speculative mood to a metaphysical interpretation of existence. Tennyson does not go so far as this. He is a poet who deals with concrete images.

Compare all this with Bashō and we see how differently the Oriental poet handles his experience. Above all, he does not "pluck" the flower, he does not mutilate it, he leaves it where he has found it. He does not detach it from the totality of its surroundings, he contemplates it in its *sono-mama* state, not only in itself but in the situation as it finds itself—the situation in its broadest and deepest possible sense. Another Japanese poet refers to the wild flowers:

> All these wild flowers of the fields—
> Dare I touch them?
> I offer them as they are
> To all the Buddhas in the
> Three thousand chiliacosms!

Here is the feeling of reverence, of mystery, of wonderment, that is highly religious. But all this is not expressly given articulation. Bashō simply refers first to his "close inspection" which is not necessarily aroused by any purposeful direction of his intention to find something among the bushes; he simply looks casually around and is greeted unexpectedly by the modestly blooming plant which ordinarily escapes one's detection. He bends down and "closely" inspects it to be assured that it is a *nazuna*. He is deeply touched by its unadorned simplicity, yet partaking in the glory of its unknown source. He does not say a word about his inner feeling, every syllable is objective except for the last two syllables, "kana." "Kana" is untranslatable into English, except perhaps by an exclamation mark, which is the only sign betraying the poet's subjectivity. Of course, a *haiku* being no more than a poem of seventeen syllables cannot express everything that went on in Bashō's mind at the time. But this very fact of the *haiku's* being so extremely epigrammatic and sparing of words gives every syllable used an intensity of unexpressed inner feeling of the poet, though much is also left to the reader to discover what is hidden between the syllables. The poet alludes to a few significant points

of reference in his seventeen-syllable lines leaving the inner connection between those points to be filled by the sympathetically
or rather empathetically vibrating imagination of the reader.

IV

Western psychologists talk about the theory of empathy or transference of feeling or participation, but I am rather inclined to
propound the doctrine of identity. Transference or participation is
based upon the dualistic interpretation of reality whereas the
identity goes more fundamentally into the root of existence where
no dichotomy in any sense has yet taken place. From this point of
view, participation becomes easier to understand and may be more
reasonable or logical. For no participation is possible where there
is no underlying sense of identity. When difference is spoken of,
this presupposes one-ness. The idea of two is based on that of one.
Two will never be understood without one. To visualize this, read
the following from Traherne's *Centuries of Meditations*:

You never enjoy the world aright, till the Sea itself floweth in your
veins, till you are clothed with the heavens, and crowned with the stars:
and perceive yourself to be the sole heir of the whole world, and more
than so, because men are in it who are every one sole heirs as well as
you."[11]

Or this:

Your enjoyment of the world is never right, till every morning you
awake in Heaven; see yourself in your Father's Palace; and look upon
the skies, the earth, and the air as Celestial Joys; having such a reverend
esteem of all, as if you were among the Angels.[12]

Such feelings as these can never be comprehended so long as the
sense of opposites is dominating your consciousness. The idea of
participation or empathy is an intellectual interpretation of the

---

[11] *Centuries of Meditations*, Thomas Traherne, 1636–1674 (London: P. J.
and A. E. Dobell), p. 19.

[12] *Ibid.*

primary experience, while as far as the experience itself is concerned, there is no room for any sort of dichotomy. The intellect, however, obtrudes itself and breaks up the experience in order to make it amenable to intellectual treatment, which means a discrimination or bifurcation. The original feeling of identity is then lost and intellect is allowed to have its characteristic way of breaking up reality into pieces. Participation or empathy is the result of intellectualization. The philosopher who has no original experience is apt to indulge in it.

According to John Hayward, in his introduction to the 1950 edition of *Centuries of Meditations*, Traherne is "a theosopher or visionary whose powerful imagination enabled him to see through the veil of appearances and rediscover the world in its original state of innocence." This is to revisit the Garden of Eden, to regain Paradise, where the tree of knowledge has not yet begun to bear fruit. The Wordsworthian "Intimations" are no more than our longings for eternity that was left behind. It is our eating the forbidden fruit of knowledge which has resulted in our constant habit of intellectualizing. But we have never forgotten, mythologically speaking, the original abode of innocence; that is to say, even when we are given over to intellection and to the abstract way of thinking, we are always conscious, however dimly, of something left behind and not appearing on the chart of well-schematized analysis. This "something" is no other than the primary experience of reality in its suchness or is-ness, or in its *sono-mama* state of existence. "Innocence" is a biblical term and corresponds ontologically to "being *sono-mama*" as the term is used in Buddhism.

I quote further from Traherne whose eternity-piercing eye seems to survey the beginningless past as well as the endless future. *Meditations* is filled with wonderful insights born of the profound religious experience of one who has discovered his primal innocence.

Will you see the infancy of this sublime and celestial greatness? Those pure and virgin apprehensions I had from the womb, and that divine light wherewith I was born are the best unto this day, wherein I can see the Universe. . . .

Certainly Adam in Paradise had not more sweet and curious apprehensions of the world, than I when I was a child.

My very ignorance was advantageous. I seemed as one brought into the Estate of Innocence. All things were spotless and pure and glorious: yea, and infinitely mine, and joyful and precious. I knew not that there were any sins, or complaints or laws. I dreamed not of poverties, contentions or vices. All tears and quarrels were hidden from mine eyes. Everything was at rest, free and immortal, I knew nothing of sickness or death or rents or exaction, either tribute or bread. . . .

All Time was Eternity, and a perpetual Sabbath. . . .

All things abided eternally as they were in their proper places. Eternity was manifest in the Light of the Day, and something infinite behind everything appeared: which talked with my expectation and moved my desire. The city seemed to stand in Eden, or to be built in Heaven. . . .

V

Compared with these passages, how prosaic and emotionally indifferent Zen is! When it sees a mountain it declares it to be a mountain; when it comes to a river, it just tells us it is a river. When Chōkei one day after twenty years of hard study happened to lift the curtain and saw the outside world, he lost all his previous understanding of Zen and simply made this announcement:

> How mistaken I was! How mistaken I was!
> Raise the screen and see the world!
> If anyone asks me what philosophy I understand,
> I'll straightway give him a blow across his mouth
>   with my *hossu*.

Chōkei does not say what he saw when the screen was lifted. He simply resents any question being asked about it. He even goes to the length of keeping the questioner's mouth tightly closed. He knows that if one even tried to utter a word and say "this" or "that," the very designation misses the mark. It is like another master's bringing out before the entire congregation a monk who asked him who Buddha was. The master then made this remark, "Where does this monk want to find Buddha? Is this not a silly question?" Indeed, we are all apt to forget that every one of us is Buddha himself. In the Christian way of saying, we are all made in the likeness of God, or, in Eckhart's words, that "God's is-ness is my is-ness and neither more nor less."[13]

It may not be altogether unprofitable in this connection to give another Zen "case" where God's is-ness is made perceivable in the world of particulars as well as in the world of absolute oneness. To us the case illustrates the Eckhartian knowledge "that I know God as He knows me, neither more nor less but always the same." This is knowing things as they are, loving them in their *sono-mama* state, or "loving justice for its own sake,"[14] that is to say, "loving God without any reason for loving." Zen may look so remote and aloof from human affairs that between it and Eckhart some may be persuaded to see nothing of close relationship as I am trying to show here. But in reality Eckhart uses in most cases psychological and personalistic terms whereas Zen is steeped in metaphysics and in transcendentalism. But wherever the identity of God and man is recognized the Zen statements as they are given below will be intelligible enough.

Hakuin (1685–1768), a great Japanese Zen master of the Tokugawa era, quotes in his famous work known as *Kai-an-koku Go* (fas. 5) a story of Shun Rofu's interview with a lay disciple well seasoned in Zen. Shun (of the Sung dynasty) was still a young man when this interview took place. It was customary for this lay disciple to ask a question of a monk visitor who wanted to enjoy the hospitality of the devoted Zen Buddhist.

Q. "How about the ancient mirror which has gone through a process of thorough polishing?"

A. "Heaven and earth are illuminated."

Q. "How about before the polishing?"

A. "As dark as black lacquer."

---

[13] Blakney, p. 180.

[14] Eckhart's idea of "justice" may be gleaned from the following passages from his "Sermon" 18 (Blakney, pp. 178–82):

"He is just who gives to each what belongs to him."

"They are just who take everything from God evenly, just as it comes, great and small, desirable and undesirable, one thing like another, all the same, and neither more nor less."

"The just live eternally with God, on a par with God, neither deeper nor higher."

"God and I: we are one. By knowing God I take Him to myself. By loving God I penetrate Him."

The layman Buddhist was sorry to dismiss the monk as not fully deserving his hospitality.

Shun now returned to his old master and asked:

Q. "How about the ancient mirror not yet polished?"

A. "Fan-yang is not very far from here."

Q. "How about after the polish?"

A. "The Isle of Parrot, Ying-wu, lies before the Pavilion of Yellow Stork, Huang-ho."

This is said to have at once opened the monk's eye to the meaning of the "ancient mirror." "The mirror" in its is-ness knows no polishing. It is the same old mirror whether or not it goes through any form of polishing. "Justice is even," says Eckhart. For "the just have no will at all: whatever God wants, it is all one to them."

Now Hakuin introduces the following *mondō*:

A monk asked Hōun of Rosozan, a disciple of Nangaku Ejō (d. 744), "How do we speak and not speak?" This is the same as asking: How do we transcend the law of contradiction? When the fundamental principle of thought is withheld, there will be no thinking of God as Eckhart tells us, "God who is in His own creature—not as He is conceived by anyone to be—nor yet as something yet to be achieved—but more as an 'is-ness,' as God really is."[15] What kind of God can this be? Evidently, God transcends all our thought. If so, how have we ever come to conceive of God? To say God is "this" or "that" is to deny God, according to Eckhart. He is above all predicates, either positive or negative. The monk's question here ultimately brings us to the same form of quandary.

Hōun, instead of directly answering the monk, retorted, "Where is your mouth?"

The monk answered, "I have no mouth." Poor monk! He was aggressive enough in his first questioning, for he definitely demanded to get an answer to the puzzle: "How could reality be at once an affirmation and a negation?" But when Hōun counterquestioned him, "Where is your mouth?" all that the monk could say was, "I have no mouth." Hōun was an old hand. Detecting at once where the monk was, that is, seeing that the monk was still unable to transcend the dichotomy, Hōun pursued with "How do you eat your rice?"

The monk had no response. (The point is whether he had a real understanding of the whole situation.)

[15] Blakney, p. 204.

Later Tōsan, another master, hearing of this *mondō,* gave his own answer: "He feels no hunger and has no need for rice."

"One who feels no hunger" is "the ancient mirror" that needs no polishing, is he who "speaks and yet speaks not." He is "justice" itself, the justice is the suchness of things. To be "just" means to be *sono-mama,* to follow the path of "everyday consciousness," "to eat when hungry and to rest when tired." In this spirit I interpret Eckhart's passage: "If I were perpetually doing God's will, then I would be a virgin in reality, as exempt from idea handicaps as I was before I was born." "Virginity" consists in not being burdened with any forms of intellection, in responding with "Yes, yes" when I am addressed by name. I meet a friend in the street, he says, "Good morning," and I respond, "Good morning." This will again correspond to the Christian way of thinking: "If God told an angel to go to a tree and pick off the caterpillar, the angel would be glad to do it and it would be bliss to him because it is God's will."

A monk asked a Zen master, "I note an ancient wise man saying: 'I raise the screen and face the broad daylight; I move the chair and am greeted by the blue mountain.' What is meant by 'I raise the screen and face the broad daylight'?"

The master said, "Please pass me the pitcher there."

"What is meant by 'I move the chair and am greeted by the blue mountain'?"

"Please put the pitcher back where it was found." This was the answer given by the master.

All these *mondō* may appear unintelligible and the reader may conclude them to be altogether irrelevant to the subject of "living in the light of eternity." It is an inevitable criticism from the point of view of an ordinary man of the world. But let us listen to what Eckhart, one of the greatest mystics in the Christian world, states about the "now-moment" which is no other than eternity itself:

The now-moment in which God made the first man, and the now-moment in which the last man will disappear, and the now-moment in which I am speaking are all one in God, in whom there is only one now.

I have been reading all day, confined to my room, and feel tired. I raise the screen and face the broad daylight. I move the chair on the veranda and look at the blue mountains. I draw a long breath, fill my lungs with fresh air, and feel entirely refreshed. I make tea and drink a cup or two of it. Who would say that I am not living in the light of eternity? We must, however, remember that all these are events of one's inner life as it comes in touch with eternity or as it is awakened to the meaning of "the now-moment" which is eternity, and further that things or events making up one's outer life are no problems here.

VI

I quote again from Eckhart's sermon:

In eternity, the Father begets the Son in His own likeness. "The Word was with God and the Word was God." Like God, it had His nature. Furthermore, I say that God has begotten him in my soul. Not only is the soul like Him and He like it, but He is in it, for the Father begets His Son in the soul exactly as He does in eternity and not otherwise. He must do so whether He will or not. The Father ceaselessly begets his Son and, what is more, he begets me not only as His Son but as Himself and Himself as myself, begetting me in His own nature, His own being. At that inmost Source, I spring from the Holy Spirit and there is one life, one being, one action. All God's works are one and therefore He begets me as he does His Son and without distinction.

Is this not a bold saying? But there is no denying its absolute truth. Yet we must not forget that the truth of Eckhart's sermon comes from setting ourselves in the light of eternity. As long as we are creatures in time and seeking our own and not God's will, we shall never find God in ourselves. When references are made to Christian symbolism such as "God," "Father," "Son," "Holy Spirit," "begetting," and "likeness," the reader may wonder in what sense Buddhists interpret these terms. But the truth is that symbols are, after all, mere symbols and when their inner signification is grasped they can be utilized in any way one chooses. First, we must see into the meaning and discard the historical or existential encumbrances attached to the symbols and then we all, Christians as well as Buddhists, will be able to penetrate the veil.

The biblical God is said to have given His name to Moses on Mount Sinai as "I am that I am." This is a most profound utterance, for all our religious or spiritual or metaphysical experiences start from it. This is the same as Christ's saying, "I am before Abraham was." "I am," that is, Christ is eternity itself, while "Abraham was," for he is in time. Those who live in the light of eternity always are and are never subjected to the becoming of "was" and "will be."

Eternity is the absolute present and the absolute present is living a *sono-mama* life, where life asserts itself in all its fullness.

4. ZEN IN THE MODERN WORLD[1]

ZEN is at present evoking unexpected echoes in various fields of Western culture: music, painting, literature, semantics, religious philosophy, and psychoanalysis. But as it is in many cases grossly misrepresented or misinterpreted, I undertake here to explain most briefly, as far as language permits, what Zen aims at and what significance it has in the modern world, hoping that Zen will be saved from being too absurdly caricatured.

In beginning, I wish to refer to a certain literary movement started on the western coast of America. I have no firsthand contact with it and to that extent I am far from being qualified to comment on the movement. But it is possible to gather something of what moves in the minds of these writers from what some critics have to say. An Eastern proverb has it: "Just one leaf falling and we know autumn is with us." Can I not then take the literary movement in San Francisco for a leaf falling from the paulownia tree as auguring a possible change in the psychological climate in Western culture? I may be going too far, but I will leave it to the judgment of the reader.

Let me quote from the Sunday *Times,* London (June 15, 1958). It reports on a gathering of the "Beat Generation," or "San Francisco Renaissance Group," which took place in a suburb of the city, and goes on to say that this group of writers, poets, painters, and musicians consists of "intellectual spivs rather than artists. They may be the harbingers of a new spiritual sense of purpose that still needs definition and translation, or perhaps they are simply unemployables from a mass educational system. . . . Zen Buddhism is its required reading, its bible."

Some American papers, too, make reference to this strange group of people relating themselves to Zen, though it seems the Americans are not so critical as the English. To quote another English opinion from *The Listener* (London, July 3, 1958):

[1] *Japan Quarterly*, October–December, 1958, pp. 452–61.

The writers sense all around them the visions of the Apocalypse and they do not know how to react. . . . They take refuge in undirected vitalism. . . . To them life itself is reduced to an immense hitch-hike, interposed·with parties, orgiastic half-hours, mild delinquency, and a studied absence of coherence. . . . They run about like hares on an aerodrome. The great machines of everyday life land and take off without paying any attention to them, and they in their turn, blinded by noise and light, are more concerned with running than with getting anywhere.

I do not know how just these remarks are, but since the writer taking it up is Mr. Alan Pryce-Jones, editor of *The Times Literary Supplement,* London, I cannot help concluding that the "Beat Generation" is not a mere passing phenomenon to be lightly put aside as insignificant. I am inclined to think it is somehow prognostic of something coming, at least to American life. I remember it was sometime last year that I read in some of the popular American magazines accounts of the San Francisco Renaissance Group in connection with Zen activities. Zen seems in some way to be responsible for it. What is there at present in the American psychology, and possibly in the Western mind generally, that is attracted to Zen?

A well-known American novelist, Nancy Wilson Ross, writes in *Mademoiselle* (New York, January, 1958) as follows:

In accounting for the present interest in Zen in the West one must look to the shaft struck into the Western mind by psychoanalysis; the grave warnings of psychologists in general about the unhappy effects of ignoring the deeper levels of the human consciousness, the unfortunate results to be seen on every side of repressing the more subtle and invisible aspects of the human being in total favor of an externalized existence.

From these remarks, I can say this about the "Beat Generation": they have probably not yet tapped the headspring of creativity. They are struggling, still rather superficially, against "democracy," bourgeois conformity, economic respectability, conventional middle-class consciousness, and other cognate virtues and vices of mediocrity. Because they are "rootless," as Simone Weil would condemn them, they find themselves floundering in the mud in their search for "the only way through into truth which is by way of one's own annihilation; through dwelling a long time in a state of extreme and total humiliation."[2] They have not yet passed through their experiences of humiliation and affliction and, I may add, revelation.

Jack Kerouac has been quoted (*The New York Times Book Review*, April 6, 1958, p. 8) as saying that "these new pure poets . . . are CHILDREN . . . childlike graybeard Homers singing in the street. They SING, they SWING." Yes, there is enough of childishness but not much of childlikeness. Spontaneity is not everything, it must be "rooted." These men have not yet developed what lies quiescent in their unconscious, especially the primary feeling for the Self. They must grow up as human beings to become conscious of the true roots of being and walk with human dignity.

Indeed, the whole world, as far as I can see, is now groping for "roots" whereby to steady itself in the course of its spiritual development. And Zen seeks first of all to reach the roots of our being, to set one's "mind at rest," to locate one's "original face," to discover where one stands. "The proper study of mankind is man," and what constitutes man is his mind or heart.[3] The *kokoro* is no other than the Self; they are interchangeable terms, and in Zen they are indiscriminately used. To know the Self is thus made the primary object of Zen study. What is man? What is the "I"? What is the root of this existence? When a pupil came to a master to be informed about Zen, the master did not give him any specific information, but simply put this question to him: "What is that which thus comes to me?" To answer this question, it is said, took the pupil eight long years. Then the answer was, "To say it is a something misses the mark!" Whatever superficial commotions we may observe in our modern life, literary or otherwise, they are exhibitions of the fear and insecurity felt in our inmost selves, and undoubtedly this feeling is the upshot of our ignorance as to what the Self is. The men of the Renaissance Group may think they understand Zen, but unless "a word" can be uttered, as Zen masters demand of their pupils, they are still on the way and not right "there." "A word" can only be something vital, original, and thoroughly creative.

[2] *La Personne et le Sacre* (in *Ecrits de Londres*, Gallimard, 1957), as quoted in Richard Rees's *Brave Men, a Study of D. H. Lawrence and Simone Weil*, p. 45 (London, 1958).

[3] *Kokoro* or *shin* in Japanese; *hsin* in Chinese.

Whatever we may say about the idealistic interpretation of the human situation, all things, all problems relating to our life are reducible to the following Zen *mondō*[4] presented in a triple form:

Q. "What is the *saṅghārāma?*"[5]

A. "Just so."

Q. "What is the man in it?"

A. "What?! What?!"

Q. "What will you do when a visitor comes?"

A. "Have a cup of tea."

These questions when translated into modern usage are: What is the world? What is man? What is society, or the human community? The answers are typically Zen in pattern, one might say, defying logical analysis or any intelligible interpretation. But there is no doubt that they are directly to the point, and one who is at all acquainted with Zen will see that they are vibrating with life and thoroughly creative.

The first question is ontological, dealing with the problem of being. Or, we may say, it concerns the problem of the world where we live. What is this "objective" world which confronts us, into which we are born and destined to live? What is the meaning of it? The second inquires into the nature, meaning, and destiny of man who sets himself against any objective world so called. What is he? What can he do? Has he anything original in him? Is he more than an animal, more than a mere cogwheel in the great machine called "universe the unknowable"? The third is related to our human relationships. How do we carry on our communal life? How are we to behave socially, individually, collectively? All problems which arise as we go on living finally resolve themselves into one of these three. But after all the most central and most fundamental problem we as human beings pose ourselves is the second *mondō* in regard to man.

The problem of man is really the problem of Self, to "know thyself," not in opposition to, or in relation to, others, but "thyself" as an absolute Self, independent of all other selves. For when it is

---

[4] What ordinarily corresponds to philosophical discussion is carried on in Zen in the form of *mondō*: the pupil asks and the master answers, sometimes in words but frequently in action. Even when an answer is given in words it is short, cryptic. Sometimes it is just an ejaculation.

[5] "The quarters where the monks rest," that is, a monastery.

thoroughly and basically grasped, we know the world, including man's communal life. The Zen master's answer to it was "What?! What?!" Ours may not necessarily be like his, though ultimately we may have to come back to "What?! What?!"; we of modern times, no doubt, have different ways to express ourselves. And we are at present struggling very hard indeed to reach the bed rock of the Self whereby we may solve all problems secondarily issuing from the basic one. It requires a deep-searching mind and a long-suffering spirit to reach this bed rock. When it is reached and we can rest there, all human problems that can possibly arise are solved in the way Chuang-tzǔ's chef used his knife to carve through all the knotty joints. The "angry young men" (the British counter-part of the Beat Generation) are still wandering over the surface of reality and have not yet come to the Self which is verily the spring of creativity.

Modern men are indeed groping in the dark. It is a birth pang that ushers in every new age in the fields of human activity. Some of them, independent and original, revolt against liberalism and philistinism, communism and despotism, industrialism and auto-mation, science and technology—which characterize the modern world of cheap, shallow intellectualism. But those of the Beat Generation are not fully conscious of why they rebel or what they propose to do; they do not know their inner Self which is moving in the deep unconscious; they do not know that there is a some-thing in each of them, individually and collectively, prodding them on and they cannot intellectually determine what it is. But if they come to feel and find this mysterious something their "new Holy Lunacy" will cease: they will just rest satisfied with themselves and with the whole world confronting them. It goes without saying that this satisfaction is not sheer passivism or doing-nothing-ness.

Until then I am afraid all that they write or produce cannot go beyond what a British critic calls "temporary antics." Even D. H. Lawrence and Simone Weil, who are appraised as "brave men" by Richard Rees, have not in my view really penetrated into the secrets of the Self. It is quite natural that being brought up in a Christian atmosphere they could not transcend their background with all its mythological trappings. The following was all that could come out of Lawrence's lips, according to Rees, a few days before his death:

No, the Catholic Church has fallen into the same disaster as the Protestant: of preaching a moral God, instead of Almighty God, the God of strength and glory and might and wisdom: a "good" God, instead of a vital and magnificent God. And we no longer any of us really believe in an exclusively "good" God.

Rees quotes a highly refreshing phrase by G. M. Hopkins, the "freshness deep down in things," and tells us that both Lawrence and Simone Weil were believers in this freshness which cannot be reached except by a miracle. Simone Weil is said further to have believed in the "supernatural." These terms as "freshness," "a miracle," "the supernatural," "the Almighty" are acceptable and assimilable in Zen, but it is more in accord with the Oriental mentality not to bring the traditional God onto the scene; better than any God, we like an absolute mind, that is, the Self.

The Self according to Zen is a storehouse of creative possibilities where we find all stored: miracles and mysteries, natural and supernatural, ordinary and extraordinary, Almighty God and a good God, wolves and lambs, briars and roses. Everything that comes out of the storehouse of infinite creativity is eternally fresh. Even our "earthly" life is not a series of humdrumnesses, it is full of wonders and viabilities. When we are awakened to this truth, we are no more "helpless puppets in a deterministic universe," because the truth makes us see that necessity is freedom and freedom is necessity in the eternally creative and ever-freshening Self.

The modern malady indicates that we have lost our spiritual balance and feel shaky about our destiny as human beings. We are negating everything that has held us somehow together not only socially or communally but essentially as individuals. We fail at present to know where to anchor our Self in its profoundest sense. God Himself is unable to keep it allied to Him as He used to in the olden days. The ultimate affirmation is gone. The "thinking reed" has been torn away from its roots and all the thinking it does is of no avail whatever. The worst of it is that modern man refuses to acknowledge this fact and tries all the harder to "think and think" as if thinking that has lost its anchorage could keep us steady with any feeling of security.

Zen tells us: "Find your Self and you will be free and safe." But men today do not know what the Self is, and they are liable to take their egoistic small self for it. They attempt to make this small one assume the role and function of the big one. When they are told

to be spontaneous and uninhibited, they imagine they have recovered the original abode of security, and act self-assertively, indeed most arrogantly. Where there is no Self, spontaneity is licentiousness and licentiousness is sheer thraldom. To be spontaneous
one must be in touch with the fount of creativity whose essential
quality is to be itself, in its "isness." Without this experience, how
can there be freedom, autarchy, unobstructedness? As to security,
it is no problem at all. When one knows what the Self really is, one
is emancipated from all sorts of bondage and is free. When one is
free, what insecurity is there to feel? The main thing is to take hold
of the Self, which is, as Zen people would say, seeing into one's
own nature or *kokoro*.

The followers of Christianity and Judaism are concerned with
the problem of God as objectively existing or outside of us; on the
other hand, most Oriental peoples are employed in turning inwardly, within oneself, to find there the Self which is the abode of
reality. In a way I would like to equate the Self with God. In truth
they are one, the Self is God and God is the Self. But the traditional
notion of God is full of dualistic flavor and whenever the term is
used we are reminded of its mythical background. Zen is singularly free of these complications. I prefer the Self to God—the Self
that sits quietly in the deepest recesses of our individual self and
yet transcends all its limitations. We are to interview him not only
at the highest peak of Mount Sinai where "being is being," but
everywhere—in the market, on the farm, on the fishing boat, in the
battlefield, at the Lyceum, at the Coliseum. At some of these places
God may be loath to come in, but the Self enters without hesitation.
The Self knows no inhibitions, nor does he meet any resistance
wherever he may go. Rinzai calls him "the true man of no-title" and
describes him as pervading all the world, in time as well as in space.

The Self, therefore, is to be definitively distinguished from the
self, but if we take this distinction in its relative, logical sense as
mutually exclusive, we shall be committing a great mistake. In the
world of Zen there is no room for contradictions; this is due to the
specifically Zen experience which annihilates all the barriers that
are supposed to exist between such logically incompatible ideas as
subject and object, being and non-being, "I" and "thou," guilt and
innocence. After we have thus gone through this utterly devastating
and all-merging experience, we come out in this world where our
everyday thinking prevails and discover that the self is not the Self
and yet they are fused; that is, the Self works through the self, and

the self strikes its roots "deep down" to the Self to get all its nourishment and energy from this once-hidden source. Zen would now declare that A (self) is A and also not-A (Self), or that A is not-A and therefore A is A. More concretely: to one who has not yet studied Zen, a mountain is a mountain; when he begins to know something of Zen, a mountain is not a mountain; but once he thoroughly masters Zen, a mountain is again a mountain. To see a mountain as not a mountain is lunacy or dying to oneself. But we are not to stay here; we must pass on further to where again "the flowers are red and willows are green." This is really a remarkable experience, altogether transcending the human intelligence which operates efficiently only in a world of relativities. At this point the following argument may not be inappropriate.

Some say that Nature moves by leaps, that her movement is not continuous. But the fact is that it is not Nature but the mind or rather human intelligence that works in that fashion. For human intelligence, knowledge, always presupposes a dichotomy of subject and object, this and that, black and white. Where there is no opposition or no cutting into two, there is no knowledge. And this cutting creates a medium whereby a relation is established between the two. Black is known by means of white and white by means of black. When a movement is continuous and uninterrupted we fail to recognize it as a movement. Between any two given points of a movement there must be a gap or a space of time, and it is by this time gap that the mind is made conscious of a movement. A dichotomy cannot be thought of without assuming a discontinuity.

To define a line we cut it into points and make these points move from one to another. The movement is really discontinuous, it is from point to point. And a line that cannot be cut into points or parts ceases to be a line. So with consciousness: it is possible only in time, and time is eternally divided into discontinuities. Everything and anything that is finite is a chopped piece of the infinite. This chopped discreteness is not in Nature per se but in the mind which, by cutting everything in Nature into two, makes it knowable and workable and serviceable for our practical human purposes.

The relationship between Nature and its dichotomized parts finds its analogy in that between the large Self and the small selves. The small selves are individualized and as such are not the Self in its suchness. But each individual self cannot be itself without being in some sense the Self. This leads us to consider the relationship between finite numbers and infinite.

The self is a finite number and limited in every way. 2 is 2 and cannot be 3 or 4 or 10 or 100 or anything else; so with any other finite number. The Self is the Infinite—the infinite not in its serial sense but in its absolute sense. Serially an infinite has a more or less negative connotation. The Self as the Infinite not only comprises all the finite numbers infinitely following one after another, but holds in itself an infinite totality of all possible numbers, and it is this Infinite that makes possible all forms of mathematically calculable operations.

In an infinite series of finite numbers, 0 (zero) is at the ever-diminishing end, while ∞ (infinity) is at the ever-increasing end. In so far as finite numbers are concerned, they cannot reach an end in either direction, either 0 or ∞, unless they perform a leap. But practically or logically speaking, a leap is another human thought symbol ingeniously devised. For how can there be an infinite leap? A leap is a finite conception. No infinities can be made to limit themselves, for when they do they are no longer infinities; both 0 and ∞ are unattainable. In a series of finite numbers, moving in either direction—negatively or positively, retrogressively or progressively—all that we can envisage and calculate and handle in any utilizable way is limited to the finite numbers. But such handling can never take place without having an unattainable at either end. Finite numbers are possible only within this equation: $0 = \infty$.

We now come to the paradox: the world we live in is a relative, finite world, limited in every way, and I say this world is possible only when it is placed within the infinite. In a world of infinity, then, the highest is the lowest, the limited is the unlimited, 2 is 3, 3 is 4, an idiot is a saint. "I" am "thou" and "thou" art "I," "I am walking and I am riding on a water buffalo," "I, empty-handed, hold a spade," "a cloud of dust rises in a well," "the surging ocean is as smoothly leveled as the mirror," "Buddha has never entered *parinirvāna*," "we are still listening to Buddha giving his sermon on Mount Vulture." Zen literature is a storehouse of such paradoxes. But since our limited world is inhabited by logicians, positivists, and philosophers of various hues, they would most decidedly not concur with my views.

To reach this world of infinity or Self or God, Zen insists we abandon our restless pursuit after logic, intellection, or ratiocination of any form—even if temporarily—and plunge ourselves deep into the bottomless abyss of primary "feeling," the eternally unquenchable yearning for "the unknown," or "the truth that will make us free" from the bondage of all forms of limitation and finitude.

The following quotation from Simone Weil will be found in this connection highly instructive and to the point:

There is a reality beyond the world, that is to say, outside space and time, outside man's mental universe, outside any sphere whatsoever that is accessible to human faculties.

Corresponding to this reality, in the center of the human heart, is the longing for an absolute good, a longing which is always there and is never satisfied by any object in this world.

Another manifestation of this reality lies in the absurdities of paradox and the insoluble contradictions which are always the terminus of human thought when it moves exclusively in this world. . . .[6]

Now, the practical questions are: How is it possible for the human mind to conceive zero, infinity, endless continuity, uninterrupted stretches of time and space, or, according to Simone Weil, "a reality beyond the world"? How can the self, cut up and limited, ever come to conceive and even to realize the Self, unlimited, uncut, and infinite? Where do we get the concept of Self if our senses and intellect fail to see anything unlimited or infinite in their existential and experiential world? How do we or can we transcend "the absurdities of paradox and the insoluble contradictions" in which we are so helplessly involved? But somehow transcend we must, for otherwise there will be no peace of mind, no security, no freedom, for which we so desperately long. To quote further from Simone Weil:

. . . All human beings are absolutely identical in so far as they can be thought of as consisting in this central demand for good surrounded by an accretion of psychic and bodily matter. . . .[7]

The good she refers to is not moral or relative good. It is the

---

[6] Rees, *op cit.*, p. 130, quoted from Simone Weil's *Profession of Faith* in her *Etude pour une Déclaration des Obligations envers l'Etre Humain.* (In *Ecrits de Londres,* Gallimard, 1957.)

[7] Rees, *loc. cit.*

"good" that God is legendarily recorded in the Bible as having announced when after His fiat the world came out, the light separated from darkness. This "good" is the absolute good, which has no reference to moral values; it is the good of "Good morning" with which we greet each other; it is the good of Ummon (d. 949) who when asked about an "absolute present" or an absolute "Here-Now," answered, "Every day is a good (or fine) day!" (which reminds us of Eckhart's beggar).

It is evident that the solution of man's ultimate contradiction can never come from cheap, shallow intellectualism, nor from pushing up the scale of industrialization to the highest possible notch. I heartily, without reserve, concur with Simone Weil's statement: "The only way through into the truth, i.e., the truth of the Self, is by way of one's own annihilation in every possible sense." We cannot have a sense of humiliation unless we sink deeply down to the Unconscious where resides the Self, and modern men have not come to this yet. Freud and his followers have unearthed a great deal from the Unconscious, but the most vitally important point is still left untouched—the discovery of the Self.

Rinzai does not say much about himself, but the little he says is of great importance:

When I had no understanding, I was all enveloped in darkness. . . . My inside burned, my mind knew no rest. I ran from one master to another, asking about the truth (*tao*). . . .

The penetrating insight of Rinzai into the nature of man, that is Self, as seen in the following passages, is untouched by the tide of changing times. With them I conclude:

Those of you who wish to discipline yourselves in Buddha's Dharma must seek true understanding. When this understanding is attained you will not be defiled by birth-and-death. Whether walking or standing you will be your own master. Even when you are not trying to achieve something extraordinary, it will come to you by itself. . . .

Do you know where the disease lies which keeps you learners from reaching true understanding? It lies where you have no faith in your Self. When faith in your Self is lacking you find yourselves carried away by others in every possible way. At every encounter you are not your own master; you are driven about by others this way or that.

What is required is at once to cease leaving your Self in search of something external. When this is done you find your Self no different from the Buddha or the patriarch.

Do you want to know who the Buddha or patriarch is? He is no other than the one who is, at this moment, right before me, listening to my talk on the Dharma. You have no faith in him and therefore you are in quest of someone else somewhere outside. And what will you find? More words and names, however excellent. You will never reach the moving spirit in the Buddha or patriarch. Make no mistake!

5. *THE ESSENCE OF BUDDHISM*[1]

BEFORE I speak about Buddhism, I wish to say a few words about religion in general. For Buddhism is a religion, and like other religions is often considered as having no direct contact with life itself, and many think that they get along quite well without it. Some go further and say that it is mere superstition, and that whether or not heaven and hell exist is no concern of theirs. Some have gone still further, and describe religion as an opiate for the masses, a means used by capitalists and bureaucrats to make the people blindly obey their will. If this is what is thought of Buddhism as a religion, there is no understanding of the role which religion plays or should play in our daily life.

In the ordinary way of life, most of us vaguely assume that there is a world of sense and intellect and a world of spirit, and that the world we actually live in is the former and not the latter, and, therefore, that what is most real and intimate to us is the former while the latter is merely imaginary if not altogether non-existent. The world of spirit is thus relegated, though we may admit its existence, to the imagination of poets, visionaries, and the so-called spiritualists; but from the genuinely religious point of view, the world of sense is an intellectual or conceptual reconstruction of what is immediately revealed to the spirit itself. What is more real, therefore, is the spiritual world and not the sensuous world. That this is so we realize only after hard and desperate thinking, that is, after many a vain attempt to reach ultimate reality, which we fail to discover in the world of sense.

The world of sense is a realm of multitudes, where everything is subject to constant vicissitudes, and with this we are never satisfied. We desire to penetrate somehow through the ever-changing world. The so-called reality and intimacy of the sense world seem ever to drive us away from it, instead of drawing us toward it, for it fails to respond to our inward yearnings, which evidently rise from the so-called visionary world which is completely concealed from

1 *The Essence of Buddhism*, Hōzōkan 1948, pp. 3–49.

the senses. What is assumed to be visionary cannot after all be pronounced visionary; it is a most concrete, real, and substantial thing, and it is after this and no other that we find ourselves so fervently yearning.

The sense world of multitudes is meant for intellectual analysis, or we may reverse the order, and say that it is the intellect which constructs the sense world. When we think we understand the world, this means that we understand it as far as it is subject to intellection. But as intellection does not exhaust life as we inwardly live it, we always feel something in us which is not quite pacified by the intellect and looks somewhere else for a fulfilment. This is why our ordinary life is full of contradictions and conflicts. Most of us, however, ignore them, and it is only when we somehow become conscious of the fact that we for the first time sit down and begin to grapple with the situation in earnest.

As we thus go on searching after the truth, we finally come to the spiritual world, or rather the spiritual world breaks upon this world of sense-intellect. When this takes place, the whole order of things changes; the logical is no more logical, and rationality loses its significance, for now the real equals the not-real and the true the not-true. More concretely stated, water does not flow in the river, the flowers are no more red, and the willows are not green. This is the most startling event that can take place in the realm of human consciousness—this spiritual world's breaking in upon the world of sense and intellect, upsetting every form of standardized experience which prevails there. But this is not all, for here takes place another most startling event along with it, which is that these negations or contradictions, in spite of their all-smashing blow, do not at all annihilate this sense-intellect world of our everyday experience; for water continues to flow and the mountains remain towering above us.

This, however, being the unique way of the Zen master when he gives expression to the world view gained from his spiritual insight, it is not easy for most of us to grasp the meaning fully. Let us resort to our common phraseology, and we shall see that what the Zen master means is that our daily experience acquires its true significance by being related to the spiritual order of existence, and that so long as we are not in touch with this order, what we conceive to be real is not at all real, as it cannot then have any more reality than a merely dreamy existence; it is only when the spiritual world impresses itself in a lively manner upon this world that the latter obtains a new value, making our life worth something.

A warning is needed here, as these frequent references to the spiritual world are apt to lead us to think that there are really two separate, independent worlds, the spiritual and the sensual-intellectual. But we must remember that these are two phases, intellectually distinguished, of one whole world, and that it is only by not realizing this fact that we wrongly believe in two independent worlds negating each other. We can go a step further and state that this relative world in which we know we live is no other than the spirit world itself. There is, indeed, one complete undivided whole world and nothing else. It is the result of intellection that we have to speak of the spirit world as if it were a more real world than the world of sense, or, conversely, to speak of the sense world as being more actual than the spirit world. But the separation is a fiction, because what is not to be divided is divided as if divisible, and when divided the one is believed to be as real as the other.

In the one complete world, strictly speaking, no reference is possible either to the spirit or to the sense-intellect. Being absolutely one, there is here no room for terms of distinction or discrimination; indeed, no speaking, no thinking is possible here; an absolute silence is probably the only way to describe the somewhat of it. Even silence, if it is understood in contrast to sound or speech, will certainly miss the point. But as long as we are all humanly and socially constituted, we cannot remain eternally dumb; we necessarily break out into speech, and utter, "Let there be light." Light comes forth, and lo! there is also the forthcoming of darkness, and they, light and darkness, set up a world of dichotomies, and we take this world for reality. But it is an illusion created by the intellect, however inevitable the process may have been, for there is no way for us to escape this intellectualization. Nevertheless, as I say, it is an illusion because it does not truthfully represent the one as it is in itself.

The idea may be expressed in the following way too. What we truly and really have is the one spiritual world, that is, the One, undiscriminated, indeterminate, undistinguished, undifferentiated. But our human consciousness is so designed that it cannot remain in this state of oneness, of sameness; and we somehow begin to reflect upon it in order to become conscious of it, to give it a clear definition, to make it the subject of contemplation, and also to break it up into pieces so that the energy eternally sealed up in silence and inactivity will become vocal and manifest itself in the dynamics of human activities. The One, as far as we can comprehend it, has now ceased to be indeterminate, undistinguished, undifferentiated. As a result, we have now a world of infinite varieties and complexities. But we must not imagine that the breaking up of the One into the Many is a development in time process. If we do, we inevitably come to the conclusion that there was once a time when nothing but the one complete world existed by itself, and unconscious of itself, and that this went in time through the process of unfolding itself into the many-ness of things, and so on. When this way of thinking is cherished, the world of spirit is left behind in the maelstrom of phenomenal forces, and we are given up to the interplay of opposite ideas, of opposite values, of opposite traditions. We then lose our spiritual equilibrium forever; we are hopelessly and inextricably mixed up in a world of contraries.

To counteract this tragedy, we have to remember that the world of spirit is right here, we are right in it, we have never departed from it. Even when we seem to be the abject slaves of the Many and the playthings of dualistic ratiocination, the world of spirit is encircling us, is circulating through us, has its axis of movement in our workaday life. But, we may say, the spirit left behind countless ages ago is no spirit, and we shall have nothing to do with it, for it cannot possibly be of any use to us now. This intellectual illusion may lead us away from the one complete world of spirit by conceiving it as beside this world of particulars, and we cannot be too careful about the polarization, lest the intellectual illusion forever veil from us the spiritual landscape.

When we think about it, the human power of thinking is the queerest thing ever devised by—nobody knows whom; perhaps by a most evil-intentioned and at the same time most lovingly-disposed mind. It works in two opposite directions, sometimes beneficially, but more frequently disastrously. The intellectual illusion has started up this world of dualities, and because of it we are made cognizant of the final abode whence we come and whither we return, but also because of it we go astray in the meantime, wandering from one post to another. Reason is used to refute itself, to destroy the prison erected by itself. A wedge is needed to split a solid block of wood, and to get the first one in another wedge is applied, and the process will have to be indefinitely repeated.

Human life is simply a bundle of paradoxes and contradictions; intellection as such cannot get anything out of it; all it does is to become desperately muddled up with self-proposed problems.

Buddhist scholars, therefore, take up paradoxes as paradoxes and describe or explain life as the distinction of non-distinction or as the discrimination of non-discrimination. According to the intellectual scheme, the spirit world will correspond to a world of non-distinction and non-discrimination, and the sense world to a world of distinction and discrimination. But, logically speaking, non-distinction or non-discrimination, when taken by itself, makes no sense, because things are what they are by being distinguished and discriminated: non-distinction or non-discrimination must mean non-existence. The spirit world is therefore non-existent when it is made to stand by itself; it can exist only when it is considered in relation to a world of distinction. But the Buddhist conception of a world of non-distinction is not a relative one but an absolute one; it is the one absolute world which exists by itself and does not require anything relative for its support. But, we may ask, is such an existence at all conceivable by the human mind? No, not intellectually. Hence the paradoxical expression, the distinction of non-distinction and the discrimination of non-discrimination, or, reversing it, the non-distinction of distinction and the non-discrimination of discrimination.

Expressing it in another way, we can state that life as we live it is the self-identification of contradictions and not the unification or synthesizing of opposites. Red is red and not-red, hand is hand and not-hand. When we say a thing is, it is an affirmation; when we say it is not, it is a negation. This is true in the world of distinction, it is in the very nature of distinction that it is so; negation and affirmation cannot be together all at once. But it is not so in the Buddhist logic of self-identity; for here negation is not necessarily a negation, nor is affirmation an affirmation; on the contrary, affirmation is a negation and negation is an affirmation. This does not mean that negation implies an affirmation which the logician may develop later. With the Buddhists, there is no such implication, nor is there any equivocation either. This statement is a most straightforward one. We may call it a logic of self-identity which is neither unification nor synthesizing. To demonstrate the truth of this logic, if a man is a Zen master, he will hold out his hand and ask, "Why is this called a hand?" When there is no answer speedily coming, he may pick up one of the sweets before him and say, "Try this, my friend, it is delicious." Here is a distinction of non-distinction.

At the outset of this lecture, an allusion was made to ordinary people's assumption of a spiritual world as existing along with the world of sense. We now know that this assumption is at once wrong and not wrong. Intellectually, the separation of the two worlds is quite tenable; but when the two are kept separated and there is no interpenetration or interfusion between them, the dualism proves fatal because it contradicts life as it is actually lived by us. Our experience is contrary to this dualistic interpretation. For the spiritual world is no other than the sense world and the sense world is no other than the spirit world. There is one completely whole world. Therefore, when I say that the spirit belongs to the world of non-distinction and sense to that of distinction, we have to be reminded of the logic of self-identity, in which the two worlds are at once one and not-one. This is a hard statement and most difficult to understand.

The Buddhist idea of non-distinction distinguished or non-discrimination discriminated no doubt transcends our intellectual comprehension, and thereby we realize that the religious life is not to be apprehended by reasoning. But this does not mean that religion is to be altogether put aside as not falling within the ken of ratiocination, for all the talk so far carried on is based on reasoning whereby man attempts to give a consistent explanation of his experience. Irrationality is also a form of reasoning. We cannot escape it. The danger arises when experience is denied in order to put reason foremost, while the fact of life tells us that the latter grows from the former and not vice versa. Reasoning must conform to life, and when there is something in life which refuses to be dealt with by reason, it is the latter and not the former that has to make a new start. Faith lives and the intellect kills. It is for this reason that religion generally assumes an antagonistic attitude toward reasoning, and sometimes goes so far as to demand a summary disposal of it, as if it were an arch-enemy of religion. This attitude, however, on the part of religion is not judicious, for it really means religion's surrender to its "enemy." If one truly understood what is meant by non-discrimination discriminated, one would not think of going against intellection per se, for intellection is after all the handmaid of religion, whereby we can say the latter is oriented toward its own original home.

What is wrong with intellection or reasoning is that by its dualism it sets up the idea of "self" as if it were a reality to which is to be given a specially honored niche in the hall of human experience. As long as intellection is confined to its proper sphere of work, all is well, but the moment it steps out of it and invades a field which does not belong to it, the outcome is disastrous. For this stepping out means the setting up of the self as a reality, and this is sure to collide with our ethical and religious valuation of human life; it also runs contrary to our spiritual insight into the nature of things. The self, as we all know, is the root of all evils. Every religious leader teaches us to get rid of this notion, as it erects an insurmountable barrier between God and man, if the man is a Christian; or it leads him, if he is a Buddhist, toward laying up a stock of demerit and strengthening all the time the hindrance of karma. Intellection for this reason is never welcomed in the realm of religious experience. Indeed, we are often told to be transformed into a simple-hearted ignoramus, because the truth of religion, that is, the spiritual truth, is revealed only to such souls.

Buddhists often speak of the "Great Death," which means dying to the ordinary life, putting an end to the analyzing intellect, or laying aside the idea of the self. Slay, they would say, with one stroke, this meddling intellect, and throw it to the dogs. This is a strong statement, but the idea is plain; it is to transcend the intellect, to go beyond the world of distinctions. For the spiritual world of non-discrimination[2] will never open its door until the discrimi-

---

[2] It may not be amiss to note here again that the spiritual world of non-distinction and non-discrimination has no separate existence of its own. It is right here with and in this world of infinite distinctions; indeed, it is no other than this world itself. It is spoken of as if it were an independent world transcending the latter; this is because of our bifurcating intellect. If it were not for it, there would be neither distinction nor non-distinction; it is due to the intellect that we divide into two the One in which we live and move and have our being.

The world of non-distinction may be considered as having two senses: the one is relative as distinguished from the world of distinction, and the other is absolute, where distinctions of all kinds are excluded, and in this sense it is the One, the Absolute. To silence our ever-annoying and logic-loving intellect, Buddhists have such expressions as distinction of non-distinction, or non-distinction of distinction, where distinction may be replaced if desired by discrimination.

Buddhists have *shabetsu* for distinction and *funbetsu* for discrimination. *Sha* or *sa* means "difference" while *fun* or *bun* is "to divide," "to cut into two." *Betsu* is "separation." *Shabetsu* has a statical, spatial, objective, physical application, whereas *funbetsu* is more intellectual, logical, subjective. Practically, the two terms mean the same thing, and here they are used indifferently and interchangeably.

nating mind is destroyed to its foundations. Only then takes place the birth of *prajñā*, the illuminating, all-transcending wisdom. *Vijñāna*, that is, the discriminating, self-centered mind, is now enlightened and becomes *prajñā*, which will move in its own straight path of non-distinction and non-discrimination. *Vijñāna*, which can be identified with our normal consciousness, will lose its way if not guided by the light of *prajñā* in the labyrinth of interminable complexities. *Prajñā's* all-illuminating light, however, does not obliterate distinctions, but makes them stand out more boldly and clearly in their spiritual significance, for the self is now dead and sees itself reflected in the mirror of non-distinction. We must not think that *prajñā* exists in separation from *vijñāna*, or vice versa. Separation means distinction, and where there is only distinction there is no *prajñā*, and without *prajñā*, *vijñāna* becomes muddled and goes astray. *Prajñā* is the principle of non-discrimination lying underneath every form of distinction and discrimination. To understand this, that is, to get out of the cul-de-sac of intellection, the "Great Death" must, so Buddhists say, have been experienced.

Prajñā is, therefore, a knowledge that knows and yet knows not, an understanding that does not understand, a thought that is no thought. It is thoughtlessness full of thoughts. It is no-mind-ness, not in the sense of unconsciousness, but in the sense that

> The cherry trees bloom each year in the Yoshino Mountains,
> But split the tree and tell me where the flowers are!

Or

> Expecting to see her come,
> How often have I wandered on the beach,
> Where I hear no sound
> But the breeze passing through the pine needles.

No-mind-ness, or mindlessness, or thoughtlessness—these are uncouth terms, but there are no adequate English words to express the Buddhist notion of *mushin* (literally, "no-mind"), or *munen* (literally, "no-thought"). The idea is to express the unconscious working of the mind, but this unconsciousness is not to be interpreted psychologically, but on the spiritual plane where all "traces" of discursive or analytical understanding vanish. It is where our power of ratiocination reaches its limits; it is on the other side of consciousness in its broadest possible sense, including both the conscious and the unconscious. When no-mindness is thus defined, we see that real Buddhists are not treading the same path on which we dualistically-minded people usually walk.

Prajñā is thus *acintya,* "beyond thinking," or "no-thinking." All thinking involves the distinction of this and that, for to think means to divide, to analyze. *Acintya,* no-thinking, means not to divide, that is, to pass beyond all intellection, and the whole of the Buddhist teaching revolves about this central idea of no-thought, or no-thinking-ness, or no-mind-ness, or *acintya-prajñā,* showing that no spiritual truth could be grasped by ratiocination.

To repeat, the spiritual world of non-distinction and non-discrimination is not a separate existence of its own apart from the world of intellection, for if it were separate it would not be a world of non-distinction, and would have no vital connection with our daily life. What Buddhists strongly insist upon in their philosophy is the merging of the two contradictory terms: distinction and non-distinction, thinking and no-thinking, rationality and irrationality, etc. They then tell us not to do any logical thinking about the merging of opposites, for as far as formal logic goes, such merging is the height of absurdity. Instead, they tell us to experience the merging itself where no-thought is actually found interfused with all forms of thought, that is, actually to perceive the impossibility of consciousness itself when severed from its background of absolute unconsciousness—and this not psychologically but spiritually.

To experience this truth of spiritual merging means to realize the irrational rationality of non-discrimination, to perceive that two contradictory terms are self-identical, that is, A is Not-A and Not-A is A. It is to become *prajñā* itself, where there is no distinction between the subject and the object of intuition, and yet there is a clear perception of the distinction—that is, the distinction of non-distinction and the discrimination of non-discrimination. It goes without saying that this makes no sense on the rational plane; yet it is imperative to have a penetrating insight into this fundamental truth of absolute self-identity of opposites. This insight, or realization, or perception, or intuition, whatever term we may use, means the awakening of *prajñā,* the attaining of *bodhi* or enlightenment, becoming the Buddha, entering into *nirvāṇa,* being born in the Pure Land, the Western Paradise; in the Hindu philosophy it is being born for a second time; in the New Testament it is the giving up of life in order to gain it.

To state the matter in a practical manner, religion requires us to put away everything that we have for some reason or other put upon ourselves and that does not really belong to us. We put on so many clothes ostensibly to keep ourselves warm, but really to make us look more than we are. We build houses on a far greater scale than we actually require, because we desire to display our wealth or social position or political power. But these things are appendages that do not make our real stature even one tenth of an inch higher. When we deeply examine our own being, we realize that these appendages have after all nothing to do with it. When we face death, we have no time to think about them. Even what we consider to be our own body we feel like casting aside as not belonging to us.

The spiritual "man" is not dependent upon any form of externals. When taking a bath one recognizes the true man, as was once remarked by the Empress Wu of the T'ang dynasty when she treated the Buddhist monks to a bath. When there is nothing to screen oneself from outside views one comes to oneself. This is where we stand altogether free from distinctions and discriminations. While the latter are not to be despised or ignored or negated, we have sooner or later, if we aspire to perfect enlightenment, to see ourselves stripped before a spiritual mirror. To stand thoroughly naked, with no worldly titles, with no special rank, with no material accretions; to be all by oneself, to be absolutely alone—this is where Buddha speaks to Buddha, this is where "I am before Abraham was," this is where one can say, "*Tat tvam asi*" (Thou art that).[3]

---

[3] It is interesting to note that Pascal in his *Pensées* makes a distinction between the heart and the reason (269 *et seq.*), and he says that what experiences God is not the reason but the heart, that God is felt by the heart—which is faith—and not by the reason. What the reason can achieve as the last thing is "to recognize that there is an infinity of things which are beyond it." The reason's office consists in disavowing itself and submitting to feeling, that is, to the heart, "which has its reasons which reason does not know." According to Buddhist phraseology, *prajñā*, "the heart," has its own way of reasoning which is altogether beyond the demonstration or discrimination of the *vijñāna*, "the reason." The reason is always discriminative, and this prevents it from directly taking hold of reality which has its abode in the world

The Emperor Hanazono (reigned 1308–1318), a most devout Buddhist, once invited Daitō, the National Teacher (1282–1337) who founded the Daitokuji monastery in Kyoto in 1326, to a talk on Buddhism. When Daitō, properly attired in the Buddhist robe, appeared before the Emperor and had seated himself, the Emperor remarked,

"Is it not a matter of unthinkability that the Buddha-Dharma (*buppō*) should face the Royal Dharma (*ōbō*) on the same level?"

Daitō replied, "Is it not a matter of unthinkability that the Royal Dharma should face the Buddha-Dharma on the same level?"

The Emperor was pleased with the reply.

This famous *mondō* is most suggestive. The Buddhist authority (Buddha-Dharma) here represented by Daitō is the world of spirit or non-distinction in its absolute sense, and the royal or civil authority (Royal Dharma) is the world of distinction. So long as we live in the dual world of distinction, we must obey its laws. A tree is not a bamboo and a bamboo is not a tree; the mountain is high and rivers flow; the willow is green and the flower is red. In the same way, where social order obtains, the master is master and the subject is subject. Daitō was a subject and had therefore to sit below the Emperor; and the Emperor's remark was made with this in mind. Inasmuch as we stay in the world of the intellect we cannot allow the intrusion of the non-thinking, irrational spirit. And as the Emperor was living in a world of distinction, he could

---

of non-discrimination and non-distinction. Pascal says, "Faith is a gift of God; do not believe that we said it was a gift of reasoning." Faith is the taking hold of reality by non-discrimination. Buddhists would say, Pascal's "faith" or "spiritual insight" corresponds to their perfect enlightenment. What, however, most decidedly distinguishes the Buddhist way of thinking from the Christian is that Buddhists regard "the reason" as not different from "the heart," but as growing from the heart and identical with the heart, and further that this self-identity of reason and heart does not prevent each functioning in its own way—the reason as the instrument of demonstration and discrimination and the heart as the organ of intuition. The Christians would say that "God made Himself man to unite Himself to man." This being so, God is now in man and man is in God, God is man and man is God, yet God is God and man is man. This is the greatest religious mystery, the profoundest philosophical paradox, the discrimination of non-discrimination and the non-discrimination of discrimination, which constitutes the Buddhist logic of self-identity.

naturally not recognize the existence of a world above his own, and Daitō must stand below the Emperor. But Daitō's mission here was to make the Emperor have an insight into the spirit world, and as long as the Emperor stayed with his own point of view he would never be able to see how the world of non-distinction could break through into the world of distinction and there claim its place. As Zen students would say, Daitō took the Emperor's weapon away from him and used it against him. The Emperor was awakened. He realized that the Royal Dharma belonged only to the world of distinction, and that it owed its authority to the all-pervading and at the same time all-annihilating presence of the Absolute Dharma.

This most thoroughgoing interfusion, as it were, of distinction and non-distinction is impossible to understand if one stays on the place of reason and rationality. It is a world of the unthinkable, *acintya,* only revealed to the spirit. The Emperor's remark came out of a world of distinction, and his unthinkability did not go beyond it; whereas Daitō took his position in the world of absolute non-distinction and his unthinkability, therefore, was not in the same category as the Emperor's. Both used the same term, but in meaning they were poles apart. So we can see that every word has a double meaning, rational and irrational, intellectual and spiritual, differential and non-differential, relative and absolute; and it is for this reason that Buddhism is said to be very difficult to understand; but once awakened to the spiritual truth of distinction not distinguished, one will find one's sailing quite easy even over the turbulent waters of thought. Daitō's retort must have to a certain extent enlightened the Emperor, for he continued to allow Daitō to sit on the same level with him.

On another occasion, when the Emperor had an interview with Daitō the master, he asked,

"Who is he who remains companionless within the ten thousand things?"

This is a reference to the Absolute which defies analysis and has none facing it. If the Emperor had really understood the last *mondō* he had with the master, he would not have asked this. Evidently he still had something in his mind which did not give him complete satisfaction; he needed further enlightenment. The master, however, did not give him a direct answer, so to speak, but standing on the same level with his august questioner, that is, still in the world of distinction, he just moved a fan in his hand and said,

"I long enjoy being bathed in the Imperial breeze."

Here is a poetical allusion to the soft, relaxing spring breeze which we all enjoy in the same way as peace-loving people do the wise government of a spiritually-minded ruler. By the use of his fan, Daitō symbolized the spring breeze of the Absolute, and a state of spiritual tranquillity and relaxation issuing therefrom, and ascribed it to the Imperial grace. But where is the Absolute which stands without companion? The Emperor is an absolute, Daitō is another, and the present lecturer even a third; so many absolutes and yet all one in the Absolute. Distinction is non-distinction and non-distinction is distinction.

The fundamental idea of Buddhism is to pass beyond the world of opposites, a world built up by intellectual distinctions and emotional defilements, and to realize a spiritual world of non-distinction, which involves achieving an absolute point of view. Yet the Absolute is in no way distinct from the world of discrimination, for to think so would be to place it opposite the discriminating mind and so create a new duality. When we speak of an absolute, we are apt to think that, being the denial of opposites, it must be placed in opposition to the discriminating mind. But to think so is in fact to lower the Absolute into the world of opposites, necessitating the conception of a greater or higher absolute which will contain both. The Absolute, in brief, is in the world of opposites and not apart from it. This is apparently a contradiction, and can never be understood so long as we stay in a world of distinction. To go beyond this world will not help, nor to stay in it either. Hence the intellectual dilemma from which we all struggle in vain to escape.

This fruitlessness was pointed out by Daitō the master, who, remaining silent on the main issue, simply moved his fan and poetically referred to the Imperial virtue. Daitō wasted no time in attempting to convince the Emperor by argumentation, for he knew that whatever understanding one could have of the truth must come from life itself as we all live it, including even the august personage himself, and not from merely discoursing upon the Absolute. Daitō purposely evaded touching upon the subject of the companionless one whom the Emperor wished personally to interview. He had no desire to lead the Emperor along the ordinary route of reasoning; the companionless one must remain companionless, that is, beyond distinctions and discriminations, and yet persistently with them and in them. To demonstrate this Daitō resorted to a most effective gesture: the Absolute, the companionless one, not only moved with the master's fan, but is the master and the Emperor and everything else.

From this it is evident that in order to understand Buddhism, and in fact all religion, we must go beyond the domain of the intellect. The intellect's function is to discriminate this from that, to divide the one into two; therefore, when the one is demanded and not the two, something else must operate to take hold of it. Yet this one is conceivable only when it is associated with the two, while this association does not mean that the one stands against or is conditioned by the two, in which case the one will no more be an absolute one but one of the two. The one must be found in the two, with the two, and yet beyond the two, that is to say, non-distinction is in distinction and distinction in non-distinction. To state the point more directly and precisely, distinction is non-distinction and non-distinction is distinction. This is not the denial of the intellect or the stoppage of reasoning, but it attempts to reach the foundation of it by means of negation-affirmation. It is by this double process only that the intellect can transcend itself, for without this transcendence the intellect can never liberate itself from the contradictions it weaves out of its own body. In terms of Christian experience, we can say that this is living in Christ by dying to Adam, or it is Christ's rising from the dead. Paul says: "And if Christ be not risen, then is our preaching vain, and your faith is also vain (I Cor. 15:14). One must die before one can rise, and this rising is acceptable by faith and not by reasoning. The merging of contradictions, the self-identity of distinction and non-distinction, is achieved by faith, which is personal experience, the opening of the *prajñācakṣu*[4] ("the eye of transcendental wisdom"), the thinking of the unthinkable.

[4] According to Eckhart, on "True Hearing." "The eye with which I see God is the same with which God sees me." The *prajñācakṣu* is this kind of eye. The *cakṣu* has no particular reality as its object of sight; when it is said to see something, this something is no other than itself; the *cakṣu* sees itself as if not at all seeing, for its seeing is no-seeing and its no-seeing is seeing. Says Eckhart, "My eye and God's eye is one eye, and one sight, and one knowledge, and one love." When we speak of seeing in a world of discrimination, the act sets up the dualism of the seer and the object seen; the one is distinctly

Prince Shōtoku (Prince Regent, 593–622), the founder of Hōr-yūji Temple at Nara, wrote commentaries on three Mahayana sūtras: the *Saddharma-puṇḍarīka*, the *Vimalakīrti*, and the *Śrīmālā*. It is noteworthy that in all of them the unthinkability of Buddhist experience is insisted upon. In the *Śrīmālā*, the *tathāgata-garbha* ("Matrix of Tathāgatahood") is described as being buried in innumerable defilements, yet as remaining beyond their control. The *tathāgata-garbha* is the pure, undefiled spiritual world of non-discrimination, while the defiling world is that of thought and differentiation. That these two are in their nature separate and cannot be merged is self-evident as far as the human way of thinking is concerned; yet the sutras declare that the pure and the defiled are found dissolved in the *garbha*, while the *garbha* itself remains uncontaminated. This is really beyond the bounds of thinkability. But when the self-identity of distinction and non-distinction is understood, the *garbha* as the field where purity and defilement display themselves each in its own form of existence will be understood. This understanding, let it be remembered, is not on the plane of intellection, but on the spiritual plane, and it is generally known as faith. The question of faith and knowledge is sometimes quite a puzzling one, because most of us fail to sound the depths of our spiritual life, which belongs to the realm of *acintya*, the unthinkable. It is a Buddha who recognizes another. Unless our insight reaches the same level as that of the Buddha, the teaching of the *Śrīmālā* remains forever a sealed book.

Christian experience, as far as I can see, teaches the same thing; the Buddhist unthinkable corresponds to divine revelation, which is something supernatural and superrational and altogether beyond

---

separated from the other. If not for this dualism, no seeing can take place in this world of opposites, of sense and intellect. But this is not the way to Perfect Enlightenment which belongs to the world of non-discrimination where abides the Absolute One all by itself. The opening of the *prajñācakṣu* means one's coming into the presence of this Absolute, that is to say, it is where "my eye and God's eye is one eye." Here seeing is no-seeing; a distinction there is between "my eye" and "God's eye"; nonetheless there is no distinction because they are "one eye." This absolute "one eye" is a colorless one, and for this reason it discerns all color. "If my eye is to discern color, it must itself be free from all color." The *prajñācakṣu* is of non-discrimination, hence its discrimination of all particular entities. When discrimination is not discriminating and yet discriminating, we have Perfect Enlightenment.

the human power of thinkability. This revelation will never come to us as long as we are bound up by the chain of logical reasonableness. God will never reveal Himself in minds stuffed with rationalistic ideas; it is not that He dislikes them, but that He is simply beyond them. He is ever disposed to appear before us, but it is we ourselves who shun Him. In truth, divine revelation is not to be sought by our own efforts; it comes upon us by itself, of its own accord. God is always in us and with us, but we by means of our human understanding posit Him outside us, against us, as opposing us, and exercise our intellectual power to the utmost to take hold of it. The revelation, however, will take place only when this human power is really exhausted, has given up all its selfishness and ideas of distinction.

Strangely enough, but in one sense most naturally, we all, Buddhists as well as Christians, living as we do on the plane of the intellect, submit everything to intellectual test and domination, and reject as unworthy of consideration all which the intellect fails to understand. In our folly we treat Buddhism in the same way as Christians do their religion, but sooner or later we are all bound to pick up what we cast away and place it on the spiritual altar of our being. For whether we realize it or not, it was there all the time, that is, in the undiscriminating matrix of Tathāgatahood. When it comes to itself, the entire world with all its ugliness and defilement and undesirableness will be seen as revealing the glory of God. When the bird sings, we know it transmits God's voice. When the Buddha held out a golden flower, Mahākāśyapa smiled. Why? Because both were in God's Pure Land, which is ours as well as Amida's. In this Land no words are needed, all conceptualization vanishes, for who knows, knows.

The Emperor Goyōzei (reigned 1586–1616) wrote a poem on the subject:

> Smiling eyebrows are opened.
> Is it cherry or peach blossom?
> Who does not know?
> Yet nobody knows.

From the viewpoint of non-distinction nobody knows, yet everybody knows. The flower is offered and somebody smiles. Apparently no communication has passed, but something must have passed between the two minds, something lying beyond the

borderland of ratiocination. For Mahākāśyapa's smile was not an
ordinary one such as we on the plane of distinction often exchange;
it came out of the deepest recesses of his nature, where he and
Buddha and all the rest of the audience move and have their being.
No words are needed when this is reached. A direct insight across
the abyss of human understanding is indicated. Our smiles are sense
bound and on the surface of our consciousness; they are like
bubbles, they come and go, but Kāśyapa's smile is the singing of
the bird, the blossoming of the cherry, the rustling of a breeze
through the autumn leaves, the murmuring of the waters along
the winding mountain stream. "Do you wish to know the way to
enlightenment?" A Zen master kicked the dog and it yelped.
Where there is understanding no comment is needed, but where
there is no understanding no amount of argument is convincing.

To think this Unthinkable, to open the secret of existence, to
escape from the prison of rationality, to pass beyond the field of
opposites, and to rise to the higher point of view, it is imperative
to have an insight into timelessness of time which also involves
spacelessness of space. After repeatedly teaching that "however
much we try to measure Buddha-knowledge by means of thought
we can never succeed," the *Saddharma-puṇḍarīka* goes on to
state in the "Chapter on Longevity": "In the immeasurably long
past I obtained my Buddhahood, and I have been living here
for an incalculably long period of time. I am immortal." According
to history, however, Śākyamuni attained enlightenment at
Buddhagaya on the Nairanjanā River more than twenty-five centuries ago, when he was thirty-five. Ignoring this fact, he declares
in the sutra that his enlightenment took place hundreds of thousands of kalpas ago, and that he has been preaching on the Vulture
Mountain ever since. Indeed he is still there, preaching in the same
old way, surrounded by hundreds of thousands of his disciples,
and we can hear him even in these faraway islands of Japan.

The two statements are obviously contradictory as any of us can
see: That Śākyamuni after his enlightenment preached on Mount
Vulture some twenty-five centuries ago; and that his enlightenment took place even before he appeared among us, and he is still
preaching on the mount so vigorously that we can all hear it even
now. Contradictions of this sort abound through every phase of
our life, not only intellectual but emotional as well. In the latter
case contradictions appear as fears, worries, vexations, and so on.
Our emotional life is so mixed up with the intellectual that we can-

not separate the one from the other, for life is one through and through. The intellect lies dormant without the instigation of the emotions, and the latter becomes altogether muddled when not backed by the former. An intellectual clarification purged of all its dilemmas helps the mind to become calm and content, being in harmonious relation with its environment. When the clarification attains this stage, it is known as enlightenment, which is thinking the Unthinkable, discriminating the Undiscriminated, and the up-heaving of the Absolute into consciousness. This is also known as a state of fearlessness (*abhaya*) which issues from the great com-passionate heart of Kwannon, Avalokiteśvara.

The problem of the self-identity of contraries has ever been the great problem for all thinking minds, for all philosophers and religious people. Buddhists have also valiantly and in a most characteristic manner grappled with it, and have come to a definite solution of it in their doctrine of *acintya*, of no-thought or mindless-ness, which, positively stated, is the opening of the *prajñācakṣu*, or plunging into the bottomless abyss itself, as Zen Buddhists would say. The solution, however, is in one sense no solution at all, for the Unthinkable (*acintya*) remains forever unthinkable, lying beyond the ken of logic and intellection. Especially with Zen Buddhists, they do not go any further than merely stating the con-tradiction as it stands. They call a spade a not-spade, heaven not-heaven, God, not-God. When asked why, they would say: God is God, a spade is a spade, heaven is heaven; and they would make no attempt to explain these contradictory statements. The Buddhist teaching as expounded in the *Vimalakīrti*, one of the three Maha-yana sutras commented upon by Prince Shōtoku, is full of such contradictions. In truth, the Buddhist solution of the great prob-lem of life consists in not solving it at all, and they contend that the not-solving is really the solving.

When the Master Daitō saw the Emperor Godaigo (reigned 1318–1339) who was another student of Zen, the master said,

We were parted many thousands of *kalpas* ago, yet we have not been separated even for a moment. We are facing each other all day long, yet we have never met.

Here we have the same idea as expressed by Śākyamuni himself in the *Saddharma-puṇḍarīka* mentioned before. In spite of the historical fact that he attained enlightenment near Buddhagaya at a definite moment of time, he says that he was fully enlightened even before the world was created. The historical fact of his enlightenment is a record which we time-minded make with the intellect, because the intellect likes to divide, and cuts time into years and days and hours, and constructs history, whereas time itself underlying history knows no such human artificial cuttings. We are living partly in this time-space-conscious history but essentially in history-transcending time-space. Most of us would recognize the first but not the second phase of their life. Daitō the master here wishes to remind the Emperor of this most fundamental experience. Hence his paradoxical proposition. (As with Buddhists "Here" is "Now" and "Now" is "Here," the idea developed in regard to time also applies to space.)

The fact that the master and the Emperor were facing each other is a fact based upon the concept of time as infinitely divisible. But from the point of view which is only possible in the realm of non-discrimination, where no dividing of time takes place and no rational calculation is possible, historical facts have no significance. In other words, "You and I have never been in each other's presence even for a moment through all eternity," and yet "we have never been separated." Or, expressed conversely, "I have been with you all day long, but have never entered your presence." The master is viewing things from his non-discriminative point of view, which the Emperor was at first unable to understand. None of these things are understandable when given to the judgment of our everyday experience as dominated by rationalization. Buddhists must learn to disregard those "facts" so called as happening in time history, if they desire to attain enlightenment and to be with Śākyamuni on Mount Vulture.

The reason we are annoyed in our daily life and unable to escape from its annoyances is due to the inability of our intellect to go beyond itself. Here, then, is a need for a major operation to sever the knots of the intellect. A mountain is not a mountain and a river is not a river; yet a mountain is a mountain and a river is a river. Negation is affirmation and affirmation is negation. Nor is this a mere play on words. When it is so understood, it is still on the plane of intellection, and we shall never be able to get away from the vicious circle. And as long as we are in it we shall never be out of the cycle of transmigration. Therefore, we must admit that all the fears and vexations and anxieties of life are due to our failure to dive boldly and straightforwardly into the center of our being, and then to rise out of it on the plane of distinction where the problems which have harassed us no more exist. The diving and the rising, however, are not two separate acts; they are one, the diving is rising and the rising is diving. Buddhists are thus exhorted to strive not to be tied by words and other products of intellection, but to view all problems from the higher plane where no words are ever spoken, where there is only the showing of the flowers and the smiling of Mahākāśyapa. Yet words are needed to transcend words, and intellection is needed to rise above the intellect, except that this rising must not be made in a dualistic or "escapist" sense, for no such escape is here possible.

We are now in a position to say something about karma. Human suffering is due to our being bound in karma, for all of us, as soon as we are born, carry a heavy burden of past karma, which is, therefore, part of our very existence. In Japan the term is connected with bad deeds, and evil people are spoken of as bearing the karma of the past. But the original meaning of the term is "action," and human acts are valued as good, bad, or indifferent. In this sense, human beings are the only beings which have karma. All others move in accordance with the laws of their being, but it is human beings alone that can design and calculate and are conscious of themselves and of their doings. We humans are the sole self-conscious animals, or, as Pascal says, "thinking reeds." From thinking, from thinking consciously, we develop the faculty of seeing, designing, and planning beforehand, which demonstrates that we are free, and not always bound by the "inevitable laws" of Nature. Karma, therefore, which is the ethical valuation of our acts, is found only in human beings, and in fact as soon as we enter the world our karma is attached to us.

Not only are we wrapped up in our karma but we know the fact that we are so wrapped up. It may be better to say that we are karma, karma is ourself; moreover, we are all conscious of this fact, and yet this very fact of our being aware of the karma bondage is the spiritual privilege of humanity. For this privilege, implying freedom, means our being able to transcend karma. But we must remember that with freedom and transcendence there comes responsibility as well as struggle; and the struggle as an outcome of freedom means suffering. The value of human life indeed lies in this capability for suffering; where there is no suffering resulting from our consciousness of karmic bondage there is no power of attaining spiritual experience, and thereby reaching the field of non-distinction. Unless we definitely make up our minds to suffer we cannot enjoy the special spiritual privilege granted to us human beings. We must make full use of it, and, accepting the karma bondage as far as it extends, resolutely face all forms of suffering and thereby qualify ourselves for transcending them.

With the problem of karma we again encounter a contradiction, this more serious because it involves life itself; it is the contradiction of life and death. As long as we remain in the domain of intellection we may put it aside for a while as not concerning us very vitally. But when the question concerns life in its most fundamental sense, we cannot dispose of it lightly. If karma is human life itself, and there is no way to be free from it except by being deprived of life, which means self-destruction, how can there be any kind of emancipation? And without emancipation there is no spiritual life. We cannot be eternally suffering, however be the present fate of humanity. Just to be conscious of karma means no more than throwing ourselves into hell-fire. God would not visit upon us this form of punishment, however bad we may be. Is there not, after all, something in our recognition of karma which will lift us from it? But this is obviously a case of self-contradiction. We find ourselves plunged headlong into an ever-rotating whirlpool of human destiny.

The karma contradiction, as long as it is a contradiction, must be solved in the same way as its intellectual counterpart. The intellectual contradiction was solved when we entered the realm of non-distinction; so the karma contradiction is to be solved by entering the realm of no-karma. Where is this? It is where we became conscious of karma as underlying all human activities. This consciousness points to the way of liberation. The human privilege of self-judgment or self-appraisement is also the key to self-deliverance. Just because we are conscious of ourselves and know how to evaluate our deeds, we are permitted to have a glimpse into a realm where no such human judgment avails, that is, where karma is merged into no-karma and no-karma into karma.

To put the matter in another form, as long as we are human, we cannot escape from karma, for we are karma, and the latter will follow us wherever we go, like our own shadow; but because of this we are able to escape from it, that is, to transcend it. Ordinarily, we are constantly under the oppressive consciousness of karma bondage, and this fact we express in the form of the spiritual urge to rise above ourselves or to approach God by perfecting or purifying ourselves, if that is possible. Rationally speaking, being merely conscious of karma bondage may not be more than a state of contemplation; but in our heart we feel that the consciousness is far more deeply seated, and rises out of our inmost self which is somehow related to something beyond itself. Our struggle with karma, we feel, is dictated by this Unthinkable, for the contemplation itself is no more than the reflection of it. If it were not for this fact we should have no urge, no struggle, no suffering, no affliction of any kind. The consciousness of karma is thus always found linked with the urge; without this urge in the human heart there would be no karma consciousness in our minds, and therefore we know that karma is connected with no-karma. It is in fact no-karma which so persistently presses itself into the domain of karma, making the latter feel, as it were, uneasy and annoyed. This is the reason why I say that the being conscious of karma bondage most assuredly paves the way to transcending it; the very fact of our intense spiritual suffering is the promise that we can eventually rise above it. From the viewpoint of Buddhist experience, the suffering is the transcending, karma is no-karma.

The consciousness of karma bondage and the effort to shake it off manifest themselves as prayer. Prayer, logically speaking, is another form of contradiction, for it refuses to follow obediently the course of nature; in this it is altogether human. Animals have no prayer; angels and gods have no prayer either. Man alone prays because he is conscious of his impotence to rise above himself, and yet he urgently desires it. As far as Nature is concerned she pursues her own way, regardless of human desires, aspirations, or ambitions. She kills us when the body has run its course of continuance, she punishes us with all kinds of illness when we go out of the path prescribed by her. In this respect she is relentless. But from the human point of view we fervently pray for the recovery of the diseased even when our medical or scientific knowledge tells us that it is absolutely impossible. It may be a human weakness, even human folly, but it is certainly human nature to feel sad and distressed at the sight of our fellow-beings going through tortures and other forms of pain for the relief of which we are utterly helpless. The only thing we can do in these circumstances is to pray. To pray to what or to whom? We do not know, yet we pray, that is to say, we desire to see the course of nature reversed—and this is not necessarily based on egoistic impulses. This is decidedly irrational, and it is for this very reason that I say that prayer opens the way to the spiritual life, and finally places us in the domain where karma is no-karma and no-karma is karma.

To repeat: karma oppresses us all the time, yet all the time we strive to rise above it. This striving, this impulse to transcend karma, issues directly from our spiritual nature. Prayer, therefore, which is another name for the urge, constitutes the essence of the religious life. Prayer apparently does not add much to humanity, but whatever little it does, it brings out the most vital factor in the structure of human nature. For it is, after all, prayer which will shake off every possible piece of contamination attached to the human heart, and make it thoroughly pure, thoroughly free from karma consciousness. The heart thus emerging out of karma is no-karma itself. But here is the one thing we must not forget, that the heart identifying itself with no-karma never remains in that state; for the heart that is no-karma is not the human heart. The heart, as soon as it attains the state of no-karma, comes back to itself and begins to feel every suffering belonging to human nature. This heart is at once karma and no-karma in a perfect state of self-identity.

The noted Buddhist declaration that life is pain or suffering (*duḥkha*) must not be understood as a message of pessimism. That life is pain is a plain statement of fact, and all our spiritual experience, Buddhist or Christian, starts from this fact. In fact, the so-called spiritual experience is no more than the experience of pain raised above mere sensation. Those who cannot feel pain can never go beyond themselves. All religious-minded people are sufferers of life pain. The Buddha, says Vimalakīrti, is sick because all sentient beings are sick. When we are surrounded by sickness on all sides, how can we, if spiritually disposed, be free from being sick? The heart of the Compassionate One always beats with those of his fellow-beings, sentient and non-sentient.

The dissolution of karma bondage, we can see now, consists in accepting it as a fact of life experience, but with the knowledge that the bondage does not really touch our inmost being, which is above all forms of dualism. This is expressed in the Buddhist logic of self-identity by saying that karma is no-karma and no-karma is karma. Where dualism holds good, this logic does not apply, though in truth dualism is only possible on the assumption of the truth of the logic of self-identity. Buddhism, therefore, upholds the logic of self-identity as absolutely necessary for the understanding of its teaching, which is the attainment of Buddhahood.

To divide is the work of the intellect, and where intellection prevails there is always a dualism. But as it is this dualism which weaves the net of karma and catches us unawares, Buddhism is insistent on doing away with intellection; but what is most important here, as I have repeatedly said, is to remember that Buddhism rejects intellection and all its complications, not unconditionally, but with this reservation, that it gains its proper functioning only after it is thoroughly purged of illusions and presumptions, that is, after it dies to itself.

One of the illusions which the intellect sets before itself is that it is free, that it can choose. By cutting up a seamless piece of cloth called life into several parts, the intellect tries to examine them, thinking that they can be pieced together and then the original reproduced. This dividing and piecing together it claims to be its privilege, its enjoyment of freedom. But nothing is more ruinous than this to the proper status of intellection in the scheme of human life. For the intellect is not free by nature; its power to divide is really the power to kill itself. The intellect gains its freedom only when this killing of itself is accomplished. The choice of alternatives is not freedom in its real sense; to be free one must not be hampered in any possible way or in any possible sense; freedom means absolute independence. Now for the intellect, analysis, with its counterpart synthesis, is its life; but this analyzing and synthesizing means self-limitation, because the work requires something to work upon as well as someone who works. Intellection is putting one thing against another, which is opposition, and opposition is self-restriction, giving up independence and freedom. Whatever freedom the intellect may enjoy in choosing one thing out of many, it is a limited freedom and not an absolute one. And if it is not an absolute one, the spirit can never feel rested and happy with itself. It is the Buddhist logic of self-identity that can give to the spirit what it desires by transcending dualism and all its consequent issues.

It is thus most decidedly not the intellect or reason which makes us free from the bondage of karma consciousness. All that the intellect does toward spiritual liberation is that it foreshadows, however faintly, the image of freedom, whereby the heart is somehow encouraged, though it cannot yet clearly see the way to its own liberation. I have said here "encouraged," but it may be

better to say that the heart is all the more depressed: it sees something ahead and is yet utterly unable to locate it exactly. This
feeling on the part of the Unconscious is reflected in the intellect,
which will now exert all its powers in solving the problem of
"thinking the Unthinkable."

A serious question presents itself now. When karma is identified
with no-karma and the distinction between good and bad is annihilated, does this not mean moral anarchy and the disorganization
of human society? Buddhism itself will no more be, along with
its logic of self-identity. When there is no karma, good, bad, or
indifferent, there will be no moral agent who is to be held responsible for his deeds. The doctrine of karma is, according to
Buddhism, the doctrine of the moral law of causation, meaning a
moral order in human society. The physical world collapses when
causation is taken away. So with the moral world; it requires that
good deeds add to the happiness of the whole community, including the individual agent himself, whereas bad deeds detract
so much from it, and hurt the other people in every possible way.
Buddhists naturally regard this teaching of "moral causation"[5] as
the most essential for their daily guidance, spiritual as well as
moral, and when this is denied there will be no Buddhism left, in
spite of its logic of self-identity. Is it possible to say this in our
practical life, that where there is no Buddhism we really have
Buddhism? This amounts to saying that life denied is life asserted,
or that committing suicide is living a full life. According to the logic
of self-identity, the contradiction may really be no-contradiction;
but how can we apply this statement to our everyday life and be
happy in the best sense of the term? We may glibly talk about no
karma, no causation, no life, to our heart's content, but should we
make any pragmatic sense out of this evidently nonsensical diction?
This will be the point now occupying our attention.

When Hyakujō Ekai, one of the most noted Zen masters of the

---

[5] By "moral causation" Buddhists mean that a deed, good or bad, or
indifferent, brings its own result on the doer. Good people are happy and bad
ones unhappy. But in most cases "happiness" is understood not in its moral or
spiritual sense but in the sense of material prosperity, social position, or political influence. For instance, kingship is considered the reward of one's having
faithfully practiced the ten deeds of goodness. If one meets a tragic death,
he is thought to have committed something bad in his past lives even when
he might have spent a blameless life in the present one.

T'ang dynasty, had one day finished his preaching, an old man who regularly attended his sermons came to him and said, "In the days of Kāśyapa-Buddha, innumerable *kalpas* ago, I lived here on this mountain, and one day a student asked me, 'Does an enlightened man fall into cause-effect [i.e., moral causation] or not?' I answered, 'No,' and for this answer I have lived in the form of a wild fox ever since. Will you give the proper answer that I may be freed from this fox form? Does an enlightened man fall into cause-effect or not?"

The master answered, "He does not ignore[6] cause-effect." The fox man was enlightened and liberated. Next day the master performed a funeral service for the fox form left behind by the old man.

The meaning of the story is this: The enlightened man allows the law of causation, moral or physical, to take its course, that is, he submits himself to it, he does not sever himself from it, he does not make any distinction between it and himself, he becomes it, he is it. When Hyakujō says that the enlightened man does not obscure cause-effect, he means what I have stated here. The old man, on the contrary, had the law separated from him, he thought there was an external agent known as cause-effect or causation, and this visited him according as he was good or bad. He did not realize that he himself was the moral agent as well as the law, that the law was inherent in the deed, that he was the lawmaker himself. So he thought that being enlightened meant severing himself from the law, putting it away from him, so that it will no more touch him. This was "not falling into cause-effect," he reasoned. But Hyakujō was the upholder of self-identity while the old man was a dualist.

Briefly stated, man may be compared to a geometrical point where three lines converge or intersect: physical-natural, intellectual-moral, and spiritual. The point, man, may be conscious of all three, but not to the same degree of intensity and coordination. Dualists, including all the people in our common life, strongly and almost one-sidedly emphasize the intellectual-moral life at the expense of the spiritual. The result is that they cannot entirely give themselves up to their physical-natural life, nor can they completely ignore the claims the spiritual makes on them. They stand

---

[6] *Mai*, literally, "to obscure."

midway, turning sometimes this way and sometimes the other way. This wavering is a source of constant vexation and uneasiness. Yet they cannot go over to the spiritual line because it is the dualists' destiny to stay on the line they have first chosen. In spite of this fact, however, there is a persistent urge impelling the intellect to transcend itself. The urge means the intellect's leaving its own line and going over to the spiritual. This is committing suicide on the part of the intellect, but it is required of it. The transference is to be executed in the most resolute manner, as is quite evident from the nature of the case. But this process of transference, properly speaking, is not a process from one stage to another, that is, one that can be traced step after step spatially and temporally. For the very moment the intellectual-moral line is abandoned, one finds oneself on the spiritual; there is no gradation, no scaled progression, but a leap, an abrupt transference, a discrete continuity.

The intellectual-moral line cannot fall back on the physical-moral because it has diverted itself from it, and this diversion is its characteristic mark. It is the spiritual line that can revert to the physical-natural, making the latter acquire a new significance in human life. The spiritual may appear to some people to be going even so far as to identify itself with the physical-natural. What distinguishes the latter most conspicuously is its passivity, its absolute submission to the law of cause-effect. When a terrific storm sways over the woods, the trees break down, and havoc is left behind. The broken ones do not complain, nor do the destructive forces feel elated. Both are simply following supreme commands of Nature. There is something akin to it in our spiritual life. The divine will, so called, is accepted and obeyed without uttering words of dissatisfaction on the part of the spiritual man. "May Thy will be done" expresses the whole business, a state of absolute dependence or of absolute passivity, in which we see both the physical-natural and the spiritual coincide. With all this, however, there is one thing which categorically divides the spiritual from the natural, that is, man from all the rest of creation, and we must take hold of this one thing if we wish to be truly worthy of the name, Man. This means that we must live actively, vitally, living the Buddhist logic of self-identity.

The spiritually-enlightened man is therefore passive to the will of God, which is, Buddhistically stated, the law of cause-effect. With him there is really no darkening or ignoring it, no falling into it, though not in the sense upheld by the aforementioned fox man.

He simply goes along his way nonchalantly, so to speak, and fearlessly convinced of the truth which he has found in himself, though it is not of his own making. He is thus in one way quite passive, but in another way altogether active because he is master of himself. While this mastership is derived from a source beyond himself, he is given full authority to use it as he wills, that is, he uses it as if not using it; here is his active passivity or passive activity. The two opposite contradicting terms are here found unified and identified in his life of self-identity.

To put the question of "not to fall or not to obscure" in a more or less familiar form, the following line of argument may be found helpful in the understanding of the Buddhist view of cause-effect.

When the appropriate conditions are matured, an event takes place, regardless of personality. The sun shines on all, good and bad. The law uniformly operates for all, enlightened and unenlightened; for it is the nature of the law that it should govern alike the moral and the physical world. The intellect that formulates the law requires ratiocination and cannot admit irrationality. However good a man may be, his moral (or spiritual) qualification can never save him from the law. When it rains he must get wet like everybody else. The law of cause-effect is rationally formulated in accordance with rules of intellection; even the wise come under these rules, because they hold true on the spiritual plane as well as on the physical. The spirit cannot negate the intellect; what it can do is to transcend it, in the sense that it has its own government within the intellectual boundaries; and as long as it keeps this in good order it knows of no outside boundaries imposed upon it. Being its own master, the spirit makes use of the intellectual limitations and expresses itself through them while reserving its right of interpretation. No doubt it belongs to a world of distinctions but at the same time it is above it.

The spiritual world is at once of distinction and of non-distinction, and for this reason karma is no-karma as well as karma itself. Karma retains its usual signification as cause-effect, but when seen in the light of non-distinction it is no-karma. With the enlightened man, therefore, karma does not work in the same way as with the unenlightened. The latter are not yet of the spiritual world and cannot help groaning under the heavy weight of karma hindrance. The enlightened one also has his karma, but he carries it as if not at all feeling its weight; he is quite unconscious of it. It is not that enlightenment does away with karma but that enlightenment goes its free, independent way, karma or no-karma. In truth, there are no two worlds, the one of karma and the other of enlightenment. There is just one world containing, as it were, karma and enlightenment, physical-natural and spiritual-supernatural. Therefore, when a bell is struck, it rings, and we all hear it, enlightened and unenlightened, and know that it is a bell.

The only difference, and a most essential one, between the enlightened and the unenlightened, is that the enlightened man has what I might call a spiritual consciousness along with the psychological and intellectual consciousness. People of the physical world have not yet been awakened to this spiritual consciousness. They just hear the bell and recognize the sound; they stop there, their insight does not go into the spiritual; they have therefore no enlightenment. It is different with the spiritually-awakened one. But we must not imagine that he is all the time conscious of his spirituality or that his "spiritual consciousness" so called is always claiming its right to be heard on the superficial plane of consciousness. It can never be focused to a point as if it were a psychological image and distinguished from the rest of things moving in our ordinary relative consciousness. Spiritual self-consciousness is a *sui generis* kind of consciousness. It is a form of intuition unanalyzable into subject and object, into one who intuits and that which is intuited. It is an intuition in which there is no opposition of the seer and the seen; it is a case of absolute self-identification. It is an intuition which is not intuition, for it is an intuition of non-distinction distinguished and of non-discrimination discriminated.

We can see now where the old man was wrong who had to assume the fox form for five hundred lives. He committed the grave mistake of making the spiritual world stand away from the moral-intellectual world of distinction. Hyakujō, knowing where the old man's fault lay, made it clear that there is no obscuring of karma for the unenlightened as well as the enlightened. The enlightened man "falls" into cause-effect just as much as the unenlightened, but his falling is merely the paying of an old debt.

This not-obscuring of cause-effect is another illustration of the logic of *prajñā*, as is reiterated in the *prajñā* class literature of the Mahayana Buddhist sutras.[7] The *prajñā* logic is the logic of self-

---

[7] The Mahayana teaching, indeed, of whatever class, is all based on the *prajñā* logic of self-identity, where contradictions as contradictions have no place, as they are all absorbed in oneness of self-identity.

identity. *Prajñā* is *prajñā* because *prajñā* is no-*prajñā*. Extending
this further we can say: White is black because white is white; or
white is not white because white is white; or to be myself is not to
be myself, whereby I am myself. The Buddhists claim this logic to
be lying at the basis of all human experience, and by thus illogically or irrationally constructing it we come to spiritual self-consciousness. The law of cause-effect is binding for all of us, we can
never evade, obscure, or ignore it. We all fall into it, and it is only
by virtue of spiritual self-consciousness that we become no more
troubled with karma good or bad, letting cause-effect follow its
own course. The *prajñā* philosopher will declare that the being
immersed in cause-effect is transcending it, that the falling into
it is the not-obscuring of it.

I am, for example, born; I may become ill; I shall grow old and
die. I cannot ignore the wheel of cause-effect, but the fact that I
am conscious of its revolution and yet at the same time conscious
that there is something that is never touched by the law of cause-
effect, enables me to "escape from it." Thus we never fall into
causality, because we are already it. To fall into it, or to be delivered from it, presupposes that there has been a state where
there was no falling and no deliverance. When we are the wheel
itself and move along with it, there is neither falling, nor being
delivered, for the wheel and we are one. Let us, however, not
forget, in this connection as before, that here must be a spiritual
intuition or apperception as to the identity of the wheel and the
one who keeps it going all the time. With this intuition one gains
immortality, as Christians would say. Those who dance around on
the moral-intellectual plane, and can never identify themselves
with it, will never find the way to an everlasting life.

There is another Zen story illustrative of the logic of self-identity.
Someone asked a Zen master, "Summer comes, winter comes. How
shall we escape from it?"

"Why not go to the place where there is neither winter nor
summer?" answered the master.

"Where can such a place be found?" asked the inquirer.

"When winter comes you shiver; when summer comes you
perspire." This was the master's solution.

As Pascal says, man is a frail thing; the universe need not arm
itself to destroy him. One drop of poison will kill the most virtuous
man as well as the wickedest one, but neither the universe nor the

poison is conscious of its destructive power. Man alone is aware of the distinction between consciousness and unconsciousness, and he alone is self-conscious. "All our dignity consists in thought," that is, in consciousness. Our consciousness has then a great significance, and enlightenment is no more than a recognition of this fact, which constitutes our spiritual self-consciousness. Enlightenment is spiritual and not intellectual; it is not of thought, but of spirit. Becoming spiritually conscious of the facts of our everyday experience is not the same as psychologically or intellectually becoming conscious of them. The difference between this spiritual form of consciousness and our ordinary consciousness in the world of sense is not on the same plane of experience; there is something categorically differentiating the one from the other. Cold is felt by the enlightened as well as the ignorant. When a bird sings all hear it, unless one is physically deficient. But the consciousness experienced by the ignorant does not rise above the sensuous plane. To the spiritually experienced the hearing of the bird and the feeling of the cold are on the spiritual plane, which is interfused with the world of senses, and yet which must be distinguished from it when we wish to be precise about it; the enlightened man interprets his daily experience from the spiritual point of view.

When the world is thus interpreted spiritually, or when it thus reflects itself in the mirror of spiritual consciousness, it is no more an object of the sense-intellect. The world with all its sufferings, shortcomings, and dualities becomes one with the spiritual world, and for those who are enlightened, suffering is no doubt suffering, but they have absorbed it, as it were, in their spiritual consciousness where all such things as take place on the psychological-natural plane find their proper meaning in harmony with the "unthinkable" scheme of the universe. Cause-effect in this sense no longer affects them; in other words, it is never "obscured."

Pascal speaks of the thinking reed, but this thinking must not be regarded as mere cognition or contemplation; it must mean a process of becoming spiritually self-conscious. The importance of contemplation was highly stressed by the early Buddhists, but the Mahayana insists on something more. All contemplation suggests a form of dualism, for where there is an object of contemplation there must be a mind which contemplates. Being spiritually conscious is more than contemplation, though self-consciousness also suggests a form of dualism. But spiritual self-consciousness implies that there is neither the one who is conscious nor that of which the spirit is conscious. To be conscious and yet not to be conscious of any particular object is true spiritual self-consciousness. Here is the identity of object and subject, and it is from this absolute oneness that a world of multiplicity is set up. As long as we are bound by these multiplicities we cannot escape their domination, but as soon as we rise in our spiritual consciousness above them, where there is yet no separation, no distinction, no opposition between this and that we are free, and all the multiplicities hurt us no more. But as I have repeatedly explained, this does not mean the denial of the sense world, but when it is made to stand by itself, ungoverned by the spiritual world, Buddhists reject it.

It is for this reason that we assert that we are far greater than the universe in which we live, for our greatness is not of space but of the spirit. And there is nothing spiritual in the universe apart from human spirituality. The greatness of the world comes from our own greatness, and all about us acquires its greatness only from us humans. And our greatness is realized only when we become spiritually conscious of ourselves and all that goes on about us, and by this kind of self-consciousness we achieve emancipation. According to legend, when the Buddha was born he exclaimed, "Above heaven and below heaven I alone am the Honored (Fully-Enlightened) One." This shows that he had realized in himself the greatness which each one of us has within him, and this supreme affirmation is reached by going through with all kind of suffering, including intellectual and moral contradictions. The supreme affirmation is: When hot we perspire, when cold we shiver.

PART VI

Zen and Japanese Culture

Draw bamboos for ten years,
become a bamboo, then forget
all about bamboos when you
are drawing.

Georges Duthuit

1. BUDDHIST, ESPECIALLY ZEN,
CONTRIBUTIONS TO JAPANESE CULTURE[1]

APART from its insistence on the all-absorbing importance of personal experience in the realization of a final fact, Zen has the following characteristics which have exercised a great deal of moral influence in the molding of what may be designated the spirit of the East, especially of Japan.

1. Neglect of form is generally characteristic of mysticism, Christian or Buddhist or Islamic. When the importance of the spirit is emphasized, all the outward expressions of it naturally become things of secondary significance. Form is not necessarily despised, but attention to it is reduced to a minimum, or we may say that conventionalism is set aside and individual originality is asserted in its full strength. But because of this there is a forceful tone of inwardness perceivable in all things connected with Zen. As far as form is concerned, nothing beautiful or appealing to the senses may be observable here, but one feels something inward or spiritual asserting itself in spite of the imperfection of the form, perhaps because of this very imperfection. The reason is this: when the form is perfect, our senses are satisfied too strongly with it and the mind may at least temporarily neglect to exercise its more inner function. The efforts concentrated too greatly in the outwardness of things fail to draw out what inner meaning there is in them. So Tanka burned a wooden image of Buddha to make a fire, and idolatry was done away with. Kensu turned into a fisherman against the conventionality of monastery life. Daito Kokushi became a beggar and Kanzan Kokushi was a cowherd.

2. The inwardness of Zen implies the directness of its appeal to the human spirit. When the intermediary of form is dispensed with, one spirit speaks directly to another. Raise a finger and the whole universe is there. Nothing could be more direct than this in this

[1] *Essays in Zen Buddhism* (Third Series), Rider & Co., 1953, pp. 337–349.

world of relativity. The medium of communication or the symbol
of self-expression is curtailed to the shortest possible term. When
a syllable or a wink is enough, why spend one's entire life in
writing huge books or building a grandiose cathedral?

3. Directness is another word for simplicity. When all the
paraphernalia for expressing ideas is discarded, a single blade of
grass suffices to stand for Buddha Vairocana sixteen feet high. Or
a circle is the fullest possible symbol for the immeasurability of
the truth as realized in the mind of a Zen adept. This simplicity
also expresses itself in life. A humble straw-thatched mountain retreat, half of which is shared by white clouds, is enough for the
sage. The potatoes roasted in the ashes of a cow-dung fire appease
his hunger, as he casts a contemptuous look upon an envoy from
the Imperial court.[2]

4. Poverty and simplicity go hand in hand, but to be merely
poor and humble is not Zen. It does not espouse poverty just for
the sake of poverty. As it is sufficient unto itself, it does not want
much—which is poverty to others, but sufficiency to oneself. Rich
and poor—this is a worldly standard; for the inwardness of Zen
poverty has nothing to do with being short of possessions, or being
rich with the overflowing of material wealth.

5. Facts of experience are valued in Zen more than representa-
tions, symbols, and concepts—that is to say, substance is everything in Zen and form nothing. Therefore, Zen is radical em-
piricism. This being so, space is not something objectively extending, time is not to be considered a line stretched out as past,
present, and future. Zen knows no such space, no such time, and,
therefore, such ideas as eternity, infinitude, boundlessness, etc.,
are mere dreams to Zen. For Zen lives in facts. Facts may be considered momentarily, but momentariness is an idea subjectively
constructed. When Zen is compared to a flash of lightning which
disappears even before you have uttered the cry "Oh!" it is not to
be supposed that mere quickness is the life of Zen. But we can
say that Zen eschews deliberation, elaboration. When a roof
leaked, a Zen master called out to his attendants to bring in something to keep the *tatami* dry. Without a moment's hesitation, one
of them brought in a bamboo basket, while another went around
and, searching for a tub, took it to the master. The master was im-

2 Ransan, late eighth century in the reign of Tê-tsung, of T'ang.

mensely pleased, it is said, with the first monk with the basket. It was he who understood the spirit of Zen better than the one who was deliberate, though his wisdom proved far more practical and useful. This phase of Zen is technically known as "non-discrimination."

6. What might be designated "eternal loneliness" is found at the heart of Zen. This is a kind of sense of the absolute. In the *Laṅkāvatāra-sūtra* we have what is known there as the "truth of solitude" (*viviktadharma*). The experience of this seems to wake the feeling of eternal loneliness. This does not mean that we all feel solitary and long forever for something larger and stronger than ourselves. This feeling is cherished more or less by all religious souls; but what I mean here is not this kind of solitariness, but the solitariness of an absolute being, which comes upon one when a world of particulars moving under the conditions of space, time, and causation is left behind, when the spirit soars high up in the sky and moves about as it lists like a floating cloud.

7. When all these aspects of Zen are confirmed, we find a certain definite attitude of Zen toward life generally. When it expresses itself in art, it constitutes what may be called the spirit of Zen aestheticism. In this we shall then find simplicity, directness, abandonment, boldness, aloofness, unworldliness, innerliness, the disregarding of form, free movements of spirit, the mystic breathing of a creative genius all over the world—whether it be in painting, calligraphy, gardening, the tea ceremony, fencing, dancing, or poetry.

As I said before, Zen, of all the schools of Mahayana Buddhism, has given great impetus to the cultivation of the arts peculiar to the Japanese, and the above delineation may help somewhat to understand the spirit of this phase of Japanese culture. To illustrate, let me choose Japanese painting known as *sumi-e* and Japanese poetry called *haiku* and also a Zen master's instruction given to a great Samurai expert in swordsmanship.

Zen came to Japan in the twelfth century and during the eight hundred years of its history it has influenced Japanese life in various ways, not only in the spiritual life of the Samurai but in the artistic expressions of it by the learned and cultured classes. The *sumi-e*, which is one of such expressions, is not painting in the proper sense of the word; it is a kind of sketch in black and white. The ink is made of soot and glue, and the brush of sheep's or badger's hair, and the latter is so made as to absorb or contain much of the fluid. The paper used is rather thin and will absorb much ink, standing in great contrast to the canvas used by oil painters, and this contrast means a great deal to the *sumi-e* artist.

The reason why such a frail material has been chosen for the vehicle of transferring an artistic inspiration is that the inspiration is to be transferred on to it in the quickest possible time. If the brush lingers too long, the paper will be torn through. The lines are to be drawn as swiftly as possible and the fewest in number, only the absolutely necessary ones being indicated. No deliberation is allowed, no erasing, no repetition, no retouching, no remodeling, no "doctoring," no building up. Once executed, the strokes are indelible, irrevocable, not subject to future corrections or improvements. Anything done afterward is plainly and painfully visible in the result, as the paper is of such a nature. The artist must follow his inspiration as spontaneously and absolutely and instantly as it moves; he just lets his arm, his fingers, his brush be guided by it as if they were all mere instruments, together with his whole being, in the hands of somebody else who has temporarily taken possession of him. Or we may say that the brush by itself executes the work quite outside the artist, who just lets it move on without his conscious efforts. If any logic or reflection comes between brush and paper, the whole effect is spoiled. In this way *sumi-e* is produced.

It is easily conceivable that the lines of *sumi-e* must show an infinite variety. There is no chiaroscuro, no perspective in it. Indeed, they are not needed in *sumi-e*, which makes no pretensions to realism. It attempts to make the spirit of an object move on the paper. Thus each brush stroke must beat with the pulsation of a living being. It must be living too. Evidently, *sumi-e* is governed by a set of principles quite different from those of an oil painting. The canvas being of such strong material and oil colors permitting repeated wipings and overlayings, a picture is built up systematically after a deliberately designed plan. Grandeur of conception and strength of execution, to say nothing of its realism, are the characteristics of an oil painting, which can be compared to a well-thought-out system of philosophy, each thread of whose logic is closely knitted; or it may be likened unto a grand cathedral, whose walls, pillars, and foundations are composed of solid blocks of stone. Compared with this, a *sumi-e* sketch is poverty itself, poor in form, poor in contents, poor in execution, poor in material, yet we Oriental people feel the presence in it of a certain moving spirit that mysteriously hovers around the lines, dots, and shades of various formations; the rhythm of its living breath vibrates in them. A single stem of a blooming lily apparently so carelessly executed on a piece of coarse paper—yet here is vividly revealed the tender, innocent spirit of a maiden sheltered from the storm of a worldly life. Again, as far as a superficial critic can see, there is not much of artistic skill and inspiration—a little insignificant boat of a fisherman at the center of a broad expanse of waters; but as we look we cannot help being deeply impressed with the immensity of the ocean which knows no boundaries, and with the presence of a mysterious spirit breathing a life of eternity undisturbed in the midst of the undulating waves. And all these wonders are achieved with such ease and effortlessness.

If *sumi-e* attempts to copy an objective reality it is an utter failure; it never does that, it is rather a creation. A dot in a *sumi-e* sketch does not represent a hawk, nor does a curved line symbolize Mount Fuji. The dot is the bird and the line is the mountain. If resemblance is everything with a picture, the two-dimensional canvas cannot represent anything of objectivity; the colors fall far too short of giving the original, and however faithfully a painter may try with his brushes to remind us of an object of nature as it is, the result can never do justice to it; for as far as it is an imitation, or a representation, it is a poor imitation, it is a mockery. The *sumi-e* artist thus reasons: why not altogether abandon such an attempt? Let us instead create living objects out of our own imagination. As long as we all belong to the same universe, our creations may show some correspondence to what we call objects of nature. But this is not an essential element of our work. The work has its own merit apart from resemblance. In each brush stroke is there not something distinctly individual? The spirit of each artist is moving there. His birds are his own creation. This is the attitude of a *sumi-e* painter toward his art, and I wish to state that this attitude is that of Zen toward life, and that what Zen attempts with life the artist does with his paper, brush, and ink. The creative spirit moves everywhere, and there is a work of creation whether in life or in art.

A line drawn by the *sumi-e* artist is final, nothing can go beyond it, nothing can retrieve it; it is just inevitable as a flash of light-ning; the artist himself cannot undo it; from this issues the beauty of the line. Things are beautiful where they are inevitable, that is, when they are free exhibitions of a spirit. There is no violence here, no murdering, no twisting about, no copying after, but a free, un-restrained, yet self-governing display of movement—which con-stitutes the principle of beauty. The muscles are conscious of drawing a line, making a dot, but behind them there is an uncon-sciousness. By this unconsciousness Nature writes out her destiny: by this unconsciousness the artist creates his work of art. A baby smiles and the whole crowd is transported, because it is genuinely inevitable, coming out of the Unconscious. The *mushin* and *munen*[3] of which the Zen master makes so much, as we have al-ready seen elsewhere, is also eminently the spirit of the *sumi-e* artist.

Another feature that distinguishes *sumi-e* is its attempt to catch spirit as it moves. Everything becomes, nothing is stationary in nature; when you think you have safely taken hold of it, it slips off your hands. Because the moment you have it, it is no more alive; it is dead. But *sumi-e* tries to catch things alive, which seems to be something impossible to achieve. Yes, it would indeed be an im-possibility if the artist's endeavor were to represent living things on paper, but he can succeed to a certain extent when every brush stroke he makes is directly connected with his inner spirit, un-hampered by extraneous matters such as concepts, etc. In this case, his brush is his own arm extended; more than that, it is his spirit, and in its every movement as it is traced on paper this spirit is felt. When this is accomplished, a *sumi-e* picture is a reality it-self, complete in itself, and no copy of anything else. The moun-tains here are real in the same sense as Mount Fuji is real; so are the clouds, the stream, the trees, the waves, the figures. For the spirit of the artist is articulating through all these masses, lines, dots, and "daubs."

It is thus natural that *sumi-e* avoids coloring of any kind, for it reminds us of an object of nature, and *sumi-e* makes no claim to be a reproduction, perfect or imperfect. In this respect *sumi-e* is like calligraphy. In calligraphy each character, composed of strokes horizontal, vertical, slanting, flowing, turning upward and

---

[3] *Wu-hsin and wu-nien.*

downward, does not necessarily indicate any definite idea, though it does not altogether ignore it, for a character is primarily supposed to mean something. But as an art peculiar to the Far East where a long, pointed, soft-haired brush is used for writing, each stroke made with it has a meaning apart from its functioning as a composite element of a character symbolizing an idea. The brush is a yielding instrument and obeys readily every conative movement of the writer or the artist. In the strokes executed by him we can discern his spirit. This is the reason why *sumi-e* and calligraphy are regarded in the East as belonging to the same class of art.

The development of the soft-haired brush is a study in itself. No doubt it had a great deal to do with the accidents of the Chinese character and writing. It was a fortunate event that such a soft, yielding, pliable instrument was put into the hand of the artist. The lines and strokes produced by it have something of the freshness, tenderness, and gracefulness which are perceivable in animated objects of nature, especially in the human body. If the instrument used were a piece of steel, rigid and unyielding, the result would be quite contrary, and no *sumi-e* of Liang-k'ai, Mu-ch'i, and other masters would have come down to us.

That the paper is of such a fragile nature as not to allow the brush to linger too long over it is also of great advantage for the artist to express himself with it. If the paper were too strong and tough, deliberate designing and correction would be possible, which are, however, quite injurious to the spirit of *sumi-e*. The brush must run over the paper swiftly, boldly, fully, and irrevocably just like the work of creation when the universe came into being. As soon as a word comes from the mouth of the creator, it must be executed. Delay may mean alteration, which is frustration; or the will has been checked in its forward movement; it halts, it hesitates, it reflects, it reasons, and finally it changes its course—this faltering and wavering interfere with the freedom of the artistic mind.

While artificiality does not necessarily mean regularity or a symmetrical treatment of the subject, nor freedom mean irregularity, there is always an element of unexpectedness or abruptness in *sumi-e*. Where one expects to see a line or a mass this is lacking, and this vacancy instead of disappointing suggests something beyond and is altogether satisfactory. A small piece of paper, generally oblong, less than two feet and a half by six feet, will now include the whole universe. The horizontal stroke suggests immensity of space and a circle eternity of time—not only their mere unlimitedness but filled with life and movement. It is strange that the absence of a single point where it is conventionally expected should achieve this mystery, but the *sumi-e* artist is a past master in this trick. He does it so skilfully that no artificiality or explicit purpose is at all discernible in his work. This life of purposelessness comes directly from Zen.

Having seen something of the connection *sumi-e* has with Zen, let me proceed to make my remarks on the spirit of "Eternal Loneliness." I know that my lecture is altogether inadequate to do justice to what Zen has really done in its peculiar way for the aesthetic side of Japanese life. So far we can say, Zen's influence in Far Eastern painting has been general, as it is not limited to the Japanese, and what I have described may apply equally to the Chinese. What follows, however, can be regarded as specifically Japanese, for this spirit of "Eternal Loneliness" is something known pre-eminently in Japan. By this spirit, or this artistic principle, if it can be so designated, I mean what is popularly known in Japan as *sabi* or *wabi* (or *shibumi*). Let me say a few words about it now, using the term *sabi* for the concept of this group of feelings.

Sabi appears in landscape gardening and the tea ceremony as well as in literature. I shall confine myself to literature, especially to that form of literature known as *haiku*, that is, the seventeen-syllable poem. This shortest possible form of poetical expression is a special product of the Japanese genius. This made a great development in the Tokugawa era, more particularly after Bashō.

He was a great traveling poet, a most passionate lover of nature —a kind of nature troubadour. His life was spent in traveling from one end of Japan to another. It was fortunate that there were in those days no railways. Modern conveniences do not seem to go very well with poetry. The modern spirit of scientific analysis leaves no mystery unraveled, and poetry and *haiku* do not seem to thrive where there are no mysteries. The trouble with science is that it leaves no room for suggestion, everything is laid bare, and anything there is to be seen is exposed. Where science rules the imagination beats a retreat.

We are all made to face so-called hard facts whereby our minds are ossified; where there is no softness left with us, poetry departs; where there is a vast expanse of sand, no verdant vegetation is made possible. In Bashō's day, life was not yet so prosaic and hard-pressed. One bamboo hat, one cane stick, and one cotton bag were perhaps enough for the poet to wander about with, stopping for a while in any hamlet which struck his fancy and enjoying all the experiences, which were mostly the hardships of primitive traveling. When traveling is made too easy and comfortable, its spiritual meaning is lost. This may be called sentimentalism, but a certain sense of loneliness engendered by traveling leads one to reflect upon the meaning of life, for life is after all a traveling from one unknown to another unknown. In the period of sixty, seventy, or eighty years allotted to us we are meant to uncover if we can the veil of mystery. A too smooth running over this period, however short it may be, robs us of this sense of Eternal Loneliness.

The predecessor of Bashō was Saigyō of the Kamakura period (1186–1334). He was also a traveler monk. After quitting his official cares as a warrior attached to the court his life was devoted to traveling and poetry. He was a Buddhist monk. You must have seen the picture somewhere in your trip through Japan of a monk in his traveling suit, all alone, looking at Mount Fuji. I forget who the painter was, but the picture suggests many thoughts, especially in the mysterious loneliness of human life, which is, however, not the feeling of forlornness, nor the depressive sense of solitariness, but a sort of appreciation of the mystery of the absolute. The poem composed by Saigyō on that occasion runs:

> The wind-blown
> Smoke of Mount Fuji
> Disappearing far beyond!
> Who knows the destiny
> Of my thought wandering away with it?

Bashō was not a Buddhist monk but was a devotee of Zen. In the beginning of autumn, when it begins to rain occasionally, nature is the embodiment of Eternal Loneliness. The trees become bare, the mountains begin to assume an austere appearance, the streams are more transparent, and in the evening when the birds, weary of the day's work, wend their homeward way, a lone traveler grows pensive over the destiny of human life. His mood moves with that of nature. Sings Bashō:

> A traveler—
> Let my name be thus known—
> This autumnal shower.

We are not necessarily all ascetics, but I do not know if there is not in every one of us an eternal longing for a world beyond this of empirical relativity, where the soul can quietly contemplate its own destiny.

When Bashō was still studying Zen under his master Bucchō, the latter one day paid him a visit and asked, "How are you getting along these days?"

Bashō: "After a recent rain the moss has grown greener than ever."

Bucchō: "What Buddhism is there prior to the greenness of moss?"

Bashō: "A frog jumps into the water, hear the sound!"

This is said to be the beginning of a new epoch in the history of *haiku. Haiku* before Bashō was a mere word play, and lost its contact with life. Bashō, questioned by his master about the ultimate truth of things which existed even prior to this world of particulars, saw a frog leaping into an old pond, its sound making a break in the serenity of the whole situation. The source of life has been grasped, and the artist sitting here watches every mood of his mind as it comes in contact with a world of constant becoming, and the result is so many seventeen syllables bequeathed to us. Bashō was a poet of Eternal Loneliness.

Another of his *haiku* is:

> A branch shorn of leaves,
> A crow perching on it—
> This autumn eve.

Simplicity of form does not always mean triviality of content. There is a great Beyond in the lonely raven perching on the dead branch of a tree. All things come out of an unknown abyss of mystery, and through every one of them we can have a peep into the abyss. You do not have to compose a grand poem of many hundred lines to give vent to the feeling thus awakened by looking into the abyss. When a feeling reaches its highest pitch we remain silent, because no words are adequate. Even seventeen syllables may be too many. In any event Japanese artists more or less influenced by the way of Zen tend to use the fewest words or strokes of brush to express their feelings. When they are too fully expressed, no room for suggestion is possible, and suggestibility is the secret of the Japanese arts.

Some artists go even so far as this, that whatever way their strokes of the brush are taken by the viewer is immaterial; in fact the more they are misunderstood the better. The strokes or masses may mean any object of nature; they may be birds, or hills, or human figures, or flowers, or what not; it is perfectly indifferent to them, they declare. This is an extreme view indeed. For if their lines, masses, and dots are judged differently by different minds, sometimes altogether unlike what they were originally intended for by the artist, what is the use at all of attempting such a picture? Perhaps the artist here wanted to add this: "If only the spirit pervading his product were perfectly perceived and appreciated." From this it is evident that the Far Eastern artists are perfectly indifferent to form. They want to indicate by their brushwork something that has strongly moved them inwardly. They themselves may not have known how to give expression to their inner movement. They only utter a cry or flourish the brush. This may not be art, because there is no art in their doing this. Or if there is any art, that may be a very primitive one. Is this really so? However advanced we may be in "civilization," which means artificiality, we always strive for artlessness; for it seems to be the goal and foundation of all artistic endeavors. How much art is concealed behind the apparent artlessness of Japanese art! Full of meaning and suggestibility, and yet perfect in artlessness—when in this way the spirit of eternal loneliness is expressed, we have the essence of *sumi-e* and *haiku*.

2. GENERAL REMARKS ON JAPANESE ART CULTURE[1]

BEFORE proceeding further, we may make a few general remarks about one of the peculiar features of Japanese art, which is closely related to and finally deducible from the world conception of Zen.

Among things which strongly characterize Japanese artistic talents we may mention the so-called "one-corner" style, which originated with Baen (Ma Yüan, fl. 1175–1225), one of the greatest Southern Sung artists. The "one-corner" style is psychologically associated with the Japanese painters' "thrifty brush" tradition of retaining the least possible number of lines or strokes which go to represent forms on silk or paper. Both are very much in accord with the spirit of Zen. A simple fishing boat in the midst of the rippling waters is enough to awaken in the mind of the beholder a sense of the vastness of the sea and at the same time of peace and content-ment—the Zen sense of the Alone. Apparently the boat floats help-lessly. It is a primitive structure with no mechanical device for stability and for audacious steering over the turbulent waves, with no scientific apparatus for braving all kinds of weather—quite a contrast to the modern ocean liner. But this very helplessness is the virtue of the fishing boat, in contrast with which we feel the incom-prehensibility of the Absolute encompassing the boat and all the world. Again, a solitary bird on a dead branch, in which not a line, not a shade, is wasted, is enough to show us the loneliness of autumn, when days become shorter and Nature begins to roll up once more her gorgeous display of luxurious summer vegeta-tion. It makes one feel somewhat pensive, but it gives one oppor-tunity to withdraw the attention toward the inner life, which, given attention enough, spreads out its rich treasures ungrudgingly before the eyes.

[1] *Zen and Japanese Culture*, Bollingen Series LXIV, Pantheon, 1959, pp. 22–37.

Here we have an appreciation of transcendental aloofness in the midst of multiplicities—which is known as *wabi* in the dictionary of Japanese cultural terms. *Wabi* really means "poverty," or, negatively, "not to be in the fashionable society of the time." To be poor, that is, not to be dependent on things worldly—wealth, power, and reputation—and yet to feel inwardly the presence of something of the highest value, above time and social position: this is what essentially constitutes *wabi*. Stated in terms of practical everyday life, *wabi* is to be satisfied with a little hut, a room of two three *tatami* (mats), like the log cabin of Thoreau, and with a dish of vegetables picked in the neighboring fields, and perhaps to be listening to the pattering of a gentle spring rainfall. While later I will say something more about *wabi*, let me state here that the cult of *wabi* has entered deeply into the cultural life of the Japanese people. It is in truth the worshiping of poverty—probably a most appropriate cult in a poor country like ours. Despite the modern Western luxuries and comforts of life which have invaded us, there is still an ineradicable longing in us for the cult of *wabi*. Even in the intellectual life, not richness of ideas, not brilliancy or solemnity in marshaling thoughts and building up a philosophical system, is sought; but just to stay quietly content with the mystical contemplation of Nature and to feel at home with the world is more inspiring to us, at least to some of us.

However "civilized," however much brought up in an artificially contrived environment, we all seem to have an innate longing for primitive simplicity, close to the natural state of living. Hence the city people's pleasure in summer camping in the woods or traveling in the desert or opening up an unbeaten track. We wish to go back once in a while to the bosom of Nature and feel her pulsation directly. Zen's habit of mind, to break through all forms of human artificiality and take firm hold of what lies behind them, has helped the Japanese not to forget the soil but to be always friendly with Nature and appreciate her unaffected simplicity. Zen has no taste for complexities that lie on the surface of life. Life itself is simple enough, but when it is surveyed by the analyzing intellect it presents unparalleled intricacies. With all the apparatus of science we have not yet fathomed the mysteries of life. But, once in its current, we seem to be able to understand it, with its apparently endless pluralities and entanglements. Very likely, the most characteristic thing in the temperament of the Eastern people is the ability to grasp life from within and not from without. And Zen has just struck it.

In painting especially, disregard of form results when too much attention or emphasis is given to the all-importance of the spirit. The "one-corner" style and the economy of brush strokes also help to effect aloofness from conventional rules. Where you would ordinarily expect a line or a mass or a balancing element, you miss it, and yet this very thing awakens in you an unexpected feeling of pleasure. In spite of shortcomings or deficiencies that no doubt are apparent, you do not feel them so; indeed, this imperfection itself becomes a form of perfection. Evidently, beauty does not necessarily spell perfection of form. This has been one of the favorite tricks of Japanese artists—to embody beauty in a form of imperfection or even of ugliness.

When this beauty of imperfection is accompanied by antiquity or primitive uncouthness, we have a glimpse of *sabi*, so prized by Japanese connoisseurs. Antiquity and primitiveness may not be an actuality. If an object of art suggests even superficially the feeling of a historical period, there is *sabi* in it. *Sabi* consists in rustic unpretentiousness or archaic imperfection, apparent simplicity or effortlessness in execution, and richness in historical associations (which, however, may not always be present); and, lastly, it contains inexplicable elements that raise the object in question to the rank of an artistic production. These elements are generally regarded as derived from the appreciation of Zen. The utensils used in the tearoom are mostly of this nature.

The artistic element that goes into the constitution of *sabi*, which literally means "loneliness" or "solitude," is poetically defined by a tea master thus:

> As I come out
> To this fishing village,
> Late in the autumn day,
> No flowers in bloom I see,
> Nor any tinted maple leaves.[2]

Aloneness indeed appeals to contemplation and does not lend itself to spectacular demonstration. It may look most miserable, insignificant, and pitiable, especially when it is put up against the

---

[2] Fujiwara Sadaide (1162–1241).

Western or modern setting. To be left alone, with no streamers flying, no fireworks crackling, and this amidst a gorgeous display of infinitely varied forms and endlessly changing colors, is indeed no sight at all. Take one of those *sumi-e* sketches, perhaps portraying Kanzan and Jittoku,[3] hang it in a European or an American art gallery, and see what effect it will produce in the minds of the visitors. The idea of aloneness belongs to the East and is at home in the environment of its birth.

It is not only to the fishing village on the autumnal eve that aloneness gives form but also to a patch of green in the early spring —which is in all likelihood even more expressive of the idea of *sabi* or *wabi*. For in the green patch, as we read in the following thirty-one-syllable verse, there is an indication of life impulse amidst the wintry desolation:

> To those who only pray for the cherries to bloom,
> How I wish to show the spring
> That gleams from a patch of green
> In the midst of the snow-covered mountain village![4]

This is given by one of the old tea masters as thoroughly expressive of *sabi,* which is one of the four principles governing the cult of tea, *cha-no-yu.* Here is just a feeble inception of life power as asserted in the form of a little green patch, but in it he who has an eye can readily discern the spring shooting out from underneath the forbidding snow. It may be said to be a mere suggestion that stirs his mind, but just the same it is life itself and not its feeble indication. To the artist, life is as much here as when the whole field is overlaid with verdure and flowers. One may call this the mystic sense of the artist.

Asymmetry is another feature that distinguishes Japanese art. The idea is doubtlessly derived from the "one-corner" style of Baen. The plainest and boldest example is the plan of Buddhist

---

[3] Zen poet recluses of the T'ang dynasty. A collection of their poems known as the *Kanzan Shi* or *Sanrai Shi* or *San-in Shi* is still in existence. The pair together, Kanzan and Jittoku, has been a favorite subject for Far Eastern painters. There is something in their transcendental air of freedom which attracts us even in these modern days.

[4] Fujiwara Ietaka (1158–1237).

architecture. The principal structures, such as the Tower Gate, the Dharma Hall, the Buddha Hall, and others, may be laid along one straight line; but structures of secondary or supplementary importance, sometimes even those of major importance, are not arranged symmetrically as wings along either side of the main line. They may be found irregularly scattered over the grounds in accordance with the topographical peculiarities. You will readily be convinced of this fact if you visit some of the Buddhist temples in the mountains, for example, the Ieyasu shrine at Nikkō. We can say that asymmetry is quite characteristic of Japanese architecture of this class.

This can be demonstrated par excellence in the construction of the tearoom and in the tools used in connection with it. Look at the ceiling, which may be constructed in at least three different styles, and at some of the utensils for serving tea, and again at the grouping and laying of the steppingstones or flagstones in the garden. We find so many illustrations of asymmetry, or, in a way, of imperfection, or of the "one-corner" style.

Some Japanese moralists try to explain this liking of the Japanese artists for things asymmetrically formed and counter to the conventional, or rather geometrical, rules of art by the theory that the people have been morally trained not to be obtrusive but always to efface themselves, and that this mental habit of self-annihilation manifests itself accordingly in art—for example, when the artist leaves the important central space unoccupied. But, to my mind, this theory is not quite correct. Would it not be a more plausible explanation to say that the artistic genius of the Japanese people has been inspired by the Zen way of looking at individual things as perfect in themselves and at the same time as embodying the nature of totality which belongs to the One?

The doctrine of ascetic aestheticism is not so fundamental as that of Zen aestheticism. Art impulses are more primitive or more innate than those of morality. The appeal of art goes more directly into human nature. Morality is regulative, art is creative. One is an imposition from without, the other is an irrepressible expression from within. Zen finds its inevitable association with art but not with morality. Zen may remain unmoral but not without art. When the Japanese artists create objects imperfect from the point of view of form, they may even be willing to ascribe their art motive to the current notion of moral asceticism; but we need not give too much significance to their own interpretation or to that of the critics. Our consciousness is not, after all, a very reliable standard of judgment.

However this may be, asymmetry is certainly characteristic of Japanese art, which is one of the reasons informality or approachability also marks to a certain degree Japanese objects of art. Symmetry inspires a notion of grace, solemnity, and impressiveness, which is again the case with logical formalism or the piling up of abstract ideas. The Japanese are often thought not to be intellectual and philosophical, because their general culture is not thoroughly impregnated with intellectuality. This criticism, I think, results somewhat from the Japanese love of asymmetry. The intellectual primarily aspires to balance, while the Japanese are apt to ignore it and incline strongly toward imbalance.

Imbalance, asymmetry, the "one-corner," poverty, *sabi* or *wabi*, simplification, aloneness, and cognate ideas make up the most conspicuous and characteristic features of Japanese art and culture. All these emanate from one central perception of the truth of Zen, which is "the One in the Many and the Many in the One," or, better, "the One remaining as one in the Many individually and collectively."

Georges Duthuit, the author of *Chinese Mysticism and Modern Painting*, seems to understand the spirit of Zen mysticism. From him we have this: "When the Chinese artist paints, what matters is the concentration of thought and the prompt and vigorous response of the hand to the directing will. Tradition ordains him to see, or rather to feel, as a whole the work to be executed, before embarking on anything. 'If the ideas of a man are confused, he will become the slave of exterior conditions.' . . . He who deliberates and moves his brush intent on making a picture, misses to a still greater extent the art of painting. [This seems like a kind of automatic writing.] Draw bamboos for ten years, become a bamboo, then forget all about bamboos when you are drawing. In possession of an infallible technique, the individual places himself at the mercy of inspiration."

To become a bamboo and to forget that you are one with it while drawing it—this is the Zen of the bamboo, this is the moving with the "rhythmic movement of the spirit" which resides in the bamboo as well as in the artist himself. What is now required of him is to have a firm hold on the spirit and yet not to be conscious of the fact. This is a very difficult task achieved only after long spiritual training. The Eastern people have been taught since the earliest times to subject themselves to this kind of discipline if they want to achieve something in the world of art and religion. Zen, in fact, has given expression to it in the following phrase: "One in All and All in One." When this is thoroughly understood, there is creative genius.

It is of utmost importance here to interpret the phrase in its proper sense. People imagine that it means pantheism, and some students of Zen seem to agree. This is to be regretted, for pantheism is something foreign to Zen and also to the artist's understanding of his work. When the Zen masters declare the One to be in the All and the All in the One, they do not mean that there is a thing to be known as the One or as the All and that the one is the other and vice versa. As the One is in the All, some people suppose that Zen is a pantheistic teaching. Far from it; Zen would never hypostatize the One or the All as a thing to be grasped by the senses. The phrase "One in All and All in One" is to be understood as an expression of absolute *prajñā* intuition and is not to be conceptually analyzed. When we see the moon, we know that it is the moon, and that is enough. Those who proceed to analyze the experience and try to establish a theory of knowledge are not students of Zen. They cease to be so, if they ever were, at the very moment of their procedure as analysts. Zen always upholds its experience as such and refuses to commit itself to any system of philosophy.

Even when Zen indulges in intellection, it never subscribes to a pantheistic interpretation of the world. For one thing, there is no One in Zen. If Zen ever speaks of the One as if it recognized it, this is a kind of condescension to common parlance. To Zen students, the One is the All and the All is the One; and yet the One remains the One and the All the All. "Not two!" may lead the logician to think, "It is One." But the master would go on, saying, "Not One either!" "What then?" we may ask. We here face a blind alley, as far as verbalism is concerned. Therefore, it is said that "If you wish to be in direct communion [with Reality], I tell you, 'Not two!'"

The following *mondō*[5] may help to illustrate the point I wish to make in regard to the Zen attitude toward the so-called pantheistic interpretation of nature.

[5] This and what follows are all from the *Hekigan-shū*, case 79.

A monk asked Tōsu, a Zen master of the T'ang period: "I understand that all sounds are the voice of the Buddha. Is this right?"

The master said, "That is right."

The monk then proceeded: "Would not the master please stop making a noise which echoes the sound of a fermenting mass of filth?" The master thereupon struck him.

It may be necessary to explain these *mondō* in plain language. To conceive every sound, every noise, every utterance one makes as issuing from the fountainhead of one Reality, that is, from one God, is pantheistic, I imagine. For "he giveth to all life, and breath, and all things" (Acts 17: 25); and again, "For in him we live, and move, and have our being" (Acts 17: 28). If this be the case, a Zen master's hoarse throat echoes the melodious resonance of the voice flowing from the Buddha's golden mouth, and even when a great teacher is decried as reminding one of an ass, the defamation must be regarded as reflecting something of ultimate truth. All forms of evil must be said somehow to be embodying what is true and good and beautiful, and to be a contribution to the perfection of Reality. To state it more concretely, bad is good, ugly is beautiful, false is true, imperfect is perfect, and also conversely. This is, indeed, the kind of reasoning in which those indulge who conceive the God-nature to be immanent in all things. Let us see how the Zen master treats this problem.

It is remarkable that Tōsu put his foot right down against such intellectualist interpretations and struck his monk. The latter in all probability expected to see the master nonplused by his statements which logically follow from his first assertion. The masterful Tōsu knew, as all Zen masters do, the uselessness of making any verbal demonstration against such a "logician." For verbalism leads from one complication to another; there is no end to it. The only effective way, perhaps, to make such a monk as this one realize the falsehood of his conceptual understanding is to strike him and so let him experience within himself the meaning of the statement, "One in All and All in One." The monk was to be awakened from his logical somnambulism. Hence Tōsu's drastic measure.

Secchō[6] here gives his comments in the following lines:

---

[6] Secchō was one of the great Zen masters of the Sung, noted for his literary accomplishment. The *Hekigan-shū* is based on Secchō's "One Hundred Cases," which he selected out of the annals of Zen.

Pity that people without number try to play with the tide;
They are all ultimately swallowed up into it and die!
Let them suddenly awake [from the deadlock],
And see that all the rivers run backward, swelling and surging.

What is needed here is an abrupt turning or awakening, with
which one comes to the realization of the truth of Zen—which is
neither transcendentalism nor immanentism nor a combination of
the two. The truth is as Tōsu declares in the following:
A monk asks, "What is the Buddha?"
Tōsu answers, "The Buddha."
Monk: "What is the Tao?"
Tōsu: "The Tao."
Monk: "What is Zen?"
Tōsu: "Zen."
The master answers like a parrot, he is echo itself. In fact, there
is no other way of illumining the monk's mind than affirming that
what is is—which is the final fact of experience.

Another example[7] is given to illustrate the point. A monk asked
Jōshū, of the T'ang dynasty: "It is stated that the Perfect Way
knows no difficulties, only that it abhors discrimination. What is
meant by no-discrimination?"
Jōshū said, "Above the heavens and below the heavens, I alone
am the Honored One."
The monk suggested, "Still a discrimination."
The master's retort was, "O this worthless fellow! Where is the
discrimination?"
By discrimination the Zen masters mean what we have when
we refuse to accept Reality as it is or in its suchness, for we then
reflect on it and analyze it into concepts, going on with intellection
and finally landing on a circulatory reasoning. Jōshū's affirmation
is a final one and allows no equivocation, no argumentation. We
have simply to take it as it stands and remain satisfied with it. In
case we somehow fail to do this, we just leave it alone, and go
somewhere else to seek our own enlightenment. The monk could
not see where Jōshū was, and he went further and remarked, "This
is still a discrimination!" The discrimination in point of fact is on
the monk's side and not on Jōshū's. Hence "the Honored One" now
turns into "a worthless fellow."

---

[7] *Hekigan-shū*, case 57.

As I said before, the phrase "All in One and One in All" is not to be analyzed first to the concepts "One" and "All," and the preposition is not then to be put between them; no discrimination is to be exercised here, but one is just to accept it and abide with it, which is really no-abiding at all. There is nothing further to do. Hence the master's striking or calling names. He is not indignant, nor is he short-tempered, but he wishes thereby to help his disciples out of the pit which they have dug themselves. No amount of argument avails here, no verbal persuasion. Only the master knows how to turn them away from a logical impasse and how to open a new way for them; let them, therefore, simply follow him. By following him they all come back to their Original Home.

When an intuitive or experiential understanding of Reality is verbally formulated as "All in One and One in All," we have there the fundamental statement as it is taught by all the various schools of Buddhism. In the terminology of the *prajñā* school, this is: *śūnyatā* ("emptiness") is *tathatā* ("suchness") and *tathatā* is *śūnyatā*: *śūnyatā* is the world of the Absolute, and *tathatā* is the world of particulars. One of the commonest sayings in Zen is "Willows are green and flowers red" or "Bamboos are straight and pine trees are gnarled." Facts of experience are accepted as they are; Zen is not nihilistic, nor is it merely positivistic. Zen would say that just because the bamboo is straight it is of Emptiness, or that just because of Emptiness the bamboo cannot be anything else but a bamboo and not a pine tree. What makes the Zen statements different from mere sense experience, however, is that Zen's intuition grows out of *prajñā* and not out of *jñāna*.[8] It is from this point of view that when asked "What is Zen?" the master sometimes answers "Zen" and sometimes "Not-Zen."

We can see now that the principle of *sumi-e* painting is derived from this Zen experience, and that directness, simplicity, movement, spirituality, completeness, and other qualities we observe in the *sumi-e* class of Oriental paintings have an organic relationship to Zen. There is no pantheism in *sumi-e* as there is none in Zen. There is another thing I must not forget to mention in this connection, which is perhaps the most important factor in *sumi-e* as well as in Zen. It is creativity. When it is said that *sumi-e* depicts

---

[8] *Prajñā* may be translated "transcendental wisdom," while *jñāna* or *vijñāna* is "relative knowledge." For a detailed explanation, see my *Studies in Zen Buddhism*, pp. 85 ff.

the spirit of an object, or that it gives a form to what has no form, this means that there must be a spirit of creativity moving over the picture. The painter's business thus is not just to copy or imitate nature, but to give to the object something living in its own right. It is the same with the Zen master. When he says that the willow is green and the flower is red, he is not just giving us a description of how nature looks, but something whereby green is green and red is red. This something is what I call the spirit of creativity. . . .

3. ZEN AND SWORDSMANSHIP[1]

... I wish to give here further quotations illuminative of the intimate relationship between Zen and the sword, in the form of Takuan's[2] letter to Yagyū Tajima no kami Munenori[3] (1571–1646) concerning the relationship between Zen and the art of swordsmanship.

As the letter is long and somewhat repetitive, I have condensed or paraphrased it here, trying to preserve the important thoughts of the original, and sometimes interpolating explanations and notes. It is an important document in more ways than one, as it touches upon the essential teaching of Zen as well as the secrets of art generally. In Japan, perhaps as in other countries, too, mere technical knowledge of an art is not enough to make a man really its master; he ought to have delved deeply into the inner spirit of it. This spirit is grasped only when his mind is in complete harmony with the principle of life itself, that is, when he attains to a certain state of mind known as *mushin* (*wu-hsin*), "no-mind." In Buddhist phraseology, it means going beyond the dualism of all forms of life and death, good and evil, being and non-being. This is where all arts merge into Zen. In this letter to the great master of swordsmanship, Takuan strongly emphasizes the significance of *mushin*, which may be regarded in a way as corresponding to the concept of the unconscious. Psychologically speaking, this state of mind gives itself up unreservedly to an unknown "power" that comes to

[1] *Zen and Japanese Culture*, pp. 94–117.

[2] Takuan (1573–1645) was the abbot of Daitokuji, in Kyoto. He was invited by the third shōgun, Tokugawa Iemitsu, to come to Tokyo, where Iemitsu built a great Zen temple, called Tōkaiji, and made him its founder.

[3] Belonged to a great family of swordsmen flourishing in the early Tokugawa era. Tajima no kami was the teacher of Iemitsu and studied Zen under Takuan.

one from nowhere and yet seems strong enough to possess the whole field of consciousness and make it work for the unknown. Hereby he becomes a kind of automaton, so to speak, as far as his own consciousness is concerned. But, as Takuan explains, it ought not to be confused with the helpless passivity of an inorganic thing, such as a piece of rock or a block of wood. He is "unconsciously conscious" or "consciously unconscious." With this preliminary remark, the following instruction of Takuan will become intelligible.

TAKUAN'S LETTER TO YAGYŪ TAJIMA NO KAMI MUNENORI ON THE MYSTERY OF PRAJÑĀ IMMOVABLE

Affects Attendant on the Abiding Stage of Ignorance[4]

"Ignorance" (*avidyā*) means the absence of Enlightenment, that is, delusion. The "abiding stage" means "the point where the mind stops to abide." In Buddhist training we speak of fifty-two stages, of which one is a stage where the mind attaches itself to any object it encounters. This attaching is known as *tomaru*, "stopping" or "abiding." The mind stops with one object instead of flowing from one object to another [as the mind acts when it follows its own nature].

In the case of swordsmanship, for instance, when the opponent tries to strike you, your eyes at once catch the movement of his sword and you may strive to follow it. But as soon as this takes place, you cease to be master of yourself and you are sure to be beaten. This is called "stopping." [But there is another way of meeting the opponent's sword.]

No doubt you see the sword about to strike you, but do not let your mind "stop" there. Have no intention to counterattack him in response to his threatening move, cherish no calculating thoughts whatever. You simply perceive the opponent's move, you do not allow your mind to "stop" with it, you move on just as you are toward the opponent and make use of his attack by turning it on to himself. Then his sword meant

---

[4] Mahayana Buddhism sometimes distinguishes fifty-two stages leading up to the supreme Enlightenment (*sambodhi*). "Ignorance" (*avidyā*) may be regarded as the first of those stages and the "affects" (*kleśa*) are affective disturbances which accompany those who abide in this stage. In Japanese, "ignorance" is *mumyō* and "affects" is *bonnō*.

to kill you will become your own and the weapon will fall on the opponent himself.

In Zen, this is known as "seizing the enemy's spear and using it as the weapon to kill him." The idea is that the opponent's sword being transferred into your hands becomes the instrument of his own destruction. This is "no-sword" in your terminology. As soon as the mind "stops" with an object of whatever nature—be it the opponent's sword or your own, the man himself bent on striking or the sword in his hands, the mode or the measure of the move—you cease to be master of yourself and are sure to fall a victim to the enemy's sword. When you set yourself against him, your mind will be carried away by him. Therefore, do not even think of yourself. [That is to say, the opposition of subject and object is to be transcended.]

For beginners, it is not a bad idea to keep the mind thoughtfully applied to their own disciplining. It is important not to get your attention arrested by the sword or by the measure of its movement. When your mind is concerned with the sword, you become your own captive. This is all due to your mind being arrested by something external and losing its mastership. This, I believe, is all very well known to you; I only call your attention to it from my Zen point of view. In Buddhism, this "stopping" mind is called delusion, hence "Affects Attendant on the Abiding Stage of Ignorance."

[The swordsman's "unconscious" and the psychoanalyst's "unconscious" are not to be confused, for the former is free from the notion of the self. The perfect swordsman takes no cognizance of the enemy's personality, no more than of his own. For he is an indifferent onlooker of the fatal drama of life and death in which he himself is the most active participant. In spite of all the concern he has or ought to have, he is above himself, he transcends the dualistic comprehension of the situation, yet he is not a contemplative mystic, he is in the thickest of the deadly combat. This distinction is to be remembered when we compare Eastern culture with Western. Even in such arts as that of swordsmanship, in which the principle of opposition is most in evidence, the one who is to be most intensely interested in it is advised to be liberated from the idea.]

PRAJÑĀ IMMOVABLE

[*prajñā is* possessed by all Buddhas and also by all sentient beings. It is transcendental wisdom flowing through the relativity of things] and it remains immovable, though this does not mean the immovability or insensibility of such objects as a piece of wood or rock. It is the mind itself endowed with infinite motilities: it moves forward and backward, to the left and to the right, to every one of the ten quarters, and knows no hindrance in any direction. Prajñā Immovable is this mind capable of infinite movements.

There is a Buddhist god called Fudō Myōō (Acala-vidyārāja), the Immovable. He is represented holding a sword in his right hand and a rope in his left. His teeth are bared and his eyes glare angrily. He stands up threateningly in order to destroy the devils who try to do harm to Buddha's teaching. Though he is thus seen assuming a realistic form, he is not hiding anywhere on earth. He is the symbolic protector of Buddhism, essentially incarnating Prajñā Immovable for us sentient beings. When the ordinary people confront him, they are reminded of what he stands for and will refrain from interfering with the spread of Buddhist doctrine. The wise, on the other hand, who are approaching a state of enlightenment, realize that Fudō symbolizes Prajñā Immovable as the destroyer of delusion. He who thus becomes enlightened and carries on his life as exemplified by Fudō Myōō will not be touched even by devilish spirits. The Myōō is the symbol of immovability both of mind and body. Not to move means not to "stop" with an object that is seen. For as it is seen it passes on and the mind is not arrested. When the mind "stops" with each object as it is presented, the mind is disturbed with all kinds of thought and feeling. The "stopping" inevitably leads to the moving that is disturbance. Though the mind is thus subject to "stoppings," it in itself remains unmoved, however superficially it may seem so.

For instance, suppose ten men are opposing you, each in succession ready to strike you with a sword. As soon as one is disposed of, you will move on to another without permitting the mind to "stop" with any. However rapidly one blow may follow another, you leave no time to intervene between the two. Every one of the ten will thus be successively and successfully dealt with. This is possible only when the mind moves from one object to another without being "stopped" or arrested by anything. If the mind is unable to move on in this fashion, it is sure to lose the game somewhere between two encounters.

Kwannon Bosatsu (Avalokiteśvara) is sometimes represented with one thousand arms, each holding a different instrument. If his mind "stops" with the use, for instance, of a bow, all the other arms, 999 in number, will be of no use whatever. It is only because of his mind not "stopping" with the use of one arm but moving from one instrument to another that all his arms prove useful with the utmost degree of efficiency. Even Kwannon cannot be expected to equip himself with one thousand arms on one body. The figure is meant to demonstrate that, when Prajñā Immovable is realized, even as many as one thousand arms on one body may each and all be serviceable in one way or another.

I will give another illustration: When I look at a tree, I perceive one of the leaves is red, and my mind "stops" with this leaf. When this happens, I see just one leaf and fail to take cognizance of the innumerable other leaves of the tree. If instead of this I look at the tree without any preconceived ideas, I shall see all the leaves. One leaf effectively "stops" my mind from seeing all the rest. But when the mind moves on without "stopping," it takes up hundreds of thousands of leaves without fail. When this is understood we are Kwannons.

The simple-minded bow before Kwannon, taking him for an extraordinary being simply because his one body is seen as in possession of one thousand arms and one thousand eyes. Some, however, whose intelligence does not go very far, deny the reality of Kwannon, saying, "How can one person be provided with so many arms as one thousand?" Those who know the reason of things will neither blindly believe nor hastily negate. They will discover that it is the wisdom of Buddhism to demonstrate the rationality of things by means of one object. This is also the case with other schools of teaching, especially with Shintoism. Those symbolical figures are not to be taken naïvely as they appear, nor are they to be rejected as irrational. One must know that there is reason in them. Reasons may be varied, but they all point ultimately to one truth.

Beginners all start from the first stage of Ignorance and Affects, finally reaching that of Prajñā Immovable, and when they reach the final stage they find that it stands next to the first stage. There is reason for this.

To state it in terms of swordsmanship, the genuine beginner knows nothing about the way of holding and managing the sword, and much less of his concern for himself. When the opponent tries to strike him, he instinctively parries it. This is all he can do. But as soon as the training starts, he is taught how to handle the sword, where to keep the mind, and many other technical tricks—which makes his mind "stop" at various junctures. For this reason whenever he tries to strike the opponent he feels unusually hampered [he has lost altogether the original sense of innocence and freedom]. But as days and years go by, as his training acquires fuller maturity, his bodily attitude and his way of managing the sword advance toward "no-mind-ness," which resembles the state of mind he had at the very beginning of training when he knew nothing, when he was altogether ignorant of the art. The beginning and the end thus turn into next-door neighbors. First we start counting one, two, three, and when finally ten is counted we return to one.

In musical scales, one may start with the lowest pitch and gradually ascend to the highest. When the highest is reached, one finds it located next to the lowest. In a similar way, when the highest stage is reached in the study of Buddhist teaching, a man turns into a kind of simpleton who knows nothing of Buddha, nothing of his teaching, and is devoid of all learning or scholarly acquisitions. The Ignorance and Affects characterizing the first stage are merged into Prajñā Immovable of the last stage of Buddhist discipline: intellectual calculations are lost sight of and a state of no-mind-ness (*mushin*) or of no-thought-ness (*munen*) prevails. When the ultimate perfection is attained, the body and limbs perform by themselves what is assigned to them to do with no interference from the mind. [The technical skill is so autonomized it is completely divorced from conscious efforts.]

Bukkoku Kokushi (1241–1316) of Kamakura has the poem:

> Though not consciously trying to
>   guard the rice fields from intruders,
> The scarecrow is not after all standing
>   to no purpose.

All is like this: The scarecrow in imitation of a human figure is erected in the middle of the rice paddies, it holds a bow and an arrow as if ready to shoot, and seeing this birds and animals are frightened away. This human figure is not endowed with a mind, but it scares away the deer. The perfect man who has attained the highest stage of training may be likened to it. All is left to the [unconscious or reflexive] activities of the body and limbs, whereas the mind itself stops with no objects and at no points. Nor is it to be located at any definitely designable spot. Yet it here exists all by itself, with no thoughts, no affects, resembling a scarecrow in the rice fields. It is the case of a simple-minded man whose naïve intelligence does not go very far, holds to himself, and is not self-assertive. This non-assertiveness also applies to one who has attained the highest degree of intelligence. But there are some who know a great deal, and just because of this knowledge they put themselves very much forward. We come across many such these days among people of my profession, and I am really ashamed of them.

We have to distinguish between two ways of training: one is spiritual,[5] the other practical. As I said before, as far as spirituality is concerned, it is a very simple matter when it is realized to its full extent; it all depends on how one gives up one's own Ignorance and Affects and attains to no-mind-ness.[6] This has already been developed step by step. But training in detailed technique is also not to be neglected. The understanding of principle alone cannot lead one to the mastery of movements of the body and its limbs. By practical details I mean such as what you call the five ways of posing the body, designated each by one character. The principle of spirituality is to be grasped—this goes without saying—but at the same time one must be trained in the technique of swordplay. But training is never to be one-sided. *Ri* (*li*) and *ji* (*shih*)[7] are like two wheels of a cart. . . .

[5] I do not like this term in this connection, for it has a certain odium attached to it. The original Japanese is *ri* (*li*). It ordinarily means "something transcendental," "something standing in contrast to detailed actualities," and is concerned with the innerliness or supersensuousness of things.

[6] In Japanese the whole sentence reads, "*Tada isshin no sute yō nite sōrō*," literally, "It all depends on how one gives up one's own mind." In this case "mind" is not "Absolute Mind," but "the mind one ordinarily has," that is, "the mind of ignorance and affects, which stops with an object or experience it may have and refuses to be restored to its native state of fluidity or emptiness or no-mind-ness."

[7] *Ri* (*li*) and *ji* (*shih*) are terms used very much in Kegon philosophy. *Ji* is a particular object or event, and *ri* is a universal principle. As long as these two are kept separate, life loses its freedom and spontaneity, and one fails to be master of oneself. Psychologically speaking, this is the unconscious breaking into the field of consciousness when consciousness loses itself, abandoning itself to the dictates of the unconscious. Religiously, it is dying to one's self and living in Christ or, as Bunan Zenji would say, "living as a dead man." In the case of a swordsman, he must free himself from all ideas involving life and death, gain and loss, right and wrong, giving himself up to a power which lives deeply in his inner being. *Ri* and *ji* are then in harmonious cooperation. Bunan's poem reads:

> While living
> Be a dead man,
> Be thoroughly dead—
> And behave as you like,
> And all's well.

Spark of the Flint Striking Steel

This is another way of expressing the idea "not to leave a hairbreadth interval." When a flint strikes steel, no moment is lost before a spark issues from the contact. This is likened to the mind not "stopping" with any one object, and no time being left for deliberation [for affects of any sort to assert themselves]. It does not mean just the instantaneity of events happening one after another. The point is not to let the mind "stop" with anything. Mere instantaneity is of no avail if the mind "stops" even for a moment. As soon as there is a moment's "stoppage," your mind is no longer your own, for it is then placed under another's control. When the mind calculates so as to be quick in movement, the very thought makes the mind captive. [You are no more master of yourself.]

In Saigyō's collection of poems (*Sanka-shū*) we have:

> As I understand you to be a man
>   who has grown weary of the world,
> I only think of you as not at all longing for [8]
>   a temporary shelter.

This is said to have been composed by a courtesan of Eguchi. The reference I wish to make is to the latter part of the poem containing the phrase *kokoro tomuna*, "not to have the mind 'stopped.'" For this applies most fittingly to the art of swordsmanship, which ultimately consists in not having one's mind "stopped" with any object.

In Zen Buddhism one asks, "What is Buddha?" and the master raises his fist. "What is the ultimate signification of Buddhist teaching?" and the master replies, even before the questioner fully finishes, "A spray of plum blossoms," or "The cypress tree in the courtyard." The point concerned here is not necessarily the appropriateness of the answer, but to see the mind not "stopping" with anything. Such a mind "stops"[9]

---

[8] "Longing for" is Japanese *kokoro tomeru*, of which Takuan talks so much in this letter of his to Yagyū Tajima no kami. The second part of the poem may also be translated: "I only think that you would not have your mind 'stopped' with a temporary shelter."

[9] Takuan has *utsuru* here for "stopping" or "stop." *Utsuru* is synonymous with *kokoro wo tomeru*. It literally means "drifting or shifting from one thing to another," or "one's attention being arrested by an object and being transferred onto it and staying there."

neither with the color nor with the odor. This "non-stopping" mind in its suchness is blessed as a god or honored as a Buddha, which is no less than the Zen mind or the ultimate limit of an art. An answer given after deliberation to a question such as the above may be splendid and full of wisdom, but it is after all at the stage of Ignorance and Affects (*avidyā-kleśa*).

Zen is concerned with a movement of instantaneity in which the flint emits a spark when it strikes steel. It is the same as a flash of lightning. A voice calls out "O Uemon!" and the man immediately responds to it, "Yes." Here is Prajñā Immovable. When the man is called, "O Uemon," he "stops" and deliberates, wondering, "What business can it be?" Finally, the answer is given, "What is it?" This comes from a mind abiding in Ignorance and Affects. Whenever or wherever it "stops"— this is the sign of being moved by something external, which is a delusion, and such is said to be the mind of an ordinary being belonging to the stage of Ignorance and Affects.

On the other hand, that which gives an immediate answer to the call, "O Uemon!" is the *prajñā* of all Buddhas. Buddhas and all beings are not two, nor are gods and men. God or the Buddha is the name given to such a mind [identified with *prajñā*]. The Way of the Gods, the Way of Poetry, the Way of Confucius—there may be many Ways (*tao*), but they all are ways of illustrating the One Mind.

When they just follow the letters and have no true understanding of what the One Mind (Prajñā Immovable) is, they abuse it in every possible way throughout their life. They are day and night engaged in doing good things and evil things according to their karma. They would abandon the family, ruin the whole nation, or do anything contrary to the dictates of the One Mind. They are all confused and altogether fail to see what the One Mind looks like. Unfortunately, there are only a few people who have really penetrated into the depths of the One Mind. The rest of us are sadly going astray.

But we must know that it is not enough just to see what the Mind is, we must put into practice all that makes it up in our daily life. We may talk about it glibly, we may write books to explain it, but that is far from being enough. However much we may talk about water and describe it quite intelligently, that does not make it real water. So with fire. Mere talking of it will not make the mouth burn. To know what they are means to experience them in actual concreteness. A book on cooking will not cure our hunger. To feel satisfied we must have actual food. So long as we do not go beyond mere talking, we are not true knowers.

Confucianism as well as Buddhism strives to explain what the One Mind is, but unless life itself conforms to those explanations, Buddhist or Confucian, we cannot call ourselves knowers of the Mind even though every one of us is in possession of it. The reason why those who are devoting themselves to the study of Tao are yet unable to see into its ultimate significance is due to their relying on mere learning. If they really wish to see the One Mind, a deep *kufū*[10] is needed. . . .

WHERE TO LOCATE THE MIND

The question is often asked: Where is the mind [or attention] to be directed? When it is directed to the movements of the opponent, it is taken up by them. When it is directed to his sword, it is taken up by the sword. When it is directed to striking down the opponent, it is taken up by the idea of striking. When it is directed to your sword, it is taken up by that. When it is directed to defending yourself, it is taken up by the idea of defense. When it is directed to the pose the opponent assumes,

---

10 *Kufū* has been explained elsewhere. It is not just thinking with the head, but the state when the whole body is involved in and applied to the solving of a problem. The Japanese often talk about "asking the abdomen," or "thinking with the abdomen," or "seeing or hearing with the abdomen," This is *kufū*. The head is detachable from the body, but the abdomen, which includes the whole system of the viscera, symbolizes the totality of one's personality.

It may not be uninstructive, I think, in this connection, to notice how Rodin's *The Thinker* is differentiated from Sekkaku's *Zen Master in Meditation*. Both are intently engaged in concentrating the mind on a subject of the utmost interest or significance. But Rodin's figure seems to me at least to be on the plane of relativity and intellection, while the Oriental one is somewhere beyond it. We also have to notice the difference in the posture assumed by each one of the two "thinkers." The one sits on a raised seat while the other squats on the ground. The one is less in contact with earth than the other. The Zen "thinker" is rooted in the foundation, as it were, of all things, and every thought he may cherish is directly connected with the source of being from which we of the earth come. To raise oneself from the ground even by one foot means a detachment, a separation, an abstraction, a going away to the realm of analysis and discrimination. The Oriental way of sitting is to strike the roots down to the center of earth and to be conscious of the Great Source where we have our "whence" and "whither."

it is taken up by it. At all events, they say they do not know just where the mind is to be directed.

Some would say: Wherever the mind is directed, the whole person is liable to follow the direction and the enemy is sure to take full advantage of it, which means your defeat. It is after all better to keep the mind in the lower part of the abdomen just below the navel, and this will enable one to adjust oneself in accordance with the shifting of the situation from moment to moment.

This advice is reasonable enough, but from the ultimate point of view which is held by Buddhists it is still limited, it is not the highest, it is not the supreme end of training. While being trained, the keeping of the mind in the lower region of the abdomen may not be a bad idea. But it is still the stage of reverence,[11] and it also corresponds to what Mencius advises—to get the runaway mind[12] back in its original seat. As to "the runaway mind" I have explained it in another letter for your inspection.

If you try to keep the mind imprisoned in the lower region of the abdomen, the very idea of keeping it in one specified locality will prevent the mind from operating anywhere else, and the result will be the contrary to what had been first intended. Then the question may arise: If keeping the mind shut up below the navel restricts its free movements, in what part of the body shall we keep it? I answer: "When you put it in the right hand, it will be kept captive in the right hand, and the rest of the body will be found inconvenienced. The result will be the same when you put it in the eye or in the right leg or in any other particular

---

[11] *Kei* in Japanese, *ching* in Chinese. The Confucian scholars, especially those of the Sung, consider that the feeling of reverence is of great importance in making progress in the study of Tao (the Way). But Zen-men think reverence is far from being the ultimate end of training. It is meant for beginners.

[12] *Hōshin* in Japanese, *fang-hsin* in Chinese. *Hō (fang)* means "free and unrestrained," "running wild," "gone loose," "lost," "letting go." Mencius (Book VI, "Kao-tzŭ") says that *jên* ("love") is human mind ("heart") and *i* ("*justice*") is human path. It is a pity that people leave the path and do not observe it, that people let go the mind and do not seek it. When they let loose chickens or dogs, they know they must search for them, but when they let go the mind they do not know that they must search for it. The way of learning is no more or less than searching for the heart they have let go. *Kokoro* means both mind and heart, intellect and affection, and is also often used in the philosophical sense as subject, substance, or soul. Wherever "mind" is mentioned in this letter of Takuan's, it is to be understood in its comprehensive sense.

part of the body, because then the remaining parts of the body will feel its absence."

The second question is: Where is the mind to be kept after all?

I answer: "The thing is not to try to localize the mind anywhere but to let it fill up the whole body, let it flow throughout the totality of your being. When this happens you use the hands when they are needed, you use the legs or the eyes when they are needed, and no time or no extra energy will be wasted. [The localization of the mind means its freezing. When it ceases to flow freely as it is needed, it is no more the mind in its suchness.]

[Localization is not restricted to the physical side of one's being. The mind may be psychologically imprisoned. For instance, one may deliberate when an immediate action is imperative, as in the case of swordsmanship. The deliberation surely interferes and "stops" the course of the flowing mind. Have no deliberation, no discrimination. Instead of localizing or keeping in captivity or freezing the mind, let it go all by itself freely and unhindered and uninhibited. It is only when this is done that the mind is ready to move as it is needed all over the body, with no "stoppage" anywhere.]

Zen-men talk about the right or true (shō) and the partial (hen) in their teaching. When the mind fills up the body entirely, it is said to be right; when it is located in any special part of the body, it is partial or one-sided. The right mind is equally distributed over the body and not at all partitive. The partial mind, on the other hand, is divided and one-sided. Zen dislikes partialization or localization. When the mind is kept hardened at one place it fails to pervade or flow over every part of the body. When it is not partialized after any schematized plan, it naturally diffuses itself all over the body. It thus can meet the opponent as he moves about trying to strike you down. When your hands are needed they are there to respond to your order. So with the legs—at any moment they are needed the mind never fails to operate them according to the situation. There is no need for the mind to maneuver itself out from any localized quarters where it has been prearranged for it to station itself.

The mind is not to be treated like a cat tied to a string. The mind must be left to itself, utterly free to move about according to its own nature. Not to localize or partialize it is the end of spiritual training. When it is nowhere it is everywhere. When it occupies one tenth, it is absent in the other nine tenths. Let the swordsman discipline himself to have the mind go on its own way, instead of trying deliberately to confine it somewhere.

¹³ The main thesis of Takuan's letter to Yagyū Tajima no kami is almost exhausted in the passages translated more or less literally above. It consists in preserving the absolute fluidity of the mind (*kokoro*) by keeping it free from intellectual deliberations and affective disturbances of any kind at all that may arise from Ignorance and Delusion. The fluidity of mind and Prajñā Immovable may appear contradictory, but in actual life they are identical. When you have one, you have the other, for the Mind in its suchness is at once movable and immovable, it is constantly flowing, never "stopping" at any point, and yet there is in it a center never subject to any kind of movement, remaining forever one and the same. The difficulty is how to identify this center of immovability with its never-stopping movements themselves. Takuan advises the swordsman to solve the difficulty in his use of the sword as he actually stands against the opponent. The swordsman is thus made to be constantly facing a logical contradiction. As long as he notices it, that is, as long as he is logically minded, he finds his movements always hampered in one way or another—which is *suki*,¹⁴ and the enemy is sure to avail himself of it. Therefore, the swordsman cannot afford to indulge in an idle intellectual employment when the other side is always on the alert to detect the slightest *suki* produced on your part. You cannot relax and yet keep the state of tension deliberately for any length of time. For this is what makes the mind "stop" and lose its fluidity. How then can one have relaxation and tension simultaneously? Here is the same old contradiction, though presented in a different form.

When the situation is analyzed intellectually, we can never escape a contradiction in one form or another: moving and yet not moving, in tension and yet relaxed, seeing everything that is going on and yet not at all anxious about the way it may turn, with nothing purposely designed,

---

¹³ The following several paragraphs consist mainly of extracts from Takuan's letter paraphrased in modern terms so as to be more intelligible for readers. Takuan's original texts and our explanatory interpolations may cause some confusion in the minds of readers. But we crave their indulgent patience, for a careful perusal will be rewarding not only in understanding the swordsman's psychology in relation to what may be called Zen metaphysics but also in clarifying certain aspects of psychology which come up in the study of the Oriental arts generally.

¹⁴ *Suki* literally means any space between two objects where something else can enter. A psychological or mental *suki* is created when a state of tension is relaxed.

nothing consciously calculated, no anticipation, no expectation—in short, standing innocently like a baby and yet with all the cunning and subterfuge of the keenest intelligence of a fully matured mind: how can this be achieved? No amount of intellection can ever be of any help in this paradoxical situation.

What is known as *kufū* is the only way to reach this result. The *kufū* is altogether personal and individualistic, it is to develop out of oneself, within one's own inner life. *Kufū* literally means "to strive," "to wrestle," "to try to find the way out," or, in Christian terms, "to pray incessantly for God's help." Psychologically speaking, it is to remove all the inhibitions there are, intellectual as well as affective or emotional, and to bring out what is stored in the unconscious and let it work itself out quite independently of any kind of interfering consciousness. The *kufū*, therefore, will be directed toward how to remove the inhibitions, though not analytically. If such an expression is permissible, let us say the *kufū* is to be conatively carried out—a process involving one's whole person; that is to say, it is to be totalistic, growing out of the depths of one's own being.

To make clear the immovability of the most mobile mind, Takuan distinguishes the original mind from the delusive mind, which is an intellectually bifurcated state of consciousness. The original mind is a mind unconscious of itself, whereas the delusive mind is divided against itself, interfering with the free working of the original mind.

The original mind is *honshin* and the delusive mind is *mōshin*. *Hon* means "original," "primary," "real," "true," "native," or "natural," and *mō* means "not real," "deceiving" or "deceived," "deluded" or "delusive." *Shin* is *kokoro*, that is, "mind" in its broad sense.

The delusive mind may be defined as the mind intellectually and affectively burdened. It thus cannot move on from one topic to another without stopping and reflecting on itself, and this obstructs its native fluidity. The mind then coagulates before it makes a second move, because the first move still lingers there—which is a *suki* for the swordsman—the one thing that is to be avoided with the utmost scrupulosity. This corresponds to the mind conscious of itself (*ushin no shin* in Japanese). To be conscious is characteristic of the human mind as distinguished from the animal mind. But when the mind becomes conscious of its doings, it ceases to be instinctual and its commands are colored with calculations and deliberations—which means that the connection between itself and the limbs is no longer direct because the identity of the commander and his executive agents is lost. When dualism takes place, the whole personality never comes out as it is in itself. Takuan

calls this situation "stopping," "halting," or "freezing." One cannot
bathe in solid ice, he would warn us. Consciousness and its consequent
dichotomy bring rigidity to the freely-flowing original mind, and
the delusive mind begins functioning—which is fatal to the life of the
swordsman.

The conscious mind is *ushin no shin* contrasting with *mushin no shin*,
mind unconscious of itself. *Mushin* literally means "no-mind," it is the
mind negating itself, letting go itself from itself, a solidly frozen mind
allowing itself to relax into a state of perfect unguardedness. [We
resume Takuan's own words.]

The Mind of No-Mind (*Mushin no Shin*)

A mind unconscious of itself is a mind that is not at all disturbed by
affects of any kind. It is the original mind and not the delusive one
that is chock full of affects. It is always flowing, it never halts, nor does
it turn into a solid. As it has no discrimination to make, no affective
preference to follow, it fills the whole body, pervading every part of the
body, and nowhere standing still. It is never like a stone or a piece of
wood. [It feels, it moves, it is never at rest.] If it should find a resting
place anywhere, it is not a mind of no-mind. A no-mind keeps nothing
in it. It is also called *munen*, "no-thought." *Mushin* and *munen* are
synonymous.[15]

When *mushin* or *munen* is attained, the mind moves from one object
to another, flowing like a stream of water, filling every possible corner.
For this reason the mind fulfills every function required of it. But when
the flowing is stopped at one point, all the other points will get nothing
of it, and the result will be a general stiffness and obduracy. The wheel
revolves when it is not too tightly attached to the axle. When it is too
tight, it will never move on. If the mind has something in it, it stops

---

15 *Mushin (wu-hsin)* or *munen (wu-nien)* is one of the most important
ideas in Zen. It corresponds to the state of innocence enjoyed by the first in-
habitants of the Garden of Eden, or even to the mind of God when He was
about to utter His fiat, "Let there be light." Enō, the sixth patriarch of Zen,
emphasizes *munen* (or *mushin*) as most essential in the study of Zen. When
it is attained, a man becomes a Zen-man, and, as Takuan would have it, he
is also a perfect swordsman.

functioning, it cannot hear, it cannot see, even when a sound enters the ears or a light flashes before the eyes. To have something in mind means that it is preoccupied and has no time for anything else. But to attempt to remove the thought already in it is to refill it with another something. The task is endless. It is best, therefore, not to harbor anything in the mind from the start. This may be difficult, but when you go on exercising *kufū* toward the subject, you will after some time come to find this state of mind actualized without noticing each step of progress. Nothing, however, can be accomplished hurriedly.

[We paraphrase again. Takuan here notes an ancient poem, on some phase of romantic love:]

> To think that I am not going
> To think[16] of you any more
> Is still thinking of you.
> Let me then try not to think
> That I am not going to think of you.

[Before we part with Takuan, I wish to touch upon what may be regarded as an eternal paradox, which may run like this: How can one keep the mind in this state of no-thinking when its function is to think? How can the mind be at once a mind and a not-mind? How can "A" be simultaneously both "A" and "not-A"? The problem is not only logical and psychological, it is also metaphysical. The swordsman may have it solved in the most concrete and practical way, for it is for him a matter of life and death, whereas most of us can assume a more or less intellectual attitude and remain indifferent, as it were. But, philosophically, it concerns us in various ways, and it also constitutes the crucial point in the study of Oriental thought and culture. The question has never been presented to the Western mind, I believe, in the way the East faces it.

[Tradition has it that Yagyū Tajima no kami Munenori left a poem to one of his sons expressive of the secret of his school of swordsmanship. The poem is a poor one from the literary point of view, as poems of this nature known as *dōka,* "poems of Tao," generally are. It runs thus:

---

16 "To think" is *omou* in Japanese. *Omou* means not only "to think" but "to recollect," "to long for," "to love," etc. It has an affective as well as an intellectual value. The word is almost a general term for anything that goes on in one's mind. Therefore, not to think (*omowanu*) is to keep the mind utterly empty of all contents.

Behind the technique, know that there
is the spirit (ri):
It is dawning now;
Open the screen,
And lo, the moonlight is shining in!

We may say this is highly mystical. The strangest thing, however, is:
What has the art of swordplay—which, bluntly speaking, consists in
mutual killing—to do with such content as is communicated in the poem
on the moon at the break of day? In Japan, the dawn moonlight has rich
poetical associations. Yagyū's allusion to it is understandable from this
angle, but what has the sword to do with poetry about the moon? What
inspirations is the swordsman expected to get from viewing the moon as
the day dawns? What secret is here? After going through many a tragic
scene, which the man must no doubt have witnessed, with what poetic
enlightenment is he expected to crown all his past experience? The
author is here telling us, naturally, to have an inner light on the psychology of swordsmanship. Yagyū the master knows that technique
alone will never make a man the perfect swordplayer. He knows that
the spirit (ri) or inner experience (satori) must back the art, which is
gained only by deeply looking into the inmost recesses of the mind
(kokoro). That is why his teacher Takuan is never tired of dilating on
the doctrine of emptiness (śūnyatā), which is the metaphysics of mushin
no shin ("mind of no-mind"). Emptiness or no-mind-ness may appear
to some to be something most remote from our daily experience, but we
now realize how intimately it is related to the problem of life and
death with which most of us nowadays remain unconcerned.]

[End of Takuan's Letter]

The gist of Takuan's advice to Yagyū Tajima no kami can be
summed up by quoting his reference to Bukkō Kokushi's encounter
with the soldiers of the Yüan invading army, which Takuan men-
tions toward the end of his long epistle. The incident is told in
the section following this. Takuan comments on the sword cleaving
the spring breeze in a flash of lightning:

The uplifted sword has no will of its own, it is all of emptiness. It is
like a flash of lightning. The man who is about to be struck down is

also of emptiness, and so is the one who wields the sword. None of them are possessed of a mind which has any substantiality. As each of them is of emptiness and has no "mind" (*kokoro*), the striking man is not a man, the sword in his hands is not a sword, and the "I" who is about to be struck down is like the splitting of the spring breeze in a flash of lightning. When the mind does not "stop," the sword swinging cannot be anything less than the blowing of the wind. The wind is not conscious of itself as blowing over the trees and working havoc among them. So with the sword. Hence Bukkō's stanza of four lines.

This "empty-minded-ness" applies to all activities we may perform, such as dancing, as it does to swordplay. The dancer takes up the fan and begins to stamp his feet. If he has any idea at all of displaying his art well, he ceases to be a good dancer, for his mind "stops" with every movement he goes through. In all things, it is important to forget your "mind" and become one with the work at hand.

When we tie a cat, being afraid of its catching a bird, it keeps on struggling for freedom. But train the cat so that it would not mind the presence of a bird. The animal is now free and can go anywhere it likes. In a similar way, when the mind is tied up, it feels inhibited in every move it makes, and nothing will be accomplished with any sense of spontaneity. Not only that, the work itself will be of a poor quality, or it may not be finished at all.

Therefore, do not get your mind "stopped" with the sword you raise; forget what you are doing, and strike the enemy. Do not keep your mind on the person who stands before you. They are all of emptiness, but beware of your mind being caught up with emptiness itself.

To supplement Takuan, the following story is given to illustrate the mind of "no-mind-ness":

A woodcutter was busily engaged in cutting down trees in the remote mountains. An animal called "satori" appeared. It was a very strange-looking creature, not usually found in the villages. The woodcutter wanted to catch it alive. The animal read his mind: "You want to catch me alive, do you not?" Completely taken aback, the woodcutter did not know what to say, whereupon the animal remarked, "You are evidently astonished at my telepathic faculty." Even more surprised, the woodcutter then conceived the idea of striking it with one blow of his ax, when the satori exclaimed, "Now you want to kill me." The woodcutter felt entirely disconcerted, and fully realizing his impotence to do anything with this mysterious animal, he thought of resuming his business. The satori was not charitably disposed, for he pursued him, saying, "So at last you have abandoned me."

The woodcutter did not know what to do with this animal or with himself. Altogether resigned, he took up his ax and, paying no attention whatever to the presence of the animal, vigorously and singlemindedly resumed cutting trees. While so engaged, the head of the ax flew off its handle, and struck the animal dead. The satori, with all its mind-reading sagacity, had failed to read the mind of "no-mind-ness."

At the last stage of swordsmanship there is a secret teaching which is not given to any but a fully-qualified disciple. Mere technical training is not enough, proficiency in this does not go beyond apprenticeship. The secret teaching is known among the masters of a certain school as "The Moon in Water." According to one writer, it is explained as follows, which is in truth no more than the teaching of Zen—the doctrine of *mushin:*

"What is meant by 'the moon in water'?

"This is explained variously in the various schools of swordsmanship, but the main idea is to grasp the way the moon reflects itself wherever there is a body of water, which is done in a state of *mushin* ('no-mind-ness'). One of the imperial poems composed at the Pond of Hirosawa reads:

"The moon has no intent to cast its shadow anywhere,
    Nor does the pond design to lodge the moon:
    How serene the water of Hirosawa!

"From this poem one must get an insight into the secrets of *mushin*, where there are no traces of artificial contrivance, everything being left to nature itself.

"Again, it is like one moon reflecting itself in hundreds of streams: the moonlight is not divided into so many shadows, but the water is there to reflect them; the moonlight remains ever the same even where there are no waters to hold its reflections. Again, it is all the same to the moonlight whether there are so many bodies of water, or there is just one little puddle. By this analogy the mysteries of mind are made easier to understand. But the moon and water are tangible matter, while mind has no form and its working is difficult to trace. The symbols are thus not the whole truth, only suggestive."

From all these quotations we can see that the Oriental thought and culture lay great emphasis on the realization of a psychical state of no-mind-ness (*mushin* or *munen*). When this is not realized, the mind is always conscious of its own doings—which Takuan calls "mind-stopping." For, instead of flowing, as he says, from one object to another, the mind halts and reflects on what it is going to do or what it has already done. Recollection and anticipation are fine qualities of consciousness which distinguish the human mind from that of the lower animals. They are useful and serve certain purposes, but when actions are directly related to the problem of life and death, they must be given up so that they will not interfere with the fluidity of mentation and the lightning rapidity of action. The man must turn himself into a puppet in the hands of the unconscious. The unconscious must supersede the conscious. Metaphysically speaking, this is the philosophy of *śūnyatā* ("emptiness"). The technique of swordsmanship is based on its psychology, and the psychology is a localized application of the metaphysics.

4. *ZEN AND THE ART OF TEA*[1]

1

WHAT is common to Zen and the art of tea is the constant attempt both make at simplification. The elimination of the unnecessary is achieved by Zen in its intuitive grasp of final reality; by the art of tea, in the way of living typified by serving tea in the tearoom. The art of tea is the aestheticism of primitive simplicity. Its ideal, to come closer to Nature, is realized by sheltering oneself under a thatched roof in a room which is hardly ten feet square but which must be artistically constructed and furnished. Zen also aims at stripping off all the artificial wrappings humanity has devised, supposedly for its own solemnization. Zen first of all combats the intellect; for, in spite of its practical usefulness, the intellect goes against our effort to delve into the depths of being. Philosophy may propose all kinds of questions for intellectual solution, but it never claims to give us the spiritual satisfaction which must be accessible to every one of us, however intellectually undeveloped he may be. Philosophy is accessible only to those who are intellectually equipped, and thus it cannot be a discipline of universal appreciation. Zen—or, more broadly speaking, religion—is to cast off all one thinks he possesses, even life, and to get back to the ultimate state of being, the "Original Abode," one's own father or mother. This can be done by every one of us, for we are what we are because of it or him or her, and without it or him or her we are nothing. This is to be called the last stage of simplification, since things cannot be reduced to any simpler terms. The art of tea symbolizes simplification, first of all, by an inconspicuous, solitary thatched hut erected, perhaps, under an old pine tree, as if the hut were part of Nature and not specially constructed by human hands. When form is thus once for all symbolized it allows itself to be artistically treated. It goes without saying that the

[1] *Zen and Japanese Culture*, pp. 271-289.

principle of treatment is to be in perfect conformity with the original idea which prompted it, that is, the elimination of unnecessaries.

Tea was known in Japan even before the Kamakura era (1185–1338), but its first wider propagation is generally ascribed to Eisai (1141–1215), the Zen teacher, who brought tea seeds from China and had them cultivated in his friend's monastery grounds. It is said that his book on tea, together with some of the tea prepared from his plants, was presented to Minamoto Sanetomo (1192–1219), the shōgun of the time, who happened to be ill. Eisai thus came to be known as the father of tea cultivation in Japan. He thought that tea had some medicinal qualities and was good for a variety of diseases. Apparently he did not teach how one conducts the tea ceremony, which he must have observed while at the Zen monasteries in China. The tea ceremony is a way of entertaining visitors to the monastery, or sometimes a way of entertaining its own occupants among themselves. The Zen monk who brought the ritual to Japan was Dai-ō the National Teacher[2] (1236–1308), about half a century later than Eisai. After Dai-ō came several monks who became masters of the art, and finally Ikkyū (1394–1481), the noted abbot of Daitokuji, taught the technique to one of his disciples, Shukō (1422–1502), whose artistic genius developed it and succeeded in adapting it to Japanese taste. Shukō thus became the originator of the art of tea and taught it to Ashikaga Yoshimasa (1435–90), shōgun of the time, who was a great patron of the arts. Later, Jō-ō (1504–55) and especially Rikyū further improved it and gave a finishing touch to what is now known as *cha-no-yu*, generally translated "tea ceremony" or "tea cult." The original tea ceremony as practiced at Zen monasteries is carried on independently of the art now in vogue among the general public.

I have often thought of the art of tea in connection with Buddhist life, which seems to partake so much of the characteristics of the art. Tea keeps the mind fresh and vigilant, but it does not intoxicate. It has qualities naturally to be appreciated by scholars and monks. It is in the nature of things that tea came to be extensively used in the Buddhist monasteries and that its first introduction to Japan came through the monks. If tea symbolizes Buddhism,

[2] Returned from China in 1267.

can we not say that wine stands for Christianity? Wine is used extensively by the Christians. It is used in the church as the symbol of Christ's blood, which, according to the Christian tradition, was shed for sinful humanity. Probably for this reason the medieval monks kept wine cellars in their monasteries. They look jovial and happy, surrounding the cask and holding up the wine cups. Wine first excites and then inebriates. In many ways it contrasts with tea, and this contrast is also that between Buddhism and Christianity.

We can see now that the art of tea is most intimately connected with Zen not only in its practical development but principally in the observance of the spirit that runs through the ceremony itself. The spirit in terms of feeling consists of "harmony" (*wa*), "reverence" (*kei*), "purity" (*sei*), and "tranquillity" (*jaku*). These four elements are needed to bring the art to a successful end; they are all the essential constituents of a brotherly and orderly life, which is no other than the life of the Zen monastery. That the monks behaved in perfect orderliness can be inferred from the remark made by Tei Meidō, a Confucian scholar of the Sung dynasty, who once visited a monastery called Jōrinji. "Here, indeed, we witness the classical form of ritualism as it was practiced in the ancient three dynasties." The ancient three dynasties are the ideal days dreamed of by every Chinese scholar-statesman, when a most desirable state of things prevailed and people enjoyed all the happiness that could be expected of a good government. Even now, the Zen monks are well trained individually and collectively in conducting ceremonies. The Ogasawara school of etiquette is thought to have its origin in the "Monastery Regulations" compiled by Hyakujō and known as *Hyakujō Shingi*. While Zen teaching consists in grasping the spirit by transcending form, it unfailingly reminds us of the fact that the world in which we live is a world of particular forms and that the spirit expresses itself only by means of form. Zen is, therefore, at once antimonian and disciplinarian.

2

The character for "harmony" also reads "gentleness of spirit" (*yawaragi*), and to my mind "gentleness of spirit" seems to describe better the spirit governing the whole procedure of the art of tea. Harmony refers more to form, while gentleness is suggestive of an inward feeling. The general atmosphere of the tearoom tends to create this kind of gentleness all around—gentleness of touch, gentleness of odor, gentleness of light, and gentleness of sound. You take up a teacup, handmade and irregularly shaped, the glaze probably not uniformly overlaid, but in spite of this primitiveness the little utensil has a peculiar charm of gentleness, quietness, and unobtrusiveness. The incense burning is never strong and stimulating, but gentle and pervading. The windows and screens are another source of a gentle prevailing charm, for the light admitted into the room is always soft and restful and conducive to a meditative mood. The breeze passing through the needles of the old pine tree harmoniously blends with the sizzling of the iron kettle over the fire. The entire environment thus reflects the personality of the one who has created it.

"What is most valuable is gentleness of spirit; what is most essential is not to contradict others"—these are the first words of the so-called "Constitution of Seventeen Articles," compiled by Prince Shōtoku in 604. It is a kind of moral and spiritual admonition given by the Prince Regent to his subjects. But it is significant that such an admonition, whatever its political bearings, should begin by placing unusual emphasis on gentleness of spirit. In fact, this is the first precept given to the Japanese consciousness to which the people have responded with varying degrees of success during centuries of civilization. Although Japan has lately come to be known as a warlike nation, this concept is erroneous with respect to the people, whose consciousness of their own character is that they are, on the whole, of gentle nature. And there is good reason to presume this, for the physical atmosphere enveloping the whole island of Japan is characterized by a general mildness, not only climatically but meteorologically. This is mostly due to the presence of much moisture in the air. The mountains, villages, woods, etc., enwrapped in a somewhat vaporous atmosphere, have a soft appearance; flowers are not as a rule too richly colored, but somewhat subdued and delicate; while the spring foliage is vividly fresh. Sensitive minds brought up in an environment like this cannot fail to imbibe much of it, and with it gentleness of spirit. We are, however, apt to deviate from this basic virtue of the Japanese character as we come in contact with various difficulties, social, political, economic, and cultural. We have to guard our-selves against such subversive influences, and Zen has come to help us in this.

When Dōgen (1200–53) came back from China after some years of study of Zen there, he was asked what he had learned. He said, "Not much except soft-heartedness (*nyūnan-shin*)." "Soft-hearted-ness" is "tender-mindedness" and in this case means "gentleness of spirit." Generally we are too egotistic, too full of hard, resisting spirit. We are individualistic, unable to accept things as they are or as they come to us. Resistance means friction, friction is the source of all trouble. When there is no self, the heart is soft and offers no resistance to outside influences. This does not necessarily mean the absence of all sensitivities or emotionalities. They are controlled in the totality of a spiritual outlook on life. And in this aspect I am sure that Christians and Buddhists alike know how to follow Dōgen in the appreciation of the significance of selflessness or "soft-heartedness." In the art of tea the "gentleness of spirit" is spoken of in the same spirit enjoined by Prince Shōtoku. Indeed, "gentleness of spirit" or "soft-heartedness" is the foundation of our life on earth. If the art of tea purports to establish a Buddha-land in its small group, it has to start with gentleness of spirit. To illus-trate this point further, let us quote the Zen Master Takuan (1573–1645).

TAKUAN ON THE ART OF TEA (CHA-NO-YU)

The principle of *cha-no-yu* is the spirit of harmonious blending of Heaven and Earth and provides the means for establishing universal peace. People of the present time have turned it into a mere occasion for meeting friends, talking of worldly affairs, and indulging in palatable food and drink; besides, they are proud of their elegantly furnished tearooms, where, surrounded by rare objects of art, they would serve tea in a most accomplished manner, and deride those who are not so skillful as themselves. This is, however, far from being the original intention of *cha-no-yu*.

Let us then construct a small room in a bamboo grove or under trees, arrange streams and rocks and plant trees and bushes, while [inside the room] let us pile up charcoal, set a kettle, arrange flowers, and arrange in order the necessary tea utensils. And let all this be carried out in accordance with the idea that in this room we can enjoy the streams and rocks as we do the rivers and mountains in Nature, and appreciate the various moods and sentiments suggested by the snow, the moon, and the trees and flowers, as they go through the transformation of seasons, appearing and disappearing, blooming and withering. As visitors are greeted here with due reverence, we listen quietly to the boiling water in the kettle, which sounds like a breeze passing through the pine needles, and become oblivious of all worldly woes and worries; we then pour out a dipperful of water from the kettle, reminding us of the mountain stream, and thereby our mental dust is wiped off. This is truly a world of recluses, saints on earth.

The principle of propriety is reverence, which in practical life functions as harmonious relationship. This is the statement made by Confucius when he defines the use of propriety, and is also the mental attitude one should cultivate in *cha-no-yu*. For instance, when a man is associated with persons of high social rank his conduct is simple and natural, and there is no cringing self-deprecation on his part. When he sits in the company of people socially below him he retains a respectful attitude toward them, being entirely free from the feeling of self-importance. This is due to the presence of something pervading the entire tearoom, which results in the harmonious relationship of all who come here. However long the association, there is always the persisting sense of reverence. The spirit of the smiling Kāśyapa and the nodding Sōshi must be said to be moving here; this spirit, in words, is the mysterious Suchness that is beyond all comprehension.

For this reason, the principle animating the tearoom, from its first construction down to the choice of the tea utensils, the technique of service, the cooking of food, wearing apparel, etc., is to be sought in the avoidance of complicated ritual and mere ostentation. The implements may be old, but the mind can be invigorated therewith so that it is ever fresh and ready to respond to the changing seasons and the varying views resulting therefrom; it never curries favor, it is never covetous, never inclined to extravagance, but always watchful and considerate for others. The owner of such a mind is naturally gentle-mannered and always sincere—this is *cha-no-yu*.

The way of *cha-no-yu*, therefore, is to appreciate the spirit of a naturally harmonious blending of Heaven and Earth, to see the pervading presence of the five elements by one's fireside, where the mountains, rivers, rocks, and trees are found as they are in Nature, to draw the refreshing water from the well of Nature, to taste with one's own mouth the flavor supplied by Nature. How grand this enjoyment of the harmonious blending of Heaven and Earth!

[*Here Ends Takuan*]

Had the art of tea and Zen something to contribute to the presence of a certain democratic spirit in the social life of Japan? In spite of the strict social hierarchy established during her feudal days, the idea of equality and fraternity persists among the people. In the tearoom, ten feet square, guests of various social grades are entertained with no discrimination; for, once therein, the commoner's knees touch those of the nobleman, and they talk with due reverence to each other on subjects in which they both are interested. In Zen, of course, no earthly distinctions are allowed, and its monks have free approach to all classes of society and are at home with them all. It is, indeed, deeply ingrained in human nature that it aspires once in a while to throw off all the restraints society has artificially put on us and to have free and natural and heart-to-heart intercourse with fellow-beings, including the animals, plants, and inanimate objects so called. We, therefore, always welcome every opportunity for this kind of liberation. No doubt this is what Takuan means when he refers to "the harmonious blending of Heaven and Earth," where all angels join in the chorus.

"Reverence" is fundamentally and originally a religious feeling—feeling for a being supposed to be higher than ourselves who are, after all, poor human mortals. The feeling is later transferred to social relationships and then degenerates into mere formalism. In modern days of democracy so called, everybody is just as good as everybody else, at least from the social point of view, and there is nobody specially deserving reverence. But when the feeling is analyzed back to its original sense, it is a reflection on one's own unworthiness, that is, the realization of one's limitations, physical and intellectual, moral and spiritual. This realization evokes in us the desire for transcending ourselves and also for coming into touch with a being who stands to us in every possible form of opposition. The desire frequently directs our spiritual movements toward an object outside us; but when it is directed within ourselves, it becomes self-abnegation and a feeling of sin. These are all negative virtues, while positively they lead us to reverence, the wish not to slight others. We are beings full of contradictions: in one respect we feel that we are just as good as anybody else, but at the same time we have an innate suspicion that everybody else is better than ourselves—a kind of inferiority complex.

There is a Bodhisattva in Mahayana Buddhism[3] known as Sadāparibhūta (Jōfukyō Bosatsu), "one who never slights others." Perhaps when we are quite sincere with ourselves—that is, when we are all alone with ourselves in the innermost chamber of our being—there is a feeling there which makes us move toward others with a sense of humiliation. Whatever this may be, there is a deeply religious attitude of mind in reverence. Zen may burn all the holy statues in the temple to warm itself on a cold wintry night; Zen may destroy all the literature containing its precious legacies in order to save its very existence as the truth shorn of all its external trappings, however glamorous they appear to outsiders; but it never forgets to worship a storm-broken and mud-soiled humble blade of grass; it never neglects to offer all the wild flowers of the field, just as they are, to all the Buddhas in the three thousand chiliocosms. Zen knows how to revere because it knows how to slight. What is needed in Zen as in anything else is sincerity of heart, and not mere conceptualism.

Toyotomi Hideyoshi was the great patron of the art of tea in his day and an admirer of Sen no Rikyū (1521–91), who was virtually the founder of the art. Although he was always after something sensational, grandiose, and ostentatious, he seems to have understood finally something of the spirit of the art as advocated by Rikyū and his followers, when he gave this verse to Rikyū at one of the latter's "tea parties":

> When tea is made with water drawn from the well of
> Mind
> Whose bottom is beyond measure,
> We really have what is called *cha-no-yu.*

Hideyoshi was a crude and cruel despot in many ways, but in his liking for the art of tea we are inclined to find something genuine beyond just "using" the art for his political purposes. His

---

[3] *The Saddharma-puṇḍarīka-sūtra,* tr. H. Kern, p. 356.

verse touches the spirit of reverence when he can refer to the water
deeply drawn from the well of the mind.

Rikyū teaches that "the art of *cha-no-yu* consists in nothing else
but in boiling water, making tea, and sipping it." This is simple
enough as far as it goes. Human life, we can say, consists in being
born, eating and drinking, working and sleeping, marrying and
giving birth to children, and finally in passing away—whither, no
one knows. Nothing seems to be simpler than living this life, when
it is so stated. But how many of us are there who can live this kind
of matter-of-fact or rather God-intoxicated life, cherishing no
desires, leaving no regrets, but absolutely trustful of God? While
living we think of death; while dying we long for life; while one
thing is being accomplished, so many other things, not necessarily
cognate and usually irrelevant, crowd into our brains, and divert
and dissipate the energy which is to be concentrated on the matter
in hand. When water is poured into the bowl, it is not the water
alone that is poured into it—a variety of things go into it, good and
bad, pure and impure, things about which one has to blush, things
which can never be poured out anywhere except into one's own
deep unconscious. The tea water when analyzed contains all the
filth disturbing and contaminating the stream of our consciousness.
An art is perfected only when it ceases to be art: when there is
the perfection of artlessness, when the innermost sincerity of our
being asserts itself, and this is the meaning of reverence in the art
of tea. Reverence is, therefore, sincerity or simplicity of heart.

"Purity," estimated as constituting the spirit of the art of tea,
may be said to be the contribution of Japanese mentality. Purity
is cleanliness or sometimes orderliness, which is observable in
everything everywhere concerned with the art. Fresh water is
liberally used in the garden, called *roji* (courtyard); in case
natural running water is not available, there is a stone basin filled
with water as one approaches the tearoom, which is naturally kept
clean and free from dust and dirt.

Purity in the art of tea may remind us of the Taoistic teaching
of Purity. There is something common to both, for the object of
discipline in both is to free one's mind from the defilements of the
senses.

A tea master says: "The spirit of *cha-no-yu* is to cleanse the six
senses from contamination. By seeing the *kakemono* in the *tokonoma* (alcove) and the flower in the vase, one's sense of smell is

cleansed; by listening to the boiling of water in the iron kettle and
to the dripping of water from the bamboo pipe, one's ears are
cleansed; by tasting tea one's mouth is cleansed; and by handling
the tea utensils one's sense of touch is cleansed. When thus all the
sense organs are cleansed, the mind itself is cleansed of defilements. The art of tea is after all a spiritual discipline, and my aspiration for every hour of the day is not to depart from the spirit of
the tea, which is by no means a matter of mere entertainment."[4]
In one of Rikyū's poems we have this:

> While the *roji* is meant to be a passageway
> Altogether outside this earthly life,
> How is it that people only contrive
> To besprinkle it with dust of mind?

Here as in the following poems he refers to his own state of mind
while looking out quietly from his tearoom:

> The court is left covered
> With the fallen leaves
> Of the pine tree;
> No dust is stirred,
> And calm is my mind!

> The moonlight
> Far up in the sky,
> Looking through the eaves,
> Shines on a mind
> Undisturbed with remorse.

---

[4] By Nakano Kazuma in the *Hagakure*. *Hagakure* literally means "hidden
under the leaves," that is, "to be unostentatious in practicing a life of goodness," or "not to be 'as the hypocrites [who] love to pray standing in the syna-
gogues and in the corners of the streets' " (Matt. 6: 5). It contains wise sayings
given by Yamamoto Jōchō, a recluse Zen philosopher, to his disciple, Tashiro
Matazaemon, both of whom lived on the feudal estate of Lord Nabeshima.
It consists of eleven fascicles, compiled between 1710 and 1716. The book
is also known as the "Nabeshima Rongo" in imitation of the Confucian
Analects (Rongo).

It is, indeed, a mind pure, serene, and free from disturbing emotions that can enjoy the aloneness of the Absolute:

> The snow-covered mountain path
> Winding through the rocks
> Has come to its end;
> Here stands a hut,
> The master is all alone;
> No visitors he has,
> Nor are any expected.

In a book called *Nambō-roku,* which is one of the most important, almost sacred, textbooks of the art of tea, we have the following passage, showing that the ideal of the art is to realize a Buddha-land of Purity on earth, however small in scale, and to see an ideal community gathered here, however temporary the gathering and however few its members:

The spirit of *wabi* is to give an expression to the Buddha-land of Purity altogether free from defilements, and, therefore, in this *roji* (courtyard) and in this thatched hut there ought not to be a speck of dust of any kind; both master and visitors are expected to be on terms of absolute sincerity; no ordinary measures of proportion or etiquette or conventionalism are to be followed. A fire is made, water is boiled, and tea is served: this is all that is needed here, no other worldly considerations are to intrude. For what we want here is to give full expression to the Buddha-mind. When ceremony, etiquette, and other such things are insisted on, worldly considerations of various kinds creep in, and master and visitors alike feel inclined to find fault with each other. It becomes thus more and more difficult to find such ones as fully comprehend the meaning of the art. If we were to have Jōshū for master and Bodhidharma, the first Zen patriarch, for a guest, and Rikyū and myself picked up the dust in the *roji,* would not such a gathering be a happy one indeed?

We see how thoroughly imbued with the spirit of Zen is this statement of one of the chief disciples of Rikyū.

The next section will be devoted to the elucidation of *sabi* or *wabi,* the concept constituting the fourth principle of the art of tea, "tranquillity." In fact, this is the most essential factor in the

tea art, and without it there can be no *cha-no-yu* whatever. It is in
this connection, indeed, that Zen enters deeply into the art of tea.

3

I have used the term "tranquillity" for the fourth element making
up the spirit of the art of tea, but it may not be a good term for all
that is implied in the Chinese character *chi*, or *jaku* in Japanese.
Jaku is *sabi*, but *sabi* contains much more than "tranquillity." Its
Sanskrit equivalent, *śānta* or *śānti*, it is true, means "tranquillity,"
"peace," "serenity," and *jaku* has been frequently used in Buddhist
literature to denote "death" or "nirvana." But as the term is used
in the tea, its implication is "poverty," "simplification," "aloneness,"
and here *sabi* becomes synonymous with *wabi*. To appreciate
poverty, to accept whatever is given, a tranquil, passive mind is
needed, but in both *sabi* and *wabi* there is a suggestion of objectivity. Just to be tranquil or passive is not *sabi* nor is it *wabi*. There
is always something objective that evokes in one a mood to be
called *wabi*. And *wabi* is not merely a psychological reaction to
a certain pattern of environment. There is an active principle of
aestheticism in it; when this is lacking poverty becomes indigence,
aloneness becomes ostracism or misanthropy or inhuman un-
sociability. *Wabi* or *sabi*, therefore, may be defined as an active,
aesthetical appreciation of poverty; when it is used as a constituent
of the tea, it is the creating or remodeling of an environment in
such a way as to awaken the feeling of *wabi* or *sabi*. Nowadays, as
these terms are used, we may say that *sabi* applies more to the
individual objects and environment generally, and *wabi* to the
living of a life ordinarily associated with poverty or insufficiency
or imperfection. *Sabi* is thus more objective, whereas *wabi* is more
subjective and personal. We speak of a *wabi-zumai*, "the *wabi*
way of living," but when a vessel such as a tea caddy or a bowl or a
flower vase comes in for appraisal, it is often characterized as
having a "*sabi* taste," or *kanmi*. *Kan* and *sabi* are synonymous,
while *mi* is "taste." The tea utensils are, as far as I know, never
qualified as being of "*wabi* taste."

Of the following two verses the first is considered expressive of
the idea of *wabi*, while the second gives the idea of *sabi*:

Among the weeds growing along the wall
The crickets are hiding, as if forsaken,
From the garden wet with autumnal showers.
The yomogi herbs in the garden
Are beginning to wither from below;
Autumn is deepening,
Its colors are fading;
Not knowing why, my heart is filled with
    melancholy.

The idea of *sabi* is said to come primarily from *renga* masters, who show great aesthetic appreciation for things suggestive of age, desiccation, numbness, chilliness, obscurity—all of which are negative feelings opposed to warmth, the spring, expansiveness, transparency, etc. They are, in fact, feelings growing out of poverty and deficiency; but they have also a certain quality lending themselves to highly cultivated aesthetic ecstasy. The teamen will say that this is "objectively negated but subjectively affirmed," whereby external emptiness is filled with inner richness. In some ways, *wabi* is *sabi* and *sabi* is *wabi;* they are interchangeable terms.

Shukō, a disciple of Ikkyū (1394–1481) and tea master to Ashikaga Yoshimasa (1435–90), used to teach his pupils about the spirit of the tea with this story. A Chinese poet happened to compose this couplet:

In the woods over there deeply buried in snow,
Last night a few branches of the plum tree burst out in
    bloom.

He showed it to his friend, who suggested that he alter "a few branches" into "one branch." The author followed the friend's advice, praising him as his "teacher of one character." A solitary branch of the plum tree in bloom among the snow-covered woods— here is the idea of *wabi*.

On another occasion, Shukō is reported to have said: "It is good to see a fine steed tied in the straw-roofed shed. This being so, it also is specially fine to find a rare object of art in an ordinarily furnished room." This reminds one of the Zen phrase, "To fill a monk's tattered robe with a cool refreshing breeze." Outwardly there is not a sign of distinction, appearances all go against the contents, which are in every way priceless. A life of *wabi* can then be defined: an inexpressible quiet joy deeply hidden beneath sheer poverty; and it is the art of tea that tries to express this idea artistically.

But if there is anything betraying a trace of insincerity, the whole thing is utterly ruined. The priceless contents must be there most genuinely, they must be there as if they were never there, they must be rather accidentally discovered. In the beginning there is no suspicion of the presence of anything extraordinary, yet something attracts—a closer approach, a tentative examination, and, behold, a mine of solid gold glitters from among the unexpected. But the gold itself remains ever the same, discovered or not. It retains its reality, that is, its sincerity to itself, regardless of accidents. *Wabi* means to be true to itself. A master lives quietly in his unpretentious hut, a friend comes in unexpectedly, tea is served, a fresh spray of flowers is arranged, and the visitor enjoys a peaceful afternoon charmed with his conversation and entertainment. Is this not the tea rite in its reality?

Parenthetically, some may ask: "In these modern times how many of us are situated like the tea master? It is nonsense to talk about leisurely entertainment. Let us have bread first, and fewer working hours." Yes, it is true that we have to eat bread in the sweat of our face and to work a number of hours as the slave of machinery. Our creative impulses have thus been miserably downtrodden. It is not, however, just for this reason, I believe, that we moderns have lost the taste for leisureliness, that we find no room in our worrying hearts for enjoying life in any other way than running after excitement for excitement's sake. The question is: How have we come to give ourselves up to such a life as to try to keep the inner worries only temporarily suppressed? How is it that we no longer reflect on life more deeply, more seriously, so that we can have a realization of its inmost meaning? When this question is settled, let us if necessary negate the entire machinery of modern life and start anew. I hope our destination is not the continual enslaving of ourselves to material wants and comforts.

Another tea master writes: "From Amaterasu Ōmikami[5] starts

---

[5] The Ōmikami is really the sun-goddess in Japanese mythology, but the writer seems to understand her to be a male deity and, anachronistically, associates her with the art of tea.

the spirit of *wabi*. Being the great ruler of this country, he was free to erect the finest palaces, inlaid with gold and silver and precious stones, and nobody would dare to speak ill of him, and yet he dwelt in a reed-thatched house and ate unpolished rice. In every possible way, besides, he was self-sufficient, modest, and ever-striving. He was truly a most excellent tea master, living a life of *wabi*."

It is interesting to see that this writer regards Amaterasu Ōmikami as the representative teaman, who lived a life of *wabi*. This, however, shows that the tea is the aesthetic appreciation of primitive simplicity; in other words, that the tea is an aesthetic expression of the longing which most of us seem to feel in the depths of our hearts to go as far back to Nature as our human existence will permit and to be at one with her.

Through these statements, the concept of *wabi* is, I think, becoming clearer. We can say that, in a way, with Sōtan, a grandson of Rikyū, real *wabi* life starts. He explains that *wabi* is the essence of the tea, corresponding to the moral life of the Buddhists:

"It is a great mistake, indeed, to make an ostentatious show of *wabi* while inwardly nothing is consonant with it. Such people construct a tearoom as far as appearances go with all that is needed for *wabi;* much gold and silver is wasted on the work; rare objects of art are purchased with the money realized by the sale of their farms—and this just to make a display before visitors. They think a life of *wabi* is here. But far from it. *Wabi* means insufficiency of things, inability to fulfill every desire one may cherish, generally a life of poverty and dejection. To halt despondently in one's course of life because of his inability to push himself forward— this is *wabi*. But he does not brood over the situation. He has learned to be self-sufficient with insufficiency of things. He does not seek beyond his means. He has ceased to be cognizant of the fact that he is in tight circumstances. If, however, he should still abide with the idea of the poverty, insufficiency, or general wretchedness of his condition, he would no more be a man of *wabi* but a poverty-stricken person. Those who really know what *wabi* is are free from greed, violence, anger, indolence, uneasiness, and folly. Thus *wabi* corresponds to the Pāramitā of Morality as observed by the Buddhists."

In *wabi*, aestheticism is fused with morality or spirituality, and it is for this reason that the tea masters declare the tea to be life itself and not merely a thing for pleasure, however refined this may be. Zen is thus directly connected with the tea; indeed, most ancient tea masters studied Zen in real earnest and applied their attainment in Zen to the art of their profession.

Religion can sometimes be defined as a way of escape from the humdrum of this worldly life. Scholars may object to this, saying that religion aspires not to escape but to transcend life in order to reach the Absolute or the Infinite. But, practically stated, it is an escape where one finds a little time to breathe and recuperate. Zen as a spiritual discipline does this, too, but as it is too transcendental, as it were, too inaccessible for ordinary minds, the tea masters who have studied Zen have devised the way to put their understanding into practice in the form of the art of tea. Probably in this, to a great extent, their aesthetic aspirations asserted themselves.

When *wabi* is explained as above, readers may think that it is more or less a negative quality, and that its enjoyment is meant for people who have been a failure in life. This is true in some sense, perhaps. But how many of us are really so healthy as not to need medicine or a tonic of one kind or another at some time in their lives? And then every one of us is destined to pass away. Modern psychology gives us many cases of active businessmen, strong physically and mentally, who will suddenly collapse when they retire. Why? Because they have not learned to keep their energy in reserve; that is to say, they have never become aware of a plan to retreat while still working. The Japanese fighting man in those old days of strife and unrest, when he was most strenuously engaged in the business of war, realized that he could not go on always with nerves at the highest pitch of vigilance and that he ought to have a way of escape sometime and somewhere. The tea must have given him exactly this. He retreated for a while into a quiet corner of his Unconscious, symbolized by the tearoom no more than ten feet square. And when he came out of it, not only did he feel refreshed in mind and body, but very likely his memory was renewed of things of more permanent value than mere fighting.

Thus we see that "tranquillity," which is the fourth and chief factor making up the spirit of the tea, ultimately means a kind of aesthetic contemplation of poverty in the Eckhartian sense, which the teamen call *wabi* or *sabi* according to the objects to which they apply the term.

5. *LOVE OF NATURE*[1]

1

To understand the cultural life of the Japanese people in all its
different aspects, including their intensive love of Nature, which
we have spoken of just now, it is essential, as I have repeatedly
stated, to delve into the secrets of Zen Buddhism. Without some
knowledge of these the Japanese character is difficult to appreciate.
This does not, of course, mean that Zen is everything in the molding of the character and general culture of the Japanese people.
What I mean is that, when Zen is grasped, we can with some
degree of ease get into the depths of their spiritual life in all its
varied expressions.

This fact is recognized, consciously or unconsciously, by
scholars and by men in the street. The former recognize it in an
analytical and critical manner worthy of their profession; the latter
appreciate it by actually living it, in the delight they feel in listening to tales and traditions traceable somehow to the teaching of
Zen Buddhism.

That Zen has had a great deal to do in the building of Japanese
character and culture is pointed out also by foreign writers on
Japan, among whom we may mention the following.

The late Sir Charles Eliot, who most unfortunately passed away
without personally revising his valuable book, *Japanese Buddhism,*
writes (p. 396): "Zen has been a great power in the artistic, intellectual, and even the political life of the Far East. To a certain
extent it has moulded the Japanese character, but it is also the
expression of that character. No other form of Buddhism is
so thoroughly Japanese." The one significant point here is that
Zen is the expression of the Japanese character. Historically, Zen
started in China about fifteen hundred years ago, and it was not
until the latter part of the Sung dynasty (961–1280), that is, in the

[1] *Zen and Japanese Culture*, pp. 345–362.

earlier part of the thirteenth century, that Zen was brought to Japan. Thus the history of Zen in Japan is far younger than in China, but it was so adaptable to the character of the Japanese people, especially in its moral and aesthetic aspects, that it has penetrated far more deeply and widely into Japanese life than into Chinese. Hence we see that the statement made by the author of *Japanese Buddhism* is not at all an exaggeration.

Sir George Sansom, another capable English writer on Japan, makes the following observation on Zen in his *Japan, A Short Cultural History* (p. 336): "The influence of this school [i.e., Zen Buddhism] upon Japan has been so subtle and pervading that it has become the essence of her finest culture. To follow its ramifications in thought and sentiment, in art, letters, and behavior, would be to write exhaustively the most difficult and the most fascinating chapter of her spiritual history. . . ." While I may have occasion later to criticize this writer's view on the Japanese love of Nature, the point he makes here is accurate, and I am in full agreement with him.

What are the characteristic features of Zen as distinguished from the other forms of Buddhism? It will be necessary to know them before we proceed to see the relationship between Zen and the Japanese love of Nature. Naturally, it is outside our scope of study here to enter in detail into what really and essentially constitutes Zen. Much has already been done along this line, directly and indirectly, in the preceding sections. Therefore, let the following brief statements here suffice concerning the teaching and discipline of Zen, as regards its four aspects: religious, moral, aesthetic, and epistemological.

2

In the first place, let me state that Zen is not a mere ascetic discipline. When we see a monk living in a humble hut and sustaining himself on rice and pickles and potatoes, we may imagine him to be a world-fleeing recluse, whose principle of life is self-abnegation. True, there is a certain side in his life tending to this, as Zen teaches a form of detachment and self-control. But if we imagine there is nothing more in Zen, we entertain a very superficial view of it. The Zen insights go far deeper into the source of life, where

Zen is truly religious. By this I mean Zen is in close touch with Reality; indeed, Zen takes hold of it and lives it, and this is where Zen is religious.

Those who are acquainted only with the Christian or some Indian Bhakti forms of religion may wonder where really in Zen is that which corresponds to their notion of God and their pious attitude toward Him; Reality sounds to them too conceptual and philosophical and not devotional enough. In fact, Buddhism uses quite frequently more abstract-sounding terms than Reality, for instance, "suchness" or "thusness" (*tathatā*), "emptiness" or "void" (*śūnyatā*), "limit of reality" (*bhūtakoṭi*), etc. And this is sometimes what leads Christian critics and even Japanese scholars themselves to regard Zen as the teaching of a quietistic, meditative life. But with the followers of Zen these terms are not conceptual at all, but quite real and direct, vital and energizing—because Reality or Suchness or Emptiness is taken hold of in the midst of the concrete living facts of the universe, and not abstracted from them by means of thought.

Zen never leaves this world of facts. Zen always lives in the midst of realities. It is not for Zen to stand apart or keep itself away from a world of names and forms. If there is a God, personal or impersonal, he or it must be with Zen and in Zen. As long as an objective world, whether religiously or philosophically or poetically considered, remains a threatening and annihilating power, standing against us, there is no Zen here. For Zen makes "a humble blade of grass act as the Buddha-body sixteen feet high,[2] and, conversely, the Buddha-body sixteen feet high act as a humble blade of grass." Zen holds the whole universe, as it were, in its palm. This is the religion of Zen.

Zen is often thought to be a form of pantheism. Apparently it is, and Buddhists themselves sometimes ignorantly subscribe to this view. But if this is taken as truly characterizing the essence of Zen, it altogether misses the point; for Zen is most decidedly not pantheistic in the same measure as Christianity is not. Read this dialogue between Ummon and his disciple.

Monk: "What is the Pure Body of the Dharma?"

Master: "The hedgerow."

[2] The Buddha-body is traditionally regarded as gold-colored and sixteen feet in stature.

Monk: "What is the behavior of the one who thus understands?"
Master: "He is a golden-haired lion."[3]

When God is the hedgerow dividing the monastery grounds from the neighboring farms, there is perhaps a faint suggestion of pantheism, we may say. But what about the golden-haired lion? The animal is not a manifestation of anything else, he is supreme, is autonomous, he is king of the beasts, he is complete as he is. No idea is suggested here of the manifestation of anything in any form.

"The golden-haired lion," as it stands in Ummon's statement, may not be quite intelligible, even with this short explanatory comment, to those who are not used to the Zen way of expression. To help them I may quote another Zen *mondō*:

Monk: "I understand that when a lion seizes upon his opponent, whether it is a hare or an elephant, he makes an exhaustive use of his power. Pray tell me what this power is."

Master: "The spirit of sincerity" (literally, the power of not-deceiving).[4]

"Sincerity," that is, "not-deceiving" or "putting forth one's whole being," is, according to Rinzai,[5] "the whole being in action" (*zentai sayū*), in which nothing is kept in reserve, nothing is expressed under disguise, nothing goes to waste. When a person lives like this, he is said to be a golden-haired lion; he is the symbol of virility, sincerity, whole-heartedness; he is divinely human; he is not a manifestation but Reality itself, for he has nothing behind him, he is "the whole truth," "the very thing."

This Zen way of understanding life and the world must be distinctly comprehended, as it is important when later the fact is demonstrated that there is nothing of symbolism in the Japanese love of nature.

If it is necessary to apply to Zen some form of classification, Zen may be pronounced a polytheism, although this "many" (*polys*) is to be taken as corresponding to the "sands of the Gaṅgā."

---

[3] *Hekigan-shū*, case 39.

[4] "Transmission of the Lamp" (*Dentō-roku*), fasc. 27. The master's name is missing.

[5] *Sayings of Rinzai*. His analects known as the *Rinzai-roku* are considered by some the supreme specimen of Zen literature.

(*gaṅgānadīvālukā*). Not a few thousands of gods, but hundreds of thousands of *koṭis* of gods. In Zen, each individual is an absolute entity, and as such he is related to all other individuals: this nexus of infinite interrelationships is made possible in the realm of Emptiness because they all find their being here even as they are, that is, as individual realities. This may be difficult to grasp for those who are not trained in the Buddhist way of thinking. But I have here no time to stop and explain the whole system from its beginning, and I must hurry on to the main subject.

In short, Zen has its own way of handling Reality, and this Zen way of handling Reality constitutes the inner meaning of the Japanese love of Nature. For the Japanese love of Nature is not to be understood in the sense in which it is ordinarily understood. This will be made clearer as we proceed.

3

Zen is ascetic when it plays the role of a moral discipline in the sense that it aims at simplicity in all its forms. It has something of the stoicism in which the Samurai class of Japan has been reared. The simplicity and frugality of the Kamakura life under the Hōjō regime in the thirteenth century no doubt owes its initial motives to the influence of Zen. Furthermore, the moral courage and indomitable spirit of Hōjō Tokimune (1251–84), without whom the history of Japan would probably have taken quite a different course, were fostered by the teaching of Zen under the Chinese masters, who, by the invitation of the Hōjō government, found their shelter then in Japan. Tokiyori (1227–63), father of Tokimune, was also a great Zen devotee, and it was, indeed, under his direction that Tokimune visited the Zen monasteries, where he went through a moral and spiritual training, making himself thereby one of the greatest figures in the annals of Japan.

In Zen we find Chinese pragmatism solidly welded with Indian metaphysics and its high-soaring speculations. Without this perfect welding of the two highest forms of Oriental culture, it is very unlikely that Zen could have grown even in the congenial and, therefore, fruitful soil of Japan. And Zen came to Japan at the most opportune time in its history, because it was then that the old schools of Buddhism in Nara and Kyoto had proved ineffectual to usher in a new spiritual era. It was most fortunate for Zen that it found in the very beginning of its career in Japan such able disciples as Hōjō Tokiyori and Tokimune. So far, the meaning of the part the Hōjō family played in the cultural, political, and economic history of Japan has not been fully appreciated. This was chiefly due to those of militaristic bias, who tried to interpret history in their own crooked style. As Japanese scholars, however, begin to study it from a new point of view, which is now possible through the tragic experience of recent years, they will surely come to realize the significance of the Kamakura era, of which Yasutoki, Tokiyori, and Tokimune were the most remarkable representatives. And the significance of Zen in this period, as one of the most effective molding agencies of the Japanese character, will also be understood.

What is the most specific characteristic of Zen asceticism in connection with the Japanese love of Nature? It consists in paying Nature the fullest respect it deserves. By this it is meant that we may treat Nature not as an object to conquer and turn wantonly to our human service, but as a friend, as a fellow-being, who is destined like ourselves for Buddhahood. Zen wants us to meet Nature as a friendly, well-meaning agent whose inner being is thoroughly like our own, always ready to work in accord with our legitimate aspirations. Nature is never our enemy standing always against us in a threatening attitude; it is not a power which will crush us if we do not crush it, or bind it into our service.

Zen asceticism consists not necessarily in curbing or destroying our desires and instincts but in respecting Nature and not violating it, whether our own Nature or the Nature of the objective world. Self-mortification is not the proper attitude we may take toward ourselves, nor is selfish utilization the justifiable idea we may conceive toward Nature in any sense. Therefore, Zen asceticism is not at all in sympathy with the materialistic trends so much in evidence all over the world, in science, industrialism, commercialism, and many other movements of thought.

Zen proposes to respect Nature, to love Nature, to live its own life; Zen recognizes that our Nature is one with objective Nature, not in the mathematical sense, but in the sense that Nature lives in us and we in Nature. For this reason, Zen asceticism advocates simplicity, frugality, straightforwardness, virility, making no attempt to utilize Nature for selfish purposes.

Asceticism, some are afraid, lowers the standard of living. But, to speak candidly, the losing of the soul is more than the gaining of the world. Are we not constantly engaged in warlike preparations everywhere in order to raise or maintain our precious standard of living? If this state of affairs continues, there is no doubt of our finally destroying one another, not only individually but internationally. Instead of raising the so-called standard of living, will it not be far, far better to elevate the quality of living? This is a truism, but in no time of history has such a truism been more in need of being loudly declared than in these days of greed, jealousy, and iniquity. We followers of Zen ought to stand strongly for the asceticism it teaches.

4

[The aesthetic aspect of Zen teaching is closely related to Zen asceticism in that there is in both the absence of selfhood and the merging of subject and object in one absolute Emptiness (*śūnyatā*).] This is a strange saying, but, as the basic teaching of Zen, it is reiterated everywhere in Zen literature. To explain this is a great philosophical task, full of intellectual pitfalls. Not only does it require arduous and sustained thinking, but frequently this very thinking is apt to lead to grave misconceptions of the true meaning of Zen experience. Therefore, as already hinted, Zen avoids abstract statements and conceptual reasoning; and its literature is almost nothing but endless citations of the so-called "anecdotes" or "incidents" (*innen* in Japanese) of "questions-and-answers" (known as *mondō*). To those who have not been initiated into its mystery, it is a wild and unapproachable territory of briars and brambles. The Zen masters, however, are not yielding; they insist on having their own way of expressing themselves; they think that in this respect they know best, and they are in the right because the nature of their experience is determinative as regards their method of communication or demonstration. If I cite the following *mondō* to illustrate Zen aestheticism, I hope you will not take me as purposely mystifying my position.

While Rikkō, a high government official of the T'ang dynasty, had a talk with his Zen master Nansen,[6] the official quoted a saying of Sōjō,[7] a noted monk scholar of an earlier dynasty:

Heaven and earth and I are of the same root,
The ten-thousand things and I are of one substance

and continued, "Is not this a most remarkable statement?" Nansen called the attention of the visitor to the flowering plant in the garden and said, "People of the world look at these flowers as if they were in a dream."

This "story" or *mondō* eloquently describes the aesthetic attitude of Zen toward objects of Nature. Most people do not really know how to look at the flower; for one thing they stand away from it; they never grasp the spirit of it; as they have no firm hold of it, they are as if dreaming of a flower. The one who beholds is separated from the object which is beheld; there is an impassable gap between the two; and it is impossible for the beholder to come in touch inwardly with his object. Here is no grasping of actual facts as we face them. If heaven and earth, with all the manifold objects between them, issue from the one root which you and I also come from, this root must be firmly seized upon so that there is an actual experience of it; for it is in this experience that Nansen's flower in its natural beauty appealed to his aesthetic sense. The so-called Japanese love of Nature becomes related to Zen when we come to this experience of Nature appreciation, which is Nature living.

Here we must remember that the experience of mere oneness is not enough for the real appreciation of Nature. This no doubt gives a philosophical foundation to the sentimentalism of the Nature-loving Japanese, who are thus helped to enter deeply into the secrets of their own aesthetic consciousness. Sentimentalism to that extent is purified, one may say. But the feeling of love is possible in a world of multiplicity; Nansen's remark falls flat where there is only sameness. It is true that people of the world are

---

[6] *Hekigan-shū*, case 40.

[7] Sōjō (384–414). Sōjō, one of the four principal disciples of Kumārajīva (who came from Kucha, Central Asia, to Chang-an, China, in 401), wrote several essays on Buddhism. The quotation is from one of them. Its source is in the *Chuang-tzŭ*, II.

dreaming, because they do not see into the real foundation of existence. The balancing of unity and multiplicity or, better, the merging of self with others as in the philosophy of the Avataṃsaka (Kegon) is absolutely necessary to the aesthetic understanding of Nature.

Tennyson says:

> Little flower—but if I could understand
> What you are, root and all, and all in all,
> I should know what God and man is.

The beauty of the little flower in the crannied wall is really appreciated only when it is referred to the ultimate reason of all things. But it goes without saying that this is not to be done in a merely philosophical and conceptual way, but in the way Zen proposes to accomplish it: not in a pantheistic way, nor in a quietistic way, but in the "living" way as has been done by Nansen and his followers. To do this and to appreciate Nansen truly, one must first greet Rikkō and be friendly with him; for it is in this way that one can feel the force of the remark made by Nansen. The genuine beauty of the flower as he saw it is for the first time reflected in one's soul-mirror.

The aesthetic appreciation of Nature always involves something religious. And by being "religious" I mean being "superworldly," going beyond the world of relativity, where we are bound to encounter oppositions and limitations. The oppositions and limitations which confront every movement of ours, physical and psychological, put a stop, also, to the free flow of our aesthetical feeling toward its objects. Beauty is felt when there is freedom of motion and freedom of expression. Beauty is not in form but in the meaning it expresses, and this meaning is felt when the observing subject throws his whole being into the bearer of the meaning and moves along with it. This is possible only when he lives in a "superworld" where no mutually excluding oppositions of which we are always too conscious in this world of multiplicities are taken up even as they are into something of a higher order than they. Aestheticism now merges into religion.

Sir George Sansom makes this comment concerning the Zen love of Nature (*Japan, A Short Cultural History*, p. 392): "But the Zen artists and the Zen poets—and it is often hard to say where their poetry ends and their painting begins—feel no antithesis between man and Nature, and are conscious even of an identity rather than a kinship. What interests them is not the restless movement on the surface of life, but (as Professor Anezaki puts it) the eternal tranquillity seen through and behind change." This is not Zen at all. Both Professor Anezaki and Sir George Sansom fail to grasp the true Zen attitude toward Nature. It is not an experience of identification, nor is it the feeling of "eternal tranquillity" they dream of. If the poets and the artists linger with that which is felt "through and behind change," they are still walking hand in hand with Rikkō and Sōjō, they are far, far from being friends of Nansen. The real flower is enjoyed only when the poet-artist lives with it, in it; and when even a sense of identity is no longer here, much less the "eternal tranquillity."

Thus I wish to emphasize that Zen does not see any such thing as is designated "the restless movement on the surface of life." For life is one integral and indivisible whole, with neither surface nor interior; hence no "restless movement" which can be separated from life itself. As was explained in the case of Ummon's "golden-haired lion," life moves in its complete oneness, whether restlessly or serenely, as you may conceive it; your interpretation does not alter the fact. Zen takes hold of life in its wholeness and moves "restlessly" with it or stays quietly with it. Wherever there is any sign of life at all, there is Zen. When, however, the "eternal tranquillity" is abstracted from "the restless movement on the surface of life," it sinks into death, and there is no more of its "surface" either. The tranquillity of Zen is in the midst of "the boiling oil," the surging waves, and in the flames enveloping the god Acala.

Kanzan was one of the most famous poet lunatics of the T'ang dynasty—Zen often produces such "lunatics"—and one of his poems reads:

> My mind is like the autumnal moon;
> And how clear and transparent the deep pool!
> No comparison, however, in any form is possible,
> It is altogether beyond description.

Superficially, this poem may suggest the idea of tranquillity or serenity. The autumnal moon is serene, and its light uniformly pervading the fields and rivers and mountains may make us think of the oneness of things. But this is where Kanzan hesitates to draw any comparison between his feelings and things of this world. The reason is sure to take the pointing finger for the moon, as our worthy critics frequently do. To tell the truth, there is here not the remotest hint of tranquillity or serenity, nor of the identity of Nature and man. If anything is suggested here, it is the idea of utmost transparency which the poet feels through and through. He is entirely lifted out of his bodily existence, including both his objective world and his subjective mind. He has no such interfering mediums inside and outside. He is thoroughly pure, and from this position of absolute purity or transparency he looks out on a world of multiplicity so called. He sees flowers and mountains and ten thousand other things, and will pronounce them beautiful and satisfying. "The restless movements" are appreciated just as much as "the eternal tranquillity." It goes entirely against the spirit of Zen and the Japanese idea of love of Nature to imagine that the Japanese Zen poets and artists avoid the restlessness of a world of multiplicity in order to get into the eternal tranquillity of abstract ideas. Let us first get an experience of transparency, and we are able to love Nature and its multifarious objects, though not dualistically. As long as we harbor conceptual illusions arising from the separation of subject and object and believe them final, the transparency is obscured, and our love of Nature is contaminated with dualism and sophistry.

To quote another poet of Zen, this time a Japanese and the founder of a great Zen monastery called Eigenji in the province of Ōmi—his name is Jakushitsu (1290–1367):

> The wind stirs the flying waterfall and sends in refreshing
>   music;
> The moon is risen over the opposite peak and the bamboo
>   shadows are cast over my paper window:
> As I grow older, the mountain retreat appeals all the more
>   strongly to my feeling;
> Even when I am buried, after death, underneath the rock,
>   my bones will be as thoroughly transparent as ever.

Some readers may be tempted to read into this poem a sense of solitude or quietness, but that this altogether misses the point is apparent to those who know at all what Zen is. Unless the Zen artist is saturated with the feeling Jakushitsu graphically expresses here, he cannot expect to understand Nature, nor can he truly love Nature. Transparency is the keynote to the Zen understanding of Nature, and it is from this that its love of Nature starts. When people say that Zen has given a philosophical and religious foundation to the Japanese love of Nature, this Zen attitude or feeling must be taken fully into consideration. When Sir George Sansom surmises that "they [aristocrats, monks, and artists] were moved by a belief that all Nature is permeated by one spirit," and that "it was the aim of the Zen practitioner in particular, by purging his mind of egotistic commotions, to reach a tranquil, intuitive realization of his identity with the universe," he ignores the part Zen has really contributed to the Japanese aesthetic appreciation of Nature. He cannot shake off the idea of "eternal tranquillity" or of a spiritual identity between subject and object.

The idea of "spiritual identity" by which our egotistic commotions are kept quiet and in which eternal tranquillity is experienced is an alluring idea. Most students of Oriental culture and philosophy grasp at it as giving them the key to the inscrutable psychology of the Eastern peoples. But this is the Western mind trying to solve the mystery in its own way—in fact, it cannot do anything else. As far as we Japanese are concerned, we are unable to accept without comment this interpretation offered by the Western critics. Plainly speaking, Zen does not acknowledge "one spirit" permeating all Nature, nor does it attempt to realize identity by purging its mind of "egotistic commotions." According to the author of this statement, the grasping of "one spirit" is evidently the realization of identity that is left behind when the purgation of egotism is effected. While it is difficult to refute this idea convincingly as long as we are arguing along the logical line of Yes and No, I will try to make my point clearer in the following paragraphs.

5

It is now necessary to say something about Zen epistemology. The term may sound too philosophical, but my object here is to make some plain statements about the facts of Zen intuition. What Zen is most anxious to do in its own characterization is to reject conceptual mediumship of any kind. Any medium that is set up before Zen in its attempt to understand the facts of experience is sure to obscure the nature of the latter. Instead of clarifying or simplifying the situation, the presence of a third party always ends in creating complexities and obscurations. Zen therefore abhors mediums. It advises its followers to have direct dealings with their objects, whatever they may be. We often speak of identification in our Zen discipline, but this word is not exact. Identification presupposes original opposition of two terms, subject and object, but the truth is that from the very first there are no two opposing terms whose identification is to be achieved by Zen. It is better to say that there has never been any separation between subject and object, and that all the discrimination and separation we have or, rather, make are later creations, though the concept of time is not to be interposed here. The aim of Zen is thus to restore the experience of original inseparability, which means, in other words, to return to the original state of purity and transparency. This is the reason conceptual discrimination is discredited in Zen. Followers of identity and tranquillity are to be given the warning: they are ridden by concepts; let them rise to facts and live in and with them.

Chōsha,[8] of the T'ang dynasty, one day came back from a walk in the mountains. When he reached the monastery gate, the head monk asked, "Where have you been all this time, Reverend Sir?"

Replied the master, "I am just back from my mountain walk."

The monk pursued, "Where in the mountains?"

"I first went out in the field scented with grasses and then walked home watching the flowers fall."

Is there any expression here suggestive of "tranquillity that is behind and through change"? or of identity that is perceptible between Chōsha and the grasses and flowers among which he walked up and down?

Chōsha one evening was enjoying the moonlight with his friend Kyōzan.[9] Kyōzan, pointing at the moon, said, "Each person without exception has this, only that he fails to use it." (Is this a suggestion of "one spirit" or of "tranquillity"?)

[8] That is, Chōsha Keishin, a disciple of Nansen. The story is from the *Hekigan-shū*, case 36.

[9] Kyōzan Ejaku was a disciple of Isan Reiyū. *Ibid.*, Engo's notes.

Chōsha said, "Just as you say; and may I ask you to use it?" (As long as "identity" or "tranquillity" blinds your eyesight, how can you "use" it?)

Kyōzan: "Let me see how you use it." (Did he then enter into Nirvana eternally serene?)

Chōsha then kicked his brother monk down to the ground. Kyōzan, quietly rising, remarked, "O brother monk, you are indeed like a tiger." (When this tiger, like the golden-haired lion, roars, one ghostly "spirit" so valued by the critics vanishes, and "tranquillity" is no more.)

A strange yet lively scene enacted by the Zen poets, who were supposed to be enjoying the serenity of a moonlit eve, makes us pause and think about the significance of Zen in regard to its relation to the Japanese love of Nature. What is really here that stirs up the two apparently meditative and nature-loving monks?

The epistemology of Zen is, therefore, not to resort to the mediumship of concepts. If you want to understand Zen, understand it right away without deliberation, without turning your head this way or that. For while you are doing this, the object you have been seeking for is no longer there. This doctrine of immediate grasping is characteristic of Zen. If the Greeks taught us how to reason and Christianity what to believe, it is Zen that teaches us to go beyond logic and not to tarry even when we come up against "the things which are not seen." For the Zen point of view is to find an absolute point where no dualism in whatever form obtains. Logic starts from the division of subject and object, and belief distinguishes between what is seen and what is not seen. The Western mode of thinking can never do away with this eternal dilemma, this or that, reason or faith, man or God, etc. With Zen all these are swept aside as something veiling our insight into the nature of life and reality. Zen leads us into a realm of Emptiness or Void where no conceptualism prevails, where rootless trees grow and a most refreshing breeze sweeps over all the ground.

From this short characterization of Zen we can see what Zen's attitude toward Nature is. It is not a sense of identity nor of tranquillity that Zen sees and loves in Nature. Nature is always in motion, never at a standstill; if Nature is to be loved, it must be caught while moving and in this way its aesthetic value must be appraised. To seek tranquillity is to kill Nature, to stop its pulsation, and to embrace the dead corpse that is left behind. Advocates of tranquillity are worshipers of abstraction and death. There is nothing in this to love. Identity is also a static condition and decidedly associated with death. When we are dead, we return to the dust where we started, we are then identified with the earth. Identification is not the thing to covet highly. Let us destroy all such artificial barriers we put up between Nature and ourselves, for it is only when they are removed that we see into the living heart of Nature and live with it—which is the real meaning of love. For this, therefore, the clearing away of all conceptual scaffolds is imperative. When Zen speaks of transparency, it means this clearing away, this thorough wiping of the surface of the mind-mirror. But, in point of fact, the mirror has never been obscured, and no need has ever been felt for wiping it clean; but because of such notions as identity, tranquillity, one spirit, egotistic commotions, and so on, we are compelled to set up a general sweeping operation.

After these interpretations, some may declare Zen to be a form of Nature mysticism, a philosophical intuitionalism, and a religion advocating stoical simplicity and austerity. However this is, Zen gives us a most comprehensive outlook on the world, because the realm of Zen extends to the very limits of thousands of *koṭis* of chiliacosms, and even beyond them all. Zen has a most penetrating insight into Reality, because it sounds the very depths of all existence. Zen knows a most thoroughgoing way of appreciating the genuinely beautiful, because it lives in the body of the beautiful itself, known as the golden-colored Buddha-body with the thirty-two major and eighty minor marks of superhumanity. With these as the background, the Japanese love of Nature unfolds itself as it comes in contact with its objects.

WRITINGS IN ENGLISH

OF

DAISETZ T. SUZUKI

Writings in English
of
Daisetz T. Suzuki[1]

I. Original Works

1. *Outlines of Mahayana Buddhism*
   London: Luzac & Co., 1907.
2. *A Brief History of Early Chinese Philosophy*
   London: Probsthain, 1914.
3. *Essays in Zen Buddhism, First Series*
   London: Luzac & Co., 1927.
   Republished: London: Rider & Co., 1949, 1958.
4. *Studies in the Laṅkāvatāra Sūtra*
   London: George Routledge & Son, 1930.
   Republished: 1958.
5. *Essays in Zen Buddhism, Second Series*
   London: Luzac & Co., 1933.
   Republished: London: Rider & Co., 1950, 1958.
6. *Essays in Zen Buddhism, Third Series*
   London: Luzac & Co., 1934.
   Republished: London: Rider & Co., 1953, 1958.
7. *The Training of the Zen Buddhist Monk*
   Kyoto: Eastern Buddhist Society, 1934.
8. *Index Verborum to the Laṅkāvatāra Sūtra*
   (Sanskrit-Chinese-Tibetan, Chinese-Sanskrit, and Tibetan-Sanskrit)
   Kyoto: The Sanskrit Buddhist Texts Publishing Society, 1934.
9. *An Introduction to Zen Buddhism*
   Kyoto: Eastern Buddhist Society, 1934.
   Republished: London: Rider & Co., 1949, 1957, 1960.

[1] For a more complete listing consult *A Bibliography on Japanese Buddhism*, edited by Bandō, S., *et. al.*, Tokyo, 1958.

10. *Manual of Zen Buddhism*
    Kyoto: Eastern Buddhist Society, 1935.
    Republished: London: Rider & Co., 1950, 1956.
11. *Buddhist Philosophy and Its Effects on the Life and Thought of the Japanese People*
    Tokyo: Kokusai Bunka Shinkōkai, 1936.
12. *Outline of Japanese Buddhism*
    Tokyo: International Buddhist Society, 1937.
13. *Japanese Buddhism*
    Tokyo: Board of Tourist Library, 1938.
14. *Zen Buddhism and Its Influence on Japanese Culture*
    Kyoto: Eastern Buddhist Society, 1938.
    Revised and republished as *Zen and Japanese Culture*
    Bollingen Series LXIV, New York, Pantheon Books Inc., 1959.
15. *The Essence of Buddhism*, Imperial Lectures
    London: Buddhist Society, 1947.
    Kyoto: Hōzōkan, 1948.
16. *Living by Zen*
    Tokyo: Sanseido, 1949.
    Republished: London: Rider & Co., 1950.
17. *A Miscellany on the Shin Teaching of Buddhism*
    Kyoto: Higashi-Hongwanji, 1949.
18. *The Zen Doctrine of No-Mind*
    London: Rider & Co., 1949, 1958.
19. *Studies in Zen*
    London: Rider & Co., 1955, 1957.
20. *Zen Buddhism*
    New York: Anchor Doubleday, 1956.
21. *Mysticism: Christian and Buddhist*
    New York: Harper & Bros., 1957.
22. *Zen and Japanese Buddhism*
    Tokyo: Japan Tourist Bureau, 1958.

II. Translations

1. *The Laṅkāvatāra Sūtra*
   (Original Sanskrit text into English)
   London: George Routledge & Son, 1932.

2. *Asvaghosha's Discourse on the Awakening of Faith in the Mahayana*
   (From Chinese into English)
   Chicago: Open Court Publishing Co., 1900.
3. *Sermons of a Buddhist Abbot*
   (From the Japanese into English)
   Chicago: Open Court Publishing Co., 1906.

III. Essay Contributions

1. *Studies on Buddhism in Japan,* "Some Aspects of Zen Buddhism; illustrated by selections from the Hekiganshū, 'the first book of the Zen school of Buddhism' " Tokyo: 1939, Vol. I, pp. 1–35.
2. *History of Philosophy Eastern and Western,* "Japanese Thought" London: Allen & Unwin Ltd., 1952, Vol. II, pp. 596–606.
3. *Moral Principles of Action,* Edited by Ruth Nanda Anshen, "Ethics and Zen Buddhism"
   New York: Harper & Bros., 1952, pp. 606–614.
4. *Symbols and Values: An Initial Study,* 13th Symposium of the Conference in Science, Philosophy and Religion, "Buddhism and Symbolism"
   New York: Harper & Bros., 1954, pp. 149–154.
5. *Natural Law Institute Proceedings,* 1951, Vol. V, at the University of Notre Dame, "The Natural Law in the Buddhist Tradition"
   Indiana: University of Notre Dame Press, 1953, pp. 91–115.
6. *Philosophy East and West,* Edited by Charles A. Moore, "An Interpretation of Zen-Experience"
   New Jersey: Princeton University Press, 1944, 1946, pp. 109–129.
7. *Essays in East-West Philosophy,* Edited by Charles A. Moore, "Reason and Intuition in Buddhist Philosophy"
   Honolulu: Hawaii University Press, 1951, pp. 17–48.
8. *Eranos Jahrbuch XXII,* "The Role of Nature in Zen Buddhism" Zurich: Rhein-Verlag, 1953, pp. 291–321.
9. *Eranos Jahrbuch XXIII,* "The Awakening of a New Consciousness in Zen"
   Zurich: Rhein-Verlag, 1954, pp. 275–305.

10. *Modern Trends in World Religions,* Edited by J. M. Kitagawa,
    "Zen Buddhism"
    Open Court Publishing Co., 1959, pp. 261–279.
11. *New Knowledge in Human Values,* Edited by A. H. Maslow,
    "Human Values in Zen"
    New York: Harper & Bros. 1959, pp. 94–105.
12. *Zen Buddhism and Psychoanalysis,* Edited by Erich Fromm,
    "Lectures on Zen Buddhism"
    New York: Harper & Bros., 1960, pp. 1–76.

IV. Articles in Journals

1. *Monumenta Nipponica,* "Zen Buddhism," Vol. I, No. 1, 1938,
   pp. 48–57.
2. *Philosophy East and West,* "The Philosophy of Zen," Vol. I,
   No. 2, July, 1951, pp. 3–15.
3. *Philosophy East and West,* "Zen—a Reply to Hu-Shih," Vol. III,
   No. 1, April, 1953, pp. 25–46.
4. *Philosophy East and West,* "Zen and Pragmatism—A Reply,"
   Vol. IV, No. 2, July, 1954, pp. 167–74.
5. *Review of Religion,* "Enlightenment," Vol. XVIII, March, 1954,
   No. 3–4, pp. 133–44.
6. *Japan Quarterly,* "The Oriental Way of Thinking," Vol. II, No.
   1, January–March, 1955, pp. 51–58.
7. *Japan Quarterly,* "Zen in the Modern World," Vol. V, No. 4,
   October–December, 1958, pp. 452–61.
8. *Art News Annual,* "Sengai: Zen and Art," Vol. XXVII, 1958, pp.
   114–20 continued pp. 193–96.
9. *Evergreen Review,* "Aspects of Japanese Culture," Vol. II, No.
   6, Autumn, 1958, pp. 40–56.

Glossary

NOTE

This glossary of names and terms in Japanese or Chinese with their respective equivalents has been especially prepared for this volume by Dr. Daisetz Suzuki and his associates as a further aid to the reader.

LIST OF NAMES AND TERMS IN JAPANESE OR CHINESE

WITH THEIR RESPECTIVE EQUIVALENTS INCLUDED IN

BRACKETS

"A"

1. Amaterasu Ōmikami　天照大神

2. Anezaki Masaharu　姉崎正治

3. Ashikaga Yoshimasa　足利義政

"B"

4. Baen
   [Ma Yüan]　馬遠

5. Banzan Hōjaku
   [P'an-shan Pao-chi]　盤山寶積

6. Bashō　芭蕉

7. Baso Dōichi
   [Ma-tsu Tao-i]　馬祖道一

8. Bodai-daruma
   [P'u-ti Ta-mo]　菩提達磨

9. Bokujū Chin Sonshiku
   [Mu-chou Chên Tsun-su]　睦州陳尊宿

10. *bonnō*
    [*fan-nao*]　煩惱

11. Bucchō 佛頂

12. *buji*
[*wu-shih*] 無事

13. Bukkō Kokushi
[Fu-kuang Kuo-shih] 佛光國師

14. Bukkoku Kokushi 佛國國師

15. Bunan Zenji
(Shidō Bunan) 無難禪師（至道無難）

16. *buppō*
[*fu-fa*] 佛法

17. Busseki Ian Shin
[Fu-chi I-an Chèn] 佛蹟頤庵眞

18. *byōdō*
[*p'ing-têng*] 平等

19. *byōdō soku shabetsu*
[*p'ing-têng chi ch'a-pieh*] 平等卽差別

"C"

20. Chang-an
[Chōan] 長安

21. *ch'an-na*
[*zenna*] 禪那

22. *cha-no-yu* 茶ノ湯

23. Chê-chiang
[Sekkō] 浙江

24. Chên-kuan, period of T'ang
[Teikan] 貞觀

25. Chia-hsing
[Kakō] 嘉興

26. Chiang-ning [Kōnei] 江寧

27. Ch'i-chou [Kishū] 蘄州

28. Chigi [Chih-i] 智顗

29. chih [chi] 知

30. chih-mo [chimo] 只麼

31. Chikō [Chih-huang] 智隍

32. Chimon Kōso [Chih-mên Kuang-tsu] 智門光祚

33. chin [kin] 斤

34. Ch'ing, district of [Seishū] 青（青州）

35. Ch'ing-p'ing Ling-tsun [Seihei Reishun] 清平令遵

36. Chin-shan [Kinzan] 金山

37. chiu [sake] 酒

38. Chiyaku Sanzō [Chih-yüeh San-ts'ang] 智藥三藏

39. chi-yüan [kien] 機緣汁

40. Chōben [Chao-pien] 趙汴

41. Chōkei Eryō
[Ch'ang-ch'ing Hui-lêng]　慧　慶　長　稜規

42. *Chokushu Shingi*
[Chih-hsiu Ching-kuei]　勅　修　清　規

43. Chōsetsu
[Chang-shuo]　張　説

44. Chōsha Keishin
[Ch'ang-sha Ching-ch'ên]　長　沙　景　岑

45. Chū the National Teacher (Chū Kokushi)
[Chung Kuo-shih]　忠 (忠國師)

46. *ch'uan*
[aegu]　喘

47. Chuang-tzŭ
[Sōji]　莊　子

48. *chüeh-kuan*
[kakkan, kakkwan]　覺　觀

49. *ch'ü-hsiang*
[shukō]　趣　向

50. Chung-tsung, Emperor
[Chūsō]　中　宗

"D"

51. *Daie Fusetsu*
[Ta-hui P'u-shuo]　大　慧　普　説

52. Daie Sōkō
[Ta-hui Tsung-kao]　大　慧　宗　杲

53. *daigi*
[ta-i]　大　疑

54. Daigu Shūshi
[Ta-yü Shou-chih]　大　愚　守　芝

55. *Daihishu*
[*Ta-pei-chou*]
大悲呪

56. Daiju Ekai
[Ta-chu Hui-hai]
大珠慧海

57. *daimoku*
大題目

58. Dai-ō Kokushi
大應國師

59. Daitō Kokushi
大燈國師

60. Daitokuji
大德寺

61. *Dentō-roku*
[*Ch'uan-têng Lu*]
傳燈錄

62. *Dōfuku*
[Tao-fu]
道副

63. Dōgen (Japanese)
道元

64. Dōgen (Chinese)
[Tao-yüan]
道原

65. Dōgo Enchi
[Tao-wu Yüan-chih]
道悟圓智

66. Dōiku
[Tao-yü]
道育

67. *dōka*
道歌

68. Dōkan
[Tao-huan]
道桓

69. Dōkō
[Tao-kuang]
道光

70. Dokuhō Kizen
[Tu-fêng Chi-shan]　　毒峯季善

71. Donrin
[T'an-lin]　　曇琳

72. Dōsen
[Tao-hsüan]　　道宣

73. Dōshin
[Tao-hsin]　　道信

"E"

74. Eigenji　　永源寺

75. Eisai　　榮西

76. Ejō (Nangaku)
[Huai-jang] (Nan-yüeh)　　懷讓（南嶽）

77. Eka
[Hui-k'o]　　慧可

78. Engakuji　　圓覺寺

79. Engo Bukkwa
[Yüan-wu Fu-kuo]　　圓悟佛果

80. Enkan Saian
[Yen-kuan Ch'i-an]　　塩官齊安

81. Enō
[Hui-nêng]　　慧能寺

82. Erinji
[Hui-lin-ssŭ]　　慧林

83. Eshō, period of T'ang
[Hui-ch'ang]　　會昌

98. Genjō (Genjō Sanzo)
[Hsüan-tsang]
(Hsüan-tsang San-ts'ang)
玄 奘 （玄奘三藏）

99. Genkaku
[Hsüan-chiao]
玄 覺

100. Gensaku
[Hsüan-t'sê]
玄 策

101. Gensha Shibi
[Hsüan-sha Shih-pei]
玄 沙 師 備

102. geta
下 駄

103. gi
[i]
疑

104. gidan
[i-t'uan]
疑 團

105. gijō
[i-ch'ing]
疑 情

106. Godaigo, Emperor
後 醍 醐 天 皇

107. Gojō, Bridge
五 條 陽

108. Gonyō
[Yen-yang]
嚴 陽

109. goroku
[yü-lu]
語 録

110. Goso Hōen
[Wu-tsu Fa-yen]
五 祖 法 演

111. Goyōzei, Emperor
後 陽 成 天 皇

112. Gozuzen
[Niu-t'ou Ch'an]
牛 頭 禪

113. Gunin
[Hung-jên]　弘忍

114. Gutei
[Chü-chih]　俱胝

115. Gyōshi Seigen
[Hsing-szǔ Ch'ing-yüan]　行思青原

"H"

116. Hagakure　葉隠

117. *haiku*　俳句

118. Hakuin Ekaku　白隠慧鶴

119. Hakuzan Oshō
[Po-shan Ho-shang]　博山和尚

120. *Hakuzan Oshō Sanzen Keigo*
[*Po-shan Ho-shang San-ch'an
Ching-yü*]　博山和尚参禅警語

121. Hanazono, Emperor　花園天皇

122. *hannya-haramitsu*
[*pan-jo-po-lo-mi*]　般若波羅密

123. Han-shang
[Kanjō]　漢上和尚

124. Heiden Oshō
[P'ing-t'ien Ho-shang]　平田和尚

125. *Hekigan-shū*
[*Pi-yen Chi*]　碧巖集

126. *hen*　偏

127. Hirosawa, Pond of 廣澤

128. Hōen Gosozan
(*See* Goso Hōen)

129. Hofuku Jūten 保福從展益欽宗賴時
[Pao-fu Ts'ung-chan]

130. Hōgen Moneki 法眼文
[Fa-yen Wên-i]

131. Hōji Bunkin 報慈文士勇
[Pao-tz'ŭ Wên-ch'in]

132. Hōjō Tokimune 北條時仁

133. Hōjō Tokiyori 北條時寺

134. Hōjō Yasutoki 北條泰

135. Hokke 法華居
[Fa-hua]

136. Hō-koji 龐居寧
[P'ang Chü-shih]

137. Honei Ninyū 保寧心
[Pao-ning Jên-yung]

138. *honshin* 本隆

139. Hōryūji 法

140. Hōsen
(*See* Shōsan Butsue Hōsen)

141. Hōshi 保誌
[Pao-chih]

142. *hōshin*
[*fang-hsin*]
放 心

143. *hossu*
[*fu-tzǔ*]
拂 子

144. Hōun Roso (zan)
[Pao-yün Lu-tsu] (shan)
寶 雲 魯 祖 (山)

145. Hōyū (Gozu Hōyū)
[Fa-yung] (Niu-t'ou Fa-yung)
法 融 (牛頭法融)

146. Hsien-tsung, Emperor
[Kensō]
憲 宗

147. *hsin*
[*kokoro, shin*]
心

148. Hsin-chou
[Shinshū]
新 州

149. *Hsin-hsin-ming*
[*Shinjinmei*]
信 心 銘

150. Hsing
[Sei]
姓

151. *hsing*
[*shō*]
性

152. Huang-ho (lou)
[Kōkaku] (rō)
黃 鶴 (樓)

153. Huang-mei Shan
[Ōbaisan]
黃 梅 山

154. *hua-t'ou*
[*watō*]
話 頭

155. *Hui-yüan Hsü-lioh*
[*Egen Zokuryaku*]
會 元 續 略

156. Hu-pei, district of
[Kohaku]
湖 北

157. Hyakujō Ekai
[Pai-chang Huai-hai]　海槃 懷涅 大大 百

158. Hyakujō Nehan
[Pai-chang Nieh-p'an]　百

"I"

159. *i*
[*gi*]　義

160. Ian Shin Busseki
(*See* Busseki Ian Shin)

161. *ichinen*
[*i-nien*]　念情 一

162. *i-ch'ing*
[*gijō*]　疑

163. Ieyasu, Shrine　家 康鳳

164. I-fêng
[*Gihō*]　儀 休

165. Ikkyū Sōjun　一 緣 宗 純

166. *innen*
[*yin-yüan*]　因 那

167. Ino
[*Wei-na*]　維 宗

168. Inshū
[*Yin-tsung*]　印 山

169. Isan Reiyū
[*Wei-shan Ling-yu*]　潙 心 靈 祐

170. *isshin*
[*i-hsin*]　一

"J"

171. *jaku* 寂

172. Jakushitsu 寂室

173. *jên*
    [*jin*] 仁

174. *ji*
    [*shih*] 事

175. *Ji*, Sect (Ji-shū) 時（時宗）

176. Jinne
    [Shên-hui] 神會

177. Jinshū
    [Shên-hsiu] 神秀

178. *jiriki* 自力

179. Jittoku
    [Shih-tê] 拾得

180. Jō (Jō-jōza)
    [Ting] (Ting Shang-tso) 定（定上座）

181. Jōdo
    [Ching-t'u] 淨土

182. Jōfukyō Bosatsu
    [Ch'ang-pu-ch'ing P'u-sa] 常不輕菩薩

183. Jōkyō
    [Ching-kung] 淨恭

184. Jō-ō 紹鷗

185. Jōrinji
    [Ting-lin-ssŭ] 定林寺

186. Jōshū Jūshin
[Chao-chou Ts'ung-shên]　趙州從諗

"K"

187. *Kai-an-koku Go*　槐安國語

188. Kaisū
[Ch'i-sung]　契嵩

189. *k'ai-wu*
[*kaigo*]　開悟

190. *kakemono*　掛物

191. Kamakura, period　鎌倉

192. *kan*
[*k'an*]　看

193. *kanmi*　甘味

194. Kanzan
[Han-shan]　寒山

195. Kanzan Kokushi　關山國師

196. *Kanzan Shi*
[*Han-shan Shih*]　寒山詩

197. Kegon
[Hua-yen]　華嚴

198. *kei*
[*ching*]　敬

199. Kei, the librarian
[Ch'ing]　慶

200. Keishin
(*See* Chōsha Keishin)

201. Keisō
[Ch'i-ch'ung]
契宗

202. *kenshō*
[*chien-hsing*]
見性

203. Kensu Oshō
[Hsien-tzǔ Ho-shang]
蜆子和尚

204. *kesa*
[*chia-sha*]
袈裟

205. *kinhin*
[*ching-hsing*]
經行

206. *ko*
[*chü*]
舉

207. Kō (Kō-koji)
[Hsiang] (Hsiang Chü-shih)
向 (向居士)

208. *kōan*
[*kung-an*]
公案

209. Koboku Gen
[K'u-mu Yüan]
枯木元

210. Kōhō Gemmyō
[Kao-fêng Yüan-miao]
高峰原妙

211. Koin Jōkin
[Ku-yin Ching-ch'in]
古音淨琴

212. *kokoro*
(See *hsin*)

213. *kokoro wo tomeru*
心ヲ止メル

214. Kōrin
[Hsiang-lin]
香林

215. *koromo*
衣

216. Kōshōji
興聖寺

217. Kōshū Tenryū
[Hang-chou T'ien-lung]
龍 天 州 杭

218. *ku*
[*chü*]
句

219. Kuang-chou
[Kōshū]
州 廣

220. *kufū*
[*kung-fu*]
夫 工

221. Kūkoku Keiryō
[K'ung-ku Ching-lung]
隆 景 谷 空

222. *kung-fu*
(See *kufū*)

223. Kwannon, Kannon
[Kuan-yin]
音 觀

224. *kwatz!*
[*ho!*]
喝

225. Kyōgen Chikan
[Hsiang-yen Chih-hsien]
閑 智 嚴 香
寂 慧 山 仰

226. Kyōzan Ejaku
[Yang-shan Hui-chi]

"L"

227. *Lao-shang-shih*
[*Rōshōshi*]
氏 商 老

228. Lao-tzŭ
[Rōshi]
子 老

229. Liang-k'ai
[Ryōkai]
楷 梁

230. Li-chou
[Reishū]
州 澧

231. Lieh-tzŭ
[Resshi]
子 列

232. *Lin-chi Lu*
   [*Rinzai-roku*]
   臨濟録

233. Li-yang, district of
   [Reiyō]
   澧陽山

234. Lu, Mount
   [Rozan]
   盧山

235. *lu*
   [*roku*]
   録

236. Lung-t'an
   (*See* Ryūtan)

"M"

237. *mai*
   [*mei*]
   昧

238. *mien-pi*
   [*mempeki*]
   面壁

239. Minamoto Sanetomo
   源實朝

240. Mino, Province
   美濃

241. *mokugyo*
   [*mu-yü*]
   木魚

242. *Momo wa yō-yō tari*
   桃八天 夭タリ

   Sono hana shaku-shaku tari
   其華灼 灼タリ

243. *mondō*
   [*wên-ta*]
   問答

244. Monju
   [Wên-shu]
   文殊

245. *mōshin*
   [*wang-hsin*]
   妄心

246.	*mu* [*wu*]	無			
247.	Mu-ch'i [Mokkei]	牧	溪		
248.	*mui* [*wu-wei*]	無	爲		
249.	Mujaku [Wu-chu]	無	著		
250.	Mumon Ekai [Wu-mên Hui-k'ai]	無	門	慧	開
251.	*mumyō* [*wu-ming*]	無	明		
252.	*munen* [*wu-nien*]	無	念		
253.	*mushin* [*wu-hsin*]	無	心		
254.	*mushin no shin*	無	心 ， 心		
255.	Musō Kokushi	夢 窓 國 師（夢窓疎石			
256.	*myō* [*miao*]	妙			
257.	Myō-jōza [Ming Shang-tso]	明	上	座	
258.	Myōshinji	妙	心	寺	
259.	Myōsō (Myōsō Zennin) [Miao-tsung] (Miao-tsung Ch'an-jên)	妙	總（妙總禪人		

"N"

| 260. | *Nabeshima Rongo* | 鍋 | 島 | 論 | 語 |

261. Nakano Kazuma 中野數馬

262. *Nambō-roku* 南坊録

263. *namu-amida-butsu* 南無阿彌陀佛

264. Nangaku Ejō
[Nan-yüeh Huai-jang] 南嶽懷讓

265. Nan-in Egu
[Nan-yüan Hui-yung] 南院慧顒

266. Nansen Fugwan
[Nan-ch'üan P'u-yüan] 南泉普願

267. Nan-yang
[Nanyō] 南陽

268. Narenyasha
[Na-lien-yeh-shê] 那連耶舍

269. *nazuna* 薺

270. *nembutsu*
[*nien-fu*] 念佛

271. Nichiren 日蓮

272. *nien-fu*
(See *nembutsu*)

273. *niu*
[*gyū*] 牛

274. *nyūnan-shin*
[*jou-juan-hsin*] 柔軟心

"O"

275. Ōbaku Kiun
[Huang-po Hsi-yün] 黃蘗希運

276. ōbō 王法

277. Ogasawara, School 小笠原流

278. ohachi 鉢

279. Om, Ma-ku-ra-sai, Svāhā 唵摩休羅細婆婆訶
[Om, Mo-hsiu-lo-hsi, Svāhā]

280. omou 思

281. omowanu 思ハヌ

282. Ōmu (shū)
(See Ying-wu)

283. Orategama 遠羅天釜

"P"

284. Pai-kao-tzǔ 伯高子
[Hakkōshi]

285. Pao-lin 寶林
[Hōrin]

286. Pao-lin-Ch'uan 寶林傳
[Hōrinden]

287. Pieh-Chi 別記
[Bekki]

288. pi-kuan 壁觀
[hekkan, hekkwan]

289. pi li wan jên 壁立萬仞
[heki-ryū-ban-jin]

290. p'ing-ch'ang hsin 平常心
[heijō-shin]

291. Ranran
[Lan-tsan]　　懶　瓚

292. *renga*　　　　煉　瓦

293. *ri*, "furthering"　利
[*li*]

294. *ri*, "reason", "spirit"　理
[*li*]

295. Rikkō (Rikkō Taifu)　陸　亘　(陸亘大夫)
[Lu-kêng] (Lu-kêng Ta-fu)

296. Rikō　　　　李　翺
[Li-ao]

297. Rikyū　　　　利　休

298. Rinzai Gigen　　臨　濟　義　玄
[Lin-chi I-hsüan]

299. *Rinzai-roku*
(See *Lin-chi Lu*)

300. Ri Senkyō　　　李　宣　敫
[Li Hsüan-chiao]

301. Ri Shunkyoku　　李　遵　勗
[Li Tsun-hsü]

302. *roji*　　　　　露　地

303. Ryū Shōkō　　　劉　相　公
[Liu Hsiang-kung]

304. Ryū Sōgen　　　柳　宗　元
[Liu Tsung-yüan]

305. Ryūtan Sōshin　　龍　潭　崇　信
[Lung-t'an Ch'ung-hsin]

321. Seigen Ishin
[Ch'ing-yüan Wei-hsin]　信惟原青

322. Seigen Gyōshi
[Ch'ing-yüan Hsing-szŭ]　思行原青

323. Seihei Reishun
(See Ch'ing-p'ing Ling-tsun)

324. Seiryō
[Ch'ing-lung]　龍青

325. Sekiden Hōkun
[Shih-t'ien Fa-hsün]　薰諸遷　法慶希　田霜頭恪　石

326. Sekisō Keisho
[Shih-shuang Ch'ing-chu]　石

327. Sekitō Kisen
[Shih-t'ou Hsi-ch'ien]　石

328. Sekkaku
[Shih-k'o]　石

329. Sen no Rikyū　休存　利　丶　千

330. Seppō Gizon
[Hsüeh-fêng I-ts'un]　義　峯心　雪

331. sesshin
[chieh-hsin]　接

332. shabetsu
[ch'a-pieh]　別　差

333. shabetsu soku byōdō
[ch'a-pieh chi p'ing-têng]　等平即別　差

334. shaku-shaku
[cho-cho]　灼林　灼

335. Shao-lin-ssŭ
[Shōrinji]　寺　少

#	Term	Characters
336.	*shê-li* [shari]	舍利
337.	*Shêng-chou Chi* [Seichū-shū]	聖胄集
338.	*shibumi*	澁味
339.	Shifuku Nyohō [Tzŭ-fu Ju-pao]	資福如寶
340.	*shih* [shi]	詩
341.	*shih-mo* [shimo]	是麼
342.	Shiko Rishō [Tzŭ-hu Li-tsung]	子湖利蹤
343.	*Shikyōryōrō* [Chih-ch'iang-liang-lou]	支彊梁樓
344.	*shin* (See *hsin*)	
345.	Shin, Sect (-shū)	眞 (宗)
346.	Shingon	眞言
347.	*shinjin ketsujō* [hsin-hsin-chüeh-ting]	信心決定
348.	Shinjō Kokumon [Chên-ching K'ê-wên]	眞淨克文
349.	Shinkō [Shên-kuang]	神光
350.	*Shinnyo Dōnin* [Chên-ju Tao-jên]	眞如道人

351. Shinrō
[Chên-lang]
振朗

352. *shippe*
[*chu-pi*]
竹篦

353. *sho*
[*shu*]
書

354. *shō*
正

355. Shōdai Erō
[Chao-t'i Hui-lang]
招提慧朗

356. shōgun
將軍

357. Shōichi Kokushi
聖一國師

358. Shōju Rōnin
正受老人

359. Shōkō
[Shêng-kuang]
勝光

360. Shōrinji
(*See* Shao-lin-ssǔ)

361. Shōsan Butsue Hōsen
[Chiang-shan Fu-hui Fa-ch'üan]
蔣山佛慧泉

362. Shōtoku, Prince (Taishi)
聖德太子

363. *shū*
[*chi*]
集

364. Shuan Nantai
[Shou-an Nan-t'ai]
守安南台 (南台守安)

365. Shukō (Japanese)
珠光

366. Shukō
(*See* Unsei Shukō)

367. Shūmitsu
[Tsung-mi]
宗密

368. Shun, Emperor
[Jun]
順

369. Shun Rofu
[Shun Lü-fu]
舜呂夫

370. *shuo*
[*setsu*]
說

371. Shūyusan
[Shu-yü-shan]
茱萸山

372. Shuzan Shōnen
[Shou-shan Hsing-nien]
首山省念

373. Sōdō
[Tsung-tao]
宗道

374. Sōji
[Tsung-ch'ih]
總持

375. Sōjō
[Sêng-chao]
僧肇

376. Sōkan
[Tsung-chien]
宗鑑

377. Sokei
[Tsu-ch'ing]
祖慶

378. *sokkon*
[*chi-chin*]
即今

379. *soku*
[*chi*]
即

380. *sono-mama*
其儘

381. Sōsan
[Sêng-ts'an]
僧璨

382. Sōtan
宗旦

383. Sōtō
[Ts'ao-tung]
曹洞

384. Sotōba
[Su Tung-p'o]
蘇東坡本紹無

385. Sōzan Honjaku
[Ts'ao-shan Pên-chi]
曹洞山本紹無 寂琦學

386. Sozan Jōki
[Ch'u-shan Shao-ch'i]
楚山微

387. Suibi Mugaku
[Ts'ui-wei Wu-hsiao]
翠微

388. *suki*
隙

389. *sumi-e*
墨絵

390. Suruga
駿河

391. Szŭ-ch'uan
[Shisen]
四川川

"T"

392. *Ta-ch'êng pi-kuan*
[*Daijō Hekkan*]
大乗壁観

393. Ta-chien
[Taikan]
大鑑

394. *Tada isshin no*
    sute yō nite sōrō
唯一心ノ様ニテ候捨テ

395. Tai-in
[T'ui-yin]
退隠

396. *taikyū*
[*t'i-chiu*]
體究

397. Takkan Kinzan
[Ta-kuan Chin-shan]
達観金山（曇穎）

398. Takuan	澤	庵		
399. Ta-kuei-shan [Dai-isan]	大	潙	山	
400. Tanka Tennen [Tan-hsia T'ien-jan]	丹	霞	天	然
401. Tao, *tao* [*dō*]	道			
402. *tariki*	他	力		
403. Tashiro Matazaemon	田	代	又	左衛門
404. *tatami*	疊			
405. Tei Meidō [Ch'êng Ming-tao]	程	明	道	
406. *teiki* [*t'i-ch'i*]	提	起		
407. *teishō* [*t'i-ch'ang*]	提	唱		
408. *teitetsu* [*t'i-tuo*]	提	掇		
409. *teizei* [*t'i-ssŭ*]	提	撕		
410. Tendai [T'ien-t'ai]	天	台		
411. *ten-jin* [*tien-hsin*]	點	心		
412. Tenki Zui [T'ien-ch'i Shui]	天	琦	瑞	
413. Tenryūji	天	龍	寺	

414. *tien-hsin*
(See *ten-jin*)

415. T'ien-t'ai
(*See* Tendai)

416. Tōfukuji 東福寺

417. Tōkaiji 東海寺

418. *tokonoma* 床間

419. Tokugawa, era 徳川

420. Tokugawa Iemitsu 徳川家光

421. Tokusan Senkan 徳山宣鑑
[Tê-shan Hsüan-chien]

422. *tomaru* 止

423. *Tongo Yōmon Ron* 頓悟要門論
(*Tongo Nyūdō Yōmon Ron*)
[*Tun-wu Yao-mên Lun*]
(*Tun-wu Ju-tao Yao-mên Lun*) (頓悟入道要門論)

424. Tōsan Ryōkai 洞山良价
[Tung-shan Liang-chieh]

425. Tōsu, monastery 投子
[T'ou-tzŭ]

426. Tōsu Daidō 投子大同
[T'ou-tzŭ Ta-t'ung]

427. Toyotomi Hideyoshi 豊臣秀吉

428. Ts'ao-ch'i 曹溪
[Sōkei]

429. Ts'êng-tzŭ
[Sōshi]
曾子

430. *tso-ch'an*
[*zazen*]
坐禪

431. *Tso-ch'an I*
[*Zazen-gi*]
坐禪儀

432. *tsukemono*
漬物

433. *tun*
[*ton*]
頓

434. Tun-huang
[Tonkō]
敦煌

"U"

435. Ummon Bun-en
[Yün-mên Wên-yen]
雲門文偃

436. *Ummon-roku*
[*Yün-mên Lu*]
雲門録

437. Ungo Dōyō
[Yün-chü Ta'o-ying]
雲居道膺

438. Unsei Shukō
[Yün-hsi Chu-hung]
雲栖株宏

439. *ushin no shin*
有心ノ心

440. *utsuru*
移

"W"

441. *wa*
和

442. *wabi*
佗

443. *wabi-zumai* 佗 佳 居

444. *wei-yin-wang*
[*ionnō*] 威 音 王

445. *wên-ta*
(See *mondō*)

446. *wu*
(See *satori*)

447. Wu, Emperor
[*Butei*] 武 帝

448. Wu, Empress
[*Bukō*] 武 后 (則天武后)

449. *wu-chi*
[*mukyoku*] 無 極

"Y"

450. Yagyū Tajima no Kami Munenori 柳 生 但 馬
守 宗 矩

451. Yakusan Igen
[Yüeh-shan Wei-yen] 藥 山 惟 儼

452. Yamamoto Jōchō 山 本 定 朝

453. *yawaragi* 軟

454. Ying-wu (chou)
[Ōmu] (shū) 鸚 鵡 (洲)

455. Yōgi Hōe
[Yang-ch'i Fang-hui] 楊 岐 方 會

456. Yōka Genkaku
[Yung-chia Hsüan-chiao] 永 嘉 玄 覺

457. *Yoku mireba nazuna hana saku*
     kakine kana　よくみれば薺花さ
     　垣ねかな

458. Yoshino, Mt.　吉野山

459. *yō-yō*
     [*yao-yao*]　夭夭

460. Yüan, period
     [Gen]　元

461. *yüeh-shih*
     [*yakuseki*]　藥石

462. Yuishiki
     [Wei-shih]　唯識

　　　　　"Z"

463. *zagu*
     [*tso-chü*]　坐具

464. *zazen*
     (See *tso-ch'an*)

465. *zen*
     [*ch'an*]　禪

466. *zendō*
     [*ch'an-t'ang*]　禪堂

467. Zengen
     [Chien-yüan]　漸源

468. Zenkan Sakushin
     [*Ch'an-kuan-ts'ê-chin*]　禪關策進

469. Zenke Kikan
     [*Ch'an-chia Kuei-chien*]　禪家龜鑑

470. *zentai sayū*
     [*ch'üan-t'i tso-yung*]　全體作用

Index

INDEX

The names of Chinese Zen figures are transliterated both in the text and in the index in accordance with the Japanese way of pronouncing them. Transliterations according to the Chinese way of pronouncing them are given in the preceding glossary.

A

537